Short Stories
for Students

National Advisory Board

Short Stories for Students

Presenting Analysis, Context, and Criticism on
Commonly Studied Short Stories

Volume 24

Ira Mark Milne, Project Editor

Foreword by Thomas E. Barden

THOMSON

GALE

Detroit • New York • San Francisco • New Haven, Conn. • Waterville, Maine • London

Short Stories for Students, Volume 24

Project Editor
Ira Mark Milne

Editorial
Anne Marie Hacht

Rights Acquisition and Management
Margaret Chamberlain-Gaston, Edna Hedblad, Lisa Kincade

Manufacturing
Rita Wimberley

Imaging and Multimedia
Lezlie Light, Mike Logusz, Kelly A. Quin

Product Design
Pamela A. E. Galbreath

Vendor Administration
Civie Green

Product Manager
Meggin Condino

ISBN-13: 978-0-7876-7032-0
ISBN-10: 0-7876-7032-4
ISSN 1092-7735

Printed in the United States of America
10 9 8 7 6 5 4 3 2 1

Table of Contents

Why Study Literature At All?

Short Stories for Students is designed to provide readers with information and discussion about a wide range of important contemporary and historical works of short fiction, and it does that job very well. However, I want to use this guest foreword to address a question that it does *not* take up. It is a fundamental question that is often ignored in high school and college English classes as well as research texts, and one that causes frustration among students at all levels, namely why study literature at all? Isn't it enough to read a story, enjoy it, and go about one's business? My answer (to be expected from a literary professional, I suppose) is no. It is not enough. It is a start; but it is not enough. Here's why.

First, literature is the only part of the educational curriculum that deals directly with the actual world of lived experience. The philosopher Edmund Husserl used the apt German term *die Lebenswelt*, "the living world," to denote this realm. All the other content areas of the modern American educational system avoid the subjective, present reality of everyday life. Science (both the natural and the social varieties) objectifies, the fine arts create and/or perform, history reconstructs. Only literary study persists in posing those questions we all asked before our schooling taught us to give up on them. Only literature gives credibility to personal perceptions, feelings, dreams, and the "stream of consciousness" that is our inner voice. Literature wonders about infinity, wonders why God permits evil, wonders what will happen to us after we die. Literature admits that we get our

hearts broken, that people sometimes cheat and get away with it, that the world is a strange and probably incomprehensible place. Literature, in other words, takes on all the big and small issues of what it means to be human. So my first answer is that of the humanist: we should read literature and study it and take it seriously because it enriches us as human beings. We develop our moral imagination, our capacity to sympathize with other people, and our ability to understand our existence through the experience of fiction.

My second answer is more practical. By studying literature we can learn how to explore and analyze texts. Fiction may be about *die Lebenswelt*, but it is a construct of words put together in a certain order by an artist using the medium of language. By examining and studying those constructions, we can learn about language as a medium. We can become more sophisticated about word associations and connotations, about the manipulation of symbols, and about style and atmosphere. We can grasp how ambiguous language is and how important context and texture is to meaning. In our first encounter with a work of literature, of course, we are not supposed to catch all of these things. We are spellbound, just as the writer wanted us to be. It is as serious students of the writer's art that we begin to see how the tricks are done.

Seeing the tricks, which is another way of saying "developing analytical and close reading skills," is important above and beyond its intrinsic literary educational value. These skills transfer to other fields and enhance critical thinking of any kind. Understanding how language is used to construct texts is powerful knowledge. It makes engineers better problem solvers, lawyers better advocates and courtroom practitioners, politicians better rhetoricians, marketing and advertising agents better sellers, and citizens more aware consumers as well as better participants in democracy. This last point is especially important, because rhetorical skill works both ways when we learn how language is manipulated in the making of texts the result is that we become less susceptible when language is used to manipulate us.

My third reason is related to the second. When we begin to see literature as created artifacts of language, we become more sensitive to good writing in general. We get a stronger sense of the importance of individual words, even the sounds of words and word combinations. We begin to understand Mark Twain's delicious proverb "The difference between the right word and the almost right word is the difference between lightning and a lightning bug." Getting beyond the "enjoyment only" stage of literature gets us closer to becoming makers of word art ourselves. I am not saying that studying fiction will turn every student into a Faulkner or a Shakespeare. But it will make us more adaptable and effective writers, even if our art form ends up being the office memo or the corporate annual report.

Studying short stories, then, can help students become better readers, better writers, and even better human beings. But I want to close with a warning. If your study and exploration of the craft, history, context, symbolism, or anything else about a story starts to rob it of the magic you felt when you first read it, it is time to stop. Take a break, study another subject, shoot some hoops, or go for a run. Love of reading is too important to be ruined by school. The early twentieth century writer Willa Cather, in her novel *My Antonia*, has her narrator Jack Burden tell a story that he and Antonia heard from two old Russian immigrants when they were teenagers. These immigrants, Pavel and Peter, told about an incident from their youth back in Russia that the narrator could recall in vivid detail thirty years later. It was a harrowing story of a wedding party starting home in sleds and being chased by starving wolves. Hundreds of wolves attacked the group's sleds one by one as they sped across the snow trying to reach their village. In a horrible revelation, the old Russians revealed that the groom eventually threw his own bride to the wolves to save himself. There was even a hint that one of the old immigrants might have been the groom mentioned in the story. Cather has her narrator conclude with his feelings about the story. "We did not tell Pavel's secret to anyone, but guarded it jealously as if the wolves of the Ukraine had gathered that night long ago, and the wedding party had been sacrificed, just to give us a painful and peculiar pleasure." That feeling, that painful and peculiar pleasure, is the most important thing about literature. Study and research should enhance that feeling and never be allowed to overwhelm it.

Thomas E. Barden
Professor of English and
Director of Graduate English Studies
The University of Toledo

Introduction

Purpose of the Book

The purpose of *Short Stories for Students* (*SSfS*) is to provide readers with a guide to understanding, enjoying, and studying short stories by giving them easy access to information about the work. Part of Gale's "For Students" Literature line, *SSfS* is specifically designed to meet the curricular needs of high school and undergraduate college students and their teachers, as well as the interests of general readers and researchers considering specific short fiction. While each volume contains entries on "classic" stories frequently studied in classrooms, there are also entries containing hard-to-find information on contemporary stories, including works by multicultural, international, and women writers.

The information covered in each entry includes an introduction to the story and the story's author; a plot summary, to help readers unravel and understand the events in the work; descriptions of important characters, including explanation of a given character's role in the narrative as well as discussion about that character's relationship to other characters in the story; analysis of important themes in the story; and an explanation of important literary techniques and movements as they are demonstrated in the work.

In addition to this material, which helps the readers analyze the story itself, students are also provided with important information on the literary and historical background informing each work. This includes a historical context essay, a box comparing the time or place the story was writ-

ten to modern Western culture, a critical overview essay, and excerpts from critical essays on the story or author. A unique feature of *SSfS* is a specially commissioned critical essay on each story, targeted toward the student reader.

To further aid the student in studying and enjoying each story, information on media adaptations is provided (if available), as well as reading suggestions for works of fiction and nonfiction on similar themes and topics. Classroom aids include ideas for research papers and lists of critical sources that provide additional material on the work.

Selection Criteria

The titles for each volume of *SSfS* were selected by surveying numerous sources on teaching literature and analyzing course curricula for various school districts. Some of the sources surveyed include: literature anthologies, *Reading Lists for College-Bound Students: The Books Most Recommended by America's Top Colleges*; *Teaching the Short Story: A Guide to Using Stories from around the World*, by the National Council of Teachers of English (NCTE); and "A Study of High School Literature Anthologies," conducted by Arthur Applebee at the Center for the Learning and Teaching of Literature and sponsored by the National Endowment for the Arts and the Office of Educational Research and Improvement.

Input was also solicited from our advisory board, as well as educators from various areas. From these discussions, it was determined that each volume should have a mix of "classic" stories (those works commonly taught in literature classes) and contemporary stories for which information is often hard to find. Because of the interest in expanding the canon of literature, an emphasis was also placed on including works by international, multicultural, and women authors. Our advisory board members—educational professionals—helped pare down the list for each volume. Works not selected for the present volume were noted as possibilities for future volumes. As always, the editor welcomes suggestions for titles to be included in future volumes.

How Each Entry Is Organized

Each entry, or chapter, in *SSfS* focuses on one story. Each entry heading lists the title of the story, the author's name, and the date of the story's publication. The following elements are contained in each entry:

- **Introduction:** a brief overview of the story which provides information about its first appearance, its literary standing, any controversies surrounding the work, and major conflicts or themes within the work.

- **Author Biography:** this section includes basic facts about the author's life, and focuses on events and times in the author's life that may have inspired the story in question.

- **Plot Summary:** a description of the events in the story. Lengthy summaries are broken down with subheads.

- **Characters:** an alphabetical listing of the characters who appear in the story. Each character name is followed by a brief to an extensive description of the character's role in the story, as well as discussion of the character's actions, relationships, and possible motivation.

  Characters are listed alphabetically by last name. If a character is unnamed—for instance, the narrator in "The Eatonville Anthology"—the character is listed as "The Narrator" and alphabetized as "Narrator." If a character's first name is the only one given, the name will appear alphabetically by that name.

- **Themes:** a thorough overview of how the topics, themes, and issues are addressed within the story. Each theme discussed appears in a separate subhead, and is easily accessed through the boldface entries in the Subject/Theme Index.

- **Style:** this section addresses important style elements of the story, such as setting, point of view, and narration; important literary devices used, such as imagery, foreshadowing, symbolism; and, if applicable, genres to which the work might have belonged, such as Gothicism or Romanticism. Literary terms are explained within the entry, but can also be found in the Glossary.

- **Historical Context:** this section outlines the social, political, and cultural climate *in which the author lived and the work was created.* This section may include descriptions of related historical events, pertinent aspects of daily life in the culture, and the artistic and literary sensibilities of the time in which the work was written. If the story is historical in nature, information regarding the time in which the story is set is also included. Long sections are broken down with helpful subheads.

- **Critical Overview:** this section provides background on the critical reputation of the author and the story, including bannings or any other public controversies surrounding the work. For older works, this section may include a history of how the story was first received and how perceptions of it may have changed over the years; for more recent works, direct quotes from early reviews may also be included.

- **Criticism:** an essay commissioned by *SSfS* which specifically deals with the story and is written specifically for the student audience, as well as excerpts from previously published criticism on the work (if available).

- **Sources:** an alphabetical list of critical material used in compiling the entry, with bibliographical information.

- **Further Reading:** an alphabetical list of other critical sources which may prove useful for the student. Includes full bibliographical information and a brief annotation.

In addition, each entry contains the following highlighted sections, set apart from the main text as sidebars:

- **Media Adaptations:** if available, a list of film and television adaptations of the story, including source information. The list also includes stage adaptations, audio recordings, musical adaptations, etc.

- **Topics for Further Study:** a list of potential study questions or research topics dealing with the story. This section includes questions related to other disciplines the student may be studying, such as American history, world history, science, math, government, business, geography, economics, psychology, etc.

- **Compare and Contrast:** an "at-a-glance" comparison of the cultural and historical differences between the author's time and culture and late twentieth century or early twenty-first century Western culture. This box includes pertinent parallels between the major scientific, political, and cultural movements of the time or place the story was written, the time or place the story was set (if a historical work), and modern Western culture. Works written after 1990 may not have this box.
- **What Do I Read Next?:** a list of works that might complement the featured story or serve as a contrast to it. This includes works by the same author and others, works of fiction and nonfiction, and works from various genres, cultures, and eras.

Other Features

SSfS includes "Why Study Literature At All?," a foreword by Thomas E. Barden, Professor of English and Director of Graduate English Studies at the University of Toledo. This essay provides a number of very fundamental reasons for studying literature and, therefore, reasons why a book such as *SSfS*, designed to facilitate the study of literture, is useful.

A Cumulative Author/Title Index lists the authors and titles covered in each volume of the *SSfS* series.

A Cumulative Nationality/Ethnicity Index breaks down the authors and titles covered in each volume of the *SSfS* series by nationality and ethnicity.

A Subject/Theme Index, specific to each volume, provides easy reference for users who may be studying a particular subject or theme rather than a single work. Significant subjects from events to broad themes are included, and the entries pointing to the specific theme discussions in each entry are indicated in **boldface**.

Each entry may include illustrations, including photo of the author, stills from film adaptations (if available), maps, and/or photos of key historical events.

Citing Short Stories for Students

When writing papers, students who quote directly from any volume of *SSfS* may use the follow-

ing general forms to document their source. These examples are based on MLA style; teachers may request that students adhere to a different style, thus, the following examples may be adapted as needed.

When citing text from *SSfS* that is not attributed to a particular author (for example, the Themes, Style, Historical Context sections, etc.), the following format may be used:

"The Celebrated Jumping Frog of Calavaras County." *Short Stories for Students*. Ed. Kathleen Wilson. Vol. 1. Detroit: Gale, 1997. 19–20.

When quoting the specially commissioned essay from *SSfS* (usually the first essay under the Criticism subhead), the following format may be used:

Korb, Rena. Critical Essay on "Children of the Sea." *Short Stories for Students*. Ed. Kathleen Wilson. Vol. 1. Detroit: Gale, 1997. 39–42.

When quoting a journal or newspaper essay that is reprinted in a volume of *Short Stories for Students*, the following form may be used:

Schmidt, Paul. "The Deadpan on Simon Wheeler." *Southwest Review* Vol. XLI, No. 3 (Summer, 1956), 270–77; excerpted and reprinted in *Short Stories for Students*, Vol. 1, ed. Kathleen Wilson (Detroit: Gale, 1997), pp. 29–31.

When quoting material from a book that is reprinted in a volume of *SSfS*, the following form may be used:

Bell-Villada, Gene H. "The Master of Short Forms," in *García Márquez: The Man and His Work*. University of North Carolina Press, 1990, pp. 119–36; excerpted and reprinted in *Short Stories for Students*, Vol. 1, ed. Kathleen Wilson (Detroit: Gale, 1997), pp. 89–90.

We Welcome Your Suggestions

The editor of *Short Stories for Students* welcomes your comments and ideas. Readers who wish to suggest short stories to appear in future volumes, or who have other suggestions, are cordially invited to contact the editor. You may contact the editor via E-mail at: **ForStudentsEditors@thomson.com.** Or write to the editor at:

Editor, *Short Stories for Students*
Thomson Gale
27500 Drake Road
Farmington Hills, MI 48331-3535

Literary Chronology

1926: Richard Yates is born on February 3 in Yonkers, New York.

1931: Ella Leffland is born on November 25 in Martinez, California.

1934: David Malouf is born on March 20 in Brisbane, Australia.

1940: American novelist and short-story writer Bharati Mukherjee is born on July 27 in Calcutta, West Bengal, India.

1941: John Edgar Wideman is born on June 14 in Washington, D.C.

1945: Deborah Eisenberg is born on November 20 in Chicago, Illinois.

1946: Julian Barnes is born on January 19 in Leicester, England.

1954: Andrea Barrett is born on November 16 in Boston, Massachusetts.

1956: Chitra Banerjee Divakaruni is born on July 29 in Calcutta, India.

1958: Jill McCorkle is born July 7 in Lumberton, North Carolina.

1961: Kate (Ann Katherine) Walbert is born in New York City.

1970: Adam Haslett is born on December 24 in Portchester, New York.

1970: Gina Ochsner is born and is adopted as an infant by Dick and Gayle Withnell.

1972: Yiyun Li is born in Beijing, China.

1976: Ella Leffland's "Last Courtesies" is published.

1988: Bharati Mukherjee's "The Middleman" is published.

1992: Richard Yates dies of complications arising from surgery on a hernia on November 7 at the VA hospital in Birmingham, Alabama.

1993: Deborah Eisenberg's "Someone to Talk To" is published.

1995: Chitra Banerjee Divakaruni's "Meeting Mrinal" is published.

1996: Julian Barnes's "Melon" is published.

1996: Andrea Barrett's "The English Pupil" is published.

1998: Kate Walbert's "Paris 1991" is published.

2000: David Malouf's "Great Day" is published.

2001: Jill McCorkle's "Fish" is published.

2001: Richard Yates's "The Canal" is published.

2002: Adam Haslett's "The Good Doctor" is published.

2002: Gina Ochsner's "The Necessary Grace to Fall" is published.

2003: Yiyun Li's "Immortality" is published.

2003: John Edgar Wideman's "What We Cannot Speak About We Must Pass Over in Silence" is published.

Acknowledgments

The editors wish to thank the copyright holders of the excerpted criticism included in this volume and the permissions managers of many book and magazine publishing companies for assisting us in securing reproduction rights. We are also grateful to the staffs of the Detroit Public Library, the Library of Congress, the University of Detroit Mercy Library, Wayne State University Purdy/Kresge Library Complex, and the University of Michigan Libraries for making their resources available to us. Following is a list of the copyright holders who have granted us permission to reproduce material in this volume of *SSFS*. Every effort has been made to trace copyright, but if omissions have been made, please let us know.

COPYRIGHTED EXCERPTS IN *SSFS*, VOLUME 24, WERE REPRODUCED FROM THE FOLLOWING PERIODICALS:

AGNI Online (www.agnimagazine.org), 2003 for "Creature of Habit: An Interview with Jill McCorkle," by Sherry Ellis. Reproduced by permission of the author.—*The Barcelona Review*, March-April, 2004 for "Interview with Adam Haslett," by Sherry Ellis. Copyright © 2004 by *The Barcelona Review*. Reproduced by permission.—*The Christian Science Monitor*, October 11, 2005 for "A Glimpse into China's Heart," by Jennifer Moeller. Copyright © 2005 The Christian Science Publishing Society. All rights reserved. Reproduced by permission from *Christian Science Monitor (www.csmonitor.com)*—*Harper's Magazine*, July, 2001. Copyright © 2001 by Harper's Magazine. All rights reserved. Reproduced from the July issue by special permission.—*The Iowa Review*, v. 20, fall, 1990 for "An Interview with Bharati Mukherjee," by Michael Connell, Jessie Grearson, and Tom Grimes. Copyright © 1990 by The University of Iowa. Reproduced by permission of the authors.—*The Nation*, v. 262, January, 1996. Copyright © 1996 by *The Nation Magazine*/The Nation Company, Inc. Reproduced by permission.—*The New Republic*, June 24, 1996. Copyright © 1996 by The New Republic, Inc. Reproduced by permission of *The New Republic*.—*Ploughshares*, v. 27, spring, 2001 for a review of "The Collected Stories of Richard Yates," by Stewart O'Nan. Copyright 2001 Ploughshares, Inc. Reproduced by permission of the author.—*South Asian Journalist's Association Online*, February, 1999 for "Essay on Chitra Banerjee Divakaruni and Some of Her Works," by Arthur J. Pais. Reproduced by permission of the author.—*Washington Post*, November 27, 2005 for "Cultural Revolutions: A Debut Collection of Stories Explores the Complexities of Life in Modern China," by Rodney Welch. © 2005 The Washington Post Company. Reproduced by permission of the author.—*The Women's Review of Books*, v. 13, March, 1996. Copyright 1996 Women's Review, Inc. Reproduced by permission.—*World Literature Today*, v. 64, spring, 1990; v. 74, autumn, 2000. Copyright ©1990, 2000 by *World Literature Today*. Both reproduced by permission of the publisher.

COPYRIGHTED EXCERPTS IN *SSFS*, VOLUME 24, WERE REPRODUCED FROM THE FOLLOWING BOOKS:

Bailey, Blake. From "Richard Yates," in *Dictionary of Literary Biography*, Volume 234, *American Short-Story Writers Since World War II, Third Series*. Edited by Patrick Meanor and Richard E. Lee. The Gale Group, 2001. Reproduced by permission of Thomson Gale.—Beuka, Robert A. From "Jill McCorkle," in *Dictionary of Literary Biography*, Volume 234, *American Short-Story Writers Since World War II, Third Series*. Edited by Patrick Meanor and Richard E. Lee. The Gale Group, 2001. Reproduced by permission of Thomson Gale.—Childs, Peter. From *Contemporary Novelists: British Fiction Since 1970*. Palgrave MacMillan, 2005. Copyright © Peter Childs 2005. Reproduced with permission of Palgrave Macmillan.—Doerksen, Teri Ann. From "Bharati Mukherjee," in *Dictionary of Literary Biography*, Volume 218, *American Short-Story Writers Since World War II, Second Series*. Edited by Patrick Meanor and Gwen Crane. Gale Group, 1999. Reproduced by permission of Thomson Gale.—Mandal, Somdatta. From "Chitra Banerjee Divakaruni," in *Dictionary of Literary Biography*, Volume 323, *South Asian Writers in English*. Edited by Fakrul Alam. Gale, 2006. Reproduced by permission of Thomson Gale.—Moseley, Merritt. From "Julian Barnes," in *Dictionary of Literary Biography*, Volume 194, *British Novelists Since 1960, Second Series*. Gale Research, 1998. Reproduced by permission of Thomson Gale.—Rooney, Brigid. From "David Malouf," in *Dictionary of Literary Biography*, Volume 289, *Australian Writers, 1950-1975*. Edited by Selina Samuels. Gale, 2004. Reproduced by permission of Thomson Gale.—Samuels, Wilfred D. From "John Edgar Wideman," in *Dictionary of Literary Biography*, Volume 33, *Afro-American Fiction Writers After 1955*. Edited by Thadious M. Davis and Trudier Harris. The Gale Group, 1984. Reproduced by permission of Thomson Gale.—Werner, Robin A. From "Deborah Eisenberg," in *Dictionary of Literary Biography*, Volume 244, *American Short-Story Writers Since World War II, Fourth Series*. Edited by Patrick Meanor and Joseph McNicholas. The Gale Group, 2001. Reproduced by permission of Thomson Gale.

COPYRIGHTED EXCERPTS IN *SSFS*, VOLUME 24, WERE REPRODUCED FROM THE FOLLOWING WEBSITES OR OTHER SOURCES:

From *Contemporary Authors Online*. "Adam Haslett," www.gale.com, Gale, 2003. Reproduced by permission of Thomson Gale.—From *Contemporary Authors Online*. "Andrea Barrett," www.gale.com, Gale, 2003. Reproduced by permission of Thomson Gale.—From *Contemporary Authors Online*. "Ella Leffland," www.gale.com, The Gale Group, 2001. Reproduced by permission of Thomson Gale.—From *Contemporary Authors Online*. "Julian Barnes," www.gale.com, Thomson Gale, 2006. Reproduced by permission of Thomson Gale.—From *Contemporary Authors Online*. "Kate Walbert," www.gale.com, Thomson Gale, 2004. Reproduced by permission of Thomson Gale.—Kurth, Peter. "The Salon Interview," *Salon.com*, December 2, 1998. This article first appeared in *Salon.com*, at http://www.salon.com. An online version remains in the Salon archives. Reprinted with permission.

Contributors

Bryan Aubrey: Aubrey holds a Ph.D. in English and has published many articles on contemporary literature. Entries on *The English Pupil, Immortality, The Middleman,* and *The Necessary Grace to Fall.* Critical essays on *The English Pupil, Immortality, Last Courtesies, The Middleman,* and *The Necessary Grace to Fall.*

Timothy Dunham: Dunham has a master's degree in communication and a bachelor's degree in English. Critical essay on *What We Cannot Speak About We Must Pass Over in Silence.*

Joyce Hart: Hart is the author of several books. Entry on *Last Courtesies.* Critical essay on *Last Courtesies.*

Anna Maria Hong: Hong is a poet and the editor of a fiction and memoir anthology. Critical essays on *The Necessary Grace to Fall* and *Paris 1991.*

David Kelly: Kelly is an instructor of creative writing and literature at two schools in Illinois. Entries on *The Canal* and *Melon.* Critical essays on *The Canal* and *Melon.*

Melodie Monahan: Monahan has a Ph.D. in English and operates an editing service, The Inkwell Works. Entry on *The Good Doctor.* Critical essay on *The Good Doctor.*

Wendy Perkins: Perkins is a professor of American and English literature and film. Entries on *Great Day* and *Paris 1991.* Critical essays on *Great Day* and *Paris 1991.*

Laura Pryor: Pryor has a B.A. from the University of Michigan and twenty years experience in professional and creative writing with special interest in fiction. Entry on *Someone to Talk To.* Critical essay on *Someone to Talk To.*

Claire Robinson: Robinson is a former teacher of English literature and creative writing and, as of 2006, is a full-time writer and editor. Entries on *Meeting Mrinal* and *What We Cannot Speak About We Must Pass Over in Silence.* Critical essays on *Meeting Mrinal, Someone to Talk To,* and *What We Cannot Speak About We Must Pass Over in Silence.*

Carol Ullmann: Ullmann is a freelance writer and editor. Entry on *Fish.* Critical essays on *Fish* and *Last Courtesies.*

The Canal

Richard Yates
2001

"The Canal" is a short story by Richard Yates, an author many literary critics in the early 2000s consider one of the great fiction writers of the twentieth century, even though he was practically forgotten by the reading public at the time of his death in 1992. Yates's most famous work, his 1961 novel, *Revolutionary Road*, is an examination of the search for meaning in mid-1950s America. In "The Canal," Yates visits the same terrain, presenting a man who is trying to reconcile memories of World War II combat with the mundane reality of urban socializing, a problem many veterans faced when they returned home and entered the business world.

The story concerns two couples at a cocktail party. When the two husbands discover the fact that they both were present at a certain military action in 1945, one man wants to compare the details of their war zone experiences while the other man would prefer to forget them. For Tom Brace, the fight at the canal signifies his luck and courage in the face of danger; for Lew Miller, the same proof of his fumbling, incompetence, and humiliation. With characteristic precision of detail and the peripheral bafflement of the two wives who try in vain to comprehend war, Yates portrays a man who is doomed to be haunted by events that he hardly understood at the time.

This story was not published during Yates's lifetime but was included in *The Collected Stories of Richard Yates* (2001), a book that increased its author's reputation in the years since his death.

Richard Yates © Jerry Bauer. Reproduced by permission

speechwriter for Robert Kennedy, who was then the U.S. attorney general. When Kennedy's brother, President John F. Kennedy, was assassinated in 1963, Yates left government life: he went to Hollywood to write screenplays for a brief while then he became an instructor at the University of Iowa's Writers' Workshop. He remarried in 1968, to Martha Speer. After seven years, he left Iowa when he was denied tenure. He taught at several Midwestern universities before returning to New York City. After the dissolution of his second marriage in 1974, he moved to Boston, where he wrote four books between 1976 and 1986.

In 1991, after spending more time in Hollywood, Yates took a position at the University of Alabama. Though the position was temporary, he found, after a two-year stint, that he was too ill with emphysema to leave Tuscaloosa. He was working on a novel about his time as Kennedy's speechwriter when he died at the VA hospital in Birmingham on November 7, 1992, of complications arising from surgery on a hernia. Yates's short story, "The Canal," appeared in print for the first time in *The Collected Stories of Richard Yates*, which was published by Holt in 2001.

Author Biography

Richard Yates was born in Yonkers, New York, on February 3, 1926, to a middle-class family. His parents were divorced when he was two years old. Yates was raised by his mother, a sculptress, and by his older sister. He attended Avon Old Farms School as a teenager and left to serve in World War II immediately after graduation. After his discharge from the army, he was diagnosed with tuberculosis and spent more than a year in a sanatorium run by the Veterans' Administration. He married his first wife, Sheila Bryant, in 1948, and they moved to France after his release from the hospital.

In 1953, *Atlantic Monthly* accepted one of his short stories, and Yates's writing career began. Yates returned to the United States and worked as a freelance writer of advertising copy while working on his novel *Revolutionary Road*. In the following years, he taught creative writing and wrote. Yet he was dragged down by depression and alcoholism, which ended his marriage in 1959.

Revolutionary Road was an instant success when it was published in 1961, and as of the early 2000s, it was considered one of the great American novels of the twentieth century. The celebrity that it brought to Yates led to his serving as a

Plot Summary

"The Canal" starts at a cocktail party in 1952. Two couples, the Millers and the Braces, are in the middle of a long conversation that has already been going on for about an hour when the story begins. Lew Miller and Tom Brace work for the same advertising firm. As the story opens, Lew Miller tells Tom Brace the division that he was in during World War II, and Brace, who has been telling a war story about the advance across a canal in Europe in March of 1945, recalls the divisions involved and realizes that Miller's division was in the same action. With this link established between them, Brace starts a more personal conversation with Miller, while the wives, who do not understand the experience of being in war, stand aside and remark with wonder on the coincidence. Brace presses Miller for details about his experience of what he calls, almost casually, "the canal deal."

Unlike Brace, Miller does not look back upon his war experience with fascination or wonder. He has a difficult time remembering the details at all, having spent most of his time in the army in North Carolina, working in public relations. For most of the war, he had a desk job stateside; he only joined the infantry in 1944. In all, then, his army experience was easier, in general. Concerning the night at the canal, he recalls that his division was somewhat removed from direct action. He was one of a line of soldiers further upstream, where there was less enemy resistance, and their orders were to deliver spools of communications wire to the other side, while Brace's division faced head on central artillery fire.

Miller recalls the events of the night at the canal, although he does not speak about them because what he remembers does not make a good story or show him in a positive light, while Tom Brace's story spotlights Tom's heroic actions. While Miller's division was crossing the canal on a partly submerged footbridge, Brace's division crossed in boats that made them easy targets. While Miller climbed a wall and ran to his destination when he reached the other side, Brace still had to face gunfire until he was able to get near enough to the enemy to throw a grenade that killed the German artillery soldiers.

Mentally reviewing the events that he has mostly forgotten or suppressed for years, Miller thinks of his panic and humiliation as a minimally competent soldier. He recalls being berated for losing his raincoat by his commanding officer, a skinny nineteen-year-old boy named Kavic. Walking in a line along a road toward the canal and under fire, Miller recalls the difficulty of following Shane, the soldier in line ahead of him: when they were crawling to avoid gunfire, the only way Miller could keep track of the man ahead of him was by feeling for the bottom of his boot. This method failed him when, just as they stood to run, the agonized screams of a man who had been shot distracted him. When he turned back to the advancement, Miller realized he had lost track of the men in his division. He looked around for them, asking other soldiers, but no one could tell him where his men were, so he crossed the canal and climbed up the ladders along the retaining wall on the other side. Wandering around on the far bank, Miller ran into the assistant squad leader and was reunited with his division. He was ordered to report to Kavic, who reprimanded him for getting separated, calling him "more [g——d——] trouble than all the rest of the men in this squad put together." Miller does not relate this humiliation at the cocktail party, but he does tell what happened after that: having accomplished their mission of carrying the wire across the canal, his squad went to a safe house away from the action, where they slept in shifts for about twenty-four hours.

Tom Brace is amazed to hear that Miller's outfit had the leisure to sleep, since his canal crossing put him right into artillery fire. Nancy Brace, Tom's wife, asks if his killing the artillery soldiers earned him a Silver Star. Brace dismisses Nancy's question with a wink, patronizing her supposedly superficial focus on the decoration, but Betty Miller gushes that he probably "should have gotten *several* Silver Stars." Of his success as the grenades he threw hit their target, Tom says, "I want to tell you, I've never been so lucky."

The conversation is interrupted by the hostess who jokes about preparing for the next war, a joke that she repeats several times in a bout of drunken silliness. The Millers and the Braces use this disruption as an excuse to say goodnight and leave the party. The men retrieve their coats, and Lew Miller feels embarrassed about his own, noting that it looks dirty and wrinkled in Tom Brace's hand.

The rainy night makes Betty Miller fear they will not find a taxicab. Able to save the moment, Brace leaps forward into the rain and hails one, showing himself to be, as he was in his war stories, competent and in control. He tells the Millers to take that cab, that he will find another one, and, while they are still objecting, Brace runs off up the block to hail the next cab.

While they are riding home, Betty Miller talks about Tom Brace. Although she hung on his story and complimented him while he was telling it, in the cab she says that she thinks both of the Braces are conceited. She then turns on her husband, criticizing him for letting Tom Brace "*eclipse*" him for the whole evening and pointing out that Lew always lets others outshine him. She is totally unaware of all the thoughts her husband has had during the party. The story ends as Lew tells his wife, "for God's sake shut up."

Characters

Nancy Brace

By contrast to her husband's powerful personality, Nancy's personality does not develop very clearly in this story. However, she admits she can imagine his war experiences because he is able to describe them so vividly. This statement cannot be taken too seriously, though, because Nancy's understanding shows nothing close to an understanding of the horrors of warfare: several times, she comments on how "marvelous" it must have been.

Tom Brace treats his wife's support in a fond but belittling manner. When she makes a point of mentioning the Silver Star that he won, he acts as if her interest in the medal misses the more serious aspects of the story, attributing her lack of understanding to the fact that she is a woman. During much of the conversation, Nancy is gone to retrieve drinks for both couples, having heard Tom's stories over and over already, but she still acts upon her return as if she would have been very interested in hearing the parts that she missed. She is a doting wife who is taken for granted by a husband who has lived a successful life and expects the best.

Tom Brace

Handsome, athletic, Tom Brace is one of the two main characters of this story. He is the force that drives it, as his curiosity about Lew Miller's war experience and his willingness to prod Miller for information about it forces Miller to remember details that he has suppressed for years.

Brace is a forceful, tactless man. He is an account executive for an advertising firm, a salesman, which indicates that he is an outgoing person who is used to convincing people to do what he wants.

Yates implies that Brace is something of a boor, monopolizing the conversation with stories of his former glory, reveling in the bygone days when he was a war hero. At the end of the story, Betty Miller calls him "conceited," though there is no way of telling whether she is giving her true assessment of him or is just trying to build up her husband, who pales in comparison to Brace. More telling is the fact that at the start of the story the subject is already on the night at the canal, even though, at that point, no one knows that Brace and Miller both experienced that particular event: Brace has been telling his army stories even though he has no reason to believe that they are relevant to anyone else in the conversation.

Brace is presented as having a streak of genuine selflessness in him. When telling of his attack on the German gunmen that threatened his squad, he gives ample credit to the machine gunner who provided him with cover. When he runs into the rain to capture a cab, a feat which had just been pronounced impossible by Betty Miller, he chivalrously turns it over to the Millers, and when they try to reject his generosity, he cuts the conversation short by running off to hail another cab.

Yates also shows that, despite his good looks, confidence, and heroism, Brace is fixated on the war. He is obsessive about the details of Miller's experience, focusing on the calibers of guns and the type of resistance that was being put forward further up the canal from him. When Miller gives the number of the outfit he served in, Brace is able to recall exactly where that outfit was situated during the canal crossing, which Miller himself is unable to do. It is clear that Brace has studied the details of that maneuver, that he has thought a lot about the whole war, quite possibly to confirm the difficulty that he himself overcame and describes so humbly.

The Hostess

Near the end of the story, the conversation about the canal crossing is interrupted when the party's hostess joins her guests. She is drunk and jokes several times about the pointlessness of talking about the last war when there is always the next war to be planned.

Kavic

Lew Miller recalls being reprimanded several times by Kavic, his squad's leader. Yates describes Kavic as a "scrawny, intensely competent, nineteen years old," implying that in any social situation other than the army, Kavic would be considered Miller's inferior by far.

Not only does Kavic shout at Miller, but he does so with exhausted patience, as if he finds it difficult to believe that anyone could be as inept or mindless as Miller is. He berates Miller for losing his raincoat and for losing his way in the dark. Kavic overreacts to events that actually come out all right in the end, and Miller is both indignant and shamed by having to take reprimands from such an unimposing authority. Yet, Miller still realizes that, on some level, Kavic is right: he should not lose equipment or get lost. It would be easy for Miller to forget his own shortcomings during the fighting by blaming the army for making a boy like Kavic his superior, but instead Miller accepts responsibility for his actions. That said, Kavic is contrasted with other soldiers and a lieutenant who act and speak politely to Miller.

Betty Miller

Betty Miller is aware that her husband, Lew, did not see much action during the war, but she is also protective of his reputation. Therefore, she looks for ways in which to build up his self-esteem. The story opens with her interrupting a war story by Tom Brace to ask if the division Brace is describing is the same one in which Miller served. Though it is not, they find that Miller's division was at the same action Brace is describing, though on the periphery of the attack. Betty's failed attempt to connect Lew to Brace's story serves to emphasize the contrast between Brace's "lucky" heroics and Miller's recollection of his own awkward, plodding functionality.

During the conversation, Betty draws out details about Tom Brace's experiences at the canal, asking him about his actions and exclaiming, "My *God*" at particularly dangerous moments in his tale. In the cab on the way home, though, she denounces both Tom and his wife as "those damn conceited Brace people," and she berates her husband for allowing them to "*eclipse*" him. Betty may actually be interested in Tom Brace's exploits, only pretending to be dismissive of him later, to show her husband that she is not impressed by the other man's actions. Or she may actually have found his war stories as irritating as her own husband's self-deprecating reserve.

Lew Miller

The story is told from Lew Miller's perspective, including his memories of the canal crossing which he does not verbalize. Miller is a copywriter for an advertising agency, working at a creative but unglamorous job. At the cocktail party, in conversation with Tom Brace, an account executive at the agency, and listening to his dramatic telling of a war story, Miller is forced to remember his own version of that story, the one he experienced himself. While the one veteran enjoys recalling his "lucky" advance across the canal, Lew Miller would prefer not to revisit the humiliating and scary experience he had in the same advance.

In the army, Miller served mostly in a public relations squad stationed in North Carolina. Late in World War II, he was sent to Europe. As Brace tells his war story, Betty Miller tries to introduce Lew Miller's own service and make it sound as if his military experience is comparable, an effort that has the opposite effect on her husband.

In Europe, Miller served as a private, a rifleman replacement. One vivid memory of the day and night at the canal is that he lost his raincoat that afternoon, and he had to suffer the indignity of being given a patronizing reprimand by the nineteen-year-old squad leader, who talked to him as if he were a fool or a child. While other soldiers at the canal, like Tom Brace, would remember charging into enemy gunfire, Miller remembers the confusion under fire of trying to follow the man in front of him in the night. While other soldiers were

responsible for killing the enemy, his squad only had to deliver communications wire. While Brace was able to keep his wits about him enough to make a "lucky" throw that kills a German gunner, Miller is distracted enough by a soldier's cries to lose contact with his squad, which prompted another belittling reprimand from the squad leader when he rejoined them.

As a result of this cocktail party, Miller shrivels into himself with self-consciousness. He notices how handsome and athletic Brace is; when Brace holds Miller's topcoat out to him, the coat itself takes on his poor self-esteem, looking wrinkled and dirty in his hand.

In the cab on the ride home, Betty gives him a chance to salvage his self-esteem by belittling Brace as a conceited bore, but Miller refuses to go along with her. Instead, he tells his wife to "shut up."

Shane

Shane is in front of Lew Miller in line as they advanced toward the canal. Miller could just barely keep sight of Shane, and, when a loud wail from an injured soldier distracted him, he turned back to find that he had lost track of Shane, severing his connection to his squad.

Wilson

Wilson is the assistant squad leader, after Kavic, a somewhat ridiculous authority figure. He is overweight, a farmer from Arkansas, not exactly the kind of keen military mind that inspires confidence. Unlike Kavic, Wilson is not belligerent toward the troops under him: he seems to have no particular agenda in mind, and instead shows himself to be just following Kavic's orders. When Miller runs into Wilson at the far side of the canal, Wilson does not reprimand him for having gotten separated, but later he brings him an order that he is to see Kavic, who does the reprimanding.

Themes

Memory

Yates dramatizes in this story how individuals remember shared experiences (perhaps especially of war) in separate ways and how those different ways of remembering determine or express the person's sense of self. Tom Brace selects from all his military experience in order to shape his story. Soldiers have many experiences in military service,

Topics For Further Study

- Tom Brace recalls vividly details about the night at the canal in March 1945, at the end of World War II, while Lew Miller would prefer not remembering anything about his night there. Talk to at least three people who have served in the military and from your interviews draw a conclusion about whose experience is more common. From your findings, develop a questionnaire that will help returning service people record their experiences, along with an explanation of why you think your particular questions would be useful.

- Recall a time when you did something that others assumed was more exciting than it was. Write a story that compares the experience that you had with the experience that others think you should have had.

- Nancy Brace and Betty Miller find it hard to understand what their husbands went through at the canal. Look through some books about war at your library, and make a list of five or more that you think they should read, with a short explanation about why you think each one would help them understand.

- One point implied in this story is that people tend to forget about wars soon after they are over. Read about the official memorials in Washington, D.C., commemorating World War I, World War II, the Korean War, the Vietnam War, and the Persian Gulf War. Write a brief description of each, and explain which you think is most effective.

- Why do you think Yates gave Miller and Brace the jobs that they hold at the advertising firm where they work? Explain what a copywriter and an account executive do and how these two jobs would be suitable to these men.

but only some of them offer material for good stories in later civilian life. Tom's story about the night at the canal conveys a picture of himself as lucky, agile, and courageous. Now an account executive at an advertising agency, a salesman, Tom uses his charisma to draw attention to himself and to influence others. His war story in a sense advertises him as a certain kind of man, an image he wants to project. His repeating his favorite war stories helps enliven the present situation, where he dominates a conversation at a cocktail party. That he drinks a lot at that party suggests he may use alcohol to insulate himself and reduce his inhibitions at the same time. It is implied that the Braces and the Millers do not know each other very well, and keeping a conversation going with strangers may be uncomfortable or difficult.

Lew Miller's memories of that night at the canal similarly reinforce his sense of himself, and yet in the present at the cocktail party, what he remembers of that night emphasizes what he wishes no one would see in him. In addition to showing how complex a given military action is and how

people engaged in it may have very different tasks and perceptions of it, Miller's memory reinforces his sense of his own physical inferiority and timid personality. Miller is a man more suited for desk work; he is ill-suited for manual work or military action. He is not athletic or agile. What he remembers of that night convinces him that he lacks those traits traditionally associated, particularly in romantic literature and in the movies, with combat. In each case, the memory of the man is an expression of his self-concept. The tour of military service entails many experiences across months, even years of service, and the selected memories work to highlight the man's positive sense of self or to emphasize the man's sense of personal inadequacy. Either way, memory of past performance contributes to the way these men present themselves in a social situation.

Self-Aggrandizement

Self-aggrandizement is the act of exaggerating one's own importance. In this story, to some extent, Tom Brace is self-aggrandizing when he tells his war story which shows himself in a positive light, when he dominates the conversation and yet appears to eschew compliments that come from his wife and Betty Miller.

The story Brace tells suggests that he was heroic in combat. At the canal, while Miller recalls having muddled across a bridge in the dark, Brace remembers how he and his squad rowed across in boats, in direct artillery range. Brace was in the first boat. They were fired upon when they were about halfway across. The men in his boat led the assault once the canal was crossed, with a machine gunner armed with a Browning automatic rifle (B.A.R.) keeping the enemy distracted while Brace moved close enough to throw a hand grenade at the German guns firing on them. Though some of the men in his squad drowned in the crossing and others were shot, quite a few probably were saved by Brace's being able to throw a grenade and take out the enemy artillery. Luckily for Brace now, his wife is the one brings up his being awarded a Silver Star for his deed.

Clearly, Brace has an ongoing fascination with the war. He initiates the discussion with Lew Miller and specifically recalls troop locations and gun calibers. When his wife says, "I never get tired of Tom's war stories," it is clear that she has heard many stories, often repeated. The insistence on re-living the time when he proved himself to be heroic may be a sign that Brace needs attention and approval, but Yates also includes evidence to suggest an alternate interpretation, that he is not needy at all. He is generous in sharing the glory for his successful assault at the canal with the B.A.R. man who provided him cover, emphasizing what a good soldier that man was. That in itself might be false humility, but Brace has been professionally successful since the war, so the question remains about why he needs to relive old victories. He is athletic, handsome, and confident. He generously runs out into the rain to hail one taxi for the Millers and then another for him and his wife. He seems self-confident, but his continual return to his wartime success may hint that something is missing in his present life for which he is compensating. In any event, in the story, Betty Miller has the final word: he is conceited and self-aggrandizing.

The Subjectivity of Interpretation

This story suggests that interpretation is subjective. Readers see the memory that Lew Miller has but does not share at the cocktail party, a memory that shows him in a negative light. But Yates also provides details about Miller's past which

Miller does not emphasize, which might modify Miller's judgment of himself. For example, Miller dwells on the anger of his commanding officer, on feeling demeaned by him in front of the other soldiers. He is ashamed of the small failures, his losing his raincoat, his getting separated from his men, and over all, he remembers Kavic's caustic criticism. He does not dwell on the fact that his men also caught direct artillery hits, which caused them to roll off the road into the ditches and plausibly contributed to their line getting broken. Then, too, Miller had spent "most of his service at a public-relations desk in North Carolina" before he was transferred into the infantry in 1944, toward the end of the war. Desk work for three years did not prepare him for the intense physical strain of infantry combat. Also, Kavic may be in charge at age nineteen because he has seen more action than Miller has before the night at the canal. Like Brace, Miller remembers good things about his fellow soldiers, how a lieutenant spoke politely to him, how the men at the wall gave each other a hand as they climbed over it. But these details do not work to sabotage Miller's self-esteem, and so he does not dwell on them. Similarly, in the untold memories Brace has, there may be more than a few that do not show him in a heroic light, yet those details of his military experience he chooses not to describe, or he may have selectively forgotten what he does not want to remember. Over the years, memory fashions the stories, refining, deleting, all to serve the teller's purpose and as an expression of the teller's subjective view of the past and of himself.

Style

Point of View

Point of view is the angle from which the action of the story is seen. In this case, the story is told in third-person, limited omniscient point of view. The story is told in the third person, and readers are given the inner thoughts of one character, but not the inner thoughts of others. In "The Canal," readers are allowed to know Lew Miller's thoughts. Most of his memory about the night at the canal is not spoken aloud to Tom and Nancy Brace. The story moves from the past to the present and from Brace's narrated story to the story Miller recalls but chooses not to narrate. As the story progresses, the contrast heightens between the two men: Brace becomes more heroic, more competent, the longer he talks; Miller becomes more focused on his own inadequacy as he reviews his own memory of that night. At one point, the story cuts away from the cocktail party while Miller and Tom Brace are discussing the guns that were aimed at Brace's squad. The text includes a long vignette of almost three pages, including dialogue, all depicting Miller's attempts to follow the man marching in front of him and his becoming lost, crossing the canal, and eventually rejoining his squad. These are his thoughts, as Brace speaks. Then Brace asks, "So what happened after you got to the other side?" The readers know what happened, but Brace, who has so far been talking most of the time, is only now ready to hear Miller's story. Miller and his men drew fire on the road as they approached and that contributed to Miller's getting separated from his squad. Miller could make a story of that approach and the cries of injured men and how the soldiers helped each other, but that part he neglects in order to focus privately on his own inadequacy. Miller remembers certain parts of the canal crossing and what he focuses on now does not make a story he would want to tell. In these ways, the story is shaped and interpreted via the point of view of the person through whose eyes the action is seen.

Foil Characters

Juxtaposed contrasting characters serve to underscore each other's distinctive traits. In "The Canal," Tom Brace and Lew Miller are presented as opposites in style and experience: Brace is an extrovert, who enjoys telling complimentary stories about himself; Miller is reserved, perhaps even introverted, and, according to his wife at least, he tends to allow others to eclipse him. Brace is tall, athletic, and talkative, while Miller is less physically capable and tends to be a listener. Miller wants to forget the war, and Brace wants to remember certain details of it. Because they are so different, they draw each other out, making readers more aware of each character's personality traits by seeing those traits missing in the other.

The wives, though, are not so explicitly contrasted. At least at the party, which is the only view the story provides of her, Nancy Brace is a big supporter of her husband's war stories, hanging on his every word and explaining that he makes her feel as if she were there. At the party, Betty Miller seems both admiring of Tom and quietly supportive of her husband. She acts as though she envies Betty, wishing that her husband would talk more, even though she knows that he saw little action during the war. In Betty's comment that "Lew never talks about the war," Miller sees his wife as romanticizing him as "a faintly tragic, sensitive husband,

perhaps, or at any rate a charmingly modest one." Miller sees this as proof of her love, though he resolves to tell her privately that she must "stop making him a hero whenever anybody mentioned the war." So publicly, both wives appear supportive and loving. Yet the conversation in the cab between the Millers suggests otherwise: Betty attacks Tom Brace and his wife and then she attacks her husband, too. Whether Nancy has this same duplicity is left open to conjecture. It is possible that she also has her private resentment: she listens repeatedly to Tom's stories, and perhaps repeatedly in public, he dismisses her. If this reading is logical, then the wives serve less as foil characters than the husbands.

Historical Context

The Last Days of World War II

Yates does not say where the battle described in the story took place, but it is possible that it took place in Germany, given that it occurred in March of 1945 and involved American troops advancing against the Germans.

The conflict that Yates describes has some similarity to the battle for Remagen on March 7, 1945. Remagen is a city in the Rhineland-Palatinate region of Germany, along the Rhine River, just south of Cologne. After the Battle of the Bulge in December of 1944, as Allied forces pushed their way into Germany, the Rhine provided the German army with a natural barrier of defense. The Ludendorff Bridge at Remagen was the last remaining bridge, a valuable asset for the invading army as it moved heavy equipment in its advance toward the capitol, Berlin. The Allies used the bridge, despite German efforts to destroy it before the Allies arrived. After the Allies' conquest on March 7, the bridge withstood ten more days of German air assault before collapsing. The fictional conflict in this story takes place at a canal and not at the Rhine River, but this area of Germany is full of canals dating back hundreds of years. Moreover, the strategic importance of the battle at Remagen indicates that it had some influence on Yates in conceiving the conflict in the story.

The war in Europe only persisted a few weeks after the canal assault in this story took place. In late April, the last of the German army was cut in two by American and Soviet troops, devastating its chances of survival. In Berlin, Adolph Hitler, the German chancellor who had pursued dominance over Europe and Africa, committed suicide on April 30. By May 7, the remaining commander of the German army signed an unconditional surrender. May 8 is celebrated as Victory in Europe Day, or V-E Day.

Postwar Corporate America

In the late 1940s and early 1950s, the United States enjoyed a level of economic stability that had not been known since the start of the Great Depression in 1929. The U.S. economy thrived, having the distinct advantage of profiting from wartime spending. Since bombing had caused damage throughout countries that had previously been economic powerhouses, such as Great Britain, France, Germany, and Japan, the United States had a distinct advantage.

The booming manufacturing economy led to the development of a new corporate culture. The war years had led to innovations in both product development and in public relations, and this, along with the easy access of money for research and development, gave U.S. businesses new opportunities for expansion. In addition, the postwar boom in college education for returning veterans led companies toward structuring their internal workings around scientific principles.

A corporate culture and worldview arose that was specifically associated with the 1950s. If that decade was later seen as conformist and self-satisfied, it may be because the previous decades had been so difficult, shaped as they were by a global economic depression followed by World War II. People who might have held blue-collar jobs or worked as manual laborers before the war (provided that they could find jobs in the 1930s) had an opportunity, after the war, to move into respected white-collar office positions. The corporate culture made it possible for these people to move up into jobs requiring intellect and verbal skills in the same way that, half a century earlier, Henry Ford's theory of division of labor had made it possible for unskilled farm workers to hold assembly line factory jobs, building automobiles.

The advertising agency came to be seen as the epitome of the corporate culture. Referred to throughout the 1950s by the general, sometimes disparaging term, Madison Avenue, due to the large concentration of the country's most prominent advertising firms on that street in New York City, advertising was seen by cynics as the ultimate end product of corporate culture: a huge industry that produced nothing but images, creating fears in its

viewers intended to manipulate them into buying products. Books such as Sloan Wilson's *The Man in the Gray Flannel Suit* (1955); William Whyte's *The Organization Man* (1956); and Vance Packard's *The Hidden Persuaders* (1957) and *The Status Seekers* (1959) described a corporate culture, epitomized by Madison Avenue, that was mercilessly conformist. Madison Avenue men were characterized as group thinkers who spent their days worrying about job security, advancement, and social status, feting clients over martinis at lunch and comparing themselves to coworkers at cocktail parties at night. It is significant that the main characters in "The Canal" are coworkers at an advertising firm, given that the advertising firm came to represent the drive for consumerism, competition, and conformity in the 1950s.

Critical Overview

During his lifetime, Richard Yates was read and respected by other writers to a much greater degree than he was read by the general public. His 1961 novel, *Revolutionary Road*, sold well, and over the years, it continued to be widely known, mostly due to its being assigned in literature classes. But from 1961 until Yates died in 1992, his literary career was a long slide into oblivion.

In 2001, though, *The Collected Stories of Richard Yates* was published, sparking admiration from all corners of the literary world. "The Canal" first appeared in print in this book, though many of the other stories from the collection had been previously published. *Esquire* magazine named the collection one of the "Best Books of 2001," noting, "It's simply criminal that [these stories] were out of print so long." Christine DeZelar-Tiedman, writing in the *Library Journal*, warns readers that Yates's worldview can be bleak but tells them out-right that "Despite the general pessimism of the stories, they never seem contrived or self-indulgent." She goes on to recommend the collection for all academic and larger public libraries. In *Booklist*, Brad Hooper goes even further with his praise, asserting that "No public library catering to short story lovers should be without this career-encompassing collection of the work of an important American story writer." He ends his review by noting that Yates "deserves a wider audience among contemporary fiction readers."

The admiration for this book is best summed up by John de Falbe, who wrote a long review of it for *The Spectator*. "Though many aspects of the

Marilyn Monroe with friends and journalists at a cocktail party in 1955 © Bettmann/Corbis

world he describes have gone, the stories transcend time," de Falbe writes. "They are about loneliness and loss, failure and dreams, dignity and grace. They are tough, unsentimental, compassionate and beautiful in their apparent simplicity."

Criticism

David Kelly

Kelly is an instructor of creative writing and literature at two schools in Illinois. In this essay, Kelly argues that the independence of thought shown by Betty Miller marks this as a story against gender stereotyping.

From the perspective of the twenty-first century, Richard Yates's short story "The Canal" offers a look at the post-World War II years that is both familiar and revealing, particularly in the ways that Yates treats the subject of gender relations. There is a tendency in the early 2000s to over-generalize the roles of women in the 1950s, to see their place in society as auxiliary at best, and Yates's story plays to that perspective by focusing on the men. Still, his female characters are not just extras in a drama that hardly concerns them but are indeed primary forces in giving meaning to the war story (or stories) that are considered in "The Canal."

The main focus of this story is the cocktail party conversation between two men, Lew Miller and Tom Brace, about their experiences during the war, especially in a particular conflict in which they both took part some seven years earlier. Brace was in the thick of enemy gunfire and had the chance to distinguish himself as a soldier, killing several Germans, winning a medal and probably saving the lives of some of the men who served under him, though he is too modest to say so: he is the one who initiates the conversation and drives it forward with his insatiable curiosity about events of that day. Miller has mostly suppressed the events of that conflict: prodded by Brace, he recalls losing equipment, becoming separated from his squad in the dark, and being mercilessly reprimanded by his squad leader.

It is as important to the story that Brace's war experience be idealized as it is that Miller's be as humiliating as possible, because this is, at its core, the story of Miller's looking back at a certain moment which he would rather not revisit. His humiliation is rounded out by the presence of women. The wives listen to their husbands' conversation with apparent awe and admiration, even though what Miller is willing to say varies noticeably from what he thinks about the night at the canal. Both women prompt the men to tell their war stories and express fascination about an aspect of life that they never lived and never will. Though they are peripheral to the main thrust of the story, Yates develops their characters subtly.

Nancy Brace sets the standard for wifely behavior in this story, taking on the role of subordinate to her husband, acting as his assistant and biggest admirer. In this way, she comes close to the stereotypical 1950s wife. Nancy reminds Brace of details he has missed, and she marvels at his feats. She compliments his storytelling ability as being so varied that she could listen to his tales over and again and being so vivid that she feels she has lived his war experience. It is all nonsense, of course, as she proves by describing the experience of combat as "marvelous." If the whole conversation that "The Canal" centers on is just one long display of Tom Brace on his "luck" night at the canal, then it is a conversation that could not proceed without Nancy as the audience.

In return for her support, Brace treats Nancy with dismissive indulgence. With such a complimentary audience, it is perhaps easy for him to take

> "The fact that Betty Miller is so free with her praise for Brace indicates that she does not see this as a competition at all, that she is an impartial audience, an independent thinker."

her for granted. When the maid does not come at his summoning, Nancy fetches drinks for the couples, for which he thanks her, but abruptly. When she brings out that his actions earned Brace a Silver Star, he uses the opportunity to underline at her expense his own presumed disinterest in the honor. He points out that a medal is a silly thing to care about, winking at Miller and asking patronizingly, "Isn't that just like a woman?" Though Nancy says that her husband's repetitive war stories are meaningful to her, he assumes that, because she is a woman, she can never grasp their meaning.

Throughout the story, Betty Miller's behavior seems to parallel that of Nancy Brace. She, too, tries to build up her husband's military career, even though she has far less to work with and is met with resistance from Miller. The story begins with Betty cutting into Tom Brace's monologue about his war experiences to point out that Lew Miller was in the war too and has his own tales to tell. When Miller discusses his service, she attempts to clarify for the Braces that he was an officer, but he shoots down her clarification by saying that he was only an officer stateside and served as a private when he was in combat. As Miller sees it, she glorifies his military career precisely because he never talks about it, having built what he thinks is "a special kind of women's-magazine romanticism" around it. Unlike Brace, who relies on his wife's encouragement, Miller discourages his wife's promoting him.

Yates presents Betty Miller as a complex character with too many contradictions for her to be easily interpreted as either building her identity around her husband's experiences or not. Throughout the story, she is generous with her praise for Tom Brace,

What Do I Read Next?

- Sloan Wilson's 1955 novel, *The Man in the Gray Flannel Suit*, captures the mood of young advertising executives (like Tom Brace in this story). It is funny, poignant, and filled with mixed emotions about the struggle to succeed in commercial America and the fear that such success comes at the expense of one's soul.

- Yates's best known work is his 1961 novel, *Revolutionary Road*, about a young husband and wife in the fifties who are upwardly mobile but eaten away by insecurity and discontent. It has been in print since its initial publication and is available as of 2006 from Vintage Contemporary.

- Yates's short story, "The B.A.R. Man," is about an army veteran, John Fallon, who works as a clerk at an insurance company and remembers his former glory in the war. He recalls that he was often referred to as "a damn good B.A.R. man," using the exact words that Tom Brace in "The Canal" uses to refer to a fellow soldier, implying that he might be the same character. This story is included in *The Collected Stories of Richard Yates* (2001).

- Yates is believed to have been a major influence on Raymond Carver, a master short story writer who also dealt sparingly with domestic issues. Carver's story, "What We Talk About When We Talk About Love," concerns a situation similar to the one described in "The Canal," with two couples talking about love instead of war. It is available in a collection by the same name, published by Knopf in 1989.

- Another writer who examined the discontents of postwar suburbia is John Cheever. Cheever's story "The Country Husband" offers a meticulous look at the times and begins with a surrealistic scenario that mirrors the problem of Lew Miller in this story: a man returns home after being in a plane crash, but his family, having heard no news of the crash, does not see the significance of what happened to him. First published in 1954, it is frequently reprinted in literary anthologies and is included in *The Stories of John Cheever*, published by Knopf in 2000.

- Critics regularly point out how Yates's precise, illuminating writing style resembles that of F. Scott Fitzgerald, one of the great writers of the twentieth century. No one Fitzgerald story is particularly like those by Yates, but Fitzgerald's stories are available in *Short Stories of F. Scott Fitzgerald: A New Collection*, published by Scribner in 1995.

---

often blurting out her admiration for his story that he clearly intends his audience to admire. If she sees this conversation as a competition between Brace and Miller, where one's achievement attempts to overshadow the other's, then she would have a natural interest in tempering her enthusiasm: the flip side of her attempts to get Miller to open up about his war experiences may be to get Brace to say less about his own. The fact that Betty Miller is so free with her praise for Brace indicates that she does not see this as a competition at all, that she is an impartial audience, an independent thinker.

On the other hand, Betty lets go of her social mask once the Millers are in a taxicab, driving away from the Braces. In private conversation with her husband, she pronounces that Nancy and Tom Brace are conceited. This comment may indicate that she feels hurt about losing the competition on which husband served more nobly in the war: if so, it would mean that her own ego is tied to Lew Miller's achievements, affirming the 1950s stereotype of the dependent woman. Her outburst in the cab may also be an invitation to her husband, intending to draw out his own anger. If she believes that Miller has been waiting all night to badmouth the Braces with her, she proves to be mistaken: she apparently does not understand him well at all.

It is clear that Yates has given Lew and Betty Miller separate interests, and, in doing so, he has subverted traditional gender expectations. A traditional wife could be thought to be, like Nancy Brace, supportive of her husband, building her ego as she builds his and losing status when he loses social ground. To some extent, the Millers have that kind of relationship, too. They can also be understood as a conflicted, mismatched couple, where one partner gains self-esteem by belittling the other. If Betty Miller were angry with her husband, disappointed when he does nothing to promote himself, their marriage might be seen to fit this formula. Instead, their marriage is a mixture of both: she wishes the best for him, she dislikes his competitor, but she does not hold Miller's defeat in the social arena against him. Yates has made their relationship too complex and real for that.

Understanding Betty Miller is a bit easier because readers are also presented with Nancy Brace, who is a standard for loyal wifely behavior. Even so, Betty Miller is not an easy person to understand. Because this story focuses on Lew Miller, his memories and his thoughts, there is enough temptation to not try to decipher Betty at all, and the fact that she does not fit into standard patterns or expectations discourages getting to know her.

A clue about Betty might be provided in the drunken words of the party's hostess, who repeats, thinking that she is clever, that they should be preparing for "the next war" instead of focusing on the last. As a woman, Betty Miller is as detached from World War II as Lew Miller wishes, unsuccessfully, that he could be himself. She does give a fair effort toward understanding it, either through her own husband's stories or through Brace's, but finds herself unable to feel drawn in as Nancy Brace does. That leaves her looking toward the future in a way that her husband does not, giving her an independent identity that in some sense subverts the stereotype of the good wife.

Source: David Kelly, Critical Essay on "The Canal," in *Short Stories for Students*, Thomson Gale, 2007.

Stewart O'Nan

In the following review, O'Nan praises Yates's collection of stories as "flawless," and comments on the author's deft use of characters on the fringe of society, their illusions, and their disappointment that follows the empty promises of the American dream.

In the years since his death, Richard Yates has been that saddest of literary celebrities, the beloved but forgotten author. What's most shocking about this is that he wrote not one but three great books.

> Yates's fifties stories of young and insecure Americans coming to grips with their less-than-ideal lives presages the work of Raymond Carver, Andre Dubus, and Tobias Wolff."

His early masterpiece, *Revolutionary Road*, has barely remained in print, and his other brilliant novel, *The Easter Parade*, is currently "indefinitely out of stock." His third great book, *Eleven Kinds of Loneliness*, is included in this omnibus collection, along with his later stories from *Liars in Love*, and nine previously uncollected pieces. Michael Chabon isn't alone when he says he hopes this book will do for Richard Yates what Knopf's big red collection did for John Cheever.

It may, and deservedly. The work is there, and still fresh, perhaps even definitive. Yates's fifties stories of young and insecure Americans coming to grips with their less-than-ideal lives presages the work of Raymond Carver, Andre Dubus, and Tobias Wolff. In his signature piece "The Best of Everything," two working-class lovers realize their impending marriage won't solve their problems— that in all probability it will only add to them. Yates's language is stripped down, his tone—like their lives—flat and emotionless: "She tried to sound excited, but it wasn't easy." "Somehow he'd expected more of the Friday before his wedding." That vague sense of letdown colors the story a dingy gray. The characters' mix of hope and resignation is unsettling, yet rings true.

Like those later, more famous writers, Yates is most at home with unheroic characters, people on the fringes—lonely shopgirls and troubled kids, tubercular patients and disgruntled vets. No matter how downtrodden his people are, they still want to believe in their own unrecognized promise. Yates's subject is disappointment, the bitterness that follows our losses, and often our complicity in those failures, our most cherished pretensions leading us astray. His little characters dream big, all the time fearing they're impostors, terrified of being found out. And the world does strip them of their illusions, again and again, sometimes cruelly. Middle-class life is spiritually vacant and economically precarious, the promises America makes are hollow, and yet Yates's people still chase after their impossible, often secondhand ideals.

This is true of the later stories as well. Though Yates wrote well into the mid-eighties, his frame remains the Eisenhower and Kennedy years, his focus the discrepancies between everyday life and the false promises of Wall Street and Hollywood, how we fall for the fleeting illusions of romantic love and money and fame—fitting for someone whose favorite author was Fitzgerald.

And it's all done in a straight-ahead, lucid style, so plainspoken that for a while in the sixties and seventies he was scorned as old-fashioned, behind the times. The eighties vindicated him, but, far from being conservative, his work is subversive, telling us truths we'd rather not contemplate.

As a package, the book is flawless, Richard Russo's introduction strikes exactly the right note, with its anecdote about his mother's never-achieved dream house. The addition of the nine uncollected stories is a bonanza for Yates fans. The best of them, "Evening on the Cote d'Azur," ranks with his finest work (appearing here in *Ploughshares* back in 1976), and even the lesser efforts give the reader a peek at a writer warming to his material. The editor has wisely included them after the published stories rather than before—a mistake that makes the first hundred pages of *The Complete Stories of Flannery O'Connor* a torture.

Even better, Holt has plans to reissue *The Easter Parade* and several other titles in the coming seasons. It's good news for writers and readers who love the widely anthologized "Builders" and "Oh, Joseph, I'm So Tired." It's just a first step, but, with luck, maybe Richard Yates will receive his due.

Source: Stewart O'Nan, Review of *The Collected Stories of Richard Yates*, in *Ploughshares*, Vol. 27, No. 1, Spring 2001, pp. 217–18.

Lee Siegel

In the following essay, Siegel discusses Yates's chronicling of characters "mired in memory" and living the "quiet desperation of unacknowledged lives," his sympathy for his characters, his style, and his neo-naturalistic outlook.

The Culture of Retrieval is inescapable today. There are the ubiquitous memoirists retrieving their early lives, and the songs barely a decade old being remixed, and the children of famous writers and directors and entertainers taking up their parents' occupations (and drawing on their parents' professional connections). We have had *Jane Eyre* the musical, recently on Broadway, a stage revival of *The Producers*, also on Broadway, and a revival of *Hair* (can you imagine?) off-Broadway. There's *The Golden Bowl* on film, a rewrite (if it successfully makes its way through litigation) of *Gone with the Wind*, and at least three small publishers bravely dedicated to reprinting forgotten works by forgotten authors. Americans disrespect the past? Yes and no. We adore the past so intensely that we refuse to let it die, but in fact our indiscriminate homage to it can be a form of disrespect. We are caught in a cycle more inane than vicious. Weakly stimulated by the present, we compulsively return to the past, which has the effect of eclipsing the present, which makes us return to the past.

The inescapability of the past was a thematic obsession of the novelist and short-story writer Richard Yates, and so the publication of the collected short stories—along with the reputation of *Revolutionary Road* and *The Easter Parade*—fits nicely into all this relentless retrospection. It was Yates, in fact, who introduced into American fiction the theme of inertia as catalyst. Portraying characters arrested by their personal histories, mired in memory and thus destined for the most irrationally self-defeating action, he shifted fiction from the Hemingway track back to the Frank Norris track, from realism back to naturalism. That is to say, he brought American fiction from the drama of free will back to the crisis of determining circumstances. In Yates's fiction, childhood and adult memories of what parents wrought exert the same power over the characters' destinies that economic forces did in Norris's *McTeague* or Theodore Dreiser's *Sister Carrie*.

Strangely, you won't ever hear Yates mentioned in connection with the American naturalists. He has most often been compared with Hemingway, the great American realist. And he is an acknowledged influence on the style and sensibility of an entire line of writers—from Raymond Carver through Ann Beattie, Andre Dubus, Tobias Wolff, Richard Russo, Richard Ford, and Jayne Anne Phillips—who consider themselves to have been fathered by Hemingway and, as it were brought up by Yates. These writers have long and eloquently regretted the latter's lapsed reputation and the unavailability (until now) of his work, pointing to his plain, unobtrusive prose and to his bleak take on life (traits that can be traced, in their view, to Hemingway's lapidary sentences and to his Lost Generation pessimism). The present decision—on the part of three separate publishers—to bring Yates back into print can probably be traced to the noble efforts of these writers on his behalf. In 1999, in *Boston Review*, the Yates champion Steward O'Nan predicted that:

> Eventually the books will make it back in print, just as Faulkner's and Fitzgerald's did, and Yates will take his place in the American canon. How this will come about it's impossible to say. Writers and editors are keenly aware of his situation, so perhaps his Malcolm Cowley is just moving up through the ranks at Norton or Doubleday.

Happily, Yates's books are indeed passing back into print. Inevitably, the response will be less a reconsideration than an uncritical celebration, since everybody loves a comeback, and since it is hard to resist an opportunity to redeem a writer whose work was often neglected during his lifetime. But if Yates was a writer of enormous talent, he had no less enormous limitations. By sentimentally ignoring those limitations, we miss the chance to see which of them occur as the necessary outgrowth of his gifts and which occur when his gifts falter.

First, there is Yates's style. His prose is so easy and natural and transparent that it suggests a profound humility before life's inscrutable sadness. Almost ego-less, it recalls Kafka's remark that writing is a form of prayer. And Yates's language bestows upon his men and women, tortured and silenced by life as they are, what might be called a clemency of accurate observation. At times he writes less like an artist than like a witness. His cool humble chronicling of his characters' slow doom (and his characters are almost uniformly doomed) can read like a redemptive freedom in an after-life of art, as in the following passage from *The Easter Parade*, a novel that follows the long, unhappy lives of two sisters, Emily and Sarah Grimes:

> It took only a couple of days for Howard to move his belongings out of the apartment. He was very apologetic about everything. Only once, when he flicked the heavy silken rope of his neckties out of the closet, was there any kind of scene, and that turned into such a dreadful, squalid scene—it ended with her falling on her knees to embrace his legs and begging him, begging him to stay—that Emily did the best she could to put it out of her mind.

The casually cruel flicking of the heavy silken ties is wonderful: Howard is leaving Emily for a younger woman, one who better satisfies his vanity. The repetition of "begging him," representing an abandonment of stylistic neutrality, is the only

> **"** Such an unyielding machinery of pessimism eventually shades into caricature, in much the way that Yates's characters themselves often shade into stereotype. Sometimes it seems that all it would take to bring a liberating light into Yates's world is the sudden appearance of a therapist, or a landscape architect."

slightly false aesthetic note in the passage. Here, Yates's art—the art of the unaverted eye—briefly stumbles on his compassion. This is one of those fascinating moments when literary style becomes a moral, even a philosophical dilemma, no less than the question of whether a photojournalist should intervene on behalf of an innocent subject.

Such a style can be emotionally consoling in the way that it calmly reflects back to us an image of familiar pain, relieving our suffering with the sense that we do not suffer alone, but it is not always spiritually satisfying. Yates's style is very closely tied to the feelings it evokes. Hemingway's, by contrast, evokes an emotion of which he simultaneously makes intellectual sense. His style is no less unobtrusive to the eye, but it is a poeticized plainness, which rubs his character against the reader's mind until the shape of each individual approaches the originality of a new idea. The reason we remember Hemingway's characters is that we've never seen them before; the reason we are moved so powerfully by Yates's characters, who then pass from our minds so quickly, is that we know them so well. Of course, Hemingway was a stoic, and stoicism is an idea that rules the emotions. Yates was a pessimist, and pessimism is a feeling that fends off thought.

In "The B.A.R. Man," now reprinted in *The Collected Stories*, Yates imagines with exquisite pacing and nuance the slow deterioration of an embittered and frustrated ex-soldier, John Fallon. But Fallon's eventual detonation flows from his predictable personality, and it conforms to the feeling that this near stereotype arouses in us. Fallon's fate is, typically, pronounced a certainty from the very first sentence: "Until he got his name on the police blotter, and in the papers, nobody had ever thought much of John Fallon."

The Collected Stories contains seven heretofore unpublished pieces, along with two that appeared in *Ploughshares* in the seventies, but the bulk, and heart, of the book consists of Yates's two story collections, *Eleven Kinds of Loneliness* (arguably his best-known work) and *Liars in Love*. The short form, with its special intensity, throws Yates's virtues and his deficiencies into stark relief. His truly magical storytelling whisks the attention from sentence to sentence, and not a word is wasted. Yet the stories often depend for their unfettered momentum on characterization that verges on stereotype. (Ralph and Gracie in "The Best of Everything" at times seem to be walking and talking on the set of *The Honeymooners*: "Whaddya—crazy?")

Yates's admirable sympathy for the plight of "ordinary people"—secretaries, cabdrivers, office clerks—is often dampened by a narrow emphasis on their ordinariness. The defensively arrogant young writer who narrates "Builders," from *Eleven Kinds of Loneliness*, might take himself to task for regarding Bernie—the cabdriver who has entangled him in his literary fantasies—as a vulgar, obnoxious, intellectually limited "Philistine," imprisoned "in the pathetic delusions of a taxicab driver." But at the end of the story, Bernie is still a pathetic Philistine while the narrator has become a minor hero simply by virtue of his realization that he has been a minor [s——t]. There is something mildly vindictive about Yates's vindications of ordinary people, a streak of schadenfreude running through his horror at their ordeal. Even Yates's famous unflinching depiction of life's cruelty has its flawed underside. His honesty can be less like an artist's truthfulness than like a psychiatrist's candor. Each tale in *Eleven Kinds of Loneliness* is like a deeply affecting icon expressing a variation on a brute existential fact of life. Yet it is as if the loneliness had been gouged raw and bleeding from the body of life, and then processed into art by Yates's systematic pessimism. We are left with the powerful reiteration of an experience rather than its transformation. We are left, like analysands, alone with the harsh illumination of isolated facts.

Call Yates's outlook, and that of his epigones, neo-naturalism. For him, it was the family, rather than the mine, or the factory, or the stockyards, that pulled destiny's strings. Pascal said that people could avoid all the trouble in their lives if they simply stayed in their own rooms. In Yates's world, people can't leave their childhood rooms, no matter how widely they travel the world as adults. This is not their trouble; rather, their trouble is a *fait accompli*, which it is their fictional duty to live out.

The short story "A Glutton for Punishment" is representative in this regard. It tells the tale of a man who as a boy so loved to feign death when playing cops and robbers with other children that he courts and welcomes failure all his life. The internal process driving Yates's characters is frequently so simple that it recalls that old desk gadget with the row of metal balls hanging on strings; by lifting the ball on one end and sending it swinging into the other, the ball at the far end is propelled into the air without moving the ones in between. Indeed, Yates's fictional circumstances are just like those motionless, intermediary balls. They have no weight, no meaning in themselves, except to serve as the kinetic conduit between cause and effect, between past and present, or future, events. Between the first sentence and the last.

The Easter Parade carries this forced march to an extreme. The novel's first sentence is, "Neither of the Grimes sisters would have a happy life, and looking back it always seemed that the trouble began with their parents' divorce." One reads the novel waiting for this judgment—seemingly so cynical as to be naive—to be surprised by some kind of irony or extenuation, but what one encounters instead is a straightforward fictional syllogism that inexorably bears out its premise. Two girls are born to a transient alcoholic mother who is unable to maintain a relationship after the end of her marriage. Sarah Grimes marries an abusive husband and dies an alcoholic; Emily Grimes moves from apartment to apartment, and from job to job, unable to maintain an emotional relationship. *The Easter Parade* boasts what must be the only first sentence in the history of the novel that is also a sentencing.

Such a stranglehold of the personal past is a romanticism in retreat, and Yates stands out among postwar American writers for the breadth of his disappointed romanticism and the distance of his retreat. Bellow, Ellison, Updike, Salinger, Cheever, Malamud, Mailer, Roth, et al., all searched everyday life for a different form of heroism, for a quotidian stoicism, for grace under new kinds of pressure. Yates gave up on everyday life.

When did disappointment become a dominant theme in literature? We cannot say that Dante is disappointed with his life as he wanders through that dark wood. It would be absurd to call Don Quixote disappointed by his futile search for Dulcinea, or Faust disappointed in his quest for absolute happiness and power. Defining events happen in those fictional worlds, and disappointment becomes a describable issue in a world where nothing defining happens. Disappointment attracted literature's attention when the modern world became ordered beyond the individual's comprehension, and when inner life—middle-class, bourgeois life—began to compensate for the lack of outer efficacy. As a response without recourse, an aborted action converted into a mood, disappointment has no outlet, only a terminus. That's why the first and greatest novel of disappointment, *Madame Bovary*, ends with the heroine's suicide.

Since disappointment is a purely mental state, it is one of the more unexpected developments in literature that disappointment should also be one of the great themes of realist fiction. Unmoored as it is from the external world, the mood of disappointment required a new technique. Flaubert invented one. First, he set *Madame Bovary* in the suburbs (back then, they called them "the provinces"), thus providing a reality more easily correlated to a static interior mood than the city could be. Then, in *Madame Bovary*'s celebrated Agricultural Fair scene, he introduced the essentially theatrical device of the ironic contrast into the novel. By juxtaposing the high-flown romantic sentiments that Rodolphe, the adulterous Emma's lover, declares to her, against a local provincial official's pompous speech, and putting alongside this the smell of cow manure, Flaubert incorporated outer reality into the mood of disappointment. He invented a dynamic environment in which to portray the arrest of personal motion.

Yates called *Madame Bovary* one of his two favorite novels (*The Great Gatsby* was the other), and *Revolutionary Road* is a distinct echo of it. Published in 1961, at the height of the postwar exodus from the cities, *Revolutionary Road* was part of a flood of fictions chronicling life in the suburbs that were quickly expanding around New York City. Like Flaubert's work, most of these novels and short stories identified the suburbs with the extinction of human vitality. I can't think of any novel, though, that presents life in the suburbs with as black a monotone as *Revolutionary Road*, the story of Frank and April, a young couple whose dreams founder on their illusions. Of course, novelists instinctively disdain the suburbs for the simple reason that the novel was born in the modern city and the suburbs offer a far more limited field of operations. If it's true, as Irving Howe once wrote, that the troubles of life are the convenience of literature, then the convenience of the suburbs puts a definite crimp in subject matter.

Then, too, in postwar America, the suburbs held out the very same *promesse de bonheur* that romantic novels once dangled before Emma Bovary. If art's job is to puncture deceit with illusion, any writer who takes on the suburbs as an end in itself rather than as a fictional means to incalculable ends will turn out one hostile Ironic Contrast after another. In fact, writers like Updike and Cheever used the suburbs the way Hemingway used the battlefield: not simply as a place but as a place of unfolding. Even Roth's *Goodbye, Columbus*, corrosive satire that it is, allows its characters to do what they would—or what they could—with their environment. Yates portrays the suburbs as an enveloping condition:

> The Revolutionary Hill Estates had not been designed to accommodate a tragedy. Even at night, as if on purpose, the development held no looming shadows and no gaunt silhouettes. It was invincibly cheerful, a toyland of white and pastel houses whose bright, uncurtained windows winked blandly through a dappling of green and yellow leaves. Proud floodlights were trained on some of the lawns, on some of the neat front doors and on the hips of some of the berthed, ice-cream colored automobiles.
>
> A man running down these streets in desperate grief was indecently out of place.

In other words, if their histories don't get Yates's characters, their environment will. Frank, like his father, dies spiritually in a soulless job; April, like her father, dies by her own hand; and all this happens in their house on Revolutionary Road, where America's revolutionary promise withers and dies in the coarse, materialistic suburbs.

Such an unyielding machinery of pessimism eventually shades into caricature, in much the way that Yates's characters themselves often shade into stereotype. Sometimes it seems that all it would take to bring a liberating light into Yates's world is the sudden appearance of a therapist, or a landscape architect.

Yates is a virtuoso craftsman, and his mature style is enviable. We are fortunate to have him back in print. But the quality of his moral outlook will determine his place in American letters. The best place to begin puzzling out the ethic of Yates's aesthetic is *The Easter Parade*, in which Yates suppresses the bloated poeticizing of *Revolutionary Road*, allowing his themes to arise effortlessly from the final pages of the novel.

After a life of unrelieved disappointment, Emily Grimes arrives at the New England home of her nephew, Peter. A newly ordained minister who has recently married and fathered a daughter. Peter is the only person in the Grimes family who seems to have come through. He has escaped his own abusive father and alcoholic mother and made a separate life for himself in a small college town. Sensing that his "Aunt Emmy" has reached the end of her rope, he invites her to stay with his family for an indefinite period of time.

The great naturalist heroines, Zola's Thérèse Raquin, Stephen Crane's Maggie, Dreiser's Carrie, went down swinging. Desire leads Thérèse to murder, and the passionate decay of desire into hatred leads her to suicide; Maggie desperately turns to crime and prostitution to survive; Carrie is borne up by the destruction of the men who seduce her. Even ill-fated Emma Bovary, whom "Aunt Emmy" is meant to put us in mind of, took a willful solace in her illusions—then, too, she summons her own destruction by plunging headlong into her chosen escape. Emily Grimes, on the other hand, has to be the most passive heroine in the history of literature. She does not, in the course of the entire novel, express a single desire of her own, except, pathetically, the desire not to be hurt or disappointed.

Emily is a saint in a world without a God, and so her saintliness has no dignity and her suffering holds no meaning. One wonders whether Yates is pulling the rug out from under the religious impulse itself. The novel, after all, takes its title from the idea of resurrection. Yates, however, offers us a parody of resurrection: a beautiful, hopeful photograph of Emily's sister, Sarah, and her future husband, Tony, taken on Easter Day at the time of their courtship, reappears toward the end of the novel, after the revelation of Tony's wife-beating and Sarah's inherited masochism and alcoholism. It's as if Yates had replaced the idea of resurrection with the concept of the return of the repressed.

The fate of Emily seems, on the surface, more ambiguous. On the brink of a nervous collapse, she tries to turn back from Peter's house and hospitality at the last minute. Peter comes down his driveway after her, and Emily hears "a jingle of pocketed coins

or keys." An instant later, when Peter suddenly realizes the extent of her distress, he asks her if she's tired and then stands "looking at her in a detached, speculative way now, more like an alert young psychiatrist than a priest."

> "Yes, I'm tired," she said. "And do you know a funny thing? I'm almost fifty years old and I've never understood anything in my whole life."
>
> "All right," he said quietly. "All right, Aunt Emmy. Now. Would you like to come in and meet the family?"

Considering that the Grimes sisters' "trouble began with their parents' divorce," Peter's invitation to enter yet another family romance could be read—indeed, almost demands to be read—as the bitterest of ironies. But since he seems happily married, with his family intact, perhaps Emily does stand, if unsteadily, at the threshold of redemption. Yet is it the redemption of religious grace or the promise of "alert" psychoanalytic "understanding" that offers no love or sympathy? Are those the jingling keys to heaven's gate (as Peter's name suggests), or are they the coins of selfishness and greed? It hardly seems to matter. The expectation of grace in a world without God and mere psychiatric understanding in a world without grace are like two sides of an obscene joke. That is Yates's zero-degree ethos.

Such unsparing sobriety makes up the solidity of Yates's achievement. Yates knew how to rivet the reader's attention on the quiet desperation of unacknowledged lives. His unpardonable failure (and perhaps his secret satisfaction) was never to give his implausibly ordinary men and women the freedom to respond.

Source: Lee Siegel, "The Second Coming of Richard Yates," in *Harper's Magazine*, July 2001, pp. 82–87.

Blake Bailey

In the following essay, Bailey gives a critical analysis of Yates's life and work.

For most of his career, Richard Yates seemed always on the brink of gaining the fame he so richly deserved. His first novel, *Revolutionary Road* (1961), was immediately hailed as a masterpiece of realism, a definitive portrait of postwar suburban malaise. William Styron called it "a deft, beautiful novel that deserves to be a classic," and Tennessee Williams said "if more is needed to make a masterpiece in modern American fiction, I am sure I don't know what it is." The novel was nominated for a National Book Award and sold ten thousand copies in hardback, eminently respectable for a literary first novel, all the more so for a novel that many found almost unbearably depressing. "You see yourself here," wrote Fred Chappell in 1971. "When you have an argument with your wife, or with someone who is a bit less articulate than you . . . you begin to hear Frank Wheeler standing inside your voice, expostulating with false earnestness. A glib pompous fat voice with an undertone of hysteria, and it echoes hollow and ridiculous in the most comfortably furnished room."

Yates was also a master of the short story, and many believe that his first collection, *Eleven Kinds of Loneliness* (1962), is an even greater achievement than *Revolutionary Road*. Years after it was first published, *The New York Times Book Review* (1 November 1981) declared it "almost the New York equivalent of *Dubliners*," and pointed out that "the mere mention of its title is enough to produce quick, affirmative nods from a whole generation of readers." On the cover of the 1989 Vintage edition, the writer Ann Beattie called the book "sharply focused, beautifully written and powerfully moving. Deservedly it has become a classic."

But neither a "classic" novel nor a "classic" collection of short stories—and arguably there were more to come—was enough to elevate Yates's reputation among those of the greatest American writers, perhaps because it was only his fellow writers who recognized the magnitude of his achievement. Throughout Yates's career, his more-fortunate colleagues such as Kurt Vonnegut, Styron, Frank Conroy—and others, some of them former students of Yates—were tireless in their efforts to promote his work. With their help he received any number of prestigious grants and awards from the National Endowment of the Arts, the Rockefeller, Rosenthal and Guggenheim foundations, and the National Institute of Arts and Letters. Despite such consistent achievement and critical appreciation, however, Yates's books tended to sell a little more poorly each time they were published, while Yates himself continued to live in tiny furnished apartments in the cities where he happened to have jobs—New York, Washington, Iowa City, Boston, Los Angeles, Wichita, and finally Tuscaloosa. Sometimes the strain, financial and otherwise, became too much, and Yates would disappear into the alcoholism and mental illness that plagued him throughout his adult life, often resulting in long periods of institutional care. A few years before his death, the critic and novelist Carolyn See observed, "He's not going to get the recognition he deserves, because to read Yates is as painful as getting all your teeth filled down to the gum with no anesthetic."

" Perhaps Yates's favorite subject is the depths to which people can deceive themselves into thinking they are somehow special, set apart from the herd."

An absolute realist both in terms of subject and style, what mattered most to Yates was what Hemingway liked to call "writing well and truly"—with extra emphasis, perhaps, on the second adverb. "Dick Yates never compromised with less than the perfect word or less than the whole truth," said his friend E. Barrett Prettyman Jr. The "whole truth" as Yates saw it, however, was hardly conducive to attracting a wide readership. His characters tend to be quietly desperate members of the middle class: attractive, well-educated people who cannot abide their mundane lives in prosperous, postwar America. Trapped in tedious, white-collar jobs, they try to escape from an oppressive sense of their own anonymity by constructing romantic self-images; they convince themselves that they are more creative, intellectual, and sophisticated than most of their bourgeois counterparts, and thus deserve better things. Inevitably, such willful delusion leads to frustration and even disaster, as Yates's characters are made to face the awful truth of who they are and what they have allowed their lives to become.

Richard Walden Yates was born on 3 February 1926 in Yonkers, New York, the son of Vincent Matthew Yates and Ruth (née Maurer) Yates. Both parents were aspiring artists, the mother in particular, and would later serve as models for the manqué strivers who populate Yates's fiction. Vincent Yates studied to be a concert tenor, but was unable to make a living at it, and later became a salesman for General Electric in Schenectady, New York. Ruth Yates fancied herself a sculptor and cultivated her slender talent with what her son considered a foolish and irresponsible tenacity. After she divorced her husband in 1929, she continued to depend on him to subsidize her sculpting career, often at the expense of supporting her children. Yates's mother appears again and again in his fiction, portraits that reflect both his compassion and sometimes scathing bitterness. The importance of this relationship can hardly be overemphasized: it instilled in Yates an overwhelming impulse to expose not only the self-deceit of others, but of himself as well, forcing him to examine his motives, in life as in art, with pitiless objectivity.

Yates's mother insisted on sending her son to a proper New England boarding school, despite the fact that her former husband was hardly in a position to pay for such a wild extravagance. He finally relented when she was able to arrange a scholarship for Richard to Avon Old Farms School—a "funny little school" in Connecticut that was known for accepting misfits whom other schools would not take. Yates's school days are memorialized in his 1978 novel, *A Good School*, where he appears as the inept, disheveled, but somewhat resilient poor boy Bill Grove (a Yates persona who also appears in "Regards at Home" and the 1986 novel *Cold Springs Harbor*). Like Grove, Yates gradually gained a measure of social acceptance at Avon, and during his last two years he was editor of the school newspaper; this experience, he later claimed, was the beginning of his long apprenticeship as a writer.

After his graduation in 1944, Yates was drafted into the army along with most of his classmates. Like Robert Prentice in Yates's autobiographical novel, *A Special Providence* (1969), Yates got off to an awkward start as an eighteen-year-old infantry private in Belgium and France. Tall (six-foot-three inches), skinny, and clumsy, he tried to compensate for his physical shortcomings by flaunting his prep-school wisdom, which invariably provoked the ridicule of his older and less privileged comrades. Eventually Yates learned to keep silent and try to prove himself as a man of action rather than intellect. During the Battle of the Bulge he contracted pleurisy, but refused any immediate medical attention until he collapsed and was taken away by an ambulance. His weakened lungs left him a semi-invalid for the rest of his life.

On his return to New York in 1946, Yates took an apartment in the Village, where he planned to read as much as possible and live the life of a "knockabout intellectual," à la Frank Wheeler in *Revolutionary Road*. As he later reminisced in an article for *The New York Times Book Review* (19 April 1981), "At twenty . . . I embarked on a long binge of Ernest Hemingway that entailed embarrassingly frequent attempts to talk and act like characters in the early Hemingway books. And I was

hooked on T. S. Eliot at the same time, which made for an uncomfortable set of mannerisms." In 1948 he met his first wife, Sheila Bryant, at a party in the Village. Sheila, like Frank Wheeler's wife April, had nursed modest acting ambitions prior to marriage, but was content to sacrifice this aspect of her Village identity for the pleasures of domesticity. But the marriage proved difficult from the start: Yates was soon fired from his job as a rewrite man for the United Press, and his pregnant wife was forced to take secretarial jobs to pay the bills.

Shortly after his daughter Sharon was born in 1950, Yates contracted tuberculosis and spent almost two years in veterans hospitals. As his friend and publisher Seymour Lawrence put it, Yates used the time "to read and read and read. Those hospitals were his Harvard, Yale, and Princeton." Yates's most important discovery was Flaubert: "*Madame Bovary*," he wrote in 1981, "seemed ideally suited to serve as a guide, if not a model, for the novel that was taking shape in my mind. I wanted that kind of balance and quiet resonance on every page, that kind of foreboding mixed with comedy, that kind of inexorable destiny in the heart of a lonely, romantic girl." The novel that was taking shape in Yates's mind, of course, was *Revolutionary Road*, though its slow gestation from draft to painstaking draft took many more years of exhausting, Flaubertian toil. Meanwhile, Yates benefited in another way from his long convalescence, as the experience provided material for two memorable short stories set in tuberculosis wards, "No Pain Whatsoever" and "Out with the Old", that later appeared in his collection, *Eleven Kinds of Loneliness*.

After he was discharged from the hospital, Yates received a veteran's disability pension that allowed him to quit his job and live abroad for two years. It was here that his artistic career began in earnest. As he later put it, "I had nothing to do but write short stories and try to make each one better than the last. I learned a lot." While in Europe, Yates wrote several drafts of at least two dozen stories, eight of which he managed to sell to magazines. The first of these, "Jody Rolled the Bones", was accepted in 1953 by the *Atlantic Monthly* and won the "Atlantic Firsts" award. More important, it attracted the attention of a young editor at the Atlantic Monthly Press, Seymour Lawrence, who encouraged Yates to put aside story-writing and start a novel. In 1956 Yates submitted 130 pages of a draft titled *The Getaway*, about a restless suburban couple who longs to escape to Europe and "discover themselves." Lawrence recommended a contract, but his associates at Atlantic/Little, Brown were less impressed, calling the novel "one of the many imitators of *The Man in the Gray Flannel Suit*." Four years and several drafts later, the book, now titled *Revolutionary Road*, was finally accepted. It was immediately recognized as the work of a major talent, and Yates's life was forever changed. On the one hand, the strain of perfecting the novel—of making "every sentence right, every comma and semicolon in place," as Yates wrote to Lawrence—had taken a toll on his marriage, and he and Sheila were divorced in 1959; but his labors paid off, and in the years ahead Yates would be offered prestigious jobs, anthologies to edit, and the acclaim of his fellow writers.

Eleven Kinds of Loneliness was published the following year, and it consolidated Yates's reputation as a prose stylist and astute observer of postwar American society. As the title suggests, most of the stories are variations on Yates's lifelong themes of disillusionment and isolation—"exercises in the building up and tearing down of expectations," as Jerome Klinkowitz put it in 1986. The first two stories are early treatments of Yates's preoccupation with class differences. In "Doctor Jack-o'-lantern", a well-meaning young teacher tries to make a welfare child named Vincent Sabella feel at home in a suburban Long Island school. Her fourth-graders, however, are already adept at noting the indicators of class, and subject the squirming Vincent to a silent, withering appraisal of his "absurdly new corduroys, absurdly old sneakers and a yellow sweatshirt, much too small, with the shredded remains of a Mickey Mouse design stamped on his chest." When Vincent tries to win their approval by claiming to have seen a movie on everybody's lips, *Dr. Jekyll and Mr. Hyde*, he is ridiculed for his funny accent and obvious lying: "I sore that pitcha. Doctor Jack-o'-lantern and Mr. Hide." After Miss Price privately admonishes him about the importance of telling the truth, he vents his humiliation by scrawling obscenities in an alley behind the classroom. A prissy girl tells the teacher what Vincent has done, and the bewildered Miss Price wonders how to proceed—"sorting out half-remembered fragments of a book she had once read on the subject of seriously disturbed children. Perhaps, after all, she should never have undertaken the responsibility of Vincent Sabella's loneliness." She makes another attempt to reach the boy with a gentle speech about how much he has hurt her, and this seems to have the desired effect. Abjectly remorseful, Vincent leaves the classroom and is accosted by two popular boys, whom he tells with pathetic bravado that the teacher "din say

nothin' . . . She let the ruler do her talkin' for her." The boys are duly impressed, until Miss Price discredits Vincent with a benignly cheerful greeting. This time the boys are unforgiving, and they run away jeering "So long, Doctor Jack-o'-lantern!" Now hopelessly alienated from his more privileged peers, Vincent returns to the alley behind the classroom and draws a grotesque nude over the title "Miss Price."

"The Best of Everything" is another study of miscommunication between people of different social backgrounds. Grace is a sensitive office girl who has been educated in the ways of refined snobbery by her sophisticated roommate, Martha. When Grace is courted by a loutish young man of humble means named Ralph, the roommate dismisses him as the sort of guy who says "terlet" for "toilet" and whose mother keeps "those damn little china elephants on the mantelpiece." For a while Grace obediently tries to avoid him, but he persists, and one night at an American Legion dance she decides to marry him when he croons "Easter Parade" in her ear. (This song is a central motif in Yates's later novel of the same name, where it serves a similar purpose of evoking an ideal of romance that is inevitably shattered by reality.) When her roommate realizes that Grace's mind is made up, she tries to make amends for her earlier insensitivity by giving the couple a chance to be alone together in the apartment. Perhaps in homage to Martha's generosity, Grace decides to do the "sophisticated" thing by giving herself to Ralph before the wedding, and waits for him in a negligée. Ralph, however, has been out with the boys and can only "stay a minute" before he rejoins them. On his way out he says to his disappointed, but now quite resigned, bride-to-be, "I'm fulla beer. Mind if I use ya terlet?"

A more subtle handling of similar themes is found in "A Really Good Jazz Piano", a story Yates revised over the course of several years; it stands as one of the masterpieces of this collection. The protagonists, Carson Wyler and Ken Platt, are Yale graduates whiling away their early twenties in Europe. As with many of Yates's more-memorable characters, they are both nuanced individuals and utterly recognizable types—young men who seem to share the somewhat shallow, liberal-minded assumptions of their class and time, but who turn out to be almost as different on the inside as out: "Carson was the handsome one, the one with the slim, witty face and the English-sounding accent; Ken was the fat one who laughed all the time and tagged along." As the story opens, Ken calls his friend from Cannes, where he has spent a desperately lonely month while Carson has stayed in Paris to pursue a Swedish art student. Hoping to coax Carson into joining him, Ken announces that he has discovered a first-rate jazz pianist in one of the seaside bars: "He's a friend of mine," Ken says, and Carson assumes the man is black—"mostly from the slight edge of self-consciousness or pride" in Ken's voice when he calls the man "a friend."

Carson goes to Cannes and Ken introduces him to his discovery, Sid, who is indeed black and a superb musician. Carson (who has "the ability to find and convey an unashamed enjoyment in trivial things") sponsors the pianist for membership in the International Bar Flies, which involves a ritual of brushing each other's lapels and saying, "*Bzzz, bzzz!*" Ken, meanwhile, basks in Carson's approval for having made such a rare find—a black musician who possesses "*authentic* integrity," as Ken puts it, who practices his art in obscurity rather than "selling out" to the commercial shoddiness of America. As it happens, though, Sid is all too eager to sell out, and the two friends are appalled to find him truckling to a vulgar agent named Murray Diamond. When Sid pauses during his performance to give Carson the Bar Flies greeting, the latter humiliates him in front of the agent by sarcastically touching his shoulder and saying, "Buzz . . . Does that take care of it?" Ken is stunned by his friend's cruelty; on the verge of attacking him in the street, he is stopped by the look on Carson's face—"haunted and vulnerable and terribly dependent, trying to smile, a look that said Please don't leave me alone." One is left with the impression that the feckless Ken will benefit far more from his *Wanderjahr* in Europe than his worldly friend.

Perhaps Yates's favorite subject is the depths to which people can deceive themselves into thinking they are somehow special, set apart from the herd. In his later fiction he would usually reserve his scrutiny for the arty strivers of the middle class, but in "A Wrestler with Sharks" and "Builders" he focuses on working-class people whose humble lot in life makes them all the more susceptible to illusions of grandeur. In the first story, a former sheet-metal worker with writerly pretensions, Leon Sobel, takes a job with a dismal trade-union tabloid called *The Labor Leader*. Yates sketches this character with a few deft strokes: "He was . . . a very small, tense man with black hair that seemed to explode from his skull and a humorless thin-lipped face. . . . His eyebrows were always in motion when he talked, and his eyes, not so much piercing as anxious to pierce, never left the eyes of the listener."

The narrator, a clever young man named McCabe who considers his employment on the *Leader* as strictly temporary, regards Sobel with a kind of polite condescension as the man confides that he is already the author of nine unpublished books: "Novels, philosophy, political theory—the entire gamut," Sobel explains. "The trouble with my books is, they tell the truth. And the truth is a funny thing, McCabe. People wanna read it, but they only wanna read it when it comes from somebody they already know their name." Sobel is determined to make a name for himself by writing for the *Leader*, and after agonizing over paltry news items with such headlines as "PLUMBERS WIN 3¢ PAY HIKE," he is rewarded with an offer to write a column of his own on "labor gossip." His first (and last) effort, however, is laughably pretentious; titled "SOBEL SPEAKING," and attached to "a small portrait of himself in a cloth hat," the column proclaims its author to be "an 'ink-stained veteran' of many battles on the field of ideas, to be exact nine books have emanated from his pen." The editor rejects the piece amid much ridicule in front of the staff, and Sobel promptly quits. McCabe, sorry for his hapless former colleague, calls Sobel at home that night to suggest a possible opening at an even more dismal trade journal, but Sobel's wife answers and curtly refuses the offer. Taken aback by the woman's obvious, dignified devotion to her husband, the chastened McCabe is left "to climb guilty and sweating out of the phone booth."

In an interview for *Ploughshares* (December 1972) Yates described the last story of the collection, "Builders," as a "direct autobiographical blowout" that was sufficiently "objectified" to work as good fiction, and which emboldened him to make similar use of such material throughout his career. The protagonist, Robert Prentice (who also appears in a less successful work, *A Special Providence*, is a struggling writer who is "clearly and nakedly" a portrait of the artist as a rather callow young man. The story evokes Yates's early career in the Village, when he continued to pattern his life after Hemingway's—they both had been to war, skipped college, worked for a newspaper, and married young—though Yates's apprentice fiction showed little evidence of Hemingwayesque precocity. As Prentice/Yates remarks in the story, "it wasn't any 'Up in Michigan' that came out of my machine; it wasn't any 'Three Day Blow,' or 'The Killers'; very often, in fact, it wasn't really anything at all. . . ."

Prentice finally gets a break of sorts when he answers an ad placed by a middle-aged cabbie named Bernie Silver, who offers an "unusual free-lance opportunity" to a writer with "imagination." The man proposes that Prentice ghostwrite a series of stories featuring a romanticized version of himself, Bernie Silver, as a heroic cabbie who changes the lives of his clients with bits of wise advice given in the nick of time. The "builders" metaphor reflects Bernie's approach to writing a well-made story; as he lectures Prentice, "Do you see where writing a story is building something too? Like building a house? . . . Before you build your walls you got to lay your foundation—and I mean all the way down the line." Finally, says Bernie, the most important aspect of the whole enterprise is the "windows": "Where does the light come in? . . . I mean the-the *philosophy* of your story; the *truth* of it. . . ." Prentice, desperate for money, conceals his disdain for the humbling assignment and becomes an earnest "builder" of Bernie's pathetically self-aggrandizing fictions. With a craftsmanship that surprises no one so much as himself, he writes about a delinquent who is saved from a life of crime by Bernie's folksy ruminations "about healthy, clean-living, milk-and-sunshine topics," as well as a story about "a small, fragile old gentleman" who almost succumbs to lonely, suicidal despair, until Bernie convinces him that he should go live with his daughter in Michigan. Bernie is delighted with these efforts, but, predictably enough, the project goes nowhere, and the two eventually fall out over money. At the end Prentice looks back over his story and wonders whether he has built it according to Bernie's rigorous specifications; he then adds the "chimney top"—the fact that he and his wife divorced shortly after the episode in question. "And where are the windows?" he wonders. "God knows, Bernie; God knows there certainly ought to be a window around here somewhere, for all of us."

On the strength of his first two books Yates was invited in 1964 to teach at the prestigious Writers' Workshop at the University of Iowa. By most accounts, he was an excellent teacher. He had "an instinctive and profound acuity when it came to seeing the heart of a story," as his student DeWitt Henry puts it, though some speak more ambivalently of Yates's almost obsessive "hectoring about the precision of language." In any case Yates took his teaching duties seriously, and his dedication—coupled with his heavy drinking—interfered with work on his second novel, *A Special Providence*. When it was finally published in 1969, it was a failure both critically and financially; the book was never reprinted, though Yates later came to regard it as a good learning experience in the writing of

properly objectified fiction. As he said in the *Ploughshares* interview, he "never did achieve enough fictional distance on the character of Robert Prentice," and thus failed to avoid "both of the two terrible traps that lie in the path of autobiographical fiction—self-pity and self-aggrandizement."

Yates's third novel, *Disturbing the Peace* (1975), took almost as much time to finish as his second, and by the early 1970s his drinking was worse than ever. He was constantly short of money, and in 1971 he was denied tenure at Iowa. For the rest of his life Yates would have a hard time finding new teaching appointments, as word of his alcoholism and precarious mental health was passed from one campus to the next. A manic-depressive, Yates tended to mix psychotropic drugs with alcohol during times of stress, which led to frequent breakdowns as he got older. His second marriage, to Martha Speer in 1968, was a casualty of his increasingly bizarre behavior, and in 1975 the couple divorced.

Always resilient in the practice of his craft, however, Yates's chaotic private life was ameliorated somewhat by several promising developments in his career. *Disturbing the Peace* was published the same year as his divorce, and helped to restore his reputation after the failure of his second novel. He was awarded a grant from the National Institute of Arts and Letters that enabled him to quit teaching for a few years and move back to New York, where he began work on what would prove to be one of his greatest novels, *The Easter Parade* (1976), which he finished in a miraculous (for Yates) eleven months. Reviews of the book were among the best Yates ever got: once again he was applauded as one of America's foremost realists, a true craftsman holding the line against the gathering tide of tricky postmodernism.

A Good School was published to respectful reviews in 1978, when Yates moved to Boston. He took a tiny, two-room apartment on Beacon Street, which his friend Andre Dubus remembers as a spartan testament to Yates's total devotion to his art: "It was a place that should be left intact when Dick moved, a place that young writers should go to, and sit in, and ask themselves whether or not their commitment to writing had enough heart to live, thirty years later, as Dick's did: with time as his only luxury, and absolute honesty one of his few rewards."

In 1981 Yates published his second story collection, *Liars in Love*, which was widely and admiringly reviewed amid somewhat meager sales.

Most of the stories are unabashedly autobiographical; by the time they were written Yates's mother and sister had been dead for almost ten years, and he felt increasingly free to write candidly about his difficult family life as a child and young adult. Characters based on his mother had played prominent, rather unsympathetic roles in *A Special Providence* and *The Easter Parade*, but in the first and perhaps best story of this collection, "Oh, Joseph, I'm So Tired", she is portrayed with more compassion as Yates's resentment seems to have been tempered over time. (It is worth noting, however, that his final portrait of his mother in *Cold Springs Harbor* is unflattering as ever, perhaps reflecting Yates's ultimate verdict on the woman; in any case, his daughter Monica claims that Yates felt he had finally "gotten her right" in that last novel.)

"Oh, Joseph, I'm So Tired" is based on an actual incident wherein Yates's mother, in what would prove to be the biggest break of her dubious career, was given the opportunity to sculpt a bust of the newly elected Franklin D. Roosevelt in 1933. In the story Yates is quick to point out that she "wasn't a very good sculptor," and punctures the petty snobbery that lay behind her artistic aspirations: "Her idea was that any number of rich people, all of them gracious and aristocratic, would soon discover her: they would want her sculpture to decorate their landscaped gardens, and they would want to make her their friend for life." Meanwhile, the family lives in a gracious courtyard apartment, which they can scarcely afford, on Bedford Street in the Village, dominated by the mother's "high, wide, light-flooded studio." Her basic priorities are further suggested by "the roach-infested kitchen . . . barely big enough for a stove and sink that were never clean, and for a brown wooden icebox with its dark, ever-melting block of ice." The mother's best friend and pretentious alter ego is a woman named Sloane Cabot—a name she made up for herself "because it had a touch of class"—who works as a Wall Street secretary while she pursues her ambition of writing for the radio. Her meager talent and essential vulgarity are revealed by a mawkishly wishful script about an "enchanted circle of friends" who live around a courtyard in the Village, gamely enduring their genteel poverty as they await the artistic success that is just around the corner. The narrator remembers how he himself was described in the script as "a sad-eyed, seven-year-old philosopher" with a comical stutter, and reflects: "It was true that I stuttered badly . . . but I hadn't expected anyone to put it on the radio."

The mother withdraws her children from public school after they come home with lice in their hair, and arranges for them to be tutored at home by a poor Jewish violinist named Bart Kampen. The children are delighted: "Bart was probably our favorite among the adults around the courtyard. He was . . . young enough so that his ears could still turn red when he was teased by children; we had found that out in teasing him once or twice about such matters as that his socks didn't match." Kampen proves to be an excellent tutor, gentle and patient, but the arrangement comes to a disastrous end when the mother learns about an offhand remark he has made about "some rich, dumb, crazy woman" who has hired him to tutor her kids. The mother hears this gossip from a mutual acquaintance in Washington, D.C.,where she has just presented her bust to the president amid a decided lack of fanfare; with insult added to the injury of an already crushing disappointment, the narrator imagines his mother's thoughts during the long train ride back to New York: "She was forty-one, an age when even romantics must admit that youth is gone, and she had nothing to show for the years but a studio crowded with green plaster statues that nobody would buy." The mother puts on a brave front for her children's benefit, pretending that her encounter with the president was a thrilling success, but then proceeds to nurse her grievance against Kampen with alcohol. Finally she confronts him with drunken bitterness: "All my life I've hated people who say 'Some of my best friends are Jews,'" she tells the startled Kampen. "Because *none* of my friends are Jews, or ever will be." The worst of his mother's nature thus revealed, the son lies in bed and ponders his family's entangled fate: "We would probably never see Bart again—or if we ever did, he would probably not want to see us. But our mother was ours; we were hers; and we lived with that knowledge as we lay listening for the faint, faint sound of millions."

"Regards at Home" is the story of how Yates eventually liberated himself from his mother some sixteen years later. Appearing as Bill Grove, he looks back at his postwar years in the Village, when his plans "to become a professional writer as soon as possible" were constantly waylaid by the obligation to care for his indigent, aging, hard-drinking mother. Though as a child Grove had "admired the way she made light of money troubles"—she stressed the romance of their poverty by reading Dickens to them in bed—he now begins to lose patience with the "childish and irresponsible" older woman who makes little effort to support herself and with whom he is forced to share his tiny apartment. After she threatens to complicate his life further by driving away the woman Grove intends to marry, he borrows some money from the bank and gives it to his mother: "I told her, in so many words, that she was on her own."

Grove's eagerness to free himself is contrasted with the filial piety of his friend and coworker, Dan Rosenthal, a talented artist who postpones his ambitions for the sake of a dependent family. For his part, Rosenthal envies the illusive freedom of Grove's life as a would-be writer living in the Village with a pretty wife—which in fact is anything but the idyllic "bohemian" affair that Rosenthal thinks it is: Grove's wife and he fight constantly, while the mother continues to be an obnoxious presence in their lives. Finally, when Grove wangles a veteran's pension to go abroad and pursue his writing career in earnest, he comes to realize his own good—if relatively selfish—fortune: "I had luck, time, opportunity, a young girl for a wife, and a child of my own." After a farewell party on the ship, Rosenthal advises him not to "piss it all away," and Grove hurries back to his cabin to "get my mother off the boat . . . and to take up the business of my life."

The title story of *Liars in Love* takes up where "Regards at Home" leaves off, with the Yates-like protagonist—here called Warren Mathews—living in London with his wife and two-year-old daughter. By now the daily ennui and cramped quarters of their tiny basement flat have combined to worsen the couple's differences until they can hardly even bring themselves to quarrel anymore; instead they pass the time in an atmosphere of tense civility as they try to avoid "getting in each other's way. 'Oh, sorry,' they would mutter after each clumsy little bump or jostle. 'Sorry. . . .'" Presently the wife decides to return to the States with their daughter, and Warren spends his first night alone in the flat pathetically winding the crank of a cardboard music box that his daughter has left behind.

The story is one of Yates's most memorable studies of the effects of loneliness, the way it can warp a person's sense of reality. Warren's attempts to make some kind of human connection in London are forever thwarted by an inescapable feeling of alienation: "The very English language, as spoken by natives, bore so little relation to his own that there were far too many opportunities for missed points in every exchange. Nothing was clear." Desperate, Warren forces himself to pick up one of the prostitutes in Piccadilly Circus, and they return to the woman's shabby flat in northeast London; glad enough for the company, he tries "to keep an open mind" as the woman, Christine, tells well-practiced lies about her life as a prostitute and, later, about the baby whose crib occupies a conspicuous corner of the room.

Soon Warren's life is enmeshed with Christine's, which involves socializing with her fellow prostitutes as well as a jovial pimp named Alfred. At first, in true Yatesian fashion, he is able to accept the whole gloomy business with the help of some romantic self-flattery: "Nobody had to tell him what a triumph of masculinity it was to have a young whore offer herself to you free of charge. He didn't even need *From Here to Eternity* to tell him that. . . ." Ultimately, though, it occurs to Warren that the woman is maneuvering him into marriage, in the hope of giving her baby a father, and he tries to disentangle himself. She responds with an angry warning that her pimp is out to get him, but when Warren learns that this is a lie—indeed, that almost everything the woman says is a lie—he is no longer intimidated: "She was only a dumb little London streetwalker, after all." Free at last, Warren reconciles with his wife and prepares to return to New York, anxious to leave an alien world and his youthful naiveté behind.

"Saying Goodbye to Sally" returns to the theme of the title story and, to some extent, the entire collection—the lies that people tell themselves in the hope of escaping loneliness. This time the Yates surrogate is named Jack Fields, a writer whose first novel took five years to write and "left him feeling reasonably proud but exhausted almost to the point of illness." Fields's book is a critical success but sells poorly, and he is reduced to doing hackwork and drinking heavily. Before long, however, he is saved by an offer to go to Hollywood and write a screenplay based on a much-admired novel—just as Yates was in 1962, when he adapted Styron's 1951 novel *Lie Down in Darkness* for the director John Frankenheimer. The latter appears in the story as Carl Oppenheimer, "a dramatic, explosive, determinedly tough-talking man of thirty-two," who bolsters his wunderkind status by acting the role of the blustery, hard-drinking "genius" while telling F. Scott Fitzgerald anecdotes for Fields's benefit.

Fields (who "had begun to see himself, not without a certain literary satisfaction, as a tragic figure") identifies strongly with Fitzgerald, all the more so when he begins to have an affair with a pretty Hollywood secretary in her mid thirties named Sally Baldwin. Fields views the woman as a Sheilah Graham substitute—the sort of throw-away romance that a great writer on the skids, à la Fitzgerald, might enjoy as he pulls himself together to write another masterpiece. Sally lives amid the garish opulence of a friend's house in Malibu, and soon Fields finds himself immersed in a nouveau-riche ménage only slightly more appealing than Warren Mathews's circle of prostitutes in "Liars in Love". Sally's housemate and fellow divorcée, Jill Jarvis, is a dim-witted vulgarian who neglects her young son while conducting a boozy affair with an oafish engineer named Cliff Myers. Finally, when Fields has seen enough, he determines to abandon Sally and her whole milieu in a way that leaves no hard feelings, taking her out for a last romantic dinner at a fancy restaurant. He tries to play the role of the gracious, worldly charmer, but Sally is not appeased by his patronizing compliments about her dress, and makes a remark that suggests she has seen through his pretensions from the start: The dress, she says, "might be useful in helping me trap the *next* counterfeit F. Scott Fitzgerald who comes stumbling out to Movieland." In the end the two seem equally relieved to relinquish their latest illusions and get on with their lives.

Following the critical success of *Liars in Love*, Yates spent the next three years working on his most ambitious novel since *Revolutionary Road*. Indeed, *Young Hearts Crying* (1984) resembled his first novel almost too closely: it, too, was the story of a promising young couple who are gradually chastened by the world, who try to transcend the sterility of their middle-class lives with artistic achievement that never quite materializes. Critics made much of the similarity between the two books, and tended to note the relative inferiority of *Young Hearts Crying* as evidence of Yates's faltering skills: some pointed out that the novel lacked the taut craftsmanship of *Revolutionary Road*, while its protagonists almost amounted to parodies of the brilliantly conceived Frank and April Wheeler. Yates was especially upset by Anatole Broyard's review in *The New York Times Book Review* (28 October 1984), the gist of which is suggested by its derisive headline, "Two-Fisted Self-Pity". Yates and Broyard had been friends in the Village during the 1960s, and Yates saw the review as an act of betrayal.

By the mid 1980s Yates's financial situation was desperate: his books almost invariably failed to earn back their advances, a situation his publisher had been willing to tolerate because of the prestige of his name. But in recent years Yates had begun borrowing against future advances, until all parties concerned were thoroughly fed up. "Can you imagine how I feel," his agent Mitch Douglas wrote in an exasperated letter to Yates's publisher, Jackie Farber, "when Richard Yates tells me that he has lost fifteen pounds and looks like a concentration camp victim because he has had to survive the past few weeks on two eggs mixed in a glass of milk, and that he was going to have to go back in the hospital simply to have food to eat?" After the commercial failure of his last novel, *Cold Springs Harbor*, Yates moved to Los Angeles, where a former student, David Milch, offered him work writing treatments for television pilots. Though he affected to be grateful, Yates resented the flamboyant Milch, a successful television producer who apparently made little effort to conceal his role as patron and rescuer. For almost three years Yates failed to produce a salable treatment, and finally Milch ended their arrangement in 1989.

Yates's writing came to his rescue one last time. On the strength of his work in progress—a novel titled *Uncertain Times*, based on his experience as Robert Kennedy's speechwriter in 1963—his publisher offered Yates a two-book contract with an advance on signing and thirty-three equal monthly payments. The next year Yates accepted a one-year appointment to teach at the University of Alabama at Tuscaloosa. He tried heroically to attend to his teaching and get some writing done, but by then he had emphysema and could not breathe without an oxygen tank. He felt alert enough to write for only an hour or so a day, which was hardly enough for a man who typically took that long to adjust the wording of a single sentence. Finally, in November 1992, Yates traveled to the Birmingham VA hospital for minor surgery on a hernia, where he died of suffocation shortly after the operation.

"He drank too much, he smoked too much, he was accident-prone, he led an itinerant life, but as a writer he was all in place," said Seymour Lawrence, "He wrote the best dialogue since John O'Hara, and like O'Hara he was a master of realism, totally attuned to the nuances of American behavior and speech." This statement is an accurate assessment of Yates's achievement, and it is a pity that his excellent work is now in danger of being forgotten; one would like to remind the literate reading public that a body of superb books awaits their discovery, and that a singular man overcame drastic odds to write them. As Jayne Anne Phillips noted, perhaps a bit too hopefully, "Yates prevailed beyond his own lifetime, just as he intended. His work stands for him, essentially American, unassailable, triumphant."

Source: Blake Bailey, "Richard Yates," in *Dictionary of Literary Biography*, Vol. 234, *American Short-Story Writers Since World War II, Third Series*, edited by Patrick Meanor and Richard E. Lee, The Gale Group, 2001, pp. 295–304.

Sources

"The Best Books of 2001," in *Esquire*, December 2001, p. 34.

De Falbe, John, "Grace Still under Pressure," in *Spectator*, January 2002, pp. 36–37.

DeZelar-Tiedman, Christine, Review of *The Collected Stories of Richard Yates*, in *Library Journal*, March 15, 2001, p. 1230.

Hooper, Brad, Review of *The Collected Stories of Richard Yates*, in *Booklist*, March 1, 2001, p. 110.

Yates, Richard, "The Canal," in *The Collected Stories of Richard Yates*, Holt, 2001, pp. 367–79.

Further Reading

Bailey, Blake, *A Tragic Honesty: The Life of Richard Yates*, Methuen Publishing, 2004.

As of 2006, this work is considered the definitive biography of Yates, written by a man who is a preeminent Yates scholar.

Castronovo, David, and Steven Goldleaf, *Richard Yates*, Twayne Publishers, 1996.

A scholarly review of Yates's work, this survey of criticism was published after the author's death but before the publication of *The Collected Stories* helped to rejuvenate his neglected reputation.

Simon, Linda, "Twenty-Seven Kinds of Loneliness: The Short Fiction of Richard Yates," in *World and I*, Vol. 16, No. 12, December 2001, pp. 239–44.

Ostensibly a review of the *Collected Stories*, this long essay contains a good overview of Yates's work and the esteem in which he is held.

Yates, Richard, "Excerpts from the Correspondence of Richard Yates and Barbara Singleton Beury, September 1960–November 1961," in *Harvard Review*, No. 25, Fall 2003, pp. 64–77.

This series of letters written in the early sixties shows Yates at his most charming and infuriatingly nonsensical. His triumphant novel, *Revolutionary Road*, had just been published, and he was drinking heavily and driving himself toward a nervous breakdown that would send him to the Men's Violence Ward at Bellevue Hospital.

The English Pupil

Andrea Barrett

1996

"The English Pupil" by Andrea Barrett appears in Barrett's highly acclaimed collection of eight stories, *Ship Fever and Other Stories* (1996). Like all the stories in the book, this one is about science and scientists, and it focuses on the Swedish botanist Carl Linnaeus (1707–1778). Linnaeus was famous for the innovative way in which he classified and named the three kingdoms of the natural world, animal, vegetable, and mineral. His work marked the dawn of a new era in natural history. Linnaeus also sent many of his pupils on travels all over the world, where they discovered new species, used Linnaeus's methods to classify them, and brought specimens back to Sweden.

"The English Pupil" is set at Hammarby, Linnaeus's country estate in 1777, when he is old and confused and has only a few weeks to live. He looks back on his life with a mixture of pride and regret. Barrett skillfully distills a wealth of significant historical and scientific facts about Linnaeus and his followers and weaves them into a compelling narrative that explores not only Linnaeus's life and work but also the depth and complexity of the relationships between the old master and his young disciples, many of whom died on their travels.

Author Biography

Andrea Barrett was born on November 16, 1954, in Boston, Massachusetts, the daughter of Walter

Barrett and Jacquelyn Knifong. She grew up on Cape Cod, within walking distance of the ocean and always had a love of the sea.

Barrett did not finish her high school education. In the fall of her junior year, she started applying to colleges, and she left high school at the end of her junior year. She was accepted by Union College in Schenectady, New York, without a high school diploma. Barrett graduated from Union College with a Bachelor of Science degree in biology.

Barrett planned to become a biologist and enrolled in graduate studies in zoology at the University of Massachusetts. But she dropped out during the first semester. Later, she took graduate classes in medieval and Reformation theological history.

It was not until after her formal studies that Barrett started writing. She did not attend any writing school but taught herself how to write fiction through trial-and-error.

Barrett's first novel was *Lucid Stars* (1988), in which she tells the story of the breakup of an American family over a period of twenty years. In her second novel, *Secret Harmonies* (1989), Barrett tells the story of a family in rural western Massachusetts struggling to make sense of their lives.

In *The Middle Kingdom* (1991), Barrett's third novel, an unhappily married American woman on a 1986 visit to Beijing with her husband becomes fascinated with China, makes Chinese friends, and discovers a way to happiness and self-understanding. Barrett's fourth novel, *The Forms of Water* (1993), tells the story of several generations of a family living in upstate New York.

At about the time of the publication of this novel, Barrett had started to teach college creative writing courses. She was reading many short stories, a genre she had always loved, and studying them closely, in addition to reading her students' stories. She wanted to learn how to write short stories herself, and this desire was the origin of her first collection of stories, *Ship Fever and Other Stories*, which was published in 1996. All the stories in the collection, which includes "The English Pupil," are about science and scientists. *Ship Fever* won the National Book Award for fiction and put Barrett firmly in the literary limelight.

In 1997, Barrett used a Guggenheim foundation grant to do research for her next novel by traveling to Baffin Island, the largest island in the Canadian Arctic. The resulting novel was *The Voyage of the Narwhal* (1998), the story of a nineteenth-century Arctic expedition that is based on Barrett's historical and scientific research.

Andrea Barrett   AP Images

Barrett's second collection of stories, *Servants of the Map*, was published by Norton in 2002. It was a Pulitzer Prize finalist in fiction in 2003. In the same year, Barrett received the Award in Literature from the American Academy of Arts and Letters.

Barrett has taught in the MFA program for writers at Warren Wilson College in Swannanoa, North Carolina; as of 2006, she was teaching at Williams College in Williamstown, Massachusetts.

Married to biologist Barry Goldstein, Barrett enjoys a leisure interest in playing African percussion instruments. In Rochester, New York, where they lived as of 2006, she and her husband played in a local musical group.

Plot Summary

"The English Pupil" begins outside the town of Uppsala, Sweden, on a very cold late December afternoon in 1777. Carl Linnaeus, the famous naturalist, who is now seventy years old and dying, is riding in a horse-drawn sleigh. He orders his coachman to take him to his country estate, Hammarby, which lies beyond city limits. The coachman agrees only reluctantly, since he has been told by his employers not to take the sleigh outside of the city.

Linnaeus watches the landscape go by and thinks of Lappland, which he had explored when he was in his mid-twenties, learning about the natural world, which had amazed him with its beauty.

Linnaeus has suffered a series of strokes and now his once-famous memory has almost gone. He tends to forget what he is doing and where he is, he cannot remember the names of plants and animals or of places and people. His legs, one arm, his bladder and part of his face are paralyzed. He can barely speak.

When they arrive at Hammarby, Pehr, the coachman, lifts Linnaeus up and carries him into the house. Then he unhitches the horses from the sleigh and shoves the sleigh into the house, near the fireplace. He lifts Linnaeus back into the sleigh and begins to light a fire. Then after Linnaeus gestures toward his tobacco and pipe, Pehr lights the pipe and places it in Linnaeus's mouth. Linnaeus is happy to be at Hammarby; no one but Pehr knows where he is.

Linnaeus remembers his favorite dog, Pompey, who is now dead, and the names of some of his students, those whom he had taught at the university in Uppsala as well as private students who had come to Hammarby. They were of many nationalities, including an Englishman, who, Linnaeus thinks, is "still around." He remembers taking the students out to the botanical gardens in the city and keeping them there for twelve or thirteen hours at a stretch.

Pehr interrupts his thoughts, saying that his family will be looking for him. Linnaeus knows this is true and reflects that his family always wants something from him. His wife, Sara Lisa, always told him there was not enough money, and she was worried about their son, Carl Junior, who is lazy, and their three daughters, who need new clothes.

Linnaeus thinks back to his achievements in creating a system for the naming of plants. He had named almost everything, and he had become famous.

A man and a woman arrive at the house. Linnaeus thinks the woman must be his daughter Sophia, and the man may be her husband, although he has no memory of a wedding. The man then introduces himself as Rotheram, one of his pupils. Then Linnaeus's mind seems to wander, and he wonders whether the man is another student, maybe Lofling, or Christopher Ternström, or Hasselquist or Falck.

Sophia says they have been looking everywhere for him, and the young man raises him gently to a sitting position. Linnaeus's mind wanders, and he thinks back to the exploits of several of his pupils, when they and he were young. He imagines the young man is Christopher Ternström, who had sailed to the East Indies and eventually died of a tropical fever on an island off Cambodia. Then he imagines he is Fredrik Hasselquist, who had traveled widely gathering plants and animals and keeping a precise diary, and who had died when he was thirty. He remembers other students also, who had managed to return alive from their travels. He remembers a pupil named Rolander and wonders whether that is the man who is with him now. Rolander had lost his mind in Surinam and had come home with insects and seeds which he claimed to be pearls and which had been mistakenly washed away by the gardener. Linnaeus thinks he is still alive and living in Denmark on charity.

Sophia asks him why he did not come back, and the man asks Pehr how long Linnaeus has been weeping. Linnaeus wonders whether the man is Lofling, who had tutored his son, Carl Junior. Lofling had traveled widely and made a name for himself as a naturalist before dying of fever in Spain.

As Sophia asks her father if he is happy and strokes his hands, he remembers more of his "apostles," as he calls them, students who had traveled the world as an extension of himself: "extra eyes and hands and feet, observing, gathering, naming."

He remembers Pehr Forskal, who traveled to Egypt and made a fine collection of new plants in Cairo; he died of plague in Arabia. He remembers Falck, too, who had traveled to St. Petersburg and beyond. Lonely and depressed in Kazan, he had shot himself.

Outside, it has begun to rain, and the man whom Linnaeus thinks of as Rotheram says they must leave now because the rain is ruining the track.

Linnaeus again remembers the student with a similar name—Rolander, who carried on his research even though on his way to Surinam he had been struck down with dysentery. Linnaeus remembers Kahler and Hasselquist and Pehr Kalm. He remembers the principles on which his system of naming was based and which he had passed on to his pupils. His apostles, he thinks, "had taken wing like swallows, but they had failed to return." He had a theory about swallows, that in the winter, they lived below the ice in lakes, waiting for spring. He had argued with a colleague over this theory, and he relishes the fact that he triumphed over all those who had opposed his work.

Linnaeus sees in his mind a group of men on the left of the fire. He thinks they are the students he has previously thought of, but there is another man there as well, whose name was Carl Thunberg. Thunberg had traveled to Japan, where he learned about Japanese flora on the island of Deshima. Thunberg was the pupil who kept in touch with Linnaeus most regularly, sending letters and herbarium specimens home and scrupulously following Linnaeus's methods.

Linnaeus listens as the men standing around him relate some of their stories. Thunberg describes the Japanese people and their gardens; Hasselquist tells him of Palestine; Lofling describes the tropics, and Forskal describes Alexandria. Falck and Kahler also make remarks. Linnaeus silently conjures up some memories of his own.

Sophia tells him that they must leave now. Linnaeus sees his apostles holding leaves, twigs, and blossoms, all named by them on his advice. They are excitedly exchanging them among themselves. But he notices that Sophia and the English pupil do not notice the men. They are helping Pehr, the coachman, push the sleigh back outside, where a light rain is turning the snow to slush. Pehr douses the fire. The group of pupils looks displeased, and Linnaeus sees them holding the plants he had named for them.

Two sleighs make their way home from the estate. The first is Sophia's borrowed sleigh. In the second, the English pupil joins Linnaeus. In Linnaeus's mind's eye, he sees a third sleigh following them, containing the apostles. Linnaeus looks up at Rotheram and tries to express his grief over those whom death has taken from him, and the anxiety and care that are his present lot. Rotheram tells him to rest; they will be home soon.

Characters

Pehr Artedi

Pehr Artedi was a friend of Linnaeus's youth who became known for his study of fishes. He drowned in a canal in Amsterdam after a night of drinking. Linnaeus edited his book about fish.

Falck

Falck was a Linnaeus apostle. Linnaeus thinks he sees him standing by the fire. Named in the story only by his last name, the historical person was Johann Pehr Falck (1732–1774). Falck traveled to St. Petersburg, Turkistan, and Mongolia. In Kazan, according to Linnaeus's memory, he was lonely and sad and shot himself.

Pehr Forskal

Pehr Forskal (1732–1763) was a Linnaeus apostle who traveled to Alexandria, where, Linnaeus recalls, he concealed himself from marauding Bedouins by dressing as a peasant. Forskal made a collection of new plants in Cairo and traveled to Arabia, where he died of plague. Historically, he is known for being the first man to describe the plant and animal life of the Red Sea. His travel diary has been frequently republished. Linnaeus thinks he sees him standing by the fire at Hammarby.

Fredrik Hasselquist

Fredrik Hasselquist (1722–1752) was one of Linnaeus's apostles. Linnaeus remembers him as modest and poor. Hasselquist traveled widely throughout the Middle East, keeping a precise diary that Linnaeus edited. Hasselquist died in a village near Smyrna, Turkey, when he was thirty. Hasselquist's main interest was in learning about biblical plants and animals. Linnaeus thinks he sees Hasselquist standing by the fire at Hammarby and talking with some of the other apostles.

Martin Kahler

Martin Kahler was a Linnaeus apostle. Linnaeus recalls how Kahler returned from his travels with nothing, his health broken by shipwreck, fever, and poverty. Pirates stole the chest containing his collections.

Pehr Kalm

Pehr Kalm was a Linnaeus apostle. All that Linnaeus remembers of him was that he crossed the Great Lakes and walked into Canada. As a matter of historical fact, Kalm (1716–1779) traveled to North America in 1748. His work included a description of the now extinct passenger pigeon.

Carl Linnaeus

Carl Linnaeus (1707–1778) is the renowned eighteenth-century Swedish botanist. In the story, he is seventy years old and in very poor health, the result of a series of strokes. He is partially paralyzed and can hardly speak, sometimes only able to produce a syllable at a time. His memory is also failing him, and he cannot even be sure that the woman who comes to the house is his own daughter Sophia.

He passes the time by reflecting on his achievements and those of his followers, whom he calls his "apostles." He recalls when he was a vigorous man of twenty-five, he explored "Lappland" and was stunned by the beauty of the natural world. He is proud of the fame and honor his work brought him and that he managed to fend off all the attacks that were made on his work. He is also proud of the work of his apostles, but he is conscious that many of them died as a result of the travels that he inspired them to take, and this fact appears to weigh on his mind. He weeps as he recalls them, since almost all of them are dead. But in his wandering mind, he recreates some of them in his imagination, even believing that they are grouped together near the fire in the room in which he is sitting. Linnaeus does not appear to be closely attached to his family, except perhaps for Sophia; he is a man who chose to focus his life on his work rather than his family.

Sara Lisa Linnaeus

Sara Lisa is Linnaeus's wife. Linnaeus remembers how she would complain that there was not enough money to provide for their children. He thinks of her as a practical woman; she also appears to have a bad temper. Pehr fears that she will be angry, and ready to blame him, for the fact that Linnaeus has gone to Hammarby without anyone's knowledge. Linnaeus also thinks that his wife criticizes his every word. He recalls an incident in Sophia's childhood, when she dropped a tray full of dishes and he bought a new set to spare the child her mother's wrath.

Sophia Linnaeus

Sophia is the youngest of Linnaeus's three daughters. He thinks of her as unlike the others, and she is his favorite, with her "fine straight nose, her beautiful eyes." He remembers how when she was small he would take her to his lectures, and she would stand between his knees and listen. Sophia arrives at Hammarby with a young man who is probably her husband or fiancé, and they escort Linnaeus home.

Pehr Lofling

Pehr Lofling (1729–1756) was a Linnaeus apostle. Linnaeus recalls Lofling taking dictation from him when he was crippled by gout. Lofling made a name for himself in Spain where he moved in 1751. He then traveled to Venezuela, South America, and from that location, he wrote letters and sent bird specimens to Linnaeus. He died in Venezuela of fever.

Pehr Osbeck

Pehr Osbeck was a Linnaeus apostle who went to China and returned with a huge collection of new plants.

Pehr

Pehr is the coachman who drives Linnaeus in the sleigh to Hammarby. He has a wife and family to support and is worried that he will get into trouble with his employers for taking the sleigh beyond city limits. He is a quiet man who takes great care to look after Linnaeus as well as he can.

Daniel Rolander

Daniel Rolander was one of Linnaeus's apostles. He came back from Surinam with only a pot of Indian fig covered with cochineal insects, which his gardener mistakenly washed away. Rolander had lost his mind in Surinam. He thought the insects were pearls. When Linnaeus pointed out his error, Rolander was angry and left for Denmark, where Linnaeus believes he lives on charity.

Rotheram

Rotheram was Linnaeus's English pupil. Linnaeus thinks the man who arrives with Sophia at Hammarby is Rotheram, although this is probably a delusion of his failing mind. Linnaeus recalls how Rotheram fell ill several years ago, and Sophia nursed him. Rotheram was close to the whole family. Historically, although it is not given in the story, Rotheram was Dr. John Rotheram (1750–1804), an English naturalist. Rotheram was one of only two people present at the death of Linnaeus in 1778. (The other was Samuel Christoffer Duse, Sophia's husband.)

Christopher Ternström

Christopher Ternström was one of Linnaeus's apostles. Linnaeus recalls him as a passionate botanist. Ternström sailed to the East Indies in search of a tea plant and some living goldfish. He died of a tropical fever on an island off Cambodia. Linnaeus believes that he sees Ternström as one of a group of men standing by the fire at Hammarby. Although the story does not state it, Ternström (1711–1746) was the first of Linnaeus's apostles.

Carl Thunberg

Carl Thunberg was one of Linnaeus's apostles. Thunberg had traveled to Japan and was passionate about learning all he could about Japanese flora.

He spread knowledge of Linnaeus's methods amongst the Japanese. Linnaeus remembers that Thunberg introduced into Japan the treatment of syphilis by quicksilver. Linnaeus thinks he sees him standing by the fire and talking with other apostles.

Themes

Age and Youth, Present and Past

There are a series of contrasts in the story between age and youth, present and past, death and life. Linnaeus is bitterly and painfully aware of these two sets of opposing realities, and he attempts to bridge the gap between them. The contrasts bring out the irony of Linnaeus's present condition. The aged, decrepit man was once famous for his prodigious memory, and his life's work consisted of naming and classifying things in the natural world. Now his mind is so diminished that he can barely recognize his own daughter and is confused about the identity of her companion. At the height of his powers, Linnaeus was like the Biblical Adam, who gave names to all the animals (Genesis 2:19). To name something is a sign of knowledge and power and is associated also with memory: "Nomenclature is a mnemonic art"; that is to say, it assists the memory. Conversely, to forget and to no longer be able to name things accurately, is a sign of the loss of power and the inability to create order in one's environment.

A sharp contrast is drawn between Linnaeus's aged condition now and the memory of his youthful vigor, when, "wildly energetic," he explored the natural beauty of Lappland. In those long-gone days, "with the whole world waiting to be named, he'd believed that he and everyone he loved would live forever." The same contrast of age and youth is drawn regarding his apostles, whom he remembers in the fullness of their young manhood, when they went boldly off to explore the distant corners of the globe. The contrast is between the vividness of life in all its exoticism and diversity—the sheer range of the unusual experiences lived by the apostles—and the weak flame that life has become in the old man.

Almost all the apostles are dead, though, a fact that Linnaeus dwells on repeatedly. Contrary to his youthful belief, nothing lives forever, and death is everywhere recalled in this story, not only of humans but also of some of Linnaeus's beloved animals. Pompey the dog, lovingly recalled, is dead. His monkey, Grinn, a present from the queen, is dead, as is Sjup, the raccoon, and the parrot who

Topics for Further Study

- Collect four or more flowers or plants, identify them, and research how and why they acquired their names. Make a class presentation in which you show the plants, identifying them according to Linnaeus's method and discussing your findings.

- Read Barrett's story "Rare Bird," in *Ship Fever and Other Stories*, which centers on Linnaeus's theory that swallows hibernate under water. How does this story complement "The English Pupil"? What more does it tell the reader about Linnaeus, the scientific method, and the role of women in science? Make a class presentation in which you summarize the story and explain its relevance to "The English Pupil" and the history of science.

- Research the current debate between the theories of evolution and creationism. What are the main arguments on each side? On which side of the debate do you think Linnaeus would stand? Should creation science and evolution both be taught in public schools? Form a team with two or more students and debate the issue.

- What is science? What is the scientific method? How does the story illustrate the scientific method? Is science the most useful and reliable way of gaining knowledge? Research two major scientific discoveries that have changed our understanding of the world in which we live or which have greatly benefited human life. Write an essay in which you describe your findings.

sat on his shoulder at meals and the weasel who wore a bell on his neck and hunted rats. Linnaeus sits in his kitchen "surrounded by the dead." All the dear departed are recalled with a sharpness of detail that eludes Linnaeus in the present. It is as if only the past is real for him now. Because so much has been lost, the present somehow has to be transformed into the past or the past made to live again, to ease his pain. This is why he creates in his imagination a group of the apostles, as they were in life, standing around the fire, and also why his mind leaves his body and seems to become the apostles themselves and re-travel their route: one moment he is Ternström, the next he is Hasselquist. This mind travel is for him a release from the burden of being the great Linnaeus, famous and learned but now half-paralyzed and with his mind fading away. These friendships with his young apostles have meant so much to Linnaeus over the course of his life. The apostles were like extensions of himself, "his own organs: extra eyes and hands and feet." This connection suggests an underlying theme of friendship and loyalty in pursuit of mutual goals; the ideal relationship between a teacher and his students that survives in spite of mental incapacity and even death.

image suggests resurrection and a kind of immortality for the apostle who sacrificed his life in the pursuit of knowledge. This point is also conveyed by the fact that Linnaeus sees in his mind's eye the apostles holding the plants that he had named for them, including "*Artedia*" (for Pehr Artedi) and "*Osbeckia*," for Pehr Osbeck.

Linnaeus's vision of the apostles standing by the fire indicates that they still live in his mind, and he sees them holding "leaves and twigs and scraps of blossoms, all new and named by them with their teacher's advice." Once again, these images drawn from nature suggest rebirth and new life, and they also affirm the eternal bond between teacher and student.

Style

Imagery of the Natural World

The Linnaeus of the story has loved the natural world so much that it has embedded itself in his thinking and the way he uses language. When he expresses his thoughts to himself or when the narrator explains his state of mind, it is through metaphors and similes drawn from the natural world. The erosion of his memory, for example, is conveyed by a metaphor of a gradually expanding dark lake: "His mind, which had once seemed to hold the whole world, had been occupied by a great dark lake that spread farther every day and around which he tiptoed gingerly." Similarly, the facts that were once at his command now "darted like minnows across the water and could only be captured by cunning and indirection."

Because he can no longer recognize people or be fully aware of what is going on around him, Linnaeus has a habit of translating his present experience into images of nature that remain clear to him. The man who accompanies Sophia, for example, bends down to address him "like the moon falling from the sky," and when the man—Rotheram or whoever he is—introduces himself, his voice "is like the wind moving over the Lappland hills."

In a story that focuses so much on death and loss, some of the images convey continuity in nature; the individual may die, but the species lives on, and through their discoveries, the "apostles" continue to live, also. For example, Pehr Forskal dies of plague, but months later, Linnaeus receives a letter from him containing a stalk and a flower from a tree Linnaeus has always wanted to see, "the evergreen from which the Balm of Gilead was obtained." The

Historical Context

The Life and Work of Carl Linnaeus

Carl Linnaeus was born in 1707 in Sweden. His father was a Lutheran minister. Even as a child, Linnaeus was interested in botany. At the age of five, he looked after his own garden. As a young man, he studied medicine and natural history at the University of Lund and University of Uppsala, graduating with a degree in medicine from the latter. In 1730, he was appointed lecturer in botany at the University of Uppsala, and two years later he embarked alone on his journey to Lappland in northern Sweden, the natural history of which was almost unknown at the time. This is the trip referred to in "The English Pupil" and as a result of his published findings, Linnaeus became well known in Sweden. According to Arvid HJ. Uggla, Linnaeus's diary of his Lappland adventure "is one of the treasures of Swedish literature. It shows his brilliant power of quick perception and intuitive description of what he saw."

Linnaeus's reputation was further established by the publication, with the financial help of the botanist Jan Fredrik Gronovius, of his *Systema Naturae* in 1735, in which he detailed the system he had developed for the classification of plant species. The system was based on the number and arrangement of the plant's reproductive organs; a plant's class was determined by its stamens (male organs), and its order by its pistils (female organs). This system made it easy for newly discovered plants to be placed in a certain category, and it quickly became immensely influential, even though the book amounted to only seven pages in extra large folio. Two years later, in 1737, Linnaeus

Compare
&
Contrast

- **Eighteenth century:** This is a time of political turmoil for Sweden. In 1718, following the death of King Charles XII and defeat in battle, Sweden is forced to give up almost all its overseas possessions. Up to that point, it had been a formidable military power. Sweden then establishes a parliamentary government and drastically reduces the power of the monarch. This period, from 1718 to 1772, is known as the age of liberty. Natural science, culture, and the Swedish economy flourish in the longest period of peace Sweden has known since the second half of the sixteenth century.

  Today: Sweden is a liberal parliamentary democracy that has created a high standard of living for its citizens by adopting a mixed system of high-tech capitalism and extensive welfare benefits. Timber, hydropower, and iron ore are the most important elements in the economy, which depends heavily on foreign trade.

- **Eighteenth century:** Beginning in 1741, Linnaeus is responsible for the Uppsala University Botanical Garden. Under Linnaeus's influence, the garden houses more varieties of plants than any garden in the world. Linnaeus uses the garden for his scientific observations and for teaching his students.

  Today: The Linnaeus' Garden at Uppsala is a reconstruction of Uppsala University Botanical Garden as it was during Linnaeus's days. It contains approximately 1,300 species of plants and is arranged according to Linnaeus's own plan that reflects his sexual system of classification. The marsh pond contains the flower named after Linnaeus, Linnaea borealis.

- **Eighteenth century:** During this period, known as the Age of Enlightenment because of the dominant belief in the power of reason to improve the lot of humanity, naturalists believe that the world was created by God and is under His beneficent supervision. Although Linnaeus accepts that new species of plants have appeared as a result of hybridization, he believes that all species were potentially present from the beginning, in the Garden of Eden.

  Today: The theories of evolution and natural selection put forward by Charles Darwin in the nineteenth century remain profoundly influential for modern naturalists. Naturalists still continue Linnaeus's practice of classification of species, and much of his system remains in use, but the emphasis is on the evolutionary rather than fixed relationships between different groups of organisms.

---

published his *Genera Plantarum*, which described all the known species of plants.

In 1736, Linnaeus visited England, where he met the leading botanists of the day; he also traveled to Holland and then to Paris. As a result of his travels, he became a well-known figure in European scientific circles. Returning to Sweden in 1738, he practiced medicine with considerable success. In 1739, he was elected the first president of the newly established Academy of Science in Stockholm. In that year also, he married Sara Lisa Moraea, the daughter of a distinguished doctor.

Linnaeus was awarded a professorship at the University of Uppsala, Sweden's most prestigious university, in 1741. His students found him an inspiring teacher and traveled the world researching natural history, bringing back interesting plant specimens to Sweden and promoting Linnaeus's methods of classification internationally. Linnaeus referred to them as his "apostles," and many of them were among the leading scientists of the eighteenth century.

Linnaeus remained a teacher for the rest of his life, until ill-health prevented him. He also continued to publish important new works. In 1753, he published *Species Plantarum*, a description of the six thousand species of plants then known. Each species is named as simply as possible, with one word in

Carl Linnaeus The Library of Congress

addition to the generic name. Linnaeus regarded *Species Plantarum* as his greatest achievement.

In 1758, Linnaeus bought a small one-storey house at Hammarby, outside Uppsala. He liked to spend as much time as he could there, away from the bustle of Uppsala. He built a larger building at Hammarby for the sake of his children's future, which was completed in 1762.

In 1761, Linnaeus was granted a Swedish patent of nobility, and from then on, he was known as Carl von Linné. During his later years, he suffered from ill health and became increasingly pessimistic. His memory began to fail when he was sixty. In 1774, he had a series of strokes, and he died in 1778. His son Carl (the lazy one, according to "The English Pupil") succeeded to his professorship at Uppsala but had little of his father's ability.

Critical Overview

Reviewers were generous in their praise of Barrett's collection of eight short stories, *Ship Fever and Other Stories* (1996), in which "The English Pupil" appeared. Donna Seaman in *Booklist* comments that Barrett "has used science as a conduit to understanding the human psyche. . . . [Her] stories are

precise and concentrated, containing a truly remarkable wealth of psychology and social commentary." The reviewer for *Publishers Weekly* makes a similar point: "The quantifiable truths of science intersect with the less easily measured precincts of the heart in these eight seductively stylish tales."

For Thomas Mallon, in the *New York Times Book Review*, the figure of Linnaeus hovers over all eight stories as a "kind of muse." Mallon points out that in "The English Pupil," Linnaeus "still makes use of 'the thread of Ariadne' that he had strung through nature's species—only now it helps his wavering consciousness keep his daughters straight." (Mallon is referring to the passage in which Linnaeus thinks of the physical characteristics of his daughters in order to discover that the young woman visiting him is Sophia, who is unlike the others and "seemed to belong to another genus entirely.")

Lisa Schwarzbaum, who reviewed *Ship Fever and Other Stories* for *Entertainment Weekly* after it was announced that the book had won the National Book Award, also thought that Linnaeus is presented "as a kind of magnetic north to whom all scientists bend." She offers the opinion that each of the stories "is intricate and beautifully chiseled; taken together, the tales flow one to the other, linked by the author's fascination with and tender appreciation of science and scientists."

Her appreciation was shared by the reviewer for the *New Yorker*, for whom "The title novella is devastating: as with every story here, you enter right into it, and cannot entirely leave it behind."

Criticism

Bryan Aubrey

Aubrey holds a Ph.D. in English and has published many articles on twentieth-century literature. In this essay, Aubrey discusses the character of Linnaeus and the challenges he faced, as revealed in the story and historical sources, as well as his relations with his "apostles."

The writer of any short story about a historical personage is faced with the challenge of deciding at what point in the person's life the story is to take place. Will it be at the time of his or her greatest achievements, for example, or at a time of great controversy or perhaps when the person is old and is looking back at his or her achievements? Andrea Barrett chose the last of these options. Carl Linnaeus died in January 1778, only one month after the time in which the story takes place. Choosing to set the story during that dark time in his life, when Linnaeus was incapacitated by a series of strokes, supplied Barrett with the contrasts and ironies between former greatness and present impotence that make "The English Pupil" effective. Barrett also packs a great deal of historical detail into her thirteen-page story. As perhaps befits a writer on science and scientists, the facts, incidents, and ideas that the author has Linnaeus recall in the story are historically accurate, and Barrett must have done much research in order to pick out some of the most colorful incidents in his life. Just to give one example, Linnaeus and the hundreds of followers whom he led on walks through the Uppsala countryside really were accompanied by musicians as they returned triumphantly to town. Eventually, as Patricia Fara reports in *Sex, Botany, and Empire: The Story of Carl Linnaeus and Joseph Banks*, the rector of the University of Uppsala banned students from participating in these mass excursions because he thought it encouraged them to neglect their duties.

In packing her story so densely, Barrett drops a number of clues to the kind of man Linnaeus was and the challenges he faced. His description of nature as "an alphabet written in God's hand," and the motto inscribed over his bedroom door, "Live blamelessly; God is present," suggest a man imbued with a deeply religious spirit. This was indeed the case. As the son of a Lutheran country pastor, Linnaeus took his religion seriously, and his beliefs were in keeping with the spirit of the eighteenth century. He believed that the natural world was created by God and that every creature in the mineral, vegetable, and animal kingdoms had its fixed place in the chain of being, from the simplest of organisms up to the highest expression of life, the human being. Linnaeus had a literal belief in the Biblical account of creation in Genesis and thought that the Garden of Eden had been a small island at the equator on which all the world's plant species had been present. In the botanical gardens that he cultivated at Uppsala, his aim was to recreate the order and plenitude of that original divine garden, a paradise on Earth. Linnaeus, it must be remembered, lived a hundred years before Charles Darwin published *The Origin of Species* (1859), which put forth Darwin's theory of the origin and evolution of species through natural selection, which would bring into question the notion of a stable, fixed natural order created by a beneficent God.

Given the religious framework of Linnaeus's beliefs, his skill as a classifier, and his choice of

> The poignancy of the story lies in Linnaeus's sorrow and possible feelings of guilt over the fate of so many of his apostles. Has he lived blamelessly, as the inscription above his door commands him to?"

profession, it is perhaps not surprising that he thought of himself, as Heinz Goerke points out in his biography of the naturalist, as a "second Adam," a man charged by God with the naming of the three kingdoms of nature and classifying each one according to its natural hierarchy. Perhaps unsurprising also is the fact that although Linnaeus believed in the omnipotence of God and offered up the praise of a humble worshipper, there was more than a trace of arrogance in his convictions about his own role in the divine plan. He believed he had been specially appointed by God to fulfill a mission. Goerke states:

> In no other naturalist of the period does the conviction of being the Lord's elect, predestined of God, find such clear expression. For this reason, he felt sure that none of his colleagues could equal him in science, let alone excel him; to him only this task had been given.

As the story makes clear, Linnaeus had his enemies, those who attacked his work, and perhaps it was the arrogance of the man, his "autocratic procedure in the matter of nomenclature," as Goerke puts it, that irked his opponents as much as what they claimed was the unnatural and arbitrary manner of his sexual system of plant classification. A picture emerges in "The English Pupil" of a man proud of his success and his fame—his pride is obvious in his story of how the king of England built a garden called Kew and named each plant according to Linnaeus's system—and also ready to do battle with his opponents. Recalling the disagreement he had had with an English naturalist over his theory that swallows wintered beneath the lakes, Linnaeus remembers, "But always there had been people . . . who criticized his every word.

What Do I Read Next?

- Like Barrett's story, Gjertrud Schnackenberg's poem "Darwin in 1881," which can be found in her *Supernatural Love: Poems 1976–1992* (2000), examines the mind of a great scientist as his life draws to a close. Also like the story, the poem interweaves past and present as Darwin looks back on his life. He does not view it with any sense of accomplishment.

- Barrett's novel *Voyage of the Narwhal* (1998) begins in May 1855, when the *Narwhal* sails from Philadelphia to the Arctic in search of a long-lost expedition. On board is the naturalist Erasmus Darwin Wells, who sees this voyage as a chance to make his reputation. The voyage does not go according to plan, and by September, the ship is ice-locked and will have to see out the winter in the Arctic. As the weather worsens, morale sinks. The well-researched story has many twists and turns and is full of memorable characters.

- *Dr. Copernicus* (reprint, 1993), by John Banville, is a historical novel based on the life of the astronomer Nicolas Copernicus (1473–1543), who asserted that the Earth is not the center of the universe. The novel explores the effect this major discovery, which permanently altered the way humans viewed God, the world, and themselves, had on Copernicus and the Catholic Church.

- *QED: A Play* (2002), by Peter Parnell, is an exploration of the life of twentieth-century physicist Richard Feynman. Like "The English Pupil" and "Darwin in 1881," the play is set near the end of its subject's life, when Feynman has just realized that he has terminal cancer. The play, which was a hit on Broadway, captures Feynman's lively personality and explores the ideas that won him the Nobel Prize in physics.

- The Museum of Paleontology at the University of California, Berkeley, maintains a webpage at http://www.ucmp.berkeley.edu/history/linnaeus.html that includes a biography of Linnaeus, an explanation of his scientific thought, and many links to other relevant websites, including sites on which Linnaeus's botanical garden and his manor home and garden at Hammarby (the setting for "The English Pupil") can be viewed.

He had fought off all of them. The Queen had ennobled him: he was Carl von Linné now."

Most of Linnaeus's opponents were foreigners; in Sweden, he was an honored man and had no serious rivals. Although he apparently dreaded public quarrels, Linnaeus knew how to take care of himself in these intellectual conflicts, and at times, he could not only be unreasonable but also vindictive and sly. When one contemporary, a man named Johan Georg Siegesbeck, from St. Petersburg, criticized his system of naming plants, Linnaeus retaliated by naming a particularly unpleasant weed, Sigesbeckia. When Lorenz Heister, a professor of medicine and botany, attacked Linnaeus's system in letters and articles, Linnaeus gradually removed his name from the later editions of his botanical works.

But it is with Linnaeus's pupils, and his relationship with them, that the story is principally concerned. Historically, it was in 1750 that Linnaeus first described the students he dispatched to distant parts of the world as his "apostles." The term indicated that he saw their work as a missionary one. They were to take direction from him, follow his system, and make his name famous as they collected and documented the natural world as they encountered it. Scholars of Linnaeus consider the work of his apostles, since he directly inspired them all, to be part of his life's achievement.

There were seventeen Linnaeus apostles (some sources say the number was nineteen), and they traveled to all the continents. Their destinations included Arabia, China, Southeast Asia, Japan, Australia, the

Arctic, and North and South America. There was plenty of work to do, since in the mid-eighteenth century, only one tenth of the plants and animals in the world were known.

Linnaeus benefited greatly from the work of his apostles. Pehr Kalm, for example, in his work in North America, especially Pennsylvania, New Jersey, New York, and Canada, discovered many new plants and informed Linnaeus of his work, greatly increasing Linnaeus's knowledge. Linnaeus's book, *Species Planatarum* (1753), listed more than seven hundred North American species, ninety of them discovered by Kalm.

Many of these adventurous young naturalists, as "The English Pupil" makes clear, met early deaths as a result of their brave exploration of unknown lands. Some of them regretted their choice of work, and as Goerke notes, Fredrik Hasselquist reportedly cursed his teacher for starting him out on such a hazardous career. Linnaeus was also, according to Goerke, reproached by the wife of Christopher Ternström, who claimed that Linnaeus had lured her husband away from her and made her a widow.

The poignancy of the story lies in Linnaeus's sorrow and possible feelings of guilt over the fate of so many of his apostles. Has he lived blamelessly, as the inscription above his door commands him to? Only he knows. Certainly, he knows how much he owes to the apostles. At Uppsala, he remembers, his pupils would sit and listen to him lecture about the specimens they had discovered and brought home. Linnaeus may be known and revered for his vast knowledge of "Fossils, crystals, the causes of leprosy and intermittent fever," as well as exotic creatures and plants such as the mud iguana of Carolina and Siberian buckwheat and bearberries, but "all these things he had known about because of his pupils' travels."

From the evidence of the story, the bond between master and disciple was a deep one. Linnaeus still believes that he and the disciple Thunberg (whom he imagines is in the room with him) share an intimacy that only they can understand. (They exchange a secret signal, or so Linnaeus thinks.) The naturalist seems to have thought of many of the apostles as his own family. When he thinks of the death of his two-year-old son, Johannes, he places it by remembering the deaths of Hasselquist and Lofling that took place immediately before and after.

It is this awareness of loss, rather than the triumph of his many accomplishments, that weighs most heavily upon Linnaeus at the end of the story. Indeed, his final words, which are, with the

exception of one word uttered earlier, the only words of his that appear in quotation marks in the entire story, are full of despair: "The death of many whom I have induced to travel has turned my hair gray, and what have I gained? A few dried plants, accompanied by great anxiety, unrest, and care."

But the final note is a compassionate and moving one. Rotheram, the English pupil, says to the old man, "Rest your head on my arm. We will be home before you know it." The image of the old master resting his head on the arm of the disciple is an affirmation of the bond of affection between Linnaeus and all the apostles, living and dead. It also suggests the continuity of the scientific enterprise, the transmission of knowledge from one generation to the next. Individuals may die, but the quest for knowledge and understanding of the natural world goes on.

Source: Bryan Aubrey, Critical Essay on "The English Pupil," in *Short Stories for Students*, Thomson Gale, 2007.

Contemporary Authors Online

In the following essay, the critic gives an overview of Andrea Barrett's work.

Andrea Barrett is an acclaimed writer. "She crafts powerfully vivid works of fiction," lauded Samuel Baker's *Publishers Weekly* profile of Barrett. *Lucid Stars*, her first novel, spans more than twenty years in detailing the dissolution of an American family. The novel's heroine, Penny Webb, falls in love with, and is soon married to, carefree skier Benjamin Day. Almost immediately, Penny finds herself pregnant and unhappy, for Benjamin has already begun forsaking her for other women. Penny realizes a measure of consolation by attending to her twin children and indulging her interest in the stars. Benjamin eventually leaves Penny for a younger woman: He remarries, fathers a third child, and then leaves his second wife for a still younger woman. Penny, meanwhile, comes to perceive the various family members—herself, the twins, her ex-husband, his ex-wife and child, and his third wife—as similar to the shifting heavenly bodies in space. James Marcus, writing in the *New York Times Book Review*, called *Lucid Stars* "a spacious and sympathetic debut."

Secret Harmonies, Barrett's next novel, is also about family ties. Here an engaging young woman, Reba Dwyer, wallows in rural Massachusetts with her meek, introspective brother, Hank, and her handicapped sister, Tonia. After a period of rebellion, Reba parts from her family and enters a conservatory. While there, she fails to ingratiate herself

Barrett's literary focus on science is not surprising, given her course of studies in college. Barrett intended to work in the field of science; she earned a degree in biology and did graduate studies in zoology."

with her ostensibly more sophisticated fellow students and, when her father suddenly abandons the family, Reba returns home. She eventually enters into a dreary marriage with a longtime friend, whom she soon begins compromising with a series of unfulfilling sexual flings. Faced with further unhappiness, Reba finally begins to understand the necessity of coming to terms with herself and the often elusive nature of contentment. A reviewer in *Publishers Weekly* called *Secret Harmonies* "[p]oignant and atmospheric," and praised Barrett's "[e]legant, accessible writing."

In her 1991 novel, *The Middle Kingdom*, Barrett once again writes about a character overcoming unhappiness to gain a measure of understanding about self-identity and life. Overweight, thirty-year-old Grace Hoffmeier accompanies her estranged husband to Beijing and then falls ill with pneumonia. She lies in a Chinese hospital and feverishly recalls her college days, her earlier marriage, and her romance with her husband, who has continued touring Beijing with a new lover while Grace recovers from her illness. After regaining her health, Grace also finds a lover and, moreover, a job in Beijing. In addition, she learns to focus on the present, without regrets for the past or anxieties about the future. "Ms. Barrett is a solid writer, and *The Middle Kingdom* is a thoughtfully plotted book," judged Cheri Fein in the *New York Times Book Review*. "An interesting story of personal growth," commented *Library Journal* contributor Kimberly G. Allen.

In 1993 Barrett published *The Forms of Water*, a multi-generation tale about a family living in

upstate New York. The aging patriarch, Brendon Auberon, convinces his nephew, Henry, to steal a nursing-home vehicle and conduct him to the abbey where he had once lived as a monk. The journey of Brendon and Henry alarms other family members, who unite in an attempt to apprehend the old man and return him to his nursing home. During the ensuing action, various characters recall earlier, often unhappy events, many of which contributed to the dissolution of the extended family. A *Belles Lettres* reviewer described *The Forms of Water* as a "well-structured novel" and complained only about the extended summary that concludes the novel after the actual chase has ended. The reviewer added, however, that this ending, which was decried as "tedious," constituted "a small flaw in an otherwise satisfying novel." A contributor to *Publishers Weekly* praised the novel, noting that "Barrett writes with keen, finely tuned sensibilities."

Barrett followed *The Forms of Water* with *Ship Fever, and Other Stories*, her first collection of short stories. Like her novels, many of the stories in *Ship Fever* deal with family ties. "The Marburg Sisters," for example, is the tale of twin sisters, one of whom becomes a scientist while the other enters the drug culture. However, other stories are less characteristic of Barrett's novels. In "The Behavior of the Hawkweeds," for example, a woman courts a student by relating the story of botanist Gregor Mendel, who vainly renounced decades of research to gain acceptance from fellow scientists. And in "Rare Bird," which is set in the eighteenth century, a female ornithologist compromises her own values while attempting to disprove the contentions of a fellow scientist. The title tale likewise occurs in the past. Here a doctor uncovers a typhus epidemic among immigrants arriving in Canada from Ireland, a land then in chaos due to the horrific potato famine of the mid-nineteenth century. *Nation* reviewer Molly E. Rauch noted "the ambitious range" of *Ship Fever*, and Thomas Mallon wrote in the *New York Times Book Review* that the collection's "overall effect is quietly dazzling."

Ship Fever "opened up diverse new audiences for Barrett," recognized Baker, who reported: "In 1996, Barrett surprised the published world by winning the National Book Award for fiction, in a decision that startled many industry insiders. Since then, the powerful volume that garnered the prize [*Ship Fever*] . . . has won additional acclaim." It was, perhaps, because of *Ship Fever*'s general focus that many were surprised it won the prestigious award. As Katherine Livingston indicated in *Science*, "Books about science are rarely considered for literary awards." "The lit-crowd chorus who wish their favorite books were chosen instead have no cause for complaint," commented *Entertainment Weekly* contributor Lisa Schwarzbaum, calling *Ship Fever* an "admirable winner." Describing Barrett's collection of short fiction, Schwarzbaum praised: "Each [story] is intricate and beautifully chiseled; taken together, the tales flow one to the other, linked by the author's fascination with and tender appreciation of science and scientists."

Barrett's literary focus on science is not surprising, given her course of studies in college. Barrett intended to work in the field of science; she earned a degree in biology and did graduate studies in zoology. It was only while doing writer papers during her second stint of graduate studies, this time in medieval and Reformation theological history, that she began thinking of writing as a career.

In 1997 Barrett made use of a Guggenheim foundation grant to do research for her next project. Using what she experienced on a trip to Baffin Island, Barrett created *The Voyage of the Narwhal*—"a dynamic and insightful historical novel" that *Booklist*'s Donna Seaman believes "is even more prizeworthy" than *Ship Fever*. "[*The Voyage of the Narwhal*] resembles many of the stories in *Ship Fever* in its 19th-century setting and in its choice of a scientist as its protagonist. But by unfurling a larger canvas with *The Narwhal*, Barrett extends into new territory her uncanny ability to make stories of science past illuminate today's world," assessed Baker, who summarized the novel: "*The Narwhal* imagines the trails of botanist Erasmus Darwin Wells, who signs on to a polar expedition led by his sister's dashing but dangerously immature suitor. The novel's drama eventually encompasses not only how they search for a previous, lost team of explorers, but also how they navigate the sea of publicity when they return to their native Philadelphia."

Barrett did not intend her "epic of 19th-century polar exploration" to be an adventure story, noted Baker. As she related to Baker: "What I was after was much more ruminative. In fact, although the research I was drawing from is full of adventure, I think this book is much less full of adventure. Its people are painters and writers, they're thinking and mulling, they're seeing, they're looking. They're not going out and slashing polar bears to death."

Though *The Voyage of the Narwhal* was very warmly received, some critics, including a *Publishers Weekly* reviewer, have found fault with the slow pace of the story. John Skow's *Time*

assessment refers to it as a "powerful, brooding novel. . . . that moves like an advancing ice age." Rating *The Voyage of the Narwhal* as an "A-," Megan Harlan judged in *Entertainment Weekly*: "Despite the disappointingly pat finale, Barrett . . . masterfully navigates the waters of envy and egotism." Seaman used the descriptors "authoritative," "imaginative," "gripping," and "masterful" when praising the story. The *Publishers Weekly* reviewer also gave a very complimentary review, stating: "Barrett delivers a stunning novel in which a meticulous grasp of historical and natural detail, insight into character and pulse-pounding action are integrated into a dramatic adventure story with deep moral resonance."

Source: Contemporary Authors Online, "Andrea Barrett," in *Contemporary Authors Online*, Gale, 2003.

Andrea Barrett and Peter Kurth

In the following interview, Barrett discusses her success, her work, the process of writing, and the themes of science and history that are central to her writing.

When Andrea Barrett won the National Book Award in 1996 for *Ship Fever and Other Stories*, she remembered to bring the notes for her acceptance speech to the awards ceremony at the Waldorf-Astoria but forgot her glasses, stepping on emcee Calvin Trillin's foot as she walked on the stage and thinking she might vomit when she got there. "I've never been to a black-tie thing in my life," Barrett remarked later. "I didn't even go to my prom." It was a year of intense controversy for the award and its judges, who had ignored what seemed to be the hands-down favorite that season, David Foster Wallace's "Infinite Jest," in favor of Barrett's calm, lucid, supremely intelligent fictions on the theme of science and the scientific mind. After years of writing in virtual obscurity, with four novels already behind her, Barrett suddenly found herself at the center of the literary map.

Two years later, with the publication of *The Voyage of the Narwhal*, Barrett has confirmed the wisdom of the judges' decision and solidified her position as one of the most eloquent and thoughtful storytellers working today. Her tale of a 19th-century Arctic expedition and its aftermath, solidly based in historical and scientific research, has won rave reviews and, for Barrett, spectacular sales, at a time when serious fiction is thought to remain outside the realm of mass appeal. Barrett spoke to *Salon* from her home in Rochester, N.Y., where she

> " You know, that sense of starting out with a question and the haziest of ideas and just giving yourself over to the exploration and being willing to follow where that leads you and build something from what you find. That does seem to be how science works."

lives with a dog, three cats and her husband, biologist Barry Goldstein.

[*Peter Kurth*:] *Let's start with literary fame. You've had two years of it since you won the National Book Award for* Ship Fever. *How has success changed your life?*

[Andrea Barrett:] Well, the phone rings a lot more, and people are asking me to do more things. And my books are more available. That's surprising and wonderful. But it hasn't really changed things in the sense that I'm still at home writing most of the time, which is where I'm meant to be. I live in the same city. I'm married to the same guy. I've tried not to let it change things in the larger sense because I'm really happy at home writing. So that's what I'm tying to do.

Did the award take you by surprise?

It could not have taken me more by surprise. I mean, just the nomination. I don't think it's possible to be more startled on this earth than I was.

You've just finished a book tour for The Voyage of the Narwhal. *Have you found that audiences and interviewers are interested in more than just your books when they talk to you? That they want to find out what makes a literary lioness tick?*

Yes, that was something I didn't really know about before I started doing this. There were two things I didn't expect. One was the interest in me as a person. There's actually nothing interesting about me except what I write. And the other is that

people have an interest I didn't expect in the subject matter of *The Voyage of the Narwhal,* as distinct from the book itself. People are just really curious about Arctic history and the Franklin expedition and the mid-19th century. So that has been interesting and curious, too, because I'm not really an authority on these things. I'm a novelist. I find myself having really fascinating conversations with people about all sorts of aspects of exploration and Arctic history and things like that.

The Voyage of the Narwhal seems an unlikely bestseller in many ways.

I'm not sure it is a bestseller. Or not yet anyway.

It's on the San Francisco bestseller list. My publisher says if you're on any list at all, you can call it a bestseller.

[Laughs] I guess we can call it that, then. But I do agree with you. I'm very startled by its success. I didn't think it would appeal to people in that way, or not that many people. It surprises me. I'm glad—of course I'm glad. It's been an interesting education in a way and so has this whole tour business and talking to the people at readings. I think that in newspapers and things we all talk so much about how nobody's reading anymore and how the quality of writing has gone down and the quality of reading has gone down, blah, blah, blah. I start to believe it after a while. And then I go out and about and I see these people who are into reading, people who are into buying books, and I think, I just have not given people enough credit. Maybe it's still true that if you write what really interests you, other people will be interested in it, too, no matter how seemingly obscure or arcane it is. If you can make a narrative out of it.

Your interest in Arctic history goes back a long time, doesn't it?

Yes, I've been interested in it since I was a little girl. I grew up on Cape Cod. We didn't live right on the water, but I could walk to it and did every day. And that must have got this started in me somewhere. I was always within sniffing range of the ocean and usually within sight of it. I think the landscape you grow up in probably does mark you in ways you don't even understand.

Is it true you were a high school dropout?

Well, it's hard to explain, but I didn't finish high school, that's true. It was the early '70s and you could do things like that. And the fall of my junior year I just started applying to colleges hoping someone would take me. I really didn't want to be in high school anymore, so I left at the end of my junior year and just went right to Union College in Schenectady without a high school diploma.

Were you already writing?

Oh, no, that came late, way after college. I was going to be a biologist. My undergraduate degree is in biology, and I went briefly to graduate school in zoology. And I also went for a little longer but didn't finish in history. I studied medieval and reformation history and I didn't start writing until I was done with both those things.

Did you know where you were headed when you started?

I really didn't know anything, and for various reasons I couldn't go to writing school, so I was just wandering around trying to teach myself, which actually is a traditional way of learning to write. Although not here [in the United States], and not in the last 25 years. But it still works.

It seems to. You had four novels published before Ship Fever.

Uh-huh. *Ship Fever* was my fifth book.

And do you see them all as part of a piece, or did you vary your form very much?

Well, it got considerably more complicated. I think when other people look at my books they see the first four as related and then these last two as related, and they see a big break in between them. It doesn't feel that way so much to me, even though the earlier ones are contemporary and the latter two are historical. I had always relied on lots of research for the stuff of my characters and their lives. In the earlier books, I wasn't moving them so far back in time, but one of the chief characters in my fourth novel, *The Forms of Water*, is an 80-year-old ex-monk, which clearly I'm not. He has this long past in China, doing missionary work and living in a contemplative order. So I had to do the same kind of research to build and invent that character as I have had to do in these last couple of books. To me it all seems to have grown naturally, but I'm very aware that it doesn't look like that to other people.

You've been quoted as saying that Ship Fever *was a departure for you.*

In the sense that it was stories and not a novel, it was a departure. I had written very few stories before. I love short stories, and I had started to teach around the time of my fourth novel and was not only reading more stories but looking at them more intently and watching my students write them. I wanted to learn how to write them, and that's really how that book started. I never had in mind, "Oh, I'm going to make a book of stories about scientists." I just wrote some stories trying to teach myself to do certain

But science and scientists are central both in Ship Fever *and* The Voyage of the Narwhal. *Can you elaborate on that? You've said you're surprised that people are looking at* Narwhal *as an adventure story. What do you see it as?*

I guess I thought of it more as a pure encounter of people with both the landscape and ideas. I was aware that there were adventure elements, but that wasn't was driving the book for me. It was more a question of thinking about the characters and representing, through them, 19th-century ideas of evolution, of species, of how the world works, of what human beings are, whether we're a different species, and letting those ideas work themselves out in the context of the Arctic, the trip up there. That sounds very funny, I guess.

Science itself is an adventure, though.

It is, or at least I perceive it that way. Maybe that's a false and romantic perception on my part, but I just conceive of it that way, in the same way that writing is an adventure. You know, that sense of starting out with a question and the haziest of ideas and just giving yourself over to the exploration and being willing to follow where that leads you and build something from what you find. That does seem to be how science works. I think that's part of why I was so drawn to the Arctic as a field for these ideas to work themselves out in, that sense of exploration. Physical exploration being a really good metaphor for the imaginative exploration of both science and writing. It really resonated with me.

And of course the source material you'd be using from that time was itself highly literary.

Yes, in that miraculous way that almost all 19th-century material is. You know, all those scientists could write. At their worst, they wrote a clear, readable, understandable prose, and at their best it's really glorious. I think Darwin's not a great writer but he's very easy to read, and other people like [Alfred Russell] Wallace are also a good example. They were really splendid writers. From that sense it's very easy material to work with. The language itself is really exciting.

How do you keep the information straight? How do you synthesize this huge mass of historical and scientific material while developing fictional characters and narrative?

Well, that really is how I came to writing fiction. I still have this really clear memory of being in a tiny, tiny bedroom in a rented house in Belchertown, Mass. And I was supposed to be writing a very long paper about the early days of the Franciscan Order, about a schism that had come up in the order. And the sense of excitement of having a room just stacked with Xeroxed copies of articles and books and running, physically running from one to the other in a state of excitement, turning a page here and turning a page there and saying, "Oh, look, how this goes with that, and how these go together." At least for me, that excitement wasn't scholarly. It had to do with making narrative, making story, which all the best historians have always known, but somehow it took another form in me. That is where it came from.

You write very carefully.

Yes, I'm a fussy writer.

Do you do many drafts?

Many drafts. I used to alternate between longhand and typed drafts. I'd write it out in longhand and then keep appending and scribbling and crossing out. And it would get almost unreadable, and then I'd type the draft, and then I'd start scribbling on that. And that would get unreadable and I would write out a draft again because it would help to have it in my hands. I came late to using a computer, but I did use a computer to write both *Ship Fever* and *The Voyage of the Narwhal,* and actually I think I probably couldn't have written them without it. I'm sort of reluctant to admit this, but it's true. Not because of the writing process, but because I had to manage so many sources. You know, that sense of needing to leave a trail for myself of where I'm plucking things from, so I can go back later. And if I write, "Oh, they set sail on the Hermaphrodite Brig"—just being able to have a draft where I put parentheses: "Looks like this, has this many masts, learned this from book X, go back and look at the pictures." Just that mechanical ease of computers can make this possible in a way that I think I would have found hard if I could only use pen and paper.

What advice do you have for writers just starting out? Are people always asking you how they can get published?

I don't know what to tell them about getting things published. It's just really different for every person, and things are complicated in publishing right now. I know the thing that helped me the most and that usually helps other people the most is just trying to be patient. And that's the hardest thing

that you can do. We all have such a drive to start publishing right away, but for a lot of us it takes a long while to get good at this. Writing isn't rocket science. It's not conversation either. It is an art, and there is a pile of stuff to learn, and it can take a long time to learn and if you can just be patient with yourself and with the time it can take and with your own working habits . . .

And if everyone around you can also be patient . . .

That's really hard, too. I was lucky. People were really patient with me for a really long time. It was almost a full decade from when I started writing hard to when I published anything, and, yeah, I think it's hard to get through those years.

Are you still teaching writing?

Well, it's very part time. But I teach in a low-residency MFA program at Warren Wilson College, which is the first and oldest and I think best of these. I usually do one semester a year. I missed two last year, but I'm actually doing it right now, so I go for 10 days at the start of the semester, and we have all these classes and workshops and lectures and we're matched up with students. I work with them through the mail for the next six months, and I just take three students at a time. It's heaven; they're really good writers and they write like crazy and send me all their stuff and I write all over it and write huge letters to them back. I fax and phone.

Are you encouraged by your students?

I am. They're wonderful writers and part of the reason I'm drawn to that program is that I like to teach one by one and by manuscript because that's what I'm good at. I'm not good in the classroom. But I also like it because it tends to draw people who came to writing later, the same way I did. You know, they're grown-ups, they have families, they have jobs. And they've also been trying very hard to write on their own for a long time, and by the time they make their way to the program they're very good and they're gigantically motivated. So they're a blast to teach and they write really beautiful things.

What's the state of the American novel at the end of the century?

Is that a real question?

Why not? People still dither over what the novel is or should be, or if it should be anything, or can be anything.

Well, perhaps insanely optimistically, at the moment the novel looks very good to me. It seems like

The Linnaeus gardens in Uppsala, Sweden, founded by the Swedish botanist Carl von Linne

© Anders Ryman/Corbis

more people are doing more various forms than I've ever seen before. Maybe the definition of the American novel has broadened and in a good way. I see an awful lot of good novels these days in such disparate categories, everything from people wrestling with history, as I'm doing, to people doing very contemporary and experimental things, people like Nicholson Baker doing *Vox*. I'm reading W. G. Sebald's *The Rings of Saturn* right now. There are so many things a novel can be now and I love that. I love to pick up a novel and be completely surprised by both the shape and the subject matter and to think, oh, but it's still a novel, another kind of novel.

What's this I hear about your playing the drums?

Where did that come from?

I saw it on the Internet.

I do. I play African percussion music. I'm very fond of it. My teachers are largely from Senegal, some of them are from Guinea, and there's a group of people in Rochester and also Buffalo that I take lessons from and/or play with and it's actually a big part of my life. I really like it.

You're famous for keeping your works in progress quiet. I assume you're working on something new?

I'm writing some stories again. I don't know where they're going yet, but I'm always working. I'm miserable when I don't work.

Source: Andrea Barrett and Peter Kurth, "The Salon Interview," in *Salon Online*, December 2, 1998, pp. 1–7.

Molly E. Rauch

In the following review, Rauch likens Barrett to a chemist with her "meticulous" prose and stories, such as "The English Pupil," permeated with science and discovery. Rauch also praises the author's talent to portray human frailty.

Some of my favorite writers have also been scientists. Primo Levi, Vladimir Nabokov and William Carlos Williams are all excruciatingly alert to intricacy, as if the precision and patience of the scientific method had rewarded them with discovery. Andrea Barrett, author of *The Forms of Water* and *The Middle Kingdom*, may not be a scientist, but you wouldn't know it from her, prose. In her new collection of stories, *Ship Fever*, she is as meticulous as any chemist, entomologist or doctor.

In "The English Pupil," Carl Linnaeus, founder of the binomial classification system, is dying. He imagines that familiar ghosts are exchanging "leaves

> Science, for Barrett, is not the unalloyed discipline of discovery and patience. In these stories it is a hell of despair and rivalry."

and twigs and scraps of blossoms" at a cocktail party stage left, his dementia increasing as dusk falls. He will tell you that "nature [is] a cryptogram and the scientific method a key" and that "nomenclature is a mnemonic art."

In the eighteenth century, Linnaeus named the natural world—ordering it, providing a common language, setting the terms of future discovery—and he haunts Barrett's stories. While for Linnaeus names should be "clear and stable and expressive," Barrett renders the world as shifting, disappointing and curiously baffling. and though Linnaeus is dying in this story, he stands on the periphery of many others like the ghosts in his own vague imagination, quietly watching. He would, I think, be pleased by Barrett's fascination with the lives of scientists. He would also be distressed by her conviction that science is bent as much by ambition, jealousy and arrogance as it is by discovery.

In the novella "Ship Fever," Dr. Lauchlin Grant leaves Montreal to work at Grosse Isle, a quarantine station for Irish immigrants flooding North America. It is 1847, and the Potato Famine has already killed thousands. Lauchlin immediately recognizes that the "ship fever" plaguing survivors of the grueling ocean journey is typhus: "They shook with chills, their muscles twitched, some of them muttered deliriously. Other were sunk in a stupor so deep it resembled death. On the chest of a man who had tom off his shirt, Lauchlin could see the characteristic rash; on another . . . the dusky coloring of his skin." Back in Montreal, Lauchlin had longed to be prestigious and successful. But what is fame in the face of this desperate sickness? "These people needed orderlies and gravediggers and maids and cooks; not physicians, not science." Science alone is insufficient, but Lauchlin does what he knows: He tirelessly cares for the violently, repulsive ill.

Trained in Paris, where "human dissection was legal," Lauchlin has modem views of medicine. He avoids bleeding his patients, for which he is criticized. He pores over textbooks, papers and folklore in an attempt to determine whether typhus is miasmatic or contagious. He notes that where patients are crammed together, the fever spreads quickly; he also notes an "infestation of lice" among the immigrants. But Lauchlin hones his understanding of science in other ways, as if to scold Linnaeus for the futility of his ordered, compartmentalizing system:

> At night I lie on the pallet in this room for a few hours and listen to the sighs and cries and moans around me, and I wonder how it is I spent my whole life with so little understanding. In Paris, I thought of medicine as a science. I thought that by understanding how the body worked, I might cure it when diseased. What's going on here has nothing to do with science, and everything to do with politics.

In "Rare Bird," Barrett offers another politicized version of the scientific method in which Linnaeus reappears. His theory that doves hibernate under water conflicts with that of a feisty ornithologist in England, Sarah Anne Billopp, who suspects that doves in fact migrate in the winter. She sets out to disprove Linnaeus's theory, overturning in the process the notions of femininity and family within which she has lived.

Constrained by eighteenth-century upper-class expectations, the unmarried Sarah Anne finds her clothes "complicated" and "burdensome," feels her time is "shattered and lost while she defers to her brother's sense of propriety" and thirsts for intellectual companionship. She writes letters to Linnaeus and receives responses that are decidedly cold—and in Latin, no less. She captures, tests and dissects wild doves with her well-educated, widowed, science-minded friend Catherine. But as the narrative focus shifts away from Sarah Anne, she becomes less an obvious heroine that a cipher. She and Catherine disappear under mysterious circumstances, leaving the central tension between propriety and liberation unresolved.

This kind of tension sustains the ambitious range of Barrett's collection, acting like magnetism upon may of her characters. While Barrett jumps from one perspective or speaker to the next, from the pages of journals and letters to the seemingly neutral, distant voice of history, her people wrestle with the inner folds of passion, the bitter lye of disappointment and the banality of death. Resolution in these stories is often partial, halting or transparent. Still, it's not a depressing collection; it is weighted more with circumspect acceptance.

Such range can lead to flaws. The stories that take place in the past—half of this collection—suffer from stumbles into prissy formalism. In "Birds With No Feet," for example, the young explorer, Alec watches his ship explode in flames, insect collection and live menagerie trapped inside. The animals caged in the forecastle are "calling through the smoke" and Alec can do nothing but watch: "His entire life, until that moment had contained nothing so distressing."

As laughably wooden as this response may be, Barrett shines when she dives into the bloody soup of human frailty. In "The Marburg Sisters," an aging father is described with chilling frankness. His daughters know about "the dying and thinning of the skin, until the slightest blow or scratch leaves blood behind. The rubbing together of fleshless bones, the sores and bruises and rashes and welts, the loosening teeth and the bleeding gums, the clumps of hair coming out in the comb, and the alternating waves of hunger and nausea." And in "Ship Fever," Lauchlin carries corpses off the ships with acute awareness: "The eighteenth body he lifted and passed was a young woman, hardly more than a girl, who'd been dead for several days. Her feet were black and twice their normal size."

Science, for Barrett, is not the unalloyed discipline of discovery and patience. In these stories it is a hell of despair and rivalry. Above all, science is action. In "The Behavior of the Hawkweeds," a story selected for *Best American Short Stories 1995*, Antonia helps her grandfather [pin the mother leaves [of Rex begonias] to the moist sand and then transplant the babies that rooted from ribs," mirroring a time when her grandfather and Gregor Mendel, the early geneticist, worked "side by side . . . open[ing] pea flowers and preferred pollen with a camel-hair brush." When science is action it propels the lives of its practitioners; its lessons, as well, transcend the confines of the discipline.

In "The Littoral Zone," married biologist Ruby studies the shoreline, "that space between high and low watermarks where organism struggled to adapt to the daily rhythm of immersion and exposure." But Ruby's inner life reflects her discipline when she finds herself in just such a space with Jonathan, another married biologist: "that odd, indefinite zone where they were more than friends, not yet lovers." Stranded somewhere between the dream and the disappointment, Ruby and Jonathan embody the taut lines Barrett has pulled through her stones, each

with their own wrenching rhythms of immersion and exposure. Those rhythms are the sounds of a writer committed to emotion and history, to nuance and absorption. The writing, then, is also a science, shot through with the blaze of discovery.

Linnaeus would be proud.

Source: Molly E. Rauch, Review of *Ship Fever and Other Stories*, in *Nation*, Vol. 262, No. 4, January 29, 1996, pp. 32–33.

Sources

Barrett, Andrea, "The English Pupil," in *Ship Fever and Other Stories*, Norton, 1996, pp. 34–46.

Fara, Patricia, *Sex, Botany, and Empire: The Story of Carl Linnaeus and Joseph Banks*, Icon Books UK, 2003, pp. 19–46.

Goerke, Heinz, *Linnaeus*, translated from the German by Denver Lindley, Charles Scribner's Sons, 1973, p. 66.

Mallon, Thomas, "Under the Microscope," in *New York Times Book Review*, January 28, 1996, p. 24.

Review of *Ship Fever and Other Stories*, in *New Yorker*, March 25, 1996, p. 91.

Review of *Ship Fever and Other Stories*, in *Publishers Weekly*, Vol. 242, No. 49, December 4, 1995, p. 54.

Schwarzbaum, Lisa, Review of *Ship Fever and Other Stories*, in *Entertainment Weekly*, No. 355, November 29, 1996, pp. 82–83.

Seaman, Donna, Review of *Ship Fever and Other Stories*, in *Booklist*, Vol. 92, No. 9–10, January 1, 1996, p. 785.

Uggla, Arvid HJ., *Linnaeus*, translated by Alan Blair, Swedish Institute, 1957, p. 7.

Further Reading

Blunt, Wilfred, *The Compleat Naturalist: A Life of Linnaeus*, Viking Press, 1971.
    In this comprehensive, well-illustrated biography, Blunt captures Linnaeus's passion for his work and shows how his system was used by naturalists all over the world and was the foundation of modern botanical science. An appendix on Linnaean classification provides a basic survey of his work.

Farber, Paul Lawrence, *Finding Order in Nature: The Naturalist Tradition from Linnaeus to E. O. Wilson*, Johns Hopkins Introductory Studies in the History of Science series, Johns Hopkins University Press, 2000.
    Farber examines the contributions of a variety of scientists to classifying and systematizing the natural world. He covers thinkers such as Nicholas Baudin, Julian Huxley, Charles Lucien Bonaparte, Stephen

Jay Gould, and Edward O. Wilson. He also argues that the work of cataloging the natural world remains vital today as biodiversity shrinks.

Hawks, Ellison, *Pioneers of Plant Study*, 1928, reprint, Books for Libraries Press, 1969.
    The focus of this volume is biographical and historical. Hawks explores how knowledge of plants has been gained through the ages, from ancient Egypt to the end of the nineteenth century. One chapter (pp. 232–38) is devoted to Linnaeus.

Koerner, Lisbet, *Linnaeus: Nature and Nation*, Harvard University Press, 1999.
    In this scholarly biography, Koerner draws on letters, poems, notebooks, and secret diaries to tell the story of Linnaeus's life. It is an engaging, sometimes amusing, and also tragic portrait.

Fish

Jill McCorkle
2001

"Fish" is a short story by American writer Jill McCorkle. It was published in her third short story collection, *Creatures of Habit* (2001). "Fish" is the final piece of the collection, in which all the stories are set in McCorkle's fictional small town of Fulton, North Carolina. Fulton is the setting for many of Mc-Corkle's stories and novels, drawn from her own experiences of growing up in the South. McCorkle is an award-winning contemporary writer known for her ability to evoke Southern life with humor and beauty. Critics agree that her talent as a writer is only improving as she continues to write.

"Fish" is a fictional memoir about the end of a man's life, as narrated by the younger of his two daughters. Surrounded by the family, the daughter ponders stories about her father's childhood, his parents, and her own childhood memories. Despite the sad subject of a parent's dying, McCorkle's short story is uplifting in its conclusion. The title of the story is symbolic, an allusion to the symbol for Jesus Christ. This short story does not show a family torn apart by grief but instead united by love. Through her remembrances, the narrator is able to keep her father close to her heart even as he dies.

Author Biography

Jill McCorkle was born July 7, 1958, in Lumberton, North Carolina, to John Wesley Jr. and Melba Ann (Collins) McCorkle. She studied creative writing

Jill McCorkle Photograph by Tom Rankin. Reproduced by permission.

with Max Steele and Lee Smith at the University of North Carolina at Chapel Hill. In 1980, the year she graduated, McCorkle won the Jesse Rehder Prize, the university's prestigious writing award. The following year she received a master's degree in writing from Hollins College.

McCorkle submitted her first novel, *The Cheer Leader*, to Algonquin Books of Chapel Hill, a new publisher founded by one of her former professors. Energized by her first sale, she quickly wrote and submitted her second novel, *July 7th*. The first book had not yet been released, so Algonquin decided to release the novels simultaneously in 1984, a daring move that garnered McCorkle a lot of critical attention for a first-time novelist. McCorkle's career never slowed down after that. In addition to prizes won while in college, McCorkle earned the New England Booksellers' Association Award in 1993 for her body of work; was named one of *Granta* magazine's Best Young American Novelists in 1996; won the North Carolina Prize for Literature and the Dos Passos Prize for Excellence in Literature, both in 1999. Five of her eight books have been Notable Books of the Year recommended by the *New York Times Book Review*. McCorkle's *Creatures of Habit* (2001) is a short story collection which includes "Fish."

As of the early 2000s, McCorkle filled in the time between novels by writing reviews and short stories. Her reviews have appeared in the *Washington Post*, the *Atlanta Journal-Constitution*, *New York Woman*, and the *New York Times Book Review*. Her short stories have been published by high profile journals such as *Cosmopolitan* and the *Atlantic Monthly*.

McCorkle has taught writing at the University of North Carolina, Tufts University, Duke University, Harvard University, Bennington College, and Brandeis University. As of 2006, McCorkle lived outside Boston with her husband and two children.

Plot Summary

"Fish" begins with news that a man, sixty-four years old, has just found out that he is dying. The cause—whether cancer or something else—is never given. Family and friends gather to comfort the man, including a woman who nursed him back from pneumonia when he was two years old. She saved him then but cannot save him now. His younger daughter narrates this story, and she recalls her father's childhood despair that he might die as did his stillborn brother. He has two older brothers and two older sisters, but his "partner" died. This sense of loss initiated a depression that haunted him for much of his life.

The narrator's eleven-year-old nephew sits with his dying grandfather and tells him all the stories the grandfather made up for him when he was very young. All of his grandchildren are there, and their affection for him is plain to see. The youngest grandchild is the narrator's baby son. Her father asks her to hold him up high so he can see the baby: "I want to see his whole body," her father says.

The narrator recalls her father's fear of water and how, nonetheless, he would wade into the pool up to his chest (the edge within reach) to watch his younger daughter dive and to cheer for her. They also went fishing together, standing in water up to their hips, and he would warn her about all the dangers of ocean fishing. Once she caught a toadfish which swallowed her hook, and her father cut the line to free it. "But just think of the fishtales he'll have for his children and grandchildren. He will always be the one that got away." He made light of it, but his daughter saw sadness in him.

Back in the present, the narrator, along with her mother and sister, Jeannie, sing her father's favorite songs for him. They are well-known love songs from the 1930s.

The narrator remembers that, before she left for college, her father gave her advice on how to be safe, and he assured her that she's never too old to come home. True to his word, when she calls him years later and asks him to come get her because she is leaving her marriage, he overcomes his fear of flying to go to her, pack up her things, and drive her home. Now, at forty years of age, the narrator is the prepared one, ready for any possibility, taking safety precautions as if second nature. It will be her turn now to pass her father's advice on to her children.

She recounts a memory of her childhood, a time she thinks her father does not remember. Their family used to take vacations to Ocean Drive in South Carolina where they rented the bottom floor of a beachside cottage and had an obnoxious upstairs neighbor who greased his body and whistled "Red Red Robin" constantly. She and her sister, Jeannie, five and nine years old respectively, buried a note on that beach in 1963 for their future selves to return to and dig up. They remembered that day, a day that was not more outstanding than any other except that it was summer vacation and their dreams were of mansions and Cadillacs and fluffy pets. Her most vivid memory of that summer is of having to clean up Play-Doh that she pressed into the rug of the rental cottage. It was difficult to pick out all the pieces, and she knew as she was sitting there cleaning it that she would remember this experience.

Casting farther into the past, the narrator remembers her paternal grandfather. Despite hardships while growing up, such as his father's alcoholism and their repossessed belongings, her father only said nice things about his father to his children, and they grew up loving him unconditionally. As a schoolboy, the narrator's father used to play hooky to go downtown and shoot pool in a dark hall. "Your eyes were always drawn to the light." The narrator describes in frank terms her father's struggle with depression:

> How frightened you must have been the first time you could not find any light at all. The times your heart was so heavy you could not rise up from the bed. . . . And there were many people willing to let you believe that . . . your overwhelming sense of loss and sadness made you less of a man.

The narrator was astonished and dismayed to learn how little understanding people had of depression and how they disrespected her father, a result of their ignorance. She and Jeannie stayed by their father's side when he was laid up in his bedroom with depression one summer in their childhood. They were afraid to leave him, afraid for him to leave them. When he was later hospitalized, his girls were too young to be allowed inside the hospital, so he came out to hug his daughters and apologize for being there. They rode home looking at a card their father gave them "about love and joy and the birth of spring." The card, the narrator recalls, "made us sad. The only resurrection I cared about was yours."

Life was renewed for their little family when their father came home from the hospital once and for all. "You were young and had many years ahead of you." Her father said the same thing to her when she left her marriage. Less than a year later, her grandfather had a stroke and was afflicted with throat cancer. The narrator went to the hospital to see her grandfather but had to wait outside. She asked her father to read her "The Little Match Girl," her favorite story at that time because it made her cry, and she liked to cry.

> It had become a kind of hobby, this need to imagine myself or someone I loved taken away. I had to prepare myself. Even now, I feel that's what I'm doing—every word, every image is a match struck in an attempt to hold on.

As her father dies, both the narrator and her sister are aware of death's imminence, as if from a sixth sense. They gather their mother and their uncle and watch this beloved man quietly pass away with one last blink of his eyes.

The narrator has two dreams about her father after he dies. First, she dreams that she has put his limp body on a swing, tying his arms to the chains to hold him in place. She is a kid, and he is wearing a robe and slippers. People pass by and tell her that she is sick and should not be holding onto the dead. She insists repeatedly that he is not dead. Eventually, they all go away, and when she and her father are alone, he lifts his head and winks at her, saying *"You're right . . . I am not dead."*

The narrator's final recollection is of her grandfather and his collie, Bruno, and how they walked to the corner store every afternoon. "This is how I remember your father. Small and neat with a hat he politely tipped at everyone he passed." He held her hand while crossing the street. He had the same blue-grey eyes as his son. In the second dream, the narrator sees her father in a mirror. He cannot speak to her because he is using all of his energy just to be visible. Her mother and sister join her in the room. The three of them are reflected in the mirror along with her father's image, briefly making them a whole family once more. He tells her in her dream, as he did before he died: "You are my heart; that's all that there is."

Characters

Father

The narrator's father finds out he is dying at the relatively young age of sixty-four. This story of his last days is narrated by the younger of his two daughters. He is the son of a butcher whose family fell on hard times, possibly because of his father's alcoholism. He is the youngest of five, having two sisters and two brothers. As a child, he felt that his partner was missing because of a stillborn baby boy born the year before he was. He also worried that he would die because he was somehow linked to the dead baby.

Despite a sad beginning to his life, he overcame pneumonia at the age of two and continued to be courageous into adulthood: saving his cat, taking care of his father, venturing into water and onto an airplane for his daughter, and finally, facing death without flinching. He never let his phobias get the best of him although these fears were not permanently overcome.

The narrator's father was not perfect, though. He suffered from depression and was eventually hospitalized for this condition, and his long absences were painful to his family. But when he finally came home and was feeling better, the narrator remembers, "it felt like life was starting again." The end of his life is filled with family, love, and memory. The remembrances of his daughter keep his spirit alive even as his body dies. Readers see his spirit in the almost otherworldly dreams the narrator has after her father dies. His voiceless communication with her implies that she and he understand something that no one else does.

Grandfather

The narrator's paternal grandfather was a butcher by trade. He had a drinking problem that may or may not have been the cause of his family's financial hardship. The narrator hints at an uneasy relationship between father and son and even recalls a story about her father carrying home her drunken grandfather when he made a public scene at a high school football game.

The narrator's memories of her grandfather are gentle and loving despite the man's troubled life. She recalls with fondness how he held her hand when crossing the street; how he smelled of bourbon and cigarette ash; how he tipped his hat to people as he passed them on the street; how he walked to the corner store every day with his old collie, Bruno. He did not know how to talk to his son about his son's depression, but he came to see him nonetheless because there was love between them.

The grandfather died not long after his son came home from the hospital after being treated for depression. He suffered a paralyzing stroke but died from throat cancer, his voice cut off.

Jeannie

Jeannie is the narrator's older sister. She has an eleven-year-old son and possibly other children. She is present with the rest of the family while their father is dying. One of the narrator's memories of her sister is of a summer vacation at the beach in South Carolina. Jeannie was nine years old, and the narrator was five. Jeannie wrote a note about who they were and their vacation, and the two girls swore that when they were older they would come back and dig it up. Jeannie's dream for their future is of Cadillac convertibles, mansions, and handsome husbands. Now an adult, she attends her father in his last days along with her sister and mother, wrapped in love and a reality that does not include mansions and convertibles.

Jeannie's Son

Jeannie's son is eleven years old, the eldest of the grandchildren. He and his grandfather share a special bond through the stories his grandfather made up for him when he was a small boy. Now, while his grandfather is on his deathbed, Jeannie's son quietly tells these stories back him as if he can keep his beloved relative alive by keeping his stories, his words, alive.

Mother

The narrator's mother figures very little in the story. Her husband is dying, and she is present, helping her daughters care for him in his last days. With her daughters, she sings her husband's favorite songs to him, hoping to make a connection, to communicate her love when he is beyond physical communication.

Narrator

The narrator is the second daughter of a man who suddenly learns he is dying at the relatively young age of sixty-four. She has a baby boy, whom her father asks to see while on his deathbed. She was once married, but it did not work out, and her father helped her leave her husband by flying out to where she was (despite his fear of flying), packing up a rental car with her belongings, and driving straight home. She also remembers, from when she was five years old, the beach cottage that her family rented in South Carolina, although those memories are somewhat disjointed and formed of vibrant sensations: the red Play-Doh smashed into the rug; the neighbor singing "Red Red Robin" continuously; the time-capsule note. Her father used to take her swimming, although he stayed by the edge because of his fear of water. One particularly poignant memory concerns a time when they were fly-fishing, and her father helped cut loose a fish that had swallowed the hook. She could see his veiled melancholy, an echo of the fish's fate.

As the narrator, her sister, and her mother help to ease his dying, the narrator gathers these memories together as a way to keep her father close even after he is gone. She loves her father deeply.

Very Old Woman

The very old woman comes to visit the dying father. She once nursed him back to health from pneumonia when he was two years old. Now she can do nothing for him except give him comfort.

Themes

Resurrection

Resurrection means to rise from the dead or to revive. Resurrection is the narrator's primary theme in "Fish." Many of the narrator's memories over the course of the story are concerned with little moments in which resurrection has occurred or nearly occurred, for example, the father's birth a year after his stillborn brother; his childhood recovery from pneumonia; his depression and subsequent recovery as an adult; and the daughter leaving her marriage and starting her life anew. The imminence of death comes as a surprise to the father at the beginning of "Fish," but he accepts it gracefully, sad only that he will miss watching his grandchildren grow. The memories the narrator recalls are a foil against death and its finality and serve to imbue a dying man with life, reviving him momentarily to the fullness of being.

At the end of the short story, the family is not mourning the father's death so much as seeing him in a new realm of existence. The narrator dreams that she is the only one who knows her father is really still alive. Then, in another dream he joins her, her sister, and her mother in a mirrored image that temporarily brings them together again. The idea that a loved one is in a different place rather than just dead and inanimate can be comforting to those left behind. The sense of transformation after death—resurrection to a new realm of being—gives the ending of the story an uplifted note. Death becomes a beginning of something new rather than an end of the mortal life.

The title "Fish" and the theme of resurrection also resonate with the Christian religion. In the early days of the Roman Empire, practicing Christians were persecuted, and these people may have kept their identities and meetings secret by using the ichthys symbol. The word, ichthys, is Greek for "fish" and may have been appropriated as a Christian symbol for a number of reasons; one is the story in which Jesus feeds five thousand people with only a small amount of fish and bread. Another idea is that letters of the Greek word for fish serve as an acronym for Jesus Christ, Son of God, Savior.

As given in her dream, the daughter believes in her father's ongoing life despite the denial of others around her, which could be understood as a reference to Mary Magdalene. Mary Magdalene was a disciple of Jesus who witnessed his crucifixion. She later discovered the sepulcher of Jesus was empty and saw a vision of angels that reassured her of his resurrection and ascension to heaven.

Familial Love

Familial love is immediately present in "Fish" with the narrator's grief over her father's impending death and the gathering of her family to be with him, to care for him, and to be with each other. But as the narrator reflects on her and her father's past, the same strong love that ties this small family (father, mother, and two daughters) together is a thread that runs back through her father's life as well. Despite the financial hardships his parents faced, his father's alcoholism, and other unspoken tensions between father and son that the narrator alludes to, she affirms to her father, "you only said nice things and we grew up to love him." This family has stuck together and cared for each other even when it meant the narrator's father, as a young man, carrying his drunken father home from a high school football game after he caused a scene. Their love was not necessarily spoken, but it was unfailingly present.

The narrator remembers the absence of her father due to his severe depression. She did not blame

Topics For Further Study

- McCorkle is a Southern writer. All of her novels and short stories are set in or around the fictional town of Fulton, North Carolina. What landscape have you grown up in? How would you describe it to others, both those who are familiar and those who are unfamiliar with the place where you grew up? Write a story, create a movie, or record a podcast to evoke that landscape and its people.

- Depression is a serious illness that can be debilitating. Research the history, symptoms, and treatments for depression. How is depression represented in this story? Write a short research paper about what you learn.

- A good title points to the central idea or subject of a story. Form a small group with a couple other students, and discuss the title's various meanings for this story, as it connects both to the story's characters and its events.

- Give a five minute presentation about your conclusions.

- Listen to recordings of the songs mentioned in the story, such as "Blue Moon" and "When You're Smiling." Who were they written and originally performed by? When were they first recorded? What do these songs tell you about the father in the story, knowing that these were his favorite? Put on a class presentation in which you play recordings of these songs and explain their relevance in the story as a way of characterizing the father and placing him in a certain time period.

- Read the rest of McCorkle's collection *Creatures of Habit*. Does "Fish" make more sense in context with the other stories? How effective is her use of animal titles? What do you think the title of the book means? Write an essay comparing "Fish" to one or two other stories in the collection.

---

him, only feared to lose him, to lose anyone. She clung to the story "The Little Match Girl," by Hans Christian Andersen, when she was young. That story is about a child who sells boxes of matches on the street to earn money for her and her father. One cold New Year's Eve night she lights match after precious match, using them up in order to keep warm. Eventually, she dies of the cold. The narrator acknowledges that her memories are like matches struck "in an attempt to hold on."

The final scenes after her father's death are not ones of grief and mourning but instead of dreams the narrator has in which her father is alive, her family brought back together. In one she sees her father in a mirror. Her mother and sister enter the room and the three of them look at the family of four standing together in the mirror image. In this dream, her father repeats what he told her on his deathbed: "You are my heart; that's all that there is." As he dies, she whispers to him, "I'll be looking for you." The ties of love in this family are not broken by death.

Style

Metaphor

Metaphor is a figure of speech in which one subject is described in terms of a dissimilar subject, in order to suggest an analogy. McCorkle uses metaphor directly at the beginning of the story when the narrator describes her father's "metaphor for life": "You WERE TERRIFIED of the water, but you loved to step into it, chest deep, pool edge within reach." The narrator's father was a courageous man, who coped with his fears by assuring his safety. She recalls his coming in the water to cheer for her when she dove and swam around him.

The toadfish the narrator catches suggests her father's ability to continue on despite problems. The hook is lodged too deeply in the fish for her father to remove it, so he cuts the line and lets the "poor old guy" swim away. The fish had a narrow escape and will live despite the hook in his body. As if drawing a comparison to himself, the father says, "But just think of the fishtales he'll have for his children and grandchildren. He will always be the one that got away." The father has lived through difficulties as a child, had depression through his adult life, and yet he has been able to go on, relating with his children and grandchildren.

Tone

Tone is the manner of expression used by the writer to convey mood, emotion, setting, or some other desired quality. The tone used by McCorkle's narrator is at first nostalgic as she reflects on her and her father's lives. She remembers events, even those from before she was born, but these are stories of her family that have been given to her. They are an oral history of sorts. The narrator's nostalgia is also accented by grief, as she watches her father die. The moment of dying can be fraught with desperation, a chance for one last opportunity, one last interaction, one last word. The dying man's wife and children beg him to blink. It is his one remaining mode of communication, the only thing on his body he can move. He obliges them, and with one final blink of his eyes, he is dead.

"Fish" ends with a definite turn toward sadness in the tone as the narrator comes to terms with her father's death. In the end, in a dream, they are briefly reunited, and the father reassures the daughter, "You are my heart; that's all that there is." The story ends on an uplifted note as the daughter promises her father as he dies that she will be looking for him.

Direct Address and Tense

"Fish" is written in first person point of view with the narrator addressing her dying father as "you." The use of direct address conveys intimacy and privacy, a communication between the speaker and a specific person. The communication is not intended for everyone, just the one being addressed. Direct address, thus, draws the reader into what in meant for only one other person. To add immediacy to this sense of privacy, McCorkle writes the story in present tense. The narrator's memories are reported in the past tense, certain past events in the father's life are also reported in past event, but the time stretching out in the present are the hours of vigil at the dying man's bedside. The narrator says, "When you come home from the hospital this time, we know that it is the beginning of the end." Some present time later, she says, "On the afternoon you die, we keep asking for a sign, a blink, a twitch." The family wants some communication back from the father, some acknowledgement. They sing to

him; they hope he hears them. In the end, at the moment before he dies, "when your eyes were still able to blink," she says, he speaks his final words, "You are my heart; that's all that there is." The deep connection between father and daughter is conveyed. The direct address and the present tense put the reader right there in the room when the father dies, right at the moment of dying.

Historical Context

U.S. Economy in Twentieth Century

"Fish" covers much of the twentieth century in the United States. One memory is from the father's childhood in the early 1930s when the United States was in the midst of the Great Depression. The Great Depression lasted for over a decade (1929–1941), ending with U.S. involvement in World War II, which created jobs and opportunities. The postwar era was a time of economic growth as the United States soared ahead of European, war-torn countries in its productivity and exportation of goods. In the late 1970s and throughout the 1980s, the U.S. economy became stagnant and then recessed, but the 1990s saw considerable growth. The present-day setting of the story is the early 1990s, when the United States was on the cusp of significant economic expansion. This expansion was matched and stimulated by exponential growth of Internet and other information technology businesses. Silicon Valley (a nickname for the Santa Clara Valley and nearby areas in northern California where many silicon chip manufacturers are located) became famous nationwide as a place in which to live and work as these businesses thrived. During the 1990s, inflation was low (money was worth more), interest rates were low (it was cheaper to borrow money for large purchases), and consumer confidence was high (Americans were more readily spending their money). Unemployment rates fell below 5 percent, the lowest they had been for thirty years. During this time, the United States was the dominant world power, and the globalization of the U.S. economy began to increase. Democratic president Bill Clinton was elected to his first term in 1992, and by the time his second term ended in 2001, the U.S. government was running on a budget surplus for the first time in thirty years. President Clinton claimed that his 1993 tax increase was the reason for the budget surplus and the stimulated economy, but many Republicans disagreed.

Terrorism in the United States

While the narrator was young, her biggest worry was her father's depression. During the father's and daughter's lives, the United States went through several wars, but their family was not directly affected. Starting in the early 1990s, during the present-day setting of this story, terrorism unfortunately became a significant topic in the United States.

The World Trade Center—also known as the Twin Towers—in New York City was first bombed in 1993 by Islamic radicals who were opposed to the international role of the United States. There were several incidents of domestic terrorist attacks (those perpetrated by U.S. citizens) in the intervening years: the Unabomber, Ted Kaczynski (1978–1995); the Oklahoma City bombing (April 19, 1995); and the Centennial Olympic Park bombing (July 27, 1996).

The largest terrorist attack carried out on U.S. soil happened on September 11, 2001. That morning, four large airplanes fueled for cross-country flights were hijacked by a total of nineteen Arabic terrorists affiliated with Al Qaeda, an Islamic fundamentalist group led by Osama bin Laden. Between 8:46 and 10:03 a.m., two of the airplanes were forced to crash into the World Trade Center towers, one crashed into the west wall of the Pentagon in Washington, D.C., and the last crash occurred in a field in Pennsylvania after the terrorists on that plane apparently failed to achieve their target (reputed to be the White House) and were perhaps overcome by the other passengers.

Critical Overview

McCorkle broke ranks as a newly published author when Algonquin Books, her North Carolina-based publisher, simultaneously released her first two novels, *July 7th* and *The Cheer Leader* in 1984. She has been a darling of critics, garnering five *New York Times Book Review* Notable Book of the Year citations as well as other prestigious awards. As of 2006, she had three short story collections and five novels in print, all published by Algonquin.

Creatures of Habit, the collection in which "Fish" was published, was well received by critics. Joanne Wilkinson, reviewing for *Booklist*, considers McCorkle's collection to be darker than her other work, which is not a negative assessment, simply an observation. Her summation is that McCorkle "writes near-perfect dialogue and is able to create

powerful emotional moods within the space of a few paragraphs." An unsigned review from *Publishers Weekly* is equally glowing, congratulating the author on not writing to formula despite her animal-centric framework. This reviewer also writes that McCorkle has a "poet's skill" and is "at the top of her game." Jo Manning at *Library Journal* highly recommends McCorkle's collection, comparing her with classic Southern writers such as Eudora Welty and Truman Capote. Susan Millar Williams, writing for the *Woman's Review of Books*, is likewise laudatory although she also states that she could do without the animal centered titles.

Criticism

Carol Ullmann

Ullmann is a freelance writer and editor. In the following essay, Ullmann examines the function of memory in McCorkle's short story.

McCorkle's short story "Fish" is something of a memoir, capturing for the reader particular events in the lives of the narrator and her dying father. While the narrator's theme is resurrection, her method is memory. The sequence of memories is not strictly chronological, and this story does not pretend to be the narrator's autobiography. Autobiographies tend to be more committed to spanning the history of a person's entire life. Memoirs tend to be more topical, consisting of bits of experience, selected to illustrate a particular theme. In this story, the narrator characterizes her now dying father by remembering scenes and experiences with him from her childhood. Through memories she shows his courage and quick action in saving his cat, his pride and compassion in carrying his drunken father home, his thoughtfulness in keeping the relationships between his children and his grandfather free of his own issues with his father, and his struggle with depression that challenged him until he succumbed and had to be saved himself. Despite the obstacles in his life, he seems to have been a positive person and a loving father. When he finds out that he is dying, he only says, "I am sixty-four years old and I have had a good life." He is relatively young to be dying, but he has overcome so much and lived a life rich in love. Through her memories of her father, the narrator shows her love for him, and she keeps his humble and affectionate spirit alive.

Memory is evoked through the physical senses. Smell is, in many ways, the strongest memory inducer because it is complex, thorough, and visceral. Particular smells can bring back memories and connected emotions. Sometimes the memory is unconscious until a person encounters the smell that brings the memory to consciousness. The narrator recalls, while thinking about her grandfather: "I fell in love with a boy who smelled like him only to later realize that the treasured memory I carried of your father was one of straight bourbon and cigarette gone to ash." Bourbon and cigarettes are not necessarily nice smells, but the narrator has connected them with her grandfather, whom she loves, so for her those smells bring on good memories and feelings. This association of smell with the grandfather also reveals the significance for the narrator's father of having a father himself who was an alcoholic.

The eleven-year-old son of Jeannie, the narrator's sister, has his fond memories of his grandfather tied up in word and sound. He is the narrator's nephew, her father's eldest grandchild. He remembers all of the stories that his grandfather told him while he was growing up. He sits by his grandfather's bed as the older man is dying, remembering those stories and telling them back to him. The narrator says that her father and this boy have a similar ability to remember details: "It is a secret he shares with you." The stories the boy tells to his grandfather are a comfort to them both, a sign of their intimacy. Like the narrator with her memories of her father, the nephew retells these stories; telling them is his way of keeping his grandfather alive. All of his grandchildren have been given stories, and they now come to their grandfather with secrets and kisses to make him smile. The narrator can also connect to her father through a story he read to her. Her favorite fairytale as a child was Hans Christian Andersen's "The Little Match Girl." The story made her cry, and she liked crying because she felt it prepared her to lose people she loved such as her father (to depression) and her grandfather (to throat cancer). Many years later, watching her father slowly die, the narrator sees herself again as the match girl, and she concludes, "every word, every image is a match struck in an attempt to hold on." "Fish" is the narrator's metaphorical box of spent matches.

Trying to remind their father of better times, to bring him comfort, the narrator, Jeannie, and their mother sing to him even though he is past being able to respond or even blink a reply. These songs are like stylized memories of happier days. They sing his favorite songs, popular love tunes from the

> **As emotional and subjective as memory is, it is the retrieval mechanism people have by which to revisit the past."**

1930s such as "Blue Moon" and "All of Me." This music is also a comfort for the women. Even though he cannot reply, they continue to sing, feeling close to him through the music that he loved.

The narrator has a vivid memory from the summer of 1963 when she was five years old and her sister was nine. She remembers the tactile experience of cleaning red Play-Doh from the braided rug of their rented beach cottage in South Carolina. The work and the repentance involved in cleaning that rug struck her even then, young as she was, as having the potential to be an enduring memory.

> I knew even as I sat there, rubbing and picking, that I would never forget, that I would think of it often. That I would grow up to believe that rectifying a mistake is sometimes reason enough to exist.

Memory is notable for its unreliability when held up against fact. So much of what people experience through their senses is ultimately colored by a partial understanding of events, by emotion, prejudice, preference, even by attention span. Given all the filters, the actual facts concerning an event can be drastically altered as they are housed in memory, making memory a potentially unreliable way to collect history. But memory is important to one's self concept and one's sense of personal history. As emotional and subjective as memory is, it is the retrieval mechanism people have by which to revisit the past. In her memories, the narrator stores her love of her father, love that can be communicated to others when she reminisces.

The memories relived in "Fish" range from small, almost trivial events to momentous occasions. The narrator remembers how her grandfather held her hand when they crossed the street. She thinks about how her father freed his cat and how he carried his drunken father home. She recalls her

What Do I Read Next?

- *Downhome: An Anthology of Southern Women Writers* (1995), edited by Susie Mee, is a collection of fiction, spanning many decades, from powerful voices of women in the South such as Lee Smith, Zora Neale Hurston, Eudora Welty, Katherine Anne Porter, and Flannery O'Connor.

- *July 7th* (1984), one of McCorkle's first two novels, tells with humor and action the tale of an unsolved murder at a small town convenience store.

- *The Cheer Leader* (1984), one of McCorkle's first two published novels, tells the story of Jo Spencer, a young woman who is perfect and accomplished in every way until one year in college when her life spirals out of control.

- Alice Hoffman's *Practical Magic* (1995) is a novel about the Owens sisters, who are raised by their aunts who practice magic. As adults, the sisters both escape this strange life, but eventually they are drawn back to their childhood home in a small New England town for a surprising revelation.

- *Their Eyes Were Watching God* (1937), by Zora Neale Hurston, tells the story of Janie Crawford, a black woman in her forties during the late nineteenth century. Janie tells her life story (which includes three marriages) to her friend Pheoby.

Hurston was a renowned African American folklorist and author from the South.

- *Oral History* (1983), by Southern writer Lee Smith, is a novel about a young woman in college who returns to her home in Appalachian Virginia to record an oral history of her family. The story she hears includes information about a curse, murder, and suicide.

- Harper Lee's 1960 novel, *To Kill a Mockingbird*, is the story of an eight-year-old girl, her brother, and their lawyer father during the Depression in Alabama. In their town, a black man is accused of raping a white girl, and the lawyer defends the black man but loses the case due to local racial prejudice.

- *The Optimist's Daughter* (1972), by Eudora Welty, is a novel about Laurel Hand, a woman who returns home to Mississippi when her stalwart father falls ill and then dies. Laurel reflects upon her past and comes to a better understanding of her family. Welty's novel won the Pulitzer Prize in 1973.

- *The Heart Is a Lonely Hunter* (1940), Carson McCullers's first novel, is about a deaf-mute man in a 1930s Georgia mill town and the lives of four of his close acquaintances.

---

father in the hospital being treated for depression and how she and her sister visited him, wanting him to come home. Given the emotional nature of memory, not all recollections are momentous. It is what the memory comes to signify that matters most.

The narrator recalls going fishing with her father. He helped her cut loose a toadfish that had swallowed her hook and threw the fish back into the water. The narrator recalls her father clearly—the gaiety and laughter overlaying a shadow of old disappointment. He told her, "just think of the fishtales he'll have for his children and grandchildren. He will always be the one that got away." This fish

served as a metaphor for her father; both the fish and her father had a close escape from death. His stories have now become his daughter's memories.

The narrator draws on these memories as a way to keep her father's spirit alive, to figuratively resurrect him from his deathbed. On the outside, she sings to him his favorite love songs, playing to his own sense of memory in order to comfort him. Inside, she relives her memories of their lives just as her nephew relives his grandfather's stories by reciting them back to him. Their recitals are a requiem, or lament, for the dead, except for the reoccurring theme of resurrection and for the narrator's dreams at the end of the story. Through memory, she has found a part of her father—the stories of his life—that is still vibrant and alive. Although her father dies, she has not given up on his life. "You are my heart," he tells her, "that's all that there is." A few days later, she replies, "I'll be looking for you." The narrator's father will always be there, captured within his daughter's memories of him.

Source: Carol Ullmann, Critical Essay on "Fish," in *Short Stories for Students*, Thomson Gale, 2007.

Jill McCorkle and Sherry Ellis

Ellis is the editor of NOW WRITE! *a collection of fiction writing exercises published by Tarcher/Penguin in September, 2006.* Illuminating Fiction, *her anthology of author interviews, is forthcoming from Red Hen Press in September, 2007. She is at work on a novel and a collection of non-fiction writing exercises. Her author interviews have also appeared in* The Kenyon Review, The Writer's Chronicle, Glimmer Train, *and* AGNI, *as well as other literary and arts magazines. A personal writing coach, she teaches writing in Concord, Massachusetts. In the following interview, Ellis talks with the author about* Creatures of Habit, *her theme of connecting animal traits to human behavior, autobiographical threads in her stories as well as other themes, her writing process, and being a Southern writer.*

Jill McCorkle was raised in Lumberton, North Carolina. The summer after she completed second grade she transformed her father's wooden work shed into a writing room and decorated it with dress-up clothing, a tea set, and fishing gear. When she was twenty-six her first two novels, *The Cheerleader* and *July 7th*, were published to critical acclaim. She has published five additional works of fiction to date: *Tending To Virginia* (1989), *Ferris Beach* (1991), *Crash Diet: Stories* (1992), *Carolina Moon* (1996, an excerpt of which appeared in *AGNI 44*), *Final Vinyl Days and Other Stories* (1998), and *Creatures of Habit* (2001). Five of these works have been selected as *New York Times* Notable Books of the Year.

"Billy Goats," the first story in *Creatures of Habit*, was originally published in *Bomb* magazine and subsequently selected for *The Best American Short Stories 2002*. Richard Bausch called this collection "so rich, so complete an experience . . . McCorkle paints everything with such clarity, and beauty . . . With every line, she incites my awe and wonder."

> " I do believe we all crave the security of home. I think we like to believe that our loyalties are not in vain. And, I think that some of our worst reactions in life are fear-driven. A trapped or frightened animal lashes out in an attempt to survive and humans do the same."

McCorkle's short stories have been widely published in literary journals and commercial magazines, including *The Atlantic Monthly*, *Cosmopolitan*, and *Ladies Home Journal*. Her new story, "Intervention" appears in the Fall issue of *Ploughshares*. She has also reviewed books for *The New York Times*, *The Washington Post*, and the *Atlanta Journal-Constitution*.

She has received the New England Booksellers Association Award for her body of work in fiction, the Jon Dos Passos Prize for Excellence in Literature, and the North Carolina Award for Literature. In 1996 she was included in *Granta*'s celebration of the Best of Young American Novelists. She now teaches writing at Bennington College and has also taught at Harvard, Brandeis, Duke, Tufts, and the University of North Carolina.

McCorkle is frequently described as a "Southern writer," despite the fact that she has been living in Greater Boston for the past ten years with her husband and children. Recently, I joined in her living room while her three dogs relaxed nearby. Resting in the corner of the room was a large Victorian dollhouse that McCorkle built and decorated herself.

[Sherry Ellis:] In Creatures of Habit *you revisit the fictional town of Fulton. What made you decide to return?*

[Jill McCorkle:] I think I've always returned there, whatever I've named it. It's certainly my fictional hometown, which is very much like my real hometown, but not the way it looks now, the way it looked when I was a child.

I know we always look back with a nostalgic glance, but I really did have a great sense of freedom and ownership of the town in which I was raised. It was a time when children went out until the street lights came on, and if our parents had known where we were and what we were doing they would have had heart attacks. There was just all this freedom. One of my favorite places to sit was under the bridge of the I-95 overpass.

That time in my hometown marks not just the transition for me into adolescence and adulthood, but I think also represents the transition of the South into what is now most often referred to as the New South. As I was growing up, I-95 started to pass through my town. As a result, there was a huge growth spurt and suddenly there were billboards and fast-food chains. The interstate connected us in a way that I never felt connected before.

The stories in this collection are named after animals and have woven into them the common movements, characteristics, and experiences that animals and humans share. In the story "Cats" you liken an ex-husband to a misplaced cat. Later in the same story, Anne, the ex-wife, wonders, "Why else do women so easily settle in with their litters and nests; why do the females in nature blend into the background while the males remain flashy and continue life as sexual predators?" In the story "Dogs" the main characters states, "If I were a dog I would have been put down by now." How did you decide to explore this theme?

Well, it's funny. I didn't begin this collection with the idea of all the animal connections; it evolved as I was writing. I often think there are natural thematic connections when you have a whole litter of story ideas at the same time. I wasn't just writing one story and putting it down; I had many stored up, and as I was moving from story to story—sketching out what I did know—I started to see the connections. Actually the opening story, "Billy Goats," was written more as a mood piece than anything. I didn't want the characters directly connected, but I wanted there to be the sense that these people populated the same community. This is where as a writer I realize that it's so valuable for me to take notes of little things I notice in life along the way. Sometimes I hold onto them for years.

The whole idea for "Cats" was inspired by my family losing a favorite cat and actually burying him in Tupperware in my yard (I was afraid he'd explode). So, in real life there was the loss of this cat, which made me think about other cats, particularly one from childhood who was lost for weeks and ultimately found his way home. I was greatly influenced by the likes of "Thomasina and The Incredible Journey," the Walt Disney movie, and I started imagining a situation where a person is attempting a similar journey. It led to the idea of a man with early Alzheimer's who actually thinks his home is with the first wife instead of the new wife across town. What started out as a more darkly comical theme, about the cat and the Tupperware mausoleum, turned into something much sadder.

In "Tippy's Teeth," an essay you wrote for "the Algonkian"—a promotional pamphlet put out by Algonquin—you state that "human behavior is not so far removed from the most primitive animal behavior as we like to think," for example that "we all crave a sense of the den" and that "a person who is that insecure and fearful is likely—metaphorically—to lunge and bite." Can you please comment on this and offer a few examples of how you demonstrate these similarities in your stories?

I do believe we all crave the security of home. I think we like to believe that our loyalties are not in vain. And, I think that some of our worst reactions in life are fear-driven. A trapped or frightened animal lashes out in an attempt to survive and humans do the same. Dogs are put down or "sent to the country" as my Tippy was for aggressive behavior.

I was talking to a friend on a particularly stressful day and I said: "If I was a dog I'd have been put down by now." I knew even as I said it that I'd use it for a first line. As I explained in "Tippy's Teeth," I did once accidentally kill a cat by dipping it in a flea dip designed for dogs and I used that incident in my story. For me it was a kind of exorcism as I'd been haunted by the memory for years; I still can't bear to think about it.

The main character in the story "Billy Goats" recalls her life as a seventh-grader, when she and her friends prowled through their neighborhood in a pack, "a herd of kids on banana-seat bikes and minibikes," as they discuss their community, the lives and deaths of people they know, and their own vulnerability. How much of this story is based on your own childhood experience?

Very much. I felt the opening story and the closing story about the death of the father were my stories, and as close to reality as I'm going to get. The facts aren't necessarily true but the voice and the place are.

I think every town has its stories. I tell my students to write about the character in their community, that person whom everybody takes for granted, laughs about, talks about; or to think of the cases of domestic sadness you can reel off in the moment. I mean here in the town I live in now, there is a house that is referred to as "the divorce house." There's always a divorce house, a suicide house. In my home town there was a house we referred to as the murder-suicide house. When my husband and I were looking for houses I drove the realtor crazy because I kept saying there must be something with a house, if we could afford it. Was there a suicide? Was there a murder? I'm superstitious enough to be bothered by such. I guess there were enough people asking the questions because the realtors have to tell you these things. I think those are the situations and landmarks that really inform childhood; you begin to learn about what's bad and what's not right in the parental world.

Your writing has been referred to as "Southern" and is compared to Eudora Welty's. What does being a Southern writer mean to you?

Well I have no problem being called a Southern writer because clearly as soon as I open my mouth there's the proof. And the South is very much my writing home as well. Even though characters sometimes wind up in different places than where they begin.

There's certainly a wonderful tradition in history that I'm proud to be associated with. I think other characteristics of Southern writing, not that they don't apply to other writers, is that there is a lot of attention to a strong sense of place, and there is also a wonderful tradition of oral storytelling. I think that any community or group that, for whatever reason, has been cut off from the rest of the world, usually does have an oral tradition—because it's so important to make sure that the legacy is handed over. And of course in the South, not only was there the War, which of course is what everyone immediately associates with Southern people, but there were other roadblocks as well, literacy being one of the biggest. I mean, my grandmother was very fortunate that she went through the ninth grade; my grandfather only completed the third. So they could tell stories they never would have been able to write. There was a lot of power in the spoken word, and it was revered as such, I think. I think a lot of that oral tradition is classic in Southern literature. You can't get from point A to point B easily, you've got to wander off to the side and tell this story. The writer Barry Hannah tells his

version of the light bulb joke: How many Southern writers does it take to change a bulb? Two . . . one to unscrew it and the other to talk about what a good old light bulb it was.

When you were in the second grade your motivation as a writer was to get a laugh or a tear. Is this still your goal?

I think as a child it was wonderful to discover that I had this power to make myself laugh or cry, and of course that grew into wanting to have the effect on others. Often what I see or hear in the world strikes me as funny. I start with something that's making me laugh, and yet I'm enough of a realist that I never believe it's that simple; then I start looking for what's under the funny. It's a method I've used often in terms of the stories expanding to a different level. Again, the story "Cats" is a perfect example of this.

Do you think that your childhood and adult hobbies and pastimes, for example fishing and dollhouse decorating, have helped you develop qualities that a writer needs?

Oh, totally, and I always like to credit my dad with this one. He always said that he loved to sit and look at the ocean, but that if he just sat there and stared and my mother saw, she would start nagging him: "What are you doing just sitting there? Go and do something."

He said, "This is why I fish". And he said the trick is that if they ever start biting too much, you stop baiting the hook. I was his fishing buddy. We rarely caught anything, but it was just that kind of quiet thinking time, and so I did learn a lot as a writer.

It's hard to justify to the world, especially to your family, why you're just going to sit in a chair and stare like a zombie. And so my whole life I've had hobbies that are solitary in nature. You know the saying "busy hands, busy minds." As an adult I built a dollhouse. The work of putting a house together and then decorating is very similar to writing a novel; you're creating this world and you have a certain level of control over it. Most of my activities are singular. When I think about sports or activities I liked growing up—ballet, gymnastics, swimming—I realize they were actions that didn't require me to interact with others. My mind was free to roam.

Do you believe all writers need "rooms of their own"?

Yes, I do, and I think all writers already have a room of their own in terms of within the self. I find when I don't get that quiet time nothing else in life feels quite right; I think it's a constant struggle to find a room of your own. I do have an office in my home, but when there is a lot going on in I can't work. Sometimes the room of my own is the car parked in the grocery store parking lot, or wherever I can get it.

Willa Cather once said, "There are only two or three human stories, and they go on repeating themselves as fiercely as if they had never happened before." Do you agree?

I do. I think we are very limited thematically and that's why we all identify with each other's stories. It's the specific detail and history that we can bring to them that makes our work or characters lives unique.

You are quoted as having said, "I have always believed that by the ripe age of adolescence . . . our emotional baggage is packed." In your novel The Cheerleader, *a story about young women coming of age, Jo challenges stereotypes of popularity. Do you believe that Jo's and Beatrice's "emotional baggage is already packed"?*

I think the characters have more than enough to think about and unpack and to understand through adulthood. I had a professor say to me when *The Cheerleader* came out, "My god, Jill! Most of us spend all our lives trying to forget all this stuff, and you have dedicated yourself to dredging it up." And I thought, well, I guess it's sort of an exorcism. It's such a classic period of life and I am interested in young women because there are so many fears and things that happen in that little space of time, the whole body image, the everything! I have to say it, but I don't necessarily think we've come too far in taking care of it.

I feel really drawn to that age group and more than any other work, I've gotten more letters about *The Cheerleader*, mainly from seniors in high school and freshman in college, and one, a letter that I will always treasure, from a grandmother who said that the book had helped her understand her granddaughter, which really meant a lot. I guess of all my books this is the one that most consistently gets the most letters, and they always begin with "Did you read my journal?" And it feels so good, and so right, that this is such a universal phenomena. We all fit somewhere on that spectrum of Jo and Beatrice. What I had wanted to show in that novel is regardless of stereotype—positive stereotype, negative stereotype—there are real dangers in being labeled by others. I think (I hope) that this book shows that these two girls have more in common than anyone would think.

Do you pre-select the time frame in which your stories and novels will occur?

No. The only time I consciously did that was with the novel *July 7th*, when I knew was going to write about just one day.

You have often written in the first person, as in your novels Ferris Beach *and sections of* Carolina Moon. *When you write a story or a novel do you know beforehand which point of view you will use?*

I don't always know, sometimes I flounder back and forth. I feel that usually if I stick with the story and keep revising it, the story dictates which point of view best serves it; the same with tense and genre, for that matter. Very often in student work I will see a student set out to write a story in third person, present tense, and it just won't stay there: it won't be in the past, they'll flip into the present, or they'll flip into "I," and so I can always tell when the story is pulled in another direction. I think that's something you listen to.

How do your choose your titles, for example Creatures of Habit?

Titles are often the last thing to come. I was very relieved to be able to look up *Creatures of Habit*. I thought it must have been used zillions of times. I think there was only one novel years ago. It's a phrase I use a lot, to describe myself. The other one that my husband always says in reference to me is "Spontaneity has its time and its place," and that's me: I have a plan and when I'm without a plan I've sort of lost the concept and I can't see. I'm always saying, "I'm a creature of habit." In childhood I went through that obsessive-compulsive thing where you have to go back and make sure the drawer is closed; then I had years of checking the coffee maker. Now I have one that automatically cuts off. I have a system and I am a creature of habit. I had jotted down a lot of title ideas and I was reading Darwin at the time, what I could read of Darwin. I kept tripping on the word "habit."

In the story "Crash Diet," Sandra White Barkley is left by her husband for a woman who is thinner and years younger than she is, and in the story "Departures," Anna Craven, a widow, spends her free time trying to escape from the emptiness of her home. Do the themes of these stories represent a feminist perspective?

Yes, I think so. It's so interesting, I'm glad you're asking this question because people often avoid the feminist question. I have all these young students now who will say, "Well, I'm not a feminist." And I'll say, "Well, of course you are, you should be. That's why you're sitting here taking this class." Somewhere along the line the word got distorted. I don't think all my characters are knowledgeable enough or wise enough that they would necessarily see it that way, but I guess I always feel that they're coming into their own. I love that Rebecca West quote, "I've never been able to find out precisely what feminism is. I only know that people call me a feminist whenever I express sentiments that differentiate me from a doormat." So I do think they are feminists in nature in that they are finding a place in the world, and focusing on where they stand and how they affect others, rather than just how they are feeding into the lives of everyone else. It's not always pleasant. I think for someone like Anna, it's as if her limbs have been ripped off; Sandra is a bit more open about her independence, I think.

You've been living in Greater Boston for many years. Do you think that the sensibilities and styles of the North have influenced you as a writer?

Yes. If nothing else, I am always making a mental comparison to the way the experience might play out in the South. More than anything though, what I experience is how much humans—regardless of age, race, religion, geography or any other label you might choose—have in common. As a teacher—both in New England and in the South—I think the bigger differences have to do with urban or rural childhoods.

In the story "Final Vinyl Days" you write from a male perspective for the first time. Can you comment on what this experience was like for you?

That was a stretch. He was a hard character but it was a challenge I needed because I knew that one of my main characters in *Carolina Moon* was going to be a guy. Once I get inside a character and have a sense of who he is, then I don't think it matters that much. I really do think that if you find what is motivating a character emotionally, it allows you to transcend race and age and gender.

What are the greatest rewards of writing for you?

It always sounds so selfish when I think about it. For me, the greatest reward in writing is the stability and the pleasure that it brings to me. I love the act of writing. That may be why I have trouble rationalizing to everybody why I do it, because I've never come to a point where I feel like its work. I feel it is a real luxury. I think it is fantasy life.

What about the hardest parts of writing?

Sometimes it's the frustration of not being able to get there. I've never had just unlimited time to write, so I don't know how I would function that way. I've always taught and had responsibility with kids and family, so it's difficult sometimes to carve out that time. I also think that as much as writers are driven by the desire to be published and read by others, I think there's a kind of love-hate relationship—because I think the whole act of then being published is the antithesis of what your writing life is all about. I mean your writing life is cocooned and safe and then all of a sudden you're stripped and out there, and that's not always easy. I think you have to find ways to keep yourself upright and somehow attached to that center that makes you want to write anyway.

In a recent article you wrote for Food and Wine *magazine, you quote the chef of a restaurant: "I need to know the rules before I break them." Do you believe this adage apply to writers too?*

I think it applies to most endeavors. I certainly encourage students who want to write experimentally that they first go with the more conventional pieces, to show that they can do it. I think there is a lot to be learned within the basics and tradition that will only make it better as you experiment.

In another recent magazine article you wrote, this one for Real Simple, *you state that comedy and humor helps people cope with tragedy. Do you believe that as a writer, you have purposely given your fictional characters humorous situations to help them cope with the traumas in their lives?*

Absolutely. Or maybe more specifically, I believe there is always humor to be found. Even within the most hideous situations, people continue to say and do quirky things.

Who are the writers that you believe have most influenced your work?

That's a very long list. I can certainly say among contemporary writers my teachers Lee Smith and Louis Rubin and Max Steele, and in terms of just "old faithfuls" and writers I feel I've learned a tremendous amount from reading, the bulk of them being of the old southern school: Eudora Welty, Harper Lee, Carson McCullers, Truman Capote, Flannery O'Connor, Katherine Anne Porter. I would also have to say Sherwood Anderson; *Winesburg, Ohio* is one of those books that made a huge impact on me as a writer.

Justice Brandeis is quoted as having said, "There is no great writing, only great rewriting." When you have finished revising your work how similar is it to your initial draft?

It varies piece to piece, but I would say quite different, I would hope different. I would say that the first draft for me, especially with stories, is like a skeleton and then each run of revision is like transparencies in an anatomy book, you're adding the muscles and the tissues and the organs, and you begin to see how they all connect and work together. That's why I find revision so very exciting and satisfying.

Do you have a sense of knowing when something is done and when it's time to stop revising?

Sometimes it's just being so sick of a piece that I can't look at it anymore. But I feel like I know when I'm almost there, and usually that's when I ask for a reader. My editor is very good about responding. She can just zero in on little areas that need a little more or less.

What are you working on now?

Well, I've got a novel I've been working on forever, a situation about a group of friends who have come together. Talk about how many stories there are! How many times have you heard that one: women gathering to talk? And then I'm also writing some stories.

How would you describe the changes in your writing over time, for example the characters you choose, their situations and their voices?

I feel they've really changed. I have felt that my work has gotten progressively darker. I think there is still light in there, but I think that I've felt safe enough or confident enough as a writer to push my characters further than I have before. I love to see and express humor in life but I'm always curious about the underbelly of it all.

Do you think you will keep returning to Fulton?

Oh yes. I'll always go back. Actually this new novel takes place very near Fulton. Right now in my mind it's set on Bald Head Island, right off the Carolina coast.

Source: Jill McCorkle and Sherry Ellis, "Creature of Habit: An Interview with Jill McCorkle," in *AGNI Online*, 2003, pp. 1–9.

Robert A. Beuka

In the following essay, Beuka gives a critical analysis of McCorkle's life and work.

Jill McCorkle is often hailed as a leading voice in the fiction of the "New South," a chronicler of the lives of everyday people whose strong connections to family and place help them to persevere through relationship woes and the travails of their seemingly prosaic, yet emotionally complicated lives. McCorkle's writing is characterized by her adeptness at catching the voice of the common person and her keen eye for detail as she precisely captures the trappings of working-class and middle-class life. Her work is often set in the small towns of what has come to be called the "New South," locales where generationally rooted sense of place is slowly giving way to the interchangeable landmarks of late-twentieth-century America: strip malls, chain restaurants and hotels, and faceless apartment complexes. Against this bland backdrop McCorkle maps her characters' lives, imbuing what might otherwise be considered a mundane existence with vitality and depth through her balanced use of caustic wit and compassion for her characters. Noted from the outset of her career as an accomplished novelist, McCorkle has, with the publication of two short-story sequences in recent years, also established herself as a highly skilled short-story writer.

Jill Collins McCorkle was born in Lumberton, North Carolina, on 7 July 1958 to John Wesley McCorkle Jr., a postal worker, and Melba Ann (née Collins) McCorkle, a medical secretary. After graduating from Lumberton High School in 1976, McCorkle attended the University of North Carolina (UNC) at Chapel Hill, honing her writing skills under the tutelage of Max Steele and Louis Rubin and graduating with highest honors and a B.A. in creative writing in 1980. She went on to earn an M.A. in creative writing from Hollins College in Virginia in 1981. Already a promising talent in her university years, McCorkle published her first short story, "Mrs. Lela's Fig Tree", in the Fall 1979 issue of the UNC literary magazine *Cellar Door*, while her second published story, "Bare Facts", won her the Jesse Rehder Prize for fiction, the most prestigious writing award offered by UNC. Subsequently, while in the writing program at Hollins, McCorkle won the university's Andrew James Purdy Prize for fiction. After graduation she spent a brief period working as an office receptionist in New York City before relocating to Florida, where she was a teacher in the Brevard County public school system in 1982-1983. For a short time she held the position of acquisitions librarian at the Florida Institute of Technology Library in Melbourne, Florida, and in 1984 she returned to Chapel Hill, taking a job as a secretary at the medical school at UNC.

During the various moves and job changes in her postcollege years, McCorkle continued writing, completing her first novel, *The Cheer Leader* (1984), while in New York and her second, *July 7th* (1984), during her years in Florida. Her return to native grounds coincided with McCorkle's explosion onto the literary scene; in 1984, the year she returned to Chapel Hill, the relatively young publishing house of Algonquin Books made the bold decision to publish both of McCorkle's "first" novels simultaneously. This unprecedented move garnered a good deal of attention for McCorkle, and the previously unknown author had suddenly arrived, to a good deal of critical acclaim. Her new-found status as successful author soon enabled McCorkle to leave behind the world of the office receptionist, and in 1986 she accepted a lectureship in creative writing at UNC. Still, her years as a receptionist were not all for naught, for while working at the UNC medical school she met her future husband, medical student Dan Shapiro. The couple relocated to Boston in 1989, and McCorkle accepted a position teaching creative writing at Tufts University. After returning for a time to North Carolina in 1989, McCorkle and her husband moved again to Boston in 1992, and she accepted the position of Briggs-Copeland Lecturer at Harvard University. McCorkle continues to live in the Boston area with her husband and two children, where she serves on the creative-writing faculty at Bennington College, Bennington, Vermont.

McCorkle already had published four highly regarded novels and was a veteran short-story writer— having placed stories in such popular magazines as *Atlantic Monthly*, *The Southern Review*, *Cosmopolitan*, and *Seventeen*—when she published her first short-story collection, *Crash Diet*, in 1992. A collection of eleven stories that portray the relationship troubles and consequent identity crises of a series of female protagonists, *Crash Diet* garnered wide critical acclaim, winning the New England Bookseller's Award in 1993. In 1992 Brad Hooper, reviewer for *Booklist*, praised the "remarkable sensibility" McCorkle demonstrates in the collection, and in the same year Pam Houston, reviewer for *The Los Angeles Times*, called *Crash Diet* a "generous, warm and honest book." In these eleven short stories—nine of which are told in the first person—McCorkle presents several women who are struggling but undefeated, generating a sense of empathy for each through the same balance of hard-earned humor and pathos recognizable to fans of her previous novels.

The title story, which opens *Crash Diet*, offers what might be an apt metaphor for the collection as a whole: the story of a perpetually overweight, recently separated woman whose dwindling sense of self-worth is measured in the lost inches of her own shrinking body, as she embarks upon a "crash diet" in the wake of her separation and discovery of the "other woman" in her husband's life. Sandra, the first-person narrator, shows the tenacity

> " McCorkle acknowledged the importance of geography to her work in a personal interview in 1999, noting that the 'sense of place' exhibited in her stories is the primary autobiographical element she sees in her fiction as a whole."

that characterizes so many of the women in this collection with her opening words of the story, in which she handles her husband's departure with defiant nonchalance: "Kenneth left me on a Monday morning before I'd even had the chance to mousse my hair," she announces. Ultimately a survivor, like all of the women in *Crash Diet*, Sandra nonetheless struggles to find herself after the dissolution of her relationship; indeed, she is literally "losing" herself over the course of the story, as her largely unconscious yet obsessional avoidance of food causes her to lose so much weight that she eventually ends up in the hospital.

The turning point of the story comes after Sandra's release from the hospital, when the selfish Kenneth comes to visit only, it turns out, to have her sign the divorce papers. As her despondent husband informs Sandra that his relationship with the other woman has ended, Sandra signs the papers in what she refers to as "the script of a fat person." Thus liberated by her own signature, Sandra shows a newfound acceptance of herself in an observation that is characteristic of McCorkle's biting sense of humor: "some things you just can't shake; part of me will always be a fat person and part of Kenneth will always be gutter slime." The story closes, appropriately enough, with a successful dinner party thrown by Sandra, whose acceptance of food is symbolic of her newfound sense of self. In both literal and figurative terms, Sandra has learned to emphasize "growth" over "loss," finding that what remains at the end of her dissolved relationship is nothing less than herself.

The thematic concerns of "Crash Diet" resurface in several other stories as McCorkle shapes the collection around the dominant, recurring theme of women surviving troubles with men. "Man Watcher" is a loosely plotted tale that chronicles the observations of the narrator, a divorced woman named Lucinda, on the various types of men she sees. Lucinda has so honed her precise—perhaps embittered—powers of observation that she proposes to write a "book about it all, all the different types of the species. You know it would sort of be like Audubon's bird book. I'd call it *Male Homo Sapiens: What You Need to Know to Identify Different Breeds.*"

This categorizing approach also informs the stories "First Union Blues" and "Comparison Shopping", two more first-person narratives that find their protagonists immersed in unsatisfying relationships, longing for more passionate relationships from the past while facing an unrewarding present and uncertain future. In each of these stories McCorkle uses diametrically opposed male characters (the virile, romantic, reckless man of the past versus the conventionally successful, staid, unappealing man of the present) as foils to help express her narrator's longings and insecurities. Each of these tales also ends with a moment of sudden affirmation, as McCorkle's heroines offer variations on the concluding declaration of Maureen Dummer, narrator of "First Union Blues", who—after facing her relationship crises and determining to survive on her own—concludes simply, "I want to live."

The majority of the stories in this collection are also united by McCorkle's precisely realistic treatment of the New South landscape. Typically setting her tales in small southern towns, like that of her native Lumberton, where the once time-honored sense of community identity is rapidly eroding, McCorkle explores the emotional crises of her female protagonists against the background of what is becoming an indistinguishable and often alienating terrain. Amid denizens of condo "communities" and interchangeable subdivisions, McCorkle's heroines often struggle in discovering their own identity within a homogeneous environment.

In this regard the reader senses the irony in statements such as Maureen's in "First Union Blues": "before I knew it, I was . . . living in a condo with a wreath on every wall and a big hooked rug that I bought at the outlet mall over near the airport. That place has got everything you might want and then some. Everything." When McCorkle's narrators work toward defining themselves against such an uninspiring backdrop, the effort is not always successful. As Norlinda, the narrator of "Comparison Shopping", comments, noting the similarity of behavior and identity in her subdivision, "That's how it is here in Windhaven Estates; we all do the same things. . . . I'm starting to get the hang of it now, though it hasn't been easy."

McCorkle's precise brand of realism, most prominently featured in her attention to the details of the contemporary New South landscape, puts her in the company of such other masters of contemporary realism as Randall Jarrell and Bobbie Ann Mason. For many critics this facet of McCorkle's writing is what makes her stories so effective. Jack Butler, for example, in his 1992 review of *Crash Diet* in *The New York Times*, praised McCorkle's convincing, acute depiction of the New South while noting the centrality of place in the struggles of McCorkle's characters: "It is their milieu that these women seek to escape. Jill McCorkle renders it brilliantly, again and again delivering the shock of recognition. 'That's just how it *is*,' readers across the country will say to themselves in repeated delight." Others disagree, arguing that McCorkle's attention to the minutiae of contemporary existence can at times be overwhelming, undercutting the force of the story itself. Even Butler, in the same review, goes on to argue that the "repetition of similar locales and tacky detail becomes numbing after a time. It begins to seem an easy trick, relied on too often. Sometimes you feel as though you were *in* Wal Mart, not just enjoying a wickedly comic vision of the place."

Ultimately, however, McCorkle's close scrutiny of the trappings of late-twentieth-century existence serves as more than a means toward exhibiting her keen sense of humor—though in a fictional world where residents live on subdivision streets named after brands of liquor, and "Mr. Coffee" machines become symbols of life's greater concerns, her stories certainly accomplish that aim. The bulk of the stories here and in her subsequent collection, *Final Vinyl Days* (1998), demonstrate that McCorkle is profoundly concerned with the dynamics of place. Particularly for an author who grew up in a small, traditional southern town, the evolution of the small-town southern landscape in recent decades poses not only physical, but also emotional and psychological concerns. And while McCorkle traced the suburbanization of the small-town South in her 1990 novel, *Ferris Beach*, in her short fiction the landscapes of the past are for the most part already gone.

McCorkle acknowledged the importance of geography to her work in a personal interview in 1999, noting that the "sense of place" exhibited in her stories is the primary autobiographical element she sees in her fiction as a whole. Her childhood in Lumberton coincided with a profound change in the landscape of the small-town South, a period the author refers to as a "time of transition." Feeling that she grew up on the "cusp between the Old South and the New South," McCorkle sees the yearning for connection to past landscapes as a factor in much of her fiction. Indeed, as she wrote in her essay "Secret Places", included in the volume *A Place Called Home: Twenty Writing Women Remember* (1996), this need to inhabit vanished but remembered landscapes is a central facet of her fictional endeavor to begin with: "My wish would be that every scene from our lives is preserved on a neat little stage and all we have to do is step in," the author writes, concluding that her own indelible connection to the landscape of her youth is what fuels much of her writing: "It's not the place so much as what I have taken away from it; the images and smells and sounds. There is a feeling, like having a secret; it's powerful and wonderful and it's what keeps people and places alive. It's why people have the urge to go back and why they tell stories."

McCorkle's keen interest in capturing the dynamics of landscape and creating a sense of place illuminate a number of stories in *Crash Diet*, none more so than the haunting "Migration of the Love Bugs", a story that uses the seemingly aimless, never ending migratory patterns of the southern insect known as the "love bug" as a metaphor for the plight of the narrator, Alice, a woman who finds herself dislocated from her home of forty years, an apartment near Boston Common, and now living in what she describes as a "tin can" of a mobile home in a Florida retirement village. While her husband, Frank, remains incredulous to her sense of longing for the home they have left behind (he thinks of their new setting, where every mobile home has a "view of the driving range," as the Promised Land), Alice sees things differently: "I was thinking that if this was the Promised Land, Moses sure dealt me a bad hand," she muses. McCorkle credits the inspiration for this story to personal experience, noting that during her first period in Boston, when she and her husband lived off Boston Common, she had further occasion to reflect on the importance of home and a sense of place. For though the locales are reversed, again in "Migration of the Love Bugs", the author contrasts a richly depicted vision of the power of home with the desultory experience of life in a prefabricated landscape.

If such concerns over the alienating nature of the contemporary landscape, coupled with the problematic romantic relationships of her protagonists and their often humorous sense of perseverance, are the characteristics that define the typical story in *Crash Diet*, worth noting as well are those stories in which McCorkle breaks out of this mold. Two such efforts are the first-person narratives "Words Gone Bad" and "Waiting for Hard Times to End"; in each of these stories McCorkle experiments with her heroines' voices, offering narrators who stand in counterpoint to the majority of others in the collection.

In "Words Gone Bad" McCorkle tells the story of Mary, an aging African American janitor at a southern university whose dissatisfaction with the pace of social reform, and larger sense of spiritual longing, are captured in the image of the wasted words she must erase daily from the classroom blackboards. After contrasting the harsh realities of her own life with the idealism and dignity represented by the resonant words and phrases of the Civil Rights movement, McCorkle's narrator concludes that the hollowness of words themselves is tied to the larger social dilemma she faces: "there's always more words on the board, words and words and more words in their dusty slanted lines of white and yellow, erasers filled with words gone old or bad or both." Through Mary, McCorkle offers another angle of vision—her most explicitly political in the collection—on life in the New South.

"Waiting for Hard Times to End" is told by Bunny, an adolescent girl whose own coming-of-age drama is played out against her interest in the affairs of her sister, Rhonda, whom she idolizes. Rhonda has left home and, unbeknownst to the naive Bunny, is leading an increasingly desperate life of bad jobs and abusive relationships, one that will eventually end with her murder in a sleazy hotel. Enamored of what she imagines to be her sister's "glamorous" lifestyle, Bunny daily awaits the mail for another postcard from Rhonda describing her most recent adventures.

Perfectly capturing Bunny's naiveté, McCorkle builds the dramatic irony of the story, creating empathy for her narrator while suggesting the inevitability of both Rhonda's demise and Bunny's painful but necessary emergence into self-awareness and womanhood. Eventually coming to understand the painful reality behind the facade of her sister's words, Bunny determines at the end of the story to forge her own path, in a closing affirmation that is one of the most honest in the collection. Like "Words

Gone Bad", "Waiting for Hard Times to End" questions the veracity of language itself, a telling gesture in a collection of primarily first-person narratives. With these two stories McCorkle further suggests the vulnerability that lies behind the spunky facade of the majority of her narrators.

Despite her success with the first-person form, perhaps the strongest stories in this collection are the two third-person narratives, "Gold Mine" and "Departures". In each of these moving, lyrical stories, one can sense the liberating influence of the third-person perspective: freed from the necessity of creating another narrative voice, McCorkle is able to imbue her characters with a newfound depth, using the third-person form to maximum effect in portraying the sort of vulnerability that is only hinted at in the first-person narratives of the collection.

"Gold Mine" tells the story of Ruthie Kates, a mother of two who, along with her now-estranged husband, Jim, had years ago opened and lovingly restored an old motel along the main highway of a seaside town in South Carolina. The inevitable ruin of this endeavor is foretold in the first line of the story: "The day the interstate opened was the day Highway 301 and Petrie, South Carolina, died." Another rumination on the parallels between place and experience, this story offers the now nearly defunct motel as a symbol of the dissolution of the romantic relationship between Ruthie and Jim. For just as Ruthie's Goodnight Inn has been replaced by one of the generic chain hotels that have sprouted up along the new interstate, I-95, Ruthie herself has been replaced by a younger woman named Barbara: "Barbara is like I-95. She is fast and lively and young, and Ruthie is 301, miles of tread stains and no longer the place to go."

McCorkle shapes the narrative as a series of recollections Ruthie experiences over the course of a single afternoon, as she stands watch over her two young children by the pool of the nearly abandoned hotel. Contrasting the youthful optimism that had Ruthie and Jim believing their hotel—and their relationship—to be a "gold mine" with the painful experience of abandonment, McCorkle paves the way for the return of Jim that evening, a moment captured in breathtaking imagery that belies the fact that Ruthie's optimism remains tempered by pain. The use of third-person mode in this story allows McCorkle to avoid the sometimes cloying tendency in her first-person narratives toward strident self-affirmations, allowing her to create instead a tale that is at once personal and universal. As reviewer

Pam Houston notes, "Taking the biggest risk in the book, 'Gold Mine' allows the abandoned Ruthie to find her strength not through determination and independence, but through acceptance and forgiveness."

Certainly the most widely praised story in *Crash Diet* is "Departures", an elegiac story of an aging woman's ongoing attempt to come to terms with her husband's death. Three years after the passing of her husband, Walter, Anna Craven continues to mourn his departure, attempting to stave off loneliness by spending the majority of her time in crowded shopping malls and airports, "any place where she can be surrounded by people without having to interact with any of them." The story shifts between scenes of Anna alone in crowed places, where she takes solace in the people who surround her, to passages that find her recalling moments of her life with Walter. Anna's recurring recollection of youthful summers at a seaside cottage with Walter and their growing family provides a yearning, lyrical counterpoint to her life now, which despite her tendency to immerse herself in crowds, is defined by her isolation.

Critical reaction to "Departures" has been overwhelmingly positive, with the majority of reviewers noting this story as the finest one in the collection. Characteristic of the critical response is the assessment of Greg Johnson, who reviewed the story for *The Georgia Review* in 1992. Johnson sees the story as a turning point of sorts for McCorkle as a short-story writer: "Fully and compassionately imagined, 'Departures' has the force of a miniature novel, and it suggests the author's possible development out of her more facile and superficial first-person approach." Indeed, McCorkle herself has noted "Departures" as one of her favorite stories of the collection, saying that it marked a significant change for her as a writer. With its depth of emotion, its nuanced narrative voice, and its sophisticated yet understated play with narrative time frames and recurring imagery, this story does suggest McCorkle's development as a short-story writer, presaging in both its themes and its technique stories that appear in her next story collection, *Final Vinyl Days*.

While one can certainly find thematic links between *Crash Diet* and McCorkle's 1998 collection, *Final Vinyl Days*, the latter collection also reveals new directions in both form and content, developments related to changes in McCorkle's life in the intervening years. In 1992, the year *Crash Diet* was published, the author and her husband again relocated to Boston, and McCorkle left behind the southern milieu that featured so prominently in many of her earlier stories. Tending to a growing family while continuing her career in the classroom, McCorkle nonetheless in these years saw her writing career flourish; in 1993 she received the New England Booksellers' Association award for her body of work, while in 1996 her novel *Carolina Moon* was published to wide critical acclaim. *Final Vinyl Days* cemented her reputation as a short-story writer. This collection of nine stories reveals a maturing artist whose increasing mastery of the short-story form is paralleled by a heightened thematic interest in mortality, vulnerability, and the uncertainty of life.

If the title story of her previous collection suggests the dominant themes of *Crash Diet* as a whole, much the same can be said of the title story of *Final Vinyl Days*. This first-person narrative is told by a post-collegiate record store employee and college-town hanger-on—one of three male protagonists in the collection—who laments the passing of what he considers the golden age of rock and roll, as evidenced by the advent of the compact disc and the increasing irrelevance of his store and his role— seller of "classic" used vinyl albums. The story is, among other things, a miniature compendium of rock and roll history, as the narrator's mounting identity crisis and increasing string of unsatisfactory one-night stands are set to a soundtrack of classic rock references to Roy Orbison, The Beatles, and The Byrds. This characteristic alone makes the story emblematic of the collection as a whole, in that all of the stories in *Final Vinyl Days* make references to popular songs, a technique that suggests McCorkle's shaping of the collection—consciously or otherwise—in the form of a record album.

McCorkle's recurring musical references are more than a gimmicky narrative trick, however; in "Final Vinyl Days" the author makes the link between the pop music of bygone days and her protagonist's growing awareness of his mortality and the passing of time, as well as his mounting sense of alienation from the world in which he lives. And in this sense, "Final Vinyl Days" uses the musical metaphor in a way that reverberates throughout the collection, as the majority of the stories here feature characters who, often in reaction to the loss of a loved one, confront the uncertainty of a finite existence in an often confounding world. For the narrator of "Final Vinyl Days", this uncertainty takes the form of his stubborn rejection of everything new in the music world. Shaken by the deaths of his musical idols Marvin Gaye and Del Shannon,

the narrator redoubles his efforts to live his life in the past; at the close of the story he fantasizes about his college sweetheart and their "perfect 1970 romance," even as he relates his increasing penchant for one-night stands with a "series of younger and younger women," who leave a "mountain of CD covers dumped on my floor." With this telling final image, McCorkle suggests her narrator's emotional imprisonment, and this theme is one that recurs in the stories that follow "Final Vinyl Days" in the collection.

A particularly noteworthy story is "A Blinking, Spinning, Breathtaking World", which chronicles a recently divorced young mother's emotional breakdown. In the face of an impending snowstorm, the protagonist, Charlotte, takes her son to an indoor amusement/theme park called Wonderland, and both the threatening winter weather and the carnivalesque setting of the action become metaphors for Charlotte's emotional turmoil. Though at one point Charlotte had been on the point of "begging" her husband to "start all over," even willing to "pretend that he had never cheated on her," by the end of the story it becomes apparent that Charlotte's sense of isolation is as all-encompassing as it is debilitating. After suffering a panic attack at the amusement park, Charlotte hurries her son back to their car, and McCorkle closes the story by chronicling Charlotte's thoughts in the car, using the carnival metaphor once again to emphasize the uncertainty that leaves her entrapped: "There was no magic potion; no incantation to make the world stop blinking, stop spinning. She could only hope that her body would keep moving—slow step by slow step—to the lines for the rest of the breathtaking rides. But for now, she was scared frozen, scared to death."

The cold, haunting closing of this story signals a larger change of perspective in the collection as a whole; for while in *Crash Diet* McCorkle chose to conclude almost all of the stories with declarations of defiant, optimistic perseverance, in *Final Vinyl Days* the prevailing tone is less self-assured, more cognizant of the fragility of life. Part of this shift had to do with her own change of perspective; in particular, McCorkle has noted that the responsibilities of motherhood influenced her writerly perspective. Less inclined to identify with the unfettered optimism of some of her earlier protagonists, McCorkle notes that in the years preceding *Final Vinyl Days* she found herself becoming increasingly interested in offering more nuanced portrayals of vulnerable characters and their relationships. This change in perspective can be seen in such efforts as "Last Request" and "Dysfunction 101", two stories whose female characters, even as adults, suffer emotionally from their parents' legacies of infidelity and abandonment. While both protagonists vow to go on with their lives, the prevailing mood at the close of both of these stories is one of acceptance rather than defiant survival, a feeling captured by the narrator of "Dysfunction 101": "First, you recognize what was wrong . . . and then you *accept* it. This does not mean that you *agree* with it, just that you say, yes, that is what happened. And then you walk off and leave it there; it is not your mess to clean up."

Despite McCorkle's more reflective tone in *Final Vinyl Days*, the collection as a whole is still spiked by the author's trademark wit, and several stories recall the sensibility of *Crash Diet*. Among these is "Paradise", the opening story of the collection, which tells the story of the blossoming romance between a couple named Adam and Eve. Setting their initial meeting at the wedding of mutual friends in small-town North Carolina, McCorkle uses her keen eye for kitschy detail in constructing a hilariously precise rendering of the trappings of a southern wedding. The couple manage to escape this dubious Eden and—uncharacteristically for McCorkle—the story's end finds them presumably embarked on a happy life together.

Another platform for McCorkle's biting humor can be found in "Your Husband is Cheating On Us", an imaginative piece structured as a monologue from a spurned mistress directed toward her lover's wife. Now that a third woman has entered the picture, the mistress—who refers to herself as "Big Foot"—senses a sisterhood of sorts with the wife and counsels her on what she should do about her philandering husband. After deriding the new, second mistress ("she works at Blockbuster Video and wears way too much eye makeup"), Big Foot concludes, "Tell him he better shape his butt up or you are out of here, sister. Make him sweat." Although perhaps not the most successful story in the collection, "Your Husband is Cheating On Us" manages to generate an idiosyncratic sense of compassion for the brassy Big Foot and her would-be friend.

But the most adventurous stories in the collection—and ultimately the most powerful—are those in which McCorkle confronts the pain of the loss of loved ones, a recurring theme in *Final Vinyl Days* that resonates with the author's life experience. In the years that followed the publication of her previous story collection she saw the passing of several relatives and old family friends. The author

notes the dislocating effect of this kind of loss, explaining that she found herself "suddenly in a place in life where a lot of those people weren't around anymore." Particularly painful was the loss of her father, and McCorkle says that the grief she experienced at his passing found its way into her subsequent fictional work.

"Life Prerecorded", one of the finest stories in the collection, centers on the emotional struggles of a young mother-to-be whose anxiety over impending childbirth manifests itself in a series of dreams she has about now-departed loved ones. Autobiographical in nature—the author describes it as the story in the collection "closest to me"—"Life Prerecorded" recalls in both its complex structure and its often elegiac tone the gem of her first collection, "Departures". Evidencing McCorkle's increasing confidence with narrative structure, the story shifts time frames and moods rapidly, in a narrative rhythm that mirrors the emotional state of its narrator, who describes her feelings as "discombobulated."

Yet, despite her frenetic play with narrative structure, McCorkle manages to imbue the story with a lyrical tone, as the narrator's recurring memories of loved ones from her past—particularly her now-departed grandmother-coupled with her new-found friendship with an elderly widower from her apartment building, mark the story as another concerned with the importance of the past and her characters' connections to it. And while the narrator's imagined conversations with her grandmother and conjured images of her neighbor's wife may be illusions, they serve to quell her emotional turmoil, and with that perhaps McCorkle suggests that these are the necessary illusions. "What we don't know is enormous," the narrator at one point opines, a fitting comment in a story that revolves around the mystery of love and loss and the yearning for permanence.

The final two stories in the collection share some of the thematic concerns of "Life Prerecorded". The first of these, "It's a Funeral! RSVP", stands as the collection's most straightforward attempt to confront the pain and mystery of death. The story of a woman who plans "early funerals," celebrations of life for those who are about to die, "It's a Funeral" plays a cathartic role in a collection haunted throughout by the loss of loved ones. While some townspeople have taken to referring to the protagonist derisively as the "Mistress of Death," she sees her funeral catering business differently, considering the parties she throws to be offering a model of hope for the living as well as the dying. In a passage that recalls McCorkle's own life experiences in the 1990s, the narrator offers the rationale behind her new business: "I was about to turn forty and already many of my very favorite people were dead. I had children, and I wanted them to grow up with a clear vision of hope. A sense of nature and art and all that has walked this earth before them." And this adventurous story, part linear narrative and part philosophical essay, works toward establishing such a vision of hope, providing a redemptive, healing moment in the collection.

The final story, "The Anatomy of Man", extends McCorkle's philosophical excursion, closing the collection on an experimental, spiritually questing note. This inventive third-person narrative is focalized through the perceptions of a young pastor who, after closing up his church for the night, immerses himself in the baptismal pool, in what has become a ritualistic event for him. The narrative takes the form of an interior monologue, as the pastor attempts to come to grips with his spiritual uncertainty, frustrated sexuality, and longing for a renewed sense of purpose in life. Finding the greatest solace in memories of his deceased great-uncle, a man whose visionary qualities had him eventually branded insane and sent to an institution, the pastor works through these memories in an effort to understand his own fading spiritual vision. As he contemplates leaving the church, a voice comes from the darkness, advising the pastor to "Do things. . . . Keep the doors open." Fittingly, McCorkle's deus ex machina, appearing on the last page of the collection, does not provide neat closure for this story or for the collection, instead emphasizing openness.

In his 1990 review for the *Atlanta Journal* of McCorkle's novel *Ferris Beach* (1990), critic S. Keith Graham remarked that by that point, six years after her stunning literary debut, "everyone this side of Richmond recognizes Ms. McCorkle as one of the best in the new generation of Southern writers." After the success of *Ferris Beach*, with not only another novel but also two compelling short-story sequences to her credit since that time, Jill McCorkle's literary reputation has spread. A wickedly funny writer who has become more than a humorist, and a precise chronicler of the landscape of the New South whose finest work nevertheless easily transcends regional labels, McCorkle has proven herself to be nothing less than a first-rate novelist and short-story writer. Currently, McCorkle is working on a novel and another short-story collection, which is sure to be good news for fans of McCorkle's increasingly inventive and searching brand of realism.

Source: Robert A. Beuka, "Jill McCorkle," in *Dictionary of Literary Biography*, Vol. 234, *American Short-Story Writers Since World War II, Third Series*, edited by Patrick Meanor and Richard E. Lee, The Gale Group, 2001, pp. 186–196.

Sources

Manning, Jo, Review of *Creatures of Habit*, in *Library Journal*, Vol. 126, No. 12, July 2001, p. 128.

McCorkle, Jill, "Fish," in *Creatures of Habit*, Algonquin Books, 2001, pp. 227–40.

Review of *Creatures of Habit*, in *Publishers Weekly*, Vol. 248, No. 37, September 10, 2001, p. 58.

Wilkinson, Joanne, Review of *Creatures of Habit*, in *Booklist*, Vol. 97, No. 21, July 2001, p. 1982.

Williams, Susan Millar, "Small Town Girls," in *Women's Review of Books*, Vol. 19, No. 1, October 2001, p. 16.

Further Reading

Atherton, Lewis Eldon, *Main Street on the Middle Border*, Indiana University Press, 1954.

> Atherton examines the life and death of small towns in the Midwest from 1865 to 1950.

Bennett, Barbara, *Understanding Jill McCorkle*, Understanding Contemporary American Literature series, University of South Carolina Press, 2000.

> Bennett analyzes McCorkle's novels and short stories to date, including a brief overview of her life.

Spielman, David G., and William W. Starr, *Southern Writers*, University of South Carolina Press, 1997.

> Spielman photographed seventy-two Southern authors in the spaces where they create their stories. The text is written by Starr.

Zinsser, William, *How to Write a Memoir*, HarperAudio, 1999, 1 cassette.

> Zinsser explains what makes a good memoir, how to decide what to write about, and more, citing examples from famous memoir writers such as Eudora Welty and Frank McCourt.

The Good Doctor

Adam Haslett

2002

"The Good Doctor" by Adam Haslett is the second story in the collection *You Are Not a Stranger Here*, which appeared in 2002. The nine stories in this collection depict small moments in the lives of fully developed characters, some of whom are estranged or disturbed. Several deal with mental illness and several with male homosexuality. Haslett is as adept at locating his stories in England as he is with situating them in the United States, and regardless of the subject, his stories are written in a poised, elegant style. In "The Good Doctor," a young psychiatrist drives to a remote house on the Nebraska prairie to evaluate a patient whose prescriptions need renewing. Within the framework of the psychological interview, Haslett examines various topics connected with drug addiction, trauma, grief, chronic rural poverty, and disillusionment. One point the story in its entirety seems to make is that federally funded medical programs in remote areas are ineffectual in delivering the necessary sustained support to people with chronic psychiatric and medical problems, problems which are themselves often caused by the very remoteness that obstructs the delivery of the needed services.

Author Biography

Adam Haslett was born on December 24, 1970, in Portchester, New York. He received his B.A. in 1993 from Swarthmore College. The following year he spent in Provincetown, Massachusetts, on a fellowship at the Fine Arts Center. While there,

Adam Haslett   © Jerry Bauer. Reproduced by permission

he learned he had been accepted into the Iowa Writers' Workshop at the University of Iowa. He put his acceptance into the Yale University Law School on hold and moved to Iowa. He received his M.F.A. from Iowa in 1999.

Next, he returned to his original goal and pursued a degree in law at Yale University. At the same time that he was studying at Yale, Haslett was publishing short stories. On the strength of reading one of them, an editor at Doubleday offered to publish a collection of stories: thus, the nine stories that came to make up *You Are Not a Stranger Here*, which includes "The Good Doctor," were welcomed into print as a collection in 2002. This first book was well received: It was the August 2003 selection for NBC's *Today Show* Book Club. Also in 2003, Haslett received the L. L. Winship/PEN New England Award. That same year he graduated from Yale with a degree in law.

As of 2006, Adam Haslett was making his living as a writer and as an attorney. He divided his time between living in New York and London, England.

Plot Summary

Set in the barren prairie of northeast Nebraska, "The Good Doctor" tells the story of an at-home interview between psychiatrist Frank Briggs and Mrs. Buckholdt, a patient who has been using sedatives and antidepressants for four years and who has recently missed several of her clinic appointments with her regular doctor. Young and somewhat idealistic about how much he can help, Dr. Briggs drives two hours to visit Mrs. Buckholdt because he wants to evaluate her case directly. He does not believe it is healthy to continue to prescribe medication for her over the phone. Though he is trained in "biological psychiatry," a physiological method of treating psychological problems with drugs, Dr. Briggs subscribes more to the value of talk therapy. He believes that a patient needs to experience empathy from the therapist, a sense of connection and caring. He takes the trouble to drive out to the Buckholdt house because he wants to understand Mrs. Buckholdt better, to hear her story firsthand. However, when he arrives at the sagging "fifties prefab" in the middle of nowhere, he confronts a family of alienated, hardened individuals and a client more in charge of the situation than he anticipated.

The night before this interview, Dr. Briggs learned that Congress was reducing funds for the National Health Service Corps, the organization for which he works as a volunteer in exchange for his medical school debt being repaid. One year into his three-year contract, Dr. Briggs is suddenly aware that his career may be on hold and that he may come away from his current work in rural Nebraska with debt he hoped to have eliminated. At the age of thirty-two, Frank Briggs has recently ended his six-month relationship with his girlfriend, and he offers himself the dubious consolation that his patients have "romantic lives more desperate than his own." He has a headache from having drunk too much alcohol the previous night, is worried about his future, and exhausted by the one-hundred-degree heat as he pulls into the Buckholdt property.

In turn, Frank meets each of the four family members. They are separated spatially from each other and not inclined to talk. The daughter appears in the driveway, but she turns and walks away in response to his greeting. After a few knocks at the door, Jack Buckholdt opens up. Jack says the daughter "ain't a bigger talker," an understatement that clearly applies to the whole family. Dr. Briggs notes that Jack evinces some physical signs of "Hepatitis C . . . or the end of a serious drinking habit." Jack's second comment begins a pattern that characterizes the interview between Frank and Mrs. Buckholdt; Jack minimizes Frank's authority by commenting on his age. He is "young to be a doctor" and appears to be running an errand for the clinic, "the one they sent up." Jack says his wife is inside and then edges past the doctor and disappears into the yard. Dr. Briggs adjusts to the dark interior and notes the back of the son's head in the kitchen. The boy is watching an animal chase on "a muted television."

While he waits for Mrs. Buckholdt, Frank looks over her record. He thinks about his ex-girlfriend Anne and how they disagreed in their residency program about the emphasis on drug therapy for psychological problems. While other residents "joked about the numbing" that insulated them from patients' problems, Frank knew he was not adapting similarly. In fact, "he still felt like a sponge, absorbing the pain of the people he listened to." Now he reviews Mrs. Buckholdt's chart, which contains an assessment by an internist. He finds her case mismanaged. What he learns is that she first appeared at the clinic four years earlier, complaining of depression following the death of her son, Jason. She had been given antidepressants followed by benzodiazepines, "written as needed." There was no therapy, and the previous psychiatrist would not have considered making a five-hour round-trip just to check on his patient, "so he'd just kept calling in her refills." In the margin of the chart, Frank sees a little note, "*Injury may be a factor.*"

Mrs. Buckholdt's first sentence is remarkably refined: "My apologies for not greeting you at the door." She is attractive, in apparently good health, nicely dressed. Frank had expected "a disorganized person," but Mrs. Buckholdt seems "out of place here, in this house out in the middle of nowhere." She locks the door to the kitchen and sits down, facing Dr. Briggs. He begins conventionally; the director wanted him to check in on her in person. She denies eye contact, looking over his shoulder. Her response is a non sequitur: "I take it you're childless." Clearly, Dr. Briggs wants to conduct a typical assessment interview: he asks the relevant questions, and the patient answers them. But Mrs. Buckholdt asserts control, asks personal questions, chooses the subjects she discusses. She is not a weakling, a victim; rather, she is "self-possessed" with "powerful" eyes and "a strong, almost male jawline." Then she moves a certain way, and Frank sees that her four fingers have been cut off her right hand. He focuses on her face, and then he decides he will accept a glass of water.

In the kitchen, Frank greets the boy, but the boy only looks vacantly at him and then back to the television, where an animal feeds on the stomach of a deer. As he leaves the kitchen, he turns the key in the lock as Mrs. Buckholdt had and rejoins his patient. He begins again, asking her if she is still troubled by the depression she had four years before when she first came to the clinic. Again, she responds with a non sequitur: "Where is it that you grew up?" When he brings her back to the subject, gently reminding her that it would be good to use their time together to understand her situation, she still pursues personal questions about him. She explains that she likes to have "a sense of who [she's] talking with." Thus, she draws the conversation off her and onto him. Frank tells her he grew up outside Boston. Again, he tries to pull the discussion back to her depression, inquiring if it is a current problem. She directs his attention to a print of a Brueghel painting on the wall.

Then Mrs. Buckholdt begins to talk about her past, and Dr. Briggs decides to acquiesce to her choice of subjects. Mrs. Buckholdt went to college out East, where she studied art history. She loved paintings and hoped to have a better life than small-town Nebraska offered her. But her father died as she began her senior year, and she had to return home. She married Jack Buckholdt, a handsome young man who read books and had a promising job at the bank. She believed him when he talked about saving up for a couple years and then moving to California. But years went by, and they did not move. They had three children instead; the area suffered an economic depression during which the bank closed, and Mr. Buckholdt took up drinking and then lost his job.

Dr. Briggs asks Mrs. Buckholdt to describe her symptoms. She says some mornings she is afraid to get out of bed. She takes medication to help her get up and serve her children their breakfast. She admits being afraid of her son. When he asks why, she answers that taking the pills helps her. Then she returns to talking about her past. Building some kind of rapport with Dr. Briggs, she asks if he is married or if he intends to marry. Then she goes on about her plans for her first son, Jason. If she could not escape this barren place, then she was committed to helping Jason do so. She read him her art books, bought him a violin, and gave him lessons. All went well until he hit fourteen, got criticized by children at school, and destroyed his instrument. She says, "this place . . . started doing its work on him somehow. . . . The little tough guy stance, afraid of anything that wouldn't make him popular." She was depressed, feeling that she was not "really there in the room" with her own children. Then Jason and his friend Jimmy Green got hooked on methamphetamine, "the drug of choice for kids out here."

Now Mrs. Buckholdt closes in on a certain Sunday when her husband and the other two children were away, and Jason was up in his room, having gone several days and nights without sleep. He began crying; she went upstairs to discover her son, now seventeen, naked and rubbed raw and bleeding. He looked at her like she had "severed a rope he'd been clinging to for dear life." She got gauze, ointment, and Band-Aids, and tried to take care of his skin. Downstairs, she was in the kitchen chopping vegetables for soup; he came in and chopped off her fingers with a meat cleaver. Then he went out of the house, naked, and never returned. Frank listens and waits, feeling "a familiar comfort being in the presence of another person's unknowable pain." A few days later, Jason and his friend Jimmy crashed someone's truck into the wall of an overpass on the interstate. Jimmy was burned; Jason was killed. Dr. Briggs listens, mentally writing his own note into her chart: "intrusive recall . . . hypervigilence, and generalized anxiety." He thinks she has post-traumatic stress disorder. Facing Mrs. Buckholdt, "this oddly compelling woman," Frank realizes why he became a doctor: "to organize his involuntary proximity to human pain." It served him as a way to control "this opening in him" to pain in others. He seems to benefit more from the interview than she does.

Earlier, Mrs. Buckholdt discussed a Brueghel painting in the room; now, having told her story, she returns to it. It was Jason's favorite work. She recalls learning that Brueghel "was a moralizer, his paintings full of parables." She takes charge of the conclusion of the interview. She does not want Dr. Briggs to return; she will not go to the clinic. It is better when she does not think of the past. She can use the pills, but she can get along without them. As she rises and alerts her son that they must soon leave for his violin lesson, Dr. Briggs feels panic at the thought that it is over between them: "he didn't want to lose her, he didn't want the telling to end." He tries to hold on by asserting that therapy is advisable, but she cuts him off: "didn't you hear what I said?" she asks him. She has the last word. She does not need him, but he knows how much he needs her.

Characters

Anne

Anne is a psychiatrist who went through residency with Frank Briggs and visited him once in Ewing Falls, Nebraska. They had dated for six months but are now no longer a couple. Like Frank, Anne was trained in "biological psychiatry"; unlike him, she does not question this drug-based method for treating mental illness.

Dr. Frank Briggs

Frank Briggs, age thirty-two, is a new psychiatrist, having completed his residency just one year before this story begins. Now he is about to enter his second of three years as a volunteer with the National Health Service Corps, an agreement which entails his working in an underserved area in exchange for his medical school loans being repaid by the organization. Frank's immediate predicament is that the Congress has cut funds to the service, and while he is committed to this work contract, he is disheartened to know his medical school debt will not be paid as he anticipated.

Frank does not believe in the current practice of relying mostly on medication to treat psychiatric conditions. He believes that patients seek "someone to acknowledge what they [are] experiencing." His ex-girlfriend Anne accuses him of "clinging to an old myth about the value of talk." Intuitive and sensitive, Frank feels "like a sponge, absorbing the pain of the people he listen[s] to."

Jack Buckholdt

Jack Buckholdt grew up in northeast Nebraska, married, got a house, a job at the bank, and for years harbored dreams of moving to California and owning a house with a view of the ocean. He told his wife they would someday have an orange tree in their yard and museums nearby for her to enjoy. Instead, the couple lived in the barren northeast Nebraska prairie, they had three children, Jack had his work at the bank, and years passed. Financial hard times hit, property was foreclosed, and Jack took up drinking. Now he is an unemployed alcoholic with liver disease, living in a broken-down house out in the middle of nowhere.

Jason Buckholdt

First son of Mr. and Mrs. Buckholdt, Jason was his mother's hope for escape from the culture-starved Nebraska landscape where they live. Before puberty, Jason was willing to be schooled by his mother in art and to study the violin, but in his teens, he resented the mockery of his classmates, and with Jimmy Green, he became addicted to methamphetamine. Strung out on lack of sleep, he sunk into a psychotic state, and attacked his mother with a knife. Days later, Jason and Jimmy borrowed a friend's truck and crashed it into a wall of an overpass on the interstate highway. Jason died in the accident; Jimmy Green survived with burns.

Michael Buckholdt

The middle child of the Buckholdts' three children, this boy sits in the kitchen watching television with the sound off while Dr. Briggs interviews Mrs. Buckholdt. The boy is unresponsive when Dr. Briggs goes into the kitchen and speaks to him and seemingly acquiescent to Mrs. Buckholdt's confining him in the kitchen behind a locked door. When the doctor is about to leave, the son asks his mother's permission to leave the kitchen, and then he goes upstairs to get ready to go to his music lesson. The son's impassive acquiescence suggests he is also traumatized by Jason's attack and perhaps alienated too by the emotional absence of his depressive mother.

Mrs. Buckholdt

Mrs. Buckholdt, age forty-four, is the mother of three children. She and her husband, Jack, live in a run-down place in northeast Nebraska near Ewing Falls. As a young woman, Mrs. Buckholdt attended college in the East, where she studied art history. After her junior year, she returned home to Nebraska. She married Jack Buckholdt, believing in his dream of their moving to California as soon as they had the money. Years accumulated, and the dream was lost. Mrs. Buckholdt suffers from depression as a result of the death of their first son, Jason. She also suffers from post-traumatic stress disorder from Jason's attack, in which he cut off the fingers on her right hand. Now she manages to provide minimally for her two younger children, but she needs a prescription for a sedative to get through some days. Though she is resigned to her meaningless life, Mrs. Buckholdt thinks about art and cultured places out East where she once went to college and saw for herself how other people are able to live.

Daughter

The Buckholdts' daughter appears in the driveway when the doctor knocks at the door, but she does not respond to his greeting. Frank describes her as looking "eight or nine, but her rigid mouth and narrowed eyes [suggest] someone older." Explaining why she does not respond to the doctor, Jack Buckholdt says, "She ain't a bigger talker." The daughter is disconnected from the family: she stands in the driveway doing nothing. There is no place to play in this dirty yard, and the sign on the barn prohibits her from going in there: "*No Girls Allowed.*"

Jimmy Green

Jimmy Green is Jason Buckholdt's high school friend. The two get involved with methamphetamine, borrow a truck from a friend, and crash it into the wall of an overpass on the interstate highway. Jimmy survives the accident and lives in the area. Mrs. Buckholdt remarks that she sees him every once in awhile.

Themes

Chemical Drug Use and Abuse

"The Good Doctor" is much concerned with drug use and abuse. Life in this rural, economically depressed Nebraska prairie offers little opportunity or hope, and drugs become the means by which people dull disappointment and disillusionment. Jack Buckholdt promised his wife they would leave for a better life in California; Mrs. Buckholdt promised Jason he would escape poverty. When as a little boy he would cry over trouble at school, she would soothe him with a fantasy about taking him across the Atlantic so he could visit Italy and Greece. But by the time he was fourteen, Jason must have realized the only escape was through drugs. He became addicted to crystal methamphetamine. His erratic behavior, his sleeplessness, and his psychotic rubbing of his body, all indicate the effects the drug had on him. Moreover, his attacking his mother in a psychotic episode and running out of the house naked, never to return, suggests quite literally how drug addiction can maim those around the addict who love and want to care for him. The accident on the interstate is probably a direct outcome of Jason's drug abuse, and metaphorically, it hints at the sense Jason may have had of there being no escape from this place. Moreover, the story shows how drugs can be abused by medical professionals who rely on them as an easy fix to mask psychological symptoms in welfare patients. Mrs. Buckholdt is a poor woman; it is easier to sedate her than it is to face the trauma and grief of her home life. Mrs. Buckholdt uses prescription antidepressants and tranquilizers to increase her ability to function in her family, to care for her remaining two children, but the drugs do not neutralize her anxiety, lift her disillusionment, or mitigate her fear of her surviving son. The story portrays drug abuse, illegal and dangerous teenage abuse, legal and equally dangerous professional use, all against a backdrop of chronic poverty and powerlessness.

Topics For Further Study

- Write a short story based on a medical or psychological examination you have experienced, characterizing the doctor by details that slip out regarding his personal life. See if you can introduce elements in the story that reverse the common expectations about how a doctor and patient conduct themselves during an examination.

- Research drug abuse among high school students in urban and rural areas over the past twenty years. Draw a chart indicating types of substances and rates of abuse in several different types of locations over two decades. You may include a large city, a small town, a farming community, and other types of remote areas. What pattern of increase or decrease in rates of abuse does your research indicate?

- Study the subject of domestic violence. Who in the family is most likely to become violent, and who is most likely to be injured? What are the long term effects on family relationships when domestic violence has led to permanent injury or death? Write an essay describing domestic violence, explaining patterns of family abuse and providing information on services available to people who suffer from this type of violence.

- Do some research on the National Health Service Corps, using its website as a starting place. Write a summary of the information you acquire about the service, the populations it serves, and financial arrangements offered to volunteers. See if you can pinpoint when "The Good Doctor" takes place by determining the time when the service lost funding through some action in Congress. What other clues does the story provide for determining the time in which it is set?

The tonic of the moment insulates or dulls, but it cannot fix the landscape of problems which grind people into complete disillusionment and alienation.

Post-Traumatic Stress Disorder

"The Good Doctor" presents a woman who four years earlier was maimed by her son, who cut off the fingers on her right hand and who shortly thereafter was killed in an accident on the interstate. Mrs. Buckholdt experienced a life-threatening, terrifying, and shocking event when Jason amputated her fingers; that event was closely followed by his death. When Dr. Briggs interviews her, he considers that Mrs. Buckholdt may suffer from post-traumatic stress disorder (PTSD). This interpretation makes sense because she was clearly traumatized by the dismemberment and by the shock of her son's death a few days later. Dr. Briggs theorizes that if this diagnosis is correct, Mrs. Buckholdt should be prescribed sertraline (Zoloft) to help neutralize her anxiety and irrational fear. Based on this one interview, however, Mrs. Buckholdt does not seem to follow the expected profile of someone who has PTSD. For one thing, she remembers the traumatic events but can discuss them as memory and not as though she is back there all over again experiencing the same pitch of emotion she went through in the moment. Her pain and loss have left her with irrational fear of her other son and with a fear that comes over her some days and prevents her from getting out of bed. Yet she does not evince drug dependency and, in fact, asserts that she can get along without the prescriptions if Dr. Briggs does not refill them. In the face of her pain, Dr. Briggs thinks about what he would recommend and how he would describe her condition in her chart, and yet Mrs. Buckholdt shows that she can manage without his help. She has developed toughness and resolve. She knows she must care for her surviving children, and she knows she can do it if she does not look back or dwell on the past. This may be denial, yet the reader will never know. She tells Dr. Briggs not to return and refuses the offer to come to the clinic once a month.

Alienation

This story depicts the members of the Buckholdt family as individuals who do not relate to each other. Each person is shown alone: the daughter on the drive, the father wandering into the yard, the son locked into the kitchen watching a television with the sound off, and Mrs. Buckholdt herself, sitting on the couch and looking past the psychiatrist's shoulder to the wall. Mrs. Buckholdt has hardened or shut down; in order to exist in the world of this household, she has repressed all emotion. The family lives out in the middle of nowhere, hours from the nearest small town, in a dilapidated house. The father drinks, the mother lies in bed some days afraid to get up, and the children are unresponsive and detached. It is as though each person is paralyzed emotionally, estranged, unable to express what is inside. The point seems to be that drug abuse and trauma can arrest people in their abilities to interact or be open to one another. The family is beyond the help of the psychological clinic, both geographically and psychologically.

Style

Setting

"The Good Doctor" is set in northeast Nebraska, near the small towns of Atkinson, Tilden, and Ewing. The Buckholdt family lives in a "white fifties prefab, sagged on one side" with "empty prairie stretching miles in every direction." The first thing Dr. Briggs notices on the property is "the skeleton of a Chevy Nova, grass to the windows." In this remote area, stuck in chronic poverty, this wreck of a car suggests a place from which there is no transportation or escape. Even the car's name literally means "no go." Then too the heat is over one hundred degrees, "the horizon molten in air heated thick as the fumes of gasoline." Art may provide "perfect" images of "lush landscapes," but these pictures are fanciful creations, unlike anything Mrs. Buckholdt has ever seen in her Nebraska-bound life. She reports to Dr. Briggs that she took her son, Jason, to Chicago to the museums, to St. Louis to buy a violin, and she told him stories about taking a ship across the ocean to visit Athens and Rome, but one may get the sense that Jason, by the time he was fourteen or fifteen, realized there was no hope for departure. His death

in a borrowed truck that hits a wall of an overpass perfectly conveys his felt urgency to escape and the wall that prevented (or provided) it.

Allusion

An allusion is a reference to some work of art or historical event or person that lies beyond the present work; the effectiveness of an allusion depends on its being recognized by the reader. The allusion has significance of its own that is relevant to the present text; the connection between the present text and the allusion relies on the shared knowledge of the author and the reader. If something is mentioned in a work of literature, it is generally worthwhile to investigate the reference and ask oneself why this allusion was made and not another. One can assume the allusion is relevant to the text at hand.

During the interview with Dr. Briggs, Mrs. Buckholdt focuses on a print by Pieter Brueghel which hangs behind the doctor on the living room wall. She states that it is a copy of *The Fight between Carnival and Lent*, which Brueghel painted in 1559. Elsewhere during their talk, Mrs. Buckholdt mentions the artist Géricault and his paintings of Arcadia, "those huge, lush landscapes of his." Mrs. Buckholdt says the painting by Brueghel was Jason's favorite, so it provides in a sense an index to his character or to what held his attention. This painting depicts a village scene that is in every sense unlike the Buckholdt property. Whereas the Buckholdts are isolated on the prairie, the villagers in Brueghel's painting are all out in the town square interacting with one another. Great diversity is depicted: people reveling, others praying; some overindulging, others gaunt with fasting. Good and evil, abstinence of Lent and celebration of carnival, all mix together among these lively, engaged peasants. To step into Brueghel's scene would be to invite total sensation and stimulation. Addicted to methamphetamine, Jason existed in a hyper state of over-stimulation, unable to sleep or to focus. In a place practically devoid of stimulation, he rubbed himself raw. The Brueghel painting helps readers understand the imagined world Jason longed for. In a similar way, Mrs. Buckholdt's love of Géricault's landscapes conveys her longing for a world very unlike the one she inhabits, green, mountainous, moist. She loved studying art history in college because standing in front of those paintings allowed her imaginatively to escape the limitations of her life in Nebraska.

Irony

One form of irony is the discrepancy between what is expected and what actually happens. The difference between what one anticipates, between what ordinarily happens, and what in this case unfolds draws the reader's attention to a central topic or problem in the story. In some ways, the interview in "The Good Doctor" reverses what conventionally happens during a psychological evaluation. It is conventional for the doctor to ask the questions, and the patient to answer them. The doctor is in charge; as the professional helper, the doctor has choices and can suggest and administer treatment. By contrast, the patient is understood to be the one with the problem, the one who is vulnerable and needy. However, in this story, in some ways, the opposite is true. The doctor is in his patient's home, on her turf so to speak. Dr. Briggs is younger than his patient, and he seems less assertive or dominant than she appears. Instead of answering his questions, she asks her own, and when he objects politely, she is able to draw him into speaking about himself, something he knows is unprofessional and inappropriate. He comments that she has missed several appointments; she asks him if he is childless. He asks her if she was depressed after her son died; she asks him where he grew up. Dr. Briggs attempts to establish control, tries to bring her back to the subject, her psychological condition and need for medication, but she counters with another question about his past, his background, his intention to marry. It is surprising to see the repeated ways in which she takes control of the interview when one would expect the psychiatrist to have control of it. Indeed, when he asserts, "it's important for me to get a handle on your situation so we can try to help you," she apologizes yet again poses a question: "Of course. I apologize. I just like having a sense of who I'm talking with. You're from the East I take it." Mrs. Buckholdt, the patient, the one who has had a traumatic experience and may, as Dr. Briggs theorizes, suffer from post-traumatic stress syndrome, is the one who comes across as organized, "self-possessed," and in surprisingly good physical health, whereas Dr. Briggs has a headache from drinking too much alcohol the previous night, is unprepared for this interview, and, as readers learn elsewhere, he is unable to sustain a romantic relationship longer than six months. These reversals in what might be ordinarily expected direct the reader to consider both the doctor and the patient in different terms. The doctor's youth and inexperience are emphasized, and Mrs. Buckholdt's strength and ability to persevere suggest she needs less professional support than Dr. Briggs assumes. In all, she is able to describe what happened to her and to assert that she can manage, without talking to him

again and without the prescriptions, if he does not refill them. That she refuses his offer of further treatment causes Dr. Briggs to panic. Thus, irony is used to show the ineptness in the professional to address the problems of his patient. It also reveals that the patient may in some ways be stronger than the doctor.

Historical Context

National Health Service Corps

According to its website, the National Health Service Corps (NHSC) was established in 1972, as a part of the U.S. Department of Health and Human Services, a federally funded agency to address the medical and psychological needs of underserved populations, wherever they are found in the United States, from rural and mountainous areas to certain inner city communities. As of 2006, an estimated fifty million Americans are without access to healthcare services, including medical and psychological support. Since its beginning in 1972, approximately 23,000 healthcare professionals have participated in the programs that seek to deliver support services to people who normally do not have them. In 1987, Congress authorized a NHSC student loan repayment plan for medical professionals who establish and maintain a practice in a geographic location which the NHSC has identified as underserved. According to a 2000 statement by the National Association of Community Health Centers, the primary problem with NHSC is limited federal funding. That association suggested that at least five times as many practitioners are needed to begin to meet the needs of underserved U.S. populations. According to the NHSC website, in 2006, some 2,700 professionals were involved in the various programs, serving the needs of several million U.S. citizens.

Rural Substance Abuse and Poverty

Rural areas in the 1990s witnessed an increase in instances of substance abuse. According to a 2003 report published by Hazelden, rural youngsters were more likely to use some drugs than their urban counterparts. For years, many believed that drug abuse mostly occurred in urban settings and rural areas were relatively free of the problem. In fact, according to a report funded by the Drug Enforcement Administration (DEA), illegal drug use was found to be higher among rural eighth graders than those children living in cities. These rural

A Thai policeman guards bags of methamphetamine pills © Chaiwat Subprasom/Reuters/Corbis

children were 83 percent more likely to use cocaine and 43 percent more likely to use marijuana. Among twelfth graders, rural teens used inhalants, amphetamines, and cocaine more frequently than those students in the same grade living in cities. According to the Hazelden report, as drug enforcement is more effective in urban settings, illegal drug activities have moved increasingly into less enforced rural areas. To illustrate the point, Hazelden cites that the DEA in 1994 seized 263 labs which were manufacturing methamphetamines, and in 1998, it uncovered 1,627 labs with most of those located in the rural Midwest and West. The problem, in part, is that in low population areas, law enforcement must cover large distances in order to locate illegal activities but does not have sufficient money or numbers of officers to do so.

Drug abuse in rural areas correlates with poverty. In a 2002 *New York Times* article, Timothy Egan mapped out "a generations-old downward spiral in the countryside," in which "the hollowed-out economy has led to a frightening rise in crime and drug abuse." The crime is directly connected to "a methamphetamine epidemic." In this article, Allen Curtis, executive director of the Nebraska Crime Commission, is quoted as saying, "Meth

seems to be everywhere in Nebraska right now." Between 1994 and 2002, the use of this drug nationwide tripled. But its abuse in rural, thinly populated places is exceptionally high. For example, according to a survey conducted by the National Institute of Drug Abuse, in Wyoming, the state with the smallest population, estimates for 2002 suggested that 1 percent of the population required treatment for methamphetamine addiction. Abusers of methamphetamine "tend to be erratic, violent and in some cases, borderline psychotic—especially when on a sleepless binge." All of this information is relevant to Jason Buckholdt's addiction and fate.

Critical Overview

Adam Haslett's first book of short stories, *You Are Not a Stranger Here*, in which "The Good Doctor" appears, was viewed as a candidate for awards. The collection was a finalist for the 2002 National Book Award and a Pulitzer Prize for Fiction finalist in 2003. For this work, Haslett won the L. L. Winship/PEN New England Award in 2003. His collection was described in mixed terms but overall taken as a positive first publication by a new writer.

A reviewer for *Kirkus Reviews* in May 2002 writes that though the stories are "extremely uneven," the book as a whole is an "unquestionably promising debut." This review notes that some of the stories hold "some spectacular moments." About "The Good Doctor," the *Kirkus* reviewer summarizes: "a callow physician's efforts 'to organize his involuntary proximity to human pain' are unsettled by the story of a luckless family's destruction by economic failure and drug addiction." Emphasizing the collection's dark topics, a reviewer for the *New York Times Book Review* says the stories "exhale a desiccated bleakness, a despair mitigated by the characters' continuing desire to be good . . . despite hopelessness, loss, disease and frequent mental illness."

A reviewer for *Publishers Weekly* points out that "Often, Haslett convincingly interweaves the perspectives and lives of seemingly disparate individuals" and concludes that "this is a strikingly assured first effort." Tom LeClair, writing for *Book*, points out that all of Haslett's characters "are estranged," and "most of his characters have no hope." LeClair cautions that the book may not suit some readers. In all, LeClair finds the stories something of a downer, stating that "Not every reader will care or dare to enter Haslett's sometimes melodramatically painful world, but the book welcomes the courageous—and the estranged."

Criticism

Melodie Monahan

Monahan has a Ph.D. in English and operates an editing service, The Inkwell Works. In the following essay, Monahan explores setting as the inescapable trap of chronic rural poverty and drug addiction and the failure of the federal outreach program to address local needs as these are depicted in "The Good Doctor."

In Adam Haslett's short story, "The Good Doctor," setting is both an historical and a geographical context, the decades-long persistent local economic depression and a history of failure of the federally funded medical outreach program, sponsored by the National Health Service Corps, to respond effectively to local substance abuse needs. The chronic poverty and the inadequate federal program attempting to address its effects, taken together, create an insidious, deterministic context, an inertia as unnoticed as the height of the grass growing through the rusted "skeleton of a Chevy Nova," on the Buckholdt

property. Here is a story of a story of a story: a problem within a problem within a problem. It might be schematized this way: first comes the story of the interview between Dr. Frank Briggs and his patient, Mrs. Buckholdt; next is her story of her son's addiction to methamphetamine, his attack on her, and his death; and last is the economic story of chronic poverty in a remote landscape that stretches back through the history of this family and the history of the parents of this family, all in a place beyond the effective reach of professional assistance. The first two stories are symptoms of the third problem, which in this case, the patient appears to understand better than the doctor.

Chronic poverty is presented first in "The Good Doctor" in the image of the half-buried Chevy Nova, rusting on the Buckholdt property. This car, whose name means "no go" in Spanish, signals no means of escape from this "empty prairie." The sagging "fifties prefab," the "dilapidated barn," the "air heated thick as the fumes of gasoline," all make up the immediate setting or backdrop, the barren, dusty landscape, in which Mrs. Buckholdt, her alcoholic husband, Jack, and their two children exist. What is wrong with this place and these people has been wrong a long time.

Waiting for Mrs. Buckholdt in the living room, Dr. Briggs examines her chart only to see "how shoddily her case had been managed." The problem of this family, summarized in the facts about Mrs. Buckholdt, go back four years, when she first came into the clinic complaining of depression after her son died. The chart provides only brief notes; she received antidepressants then sedatives and no therapy. In this rotating-door, federally funded agency, presumably one psychiatrist after another dealt with Mrs. Buckholdt over the past four years. The last one phoned in her refills rather than investing the time in driving out to her place to see her; Dr. Briggs, the new person handling her case, takes the trouble to visit her house in the hopes that talking with her will help. The chart does not clue him in on the background. In the margin, Dr. Briggs sees "a cryptic line," that *"Injury may be a factor,"* a line that may be a warning but certainly is not all that informative and leads him to suspect incorrectly some kind of farm accident.

Immediately, however, readers are given reason to wonder if this clinic and Dr. Briggs's good intention are capable in any way of addressing Mrs. Buckholdt's case. In fact, "The Good Doctor" begins the morning after Dr. Frank Briggs gets some bad news. A volunteer with the National Health

"
The story proves the
lie of its title; here is a
case of chronic poverty and
drug addiction, of trauma,
grief, and loss, which the
'good' doctor cannot even
begin to fix."

Service Corps, Dr. Briggs has agreed to work for three years for "a paltry salary" in the northeast Nebraska boondocks in exchange for repayment of his medical school debt. The news is that agreement is about to change: Congress is cutting funding to the agency, and Dr. Briggs is being left with "the full burden of his debt." As Mrs. Buckholdt's chart shows, the program has been ineffective for some years already, and now as Dr. Briggs begins his second year of working in it, the program faces budget cuts which may make it infeasible for Dr. Briggs to continue practicing in this location. Connected to money issues is a question about methodology.

Dr. Briggs was trained in a residency program dominated by "biological psychiatry"; drugs were the preferred method for treating psychological and behavioral problems. However, though he is a medical physician and trained in physiological diagnosis, Dr. Briggs clings "to an old myth about the value of talk." Young and idealistic, he believes patients need "someone to acknowledge what they were experiencing." Frank Briggs has not developed the "numbing" his fellow doctors acquired during their training. He knows himself to be "a sponge, absorbing the pain," and he puts his faith in the healing effect of empathy. That position is fine, but how can it be applied effectively within a program which faces budget cuts in an area so remote some of the clients are hours away? In other words, reduced funding for the program constricts its reach and effectiveness and undermines the workers who face unexpected financial worries themselves. In addition, treatment method is called into question given the mission of this program to serve populations in remote areas where frequent consultation is impractical

and drug addiction widespread. Mrs. Buckholdt's case has gone unmanaged for years, and given internal difficulties in the agency and Dr. Briggs's own financial burden, how likely is it that Mrs. Buckholdt's best interests can be served in this place and at this time?

Unlike the previous psychiatrist, Dr. Briggs wants to extend himself to his patient. He is willing to drive the five-hour round-trip to her house to see for himself how she is doing and to evaluate her medications. But in their interview, Dr. Briggs encounters some surprises. The contrast between the chart and Mrs. Buckholdt herself is immediately apparent. Her first response to Dr. Briggs is refined, gracious, so unlike this most ungracious "fifties prefab" out in the middle of nowhere. She appears in good health, is nicely dressed, and has "a self-possessed demeanor." Older and in some ways in better shape on this afternoon than the doctor, who is himself suffering from a hangover, Mrs. Buckholdt takes charge of the interview.

Dr. Briggs wants to focus on her present condition, inviting her to describe her symptoms. It registers on him as off the subject when she chooses instead to question him about where he grew up and went to school, eliciting the fact that he comes from an affluent Boston suburb. The subject is germane, however, from her point of view, for she went to college back East, and she knows the difference between affluence and poverty, between being cultivated and not having a clue about how to survive in a place that offers no hope of a better life. Mrs. Buckholdt, in asking about the doctor, excuses herself for seeking personal information: "I just like having a sense of who I'm talking with. You are from the East I take it." It is not professional for the conversation to focus on the doctor rather than the patient, yet given the story Mrs. Buckholdt has to narrate, a sense of place is relevant. She knows where Dr. Briggs is coming from, both literally and professionally, and she wants him to know she can imagine the town where he grew up: "a rich town, isn't it? Tidy lawns. A country club. Kids going to college. Am I right?" These details of setting signify the context for Dr. Briggs's own development and suggest the factors that supported his becoming the psychiatrist he is. When he asks about her depression, she looks over his shoulder to a Brueghel print on the wall.

The case at hand, from this patient's point of view, is a matter of setting. It matters that she was sent back East to college, that she studied art history, that she was cultivated and saw how rich

What Do I Read Next?

- *The Collected Stories of Richard Yates* (2001) contains selections from Yates's two earlier collections *Eleven Kinds of Loneliness* (1962) and *Liars in Love* (1981), along with nine other uncollected stories. Readers who like Haslett's style may enjoy Yates's way of exploring why individuals fail to achieve meaningful relationships. The book contains an excellent introduction by Richard Russo.

- Over thirty years after her death in 1967, the stories of Mary Ladd Gavell, managing editor of *Psychiatry* magazine, were published in *I Cannot Tell a Lie, Exactly and Other Stories* (2001). Set in a time before television, these stories explore with a surface simplicity the subtle nature of family relationships.

- The elegant style of Donald Hall is at work in his collection *Willow Temple: New and Selected Stories* (2003), twelve stories in all, including one about children of alcoholic parents, another about a child who witnesses a mother's infidelity, and still others about early adulthood. In some of these, Hall traces the emptiness of life after a person is traumatized.

- Elizabeth McKensie wrote a novel in nine interlocking stories, entitled *Stop that Girl: A Novel in Stories* (2005). The stories cover the life of Ann Ransom, through her childhood, marriage, and divorce.

- In *The Center of Everything* (2003), Laura Moriarty tells the story of ten-year-old Evelyn Buchnow, who takes care of herself because her unemployed, emotionally imbalanced mother cannot care for her. Elizabeth experiences loneliness and confinement in her small Midwestern town.

---

kids live in eastern cities. It also signifies much that the death of her father called her back to Nebraska without allowing her to complete her bachelor's degree, back to a mother who thought the cost of education for a daughter was a waste of money. In this way, Mrs. Buckholdt learned what she could not find in northeast Nebraska. She married and bought into her husband's dream of escape. Investing more than she knew in the hope of a change in real estate, she and her husband bought a house in Nebraska, theoretically to save up for the move, and then they had children, the first one born quickly. Thus, the factors were in place for their remaining where they were longer than they envisioned. Perhaps imperceptibly at first, economic depression made the inertia of this place more adhesive. Mr. Buckholdt's job became one of managing foreclosures; then the bank folded, and he lost his job and began to drink. Some years later, what chance of leaving existed? Disillusioned for herself, Mrs. Buckholdt nonetheless perpetuated the narrative of escape for her son, Jason.

In her story about Jason, Mrs. Buckholdt asks Dr. Briggs: "You're a doctor in these parts . . . You must know all about methamphetamine." Dr. Briggs agrees; cases of this addiction appear in his clinic; "It had become the drug of choice for kids out here, cheaper than coke." Existing in poverty-stricken rural Nebraska, seventeen-year-old Jason Buckholdt had perhaps as high as a one in four chance of exposure to this drug. On the day of his psychotic episode, Mrs. Buckholdt had gone to his room when she heard him crying in the same tone of voice he had had as a little child; now describing that scene to Dr. Briggs, she recalls years earlier when Jason was a little boy, how she would comfort him. Significantly, she consoled him with an escape narrative: "I'd tell him how one day we'd take at trip on a boat all the way across the Atlantic and he'd see Athens and Rome and all the places where the stories I'd read him took place." Mrs. Buckholdt used the myth of eastbound travel, a fantasy of entering the setting created in fiction, to appease her little boy. She might have taught him how to deal with school or kids who made fun of his studying the violin, but instead, she gave him the myth of escape.

Unfortunately, the effectiveness of this anodyne wore off by the time Jason was fourteen. Mrs. Buckholdt states, "this place, it started doing its work on him somehow." Just as Jason entered puberty, "His father had started drinking . . . Everything was going to hell around here, prices dropping through the floor . . . And as for symptoms, yes, to tell you the truth, I was depressed. . . . Things hadn't gone like we'd planned." Given her own shrinking circumstances, she thought about the contrast between her life and the young women who attended college with her, "visiting Europe, standing in front of those pictures."

The reality is that increasingly in the late 1980s and throughout the 1990s, methamphetamine was cheap and easily available in the rural Midwest. Jason and his friend Jimmy Green were caught buying some in a parking lot in Ewing Falls, Nebraska. Jason was sent for three months to a juvenile detention center in nearby Atkinson; when he came home he was "angrier, more confused." Mrs. Buckholdt theorizes that he procured meth even while incarcerated; she asks, "how they can run a jail where children can get drugs?" Some time later, when she was home alone with Jason, who had been awake for several days and nights, a terrifying psychotic episode occurred. He was naked, sobbing, and had rubbed his flesh raw. She says, "he looked at me like I'd severed a rope he'd been clinging to for dear life, just like that, like I'd sent him down somewhere to die." She adds, "I was his mother . . . What was I supposed to do?" She wrapped him in a towel and applied ointment to his wounds. Later, in the kitchen, he grabbed a meat cleaver and "chopped [her] fingers off, the fingers [she'd] touched him with." Dr. Briggs is silent as he listens to the story, and after she finishes speaking, he remains quiet. With the truth out in the room, Mrs. Buckholdt seems "smaller and more frail, her earlier, imposing demeanor exhausted." Significantly, when he died, Jason was heading west on the interstate; the borrowed truck hit a cement wall.

Hearing her story, Dr. Briggs feels "a familiar comfort being in the presence of another person's unknowable pain." He acknowledges to himself that "More than any landscape, this place felt like home." Able to attend, to pay attention to her story, Dr. Briggs still responds clinically, mentally composing a statement for her chart as he watches her: "intrusive recall . . . hypervigilance, and generalized anxiety. Diagnosis: posttraumatic stress disorder. Treatment: a course of sertraline, one hundred milligrams daily, recommendation for psychotherapy,

eventual titration off clonazepam." Sitting quietly, he has to wonder if "the power to describe the people they listened to save [doctors] from what they heard." He thinks about the psychological vacancy of some patients, the denial of others, "the unsaid visible in their gestures, filling the air around them." Musing about his patients, thinking now about Mrs. Buckholdt's story, Dr. Briggs realizes why "he'd become a doctor: to organize his involuntary proximity to human pain."

But the illusion of being able to organize pain is immediately shattered by Mrs. Buckholdt's resolute dismissal of him. They look again at the Brueghel print, *The Fight between Carnival and Lent*, Jason's favorite work of art. The painting depicts a village square with lots of peasants engaged in various activities and at its center the "contending forces" of self-indulgence and abstinence. It is not the "lush landscapes" Mrs. Buckholdt loved; it is a painting, though, full of life. Mrs. Buckholdt is ready for Dr. Briggs to leave; she is taking her surviving son for his violin lesson. In response to the idea of leaving the house, Frank Briggs feels a visceral tightening: "the panic beginning before his mind could form the thought: he didn't want to lose her, he didn't want the telling to end." But the stories have all come to an end: he can recommend drugs and therapy, but she already knows there is no escape from the setting that controls this plot. When he demurs, she holds the door for him, asking him, "didn't you hear what I said?"

Dr. Briggs has, in fact, not heard her, if he continues to think that his remedy of drugs and talk can extricate her from the place and time that controls her life. Evidence provided at the outset also suggests that neither Dr. Briggs nor the more distant National Health Service Corps which he represents can in any way transform the remote regions in which cases such as that of Mrs. Buckholdt occur. They cannot undo the past, shift the decades' long downward spiral of economic depression, or make the barrenness in her life as lush as a painting or the California fantasy she once loved. The story proves the lie of its title; here is a case of chronic poverty and drug addiction, of trauma, grief, and loss, which the "good" doctor cannot even begin to fix.

Source: Melodie Monahan, Critical Essay on "The Good Doctor," in *Short Stories for Students*, Thomson Gale, 2007.

Adam Haslett and Sherry Ellis

Ellis is the editor of NOW WRITE! *a collection of fiction writing exercises published by Tarcher/Penguin in September, 2006.* Illuminating

Fiction, *her anthology of author interviews, is forthcoming from Red Hen Press in September, 2007. She is at work on a novel and a collection of non-fiction writing exercises. Her author interviews have also appeared in* The Kenyon Review, The Writer's Chronicle, Glimmer Train, *and* AGNI, *as well as other literary and arts magazines. A personal writing coach, she teaches writing in Concord, Massachusetts. In the following interview, the author talks about his writing process, the theme of estrangement and psychological disturbances, language and dialogue, and rhythm in his stories.*

Adam Haslett is the author of *You Are Not A Stranger Here*, a short story collection that portrays pivotal moments in the inner lives of characters who suffer from estrangement and psychological disturbance. Craig Seligman in his *New York Times Book Review* wrote, "There's not a clinker in the group, and this consistency, along with the maturity and the austerity and the exceptional tact of the writing, gives every indication that unless something goes radically haywire, *You Are Not a Stranger Here* is the herald of a phenomenal career."

In 2002 *You Are Not A Stranger Here* was a finalist for the National Book Award and in 2003 it was a finalist for the Pulitzer Prize. The story "Devotion" is included in the anthology: *The Best American Short Stories 2003* and "Notes to My Biographer" was a finalist for the National Magazine Award. In August, 2002 *You Are Not A Stranger Here* was the selection of the NBC Today Show Book Club.

Haslett completed his undergraduate studies at Swarthmore College where he studied with Jonathan Franzen. He subsequently received fellowships from the Provincetown Fine Arts Center, the Michener/Copernicus Society of America and Breadloaf. In 1999 he received his MFA from the Iowa Writer's workshop. In 2003 he won the L.L. Winship/PEN New England Award. A man of many talents and interests, in 2003 Haslett earned his law degree from the Yale School of Law.

He divides his time between New York City and England. Recently Sherry Ellis spoke with him by phone at his home in New York City.

[*Sherry Ellis:*] You Are Not A Stranger Here *is a collection of stories that contains the themes of estrangement, suffering and the desire to make connections. "You Are Not A Stranger Here" is also a line in one of your stories. How did you choose it as the title of this collection?*

" Something could have a dark ending but that doesn't mean it's a pessimistic experience to read it, because the optimism may arise in the identification the reader has with the predicament of a particular character. That usually involves some kind of emotion."

[Adam Haslett:] It did come out of a story. It was in the story first, certainly, and the story was actually titled "Wars End" when it was first published in *Bomb Magazine*. And then I ended up deciding to re-title it and I liked the title, so I used it for the book. "You Are Not a Stranger Here" was the only one that struck me as inclusive of all the others, in a sense, addressing the reader, inviting them into the book.

When did you know that the nine stories in this anthology were short stories and not novellas or novels?

I was always writing short stories. None of them were longer pieces that were cut down. They were written as short pieces, and I wrote at least two-thirds of the stories before I even conceived of them as a collection. Only the last third were written with the book in mind. At that point I had contracted to complete a manuscript.

As the story "The Beginnings of Grief" draws to a close you describe a visit between a violent teenager and a recently orphaned classmate who takes solace in physical pain. "He came on a Tuesday. Rain was falling through the naked branches of the trees onto a carpet of rotting foliage". Is the vocabulary and metaphor you use in this passage an example of what you describe as finding "the correct rhythm" in language, and can you describe the process of trial and error that you use?

To answer the process question first, the trial and error is really just a repeated reading of the sentences over and over again, to try to discern the rhythm of them, to find out if the second sentence is obeying the rhythm of the sentence before that. It is another way of describing the editing process. I think of each story as having a rhythm, an intensity, and I am always trying to find the rhythm that fits a particular story. In the first story in the book the rhythm is quite fast, and in others more deliberate. As for "The Beginnings of Grief" there is a certain kind of emotional detachment in the narrator. The ambition was to allow that detachment to filter down into the semantics of the sentences.

Do you plan the direction your stories will take before you begin writing, even if they happen to veer off somewhat differently in the process? In "The Beginnings of Grief," for example, was that specific ending planned from the beginning?

I generally have a sense of where the story is headed emotionally, i.e. I know where I want to reader to end up, the feeling I want them to end up with and the process is writing the story toward that end, hoping to get at that ideal balance you have in your head at the outset. Obviously, one's ideas develop as you go along, but the emotional key rarely changes.

Last year TBR *ran both a Spanish and a Catalan translation of "The Beginnings of Grief"; the Spanish translation of* You Are Not a Stranger Here *had just come out (Salamandra, 2003), and the Catalan version of the collection is due out April 2004 (Angl TBR's editor said: "The earlier Catalan version had been done by a class of translation under the tutelage of Matthew Tree, writer and translator. They had a hard time with 'sloppy joe,' and Matthew, who's British, had never heard the term either. Salamandra's Spanish translator, Eduardo Hojman, went with 'bocadillo,' but the Catalans tried for the more literal 'la carn picada amb tom?? et' (hamburger with tomato). 'Helicopter "wings"' gave them pause, too. But generally speaking, Matthew said what the students found tricky was maintaining the fine balance between the literary register in the story and the free use of colloquial American English, which works fine in the original but in Catalan is difficult to slip in and out of from one register to another." Might you have any general comments about the art of translation? Have you ever read any of your stories in translation?*

Let me first say I have enormous respect and gratitude to my translators. It is a greatly unappreciated art and I feel very fortunate to have had such good translators thus far. Pocia, my German

translator was particularly careful and thoughtful. Sometimes I get questions from them about particular idiomatic phrases that they are having difficulty translating into their native tongue and I try to offer more background or alternatives. In the end, it seems to me what one wants in a good translator is the same as what you want in a good writer—an ability to emphasize, a good ear, and a talent with language.

I've read some translations of my work, but am only really competent in French so can't judge most of them. The Greeks could have put a cookbook between the covers and I would have been none the wiser

Allan Gurganus once said that, "Dialogue isn't what characters say to each other, but what they do to each other." Do you want dialogue to have the effect on your characters of doing something to one another? And what other function(s) do you hope your dialogue serves?

I think I agree with Gurganus about that. You want it not to be simply giving information but to be characterizing and active. I don't know that I've thought about dialogue as a separate issue and when I work it's all part of the rhythm question, deciding when dialogue or description makes more sense.

In "Reunion" a young man with AIDS uses writing to have imaginary communication with his deceased father. In "My Father's Business" letters between psychologists are the means through which the primary character is revealed. In "Devotion" letters demonstrate sabotage in a complex, oftentimes symbiotic relationship between middle-aged siblings. What led you to use written communications in these different situations and what do you think they help you to achieve?

That's interesting. You're pointing out a connection I'd never even noticed. So I'm somewhat disarmed by the question. But now that I think about it I think particularly in "My Father's Business" and "Reunion" and less-so in "Devotion" letters give me the ability to use another written form within the story, to get at information and the world in a different way than standard realist narrative. So in a sense it's an outlet. I'm able to get things into a story that wouldn't otherwise find a way in.

In the story "The Volunteer" you explore psychopharmacological treatment and its impact on perspective and creativity. When a woman with schizophrenia decides to stop taking her medication she "wakes to colors more vivid: the Oriental carpet's swirls of burgundy and gold; dawn kindling the sky an immaculate blue." It seems from this story that you might be supportive of people who stop taking their medicine. How did you become interested in exploring this theme?

Well, I certainly don't advocate people not taking their medication; I don't really have an editorial position on that. My goal is always to take the reader as far into the minds of my characters as I can get them, and in a few of the stories in the book that means taking the reader into the lives of people facing the dilemma of whether to take medication, what it does to one and so forth. So in that story, "The Volunteer", I think it had consequences both good and bad for her. And in terms of how I came into all this I've said in other places that my father was a manic depressive and there is some family background as to the question of taking medication or not.

Many of your characters are complex, multifaceted individuals who are diagnosed with psychiatric problems. For example, in "Notes To My Biographer," Franklin Caldwell, the protagonist, is a seventy-three year old inventor who has had mental health problems since his youth. He comments on the many Robert Wagner look-a-likes he sees. How do you balance humor and pathos in your characters?

It's not easy and I'm lucky if I can. That's a very tough question to answer. I don't think there's anything deliberate or intentional about it. I get lucky with a certain voice that allows me into a certain mind like his and a certain sense of humor can come out. But combining humor and pathos is a pretty tall order and it's a very difficult thing to accomplish. I don't feel I have much control over doing it.

In an article in "The Yale Bulletin & Calendar" you are quoted as saying, "The law deals with people's exterior lives, with the uniform rights that people have, whereas in my stories I am concerned with people's interior lives, with their souls." When you are writing how do you investigate the "interiority" of your characters?

Well, it's kind of the whole shooting match for me. That's really the point—I think it's the act of imagining myself further and further inside, the act of projecting myself into the position and situation I've made up for my character, and then trying to imagine in as much detail as possible what a human reaction would be in that circumstance. So, it's the same kind of trial and error and concentration. Some days you can maintain it, and some days you can't.

You've previously discussed the differences between creative writing and law, but do you also believe there are connections between them?

There are so many different levels on which they may be related, but I don't think that the main preoccupations of each are related. I mean the exterior/interior is divided pretty clearly. But I think lawyers are fictionally very interesting characters, as people who find themselves advocating for things they may not believe themselves. Also, law is the language that power speaks through in this country, so if you want to get at the social fabric it can be an important discourse. I suppose the big, obvious thing is the story telling aspect, that when you go into in the courtroom you are really trying to tell a story; but the stories that writers and lawyers are each telling are so radically different, and hopefully a good lawyer is restrained by the facts.

"The portrayal of the dark side of human experience is not a pessimistic act," is a comment you once made. Can you further explain what you mean?

Well I guess some people's reaction is that the stories are depressing. It seems to me that response comes out of a sense that something is depressing or not because of how it ends, which to me seems too literal. Something could have a dark ending but that doesn't mean it's a pessimistic experience to read it, because the optimism may arise in the identification the reader has with the predicament of a particular character. That usually involves some kind of emotion. I think of any emotion, even sadness, as different from depression, which is really a numbness, a lack of feeling.

In "The Good Doctor" a psychiatrist visits a female patient at her home with the goal of enticing her into treatment. He finds her in a very bleak and disheartening circumstance and experiences "a familiar comfort being in the presence of another person's unknowable pain . . . more than any landscape, this place felt like home". How did you choose the title "The Good Doctor"?

The title just captured something about his intentions and what would become of them.

William Trevor has said of writing short stories, "I think it is the art of the glimpse". Can you discuss this comment in regard to your own experience of writing?

William Trevor is one of my favorites. I think he is an incredible writer. I guess I take him to mean that it's a slice of life found in a particular moment, a clarifying moment captured. Short stories have a poetic density to them that novels simply can't achieve. You can think of them as one long exhalation. It's one of the things I like about writing them; their emotional intensity is quite satisfying.

Who are the other writers that have inspired you?

As to the short story I'd say William Trevor, Joy Williams and Alice Munro. My taste in novels is all over the place, but I'm a bit of a modernist fan: Faulkner, Joyce, James, Woolf, Mann, all those folks.

You've lived, and continue to live, in England for extended periods, and several of your stories are set there. Can you give us a quick personal take on the US versus England—the people, culture, etc.

Actually, I've lived most of my life in the US. I spent three years as a kid in Britain and I visit there and Scotland a fair amount, but my social and professional life are definitely based in America. As for cultural differences I'd have to say the most pronounced is the continuing thickness of class differentiation in Britain, tied to accent mostly, that is far less on the surface in America. The United States is very divided by class, but there is almost no acknowledgement of this fact and whenever politicians even mention taxing the wealthy they are accused of "class warfare." The myth of egalitarianism runs very deep in the US, less so in Britain.

How challenging has it been for you to cope with all the praise and attention, and the resulting changes in your life?

Well, I think I had the good fortune of being in law school when a lot of it was happening, so there was a balance because of all the other things I needed to deal with and attend to. I guess I feel incredibly fortunate that the book has had the life it has and the recognition it has got, and most centrally in terms of it effecting my life I'm glad that I'm able to be able do what I plant to do, which is begin work on a new book.

Do you have any suggestions for writers who are trying to develop themselves and become part of the literary marketplace?

I was actually rejected from a lot of MFA programs and I have a fat folder from literary magazines filled with rejections, so I went through that whole process. Sometimes I think it is just endurance, spending enough time at it, arranging your life so that you can work; MFA programs are one way of doing that for awhile, though they don't suit everyone.

I guess my real break came when the woman who eventually became my editor read a story of mine in a magazine and asked to see more. That

was the beginning of the book being bought and eventually published.

And once you started to get your stories published did your writing career fall into place easily? Did you still receive many rejection letters?

Oh yes, there are always rejection letters coming. I don't think you pull a switch, and I think any other author would confirm that.

So, do you have any suggestions or words of encouragement for beginning writers who want to be published?

I guess I would say don't worry. Keep the idea of the market out of your mind for as long as possible, because it really doesn't matter when you publish something. There are people who will eventually know the difference between something that is really good, something that is carefully attended to and thought out. I have taught and my advice to my students is to keep the whole idea of marketing out you mind, until you feel you have something very strong, and then worry about it.

[*Sherry Ellis*:] *"Devotion" is included in* The Best American Short Stories 2003. *If you had been asked to choose one of your stories for this anthology which one would you have selected and why?*

I can't really say. I don't think I have an opinion on that one.

Can you talk a little more about what you're working on now?

Other than saying it is a novel, not really. I'm a little superstitious when it comes to talking about new work.

Source: Adam Haslett and Sherry Ellis, "Interview with Adam Haslett," in *Barcelona Review*, No. 41, March–April 2004, pp. 1–6.

Contemporary Authors Online

In the following essay, the critic gives an overview of Haslett's work.

Adam Haslett simultaneously applied for admission to Yale Law School as well as to a number of writing fellowships, and he was successful in both areas. Yale gave him a one-year deferral so that he could study in Provincetown, Massachusetts, and when he was accepted into the Iowa Writers' Workshop the deferral was extended by two additional years. During the second semester of Haslett's law studies, a Doubleday editor, who had read one of his short stories, offered to publish a collection. Thus, Haslett's law degree was postponed yet another year so that he could write an adequate number of new stories to take Doubleday up on their offer.

"Notes to My Biographer," the first of the nine stories in *You Are Not a Stranger Here*, was originally published in *Zoetrope*. It focuses on Frank Singer, an aged inventor and veteran suffering from mental illness who doesn't trust the medical establishment; by refusing to take his medication he makes life hell for all around him. Frank drives to California to see his gay son, Graham, who is suffering from the same inherited illness; the son does take his meds, though, for fear that not doing so will result in behaviors that would drive away his lover.

Reviewing the story for *Salon.com*, Laura Miller said, "it's not a story about the ravages of mental illness after all, but one about the price paid for mental health. More often than not, Haslett's characters find themselves contemplating a choice between subduing their demons or facing them head on; these stories are full of people deciding not to swallow their pills. . . . The twist in an Adam Haslett story is often a revelation about who is actually the stronger in a pair of characters."

Craig Seligman wrote in the *New York Times Book Review* that Haslett "may have talent to burn . . . but his prose exudes a desolation so choking that it can come only from somewhere deep inside. . . . Haslett has despair. And I don't mean the histrionic despair of discouraged youth. . . . Haslett writes like a man inured to disappointment." Seligman called "Notes to My Biographer" and the collection's last story, "The Volunteer," the "showpieces of the collection." The latter is about an ageing, institutionalized female schizophrenic and the high school volunteer who visits her. Regarding "Notes to My Biographer" Seligman wrote, "It's funny, it's awful, and it's the only one of the stories in this collection that gave me some hope that their creator might be able to draw some pleasure out of the spectacular career that . . . he's surely heading into."

Several of Haslett's stories are set in Great Britain, including "Reunion," in which a young man is dying of AIDS. Two stories that are gay-themed are "The Beginnings of Grief" and "Devotion," about a brother and sister who love the same man. Other stories that deal with mental illness include "Divination," in which a boy has the gift of prophecy but considers it a mental illness. Seligman said that this theme "supplies the ruling metaphor for the collection: a debilitating, humiliating, alienating condition . . . that can be escaped only through death; a condition, in other words, that's very much like life."

A *Kirkus Reviews* contributor called "War's End" "a hypnotically strange amalgam of Chekhov and Beckett" and "one of the finest, and most unusual, stories of recent years." A *Publishers Weekly* reviewer, however, thought this same story veers too much "toward the sentimental," though the reviewer concluded that *You Are Not a Stranger Here* is "a strikingly assured first effort." Finally, *Book* reviewer Tom LeClair said that the collection "welcomes the courageous—and the estranged."

Source: Contemporary Authors Online, "Adam Haslett," in *Contemporary Authors Online*, Gale, 2003.

Sources

Egan, Timothy, "Pastoral Poverty: The Seeds of Decline," in *New York Times*, December 8, 2002, Sec. 4, p. 1.

Haslett, Adam, "The Good Doctor," in *You Are Not a Stranger Here*, Doubleday, 2002, pp. 24–47.

LeClair, Tom, Review of *You Are Not a Stranger Here*, in *Book*, July–August 2002, p. 78.

Review of *You Are Not a Stranger Here*, in *Kirkus Reviews*, Vol. 70, No. 10, May 15, 2002, p. 685.

Review of *You Are Not a Stranger Here*, in *New York Times Book Review*, Vol. 107, No. 30, July 28, 2002, p. 14.

Review of *You Are Not a Stranger Here*, in *Publishers Weekly*, Vol. 249, No. 27, July 8, 2002, p. 32.

Further Reading

Lee, Steven, *Overcoming Crystal Meth Addiction: An Essential Guide to Getting Clean from CM Addiction*, Avalon Publishing Group, 2006.
    A psychiatrist who specializes in treating methamphetamine addiction explains the physical and psychological effects of this condition and answers many common questions people may have about the problem, its effect on family members, methods for treatment, and rates of relapse and recovery.

Pickering, Kathleen, et al., *Welfare Reform in Persistent Rural Poverty: Dreams, Disenchantments, and Diversity*, Pennsylvania State University Press, 2006.
    Readers who would like to understand better the disillusionment of the Buckholdt family may find this book of interest. It analyzes the circumstances and factors which cause chronic poverty in rural areas where there are few jobs, poor education, and low-income families that make do with little hope for improvement or escape.

Richie, Beth E., ed. *Domestic Violence at the Margins: Readings on Race, Class, Gender, and Culture*, Rutgers University Press, 2005.
    This anthology of essays covers the field of domestic violence as it occurs among various marginalized populations, in part, in an effort to challenge stereotypes

people have regarding perpetrators and victims and also to explain social and legal services which address the problem.

Rural Drug Abuse: Prevalence, Relation to Crime, and Programs, DIANE Publishing, 1994.
This study evaluates the extent of substance abuse in rural areas and its connection to crime. It also describes and evaluates programs designed to treat or prevent drug abuse specifically in rural, underserved areas of the United States.

Stamm, B. Hudnall, ed., *Rural Behavioral Health Care: An Interdisciplinary Guide*, American Psychological Association, 2003.
Readers who would like to know more about public and federal programs designed to deliver psychological services to remote and rural populations may find this book useful. Three topic areas are covered here: behavioral needs in rural areas; problems facing federal and public service agencies in delivering services, and special problems associated with certain populations in these areas.

Great Day

David Malouf

2000

"Great Day," which appeared in David Malouf's 2000 collection, *Dream Stuff*, has been singled out as one of his best stories. This well-crafted tale explores the tensions that can arise in a close-knit family; it traces each family member's need to find a harmonious balance between personal desires and external connection to the group. The story centers on one day in the life of the Tyler family as its members celebrate the seventy-second birthday of the family patriarch, Audley Tyler. The story begins on the morning of the day, which is also a national holiday, as some members of the family wait for the arrival of the entire clan. Tensions immediately arise as individuals begin to express their separate longings and the obstacles to those longings as they gather together for the celebration. The tensions are eventually resolved as all are able to renew or reestablish connections and come to an acceptance of their collective and personal experience. As the story ends, the family comes together to celebrate their sense of community at the close of their "great day."

Author Biography

David Malouf was born in Brisbane, Australia, on March 20, 1934, to George and Welcome (Mendoza) Malouf. After he was awarded a degree with honors from the University of Queensland, he relocated to England, where he was employed as

David Malouf © Jerry Bauer. Reproduced by permission

a teacher from 1959 to 1968. That year he returned to Australia where he served as a lecturer at the University of Sydney until 1977. Malouf gained recognition and several awards for his poetry written during his teaching years. In 1975, he turned to fiction with his well-received first novel, *Johnno*. In 1978, he retired from teaching and devoted himself full-time to writing.

Malouf has gained international acclaim for his work, which includes several volumes of poetry, six novels and two novellas; three short-story collections, including *Dream Stuff*, in which "Great Day," appeared; several nonfiction works; a series of libretti for opera, and a play.

Malouf has received many awards. Among these are the following: the 1974 Australian Literature Society Gold Medal and the 1974 Grace Leven Poetry Prize for *Neighbours in a Thicket: Poems*; the New South Wales Premier's Fiction Award in 1979 for *An Imaginary Life: A Novel* and the New South Wales Premier's Drama Award in 1987 for *Blood Relations*; the 1983 Book of the Year and the 1983 Australian Literature Society Gold Medal for *Fly Away Peter*; the Best Book of the Region Award, the Commonwealth Writers' Prize (Southeast Asia and South Pacific Region), the Miles Franklin Award, and the Prix Femina Prize (France)

for *The Great World* in 1991; and the 1994 Los Angeles Times Book Prize for fiction, the 1994 Commonwealth Writers' Prize (Southeast Asia and South Pacific Region), the 1995 Prix Baudelaire (France), and the 1996 IMPAC Dublin Literary Award for *Remembering Babylon*. In 1994, his *Remembering Babylon* was short listed for the prestigious Booker Prize. In 2000, the *New York Times* named *Dream Stuff* one of its Notable Books of that year, and the same year, Malouf received the Neustadt International Prize for Literature.

David Malouf lived in Tuscany, Italy, from 1978 to 1985, after which he returned to Australia.

Plot Summary

"Great Day" opens early on the morning of Audley Tyler's seventy-second birthday, which is the same day as a national Australian holiday. Angie, Audley's daughter-in-law, sits gazing out to sea while nearby, Audley is fishing. When Angie walks back to the house, she is greeted by her son, Ned, who informs her that Fran is coming with Audley's son, Clem, her ex-husband.

Angie is always "ill at ease" in the kitchen of her mother-in-law, Madge, where Angie sits drinking tea. Her daughter, Jenny, asks Angie whether Audley has caught any fish, and Ned asks why Fran and Clem are still friends after their divorce, but no one answers them. Ned agrees to go out and pick wild spinach with his sister for Madge's soup. The narrator notes that the daughters-in-law never really feel a part of the tightly knit Tyler clan.

Today, the entire family along with some neighbors will gather to celebrate Audley's birthday. Later, Audley comes back to the house with two freshly caught blackfish, and he eats breakfast. The narrator explains that Audley was an important official in the Australian government for thirty-seven years. Madge puts the fish in the sink and turns to one of the children's books she is writing, which she bases on her family's experiences.

Angie goes outside again, and Ralph, her husband, joins her. An hour later, Fran arrives followed in a separate car by Clem. The children are confused when Clem asks them whether he and Fran look like newlyweds. They know that since his car accident, "Clem *said things*, just whatever came into his head." Three years before, he swerved his car to avoid hitting a boy and crashed; the accident put him in a coma for fourteen months.

Fran used to be the girlfriend of Jonathon, Clem's brother, but she had gotten tired of his marked self-confidence. Determined that she would "save" Clem from his family, she married him, but then she left after only two years. They remained friends after the divorce, "locked in an odd dependency." She and Angie, who both feel like outsiders in the family, have become friends. Audley is the only member of the family with whom Angie feels a connection.

Clem sits in the kitchen with Madge, asking her to talk about him when he was a child since many of his memories were erased by the accident. She tells him some stories, and he admits that he does not remember them. When he asks her if she and his father loved him, Madge answers, "Of course we did," and insists that he was Audley's favorite. After Clem claims that he thought he was a disappointment to his father, Madge replies, "Maybe. Maybe that too." When he hears his father approach, he runs out the door and gives him a bear hug, telling Audley how glad he is to see him.

Later, Ned sees a group of people heading to the beach. A child from the group introduces himself to Ned, but Ned is furious that the boy has taken him unawares and rebuffs him. When he gets back to the house, Ned asks his father whether the group is allowed to make a bonfire on the beach, and Ralph tells him that they are, which angers Ned who stalks off to tell his grandfather. Ned admires Audley for his formality, which his own father lacks. After he gets no response from his grandfather, Ned goes back to the beach and spies on the group. As he leaves, he stumbles on the boy who had introduced himself and says, "Hi," to him by way of reconciliation.

Audley walks to town and heads toward the Waruna Folk and History Museum, which he often visits. The museum holds a collection of Tyler family artifacts and offers Audley a chance to reminisce about the past.

At seven-thirty, the guests begin to arrive. Jonathon, who brings a new girlfriend, is followed by "an old flame of Audley's," according to Madge. An hour later, groups of men "vigorously" argue while the women sit "on the sidelines." As Fran wanders from group to group, Clem watches her from the background. Cedric Pohl, a guest whom she has never met before, introduces himself to Fran. As they chat, she notices that he is interested in her.

Feeling that "too much might be happening too fast," Fran escapes outside where Ned, Jen, and some of their cousins are dancing to music from a stereo. Fran thinks about how during visits there she used to fill notebooks with angry epithets about the Tyler family, who she felt never fully accepted her. When Audley approaches and tells her he will get her something to drink, she feels the same desire to be a part of the family, but then, just as suddenly, she feels the same anger over her exclusion. She grabs Angie and the two escape to the beach.

As they walk along the beach, Fran admits that Cedric has asked to drive her home. Angie insists that he is "a bit of a s———," explaining that he has cheated on his wife. After they come across the group that Ned had seen on the beach, they stop and watch for a while. Fran imagines herself joining the group.

As they walk back to the house, they see a strange glow in the sky, which turns out to be the museum that has been set on fire by arsonists. When all in the house race to town, they discover that the museum cannot be saved. Audley feels oddly relieved as he stands next to his old friends and watches the museum burn, knowing that many objects connected to his past are being destroyed.

After some of them return to the house, Clem feels that something needs to be said on the occasion. He gives a disjointed speech about how everyone in the universe is connected and that "nothing ever gets *lost*." Even though Fran had already left with a group that included Cedric, Clem feels satisfied with his speech and himself. After everyone leaves, Angie and Ralph take a walk while Audley plays the piano. Later, she goes into the kitchen to clean up where she is soon joined by Audley. They talk about Clem's speech, which Audley admits moved him deeply. The story closes with a description of the glowing ashes of the museum, the bonfire on the beach, and the promise of "a new day coming."

Characters

Cedric Pohl

The night of the celebration, Fran leaves with Cedric Pohl, an attractive thirty-three-year-old. His expensive haircut, along with his propensity for travel, suggests he is wealthy. He is "a bit too sure of himself," but she responds to his need to relieve her of her obvious desperation. Little information is provided about him since he serves more as a illustration of Fran's constant need to develop new relationships.

Angie Tyler

Angie Tyler, Ralph's wife, has a sense of "stillness" and a "capacity to just sit among all that Tyler ebullience and remain self-contained." She also has a sense of darkness that gives her sympathetic connection to Audley, which is suggested by the framing technique Malouf uses in the story. The opening and closing scenes focus on the two together, separate from the rest of the family.

Audley Tyler

Audley Tyler, the patriarch of the family, whose ancestors were among the early European settlers, has a formal bearing and appears in a black suit on all occasions. Angie regards him as "a somber column," whose demeanor commands attention and respect. He is fastidious and at times gloomy with a 'tendency to withdraw." His dark side becomes ominous when he tries to disguise it with "bitter jokes and a form of politeness that at times had an edge of the murderous."

Yet he is also responsible in his position as the primary caregiver for his children and as a government official. During his years with the government, he served as a model to young, ambitious men "who saw in him the proof that you could get to the top, and stay there too, yet maintain a kind of decency." He is the one most moved by Clem's speech, and by the end of the story, he comes to recognize more than any of them the value of family. After the museum burns to the ground, he is also able to reconcile himself to the reality of death.

Clem Tyler

Clem Tyler, one of the four Tyler brothers, never felt included in his family since he did not seem to take after any of them. He has a good nature but is "slow, tongue-tied, aimless," which was exacerbated by his accident. Because of her confidence in him, Fran is the only one with whom Clem "felt entirely whole." When he is at the party, he seeks her out in order to "centre himself. Otherwise, the occasion might have become chaotic" due to the expectations others may have of him. When he cannot think clearly, he experiences moments of panic and must find a familiar object to calm himself. His obvious love and affection for his family fills him with the confidence he needs to give his speech about how connected they all are to each other and to the universe.

Fran Tyler

Fran Tyler, Clem's ex-wife, is adventurous and restless and so is attracted to new places and new men. She turns to Clem for stability. While she demonstrates a good sense of humor, it can sometimes turn cruel as when she kept journals that attacked what she considered to be the family's faults. Fran is the only one who is able to find a life outside the family that she balances with her need to remain connected to it.

Jenny Tyler

Nine-year-old Jenny Tyler, Angie and Ralph's daughter, is younger than her brother but appears worldlier. She rolls her eyes when Ned does not understand why Clem and Fran got divorced if they are still friends.

Jonathon Tyler

Jonathon Tyler, one of the four Tyler brothers, introduced Fran to the family as his girlfriend, but she soon got tired of "the assurance he had of being so much cleverer than others" and of "his sense of his own power and charm."

Madge Tyler

Madge Tyler is a messy, disorganized housekeeper, whose bluntness and "off-hand discourtesies" sometimes put off others, especially her daughters-in-law. She is self-deprecating and full of life. Her boys have inherited her "energy and rough good humour." She provides a nice counter to Audley's solemn and dignified demeanor. Madge was adopted and brought up by farmers, and she determined early on that she "belonged to no one but herself," which, according to Audley, "made life very interesting."

Ned Tyler

Eleven-year-old Ned Tyler, Angie and Ralph's son, tries to gain some measure of power in the family by being "the bearer of news," and he is disappointed when the others already know that Fran is coming with Clem. He is also disappointed that the family will not be celebrating the country's anniversary since "he wanted time to have precise turning-points that could be marked and remembered." Ned becomes intensely concerned about things and is "quick to take offense" if he feels that others are not equally concerned, as with the question of the bonfire.

Ralph Tyler

When they were young, Ralph Tyler and his brothers "had to fend for themselves, shouting one another down in the war for attention and growing up loud and confident." Ralph is shyer than his brothers but shared their same love and respect for their parents. He is easygoing, having been part of the liberal movement of the 1960s.

Themes

Dreams

The thematic focus on dreams in the story is announced by the title of the collection, *Dream Stuff*, an allusion to Shakespeare's *The Tempest* (4.1.156–58). Prospero, the central character in the play, notes the temporal nature of human life in his claim, "We are such stuff / As dreams are made on; and our little life / Is rounded by a sleep." (The passage from Shakespeare appears in Peter Pierce's article, "What Dreams May Come: David Malouf's *Dream Stuff*.) In "Great Day," this allusion suggests reflection, as Audley celebrates his seventy-second birthday, and hope as the characters are able to find comforting connections.

Fran's dream becomes a sign of the unification that the family feels at the end of the story after Clem has declared, "Anything is possible.... Nothing ever gets *lost*." She sees herself lying down with the others on the beach and recognizes the connection that she has with the Tyler family as she emerges "in out of the dark" and "into the circle of light."

Loss

Several characters in the story experience an ironic sense of loss. Paul Sharrad notes that this loss "can be both debilitating and the catalyst for creation." Clem and Fran, for example, lose a partner when they get a divorce, but the experience allows them to establish a new, supportive relationship with each other. Clem is also able to strengthen his relationship with his family while Fran finds a satisfying balance between her life inside and outside of it.

Ned loses his sure sense of right and wrong when his father and grandfather refuse to support his contention that no one should be setting bonfires on the beach. Paradoxically, he is also disappointed that his family is not celebrating the national holiday by waving flags or building their own bonfires. He disagrees with his father's conclusion that "If these fellers want an excuse for a good do, I'm not the one to deny them, but it's just another day like any other really." Ned becomes angry at the members of his family who "like things left up in the air" and who "never want anything settled."

This inconclusiveness, however, also suggests an openness and flexibility that Ned eventually

Topics for Further Study

- Write an autobiographical essay exploring tensions within your family. Note whether the tensions were resolved and if so, how.

- Read another story from *Dream Stuff*, and prepare a presentation for the class comparing and contrasting that story's use of the dream motif with that of "Great Day."

- Do some research on the national holidays of Australia and how aborigines may feel about them or observe them. Write a paper on your findings.

- Visit a small, local museum, and learn about a local family whose artifacts may be housed there. Write a paper on this family, describing its contribution to the local area and describing some of the items belonging to the family you saw in the museum.

adopts. After he watches the group on the beach, he admits "that what he really regretted was that the bonfire was not theirs," and, as a result, he is able to make a connection with the boy whom he had previously rebuffed.

Style

Imagery

The dominant image in the story is fire, which appears in the beginning as Ned watches a group on the beach build a bonfire and, at the end, when the museum is set ablaze. The fires provide an ironic tension in the story as they suggest both destruction and positive change. Both the bonfire and the museum fire represent outside forces that have the potential to disrupt the Tyler family, but at the same time, they also provide a cathartic and unifying influence.

Initially, the bonfire presents tension through Ned's response to it as he fails to get support from his family for his contention that the group on the beach is breaking the rules. His eventual acceptance of the bonfire helps Ned become less rigid in his thinking. The bonfire also enables Fran to realize her connection to the Tyler family: she imagines herself enclosed in the circle of light it offers, the same comforting "light that fills the world."

Malouf connects the bonfire to the museum fire as he describes the glowing embers of each at the story's close. Initially, the museum fire causes a similar tension in that it is the result of outside forces, here specifically more threatening ones. Yet as Audley watches the artifacts of his past be destroyed by the fire, he comes to recognize the importance of what is left behind. In both cases, the fire draws a circle of people around it, emphasizing connection between those who form the circle.

Historical Context

Australian History

The story is set on a warm day during the Australian summer. No date is mentioned, but it is most likely in January, which is Australia's hottest month. During this month, Australians celebrate two historical events: Australia's Independence Day on January 1, which honors the day the country won its independence from Great Britain in 1901; and Australia Day on January 26, which honors the date in 1788 when the first white settlement was established. Some critics have assumed that the story takes place on Independence Day, but others have inferred that it is Australia Day. Malouf never identifies the specific holiday that becomes the backdrop for the story, perhaps to place more emphasis on the reunification of family.

Historical details do play an important part, however, at the end of the story when the museum that contains many of the family's artifacts burns down. Peter Pierce, in his article on *Dream Stuff*, notes regional elements in "Great Day," arguing that while there are no aborigines in the story, and "no bonfires of theirs will ring the long continental coast in celebration," on this national holiday, Malouf asks us "to reflect on where and how far Australia has traveled since the McGiverns . . . came to the blacksoil country and other regions of Australia that they pioneered."

Aborigines, the name given to the original inhabitants of Australia, may have emigrated from Asia approximately 20,000 years ago. Though various

groups of aborigines moved there, the country remained isolated from the outside world until Europeans began to explore and settle it. Portuguese Manuel Godhino de Eredia is considered to be the first European to sight the continent in 1601, followed by Spaniard Luis Vaez de Torres in 1605. Dutch explorers later named it New Holland.

In 1770, Captain James Cook landed on the east coast and claimed the land for Great Britain. The first British settlement, soon established in 1788, was a penal colony in Port Jackson, which is now Sydney. The continent became a British dependency by 1829. During the late eighteenth and early nineteenth century, Australia became a dumping ground for anyone deemed undesirable by the British government.

In the middle of the nineteenth century, a gold strike brought an influx of people from around the world to the continent. By the mid-1800s, permanent colonization had erased the old penal settlements, and by 1901, a self-governing confederacy with its own constitution was established.

Critical Overview

Dream Stuff earned Malouf overwhelming critical praise, and "Great Day" is often singled out as the finest story in the collection. Paul Sharrad, in his article on Malouf's short prose, insists that Malouf is "Australia's leading producer of 'poetic prose.'" He finds that "the shorter work . . . relies for its impact on musical qualities such as rhythm and cadence and the modulation of evocative motifs" and allows Malouf "more consistently to tap into his creative strengths and to provide new insights into old experiences."

Rebecca Miller in her review of *Dream Stuff* for *Library Journal*, praises "these nine beautiful and often brutal stories" that "[describe] a precarious world in which the imagination, through dreams, is the only thing that can face down the losses of life." She adds, "Almost all of the stories here are superb, evocative creations." She finds, "As a whole, the collection is like a tumultuous life: it reels through surprising turns of plot, alternating between moments on the brink of death in one story and loss of innocence in another, then presses on, redeemed only by the warmth of human feeling and a glimpse of the possible."

A review in the *Economist* applauds the tone of the collection, arguing that "there is nothing

The coast of Kangaroo Island, South Australia, between Remarkable Rocks and Cape du Couedic
© T. Allofs/Zefa/Corbis

conventionally 'dreamy' about the stories themselves. Not so much as a trace of sentimentality. Not the least haziness or insubstantiality." The reviewer also admires the solid construction, the "uncompromisingly gritty and emotionally charged" subject matter, the "extent of psychological territory covered," and "physical landscape" of the stories, which is "carefully charted." The review concludes by insisting, "Such, in the hands of a latter-day Prospero like Mr. Malouf, is the stuff that dreams are made on."

Peter Pierce, in his article on *Dream Stuff*, finds "an artful casualness" in the stories and praises their focus on "the variegated stuff of dreams—longed for and summoned up. Or come unbidden, bringing peace, or disquiet," which, he claims is their "unifying metaphorical thread."

A reviewer for *Publishers Weekly* notes the regionalism of the stories, arguing that "Malouf . . . has a peculiarly Australian sensitivity to the mechanics of large families" and that his "stories show his feeling for the intense grip of the continent's space upon its people." Yet, the reviewer also insists that Malouf "[transcends] regionalism by his instinct for that odd, modulated empathy victims and outsiders can feel for their assailants" and so

"shows a rare, exploratory intelligence coupled with a compassionate view of human conduct." Singling out "Great Day," this reviewer states, "of the nine stories gathered in Malouf's latest collection, most are excellent, and one—"Great Day," the final entry—is outstanding," finding it "elegantly structured and perfectly pitched." Miller also singles out the story, which she claims is "the collection's final and most deeply crafted work" as does a review in *New Statesman* that claims, ""Great Day" [is] a charming, life-affirming account of a family gathering on the bicentenary Australia Day in 1988." While, like the other stories, it "also turns opaque, with characters making gnomic utterances," the reviewer concludes that "here and elsewhere, Malouf's fine writing does live up to its pretensions as often as not."

Criticism

Wendy Perkins

Perkins is a professor of American and English literature and film. In this essay, Perkins traces the characters' achievement of a harmonious balance.

> **❝**
> ...Fran has an epiphany of sorts, suggesting that she can be content inside the circle of the family as well as outside it, by striking a balance between the two.**❞**

In his article on David Malouf's shorter fiction, Paul Sharrad argues that Malouf's stories explore the mystery inherent in "the moment of contact between different orders of experience," specifically "the mystery of what makes people tick" and "of how some of us find intuitive balance in a world that others force into solid blocks of unfeeling certitude." These mysteries are the main focal points of "Great Day" in its chronicle of one day in the life of the Tyler clan. During the course of this day, readers get glimpses of what makes each member tick as well as their struggles with the inevitable tensions that arise in a tightly knit family structure. The day, however, becomes "great" by its close, when the characters are able to strike a balance between connection and disconnection and between the past and the future.

Ned, Angie and Ralph's son, is one of the first to feel the tensions on the morning of Audley Tyler's seventy-second birthday, which falls on a national Australian holiday. At eleven, Ned, "whose idea of the world was very different" from that of his relatives, has "a hunger for order that the circumstances of his life frustrated." At breakfast, he wonders why Clem and Fran are still friends after getting a divorce. When he does not get a satisfactory answer to this mystery, he explodes, "People never tell me anything. . . . How am I ever going to know how to act or anything if I can't find out the simplest thing?"

Later in the day, when he sees a group of people begin to set up a bonfire on the beach, he is certain that they are breaking rules and so tells one of the boys who has come up suddenly behind him to "piss off." Nat gets no satisfaction from his father who tells him, "it's a free country." Preferring the

more formal attitude of his grandfather, Ned turns to Audley but gets no response. Yet, Audley's formality tempers Ned's indignation. When he returns to the beach and watches the group set up the bonfire, Ned is able to find a balance between his need for rules, his patriotism as he watches the celebratory fire, and his introduction to a new way of thinking. His experiences this day cause him to widen his view of the world, and as a result, he is able then to greet the boy he had rebuked earlier and so establish "a kind of reconcilement."

Fran and Angie have always felt a sense of disconnection between themselves and the rest of the Tyler family, "a close-knit tribe" that "hedged against intruders." Angie was "always ill at ease in Madge's kitchen, fearful she might register visible disapproval of the mess" she finds there. Angie "always felt, down here, like a child who had been dumped on them for a wet weekend and could find nothing to do." As a result, she hangs back during family gatherings, staying on the edges of the celebrations and often leaving for a time to walk along the beach.

Fran was "never quite sure that Madge approved of her" and had married Clem because she regarded him "as a fellow sufferer among them and decided it was her role to save him." Initially, she and Angie "had been wary of one another" because "they were so unalike," but they eventually came together, feeling "so out of it at times that they would huddle in subversive pockets, finding relief in hilarity or in whispered resentment." During Audley's party, feeling overwhelmed by the crowd, the two go off together for a walk on the beach during which they criticize some of the guests.

Tension between Fran and the family has increased after the divorce, which becomes evident when the family ignores Clem's question, "Do we look like newlyweds?" Yet, Fran is able to find a tentative balance in her relationship with the family by the end of the day. Malouf solves the mystery of Fran and Clem's friendship when he notes that the two "had begun to see one another again, locked in an odd dependency. She was adventurous, what she wanted was experience, 'affairs.' Clem was the element in her life that was stable."

Fran also feels compelled to maintain her relationship with the family. She is one of those people "who'd got hooked on the Tylers," to "the illusion of belonging, however briefly, to the world of rare affinities and stern, unfettered views they represented." Her need for acceptance is illustrated in the vision she has while she and Angie watch the group on the beach drawing together by the bonfire. Fran admits, "I could sit here till I understood at last what it all means: why the sea, why the stars, why this lump in my throat." When she imagines herself lying down on the sand with the others in "a circle of light," Fran has an epiphany of sorts, suggesting that she can be content inside the circle of the family as well as outside it, by striking a balance between the two. This knowledge allows her to acknowledge her ties to Clem as well as to leave later with Cedric.

Clem, like his ex-wife, has always felt like an outsider to his family, especially after the accident, which caused him to lose much of his memory. Tension arises when he says "whatever [comes] into his head," as he does with his newlywed comment. When he sits in his mother's kitchen that morning, he tries to gain reassurance from her that she and his father loved him. Madge insists that they did and that he was Audley's favorite, but then she admits that he may also have been a disappointment to his father.

By the end of the day, though, Clem is able to accept his role in the family, which is illustrated in the speech he gives after the museum has burned down. Feeling that "something more was needed" before everyone said goodnight, he begins to talk with growing confidence to these "friends, people he loved, who would understand if what he said went astray and did not come out the way he meant." Like his wife, he experiences an epiphany this evening, recognizing a connection among all of them, which proves that "anything is possible. . . . Nothing ever gets *lost*." This recognition makes everything "all right," even though Fran had not been there. "They could go to bed now. He could. They all could. The day was over."

Audley realizes the same thing this evening after watching all his beloved family artifacts go up in smoke. Peter Pierce, in his article on the story, argues that "the destruction of the museum is cathartic" for Audley. Pierce claims that "he welcomes this destruction of the stuff of his past" because it serves as "a drastic cleansing of the sort that one's own mind and actions can seldom manage." Audley comes to recognize that his family, which represents the true importance of the past and of the present, has not been lost.

As he sits in the kitchen with Angie, reinforcing their special bond that provides her at the end of the night with her own sense of connection, Audley revels in Clem's happiness during his speech

What Do I Read Next?

- Malouf's title story in *Dream Stuff* (2000) explores the tensions between European and Australian cultures in its focus on a writer returning home to Australia.

- Malouf's "At Schindlers," in the same 2000 collection, contrasts the social and the personal as it chronicles the life of a boy who loses his father during World War II.

- *Long Day's Journey into Night*, first performed in 1956, is Eugene O'Neill's finest study of domestic interaction and offers insight into O'Neill's own tragic relationship with his family.

- The narrator in Jonathan Franzen's *The Corrections* (2001) explores the lives of his offbeat family in this bittersweet bestselling novel as he tells of his struggle to make peace with them.

and suggests, "I think he was trying to say something to *me* . . . about the fire—as well as all the rest." What Audley discovers is the importance of "attending," of paying attention to others, a virtue that they have all displayed at one point during the day that has enabled them to find a harmonious balance in their lives and an appreciation "of a new day coming," of "the light that fills the world."

Source: Wendy Perkins, Critical Essay on "Great Day," in *Short Stories for Students*, Thomson Gale, 2007.

Brigid Rooney

In the following essay, Rooney gives a critical analysis of Malouf's life and work.

David Malouf enjoys a distinguished reputation, nationally and internationally, as a writer whose lyrical mappings of identity, place, and the body also bear upon questions of belonging and national identity. Crossing successfully from poetry to prose fiction in 1975, Malouf has continued to write in a wide variety of forms and genres. He is author, to date, of at least six volumes of poetry, several editions of selected poems, six novels, two

> The stories in *Dream
> Stuff*, set entirely in
> Australia, are linked
> unobtrusively by the motif
> of dreaming."

novellas, three short-story collections, many auto-biographical and prose nonfiction publications, a series of libretti for opera, and an original play. While this range demonstrates unusual versatility, Malouf's writing also exhibits remarkable consistency in approach, preoccupation, and style. On the shortlist for the Booker Prize in 1993 for *Remembering Babylon* (1993), Malouf has been the recipient of many prestigious awards for fiction, poetry, and drama. These include the 1974 Australian Literature Society Gold Medal and the 1974 Grace Leven Poetry Prize, for *Neighbours in a Thicket: Poems* (1974); the New South Wales Premier's Literary Awards, in 1979 for *An Imaginary Life: A Novel* (1978) and in 1987 for *Blood Relations* (1988); the 1983 *Age* Book of the Year and the 1983 Australian Literature Society Gold Medal, for *Fly Away Peter* (1982); the Best Book of the Region Award, the Commonwealth Writers' Prize (Southeast Asia and South Pacific Region), the Miles Franklin Award, and the Prix Femina Prize (France) for *The Great World* (1990) in 1991; and the 1994 *Los Angeles Times* Book Prize, the 1994 Commonwealth Writers' Prize (Southeast Asia and South Pacific Region), the 1995 Prix Baudelaire (France), and the 1996 IMPAC Dublin Literary Award for *Remembering Babylon*.

Born in Brisbane on 20 March 1934 into a family of mixed British and Lebanese ancestry, Malouf's writing does not explicitly treat issues of ethnic minority or difference, instead drawing upon European heritage in ways that engage primarily with the (white) mainstream of Australian literary culture. As Bob Hodge and Vijay Mishra point out, for Malouf "Australia is not the place of exile; it is in fact the place of return." Educated at Brisbane Grammar School, Malouf graduated with honors from the University of Queensland before departing for England, where he worked as a teacher from

1959 to 1968. On his return to Australia, Malouf took up a teaching post in the Department of English at the University of Sydney. During this decade Malouf not only developed an increasingly sophisticated body of poetry but also made his mark as a novelist with the publication of *Johnno* in 1975. Reviewers heralded this first novel as an innovative contribution to Australian writing, and thereafter Malouf's novels evolved in confidence, breadth, and complexity, ultimately earning him an international readership and reputation. On winning a three-year fellowship from the Literature Board of the Australia Council in 1978, Malouf retired from teaching to commit himself full-time to writing. Living alternately in Tuscany and Sydney, Malouf has been able to harness his expatriate experience to situate Australian writing in an international frame, promoting the imaginative transformation and interpenetration of both Australian and European meanings. In the words of Martin Leer, Malouf "sees Australia as producing 'critical variants of Europe': it is 'Europe translated.'"

Though his fiction has made a greater public impact, Malouf's poetry displays an artistry considered by some (particularly his fellow poets) to source—if not eclipse—his prose writings. For Ivor Indyk, Malouf "remains a poet, writing in the medium of prose." Malouf's first significant mark as a poet was as one of the contributors to *Four Poets: David Malouf, Don Maynard, Judith Green* (later known as Judith Rodriguez), *Rodney Hall* (1962), a collection showcasing the work of newcomers to the field. Three volumes of poetry that followed—*Bicycle and Other Poems* (1970), *Neighbours in a Thicket*, and *Poems 1975-1976* (1976)—attracted considerable critical interest, establishing Malouf's as a distinctive new voice in Australian poetry.

From the outset, Malouf's poetic voice has been infused by a sense of immediacy, an intimacy of address, and, as Dennis Haskell observes, an emphasis on "presentation of the self." A critical moment in Malouf's poetry—signaling the development of a characteristic approach—occurs in his much anthologized poem "An Ordinary Evening at Hamilton" (1974):

> The garden shifts indoors, the house lets fall
> its lamp light, opens
> windows in the earth

The commingling of house and garden relays an encounter—described by Vivian Smith as "the opening out of the individual consciousness to merge with a landscape, a past, another consciousness;

a moment which becomes one of self-recognition, of which the poem is the voice"—that recurs throughout Malouf's writing. In both his poetry and his prose, attention is frequently drawn to the space of boundaries, in which the encounter between such pairs as self and other, animal and human, sea and land, nature and culture is negotiated. For Malouf, such encounters on the boundary—a place of meeting or crossing into otherness—can dissolve and transform being. The crossing of consciousness into difference is arrestingly realized in the sensuous sequence "The Crab Feast I-X," from Malouf's highly praised collection *First Things Last: Poems* (1980):

> Bent over you I dip my hand
> in the bowl, I shake my cuffs, out in the open
> and lost. Deep down
> I am with you in the dark. The secret flesh of
> My tongue enters a claw.

Observing both the gravity and inventiveness of his poems—their often "anecdotal starting point" and their "sense of intellectual searching"—Thomas W. Shapcott, in "The Evidence of Anecdote: Some Perspectives on the Poetry of David Malouf" in *Provisional Maps* (1994), argues that "process is centre-stage in Malouf's poetic world." These qualities are amply illustrated in "The Crab Feast I-X" and indeed in poems such as "Adrift," which recalls the lonely and bereft mother in old age, or "This Day, Under My Hand," with its vivid image of

> The cold Pacific banging
> an open gate. Australia
> hitched like a watertank
> to the back verandah, all night
> tugging at our sleep.

Malouf's poems sometimes prefigure his fiction, especially in their recourse to meditation and the resources of memory. As Philip Nielsen points out, "The Judas Touch," an early poem dedicated to "John Milliner: drowned February 1962," foreshadows Malouf's first novel, *Johnno*. Likewise, Laurie Hergenhan shows how elements of "The Year of the Foxes" prefigure elements of Malouf's later fiction.

Malouf's novels, however, do not merely repeat the preoccupations of his poetry in another form but also experiment with the novel as form, playing with its temporal constraints and possibilities. The intimacy of the poet's voice is modulated by and contends with the linear drive of narrative. Through the novels, Malouf explores intimate personal terrain in ways that refract and dramatize questions of Australian history and national identity. Andrew Taylor in "The Great World, History,

and Two or One" (collected in *Provisional Maps*) notes the imaginative scope of Malouf's fictional mappings of Australian history: "two hundred years of Australian history are covered almost continuously by Malouf's fiction, something not found in any other Australian novelist." Yet, Malouf's exploration of monumental or emblematic episodes in Australian history, in World Wars I and II, for example, is never directed by a strongly "historical" focus but proceeds by means of subjective experience and encounter. The linear thrust of history is interrupted and slowed by the personal experience of time and the expansion outward of the space of narration. That this strategy is conscious is evident in Malouf's typically lucid account to Helen Daniel of how he seeks to harness the narrative process in his 1996 novel, *The Conversations at Curlow Creek:*

> I'm aware of the number of times I really want to use the novel to stop time, to slow things up. You can slow up the narrative so that a second is something that can be explored maybe over pages. I like that play between movement and stillness in the novel.

In Malouf's novels, recurring scenarios cumulatively produce an elaborate network of ideas. These thoughts include, for instance, the narrated recollection of place (particularly of domestic interiors); the playing out of a dynamic between male alter egos or twinned characters (such male dyads are often triangulated by the inclusion of a third, female character); exploration of the figure or role of the artist—for example, Dante, Frank Harland, Imogen Harcourt, Ovid, and the unnamed "Great Man of Letters" in *Child's Play* (1981); and the juxtapositioning of Australia and Europe. *Johnno*, *The Conversations at Curlow Creek*, and *The Great World* all feature triangulated relations between central characters (the bonds between two men, partly in relation to a woman). Whereas *Fly Away Peter* and *The Great World* invoke the mythology of the Australian digger, *Child's Play, An Imaginary Life*, and *Harland's Half Acre* (1984) explore the writer- or artist-figure's response to exile and belonging. *An Imaginary Life*, like *Remembering Babylon*, plays upon the frontier space of empire, raising questions via an encounter with a hybrid being in the shape of the feral (lost or returned) child.

The evocation of wartime Brisbane in Malouf's first novel, *Johnno*, sparked excitement among critics about the potential for regionally focused Australian writing. In *Johnno*, Brisbane is both "the most ordinary place in the world" and timeless or mythological, standing in for that more elusively expansive geopolitical entity, Australia, "a place too big to hold in the mind." Likewise, the brevity and apparent stylistic simplicity of the novel belie its sophisticated organization and the play of ironies generated through the dynamic between its circumspect narrator, Dante, and his wayward and charismatic boyhood friend, Johnno. Dante's musing upon an old school photograph is an early instance of Malouf's recurring use of *ekphrasis*, a literary device involving the detailed written representation of a visual text such as a photograph or painting. Dante's meditation on the photograph initiates his retrospective tale, in which energies seemingly focused on Johnno frequently divert toward the narrator's own processes of creating meaning. Johnno himself functions, alternately, as a prototypical masculine adventurer—"our very own Tamberlaine and Al Capone"—and as a foil to Dante himself, as a marker pointing back to the narrator's "hypocritical niceness." The dynamic between Dante and Johnno unfolds through space as well as time, moving from adolescent adventure in Brisbane, to Johnno's departure for Africa, then Europe, followed by Dante, until their successive returns to Australia, where their separate yet linked destinies are played out in evasion, suicide, and regret. For Hodge and Mishra, "Johnno becomes, for Dante, both his uncanny mirror image and the shadow he also pursues." As Leigh Dale and Helen Gilbert argue, the ambiguities of the text tend to veil its dissidence, deferring absolute answers about the otherwise erotic dimensions of the relationship between the two men. The invocation of the epic poet Dante, moreover, introduces a significantly metafictional layer to the narrative: Dante's "survivor guilt" over Johnno coalesces with the guilty dilemma of the artist who, as Nielsen argues, must exploit "personal relationships for his own aesthetic ends."

In *An Imaginary Life*, Malouf broke new ground while continuing to refine and elaborate themes introduced in *Johnno*. Narrated by Ovid, the Roman poet exiled in old age to a remote northern outpost of empire, *An Imaginary Life* has been taken up by many readers as a meditation upon the writer's antipodean and (post)colonial positioning, and upon questions of exile and belonging. Flung out from the imperial center where distinctions between civilization and nature are tenuous, Ovid engages in a quest for meaning that brings him to the edges of selfhood, language, and existence. Encountering the mystery of a boy brought up by wolves (mythically central to imperial Roman identity), Ovid entices the boy into the village, seeking to render him tractable to human society and

language. Suffering the sudden ravages of illness, however, the villagers become superstitiously fearful, and Ovid and the boy depart, traveling beyond this last outpost into an arctic wilderness. Roles reverse, and the boy becomes Ovid's protector as he journeys toward the culmination of his quest, which is also the moment of his death. Malouf's novel—meditating upon language, spiritual and aesthetic being, and the body's experience of change—converses in imaginative and metafictional terms with the ancient Roman poet of *Metamorphoses* (completed, A.D. 8):

> Our bodies are not final. We are moving, all of us, in our common humankind, through the forms we love so deeply in each other's darkness. Slowly, and with pain, over centuries, we each move an infinitesimal space towards it. We are creating the lineaments of some final man, for whose delight we have prepared a landscape, and who can only be god.

Published in seven languages, this novel is arguably the most widely known and admired of Malouf's oeuvre (with the possible exception of *Remembering Babylon*, which bears many resemblances to *An Imaginary Life*). Both when it was first published and during the intervening years, the novel has attracted a great deal of critical attention, particularly as a text about the (post)colonial condition. For Gareth Griffiths, for example, *An Imaginary Life* suggests how texts can be "effectively open to the full complexity of the condition of postcolonial societies and the problems these societies now exhibit."

Malouf next embarked on a series of novellas and short stories. Though first published in 1981 with *Child's Play*, the novella *The Bread of Time to Come* was republished separately in 1982 under the title *Fly Away Peter*, while *Child's Play* was republished in 1982 with two short stories—"Eustace" and "The Prowler." Although in some ways entailing a strikingly different scenario, *Child's Play* is unmistakably continuous with Malouf's previous fiction. As in both previous novels, a palpably metafictional element attends the dramatization of individual power and destiny in this novella—writing and death, and art and terrorism. The narrator of *Child's Play* belongs to a terrorist cell located in a provincial Italian town; his assignment involves the assassination, for reasons unspecified, of an elderly, preeminent Italian writer—the unnamed "Great Man of Letters" in the novel, whose work-in-progress bears the title "Child's Play." As he prepares for his mission, the narrator is drawn into a quasi-oedipal struggle over the question of who determines and controls meaning, narrative, and destiny—in other words, over "authorship." The terrorist's plot, seeking dominion over its target, is caught within the larger design of the great writer's text: "But I should confess that if, through long sessions of study, I have begun to understand him a little, to observe, that is, the dangers that are inherent in the very nature of his 'trick,' he has also, and so long ago that it quite scares me, both understood and accounted for me." A *mis-en-abyme* (an infinitely regressing image) opens in the shuttle among the three "author" figures—the terrorist, the writer, and Malouf himself. Other familiar elements from the previous novel that recur in *Child's Play* include its use of retrospective narration; the twinning or doubling of characters, in the relationship between the narrator and his dead older brother; and *ekphrasis* in the narrator's use of photographs to familiarize himself with the appointed scene of death, a device that occasions a meditation on issues of narrative, time, destiny, and meaning. The ambiguous ending of the novella has been regarded as only a "qualified success," according to Nielsen, although it has also been read as a deliberate refutation of Roland Barthes's "death of the author," according to Stephen Woods. Walking "under the early blossoms" of an apple orchard, the narrator is either escaping into safety or encountering extinction. Though its significance remains opaque, this conclusion recalls the merging of self and landscape in Ovid's sublime death in *An Imaginary Life.*

In Fly Away Peter, Jim Saddler, humble rural worker, and Ashley Crowther, heir to a Queensland coastal property, are the mirroring couple whose differentiated class positioning both materially shapes their destinies during World War I and represents male bonding as something capable of transcending class difference. The approach the novel takes to the genesis of the Anzac legend, however, seems less concerned with history than with metaphysical themes—of self in process; self in response to others; and self in relation to landscape, destiny, and time. Educated in progressive land-management theories in England, Ashley observes Jim's practical knowledge of the swampland on his Queensland property and immediately employs him to record its migratory-bird life. Ashley recognizes that Jim's intimate knowledge gives him a claim over the land: "Such claims were ancient and deep. They lay in Jim's knowledge of every blade of grass and drop of water in the swamp, of every bird's foot that was set down there—in his having, most of all, the names for things and in that way possessing them." Although the narrative seems to efface the claims of indigenous people, Malouf's focus on belonging through knowledge and naming augurs the development, in his later fiction, of a more complex encounter with frontier history. New, twentieth-century technologies—plane and camera—enter the plot as ambivalent signs of the progress of modernity and of impending war. English freelance photographer Imogen Harcourt, a mature professional woman working in close partnership with Jim, triangulates the male pairing. Migratory patterns of birds prefigure the absurdity of young men's flight to their deaths on the Western Front, the terms of which are graphically and powerfully depicted in the contrasting second half of the novel. The cruelties that then unfold are resolved, momentarily, and in the consolation a grieving Imogen takes from her vision of a surfer an image that positively fuses human technology with nature.

A more lengthy and historically detailed novel, *Harland's Half Acre*, came next, featuring—like earlier works—Brisbane and rural Queensland settings, and a dually focused narration. In some sequences a third-person narrator recounts episodes in the life and career of Frank Harland, a landscape artist, son of a charismatic battler and widower, Clem. The significance of exile and belonging in the genesis of Australian art is dramatized in Frank's movements through time and space, from his early removal from the family home after his mother's death, his return to family and his efforts to guide his motherless siblings and his nephew, to his final, Ovid-like death on Bribie Island. An itinerant worker during the Great Depression years, Frank drifts in space even as his landscape paintings mature, finally reaching a wider public. The recounting of Frank Harland's life is interwoven with the first-person narrative of Phil Vernon, whose family life in Brisbane, seemingly tangential, eventually intertwines with Frank's life, leading to Phil's role as intermediary between artist and public. As a child, Phil mediates between his partially estranged grandparents, and later, between Frank and his temperamental nephew and heir, Gerald. Like Dante in *Johnno*, Phil is a surrogate for the writer, functioning as witness to events. Yet, as lawyer and family friend, he is torn between the need for professional impartiality and the demands of personal involvement. The *ekphrastic* device of the photo as trigger for narration, previously employed in both *Johnno* and *Child's Play*, recurs in a seminal scene in which the young Phil first encounters Frank's landscape paintings and finds himself primally caught by the portrait of a local woman who murdered her partner, a European immigrant. The darkness of European history is here, and elsewhere in the narrative, transplanted into Australian contexts, reversing clichés about Australian innocence in contrast to European experience. Likewise, Frank Harland's "half acre" is more than a modest slice of Australian ground; Frank's mental landscapes and artistic journey essay new strategies for making and thereby belonging to Australia.

Malouf's next published work was *Antipodes* (1985), a collection of short stories, which was followed by an autobiographical memoir, *12 Edmonstone Street* (1985). Shapcott in "The Evidence of Anecdote: Some Perspectives on the Poetry of David Malouf" describes these works, in which Malouf vividly recalls the contours of his childhood home and his encounters with Tuscany and India, as "autobiographical prose interiors." Gillian Whitlock in "The Child in the (Queensland) House: David Malouf and Regional Writing" (in *Provisional Maps*), discussing the regionally inflected exploration in the title story of the "Queenslander" (a wooden bungalow on stilts), observes how the narrative proceeds by means of its "spacial contiguities rather than a sequence of events": "Gradually this child-in-the-house narrative makes its way from verandah, through the rooms and down to 'under the house,' a space that Malouf mythologizes as a forest, as dark as anything in Grimm."

During the late 1980s Malouf turned his hand to writing for the stage. As well as a highly acclaimed libretto written for Richard Meale's opera *Voss* (1986), based on Patrick White's novel, Malouf also published his first and, to date, only original play. *Blood Relations* was Malouf's reworking of William Shakespeare's *The Tempest* (first performed, 1613; first published, 1623) and was first staged by the Sydney Theatre Company in 1987. Set at Christmastime in a family home on the tropical coast of northwestern Australia, the drama concerns the unearthing of the father's past and the transformations that this process brings. Dale and Gilbert observe that the play deploys "the edge" as a "place of negotiation," "a political space where Prospero's dream of a 'prosperous' island state, where the colonizer acts as 'husbandman' to a bountiful new world, is thwarted." Since then Malouf has produced three further librettos for contemporary opera, including Richard Meale's opera *Mer de Glace* (1991), an adaptation of Mary Shelley's *Frankenstein* (1818); Michael Berkeley's first opera, *Baa Baa Black Sheep* (1993), based on episodes from Kipling's *The Jungle Book* (1894); and most recently Berkeley's opera *Jane Eyre*

(2000), based on Charlotte Brontë's novel. Annie Patrick observes that Malouf's contribution to each libretto extends beyond mere adaptation into creation of "operatic counter-parts which not only demonstrate his ability to write for voice and the stage—[but also] his collaborative skills with a composer."

The Great World was Malouf's next full-length novel and his most detailed and expansive yet. This novel, as Nielsen remarks, offers no radical departures from Malouf's earlier work but rather consolidates and extends familiar themes and approaches. Realist and historical in genre, but often ruminative and lyrical as was the earlier fiction, *The Great World* spans a seventy-year period, focusing on Australians affected—individually and collectively—by their experiences of World War II. Among other memorable episodes, the novel depicts in harrowing terms the ordeal suffered by Australian prisoners of war at the notorious Changi camp and on the Thai/Burma railway. The title of the book refers to an abandoned theme park, "the Great World," used as makeshift quarters for a contingent of prisoners working on the Singapore docks. Thus, juxtaposing the imagined expansiveness of the world with its cruel foreshortening through war and imprisonment, "the Great World" also alludes to the shifting perspectives of its protagonists—their expectations and experiences of the wider world. Narrative focus is shared between complementary male characters, ne'er-do-well Digger Keen and self-made businessman Vic Currant, whose friendship begins in the camp in Malaya and whose destinies and personal lives thereafter entwine. Malouf's exploration, via the evolving relationship between Digger and Vic, of the ethos of mastership—that quintessentially masculine virtue associated with the Anzac legend—sympathetically rewrites this period of Australian history in personal and ironic but also mythic terms. Though a few reviews were less enthusiastic—for example, Gerard Windsor's in the *Australian Book Review* (April 1990)—most concurred with A. P. Riemer's view in *The Sydney Morning Herald* (17 February 1990) that this was "a masterly novel, a deeply satisfying work of art."

In the multiple-award-winning *Remembering Babylon*, Malouf returns to the motif of the *enfant sauvage* (wild child) first treated in *An Imaginary Life*, reversing its narrative movement. Based on an account of British sailor James (Jemmy) Merrill, who was shipwrecked in 1846 and who lived for many years with an Aboriginal tribe before returning to white settlement, Malouf's novel rewrites the imperial first-contact story of Daniel Defoe's *Robinson Crusoe* (1719). It also rewrites colonial captivity narratives, such as that of Eliza Framer, a British woman shipwrecked in 1836 on Fraser Island, off Queensland, on which White's novel *A Fringe of Leaves* (1976) was based. In mid Queensland in the 1850s (during one of the bloodiest phases of colonization), castaway ship boy Gemmy Fairley, having been rescued and nurtured by an Aboriginal tribe for sixteen years, finally returns to white society. Hovering on the fence line—the literal and symbolic perimeter of the colony—Gemmy "surrenders" to a small group of children who then mediate his encounter with the adults. With his damaged body ("smudged appearance" and "baffled, half-expectant look of a mongrel that had been whipped"), strange behavior, broken English, and obscure history, Gemmy represents a highly threatening state of being between two statuses, or liminality. As the "white blackfellow" he was "a parody of a white man," an "imitation gone wrong." Gemmy had also puzzled the Aborigines, who saw him as "half-child, half sea-calf," like Caliban in *The Tempest*. To the white settlers, Gemmy dangerously embodies that which daily eats at their security—proximity to a vast, unchartered country and to its feared Aboriginal inhabitants: "Out here the very ground under their feet was strange. It had never been ploughed." Taken in by the McIvors, Gemmy's closest link is with the children who first encountered him—Lachlan Beattie and Janet McIvor—and the narrative relays their stories, along with the varied reactions of the small community. Though widely reviewed in glowing terms, Malouf's novel also sparked a contentious critical debate about its politics. Published in the very year in which the Australian High Court replaced the legal doctrine of *terra nullius* (a legal concept meaning "the land belonging to no one" used by the British to deny the claims of the indigenous people of Australia to their native land) with that of native title (in the case of *Mabo* vs *Queensland*, No. 2), *Remembering Babylon* has been criticized for authenticating white experience and history at the expense of Aboriginal bodies, experience, and history (as Germaine Greer, Suvendrini Perera, and Garry Kinnane discuss). Others, such as Bill Ashcroft, counter this charge with the argument that the novel is subversive, representing "the very different, transformative oppositionality of post-colonial discourse" (see also Lee Spinks and Penelope Ingram).

Reception of Malouf's next novel, *The Conversations at Curlow Creek*, has generally been positive. Anthony J. Hassall praises its "passionate, poetic reimaginings" of competing versions of colonial Australia. Although replete with patterns familiar from Malouf's previous work, in this novel the representation of the violence of colonial history is arguably more direct than that of *Remembering Babylon*. The story, set in Australia in 1827, concerns the impending execution of Irish rebel and colonial bushranger Daniel Carney, who—among other crimes—has fostered insurrection against the British by local Aboriginal tribes. Also of Irish background, Michael Adair, the officer posted to supervise this execution, passes the night in the hut with the imprisoned man, while the three troopers and Aboriginal tracker who captured Carney make their camp outside the hut. Adair's recollections of his boyhood past compose much of the narrative. Adopted into a wealthy Irish family, Adair had formed a close but rivalrous bond with his foster brother, Fergus Connellan, whose identity merges during the narrative with that of Carney, the condemned man. Rivalry between the adopted brothers is complicated by the presence of a young woman, Virgilia, who was tutored alongside them. Virgilia secretly loves Fergus, while Adair secretly loves Virgilia. In contrast to the austere and conservative Adair, who is overly conscious of his lesser place in the world, Fergus is a romantic idealist who, refusing his inheritance, leaves Ireland for Australia in search of a more just society. Adair's guilt over this uneasy past oppresses him; so, too, the specter of colonial violence—in a moment of confrontation—haunts the troopers' fireside conversation outside the hut. Reconciliation, for Adair, is finally figured in two sacramental movements: in a baptismal moment when the condemned man, prior to his hanging, is permitted to wash himself in the stream, and, in the final moment of the narrative, as Adair breaks his nightlong fast: "He chews as he walks on, his saliva mixing with [the bread's] sugars and driving new light into his heart, refreshing his mouth like common speech." The narrative thus repeats a gesture familiar in Malouf's writing, moving through encounter with difference toward transformation, reconciliation, and transcendence.

As well as the less widely distributed *Untold Tales* (1999), Malouf has published two volumes of short stories—*Antipodes* and *Dream Stuff* (2000)—which show both diversity of content and thematic coherence. In *Antipodes*, which, despite positive reviews, has subsequently received little critical attention, the geographic opposition of Australian and European perspectives is, as James

Tulip suggests, one of a series of dramatic opposi- tions across a range of stories in which the romance of distance is set against the pleasures of the every- day. "Southern Skies" treats these themes, for ex- ample, through the narrator's recollections of the Professor—an esteemed family friend whose "Old Country" manners and erudition at first annoy the young male narrator, who seeks assimilation with contemporary Australia; later the Professor draws him across the threshold into a different experience of romance, vulnerability, and desire. Suburban and familial perspectives—in stories such as "The Empty Lunch-Tin" and "Bad Blood"—delicately explore the unexpected in everyday relationships. The stories in *Dream Stuff*, set entirely in Australia, are linked unobtrusively by the motif of dreaming. "Jacko's Reach," for example, concerns how the one remaining plot of wilderness in a suburb, finally resumed for development, lingers in the imagination; and the youthful narrator of "Closer" dreams of reconciling, across the closed boundary of a Pentecostal home, with the uncle whose annual visits to the property's perimeter are studiously ig- nored by his family. In this collection, Peter Pierce detects an increasing sense of "skepticism about the reality of the social world," since its various sto- ries speak "of haunting, of vanishing, of desperate attempts to put down roots and unavailing efforts to escape them—of the impact of war and of the conflicts within families."

As well as being an Australian writer of un- doubted eminence and achievement, Malouf is a formidable commentator upon his own work and an eloquent exponent in the public domain of his views, particularly of the role of the writer in con- temporary Australia. In addition to his creative works, Malouf has also produced many lectures, opinion pieces, essays, and interviews. During his 1998 ABC Boyer Lecture series (published as *A Spirit of Play: The Making of Australian Con- sciousness* [1998]), Malouf reiterates his vision of a necessarily dynamic relationship between contem- porary Australians and the land:

> We are the makers, among much else, of landscapes. We remake the land in our own image so that it comes in time to reflect both the industry and the imagina- tion of its makers, and gives us back, in working land, but also in the idealized version of landscape that is a park or garden, an image both of our human nature and our power. Such making is also a rich form of possession.

Malouf's own writing, compellingly for some readers but problematically for others, testifies to this observation. Concerned about distinguishing

his sense of "making" from negative modes of colonization, Malouf advocates "a convergence of indigenous and non-indigenous understanding, a collective spiritual consciousness that will be the true form of reconciliation" in Australia. Malouf's writing maps encounters between self and other, tensions between exile and home, and relations be- tween the individual and history—issues holding particular resonance for contemporary Australians. The transformations that, in Malouf's writing, are deployed to resolve these encounters—via death in the landscape, absorption into the other, experience of the limitless body, and immersion in the sacred—suggest the writer's belief in the efficacy and relevance of art, not merely as a powerful mode of expression, but also as a strategy of belonging.

Source: Brigid Rooney, "David Malouf," in *Dictionary of Literary Biography*, Vol. 289, *Australian Writers, 1950–1975*, edited by Selina Samuels, Gale, 2004, pp. 214–222.

Peter Pierce

In the following essay, Pierce explores the im- portance of dreams as "analogies" to the waking state, the merging of and volleying between spaces and consciousness, and the fluid impermanence of life in "Great Day" and other works in the Dream Stuff *collection.*

Towards *Dream Stuff*. The title of David Mal- ouf's first collection of short fiction, *Antipodes* (1985), specified a capacious geographic setting. This was European, specifically contemptuous British colonial shorthand for Australia, Malouf's native country. Yet, his title implied, opposite of what? Malouf showed himself more concerned with the particulars of a world disparaged sometimes as new than with critical contrasts between it and the parent cultures of Europe. For Malouf's prose fic- tion, from *Johnno* (1975) to the present, has revealed him to be, by intuition and craft, a maker of metaphors and seldom an ironist or a satirist.

Antipodes has received scant subsequent criti- cal attention. In full-length studies of Malouf's work by Philip Neilsen (*Imagined Lives*, 1990) and Ivor Indyk (*David Malouf*, 1993) and in the vol- ume *Provisional Maps: Critical Essays on David Malouf* (1994), edited by Amanda Nettelbeck, the short fiction is scarcely mentioned. Malouf's novel- las (as it is formally most accurate to style them)— *Johnno, An Imaginary Life* (1978), *Child's Play* (1982), and *Fly Away Peter* (1982)—engage the critic's interest, together with the novels that suc- ceeded them. There have been four of these as well *Harland's Half Acre* (1984), *The Great World*

(1990), *Remembering Babylon* (1993), and *The Conversations at Curlow Creek* (1996). In these books Malouf used a broader canvas, and displayed ostensibly larger ambitions to depict the peopling, the shaping of Australia (what Indyk called "The Temptation of Epic"). This was a personalized kind of historical fiction, its nature perhaps best expressed by Digger Keen, hero of *The Great World*:

> Even the least event had lines, all tangled, going back into the past, and beyond that into the *unknown* past, and others leading out, also tangled, into the future. Every moment was dense with causes, possibilities, consequences, too many, even in the simplest case, to grasp.

This comment resonates through Malouf's writing, whose latest stage is a return to the short story.

Dream Stuff (2000) appears fifteen years after *Antipodes*. Its nine stories are emphatically, almost ostentatiously set in Australia (two of those in *Antipodes* took place in Europe). The title of "Lone Pine"—a horrifying, if slightly formulaic tale of a violent intrusion into the lives of elderly travelers—summons remembrance of an Australian battle site of the Great War, at Gallipoli, in 1915. "Blacksoil Country" speaks not only of the contrary earth itself, but of all that is buried within it. Several of the stories relate tensions and accommodations made principally, of course, by women on the home front, in wartime. "At Schindlers" is set in the period of the Second World War, and Malouf's Brisbane childhood. This is the territory traversed in the early parts of *Johnno* and in his poem "The Year of the Foxes." "Brisbane ladies, rather / the worse for war, drove up in taxis / wearing a GI on their arm / and rang at our front door." "Sally's Story" is that of a willing and remunerated Australian version of a comfort woman during the Vietnam War. Others—"Dream Stuff " and "Jacko's Reach"—treat of the erasure in fact, but not in intimate memory, of an old tropical city by a new, self-consciously modern one.

This time Malouf's title, notwithstanding the studied offhandedness of its second word on the one hand, its Shakespearean allusion on the other, directs us to mental rather than physical space. It prepares for an exploration of the perplexities of individual perception, consciousness, conscience, rather than of the other kinds of burdens of social, communal life. With an artful casualness, Malouf has gathered nine stories, in each of which dreams have important, if not usually central narrative functions. At the same time they have a notable, almost discordant variety of subjects and moods. *Dream Stuff* hints at a testing stage of imaginative

 To vanish is principally to leave the social world and its obligations, the web of connections to which Malouf is so alert. The dream world is essentially an antisocial or an asocial realm. Whatever its inevitable nightmares, this is its reward, or compensation, for all that has to be endured in company."

transition through which Malouf is presently working (has worked at here) and whose next, longer issue we wait to see.

"What dreams may come" / "Such stuff as dreams are made on." Hamlet's fretful imagining of the life after death, that "bourn from which no traveller returns," makes him speculate about "what dreams may come" to trouble a hoped-for peace. At least one of Malouf's protagonists in this collection, young Jordan McGivern, might enlighten him. Prospero's magisterial declaration in *The Tempest*, "We are such stuff as dreams are made on. / Our little life is rounded by a sleep," is Malouf's enticement to his readers, besides providing the title and suggesting something of the range of the stories to follow . . .

The last and longest story in *Dream Stuff*, "Great Day," is connected implicitly to the one before it, by one of those delicate touches of Malouf's that are not hints, are barely intimations, but to which we must attend. The occasion is the seventy-second birthday of former Public Service mandarin Audley Tyler. It is also the two-hundredth anniversary of the Australian nation. Of Aborigines there are none to be seen. No bonfires of theirs will ring the long continental coast in celebration. We are asked to reflect on where and how far Australia has traveled since the McGiverns, and many others like them, came to the blacksoil country and other regions of Australia that they pioneered. The Tylers might answer confidently. They boast an old colonial lineage, a long acquaintance with power that is shown off with a complacent, ponderous ease. "In our family everything could be traced back", Audley declares.

As so often in Malouf's fiction, we find ourselves in a luminal space, where land and sea merge, shiftingly. Angie, who has married into the Tyler "clan," enjoys that fleeting time of "an expanding stillness in which clocks, voices and every form of consciousness had still to come into existence and the day as yet, like the sea, had no mark upon it." The cadences of the prose are graceful, slow-paced, sonorous, yet muted, impelling us to listen—as Angie does—to what sounds will shape themselves and end the silence. Anticipated here is the vision of Audley's damaged son, Clem, which is offered exultantly at the conclusion of this day, of making connections, of being able to hear the sounds of other life coming toward us, benignly.

As the family gathers, and readers gradually sort out their names, we learn of how Clem crashed his car while avoiding a child who was playing chicken. "The whole continent came bursting through the windscreen into his skull." In a coma for fourteen months, he was "floating out there in the absolute dark." Now partly recovered, he solicits others to help him to recover his memory, to fill in the lost details of his childhood as though it is a new story whose elements he must laboriously but delightedly learn. Once again, Malouf resorts to a topographical image for Clem's condition. His was "a relationship to the world that was to be obscure and difficult and a life that was not to shoot forward in a straight line but would move by missteps and indirections."

In the anticlimax of "Great Day," the Waruna Folk and History Museum, cluttered with items from generations of the family life of the Tylers, is burned down. Arson ensures that the town, the Tylers, have a "bonfire after all." For Audley, who fears that any bedtime, the next sleep, will be his last, the destruction of the museum is cathartic. He guesses who was responsible, but thinks sententiously and in plural terms of the criminal that "when we punish them it is to hide our secret guilt." In truth, he welcomes this destruction of the stuff of his past. It amounts to a drastic cleansing of the sort that one's own mind and actions can seldom manage. All that had seemed a certified part of family, community, national history, the mutable paradoxically fixed in objects, behind glass, on display, has proved helpless to resist its last change. That which seemed fixed was always fluid. . . .

The vanishing acts that punctuate Malouf's writing—as people seem to step off the edges of their worlds, inscrutably, or into legend—are ways of registering exactly this nexus of the fixed and the fluid. Such vanishings are luminal moments too, as when a person passes from consciousness to sleep, then into the dreamstate that Malouf explores so obliquely and intricately; or when they drown, disappear, go missing, simply—like the novelist Colin—flee. To vanish is principally to leave the social world and its obligations, the web of connections to which Malouf is so alert. The dream world is essentially an antisocial or an asocial realm. Whatever its inevitable nightmares, this is its reward, or compensation, for all that has to be endured in company.

The subtle dynamics of the relationship of the fixed and the fluid in Malouf's fiction is also a way of reckoning with another of his favored dualisms, this time of location/dislocation. Malouf has always spent a significant amount of his energy on the vivid evocation of the tactile presences of place (think of the reexploration of the old family home in his autobiography, *12 Edmondstone Street*, 1986). In *Dream Stuff* we experience the exuberant, provisional settlements of holiday time (in "At Schindlers"); translations from the city to the bush as temporary homecomings, such as Sally's to her mother's in "Sally's Story" ; Colin's return to Brisbane and the hurried retracing of his path in "Dream Stuff"; the Sodom of Sydney, the infernal, imagined, never directly known place that has swallowed up Uncle Charles in "Closer", the itinerant life of rural laborers such as the McGiverns in "Blacksoil Country."

A pattern of dislocation here contends with the desire to be settled. Remembered places, out of reach in space and time, appear more substantial and permanent than those in which homes are made and families endure. The estrangements within so many of those families as depicted in *Dream Stuff* are, in some measure, Malouf's intuition of the essential improbability and instability of the social realm, compared to the inner, the dream life. That intuition is crystallized in a passage from *Remembering Babylon* when Jock McIvor struggles to understand nothing less than a change in his perception:

> It was as if he had seen the world till now, not through his own eyes, out of some singular self, but through the eyes of a fellow who was always in company,

even when he was alone; a sociable self, wrapped always in a communal warmth that protected it from dark matters (108).

The price of such perception is that confrontation with the "dark" can no longer be dissembled, or avoided. That which seemed fixed, for McIvor, and for his successors in Malouf's fiction, will never be so again. . . .

Stories of haunting, of vanishing, of desperate attempts to put down roots and unavailing efforts to escape them, stories of the impact of war and of the conflicts within families—these are some of the distinctive elements of *Dream Stuff*. The variegated stuff of dreams—longed for and summoned up, or come unbidden, bringing peace, or disquiet—is a unifying metaphorical thread in this collection. Yet perhaps it challenges us most of all to confront a perception that now seems central to Malouf's work, a kind of gentle yet implacable skepticism about the reality of the social world. And that leads, more intensely than ever before in his work, to an apprehension of our solitariness, so that our lives in the waking world become analogies for the terrible privacies of our dreaming.

Source: Peter Pierce, "What Dreams May Come: David Malouf's *Dream Stuff*," in *World Literature Today*, Vol. 74, No. 4, Autumn 2000, pp. 751–57.

John Scheckter

In the following essay, Scheckter examines Malouf's incorporation of "play" to usurp fixed locations—whether a place or consciousness—and how this suggests impermanence. Malouf utilizes the Aboriginal culture's ability to re-imagine the world as a "challenge" to European colonialism and ideology.

In 1998, David Malouf delivered the Boyer Lectures, an annual radio series sponsored by the Australian Broadcasting Corporation, his presentations were later published as *The Spirit of Play: The Making of Australian Consciousness*. "Play," that fine postmodern term, broadens wonderfully in the postcolonial atmosphere of Australia, denoting most usefully, along with drama and other circumstances of production, the deliberate slackness that is built into a ship's rigging to let masts and spars flex without damage, where taut trim in a storm would shatter them. This play, in turn, feeds into the subtitle's similar implication of continuing process, in which "making" suggests an ongoing construction and the avoidance of a definite article suggests that multiplicity and variation have replaced the uniformity in what older fashions of national characterization

> *... the first-principle unity here described as 'nothing is lost' is nonetheless measurable in terms of responses that approach nearer to or recede farther from its implications of inclusiveness. Such a model copes with play more successfully than orders based upon categorical limitation and hierarchy."*

would have styled "*the* Australian consciousness." This maneuvering is highly representative of Malouf's style as a writer of fiction, especially in the new story collection, *Dream Stuff* (2000). But it goes more deeply than that.

The "spirit of play," of course, echoes the most common description of Aboriginal consciousness as "the spirit of place," a conjunction that Malouf wants his auditors to take seriously. To substitute "play" for "place" is to do exactly that, to play with words, to suggest intersecting modes of consciousness and methods of learning, to exchange the suppositions of permanence and objectivity implied by fixed location for admissions of contingency and self-consciousness. It is also to claim that the phrase, and the indigenous consciousness it describes, may be translated meaningfully by later participants. Even so, the notion of play, however vital and energizing to contemporary societies, has here built into it a disturbing reminder of colonial appropriation, as indeed the exploration of historical influences upon a present consciousness has been an ongoing concern in Malouf's work.

Aboriginal culture, as Malouf has referred to it recently, is most notable for types of dynamism and regeneration that challenge monopolistic European cultural definition, while suggesting, on the other hand, that the dominant culture may forget how important its own forms of rapid adaptation can be:

> This capacity to re-imagine things, to take in and adapt, might be something we should learn from, something that comes closer than a nostalgia for lost purity to the way the world actually is, and also to the way it works. It might remind us of something we need to keep in mind which is the extent to which Aboriginal notions of inclusiveness, of re-imagining the world to take in all that is now in it, has worked to include *us* (*Spirit*, 59).

This clever *re*appropriation of indigenous culture, which replaces descriptions of "timeless" tribal identity, ultimately licenses the "play" by means of the "spirit" that precedes and surrounds it. Such a process may initiate deep changes within human character, which may, for all their contingency and even violence, include redemptive possibilities for happiness and health.

Dynamism, and the continuing sense of individuality in progress, are central to the models of consciousness in Malouf's fiction. These processes of play are clear, for example, in Malouf's praise of Australian poets of his generation they

> created a body of poetry in which all the common phenomena of our Australian world—flowers and trees and birds, and helmet shells and ghost-crabs and bluebottles—had been translated out of their first nature into the secondary and symbolic one of consciousness in that great process of culture, and also of acculturation, that creates a continuity at last between the life without and the life within. It is one of the ways—a necessary one—by which we come at last into full possession of a place. Not legally, and not just physically, but as Aboriginal people, for example, have always possessed the world we live in here in the imagination (*Spirit*, 39).

Meaning is not inherent, then, but emerges through translation within the structured yet emphatically accommodative symbolism of an individual consciousness. Aboriginal process becomes a great "example" for postcolonial Australia "as it painstakingly redefines itself, reclaiming its history and implanting a home-grown culture" (Conrad, 25). But possible frameworks of translation must be limitless, as the mind moves "towards what is, in effect, a convergence of indigenous and nonindigenous understanding, a collective spiritual consciousness that will be the true form of reconciliation here" (*Spirit*, 39–40).

Reconciliation, however, cannot come easily, for uplifting translation and convergence imply their opposite, resistant or restrictive mediation by means of rationalization and solipsism. Throughout *Dream Stuff*, individuals struggle within their perceptions of the world they work to acknowledge, first, that

conscious construction of identity is very difficult; second, that self-knowledge often results in a reflexive distrust that threatens esteem and accommodation, and third, that the recognitions achieved through translation and convergence are severely limited by failures of enactment, and above all by mortality.

Dream Stuff is another playful title, an intersection of Western high culture and Aboriginal influence. Its glancing reference to *The Tempest* ("We are such stuff as dreams are made on," 4.1.156–57) embeds the postcolonial inheritance of high-cultural irony; the suggestion of the Aboriginal Dreaming or Dreamtime, the ongoing spiritual regeneration that manifests itself in seemingly continuous physical reality, characterizes an Australian present informed by converging influences and intersecting mythologies. In between, the pettiness of "stuff" is both a playful deflation and a warning that serious human possibilities can be reduced by frustration and deflection when circumstances offer enough routine, enough well-being, enough self-esteem, the easiest way to cope with the enormous burden of the convergent present is to ignore it. . . .

One of the characters in "Great Day," the last and most expansive story of *Dream Stuff*, advances such a new vision of continuity and encompassment toward its ultimate. Clem Tyler describes a reverse extension of current radio astronomy, a receiver deep in space gathering sounds from Earth that, given the distance they travel, are historical by now—a factor that places Australia in a particular position of coming-into-being:

> "What it picks up, it's made that way, is heartbeats, just that. Every heartbeat on the planet, it doesn't miss a single one, not one is missed.

> "Once upon a time, all this bit of the planet, all this—land mass, this continent—was silent, there was no sound at all, you wouldn't have known it was here. Silence. Then suddenly a blip, a few little signs of life. Then a rush, till there are millions. Only it takes such a long time for the sound to travel across all that space that the receiver doesn't even know as yet that we've arrived—us whites, I mean. But that doesn't matter because we *are* here, aren't we?

> If we imagined ourselves out there and concentrated hard enough, really concentrated, we could hear it too, all of it, the whole sound coming towards us, all of it. It's possible. Anything is possible. Nothing is lost. Nothing ever gets *lost* " (179–81).

The leap of imagination to extend the viewpoint seems both ordinary, a common extrapolation of time and space beyond direct observation, and marvelous, a view of human existence from a baseline so long that perspective becomes panoptic synchronous.

In fact, Clem's metaphor of encompassed space and time establishes the first principle necessary for building a definitional structure to liberate consciousness from the failures of self-defensiveness. Essentially nonverifiable through logical distinctions of factuality and denotation, the first-principle unity here described as "nothing is lost" is nonetheless measurable in terms of responses that approach nearer to or recede farther from its implications of inclusiveness. Such a model copes with play more successfully than orders based upon categorical limitation and hierarchy. It accommodates contemporary spatializations of fractal patterning and sensitive dependence, and temporal factors of layering and synchronicity. Validly translating scientific terms to discursive ones (Oliver, 126), it signals the collapse of rhetorical figures of analogy and simile, as the neutrality that permits the mind to look in one direction and then to look comparatively in another disappears into simultaneous affective unity; individual differentiation is retained, perhaps even accentuated—the receiver hears every heartbeat—by the breakdown of systems that previously licensed divisive generalizations based upon origin, affiliation, or activity.

With "nothing is lost" as the first principle, the territory of consciousness in *Dream Stuff* is established by Henry James's discussion of writing from experience, which Malouf cites in an interview with Ramona Koval:

> The power to guess the unseen from the seen, to trace the implication of things, to judge the whole piece by the pattern, the condition of knowing life in general so completely that you are well on your way to knowing any particular corner of it—this cluster of gifts may almost be said to constitute experience, and they occur in country and in town, and in the most differing stages of education. If experience consists of impressions, it may be said that impressions *are* experience, just as (have we not seen it?) they are the very air we breathe. Therefore, if I should certainly say to a novice, "Write from experience and experience only," I should feel this was rather a tantalizing monition if I were not careful immediately to add, "Try to be one of those on whom nothing is lost!" (James, 427).

Just try—the effort needed to apprehend unity involves extreme effort guessing and tracing patterns, separating and then synthesizing a vastness of sources including the unexpected, scrutinizing and validating the flow of impressions as they coalesce into what can be articulated as experience, followed by pushing that articulation toward the verifiability which an audience can acknowledge as meaning Play, indeed.

Clem Tyler's image of the cosmic heartbeat receiver follows a car accident—perhaps echoing the one that nearly killed Robert Hughes—in which the space and time of the continent are summed up in a terrible instant. Late at night, three years before, a Aboriginal child playing "chicken" had leaped in front of Clem's car:

> Clem swung the wheel, narrowly avoiding the boy, and the whole continent—the whole three million square miles of rock, tree-trunks, sand, fences, cities—came bursting through the windscreen into his skull. The remaining hours of the night had lasted for fourteen months. It had taken another year to locate the bit of him that retained the habit of speech.

Nearly every other character in *Dream Stuff*, except those we have seen retreating into limitation and defensiveness, pays a more or less heavy price for acquiring a sense of inclusiveness and proof from loss. . . .

Time and again, in *Dream Stuff* and in his writing "all the while," David Malouf offers narrations of broad human possibility that draw readers into wise and complex visions of human dreaming.

Source: John Scheckter, "Dreaming Wholeness: David Malouf's New Stories," in *World Literature Today*, Vol. 74, No. 4, Autumn 2000, pp. 714–48.

Sources

Barnacle, Hugo, Review of *Dream Stuff*, in *New Statesman*, May 1, 2000, p. 57.

Malouf, David, "Great Day," in *Dream Stuff*, Vintage, 2000, pp. 131–85.

Miller, Rebecca, Review of *Dream Stuff*, in *Library Journal*, June 15, 2000, p. 120.

Pierce, Peter, "What Dreams May Come: David Malouf's *Dream Stuff*," in *World Literature Today*, Vol. 74, No. 4, Autumn 2000, pp. 751–57.

Review of *Dream Stuff*, in *Economist*, Vol. 355, No. 8170, May 13, 2000, pp. 14–15.

Review of *Dream Stuff*, in *Publishers Weekly*, May 1, 2000, pp. 47–48.

Sharrad, Paul, "'A Delicate Business': David Malouf's Shorter Prose," in *World Literature Today*, Vol. 74, No. 4, Autumn 2000, pp. 759–68.

Further Reading

Banting, Erinn, *Australia: The Culture*, Crabtree, 2002.
    This work examines the diverse culture of Australia and provides a brief history of the country's development.

Day, David, *Claiming a Continent: A New History of Australia*, HarperCollins, 2001.

This comprehensive overview of Australia covers its history from settlement to the end of the twentieth century.

Dever, Maryanne, "Secret Companions: The Continuity of David Malouf's Fiction," in *World Literature Written in English*, Vol. 26, No. 1, 1986, pp. 67–74.

In this article, Dever traces thematic patterns and motifs in Malouf's fiction.

Kavanagh, Paul, "With Breath Just Condensing on It: An Interview with David Malouf," in *Southerly*, Vol. 3, 1986, pp. 247–59.

Kavanagh interviews Malouf about his theories on writing as well as his works' reflection of Australian culture and landscape.

Immortality

Yiyun Li

2003

"Immortality," a short story by Chinese writer Yiyun Li, was first published in the *Paris Review* in 2003. It was reprinted in Li's collection of short stories, *A Thousand Years of Good Prayers* in 2005. "Immortality" is set in China and is told from the point of view of an entire town as it goes through the turbulent events that affected China in the twentieth century. These events include the overthrow of the Qing dynasty (1644–1911/12); the establishment of a communist dictatorship and the personality cult of Mao Zedong; the horrors of the Cultural Revolution, in which millions died; and the massacre of prodemocracy demonstrators at Tiananmen Square, Beijing, in 1989. All these details form the backdrop to Li's highly unusual story of a boy who was born in 1949, the year that the communists came to power, and who as he grew up bore such a strong resemblance to the dictator that he was summoned to Beijing and trained to impersonate the dictator in official films and national events. With its vivid picture of life in China during the communist era, Li opens a window on a world that to Western readers may seem exotic and strange, and the tragic story she tells, of a young man who eventually falls from grace as rapidly as he first rises to fame, is a quietly compelling one.

Author Biography

Yiyun Li was born in Beijing, China, in 1972. Her father was a physicist and her mother a teacher. As a young child, Li learned how harsh the judicial

system could be in the communist country. In 1978, when she was five and a half, the police drove through her neighborhood informing all the residents by loudspeaker that they were to assemble in an open field in ten minutes. In the field, four heavily bound men were placed on a temporary stage, and a police officer announced that they were counterrevolutionaries who had been sentenced to death. The sentence was to be carried out after the men had been paraded through all the local districts. At a signal from her daycare teacher, the five-year-old Li raised her fist, and along with everyone else, shouted a slogan calling for the men to be put to death.

As Li grew up, her mother would close the windows of their house when Li's grandfather, who had fought in the nationalist army against the communists, denounced Mao Zedong, the communist leader. Li's mother warned her to be careful what she said when she was out of the house and could be overheard by others.

Li was a high school student in Beijing when in June 1989, the Chinese Army crushed the prodemocracy protesters in Beijing's Tiananmen Square, killing thousands. She later said, according to Bob Thompson writing in the *Washington Post* on December 21, 2005, that everyone in Beijing knew someone who had been at the square that night, and she compared it to the terrorist attacks on the United States on September 11, 2001.

After the Tiananmen Square incident, the Chinese government ordered that every student at Beijing University was to attend a military camp for one year for purposes of political reeducation. In 1991, Li, a freshman student at the university, found herself at a military camp in central China. Though she already loathed the communist system, her enforced military service made her feel as if she were a victim of the regime, and her anger against the system continued to grow.

After she left the army, Li studied biology, with the goal of pursuing graduate study in the United States. In 1996, Li came to the United States, even though at the time she had only limited command of English. She enrolled in a Ph.D. program in immunology at the University of Iowa. She also took an adult education class in writing.

In 2000, Li realized that her ambition was to become not an immunologist but a writer. She accepted a master's degree in immunology and, in 2001, enrolled in a creative writing course at the University of Iowa. Her teacher was James Alan McPherson, a Pulitzer Prize winner. McPherson

was deeply impressed by Li's story, "Immortality." Encouraged to continue writing, Li was admitted to the prestigious Iowa Writers' Workshop, where she completed two more master's degrees, an MFA in fiction and an MFA in creative nonfiction writing. By this time, "Immortality" had been published in the *Paris Review* (2003) and a memoir by Li had been published in the *New Yorker* (2004). Soon, Random House had offered her a contract for a collection of short stories, which was published in 2005 as *A Thousand Years of Good Prayers*. The collection, which includes the story, "Immortality," received unanimous praise from reviewers and won the Frank O'Connor International Short Story Award, the largest short story prize in the world.

As of 2006, Li lived in Oakland, California, with her husband and their two sons.

Plot Summary

"Immortality" is told in the first person plural by a narrator who represents an entire Chinese town over the course of the twentieth century. The narrator begins by going back to the time of the Chinese imperial dynasties, when members of the imperial family were served by eunuchs who attended to their every need. Eunuchs are men who have had their testicles surgically removed.

This particular town has a history of sending boys to be castrated and serve the emperor and his family. Serving in this way was considered an honorable calling, and the town is proud of the role it has played in producing what were called "Great Papas." The tradition died out, however, when the last imperial dynasty was overthrown and replaced by republics. By the 1930s, most of the Great Papas lived in poverty in temples around the Forbidden City, which was the imperial palace located at the center of the capital city, Beijing.

In the late 1940s, the communists were victorious in the civil war, and the new rulers promised everyone a prosperous life. In the narrator's town, a carpenter's wife becomes pregnant. As the baby grows inside her, she keeps looking at newspaper pictures of the communist dictator. (Historically, the dictator was Mao Zedong, although in the story he is not named.) The narrator reports that there is a saying in China that the more a pregnant woman studies a face, the greater the possibility that the child will resemble that face. So it turns out. The baby boy soon begins to resemble the dictator rather than his father, who was executed by the communists after making some indiscreet remarks about the dictator in a pub. The dictator's rule is a brutal one, but the townspeople are unaware of this, merely going along with whatever the authorities want them to believe.

The boy's mother, widowed at the age of eighteen, is given a job as a street sweeper. No one wants to marry her, and she ages rapidly. By the time the boy is ten, she looks sixty. At that time, a famine comes and lasts for three years. (Historically, this is the famine in China that occurred from 1959 to 1961.) It is partly the fault of the communists, for mismanaging the economy. But when the authorities tell the townspeople that the famine is caused by sparrows and rats that ate all their food, the citizens believe them and attempt to kill all the sparrows. (This incident is based on Mao Zedong's declaration during the famine that sparrows were pests and should be hunted down by the people.) The boy who resembles the dictator tries to sneak a sparrow into his sleeve and take it to his mother to eat, but a bigger boy grabs him and accuses him of stealing the property of the People. The boy is set upon by a mob and beaten until his mother comes to rescue him, telling the mob to look at the boy's face. The mob freezes when it realizes that the boy looks exactly like the dictator whom they are taught to revere.

After this event, no one in the town ever utters a disrespectful word about the boy's face, and the older the boy gets, the more he resembles the dictator. After he graduates from high school, the Revolutionary Committee discusses what would be an appropriate job for him. They eventually appoint him as the director of the advisory board to the Revolutionary Committee, which involves no responsibilities at all. The young man prospers, but no young woman will date him, because the word is that marrying this man will either bring the greatest fortune or the greatest misfortune.

When the dictator dies, the people in the town ostentatiously mourn. All entertainment is banned for six months. A year later, the young man, now twenty-eight, is whisked off in an official car to the capital city, where he is to audition as the dictator's impersonator. His mother is proud of him. The young man spends days in training for his new role, along with other candidates for the position. He succeeds in getting to the final round of competition, with three other men, and wins because he is the one who is adjudged to have best captured the essence of the dictator.

After this, he becomes the sole face that represents the dictator to the nation. He stars in movies about the dictator, and flies across the country appearing in televised celebrations of national holidays. The town hopes that he will marry a local young woman, but it becomes increasingly clear that this will not happen.

Time passes, and the country undergoes social changes as a result of Western influences. People can now buy Western consumer items and watch imported movies. The people in the town begin to realize that their own lives are not as happy as they had been taught to believe, and the capitalist countries are not simply waiting for the Chinese communists to liberate them through the worldwide spread of communism. Biographies and memoirs of the former dictator begin to appear that present the dictator in a bad light. Rumors spread that under his rule, fifty million people died through famine or political persecution. Doubt runs rampant through the people in the town. They are no longer interested in the stories told to them about the dictator's impersonator by his mother.

The present leader of the nation tries to reignite enthusiasm for communism, but a protest breaks out in the capital city. Thousands of people rally for democracy, but the army fires on the protesters. (Historically, this was the massacre in Tiananmen Square, in Beijing, in June 1989, in which between five hundred and seven thousand people were killed.) Shortly after that, the "big-brother country," which is their neighbor, ceases to exist. (This is a reference to the demise of the Soviet Union in 1991.) The townspeople are confused by all these rapid changes.

The dictator's impersonator, now in his forties, begins to encounter problems. He has never made love to a woman, and he starts to fantasize about his missed opportunities. He also thinks that no woman is good enough for him, since he is such a great man. He has time free now, and he takes to wandering the streets in disguise. At a stall in an alley, he buys a pornographic book and a biography of the dictator written by his physician of thirty years. The book was banned on publication abroad but has been smuggled into the country from Hong Kong and the United States. (This is a reference to the memoirs of Mao Zedong's physician, Dr. Li Zhisui, published in the United States in 1994.)

The man returns to his room and studies both books. He feels an emptiness he has never known before. He sees in the biography pictures of the dictator with attractive young nurses, and he realizes that being a great man means one can have whatever one wants in the world. He goes out in the night and finds a prostitute in a karaoke-and-dance bar. They go together to a hotel. The woman's pimp rushes into their room, impersonating a police officer. He handcuffs the man and photographs him. When the couple realizes who he is, they ask for ten times what they usually request in blackmail money. The man refuses to pay, thinking that his indiscretion will pass unnoticed. But rumors start to spread through the capital about his visit to the brothel. The incriminating pictures circulate until everyone claims to have seen them, and he is fired from his job as the dictator's impersonator. He is in any case no longer needed, since a new leader has come to power and is seeking someone who resembles him rather than the former dictator to become his impersonator.

On a winter's day, the man returns to his hometown. His mother has died, and he goes to her tomb, where he castrates himself. None of the townspeople knows why he does this, although they all remember the stories of the eunuchs of old, the Great Papas. The man lives on in the town, facing a long barren life. He sits around in the sun and walks to the cemetery at dusk, where he talks to his mother until it is dark. The townspeople pray for him to live forever, as they had prayed for the dictator.

Characters

Dictator

The dictator is not named and does not appear directly in the story, but his presence is felt everywhere. His photograph appears all the time in the newspapers during the 1950s; at that time, he is "the only superstar in the media," and the townspeople refer to him as "Our Father, Our Savior, the North Star of Our Lives, the Never Falling Sun of Our Era." Since they regard him as a surrogate father, they weep like orphans at his death. Underneath their adulation of this pseudo-divine figure, however, lies a "hidden hatred" that they dare not acknowledge.

Impersonator

The impersonator is a young man whose face resembles the face of the dictator. The resemblance is so uncanny that even as a boy he leads quite a privileged life. At school, the teachers never rebuke him, and in the team games the children play, the side without him is always willing to lose. After he leaves school, he is given a title as director of the advisory board to the Revolution Committee, but this is a fake job that involves no work at all. A year after the dictator dies, the young man is taken to the capital city where he auditions as the dictator's impersonator. He is successful and travels the country, impersonating the dictator at national celebrations. He also appears in movies as the dictator. In this role, he is adored by the masses. People want to shake his hand and get his autograph, pretty young women rush up to him with bouquets of flowers, and enthusiastic children swarm around him. When he is in his forties, however, he becomes tormented by the fact that he has never married and never even made love to a woman. He has rejected many women who would have married him because he did not think they were worthy of him, since he has come to consider himself a great man. Eventually, he falls prey to lust, buying pornographic magazines and soliciting a prostitute in a bar, only to be blackmailed by the woman's pimp. He is fired from his job as impersonator, and even though he begs for another chance, his career is over. He returns to his hometown and castrates himself by his mother's tomb. At the end of the story, he cuts a pathetic figure: "He sits in the sun and watches the dogs chasing one another, his face hidden behind dark glasses and the high collar of his coat." In the evenings, he goes to the cemetery and talks to his mother.

Impersonator's Father

The impersonator's father is a young carpenter. He marries at the time when the dictator first comes to power. This would be in 1949, when the communists triumphed in the civil war. The carpenter is described as "a hardworking man, nice to his neighbors, good to his wife." However, he meets a tragic fate. One evening he is a little drunk and makes a joke about the dictator's policy of describing women who have given birth to a certain number of babies as mother heroes. This is considered an attack on the dictator's population policy, and the carpenter is tried and executed. His son is born on the day of his death.

Impersonator's Mother

The impersonator's mother is an illiterate eighteen-year-old girl. When she is pregnant, she frequently gazes at the face of the dictator in newspaper photographs; as a result, so she believes, her son's face resembles that of the dictator. After the execution of her husband, she is given a job as a street sweeper. Although she is beautiful, none of the young men in the town offers to marry her, since she is stigmatized as the widow of a counterrevolutionary. She ages rapidly in her appearance. By the time her son is ten years old, she looks like a woman of sixty. But she is fiercely protective of her son and rescues him from the mob that attacks him. She is proud of him when he is taken away to the capital city to become an impersonator and takes credit for the fact that he looks like the dictator. She enjoys telling the townspeople stories of his new life; she also does her best to persuade him to marry one of the local girls, telling him that he needs a son. When word of the scandal about her son's visit to a prostitute reaches her, she is stricken by shame, falls ill, and dies.

Narrator

The narrator is the collective voice of the town, persisting over many generations, and referred to in the first person plural as "we." The townspeople are simple folk who cling to their old traditions at the same time as they embrace the new ideology of communism. They regard the Great Papas of the past as heroes and think of the dictator's impersonator as a hero, too, even after he disgraces himself. In their eyes, he is the greatest man in their history. The townspeople are not educated, and they have little power to think for themselves. They are obedient to authority, and they respond not as individuals but as a group. For the most part, they are tools in the hands of the dictator and the Communist Party. They are naive and appear to know little about the world beyond the borders of their town.

Themes

Mind Control

The story shows some of the negative consequences of a totalitarian system, in which the government controls every aspect of people's lives, including how they behave and what they think. The minds of the townspeople are controlled by the Communist Party, which is their only authority for what is happening both in their own town and in the wider world. They show no ability to make independent judgments for themselves or to exercise common sense. They will believe almost anything. They are convinced, for example, that the famine is caused by sparrows and rats eating the food, simply because this is what the Communist Party tells them, its propaganda transmitted to them through loudspeakers in the town.

The system under which the townspeople live wipes out individuality. They always think and behave as a group, and the group mentality can make them dangerous, as when they set upon the boy who during the famine merely wants to take a sparrow home for his mother to eat. They lose their reason, thinking that the boy is committing some offense against them all, and they become like animals: "Some of us bare our teeth, ready to eat him alive."

The townspeople are also quite ready to condemn their own people simply because the Party tells them to, as when they celebrate the execution of the young carpenter—the father of the future impersonator—for some small indiscretion which resulted in his being branded as a counterrevolutionary. The townspeople thrust their fists into the air and hail a great victory for the People and chant revolutionary songs.

Since they are easily controlled by the Party and believe fervently in the personality cult of the dictator, the townspeople are ready to make any sacrifice that is demanded of them, even their lives. When the dictator defies the Americans to drop atomic bombs on China, the ordinary people in the town work themselves into a state of great indignation about the aggression of the Americans. They are ready for the bombs to fall, so they can "prove to the dictator [their] courage, and [their] loyalty."

The tyrannous nature of the rule to which the townspeople have submitted is everywhere apparent. The Party rigidly enforces the personality cult of the dictator, even sending parents of first-graders who make the mistake of misspelling the dictator's name to labor camps. The people are terrified of doing or saying something that will get them into trouble with the government. They must make sure they express the sentiments that are officially approved. If for a moment they think anything that might call official doctrine or government practices into question, they instantly repress the thought. For example, when some of them go to see the memorial of the dictator erected after his death, they pay a "substantial fee" (the hint of exploitation is unavoidable) to buy a white paper flower to be placed at the foot of the coffin. Some of them wonder whether the flowers are collected at night and resold the next day, but "instantly we will feel ashamed of ourselves for thinking such impure thoughts in the most sacred place in the world." Another example occurs when they watch national celebrations on television and see people dancing and singing with hearty smiles on their faces "like well-trained kindergarteners." For a moment, the brainwashing is not

Topics For Further Study

- Make a class presentation with a classmate on the life and achievements of Mao Zedong. What were Mao's contributions to twentieth-century China? Does he deserve credit as a modernizer of China? Was he a tyrant on the scale of Hitler and Stalin? One person should present the positive aspects of Mao's rule and the other the negative side. Then the class should vote on whether Mao deserves to be called a great man.

- Re-read "Immortality," and write an essay in which you describe some of the ways in which traditional folk beliefs continue to exist alongside communist doctrine in the minds of the townspeople. What effect do those beliefs have on the people's behavior?

- Team up with one other student. Imagine you are both pro-democracy students in Beijing in 1989, just prior to the Tiananmen Square massacre. Write a five-point manifesto listing the kind of changes you are advocating in Chinese politics and society. Then research the history of China since 1989, and against each point in your manifesto, describe any progress or lack of progress that has been made in attaining the desired goal. Has China gone backwards or forwards in terms of democracy since 1989? Make a joint class presentation of your findings.

- In the story, the United States is perceived as an enemy of China and a potential adversary in a nuclear war. Write an essay describing how President Richard M. Nixon's visit to China in 1972 changed the relationship between the United States, China, and the Soviet Union. What was Nixon's purpose in visiting China?

---

quite perfect: "At such moments, those of us who think a little more than others start to feel uneasy, haunted by a strange fear that our people are growing down, instead of growing up." But that intuition quickly vanishes when the dictator's impersonator appears on the screen.

It is only when Western influences start to appear in China that the people start to think for themselves a little more, and doubts begin to appear. They realize the falsity of much of what they were taught in the early days of communist rule. But the communist system soon manages to reassert its hold over the people's minds. In the aftermath of the killing of pro-democracy demonstrators (this is a reference to the Tiananmen Square massacre in 1989), the people mindlessly echo the words of the new dictator, who has said that he is willing to kill two hundred thousand people in exchange for twenty years of communist stability: "Numbed by such numbers, we will echo his words and applaud his wisdom when we are required to publicly condemn those killed in the incident." This suggests that in terms of how the people's minds are controlled by the authorities, nothing much has changed since the 1950s.

Emasculation

When they first come to power, the communist leaders proclaim that communism is great, and they persuade the people that there will now be prosperity for everyone. But the story shows that in one respect at least, China continues as before. In the old days, the town used to castrate seven- and eight-year-old boys and send them to the capital city to serve the imperial family. The town is proud of its history of supplying the emperor with Great Papas, but the reader will find it hard to accept the notion that there is any honor in the practice of sacrificing boys' masculinity so that they may better serve the ambitions and whims of the country's leaders. The mutilation of the Great Papas serves as a powerful symbol of how individuals are emasculated in service of their rulers, and so it is with the young impersonator, who is a eunuch in everything but name even before he castrates himself at the end of the story. His status as a celebrity derives solely from his imitation of the dictator; in himself, he is nothing, his achievements nothing. All his power is derived from the dictator, on whom he is utterly dependent. The slightest sign of any individual expression would mean that he was no longer fit to impersonate the dictator. In this sense, he is as emasculated as the eunuchs of old, and like the eunuchs also, when he can no longer be of any use to his rulers, he is discarded. It comes as no surprise that eventually, because of sexual frustrations that derive in part from his life as an impersonator (he is too puffed up with ideas of his own greatness to accept a local young woman as a bride), he castrates himself and becomes literally a eunuch.

Style

Point of View and Setting

The point of view from which the story is told is an unusual one, since the narrator is not an individual voice but a collective one: the members of the town stretching over a period spanning many generations. This point of view effectively conveys a sense of community; the town is proud of its history of sending Great Papas to serve the imperial family, and it is through the money that the eunuchs send home that their brothers are enabled to marry and raise families. The townspeople believe that this is their great distinction in history. Were it not for the Great Papas, they would have nothing of value; after all, they are "small people born into this no-name town." The fact that not a single person in the story is given a name contributes to another effect conveyed by the collective point of view, the sense that the town is a single group and acts as a group; it does not value individuality. The people in the community all think in the same way. This is in part because the town is relatively isolated, not yet affected by modernity. In the 1950s, although the town does have at least one newspaper, it gets a lot of its information from loudspeakers placed on the roofs of the houses, which are used by the Party to disseminate news and propaganda. Even in the 1970s, when a car comes to take the young man away for his training, most of the townspeople have never seen a car before. During that period also, there is just one television set in the entire town.

Historical Context

Chinese History in the Twentieth Century

China's two thousand years of imperial rule by various dynasties, the last of which was the Qing dynasty, ended in 1912 when the army overthrew the dynasty and established a short-lived republic. This change in power was followed by a ten-year period of fragmentation in which various "warlords," provincial military leaders, competed with one another for power. This period lasted from 1916 to 1927. During the 1920s, the great struggle between the nationalist movement and the communists to gain control of China began. In the 1930s, the nationalists, led by Chiang Kai-shek (1887–1975), gained the upper hand and expelled the communists from southern and eastern China. In what became known as the Long March, the communists trekked across China and established a base in the northwest. It was during this period that Mao Zedong (1893–1976) emerged as the communist leader.

In the 1930s, the impoverished and divided nation also had to deal with the Japanese invasion, which was not finally repelled until the end of World War II in 1945. After World War II, the civil war between nationalists and communists, which had been put on hold during the previous decade because of the need to unite against the foreign invader, resumed. By 1949, the Communist Party emerged victorious and inaugurated the People's Republic of China under the leadership of Mao Zedong. Chang Kai-shek and the remaining nationalists fled to the island of Taiwan.

The communists soon formed a strong central government with a planned economy based on the five-year plans typical of the Soviet Union. In rural areas, the old feudal system was broken up, and land was taken from landowners and given to the peasants. This was a violent upheaval, and from 1950 to 1952, some 700,000 landlords and others designated as counterrevolutionaries were killed.

Despite the violence, during the 1950s, China made enormous strides in modernizing the backward economy, particularly by investing in heavy industry (iron, steel, machinery). During the first five-year plan, the annual industrial growth rate was 11 percent. But Mao was dissatisfied with the results, and from 1958 to 1960, he oversaw what was called the Great Leap Forward, a drastic reorganization of the economy aimed at raising production. The results were disastrous and contributed to the famine that afflicted China especially in 1960 and 1961, during which twenty million people died of starvation.

The Cultural Revolution

In 1966, the ten-year period known as the Cultural Revolution began, during which the country descended into chaos and near anarchy. The

Compare & Contrast

- **1950s:** According to China's census in 1953, the population of China is 583,000,000. The population rises fast as death rates fall, and birth rates are not curbed.

  1980s: In 1982, China's census reports the population to be 1,008,175,288, an increase of about 73 percent on the 1953 figure. At this time, China's population is about one-fourth of the global population.

  Today: The population of the Chinese mainland is estimated in July 2005 to be 1,306, 313, 812.

- **1950s:** Although population is rising rapidly, the communist government does not implement a population policy.

  1980s: China continues the population policy it instituted in the 1970s, when family planning was incorporated into the constitution. The fertility rate drops from 5.29 (children born/woman) in the 1950s to 2.63 in the 1980s. However, enforcement of the one-child policy is harsh. There are forced abortions, infanticide, and strict penalties.

  Today: The population policy remains but is less strictly enforced. Rights of women are more respected as China tries to strike a balance between population growth, human rights, and long-term social development. The fertility rate is estimated to be 1.72 in 2005.

- **1950s:** China's economy is centrally planned and for the most part is not open to international trade. China makes great strides in modernization.

  1980s: China focuses on market-oriented economic development, develops stock markets, and opens up to foreign trade and investment.

  Today: Economic reform has produced a more than ten-fold increase in China's gross domestic product since 1978. Living standards have improved dramatically. Although China remains a communist, one-party state, the private sector of the economy is growing, and China is a major participant in the global economy.

Cultural Revolution was put into motion by Mao as a way of outmaneuvering other communist leaders whom he had come to distrust. Mao also wanted to shake up the bureaucracy, which he thought was too slow in implementing reform. For this he enlisted the aid of millions of young people, mostly students, reasoning that they were not attached to the ways of the past and would generate the necessary revolutionary fervor. Mao invited these students, who were known as Red Guards, to tear down all the old structures of society. Mobs of Red Guards dressed in paramilitary uniforms traveled the countryside by train creating turmoil wherever they went. Educational and religious institutions were targeted. Teachers were beaten up by their students; factories and high schools were closed. People who were arbitrarily accused of being counterrevolutionaries were either imprisoned or executed. Millions died during the Cultural Revolution; some estimates put the deaths at between twenty-three and thirty-five million.

The Cultural Revolution was also the time when the personality cult surrounding Mao, which had been present since the 1940s, reached its most extreme form. Jonathan Spence explains in his book *Mao Zedong* the form the personality cult took during this time:

> Every street was to have a quotation from Chairman Mao prominently displayed, and loudspeakers at every intersection and in all parks were to broadcast his thought. Every household as well as all trains and buses, bicycles and pedicabs, had to have a picture of Mao on its walls. Ticket takers on trains and buses should all declaim Mao's thought.

Mao Zedong was regarded as the embodiment of the Chinese nation, the great leader whose wisdom unerringly steered the ship of state.

Economic Liberalization

Mao died in 1976. In the 1980s, his successor, Deng Xiaoping (1904–1997), pursued what were known as open-door economic policies, which encouraged the introduction of Western capitalistic practices to the Chinese economy. These policies were continued by Deng's successor, Zhao Ziyang (1919–2005), who became general secretary of the Chinese Communist Party in 1987. As a result, the Chinese economy began to prosper as never before. Annual growth rate during the 1980s was about 9.5 percent (compared to an average 3 percent annual growth in the United States), and Chinese consumers found that luxury items such as American clothes, stereos, automobiles, and washing machines were now within their reach.

Economic liberalization also produced demands for political liberalization. During 1989, there were massive pro-democracy demonstrations in Beijing's Tiananmen Square. In early June, one such demonstration was violently suppressed. Chinese leaders sent in troops and tanks, killing hundreds, possibly thousands, of demonstrators. Many students and others were executed or imprisoned following the shootings.

Mao Zedong   UPI/Corbis-Bettmann

Critical Overview

Li's collection of stories, *A Thousand Years of Good Prayers*, in which "Immortality" appeared, was greeted with universal acclaim. Reviewers admired Li's treatment of the different ways in which Chinese people came to terms with the dramatic changes in their society during the 1990s and also her many portraits of Chinese immigrants adapting to life in the United States. *Publishers Weekly* calls the book "A beautifully executed debut collection. . . . These are powerful stories that encapsulate tidily epic grief and longing."

Many reviewers also singled out "Immortality" for comment. Fatema Ahmed in the *New York Times Book Review* describes it as the most ambitious story in the collection, in which Li takes the reader "on a virtuoso tour" through the turbulence of China's twentieth century history. Ahmed comments that "The collective first-person narrators, reminiscent of the bereaved neighborhood boys in Jeffrey Eugenides's novel *The Virgin Suicides*, are a striking symbol of endurance; like Eugenides's narrators they, too, outlive the subjects of their story."

For Rodney Welch in the *Washington Post*, "Immortality" is the best story in the collection. Welch writes:

> The story captures 20th-century China in all of its false hopes, terrors and (speaking of violent metaphors)

emasculation, and the narrative voice is perfect: It's told by an anonymous voice in the crowd—a crowd that believes what everyone believes, which is also what it is ordered to believe from on high.

In England's *Guardian*, Michel Faber comments on the story's "disquieting blend of realism and fable." Calling it "the most overtly artful piece" in the collection, Faber writes: "The doppelganger's career in propaganda movies is handled with deadpan humour, but we are kept off-balance by a piteous parallel narrative about imperial eunuchs and by the sheer horror of quotes from the tyrant's speeches." In the *Village Voice*, Rebecca Tuhus-Dubrow describes "Immortality" as "eerie" and draws attention to the unusual point of view from which it is told: "[T]he first person plural, convey[s], better than any description could, a sense of community that subsumes its constituent selves."

Criticism

Bryan Aubrey

Aubrey holds a Ph.D. in English and has published many articles on contemporary literature. In this essay, Aubrey discusses, first, China's traditional practice, now discarded, of employing eunuchs as imperial servants; and second, the cult of personality associated with Mao Zedong.

In its short twenty-four pages, Li's story "Immortality" manages to provide a condensed yet illuminating tour of some of the most bizarre and disturbing aspects of Chinese political culture as it hurtled from one violent change to another through the twentieth century. Much of what Li describes may strike the Western reader as strange, repellant, and sinister, and it will be no surprise that the author chose to leave her homeland and live in a society where freedom and individuality are prized more highly than passive obedience to collective authority. This essay discusses two aspects of the story that are most foreign to the American mind: first, China's practice, discarded only in the early twentieth century, of employing eunuchs as imperial servants; second, the cult of personality associated with Mao Zedong and the associated limitations of thought that are demanded in a totalitarian society.

Li's account of the role of eunuchs in China's imperial dynasties, which takes up the first four pages of "Immortality" is fact not fiction. As Mary M. Anderson explains in her book, *Hidden Power: The Palace Eunuchs of Imperial China*, eunuchs were an irreplaceable part of the Chinese imperial system. Since eunuchs were unable to father children and, therefore, had no sons to whom they might seek to hand down political power, it was considered that they would be completely passive and loyal to the emperor. Only eunuchs were allowed to attend the emperor and the ladies of the imperial family as well as the emperor's large harem. One of the eunuch's duties was to ensure that no male took advantage of the concubines, since it was considered essential that all the children the concubines bore were fathered by the emperor. As Li makes clear in the story, and as Anderson confirms, some eunuchs, since they were so close to the emperor, did attain positions of power and influence, as well as accumulating considerable wealth. Eunuchs were often put in charge of young princes and would make sure that they exerted as much influence as they could on the future emperor to further their own ambitions.

Eunuchs, who could easily be spotted by their high falsetto voices and characteristic walk—leaning slightly forward, taking short steps, toes turned outward—were resented by the mandarins, the elite members of the Chinese civil service, who could not attain such personal closeness to the emperor. Anderson points out that since it was the mandarins who wrote the histories of China, it is not surprising that eunuchs were presented in such histories as having exerted a bad influence on the country. Despite the bias of the mandarins, however, Anderson regards it as undeniable that the disloyalty of powerful eunuchs, particularly those who served weak emperors who mistrusted their own political advisors and, therefore, became dependent on their eunuchs for advice, did cause great harm to China in various periods of history. This, of course, is a conclusion that the humble inhabitants of the anonymous town in "Immortality," who are proud of the eunuchs they sent to the palace, would reject as malicious fabrications. They persist in referring to castration as being "cleaned," a tidy euphemism that disguises the horrific and repellant nature of the practice.

When China's last imperial dynasty was overthrown, in the early years of the twentieth century, the practice of castrating boys for the purposes of serving the nation's leaders ended. By mid-century, the most populous nation on earth had adopted communism and was determined to modernize its society and become a great power in the world. It was during these years, from the 1950s to the 1970s, that the so-called cult of personality emerged in China, associated with the towering figure of Mao Zedong. This is the period described in "Immortality" "when the dictator becomes larger than the universe in our nation."

The personality cult was a feature of twentieth century totalitarian regimes. A single leader was elevated to quasi-divine status and was presented as the great liberator of his people. His image appeared everywhere in statues and on billboards, posters, and murals in public places, for the people to contemplate. The leader was often represented in different guises, in military uniform as revolutionary hero and in civilian clothing as gentle father of the nation. His slogans and teachings were also ever-present, either accompanying the images or quoted by Party officials as well as ordinary people. Bookstores, schools, and libraries were filled with volumes of the leader's speeches and other writings. For those living in the midst of such a cult, it became almost impossible to think of their country except in terms of the indispensable leader who was the very soul of the nation. Thus in China, as Jonathan Spence explains in his book, *The Gate of Heavenly Peace: The Chinese and their Revolutions, 1895–1980*, Mao was hailed by the masses as the "great helmsman," and little books of his sayings were distributed everywhere. When the Red Guards burned the British legation in Beijing during the Cultural Revolution, they chanted that Mao was "the red, red sun in their hearts." Spence quotes a poem written by a young female textile factory worker that refers to the time when Mao saluted the marching Red Guards from the terrace of the Gate of Heavenly Peace in 1966. The poem conveys the feeling that the great man had the keys to the future in his hands: "Chairman Mao waves his hand at the Gate of Heavenly Peace; / In an instant, history has rolled away so many centuries."

China under Mao Zedong is only one example of the cult of personality. Before Mao, Joseph Stalin (1879–1953), who wielded absolute power in the Soviet Union from the 1930s until his death, established a similar cult. Stalin was regarded as virtually a demigod; numerous places in the Soviet Union were renamed after him; writers and artists were compelled to depict him in a heroic light; and schoolchildren were taught that everything valuable and good came from their great leader. As the historian Roy A. Medvedev explains, "The deification of Stalin justified in advance everything he did, everything connected with his name, including new crimes and abuses of power. All the achievements and virtues of socialism were embodied in him."

The cult of personality was designed to convince the people that the leader was kind and just and wise and did everything for the benefit of the people. Stalin was often known as "Uncle Joe," for example, which gave him a benevolent image. The truth was markedly different, though, since both Stalin and Mao were responsible for the deaths of millions of their fellow countrymen and women. But for the most part, the brainwashed masses were unable to entertain the notion that their kind and noble leader might also be a man who ordered or condoned mass murder and was indifferent to the value of human life. This was in part because in a totalitarian state the Party controls all the sources of information, so the masses know only what they are permitted to know. But in addition to this limitation, they are trained to think in certain limited grooves. If they are presented with evidence that their leaders are not quite what they seem to be, or they suspect as much, they immediately repress the thought or reinterpret the information they have received. The classic analysis of the kind of thinking that goes on in totalitarian societies was made by the English novelist and essayist George Orwell in his novel *Nineteen Eighty-Four*, published in 1949 and set in Oceania, a future totalitarian society in

> " But for the most part, the brainwashed masses were unable to entertain the notion that their kind and noble leader might also be a man who ordered or condoned mass murder and was indifferent to the value of human life."

which the cult of personality centers on the infallible, all-knowing leader known as Big Brother. In Oceania, the people are trained from an early age in what is called "crimestop," a kind of unconscious self-censorship in which a person automatically stops short of any thought that might lead in a heretical direction. Should that process break down, the result is "thoughtcrime," which is not an actual crime or any act at all, but simply a thought that does goes against the interests of the Party. Should it be discovered, a person can be arrested for thoughtcrime. In "Immortality," there is a clear example of what Orwell meant by both these terms. When the people from the town visit the memorial to the dead dictator, they see a mass of white paper flowers around the coffin, and some of them, just for a moment, wonder if the flowers are collected each night and resold the following day. But they instantly repress the thought and feel ashamed of themselves for thinking it. In other words, just as a "thoughtcrime" pops up, "crimestop" comes into play. The people have been conditioned and are now incapable of thinking a negative thought about the Party.

Other elements in "Immortality" show how the masses have had their ability to think in a rational manner blunted by the propaganda of the Party. When they discover that their beloved leader is willing to sacrifice half the population of China to American bombs, they direct their anger not at the dictator, to whom they make ostentatious displays of loyalty, but at the United States. Perhaps even more disturbingly, later, when cracks start to appear in the monolithic cult, the people seem indifferent

What Do I Read Next?

- Li's article, "The Man Who Eats," in the *New Yorker* (September 6, 2004), is a memoir of her grandfather, a former member of the Chinese nationalist army and a formidable man who lived through three regimes, two world wars, two civil wars, famine, and revolution. The piece also contains much information about conditions of life in Beijing when Li was growing up in the 1970s.

- *China's Son: Growing Up in the Cultural Revolution* (2001), by Da Chen, is a story of how one man's life was devastated by the Cultural Revolution. Da Chen came from a landowning family and found himself an outcast in communist China. Told that he could never become more than a poor farmer, he dropped out of school. After the death of Mao in 1976, however, he realized that a college education might still be possible for him. Working long hours, he made his dream come true, earning a place at the prestigious Beijing University.

- *The Rice Room: Growing Up Chinese-American, From Number Two Son to Rock 'n' Roll* (1994) is an autobiography by Ben Fong-Torres, who was a writer and editor for *Rolling Stone* magazine during the 1960s. As a first-generation Chinese immigrant, Fong-Torres found himself immersed in a culture that was vastly different from the cultural heritage which his immigrant parents urged him to preserve. Fong-Torres describes his feelings of having a dual identity and how his attempt to forge a compromise between the old and the new affected all areas of his life.

- *The Chinese Century: A Photographic History of the Last Hundred Years* (1996), by Jonathan Spence and Annping Chin, is a collection of rare historic photographs documenting Chinese history through the century, from the lives of the famous to the millions of anonymous ordinary citizens. There is also a supplementary text that gives some historical background for the photographs.

---

to the dictator's crimes. Rumors circulate that fifty million may have died from famine and persecution during his reign, but when the people realize that this is less than the number of people the dictator was willing to sacrifice in a nuclear war, they say, in a matter-of-fact way, "So what is all the fuss about?" Still without the strength to call their leaders to account, they soon acquiesce and even applaud the statements of a later leader who says he is willing to sacrifice many thousands of lives in exchange for social stability. It seems that the long habit of subservience to authoritarian leaders is not an easy one to shake off.

Source: Bryan Aubrey, Critical Essay on "Immortality," in *Short Stories for Students*, Thomson Gale, 2007.

Rodney Welch

In the following review, Welch calls Li's collection A Thousand Years of Good Prayers *"fresh, wise, and alive, creating a fascinating, horrifying*

and heartbreaking picture of life in a country where the past never goes away."

Yiyun Li's *A Thousand Years of Good Prayers* is a remarkable debut—as acute and authentic-sounding about the domestic effect of cross-cultural change in modern China as Jhumpa Lahiri's *Interpreter of Maladies* was about India. Also like that book, it's one of those rare short story collections where you find yourself reading one perfectly realized gem after the next.

Li—who grew up in Beijing, came to America to study medicine and entered the Iowa Writers' Workshop after taking a master's degree in immunology from the University of Iowa—writes with the kind of brisk clarity you see in, say, the Japanese novelists Junichiro Tanizaki and Yukio Mishima. She gets down to business quickly, sketching characters with swift, deft strokes, immediately setting them off on journeys that are as compelling as they are tragic. There's a strong streak of Flannery O'Connor here, too; metaphors for life, faith and desire are realized through violence, and the often bloody fate of these characters has a richly revelatory power.

These natives and exiles of post-Mao, post-Tiananmen China are victims of tradition and change, of old barbarities and recent upheavals. Some of them have grown up singing love songs to the Communist Party—"The Party is dearer than my own mother," goes one; "My mother only gives me a body. It is the Party who gives me a soul"—and now see the influences of capitalism everywhere. Elderly people play the stock market, and young people leave for America, where cultural norms against divorce, homosexuality and abortion are far more relaxed.

Tradition, however, is as strong as ever and has a way of hunting these characters down. Nowhere is this more true than with marriage, which serves as a kind of binding theme of these stories. Li contrasts the failed unions of the young with the domestic hells of their parents, both becoming so accustomed to unhappiness that they make a culture of their own misery.

That's certainly the case with Sansan, the schoolteacher in "Love in the Marketplace," who receives an offer of marriage from Tu, the man she lost earlier to her best friend. Sansan's mother urges her to forget the past, but she refuses; she has banked her entire life on the all-or-nothing proposition of being Tu's first and only, a point she makes with bloody emphasis in a horrifying and starkly effective final scene. In "The Arrangement," a man holds his marriage together by avoiding it as much as possible—and leaving his sickly, frigid, vicious wife to the care of a long-suffering friend.

In the title story, a father tries to patch things up with his recently divorced, estranged daughter, whom he wants to see remarried. "Women in their marriageable twenties and early thirties are like lychees that have been picked from the tree," he advises her. "Each passing day makes them less fresh and less desirable, and only too soon will they lose their value, and have to be gotten rid of at a sale price." What he doesn't know is that his daughter sees through his illusions about his own life and knows what a sham his own marriage has been.

"After a Life" follows the dual stories of Mr. Su and Mr. Fong, elderly Chinese gents who meet each other at the "stockbrokerage" and are both mired in burdensome lives that go against prevailing convention. Mr. Fong uses Mr. Su to cover for

" These natives and exiles of post-Mao, post-Tiananmen China are victims of tradition and change, of old barbarities and recent upheavals."

an affair, which threatens to reveal the hidden secret of Mr. Su and his wife: an adult daughter with cerebral palsy, whom they keep locked away in a room for fear of revealing their shame to the neighbors. "Life is not much different from the stock market," Mr. Su thinks. "You invest in a stock and you stick, and are stuck, to the choice, despite all the possibilities of other mistakes."

"Son" vaguely calls to mind O'Connor's story "The Enduring Chill" and seems to have a touch of her faith as well; it's written with a cool objectivity that is just a shade short of openly devout. Han, living in California, returns home to China to visit his mother and discovers she has given up Marx for Jesus. Han tries to convince her that she has merely exchanged one false god for another—an argument that will not only bring terrible consequences but will force Han, who is gay, to realize that his mother is living her convictions with far more courage than he can live his own.

Several stories directly address the human costs of life under a brutal dictatorship. The best, "Immortality," follows the fate of a child who looks like Mao, which becomes first his blessing and then his curse. The story captures 20th-century China in all of its false hopes, terrors and (speaking of violent metaphors) emasculation, and the narrative voice is perfect: It's told by an anonymous voice in the crowd—a crowd that believes what everyone believes, which is also what it is ordered to believe from on high.

Each of these stories takes you to a different place, and each feels fresh, wise and alive, creating a fascinating, horrifying and heartbreaking picture of life in a country where the past never goes away.

Source: Rodney Welch, "Cultural Revolutions: A Debut Collection of Stories Explores the Complexities of Life in Modern China," in *Washington Post*, November 27, 2005, pp. 1–2.

Political protest in China with students holding a banner in Tiananmen Square, China
© Peter Turnley/Corbis

Jennifer Moeller

In the following review, Moeller applauds Li's A Thousand Years of Good Prayers *for its "insight into what lies at the heart of Chinese culture" and commends her talent for creating "well-realized characters."*

A flight from Boston to Beijing costs $900. Yiyun Li's book, *A Thousand Years of Good Prayers*, costs about $22. What do these two purchases have in common? Spending money on either may offer insight into what lies at the heart of Chinese culture.

Personally, I would suggest both.

My own trip to China a year ago was full of cultural exchange and understanding, but I left with a number of unanswered questions, such as, why do the Chinese stand in line with recycled paper flowers outside Mao's mausoleum to pay tribute to a man who died in 1976? What was it like to live during the Cultural Revolution? Are young Chinese moving away from their own cultural traditions and toward Western values?

A Thousand Years of Good Prayers provides context and understanding, but does not directly answer any of these questions. That's the beauty of it.

Li's writing and storytelling present the reader with the information necessary to understand each character, but leave stories open-ended enough that readers find much left to ponder.

This collection of 10 short, fictional stories examines and explores Chinese cultural phenomena such as eunuchs, the one-child policy, corruption, arranged marriages, the rise of religious fervor, and the stigma of single women, and then juxtaposes the Western-embracing youth with their traditional elders.

In all cases, Li draws neither negative nor positive conclusions. Instead, she places readers in a variety of characters' shoes for a moment in time, long enough for them to get at least a glimpse of the historical, emotional, and cultural contexts that lie beyond.

Li thus offers readers their own chance to grasp a Chinese thought process, yet still allows them to draw their own conclusions.

She does all of this subtly—almost unnoticeably so—through her well-realized characters. The book begins with Granny Lin, an old Chinese woman who has been laid off from her job as a government-owned factory worker. With no job and no pension, Granny Lin lets her friend arrange a marriage for her with an elderly widower.

Through statements like, "It does not say that Red Star Garment Factory has gone bankrupt, or that being honorably retired, Granny Lin will not receive her pension . . . for these facts are simply not true. 'Bankrupt' is the wrong word for a state-owned industry," Li refrains from partaking in direct political discussion.

Instead, she describes the strictly-in-denial fashion in which the Chinese government closes down a factory. The story presents a type of evasion that might surprise Westerners but is common in China.

In another story, Li explores life during the Cultural Revolution, suggesting that the people failed to grasp that the famine and suffering they experienced had anything to do with Mao's policies.

The fictional characters seem instead to believe Mao when he explains their hunger over the loudspeaker by saying, "Get rid of the sparrows and the rats; they are the thieves who stole our food and brought hunger to us."

While not directly related to each other—and without character overlap—her stories weave together easily, providing a well-rounded but fluid and thought-provoking look at Chinese society.

Growing up in Beijing, Li has captured the art of writing in a way that both explains and honors Chinese culture, while also questioning it.

In these stories, Li provides a glimpse into the oft-misunderstood lives of the Chinese people and the way their culture impacts their thoughts and decisions. Although based in fiction, Li's frequent allusions to actual historical events made me wonder if her tales explains what it was actually like to live in Zhong Guo.

Part of Chinese culture and tradition includes speaking in euphemisms and avoiding blunt confrontation that would incur the loss of 'face.'

This respectful tone of conversation employed by Li throughout *A Thousand Years of Good Prayers* provides a natural and genuinely Chinese feel to her writing—even as her stories cleverly question every aspect of tradition.

This is Li's skill, to delicately maintain balance, justifying tradition and contradicting it at the same time through her fictional account of the Chinese people's perspective and reaction to past and present.

In her last story, an older Chinese gentleman visiting his daughter in America says to a friend,

> This collection of 10 short, fictional stories examines and explores Chinese cultural phenomena such as eunuchs, the one-child policy, corruption, arranged marriages, the rise of religious fervor, and the stigma of single women, and then juxtaposes the Western-embracing youth with their traditional elders."

"'That we get to meet and talk to each other—it must have taken a long time of good prayers to get us here'."

Although I never sat down with Yiyun Li or any of the book's fictional characters, reading *A Thousand Years of Good Prayers* gave me a better understanding—even if only a fictional one—of my neighbors across the globe.

Source: Jennifer Moeller, "A Glimpse into China's Heart," in *Christian Science Monitor*, October 11, 2005, p. 16.

Sources

Ahmed, Fatema, Review of *A Thousand Years of Good Prayers*, in *New York Times Book Review*, October 23, 2005, p. 17.

Anderson, Mary M., *Hidden Power: The Palace Eunuchs of Imperial China*, Prometheus, 1990, pp. 15–18, 307–11.

Faber, Michel, Review of *A Thousand Years of Good Prayers*, in *Guardian* (London), January 7, 2006, p. 16.

Medvedev, Roy A., *Let History Judge: The Origins and Consequences of Stalinism*, edited by David Joravsky and Georges Haupt, translated by Colleen Taylor, Alfred A. Knopf, 1972, p. 362.

Orwell, George, *Nineteen Eighty-Four*, Harcourt, Brace, 1949, pp. 213, 236.

Review of *A Thousand Years of Good Prayers*, in *Publishers Weekly*, Vol. 252, No. 26, June 27, 2005, pp. 39–40.

Spence, Jonathan, *The Gate of Heavenly Peace: The Chinese and Their Revolutions, 1895–1980*, Viking, 1981, pp. 343, 346, 350.

———, *Mao Zedong*, Viking, 1999, pp. 163–64.

Thompson, Bob, "Will Her Words Fail Her? Immigration Officials Snub Literary Sensation Yiyun Li despite Her Peers' Praise," in *Washington Post*, December 21, 2005, p. C01.

Tuhus-Dubrow, Rebecca, "How Soon Is Mao? Li's Fiction Debut Is China by Way of Iowa," in *Village Voice*, October 31, 2005.

Welch, Rodney, "Cultural Revolutions: A Debut Collection of Stories Explores the Complexities of Life in Modern China," in *Washington Post*, November 27, 2005, p. BW07.

Yiyun Li, "Immortality," in *A Thousand Years of Good Prayers*, Random House, 2005, pp. 44–67.

Further Reading

Casserly, Jack, *The Triumph at Tiananmen Square*, ASJA Press, 2005.
> This is a vivid, eyewitness account by a veteran American news reporter of the Tiananmen Square massacre in 1989. Casserly also provides an account of the transformation of China in the 1980s and 1990s into a nation that manages to combine communism with free-market economics.

Li Zhisui, *The Private Life of Chairman Mao: The Memoirs of Mao's Personal Physician*, translated by Professor Tai Hung-chao, with the editorial assistance of Anne F. Thurston, Random House, 1994.
> This book is referred to in "Immortality." Li was Mao's physician for thirty years, and in this book he describes Mao's private life, including his medical conditions, such as his dependence on barbiturates, his sexual contacts with young women even when he was an old man, and many other revelations. The memoir makes an intimate but entirely unflattering portrait of a man whom Li regards as a tyrant with a callous disregard for human life.

Terrill, Ross, *Mao: A Biography*, Harper & Row, 1980.
> This very readable biography does justice to Mao's status as one of the most powerful leaders of the twentieth century. Terrill also discusses Mao's personal and political failings but does not demonize him in the way Li Zhisui does.

Yiyun Li, "What Has That to Do with Me?" in *Gettysburg Review*, Vol. 16, No. 2, Summer 2003, http://www.gettysburg.edu/academics/gettysburg_review/yli.htm (accessed May 3, 2006).
> Using the point of view of a five-year-old girl in day care, Li tells the story of a nineteen-year-old girl who expressed doubts about Mao Zedong during the Cultural Revolution. The girl was arrested and imprisoned for ten years before being executed in 1978. Li links the story to her own experience growing up in Beijing.

Last Courtesies

Ella Leffland

1976

Ella Leffland's short story "Last Courtesies" is surprisingly violent. But the violence is, at least at the beginning, more suggested than explicit. In the foreground, the protagonist Lillian suppresses violent urges, while she is described as "too polite." Throughout most of this story, Lillian is filled with fear and remorse, but she is determined to keep her emotions in check. She does go out of her way to not return rudeness expressed toward her. There are, however, moments when doing so is impossible, just as there are moments when the background violence of this story leaks through. This story is a psychological study of eccentrics. The violence erupts in ever mounting stages as the eccentricities of the characters collide, culminating in the brutality at the end.

"Last Courtesies" was first published in 1976 in *Harper's Magazine*. It was then chosen for the O. Henry Award for best short story the following year. Four years later, the story was selected as the title piece for Leffland's collection *Last Courtesies*. In a *New York Times* review of this collection, John Romano referred to Leffland as one of the "poets of alienation" but distinguished her from others "in being essentially moral as well as psychological." Romano also praised Leffland for the sympathy that she arouses for her characters without judging them.

Author Biography

Ella Leffland was born on November 25, 1931, in Martinez, California. She attended San Jose State

College, where she earned a bachelor's degree in 1953. Leffland has stated that she began writing around the age of ten, but she was twenty-eight before she had her first short story published. After that, she wrote five novels and a collection of short stories.

Leffland worked as a city hall reporter for a few years upon obtaining her college degree. Then for three years she was a copyeditor for San Francisco's *Sun Reporter*. She also worked variously as a typist, a sales clerk, a researcher, and as a kitchen helper on a Norwegian tramp steamer. While holding these jobs, she returned to writing repeatedly.

Leffland's writing is psychological in emphasis. She probes her characters' psyches, pushing them to reveal how their minds work. Her first novel, *Mrs. Munck* (1970), relates the story of a woman struggling for her independence. This story was later produced as a made-for-television movie of the same title. Diane Ladd directed the play and starred in its leading role. Leffland's *Love out of Season* was published next in 1974. Then came *Rumors of Peace* (1979), a coming-of-age story. The protagonist is a young girl living in San Francisco during World War II. In 1980, Leffland put together her collection of short stories, *Last Courtesies*.

Leffland has stated that she likes to travel, and in 1979, she went to Germany to conduct research for a new book, a study of Hermann Goering (1893–1947), who was the highest ranking military officer in the Third Reich and Adolf Hitler's designated successor. In preparation for writing her 1990 book *The Knight, Death, and the Devil*, Leffland met with many people who had known Goering.

Leffland has spent most of her life in California, and as of 2005 she lived in San Francisco.

Plot Summary

Ella Leffland's *Last Courtesies* begins with a comment about the protagonist Lillian. Vladimir, the Russian piano tuner, tells her she is "too polite." Lillian disagrees. Lillian does not push people in the bus line, but she does "fire off censorious glares." Thus, according to Lillian, she is far from being too polite. She is merely "civilized."

Only four months have passed since her aunt Bedelia's death, and Lillian misses her very much. She thinks of her aunt as an elegant woman, who can engage in intellectual discussions about Bach, Russian novelists, her well-kept garden, and topics of nature. Her aunt was also a pianist, and that was how their acquaintance with Vladimir came about. Wearing overalls that make him look like a mechanic, Vladimir has tuned their Steinway grand piano. He used obscenities whenever Bedelia was not present. He spoke his mind and was known to insult his clients for not taking better care of their pianos. Rumor has it that he poured buckets of urine on dog-walkers who allowed their pets to defecate underneath his windows, and it is said that he had several times been institutionalized. But Aunt Bedelia enjoyed him.

One night, Lillian told her aunt that "Vladimir was brilliant but unsound." Bedelia asked how her niece came to this conclusion. But every detail that Lillian offered, Bedelia turned around to Vladimir's advantage. That was Bedelia's manner, to see the best in people. Lillian felt inadequate, as though she lived in Bedelia's shadow. She felt left out of the friendship between Bedelia and Vladimir, but no matter how long Lillian lives (her aunt has died at age ninety-one), Lillian suspects she will never gain the grace her aunt possessed. Bedelia was the "last survivor of a fair, legendary breed."

Before she died, Aunt Bedelia invited Vladimir over for dinner. She prepared the meal herself, picked flowers from the garden for a centerpiece, and donned jewelry that she usually wore only for special holidays. None of this was wasted on Vladimir. He noted and admired everything. Bedelia and Vladimir spent the evening talking about lofty subjects, covering their travels to exotic places and the finer points of music theory as it related to classical masters. Then Vladimir "flung himself into Bach" on the grand piano. With Bedelia, Vladimir was a cosmopolitan gentleman. But with Lillian alone, he was vulgar, even aggressive.

Although Lillian doubted it, Bedelia thought that Vladimir might be enamored of Lillian. After Bedelia's death, Vladimir spends a lot of time at the apartment. Lillian consoles him, and Vladimir, in turn, tries to counsel Lillian regarding her future. Vladimir tells Lillian that if the butcher gives her a bad cut of meat, she should "give them the finger." He also tells her she should get married, not out of desire but rather for protection.

Lillian swears she does not need protection, that she can take care of herself. She uses the example of how she has complained about her new upstairs neighbor. There is a lot of noise all times of the day and night coming from that apartment—everything from music, laughter, and loud shrieks, to squeaky bedsprings in the night. On the front steps one day Lillian happens to bump into the young woman, Jody, and manages to politely request that she turn down her music after 10:00 p.m. It is a rule, Lillian informs her. The girl promises to comply, but she does not really alter her lifestyle. When Vladimir comes to visit, Lillian tells him about her annoyance with Jody. Vladimir begins to curse at the girl upstairs, but Lillian asks him to stop. He is acting too judgmentally, she informs him. His tactics are too brash; Bedelia would never have encouraged him to act in this way, Lillian reminds him. But Vladimir says that he is only doing what everyone does. He suggests that Lillian thinks he is demented. He tells her: "I am one of the many! I am in the swim!" In other words, it is Lillian who is out of sync. He then relates a news story about a woman found murdered and her body cut to bits in an alley not far away, reminding Lillian of dangers that face a woman who lives alone.

Lillian worries about Vladimir. She asks a co-worker who knows of him what she thinks. The co-worker believes that Vladimir is on the verge of being committed again. At home, Lillian is frightened, and she misses the comfort of her aunt's presence. Later Jody phones Lillian to ask her to go upstairs to see if the gas stove is turned off. Lillian sees a mess in Jody's apartment, but the stove burners are off. Lillian snoops a little through Jody's apartment, noticing notes left for "Jamie" and is surprised to find books written by "Dostoevsky, Dickens, Balzac, Melville." Lillian thinks to herself how odd it is "that the girl had this taste in literature, yet could not spell the simplest word and had never heard of a comma." As Lillian is about to leave, she is caught off guard by the unexpected appearance of the young man, Jamie. He invites Lillian to have a cup of coffee. She refuses. He tries to start a conversation, during which Lillian watches him spear a cockroach and then squash another one with a butter knife.

Lillian gradually loses her civility. She almost walks off her job; on the way home from work, she is tempted to smack an old man for stepping on her foot and to smile at the news of a motorist being killed by a sniper. She takes a hot bath, hoping it will restore her good nature. But she continues to have trouble sleeping because of the noise from Jody's apartment and is newly troubled when another woman in the neighborhood is gruesomely murdered. Lillian begins taking sleeping pills.

Lillian sometimes watches Jody and Jamie, when they are in the garden, sunning themselves. Sometimes she sees Jamie by himself. She thinks Jamie is in love with Jody and depressed because Jody often leaves him alone.

Vladimir comes over one night and again curses the noisy neighbor; he tells Lillian that he has found her a prospective husband. He says Jody is a prostitute, which Lillian does not believe. She thinks Vladimir is crazy. She tells Vladimir, "You exaggerate everything, I'm afraid." Vladimir, in turn, believes that Lillian is blind. He is worried for her. But Lillian responds: "To live each moment as if you were in danger—is demeaning." Vladimir tries to shake Lillian out of what he thinks is blind denial. But in doing so, he frightens her. She screams at him, and he eventually leaves. Lillian locks the door behind him. She goes to the hallway to phone for help, the police, her doctor, a friend, anyone. She then hears a knock on the door. The knocking stops, and Lillian stumbles over Vladimir's jacket that is lying on the floor. She hears him try to start his car. She feels his wallet in the pocket of his jacket. Then she hears more knocking on her door. She knows that without his wallet he does not have money to call for help, but she cannot manage enough courage to open the door. Then she thinks about the Vladimir that her aunt knew, the gentleman. She thinks about how Vladimir sits in his car outside her apartment, keeping an eye on her. She wonders how he will get home. Then the knocking stops, and she goes to the front window to see him walking away.

She stands there stunned for a long time when she finally realizes that someone is again knocking on the door. She turns on the porch light and unlocks the door. It is Jamie. She begins to panic when she notices Jamie's unusual stare, but she talks herself out of it, believing that her nerves are just jangled. And in that moment of hesitation, Jamie lunges at her. She feels a "painless blow, followed by dullness, a stillness deep inside her." And as colors first fill the room and then slowly fade, Jamie wrenches the knife from Lillian's body.

Characters

Aunt Bedelia

Bedelia, aunt of the protagonist Lillian, has already died when the story begins, but there are flashback scenes in which the narrator describes the elderly woman with whom she lived. Intelligent, gracious, and refined in an old-fashioned way, Bedelia is well educated in the arts and well traveled. She brings out the best in people, such as the piano tuner Vladimir, whom she befriends. Whereas Lillian believes that Vladimir is crass and belligerent, Bedelia emphasizes his knowledge and interests. When Vladimir is with Bedelia, he strives to be a gentleman, and he and Bedelia enjoy each other. Bedelia is a role model for Lillian. However, Lillian does not have the confidence to aspire to her aunt's social grace and civility. After Bedelia's death at age ninety-one, Lillian's life slowly disintegrates.

Jamie

The psychopath Jamie hangs around Jody's apartment and is thought to be her boyfriend. Lillian first meets Jamie when she goes to Jody's apartment to make sure Jody's stove is turned off. He startles Lillian, coming upon her quietly without announcing himself. He invites her to sit down and talk to him, but Lillian is reluctant. While she stands there, however, she watches Jamie use a butter knife to kill two cockroaches. Jamie is a morose figure, often seen standing in the rain. He is, in fact, the so-called "rain man," who has murdered two women in Lillian's neighborhood and mutilated their bodies.

Jody

Jody lives in the apartment over Lillian's. She is young, outgoing, and unaware of how much she disturbs Lillian with all her noise. Jody's apartment is a mess, which Lillian notes when she enters it to check on the stove. But in the midst of the mess, Lillian sees books that suggest Jody is well educated. Jody, who has one or more sexual partners visit her at night, explores yoga and classical literature. Jody also appears to have a relationship with Jamie, who hangs around her apartment even when she is not there.

Lillian

Lillian, the protagonist, is a plain middle-aged woman, now widowed. However, she feels like a spinster. Vladimir tells her she is too polite, an attribute that she denies. She avoids confrontation, a habit that she describes as being civilized. She misses Aunt Bedelia but denies that her aunt protected her. Vladimir suggests that Lillian get married in order to have in a new husband the protection that Bedelia once provided. Lillian suspects that Vladimir is attracted to her and is often frightened by him. She is actually frightened by a lot of things and has trouble sleeping because of her fear as well as the noise from her upstairs neighbor Jody. Lillian has a certain innocence or naivety. Her instincts, possibly dulled by her lack of self-confidence, turn her in the wrong directions. She stores up her anger, directing it toward unsuspecting people, such as her wanting to slap a stranger in a bus line for stepping on her toes, when in fact she is angry at Jody for all the noise she makes.

Rain Man

See *Jamie*

Vladimir

Vladimir, a White Russian who fled war-torn Prague with his parents in 1917 and eventually immigrated to the United States, is educated in the classics and plays the piano. He works as a piano tuner, and that is how he meets Bedelia. She owns a piano and shares her knowledge with him whenever he appears in her apartment. Vladimir is probably the most outwardly peculiar of the eccentric characters that fill this short story. He is physically unkempt, can be vulgar in his actions and speech, and has himself committed to a mental institution from time to time. But at the level of his heart, he is all love. He is fascinated with Aunt Bedelia because of her charm and cultivation and because she connects with him in positive ways. When she dies, he continues to go to the apartment to mourn her and on her behalf to watch out for her niece. Vladimir suggests that Lillian get married after Aunt Bedelia dies, but he takes himself out of the running, stating that he does not like women. At one point, Vladimir even suggests that he has found a man for Lillian to marry, but nothing comes of this.

Vladimir spends the latter part of this story worrying about Lillian. It is not clear if he watches over her for her own sake or out of respect for his feelings for Aunt Bedelia. But at night, he sits in his car and watches Lillian's apartment. He wants to protect her from the murderer who lurks in the neighborhood. However, when he tries to warn Lillian of the danger, he becomes so irrational that Lillian fears Vladimir more than she fears the unknown murderer. Vladimir's warnings and his attempts to save Lillian are in vain, and in his last appearance in the story, he knocks on the door, which Lillian refuses to answer.

Themes

Alienation

In one way or another, all of the characters in Leffland's short story "Last Courtesies" live isolated lives. The least alienated may be Jody, even

Topics For Further Study

- Choose a neighborhood in San Francisco (such as Haight-Ashbury, Mission District, North Beach, Pacific Heights, or even the sister-city Oakland) and research what the chosen district was like in the 1970s and how it has since changed. Have there been major renovations? Have buildings been added? How has the population changed? How do the 1970 prices of homes in this area compare to prices in early 2005?

- Create a diary, writing it as if you were the protagonist Lillian. Have the diary begin with the death of Lillian's aunt and proceed through about six months to the night just before Lillian's murder. What are her private reactions to her aunt's passing? What are her thoughts about Vladimir? How does she express her anger and frustration about Jody? And what does she think about Jamie?

- Choose a piece of music by one of the composers mentioned in this short story (Bach, Wagner, Scarlatti, etc.). Collect information about the chosen piece, noting when it was composed, what the life circumstances of the composer were at the time the piece was written, how the music was received by critics and audiences, and any theoretical discussion of it that you find meaningful. Next present the music to your class, providing as much interesting background information as you can find to help captivate your audience. The more colorful anecdotes you provide, the better.

- Read Ken Kesey's *One Flew over the Cuckoo's Nest* (1973). How does the protagonist Randle Patrick McMurphy compare to Vladimir in Leffland's "Last Courtesies?" Do McMurphy and Vladimir have similar personality traits? Do they socialize in similar or different ways? What are their views of women? How do they react to things they do not like? Compare their styles of dress and behavior. Compare their levels of intelligence. How does each character help the author convey the story's main point?

---

though she is described as having many male suitors come to her apartment each night (and Vladimir calls her as a prostitute). On one level, Jody appears to be the most social, but her emotions, in order to handle her way of life, must be guarded. She thus isolates herself from those feelings. If she is indeed a prostitute, then Jody also removes herself from acceptable social practices and a committed relationship. If Lillian is the most socially aware of the characters, then Jody's lack of concern for Lillian's comfort, demonstrated by playing loud music at night, can be seen as symbolic of how alienated she feels. Jody separates herself from Lillian's humanity, not thinking of Lillian as a person who needs sleep. Jody is the only person who really matters and in this sense she does not connect with others.

Jamie is a rather morose figure, often seen alone, waiting for Jody to reappear. He stands outside her apartment, often in the rain, just staring.

The secret revealed at the ending is that Jamie is a serial killer. Intensely alienated, Jamie is in fact a sociopath, capable of gruesome acts.

Vladimir experiences an immigrant's alienation, trying to live in a foreign culture, trying to communicate in a second language. He acts out his frustration and anger is socially unacceptable ways, but he is in truth a cultivated individual who can connect to others through shared appreciation of the arts. Aunt Bedelia sees the best in Vladimir, and this view of him encourages him to communicate. Others, however, are put off by his eccentricities; therefore, Vladimir withdraws from them.

Lillian assumes she has the best social skills of all the characters. But she may be the most isolated. She knows how to act as if she is part of the social group, but she has little or no connections with others. She lives alone, and her attempts at socializing fail. She does not know how to carry on a conversation. She is unable to assert herself with Jody. She feels roughly treated by others and harbors hostility. Lingering grief over her aunt's death and the loss of the social insulation Bedelia provided, Lillian feels exposed and powerless.

Eccentricities

Eccentricities abound in this short story. Of all the characters, Vladimir is the most explicitly eccentric. He does not care about his odd clothes, his shocking language, what social conventions he breaks. Vladimir does what he wants. He is not ignorant of common practices but rather chooses to ignore them. Aunt Bedelia is eccentric in another way. She is a woman of times-gone-by. Her formal education sets her apart from most people. She is excessively particular and refined. Lillian, on the other hand, is eccentric in a more monotonous way. She is plain, soft-spoken, and submissive. Her eccentricities are those of boredom gone to an extreme. She does very little for herself in her dress, her attitude, her respect for herself. Her routine is based on sameness and dullness. But underneath this mask is a fanatic, who smiles, sometimes, at the pain of others. Eccentricities in these characters make them appear unique and, in many ways, fascinating because they are not one-dimensional or stereotypical figures.

Violence

From the actions of Jamie, squashing cockroaches, to the thread of murders that runs through this story, violence is an underlying current. Violence is suggested, as in news stories that are mentioned and in some of Lillian's thoughts when she grows tired of being so passive. Violence is present in the anecdotes told about Vladimir, who takes out his anger on strangers. Actual violence explodes in several scenes, for instance when Vladimir and Lillian try to make sense of one another toward the end of the story and in their anger slap one another. Then there is the final act of violence when Jamie kills Lillian. Although this strain of violence runs through the story, however, very little of it is detailed. Thus the violence is felt under the surface rather than being fully displayed. Readers sense it rather than witness it.

Fear

Although Vladimir is fearful for Lillian, it is Lillian herself who manifests the most fear in this story. She claims she is not too shy, but she is definitely easily intimidated. She tries to confront Jody in an attempt to get her upstairs neighbor to turn down her music, but the confrontation brings little result.

Lillian leaves it like that. Her fear in this instance is based on her understanding of social grace. She does not want to "make a scene." When Vladimir comes over for a visit and hears all the racquet, he becomes inflamed. But Lillian tries to quiet him. She does not want him to confront her neighbor. Lillian would rather suffer through the noise.

Lillian is also afraid of Vladimir. She has heard rumors of his having been institutionalized and fears his irrationality. Lillian is a straightforward kind of woman, hoping always to present herself in a simple and uncomplicated way. Vladimir is just the opposite. He acts out his emotions immediately without giving them much reflection. In contrast, Lillian, who is afraid of her own emotions, holds her feelings in, controlling every one of her actions no matter how she feels. In the end, her fear blinds her. Instead of trusting Vladimir who is trying to protect her, she is afraid of him and does not allow him back into her house. Instead, she opens the door to Jamie, the only character in this story she should have feared.

Style

Suspense

Suspense in this short story is created out of fear of others. Vladimir is so eccentric he is hard to understand. His emotions are unstable and some of his actions are unsociable. He is as likely to explode as he is to read poetry or play a piano composition by Bach. So when the story focuses on the unpredictable Vladimir, readers feel a sense of the unknown, which contributes to the suspense.

The initially peripheral neighborhood murders also cause suspense. Two women are killed and their bodies mutilated. The reader wonders if Jody or Lillian will be next. The reader wonders who is the murderer. As the suspense builds, readers may suspect Vladimir is the criminal. He admits not liking women, and he is the most obviously irrational person in the story. So his visiting Lillian engenders concern for her safety. When Lillian opens the door, the brief relief that it is not Vladimir standing there is followed by the discovery that Jamie is the "rain man." He shoves Lillian to the floor, and the third murder occurs.

Foreshadowing

Foreshadowing consists of details that hint at the outcome; other hints about the outcome can deliberately mislead a reader in order to extend the suspense. Vladimir warns Lillian about taking precautions to protect herself. But the unpredictable and explosive Vladimir appears not to be trusted; his anger is threatening. While Vladimir commands reader attention, however, Leffland points to the real murderer. That occurs in the scene in which Jamie uses a knife to spear and then squash two cockroaches. Lillian is disgusted by this act, but she does not consider its potential meaning, and at the last moment when she possibly could save her life, she opens the door to Jamie.

Anti-hero

The anti-hero is a main character who has traits quite opposite to a conventional hero. The anti-hero is inept, clumsy, perhaps dishonest. He fails to solve the problem, is unable to master the situation. Though Vladimir is not the protagonist, he has some traits of the anti-hero. Vladimir tries to save Lillian (which is heroic in its intention) but he fails to do so. His short stature, his dress, demeanor, actions, all are contrary to what a stereotypical hero is. He is sloppy, crass, worrisome, and ineffectual. He tries to help Lillian, but he just makes her circumstances worse. He yells at Jody but is ignored. He tells Lillian all the wrong things: she is too shy; she is not a beauty; she looks like a prostitute when she puts on makeup. When she fails to comprehend him, he slaps her. He sits in his car, watching over Lillian with devotion. But on the night when he should have been there, he leaves just as the perpetrator arrives.

Historical Context

1970s in the United States

During the 1970s, a new generation of young adults examined, criticized, and in some cases totally discarded the former generation's ways. Established concepts about friendship, sexuality, marriage, race relations and ethnicity, war, and women's rights were challenged and transformed. The ongoing Vietnam War (1959–1975), which was ultimately lost by the United States, caused disillusionment and anger among men who were eligible for the draft. It was a time of experimentation and protest, which were expressed in literature, lifestyles, and in political resistance. There were divisions between the younger generation and the older one, as well as between the more radical and more conservative members of the youth movements. Because of this upheaval, young

people particularly felt a new alienation from their government and their political leaders. Those who wanted change opposed those who wanted no change. Authority was questioned, laws challenged or ignored.

The culture shifted in various ways during the 1970s. On an environmental level, the 1970s saw the removal of lead from gasoline because of the recently recognized effects of lead poisoning in children. The first Earth Day was held, calling attention to environmental pollution. President Nixon signed the first Clean Air Act, and the dangers of second-hand smoke were revealed. The Environmental Protection Agency was created. On the social level, streaking (running naked at a popular event or in a public space) became a fad and so did drinking bottled water. Disco music was in and Elvis Presley died. The Beatles produced their last album as a group, and Janis Joplin and Jimi Hendrix died from drug overdoses. The first International network for the general public was created, and Sony's Walkman came on the market.

Public cynicism regarding elected officials grew as people learned of the Watergate break-ins. President Nixon subsequently resigned under threat of impeachment. Four students were shot at Kent State University as National Guard troops tried to quell a student demonstration against the Vietnam War. Then governor of Alabama, George Wallace led a demonstration against racial integration of his state's schools. The Chicago 7, a group of protest organizers who met in Chicago during the Democratic National Convention, were found innocent of inciting riots. President Carter pardoned all draft dodgers, who had left the country to avoid serving in the military. The Supreme Court reinstated the death penalty, and in *Roe v. Wade* made abortion legal.

White Russians

The Russian Civil War (1918–1921) involved various militant groups, including the Bolsheviks (the Marxists under Lenin), the Green Army (the anarchists), the Red Army (communists), and the White Army, which opposed the other three. The White Army was a loose, unorganized group of Russians who supported the czar. Some of those associated with the White Army (also called White Russians) leaned toward democracy and were backed by European nations as well as Japan and the United States. People from Ukraine, Siberia, and Crimea provided additional troops and supplies for the Whites, but the army was never able to unify and did not pose sufficient force to make much difference in Russia. Many White Russians fled the

Compare
&
Contrast

- **1970s:** Russia is part of the Soviet Union, which invades Afghanistan.

  Today: After the breakup of the Soviet Union, Russia becomes an independent country, which watches as the United States invades Afghanistan.

- **1970s:** San Francisco Opera begins its presentation of annual free concerts in Golden Gate Park. These concerts feature artists from the Opera's season-opening weekend. The event draws some 20,000 listeners.

  Today: The San Francisco Opera opens its eighty-third summer season with Russian composer Pyotr Ilyich Tchaikovsky's *Queen of Spades*, a suspenseful, psychological thriller.

- **1970s:** People in the United States are divided by the Vietnam War. More than 58,000 U.S. soldiers have been killed. Protestors march in the streets by the thousands.

Today: The country is divided over the economy, politics, and the U.S. invasion of Iraq. As of late 2006, nearly three thousand U.S. soldiers have been killed in Iraq and tens of thousands of Iraqis have been killed. Casualties have numbered in the tens of thousands on both sides. Protestors demonstrate worldwide against the war, but the number of protestors in the United States are fewer than those in Europe who protest the war.

- **1970s:** The Haight-Ashbury section of San Francisco is the West Coast headquarters of the counter-culture movement, a place where hippies don flowers in their hair and musicians such as the Grateful Dead play.

  Today: Haight-Ashbury (also called the Upper Haight) is a tourist attraction, with vintage clothes stores, alternative music stores, used book stalls, and inexpensive places to eat.

country, regrouping in places such as Paris, Berlin, and Shanghai. Networks among these groups developed and were maintained until World War II. After that, many so-called White Russians immigrated to the United States.

Critical Overview

"Last Courtesies" won the O. Henry Award in 1977, shortly after the short story's first appearance in print, in a 1976 *Harper's Magazine*. When the collection *Last Courtesies* was published in 1980, John Romano, for the *New York Times*, described the collection as a series of "sad tales" which contain characters who are "profoundly alone," are suffering, and "cannot make [themselves] understood." However, Romano modified his statement by asserting that even though Leffland's characters suffer these problems, readers are not, at first, fully aware of the characters' anguish because, according to Romano,

"the narrator is always there with them." Romano further explained that the reader is not completely taken into the characters' pain because Leffland's "authorial presence is distinctly caring," and her "imagination is always bound up with sympathy."

In a 2003 article, written for the *Kenyon Review*, Henry Alley completes a comprehensive overview of the various winners of the O. Henry Award, comparing them to the times in which they were written. In reference to Leffland's short story, Alley states that "Last Courtesies" "belongs distinctly to the seventies, because the complex protagonist Lillian cannot locate, exactly, where the crack in the world is." Leffland's story reflects the fact that the decade was one of cultural revolution, a time of fast changes and discordances.

In the early 2000s, the collection has not received much critical attention. But Leffland's writing in general has. She was described as a "really good" novelist, for instance, in Carolyn See's *Washington Post* review of another Leffland

A piano is a prominent feature in Ella Leffland's "Last Courtesies" Francoise Gervais/Corbis

work. Also, Sybil S. Steinberg, writing for *Publishers Weekly*, asserted that Leffland's writings demonstrated the "breadth and seriousness" of the author's imagination. Finally, critic Donna Seaman, writing for *Booklist*, commenting on Leffland's *Breath and Shadows*, found that Leffland "writes with a grandeur and an omnipotence reminiscent of nineteenth-century fiction." Seaman also found that this particular book was a "wise and poetic novel as enchanting and resonant as a fairy tale."

Criticism

Joyce Hart

Hart is the author of several books. In the following essay, Hart looks at the relationship between the protagonist Lillian and the piano tuner Vladimir in Leffland's short story.

In the short story "Last Courtesies," author Ella Leffland has created characters that stand diametrically opposed to one another. Sharp differences are most exaggerated in the contrast between the protagonist Lillian and the piano tuner Vladimir. Only the relationship between Lillian and

Vladimir spans the entire story. As a matter of fact, the continual back-and-forth dialogues, confrontations, and contradictions between them hold this story together, create the tension, and make "Last Courtesies" what many reviewers refer to as a psychological study.

Pointing out the significance of these two characters and their contrary relationship, Leffland begins her story with one of the couple's many disagreements. Vladimir sums up Lillian's personality and the reason why she has so many difficulties. "Lillian, you're too polite," he says. Lillian immediately contradicts him. But even more telling than this is the way, right from the beginning, that Leffland presents this information. She gives Vladimir's comment as a direct quotation, but for Lillian's response, Leffland has the narrator describe the protagonist's thoughts. Lillian, in other words, keeps them to herself. She does not agree with Vladimir but for some common courtesy, some social restraint that Lillian has imposed upon herself, she does not believe it is correct to express to Vladimir how she feels. Or maybe she is just not confident in her own assessment of herself. Whatever the reason, Vladimir displays an aspect of his personality, saying what is on his mind no matter how unacceptable it may be, and Lillian supresses hers, keeping her feelings concealed.

Social courtesies are important to Lillian. She believes, according to the narrator, that "the world owed itself," in the least, human courtesies. Without these social amenities, Lillian thinks, the world would collapse. In her mind, she obeys what she believes are proper social graces. Courtesies come before all else.

Not so for Vladimir. This man has a reputation for doing the socially unacceptable. He uses foul language; curses piano owners who do not take care of their musical instruments; and it is said that he even once knocked down a relative in the course of a discussion about the German composer Richard Wagner (an anti-Semite whose music was a favorite among the Nazis). Vladimir also scares off mothers and their young children, and, at his worst, is reported to have thrown buckets of urine on dog owners who make the mistake of stopping under Vladimir's windows to allow their pets to relieve themselves. But according to others the worst of all Vladimir's social disgraces is the fact that he has been "institutionalized several times." Even though he admits himself to mental facilities voluntarily, this part of his past terrifies Lillian. She wants to fit in, and to her, Vladimir's giving himself over to

> "Lillian imagines that
> there is some universal
> audience that is viewing her
> everyday performance. This
> audience is extremely
> judgmental, and if she does
> not pass their tests, she
> will be disgraced."

medication, a strictly controlled environment, and subsequent loss of freedom proves that he knows he does not fit in and that he may cause harm to himself or to others. Lillian could be correct in feeling this way. But another possible reason that Vladimir turns himself in is that he becomes, at certain times, so fed up with society he needs a sabbatical from it.

Ironically, Vladimir believes that he fits quite well in society, at least most of the time. He thinks that he is just like most people—aggressive, vile, loud, and outspoken. Vladimir tells Lillian that it is she who is really out of step, despite the fact that she strives every day to fit in. Of course, Lillian disagrees with this point, too.

About midway through the story, Vladimir tells Lillian that she is too soft. He describes himself in contrast as "an armored tank." This is his way of taking care of himself in an uncaring, deceitful society that will take advantage of those who are weak. Lillian's softness makes her vulnerable, Vladimir believes, so he advises her to get married. "I have no desire to marry," Lillian tells him. But Vladimir scoffs at her reply. This world is not for desires, he informs her, and she had better stop living through her heart and start living through her head. "Think of your scalp!" he warns her. But Lillian really does not live through her heart. If she did, she might be better off than she is. Lillian lives neither through her heart nor her head. She lives through her imagination. Lillian imagines that there is some universal audience that is viewing her everyday performance. This audience is extremely judgmental, and if she does not pass their tests, she will be

disgraced. She cannot always put her finger on who this audience is or what their rules are, but she has some vague ideas. When she transgresses (such as the time she wants to slap a stranger in the bus for stepping on her foot), she is remorseful.

Vladimir is right: Lillian is too soft. No matter how much she tries to deny this, her actions confirm Vladimir's observations. She plays the victim role quite well. For instance, she allows Jody, her upstairs neighbor, to nearly drive her crazy with loud noises both day and night. Yes, Lillian does complain to Jody but to no avail. Lillian might know how to ask for changes in her neighbor's behavior, but she does not know how to insist. She does not know how to do more than complain, how to take a problem and stick with it until she comes up with a solution. Lillian's idea of solving a problem is to wish it away and then hide or suffer while it persists. When Vladimir steps in, trying to help, Lillian is anything but thankful. Vladimir attempts to fill the gaps in Lillian's personality. He is loud and demanding. But this embarrasses Lillian. She is humiliated by his social transgressions. If Lillian had allowed Vladimir full rein, if she had stepped back or even encouraged him, she might have finally enjoyed a good night's sleep without resorting to sleeping pills. But instead, she now has Vladimir to worry about.

There is another area in which these two characters contrast. That is in their instincts. Lillian's instincts are as off-the-mark as Vladimir's are on. She refuses to judge Jody and Jody's companion Jamie in an unfavorable light. "They're people, Vladimir," Lillian tells him. "Human beings like ourselves." Of course, Vladimir has fun with that statement. He says Jody and Jamie are people from the sewers: "The sewers are vomiting them up by the thousands to mix with us." They are "weak, no vision, no guts." Then Vladimir states that Jody and Jamie represent "the madness of our times." Intriguingly Vladimir describes Jody and Jamie, in part, the same way he does Lillian—weak and no guts. Moreover, he uses the term madness, one that others use to describe him.

So is there any reasonableness in either Lillian or Vladimir? Is it found in Lillian who suppresses all her emotions, denying herself the pleasure of expression and driving her into the role of victim? Or is it found in Vladimir, who makes a lot of noise but pushes people away from him because of it? These characters both appear to be searching for something. Lillian is caught between wanting Vladimir, for example, and being reviled by him.

What Do I Read Next?

- Before publishing the collection of short stories *Last Courtesies* (1980), Leffland wrote *Rumors of Peace* (1979), a coming-of-age novel for which Leffland is well known. Leffland tells the story of Susie, a teenaged girl living in San Francisco during World War II who copes with her own personal maturation and the terror of war. The protagonist is a bright person, whom her teachers have labeled a troublemaker.

- *Shiloh and Other Stories* (1982) was written by Bobbie Ann Mason, a contemporary of Leffland and a well-known American short story writer. This respected collection of short stories won the PEN-Hemingway Award. In this collection, Mason creates characters placed in a familiar setting for her—western Kentucky, where she grew up. The characters face challenges as their community is modernized.

- For an overview of short story authors and their work, a good place to start is *The Best American Short Stories of the Century* (2000), edited by John Updike. The collection includes stories by Willa Cather, Katherine Anne Porter, Annie Proulx, Ann Beatie, and Susan Sontag, among others.

- Joyce Carol Oates edited *Telling Stories: An Anthology for Writers* (1998), which presents works of such writers as Anton Chekov, Gish Jen, Thom Jones, Stephen King, and Ovid, along with comments by Oates on matters of style and teaching literature.

She invites him for dinner not because she wants to see him (or at least not because she can admit to herself that she wants him) but because "it would be too rude" not to. And yet, at the moment that Vladimir mentions that he senses "sex boiling" around her, Lillian silently hopes that Vladimir's "hands would leap on her." And then there is Vladimir, who sincerely cares about Lillian. He sits in his car all night worrying about her and yells at her and shakes her, trying to wake her up to the potential danger that he feels is nearby. He is constantly advising her on how to act, how to dress. But then he adds: "I have always regretted . . . that you resemble the wrong side of your family." This man is definitely not a romantic. When he tries to demonstrate his emotions for her, he fiercely grabs her wrists and slaps them together in a tight grip that causes her pain, and then he slams his two open hands against her cheeks. This, of course, frightens Lillian, who absolutely—both figuratively and physically—slams the door on him.

Had Lillian and Vladimir worked out their differences, they might have enjoyed themselves as a couple. Vladimir might have saved Lillian's life, and for her part, Lillian might have made Vladimir a little more socially tame. But then if that had happened, it would have been a different story.

Source: Joyce Hart, Critical Essay on "Last Courtesies," in *Short Stories for Students*, Thomson Gale, 2007.

Bryan Aubrey

Aubrey holds a Ph.D. in English and has published many articles on contemporary literature. In this essay, Aubrey discusses characterization and narrative technique in "Last Courtesies."

"Things fall apart; the centre cannot hold; / Mere anarchy is loosed upon the world," wrote W. B. Yeats in "The Second Coming," and these lines might serve as an epigraph for Leffland's story, "Last Courtesies." The story is at once a lament for a vanishing world of civility and an intriguing character study. It is also a carefully crafted story, with well disguised ironies, that reaches a climax worthy of a suspense thriller.

Conflict between the older and the younger generations is hardly a new theme in literature or in life. The world is always changing, and change can be disturbing to those who have become set in their ways. The physical energy of the young, their

" The scene in which
the excited and almost
deranged Vladimir visits
Lillian on a dark and rainy
night is masterful, building
quickly in menace and
horror, and full of irony
that only becomes apparent
at the end."

unwillingness to accept limitations, and their natural impatience with established ways of doing things will always sit ill with those who have learned by experience the need to compromise, to accept authority, to live in a way that respects the rights of others. The young are always, in their own eyes, the center of the universe; the old are not permitted such a privilege. The new, uncouth world in which they suddenly find themselves, that mocks everything they have learned to value and respect, leaves them with few options, since time will not travel backwards, and the turning wheel of life (a notable image in the story) will not stand still. They can retreat into splendid, dignified isolation, like Aunt Bedelia; they can indulge in impotent rages, like Vladimir, or suffer largely in silence, like Lillian, but whatever they choose to do it will not affect the young, who will continue to be noisy, indulge in uninhibited sex, and generally act in ways that make their elders believe the world they loved has gone to the dogs, and they are powerless to change it.

In "Last Courtesies," it is ancient Aunt Bedelia who is least affected by the decay of the civilization around her. She has "sealed herself off in a lofty, gracious world" rooted in the past. Her serene detachment acts as a foil for Lillian's neurotic, lonely desperation. By her ability to rise above all pettiness and spite and maintain an "immense calm," Bedelia mocks the struggles of her floundering niece. Aunt Bedelia is a woman of intelligence, education, and high culture, the "last survivor of a fair, legendary breed" (as Lillian sees her). Through some miracle, attained perhaps by a

combination of strong will and a naturally optimistic temperament, Aunt Bedelia has managed to preserve her ability to experience the spontaneous joy of life despite her physical ailments and frailty. It is this quality that enables her to win and retain the devotion of the rough diamond, Vladimir. She also achieves that most blessed of all human experiences—a good death. This is also a wonderfully comic moment in the story. Aunt Bedelia dies splendidly on cue, as Beethoven's Ninth Symphony, which is playing on the phonograph, reaches its climax. There cannot be many people who have been ushered into heaven to the strains of "Freude, schöner Götterfunken" ("Joy, lovely divine spark") but Aunt Bedelia is one of them, thereon to haunt the remainder of the story as a silent, saintly reproach to the inadequacies of the other actors in this unnamed metropolitan hell that bears a distinct resemblance to New York City.

One advantage that Aunt Bedelia has is economic means. Whether it is through her own savings or inherited wealth, or because the steady, wage-earning Lillian supports her, she appears to be free of monetary pressures. She is, in a sense, free to be free. As a "sheltered soul" (Lillian's description of her) she can afford to freeze time at the point that suits her and continue to live in a world she understands and which nourishes her spirit. Poor Lillian has no such luxury. She must work to survive in a boring but nonetheless demanding job ("Italian and German required"), she must walk the dirty streets, get shoved in bus queues and deal with the sullen trades people. She cannot disengage herself from what she knows is the "world's madness— its rudeness, its litter, its murders." Lillian's dismay at what city life has become in the 1970s means that in her mind she can live anywhere but the present, which no longer has any room or place for her. In one sense, with her boxy suits and her "tight 1950s hairdo," she is already twenty years out of date. She was a youngish widow then but she refused to move on. She still regards television as a "philistine invention" and refuses to buy one. But while she has stood still, the world has not. And now her mind, recoiling from the desolation of the present, keeps taking her back even further. As she wanders through the desert of the great metropolis, images of her personal lost paradise—her marriage to George, which ended tragically when he was killed during World War II—drift into her mind, reminding her with horrible finality of the love and the pleasure that can never return. She is filled with

an intolerable longing for the past . . . for the face of her young husband . . . odd, but it never seemed to rain in her youth, the green campus filled the air with dizzying sweetness, she remembered running across the lawns for no reason but that she was twenty and the sun would shine forever.

Now she is fifty-seven and it seems that the sun does not shine at all.

After Aunt Bedelia dies, Lillian is faced with a direct assault on her privacy and her civilized values by her good-natured but inconsiderate neighbor Jody—a creature who is so different from Lillian that they may as well have come from different planets. Lillian's encounters with Jody and her waif-like boyfriend Jamie test to the full the tolerance and courtesy on which Lillian prides herself. She emerges from the test with her honor intact. In her complaints about the noise from the apartment above, she is the very model of decorum and quiet good manners. Even though she comes under increasing strain and has to take sleeping pills to get through the night, her principles of decency stand firm. The only time she is close to letting herself down comes one day when, after a sleepless night, she almost walks out on her job and almost slaps a man who inadvertently steps on her foot in the bus queue. She soon recovers her poise, with the help of that old standby for troubled souls, the hot bath.

The author uses this period of maximum stress in Lillian's life to carefully remind the reader that there is a serial killer on the prowl in the neighborhood. A second woman has been slashed to death by the man the newspapers dub "rain man," and Lillian, alarmed, even takes to shining a flashlight under her bed at night before saying the Lord's Prayer. (This is another of the delightful touches of humor that Leffland manages to introduce into what is in the end a tragic tale.)

From that point on, the narrative is perfectly controlled to produce the surprising yet inevitable climax. The scene in which the excited and almost deranged Vladimir visits Lillian on a dark and rainy night is masterful, building quickly in menace and horror, and full of irony that only becomes apparent at the end.

Vladimir presents an ugly picture; his emotions are at boiling point and he seems about to lose control. A deep-seated hatred of women seems to be forcing itself to the surface of his psyche, and the scene simmers with repressed sexuality and violence. When he points at Lillian she notices his outstretched hand and wonders, "what if it reached farther, touched her?" The ominous signs then multiply rapidly. Vladimir says he knew that the rain man would claim a second victim; he "smells blood on the wind!" (how? the reader may wonder, startled at the lurid image). Then Vladimir reveals that every night he has been sitting outside in his car, watching her apartment, which sets off alarm bells in the reader's mind, if not yet in Lillian's. After that, Vladimir appears to calm down but then he scrutinizes Lillian with his "small glittering eyes"—in context, another disturbing image. He abuses her for wearing makeup ("You've got [f——]ing gunk on! Rouge!"); she sees hatred in his eyes, and he repeats his censure of her, referring to her "stinking whore-rouge." When she denies she has any desire for a man, and he responds that he "senses sex boiling around" in her, her blush and her conviction that "his hand would leap on her" create a moment of startling eroticism combined with an undercurrent of violence.

What seems to unhinge Vladimir completely is the moment Lillian stands up for herself and repudiates his extreme views about the degenerate nature of society and the danger Lillian is in. She responds by saying that she refuses to live each moment as if she were in danger. There is a double irony here, since Lillian is in danger but does not realize it, but she is not in danger from Vladimir, in spite of the fact that at this moment he suddenly seems to present a mortal threat to her. When he grabs her wrists and goes into demented lyric ecstasy about the fountains of blood that spurt up from the helpless victims of the rain man, Lillian and the reader suddenly realize, in one moment of horror, the awful truth (or so it seems): Vladimir is the rain man. Now it all makes sense. Of course. There have been enough warning signs. Vladimir was characterized as insane all along, as Lillian acknowledges before this moment of crisis is upon her ("what was Vladimir, after all? Insane"). He has been committed, or committed himself, to mental institutions on several occasions in the past. Earlier in the story, Lillian worried about "the violence of Vladimir's emotions"; and he admitted then that he loathed women ("Full of rubbishy talk!"), which seemed innocuous enough at the time but in light of later events takes on an ominous note.

But of course, understandable though Lillian's reaction is in this moment of panic and fear, Vladimir is not the rain man. She, and the reader as well, have been well fooled. As far as murder is concerned, Vladimir is a red herring, and the author, like any good writer of a mystery or a suspense thriller, has meticulously prepared readers to take the bait, and in doing so they have forgotten not only Bedelia's judgment of Vladimir as a "man of integrity" (and Bedelia, that wise old soul, is never wrong) but also Jamie, the seemingly ineffectual, innocuous, rather pathetic figure—until he emerges from the rain and the shadows to make the fatal knife thrust.

All good stories reward a second reading, and it is on re-reading "Last Courtesies" that we are likely to notice how much we missed, or failed to evaluate correctly, regarding Jamie. His first appearance occurs when he appears seemingly out of nowhere as Lillian is about to leave Jody's apartment. Lillian suddenly sees a man standing in the doorway, and she screams. But the tension is immediately undercut by the description of him as a "boy," even quite a wholesome one, with his "butter-yellow locks flow[ing] in profusion." But there is one detail here that, in light of the story's climax, chills the blood: this boy *comes in from the rain.* Everything—his clothes, his hat, his hair—is "dripping with rain." *Enter the rain man.* Only now do we remember also that in the last scene, it is also raining, and Lillian spies Jamie from her window standing around in the rain, apparently masturbating under his coat. Then he sits still on a tree stump, for no apparent reason, getting soaked. This is so strange and unusual that Lillian remarks on it: "It was beyond her, why anyone would sit still in a downpour." Not so strange, apparently, for the rain man.

The author plants another clue in the scene mentioned above, in which Jamie invites Lillian to have coffee in Jody's apartment. Jamie is carefully presented in a way that makes him seem harmless: he is "a slight youth with neat little features" who speaks with a "childlike spontaneity" and looks lonely and forlorn. Certainly not the stuff of which serial killers are made. He even seems friendly towards Lillian. And yet—note how he deals with the cockroaches that scamper around the apartment: "Fumbling with a bread knife, he picked it up and languidly, distantly, speared a cockroach with the point. Then with the side of the knife, he slowly, methodically, squashed the other one." After he has done this, he slowly mashes the bugs to pulp. On first reading, this appears to be no more than childish—disgusting perhaps, but not alarming. But in light of what happens later, it becomes a gruesome foreshadowing, enacted in front of Lillian's own eyes, of what this seemingly unthreatening boy will eventually do to her. In similar fashion, the fact that Lillian, on the fateful day, spots Jamie in the garden wearing a black cloak seems at first no more than a self-conscious attempt at bohemianism on his part, but Lillian's characterization of him as "this little would-be Dracula" carries more menace than she realizes.

The crowning irony of Jamie's quiet lurking in this story is that Vladimir practically tells Lillian who she should be afraid of: "Probably he [Jamie] pops pills and lives off his washerwoman mother, if he hasn't slit her throat in a fit of irritation! It's the type, Lillian! Weak, no vision, no guts!" But Lillian takes no notice, and neither does the reader, caught up in Vladimir's increasingly wild rant.

Having worked in her subtle, easily overlooked clues, and with her red herring firmly in place, the author is now free to spring the surprise that in retrospect seems inevitable. She also has time to emphasize the most biting irony of all, that also sums up the theme of the story. Lillian's "courtesies," that she preserves to the last in the hope of keeping herself above the decadence that swims all around her, are what finally lead to her death: she refuses to slam the door on the intruder without a few polite words of regret, thus giving him the few seconds he needs to do his work. In this dark new world, politeness is the kiss of death.

Source: Bryan Aubrey, Critical Essay on "Last Courtesies," in *Short Stories for Students*, Thomson Gale, 2007.

Carol Ullmann

Ullmann is a freelance writer and editor. In the following essay, Ullmann examines the theme of courtesy as exhibited and understood by the characters of Leffland's short story "Last Courtesies."

Leffland's short story "Last Courtesies" explores themes of civility and rudeness through four of the major characters: Aunt Bedelia, her niece Lillian, their friend Vladimir, and a neighbor's boyfriend named Jamie. Bedelia is a consummate judge of character. Vladimir is also a good judge; however, Lillian is trying too hard to be courteous and looking for courtesy from others to pay attention to a person's true nature. To her, Vladimir is vulgar and overly impassioned whereas Jamie is a morose, vaguely rude "pretty boy." Even while she comes to trust Vladimir because of his connection to her aunt, she cannot see Jamie, with all his strangeness as well as his brief courtesies, as a serial killer. The common courteousness of an age which has passed serves now only to permit the trampling of the undiscerning individual by modern society.

Aunt Bedelia is the eldest character in Leffland's short story. In the story line she is recently deceased and therefore present only in memory and flashback. She is drawn as a person of exquisite opinion by both her niece Lillian and her good friend Vladimir: "'Your aunt was a genius at judging people.'"

Although she is old-fashioned by the time of her death, Bedelia's personal bearing and insight into the nature of individuals makes her stand out as singularly capable. "[A]unt had sealed herself off in a lofty, gracious world; she lived for it, she would have died for it if it came to that." She does not directly contrast with the modern world so much as stand calm in the midst of a frenetically changing world, neither apparently noticing the other.

Bedelia is the undeclared model of civility in this short story. She is refined in her tastes, particularly in regards to classical music. She is never driven to passion by anyone's behavior, maintaining an unruffled, peaceful demeanor. This is especially apparent when Lillian (who is not an unbiased point-of-view character) is faced with what she considers to be an unlikely but deep friendship between Bedelia and Vladimir. Lillian is puzzled by their relationship because of her prejudice against Vladimir based on his rude language, which she sees as a strong contrast to her aunt's refinement, almost entirely missing the ways in which the two complement each other well. Their friendship is nevertheless maintained for the remainder of Bedelia's life. Lillian ultimately feels she can trust Vladimir because she has such consummate belief in her aunt's assessment of character, which is perhaps one of the few things on which Lillian and Vladimir can implicitly agree.

Lillian, Bedelia's middle-aged niece, relies on her aunt a great deal as a buffer against the modern world. She clings to the memory her aunt's peacefulness but regards the modern world as decaying: "[S]he thought she could hear the world's madness—its rudeness, its litter, its murderers—beat against the house with the rain." In this way she departs from her aunt's perfect composure of mind.

The narrator describes Lillian's repressed incivilities this way: "She had almost walked off her job, almost struck an old man, almost smiled at murder. A feeling of panic shot through her; what were values if they could collapse at the touch of a sleepless night?" Despite her fear over the potential loss of values, shortly thereafter she has morbid and unrepentant thoughts about her frustration regarding her neighbor: "Perhaps the girl's insanely late hours were boomeranging, and would soon mash her down in a heap of deathlike stillness (would that Lillian could implement this vision)." Lillian need not guard herself against stuffiness so much as insincerity.

> "Lillian fails her final opportunity to tap into her intuition, to leave courtesy behind, even momentarily; however, this failure does not lead to a bruised insole or wet newspaper...."

Lillian is civil to a fault but clearly lacks her aunt's facility for judging character. She seems only to be able to look at the surface, at manners and social behavior, which is evident in her private thoughts about Jody, Jamie, and Vladimir. Lillian, for example, is astonished, annoyed, and even disgusted by Jody but does not believe her to be a prostitute when Vladimir declares she is. Lillian's excuses on Jody's behalf are based on what she has perceived as civilized qualities in Jody's character—taking classes, reading Dostoevsky, having a boyfriend—as if being civilized and having sex for money is an impossible combination.

Jamie shows Lillian some surface warmth—smiles and offers an invitation for coffee—and at the same time is so turned inward that he can hardly see her, interact with her. Despite his faults, in Jamie Lillian sees his youth, his attempts at courtesy, and never perceives the deadly, troubled soul barely contained therein. Lillian, appalled by her appalling neighbors, tries to pull back and see things as her aunt might have:

> [S]he wondered what Bedelia would have thought of Jody and Jamie. And she remembered how unkempt and disconcerting Vladimir had been, yet how her aunt had quickly penetrated to the valuable core while she, Lillian, fussed on about his bad language. . . .[I]t was hard to tell with Bedelia, which facet she might consider the significant one . . . she often surprised you . . . it had to do with largeness of spirit.

Lillian respects Bedelia's insight even if she does not understand how she comes by it. Even as her aunt carries on an intense friendship with Vladimir, Lillian focuses negatively on his vulgar language, passionate outbursts, and spotty reputation. She cannot, until the very end of the story, reconcile his appearance and behavior with the good, discerning, protective soul beneath the surface; however, her breakthrough in understanding Vladimir for herself is not enough to save Lillian. She declares to Vladimir, "'To live each moment as it you were in danger—it's demeaning. I will not creep around snarling like some four-legged beast. I am a civilized human being.'"

The story opens with Vladimir's admonishment: "'Lillian, you're too polite.'" To this he also adds: "'You need a protector, now Bedelia's gone!'" He repeats these sentiments every time he speaks with Lillian. Vladimir, though of a kind with Bedelia, is living in and aware of the modern world. Rather than react to the changing world with indifference (as Bedelia seems to do), or bitterness (as Lillian does), Vladimir fights back. It is the way he knows to survive—and survival is how he perceives life to be. He respects and loves the courtesy of the bygone era, in which he and Bedelia indulge in their friendship, but keeps one foot in reality, and, consequently, is vulgar and rude.

Vladimir is the most interesting character in this story because of the author's slow revelation of his full personality. If the reader trusts Bedelia from the beginning, as Lillian does, then one is assured of Vladimir's good intent toward Bedelia and Lillian. But the deceased Bedelia's opinions are peppered by Lillian's second-guesses. Early on, the reader is left to wonder whether Vladimir's character has been fully comprehended.

When the story opens, Bedelia is dead and Vladimir is visiting Lillian. They are not really friends—more like quarreling relatives who reluctantly care for each other—sharing only the common bond of her aunt. Lillian tolerates his visits out of her own overpowering sense of civility, as well as duty to her aunt's memory. Vladimir's motives are less clear, although being in or near Bedelia's home appears to help him mourn and feel close to his dead friend.

Over the course of the story, Vladimir pushes Lillian to remarry although she has lived most of her life as a widow. She cannot understand what he's really trying to say, although he says it plainly enough—that she needs a protector. Lillian even believes at times that he is suggesting himself as her partner. Vladimir is impatient with her and her civility, urging Lillian time and again to stand up for herself and discard courtesy in favor of a show of strength. He fears for her safety. Why, is never clearly delineated. Perhaps, like Bedelia, Vladimir has that old-fashioned insight and understands that a woman with Lillian's innocence is unsafe unless she has someone with whom to live who can look after her.

Vladimir's admonishments to Lillian to stand up for herself, to protect herself, foreshadow Lillian's violent death. She thinks he is overreacting—she declares that she is civilized and will not live in such a paranoid state—but misses the discerning insight of Vladimir's own character by being caught up in prejudice toward his rougher aspects.

While arguing about Jody and Jamie, Vladimir dismisses Lillian's judgment as bearing no resemblance to her aunt's:

> "The difference between instinct and application. Between a state of grace and a condition of effort. Dear friend Lillian, tolerance is dangerous without insight. . . . It is fatal to try to carry on a dead art—the world has no use for it! The world will trample you down! Don't think of the past, think of your scalp!"

This turns out to be Vladimir's penultimate passionate plea for Lillian to guard herself. *He* has been protecting her, watching her apartment nightly from the street, but frustration and perhaps a little madness break through and he is driven away into the rainy night, leaving Lillian unguarded. Ultimately, Vladimir and Lillian's failure to connect and understand each other means that his entreaties are lost on her. Soon thereafter she opens her front door to Jamie and, despite her own visceral feeling that something is wrong, she refuses her instinct, suppressing exhaustion and panic long enough to make a polite excuse—which is long enough for the deranged young man to leap to the attack.

Jamie's arrival in the story is ominous. He appears without a sound in Jody's apartment in the middle of the night while Lillian is there alone. Lillian is frightened but she fights her intuition concerning this young man almost from the first, employing both courtesy and an acceptance meant to mimic Bedelia's judgment of character. "And he looked, all at once, so lonely, so forlorn, that even though she was very tired, she felt she must stay a moment longer."

His strange mixture of youth and sloth, beauty and moroseness, does not disturb Lillian, even as he casually disembowels a cockroach with a butter knife at the kitchen table. His small gestures of warmth override, for Lillian, all else, so rare a commodity these small gestures seem to be in young man. She sees his "pretty boy" looks and his alternately sad visage as a sign of his humanity, neglecting her own instincts that something deeper is wrong.

Lillian focuses her efforts of understanding instead on Jamie's girlfriend, Jody, who is a noisy, thoughtless neighbor. Lillian is so stressed over Jody's behavior and Vladimir's intensity that she is unaware of how Jamie's strangeness is beyond the pale even within a modern context. In part Lillian wants to be insightful as Bedelia was, but she lacks the ability to discern, swinging so far toward acceptance that she cannot see any danger.

In the final scene of the story, Jamie stands out in the rain, dressed in a black cape, mournfully watching his girlfriend's windows as she entertains a customer. Lillian spies him out in the garden and feels sad for him but also more than a little unsettled. Even Vladimir's superior character insight does not pick out Jamie as the serial killer "rain man" or he would presumably have warned Lillian more specifically or at least not left her building that night, having seen "'that pea-brained boyfriend . . . in his secondhand ghoul costume'" haunting the premises.

Lillian fails her final opportunity to tap into her intuition, to leave courtesy behind, even momentarily; however, this failure does not lead to a bruised insole or wet newspaper:

> [T]he rain muffled his voice; though she caught an eerie, unnatural tone she now sensed was reflected in the luminous stare. With a sudden feeling of panic she started to slam the door in his face. But she braked herself, knowing that she was overwrought; it was unseemly to use such brusqueness on this lost creature because of her jangled nerves.

In that moment of blind courtesy, Lillian is finally trampled by the modern world.

Source: Carol Ullmann, Critical Essay on "Last Courtesies," in *Short Stories for Students*, Thomson Gale, 2007.

Contemporary Authors Online

In the following essay, the critic gives an overview of Leffland's life and work.

Ella Leffland once told *CA*: "I started writing at about ten, and all I can say is that it's gotten harder ever since." She sent a story to the *New Yorker* when she was fourteen. After mailing submissions to them for the next fourteen years, they finally published "Eino," a story she sent in after her second trip to Europe. Now the author of several novels and an acclaimed collection of short stories, she is known for her ability to draw insightful portraits of people variously caught between the expectations of others and the desire to satisfy their own needs. In some of her works, loyal and accommodating characters recognize their need

> *In some of her works, loyal and accommodating characters recognize their need for approval and take courageous steps toward emotional independence; in others, Leffland has examined the loneliness of characters whose independence has alienated them from other people."*

for approval and take courageous steps toward emotional independence; in others, Leffland has examined the loneliness of characters whose independence has alienated them from other people. Leffland's analytical approach to social relationships stems from her dual cultural heritage as a Californian who was raised in a Danish household. *The Knight, Death and the Devil*—her novel based on the life of Nazi Reichsmarschall Hermann Goering—intensified her interest in the relationship of individuals to society.

Leffland's first novel *Mrs. Munck* is a close examination of the psychology behind a woman's reclusive life as the caretaker for an invalid man who has abused her in the past. She expects it will be easy for her to take revenge while he is under her care. As the novel progresses, Rose begins to understand why she has trapped herself into this bitter relationship and makes decisions that will free her. Leffland builds suspense by slowly unfolding this intensely personal drama. Though some reviewers felt it unfolded too slowly, *New York Times* reviewer Christopher Lehmann-Haupt praised Leffland's first novel, stating that "anyone with the smallest spark of indignation over the second-class status of women in modern society is going to read Leffland's novel with eyes blazing, adrenalin flowing and heart pounding."

Leffland told *Publishers Weekly* interviewer Sybil Steinberg that her intention in writing *Mrs. Munck* was "to show . . . a woman—that is, specifically a female character—from the inside of her heart and mind. I wanted her to start off a free soul, an individual, unstamped by convention. . . . I wanted to give this girl a universality, and then show the difficulty she has in preserving it, in escaping from the roles thrust upon her. That's what I was *trying* to do, but I didn't succeed. I don't think Rose Munck makes it, but if not, she makes an attempt, and I'm not sorry to see her in print."

Stories in Leffland's collection *Last Courtesies and Other Stories* "deal with loneliness and alienation, people who cannot make themselves understood," Wayne Warga writes in the *Los Angeles Times*. The cast in this volume includes a mother who neglects her child, a craftily abusive hostelkeeper, a self-centered American tourist, and a womanizer. "What saves one from a sort of terminal dismay [after reading them] is the art with which the stories are rendered, the sort of affection she has for her characters and her ability to include us in this relationship," Warga continues. John Romano explains in the *New York Times Book Review* that although many of Leffland's characters "are deep and thorough joys to hate" for their condemnable behavior, "the principle business of these stories is bestowing sympathy." The title story won the O'Henry Prize for short fiction in 1977. Romano, who remarks that Leffland "befriends" her subjects by writing about them, concludes that aside from Leffland, "There is not a contemporary writer of short stories from whom truth of feeling, splendidness of insight, and a human beauty both aching and real can more confidently be expected."

Though Leffland's interest in how characters measure their responsibility to others remains constant, her fiction covers a wide range of tone and subject matter. In contrast to the bleak lives portrayed in *Last Courtesies*, says Warga, the novel *Rumors of Peace* is "about growing up in Northern California during World War II, packed with the aches and pains of adolescence and emotionally armed by the impact of the war." Suse, a girl from a happy family, nurses her fear and rage by following daily news reports of the war and calms herself to sleep by picturing dead and wounded Japanese soldiers. This obsession is interrupted by her infatuation with a Jewish refugee some time after reading *Madame Bovary*, and by her friendship with two sisters, Peggy and Helen Maria. Peggy becomes a social climber; Helen Maria studies Greek history and becomes an asset to Suse's understanding of world events. "Suse . . . brings to life Leffland's concern with the nature of moral growth," Linda B. Osborne observes in the *Washington Post Book World*. Throughout the novel, Suse grapples with questions about war that lead her into the enigmatic heart of human nature: "Why do diplomats argue with detached elegance while soldiers die? Why do some people persecute others? Why does mankind repeat the mistakes of war? Finding no answers from adults, she attacks these questions with her own curiosity, stubbornness, and anger," Osborne relates. And when the bombing of Hiroshima ends the war, Suse understands that the event "brings no resolution to the puzzle of war itself," leaving Suse in a world full of moral questions where the opposition is not so clearly defined, the reviewer adds.

Like the young heroine of her *bildungsroman*, Leffland was deeply affected by the human cost of the war that came no nearer to her childhood home than Pearl Harbor. During World War II, Leffland was terrified of dying in a bombing raid. She felt intense loathing for the German invaders who were trampling her ancestral homeland. Leffland was still a girl when she became fascinated with Goering, who loomed larger than life in stories told by European relatives. Her fascination later culminated in obsession. On a trip to Yugoslavia in 1977, the author took a side trip to Germany where she visited the places where Goering had lived as a child, had risen to power, and had been condemned for war crimes. After finishing *Rumors of Peace*, she studied German and began concentrated research on Goering, gathering biographical information and the names of people who could answer her questions.

In 1979, Leffland went to Germany looking for materials on Goering and was aided by his nephew, who had amassed a room full of Goering memorabilia. She was also fortunate to find a man who had once served as Goering's bodyguard, who put her in touch with others who had known the Reichsmarschall. Leffland's book makes use of many of the facts she discovered on that trip, she told *Publishers Weekly* interviewer Sonja Bolle: "The book is as truthful as I could make it. . . . But I was free to invent where there were no facts, and of course to omit or to change facts, because of the necessity of making a novel as balanced and believable as possible. In the course of my research, I am sure there must be things I misinterpreted or misunderstood. But I came across inaccuracies in history books, too." She also told Bolle, "I hope that my presentation of Goering shows the sides of him that are overlooked in the various biographies."

Critics concur that Leffland's portrait of the creator of the Gestapo and the death camps is as balanced and insightful as her treatment of fictional characters. Though she takes no pains to mask Goering's dark side, she presents him also as a charismatic leader, a loyal friend, an animal lover, and a discerning art critic. He was vulnerable as well as powerful, and eventually lost his position as Hitler's adviser. Don G. Campbell notes in the *Los Angeles Times Book Review* that Leffland's Goering "emerges as probably the most . . . popular, and perhaps the brightest mind in that twisted inner circle of perverted talents surrounding Hitler. . . . We are left to wonder: What turns would those massive talents have taken against a different historic background?" A *Publishers Weekly* reviewer concludes that although Leffland's subject "remains essentially an enigmatic and unappealing character, the growth of his complicity in his country's moral depravity makes absorbing reading."

The Knight, Death and the Devil sheds light not only on the life of Goering, but on the political movement in which he played a prominent role. Thomas Keneally remarks in the *New York Times Book Review*, "Among other things, [Leffland] gives us a credible sense of why Nazism inflamed so many imaginations. We feel with Goering and others the drag of that dark seduction, the sense of 'entrance to something extraordinary, something absolutely new and breathtakingly alive.' Ms. Leffland's handling of such Nazi dramas as the creepy reconciliation of randy Dr. Goebbels, Minister for Propaganda, and his wife, Magda—a couple 'lodged deeper than ever in the core of the mythos'—is impeccable."

Chicago *Tribune Books* critic Joseph Coates places Leffland's book among those novels that inform more effectively than the more formal works of history or political science. Coates explains, "By brilliantly dramatizing [the] process—in which victims become oppressors, then victims of their own oppression—Leffland has given us an epic for our century, a tragedy with the narrative tug of a riptide that sweeps the reader through 50 years of mankind's worst moments. Seldom has history been so compelling, or appalling." Keneally concludes, "Those who have spent either much or little time looking at this era will be fascinated by the richness of [Leffland's] picture and the authenticity of this massive work."

Source: Contemporary Authors Online, "Ella Leffland," in *Contemporary Authors Online*, The Gale Group, 2001.

Sources

Alley, Henry, "The Well-Made World of the O. Henrys, 1961–2000," in *Kenyon Review*, Vol. 25, No. 2, April 1, 2003, p. 36.

Romano, John, Review of *Last Courtesies*, in *New York Times*, October 5, 1980.

Schiller, Johann von, "Ode to Joy," quoted in Grout, Donald Hay, and Claude V. Palisca, *A History of Western Music*, 5th ed., W. W. Norton, 1996, p. 559.

Seaman, Donna, Review of *Breath and Shadows*, in *Booklist*, Vol. 95, No. 15, April 1, 1999, p. 1386.

See, Carolyn, "A Look into Life's Myths, Reality and Why We Live the Way We Do," in *Washington Post*, April 9, 1999, p. C2.

Steinberg, Sybil S., Review of *Breath and Shadows*, in *Publishers Weekly*, Vol. 246, No. 3, January 18, 1999, p. 325.

Yeats, W. B., "The Second Coming," in *W. B. Yeats: Selected Poetry*, edited by A. Norman Jeffares, Macmillan, 1972, p. 99.

Further Reading

Eidam, Klaus, *The True Life of Johann Sebastian Bach*, Basic Books, 2001.
> Leffland's short story refers to music and includes discussions about the great classical composers. Eidam's biography of Bach has been described as a revitalized account of the composer's life. The author's meticulous research separates the truth from the myth of Bach's life.

Fiedler, Johanna, *Molto Agitato: The Mayhem behind the Music at the Metropolitan Opera*, Anchor, 2003.
> The protagonist in Leffland's short story works for the Opera House and mentions the chaos she encounters on her job. Here is a true-life experience of behind the scenes at another opera house. Fiedler (daughter of famed conductor Arthur Fiedler) worked as the press representative of the Met in New York.

Freeborn, Richard, *Dostoevsky: Life and Times*, Haus Publishing, 2003.
> Dialogues between Leffland's characters include discussions of Russian writers. One of the more important of these writers is Fyodor Dostoevsky, author of such novels as *The Brothers Karamazov*, *Crime and Punishment*, and *Notes from the Underground*. This is the story of this great Russian author's life.

Ilyin, Olga, *White Road: A Russian Odyssey, 1919–1923*, Holt, Rinehart, and Winston, 1984.
> This is one family's account of living through the Bolshevik revolution in Russia. This book might provide readers a better understanding of Leffland's character Vladimir, given what many white Russians experienced before they came to the United States.

Meeting Mrinal

Chitra Banerjee Divakaruni

1995

"Meeting Mrinal" by Chitra Banerjee Divakaruni is the last story in the collection *Arranged Marriage*, which was published in 1995. Most of the stories in the collection examine the experiences and perspectives of Indian women who have immigrated to the United States, often through a traditional arranged marriage. The stories show women who find themselves caught between two cultures, the restricted but comforting Indian culture of their birth and the freer but ruthless Western culture. The protagonist of "Meeting Mrinal" is Asha, an Indian-born woman who immigrates to the United States to join her Indian husband (acquired through an arranged marriage). In her new home, she leads the life expected of a traditional Indian wife until an event occurs that forces her to move beyond her accustomed role: Her husband leaves her for a younger white woman. The story opens at this point, recounting Asha's attempts to come to terms with her feelings of failure and her need to carve out an independent life in an alien culture. This process reaches a crisis during a meeting with Mrinal, a childhood friend from India who is now a successful businesswoman. Divakaruni explores the immigrant search for identity and coherence in the adopted culture, in which the traditional assumptions do not work and the new ways require unexpected and sometimes painful growth.

Author Biography

Chitra Banerjee Divakaruni was born on July 29, 1956, in Calcutta, India, the daughter of R. K. and

Tatini Banerjee. One of her earliest memories is that of her grandfather telling her stories from the ancient Indian scriptures, the *Ramayana* and the *Mahabharata*. She noticed that unlike the male heroes, the main relationships the women had were with men; they never had any important women friends. This realization was to greatly influence Divakaruni's writing, which focuses on women's relationships.

Divakaruni was brought up and continued to be in adulthood a devout Hindu. As a child, however, she attended a convent school run by Irish nuns. She gained a bachelor's degree from Calcutta University in 1976 and, in the same year, immigrated to the United States. In 1978, she received a master's degree from Wright State University in Dayton, Ohio, and in 1985, she received a Ph.D. from the University of California, Berkeley. She began to write fiction after graduating from Berkeley.

Divakaruni has drawn on her own experiences as an immigrant and those of other immigrant Indian women in her poetry, short stories, and novels. Her poetry collection, *Black Candle* (1991), recounts stories of women from India, Pakistan, and Bangladesh. *Arranged Marriage* (1995), a collection of short stories which marked her first foray into prose and which includes "Meeting Mrinal," portrays immigrant Indian women who are caught between two cultures: the Indian culture of their birth and the Western culture of their adopted country, the United States. Her novel *The Mistress of Spices* (1997), a blend of poetry and prose, draws on Indian mystical and cultural traditions to portray a woman who has acquired immortality through a rite of fire and the knowledge of how to use spices for healing. Eventually, she is forced to choose between her own culture and that of the non-Indian man she comes to love.

In 1999, Divakaruni published a novel, *Sister of My Heart*. The book explores the conflicts between Indian people who embrace their traditional culture and those who embrace new Western ideas. Divakaruni published another collection of poetry, *Leaving Yuba City*, in 1997. These poems also deal with immigrant women and their struggles to find an identity in their new country.

When asked why she writes, according to the quote posted on the Random House website, Divakaruni replied, "There is a certain spirituality, not necessarily religious—the essence of spirituality—that is at the heart of the Indian psyche, that finds the divine in everything. . . . It was important for me to start writing about my own reality and that of my community."

While arranged marriages have formed a major theme in her work, Divakaruni herself opted for love; on June 29, 1979, she was married to S. Murthy Divakaruni. As of 2006, the couple had two sons, Abhay and Anand. As of 2006, she lived in Sunnyvale, California, and was a professor of creative writing at Foothill College, Los Altos, a position to which she was appointed in 1989. Divakaruni is active within the Asian American community. In 1991, she established Maitri, a hotline for South Asian women who suffer domestic abuse.

Divakaruni has received many awards for her work. In 1996, for *Arranged Marriage*, she received the PEN Oakland Josephine Miles Prize for Fiction, the Bay Area Book Reviewers Award for Fiction, and an American Book Award from the Before Columbus Foundation. *The Mistress of Spices* was named a best book of 1997 by the *Los Angeles Times* and a best paperback of 1998 by the *Seattle Times*. For poems that were later collected in *Leaving Yuba City*, she won a Pushcart Prize (1994), an Allen Ginsberg Poetry Prize (1994), and a Gerbode Foundation Award (1992).

Plot Summary

When "Meeting Mrinal" opens, Asha, the Indian-born protagonist, who now lives in California, is somewhat guiltily preparing a ready-made pizza for her teenage son, Dinesh. Asha's husband, Mahesh, with whom she had an arranged marriage in India, has left her for a younger white woman. Though Asha used to spend hours preparing complex Indian meals from fresh ingredients for the family, she has almost given up cooking since Mahesh left. She now spends her time studying library science in order to get a full-time job and getting fit in an exercise class. Since Mahesh left, Asha and Dinesh no longer talk much. He shuts himself in his room, listening to or playing music.

One day, Asha gets a telephone call from Mrinal, a childhood friend from India whom she has not seen for nearly twenty years. Mrinal is now a successful businesswoman living in Bombay. She is coming to San Francisco for a conference and wants to meet Asha and her family. Asha has always had a competitive relationship with the glamorous, career-driven, and unmarried Mrinal and inwardly feels inferior to her. Asha's delight at hearing from her friend soon gives way to fear and shame at the thought of admitting that her husband has left her. Asha feels particularly defensive as

Media Adaptations

- Chitra Banerjee Divakaruni's first novel, *The Mistress of Spices*, was made into a film, released in 2005. The film was directed by Paul Mayeda Berges and stars Aishwarya Rai as Tilo. As of February 2006, the distributor was Entertainment Film Distributors.

Mrinal had counseled her against agreeing to an early arranged marriage, advising her to finish college and get a job. Asha talks to Mrinal as if her marriage is still intact but makes up excuses to get out of meeting her, saying that Mahesh is out of town, that she is busy, and that Dinesh has pressing engagements. Finally, she realizes that she cannot disappoint her friend and sets up a meeting.

Dinesh is angry with his mother for lying to Mrinal. He asks why she could not tell the truth: Mahesh got tired of her and left her for another woman. Asha slaps Dinesh, claiming to object to his swearing, but in reality, she is inwardly furious at his voicing an uncomfortable truth. For the next few days, Dinesh avoids Asha. She tries to win him over by cooking his favorite Indian dish and apologizing, but he says he has already eaten and coldly dismisses her attempts at reconciliation.

Asha rummages for an outfit for her meeting with Mrinal, worrying that all her clothes are too garish or too drab. She recalls the day when Mahesh told her that their marriage was over. Asha could scarcely believe what she was hearing, as she thought back to their apparently happy family life. When Asha asked him whether he had ever been happy with her, Mahesh said that he thought he had, but he did not know what real happiness was. Asha fought against the divorce, even buying a sexy negligee to try to win Mahesh back, but he moved out the same night.

Asha is nervous about meeting Mrinal. She reflects that Mrinal has the perfect life: She assumes simplistically that Mrinal has "*money, freedom, admiration*," and "*she doesn't have to worry about pleasing anyone.*" Asha's envy is mixed with a feeling of comfort at the thought of Mrinal's success, despite the fact that it makes her own life seem cluttered and ordinary.

When Asha enters the restaurant, she sees Mrinal sitting at one of the tables, looking glamorous. Asha looks in vain for a sign that Mrinal is secretly unhappy. As the two women embrace, Asha notices a ring on Mrinal's finger and asks if is an engagement ring, but Mrinal says she bought it for herself. Asha is impressed by this independent act. Mrinal begs Asha to tell her about Mahesh and Dinesh. Asha does so, without revealing that her marriage is over. Mrinal sadly says that Asha is lucky to have such a wonderful husband and son. She reveals that she herself is unhappy and begins to cry. She admits that she had planned to pretend that everything was fine with her life, but when she saw the love for her family shining in Asha's face, she could not keep it up. The two women part without Asha's revealing her own secret.

Asha drives home. She closes the garage door behind her but does not switch off the engine. As the garage fills with fumes, she weeps for Mrinal's and her own loneliness and also for their profound disillusionment. The idea of Mrinal's perfect life had made her own sorrows easier to bear, but now as that perfection has been shown to be a mirage, she feels as though she has nothing to sustain her.

Suddenly realizing that suicide is not the answer, Asha turns off the engine and stumbles out of the garage. Dinesh appears. Full of concern for his mother, he helps her to the bathroom, where she vomits. She reflects that though she has always tried to be the perfect wife and mother, she has lost her husband, lied to her friend, and vomited over the sink in her son's presence. Then, an image takes shape in her mind: a beautiful clay bowl from her art appreciation class. There is a tiny flaw on the lip. Her teacher had said that this was a deliberate flaw that the master potter left in all his works in the belief that it made them more human and more precious.

When Dinesh asks his mother how the meeting with Mrinal went, Asha admits that she "made a mess of things." She offers to tell him about it over some hot milk with pistachios. Smiling, he agrees. As she prepares the milk, she plans the letter she will write to Mrinal to tell her the truth. She knows that she and Dinesh will not always agree, but they solemnly raise their glasses to their "precious, imperfect lives."

Characters

Asha

Asha is an Indian-born woman and the protagonist of "Meeting Mrinal." Brought up in India, Asha leaves college early and agrees to an arranged marriage to Mahesh, an Indian man who has immigrated to the United States. Asha moves to California to join her husband, and they enjoy a seemingly happy married life. Asha throws herself into traditional wifely activities such as cooking elaborate meals for the family. When the novel opens, Mahesh has just left Asha and their teenage son, Dinesh, for a younger white woman, Jessica. Asha is forced to move beyond her accustomed role as a wife and mother and forge an independent life in an alien culture that offers more freedom but also poses more challenges than her culture of origin in India. She is afflicted by a sense that she has failed in her traditional role as a wife and that she is too gauche and unsophisticated to fit into the harsh, fast-moving Western culture that beckons.

A turning point for Asha comes when she meets a childhood friend, Mrinal, with whom she has always had a competitive relationship and to whom she feels inferior. Mrinal has succeeded in those areas that Asha finds threatening, having built a successful career and an independent life. Asha finds herself lying to Mrinal, pretending that her marriage is fine. When Mrinal admits that she is unhappy at her lack of a loving family life, Asha falls into despair. She attempts suicide but, when she reaches her lowest point, is finally able to let her mask of motherly control drop and accept help from her son. For the first time, Asha's relationship with Dinesh is one of truth and honesty, and she prepares to tell Mrinal the truth about her marriage. Asha's journey has taken her from desperately working to maintain the pretence of a happy marriage to an acceptance that while no one's life is perfect, every life is infinitely precious.

Dinesh

Dinesh is the teenage son of Asha and Mahesh. As is typical of the American-born children of immigrants, he has become much more assimilated into Western culture than his parents. He favors T-shirts emblazoned with gruesome slogans, wears an earring, and has his hair cut into a brush-like style. He talks to his mother very little since his father left and treats her with the withdrawn politeness of a stranger. However, the anger he feels at the breakup is suggested by his habit of locking himself in his room and playing hard rock music at full volume

and by the fact that he can only refer to his father as "*him*."

Dinesh's anger surfaces when he overhears Asha lying to Mrinal on the telephone about the state of her marriage. He does not understand why his mother cannot tell the truth. She tries to win him round by cooking his favorite meal and calling him by his baby name, Dinoo. The tactic fails because Dinesh is no longer a child and is thoroughly impatient with all kinds of lies, including those that are told to children to make them feel safe in an uncertain world. The fact that he moved into the master bedroom when his father left is symbolic of his claiming new status as an adult.

The crisis between Dinesh and his mother is resolved when she attempts suicide. Dinesh moves into the adult role of protector, becoming, as Asha notes, "*motherly*," and helps her to the bathroom, where she vomits. Dinesh has seen his mother drop her pretences and descend to the role of a helpless child, and he has heard her honestly admit that she made a mess of her meeting with Mrinal. Now that he is being treated as an equal and trusted with the truth, he is at last able to show his love for his mother. He smilingly accepts her offer of pistachio milk, and together, they drink to their "precious, imperfect lives."

Jessica

Jessica is Mahesh's red-haired secretary, a white woman who is younger than Asha. Mahesh falls in love with Jessica and leaves Asha for her. She does not appear in the story.

Mahesh

Mahesh is Asha's ex-husband. At the time the story opens, he has already left Asha for a younger white woman, Jessica, so he is only presented through the memories of Asha. After his arranged marriage to Asha, Mahesh quickly settled into the role of dutiful husband, gazing adoringly at the baby Dinesh and choosing Asha's outfits when they would go out. Mahesh had thought he was happy in his marriage until he fell in love with Jessica; it was then that he realized he did not know what happiness was.

Mrinal

Mrinal is Asha's close friend from childhood. She provides a contrast to Asha. While Mrinal has stayed in India, she has turned her back on Indian conventions and chosen a more Western way of life. She has remained unmarried, forging a highly successful career. Mrinal is intelligent, glamorous, and wealthy. When she meets Asha, she is as determined as her friend to pretend that her life is perfect, but when she sees Asha's love for her family shining in her eyes, she can no longer maintain the pretence and admits that she is lonely and unhappy. Mrinal is proof that however impressive a person's life looks on the outside, much grief and anxiety can lurk beneath the glossy surface.

Themes

Women Caught between Two Cultures

"Meeting Mrinal" shows the predicament of Asha, a woman who grew up in India, had an arranged marriage according to Indian tradition, and then had to adapt to a new lifestyle and culture as a divorced woman. The first change, taking place before the story opens, comes when she immigrates to the United States, a harsher culture full of "failing grades, drugs, street gangs, AIDS." However, the cultural shock is cushioned by the fact that she is able to sustain the traditional Indian role of wife and mother, albeit with a part-time job. This cushion is suddenly taken away from her when her husband informs her that their marriage is over. In the Indian tradition, the family is a woman's support system. If the family is no longer intact, she loses that support and must make decisions on her own—a situation that is much more the norm in Western society.

The divorced Asha faces both external and internal challenges. Externally, she considers moving out of the marital home and trains for a full-time job; she joins a fitness class and gives up cooking elaborate Indian meals for herself and her teenage son, relying instead on takeouts. Internally, she must come to terms with the failure of her marriage, a role to which she had committed her entire being for years, and become an independent woman in her adopted country. The prospect daunts her because she feels poorly equipped for her new role. Comparing herself with Mrinal as the epitome of what she must become, she finds herself lacking. She feels dowdy, incompetent, and ill-at-ease with the hustle and sophisticated gloss of life in the West.

Mrinal has made the opposite life choices to Asha. Mrinal remained in India, yet she rejected the traditional Indian wifely role and acquired the trappings of the successful westernized woman. She has a powerful and lucrative job, beautiful clothes, and a lovely home. However, her achievements have come with a price: she is lonely and childless.

In the flawed lives of Asha and Mrinal, Divakaruni shows that both the traditional Indian female role and the modern Western female role entail their own sacrifices, problems, and uncertainties; neither choice is better or more complete than the other. She also dramatizes a basic irony: the Indian woman who remains in India actually develops a more Western-style life for herself; the Indian woman who comes to the United States attempts to sustain a traditional Indian lifestyle and only departs from it when her marriage fails and she is forced to be on her own.

Women's Relationships

On her website, Divakaruni writes, "Women in particular respond to my work because I'm writing about them, women in love, in difficulties, women in relationships. I want people to relate to my characters, to feel their joy and pain, because it will be harder to [be] prejudiced when they meet them in real life." "Meeting Mrinal" shows the richness, conflicts, and complexities that mark Asha's relationships with her female friend, with her husband and child, and with Western society in general. Asha's relationship with Mrinal is particularly loaded with significance. Though Asha loves her friend, her perception of Mrinal as someone who has succeeded in all the ways in which she herself has failed adds a level of competitiveness, defensiveness, and dishonesty to their relationship. Each woman wants to be admired by the other. At their meeting, Asha cannot admit that her marriage has failed, and Mrinal tries to resist admitting that she is unhappy with her single, childless state, only giving in when her emotions break through her resolve to maintain the veneer of perfection. The pursuit of acceptable appearance which fails in both cases illustrates how people are aware of being judged by others by certain exterior characteristics and how the fear of judgment prevents them from being honest about the realities of their lives.

Asha's relationship with Dinesh is also compromised by a lack of truth: mother and son no longer talk. The more Dinesh withdraws, the more Asha attempts to compensate for what she sees as her failure as a mother by engaging in traditional motherly behavior such as preparing his favorite meals. The cycle of deception is broken by Asha's acceptance of Dinesh's support when she reaches her lowest point of half-heartedly trying to commit suicide and by her admission to him that she "made a mess" of her meeting with Mrinal. When she promises to tell him about it, it is clear that she is ready to trust him with the truth and move into a

Topics For Further Study

- How do the cultures of India and the United States differ in "Meeting Mrinal"? Do some additional research to find more differences between the two cultures. Write a report on your findings based on both the story and your additional research.

- Interview two people who have immigrated to your country and who come from an ethnic or national background different to your own. You may find it easier to tape-record your interviews, though it is a legal requirement that you first obtain the permission of your interviewees. One of these people might be a first-generation immigrant (who has moved to your country from elsewhere) and the other a second-generation immigrant (a person born in your country of parents who immigrated). Recount their experiences, both positive and negative. Compare the experiences of the two people, considering in what ways each person's experience was easier or more difficult.

- Interview a woman or girl of Indian ethnic background about her experiences of her original culture and that of the country where she now lives. Write an essay describing your findings.

- Choose an area of your country which has a history of immigration and one ethnic or national immigrant group that has immigrated to that area. Trace the historical factors that influenced the group to settle there and identify the ways in which the group has influenced the development of the area.

- Interview an immigrant to your country about their experiences of immigration. Investigate reasons why they left their country of origin, the expectations they had of their destination country, what they found when they arrived, and how their lives have evolved since immigrating. Based on your findings, write either a report, or a first-person account, in the form of a play, short story, or diary entry suitable for reading aloud or radio broadcast.

- Choose from one of the following two assignments. Interview a woman of Indian or other Asian origin who has had an arranged marriage, and a woman of the same origin who has had a non-arranged, love marriage. Write a report comparing and contrasting their experiences. You will need to bear in mind the potential sensitivity of the subject and treat your sources with the degree of confidentiality they request. Or research the topic of arranged marriage. Include an examination of any studies on the topic and consider how the custom is changing with the times. Write a report on the advantages and disadvantages of the system of arranged marriage.

---

more equal relationship with him. The irony here is that openly admitting to personal limitations enhances relationships, while pretending to be something one is not prevents intimacy.

Familial, Cultural and Social Expectations of Women

Why is Asha determined to project an image of the perfect life? It would be unfair to blame the men in her life for imposing their expectations onto her. Neither man is a demanding tyrant: Dinesh does not worry where his meals come from; Mahesh, in love with his secretary, has become tired of the husbandly role of choosing outfits for his wife and pretending to desire her sexually. Asha tries so hard to be the perfect wife and mother not because of her husband and son want that but because the culture in which she developed conditioned her to do so. As a girl and young woman, Asha was taught that she should cook elaborate meals for Mahesh and Dinesh, put her family before her career, dress to please Mahesh at social engagements, and keep him happy in the bedroom.

Also, Asha makes her own choices. She is no longer in India, and even if she were, many Indian women now choose to ignore gender-linked cultural conventions, as Mrinal does. In reality, Asha is both a product of her culture and a person who reacts to it. She has chosen to focus on pleasing and nourishing her family. Her choice is backed by centuries of cultural conditioning, but it is still her choice. Asha is as free as Mahesh or Mrinal to act independently, but doing so would entail moving out of her comfort zone, as is made clear from her response to the plush restaurant where she meets Mrinal: "As I awkwardly followed the maître d' I knew I didn't belong here, and that every person in the room, without needing to look at me, knew it too." Eventually, she is forced by Mahesh's departure to drop the Indian wifely role and to see more deeply into the vagaries of her own experience. She has to learn the hard way that nothing assures one of happiness, and unforeseen events require one to adapt.

As the example of Mrinal shows, Western culture brings its own set of expectations which are just as onerous, in their own way, as those of traditional India. Many women feel that they are expected to be glamorous, physically fit, financially successful, and polished in social situations. Mrinal has achieved these traits, but at the price of loneliness. Finally, both women admit that they are unable to fulfill all the expectations they have embraced, but these admissions, far from being defeats, have the cautiously optimistic air of new beginnings, and they provide for greater intimacy and sincerity within their relationships.

James Bond

When Asha and Mrinal were childhood friends, they were both fans of James Bond, the suave, all-powerful, and womanizing fictional spy created by the English novelist Ian Fleming (1908–1964) and popularized in a series of Hollywood films. For Asha and Mrinal, Bond was a symbol of a romanticized image of the West, full of "golden guns and intricate machines and bikini-clad beauties." They vow that if they ever make it to the West, they will celebrate by drinking Bond's favorite drink: vodka martini, shaken not stirred. Indeed, when Mrinal meets Asha in the restaurant, she orders this drink for them both. At the beginning of the meeting, Mrinal seems to Asha to belong to this idealized world of affluence and power. Only when Mrinal bursts into tears and admits that she is not happy does the truth begin to push its way through the fiction. Mrinal has been forced into this revelation by her realization of the lack of love in her life, an element that Asha does have in her relationship with Dinesh. One of James Bond's defining characteristics is his lack of a love life (as opposed to a sex life, which he does have) or a family. Mrinal's story suggests that Bond is a character deserving of pity rather than blind admiration. Moreover, in using Bond as a desirable image, Divakaruni cautions people not to measure their own lives in terms of the slick ideals promoted by any culture.

Style

Setting

The story is set in two locations: India, where Asha was brought up and married and which is presented only in her memories and California in the United States, where she now lives. As well as being two separate countries, India and the United States have two different cultures and sets of social expectations. Asha's Indian upbringing teaches her to be a certain kind of wife and mother, whereas the United States challenges her to break away from these traditional roles and forge an independent life. The United States is presented in both negative and positive aspects: the negative, chaotic side is represented by Asha's fear of "failing grades, drugs, street gangs, AIDS" that lie in wait for Dinesh, and the positive side is represented by the greater freedom and power that beckons to the newly divorced Asha.

The plush restaurant where Asha meets Mrinal brings out Asha's insecurity about affluent Western society: she feels that she does not belong there and that every person in the room knows it. She is more comfortable with inexpensive places like Chuck E. Cheese or the Chinese takeout.

Characterization and Point of View

Asha and Mrinal are contrasting characters who represent the different choices facing Indian women (and to varying degrees, women of all nationalities): to follow the traditional route of marriage and children (Asha) or to stay single and pursue professional success (Mrinal). Far from being stereotypes, however, both characters suffer conflicts and doubts amid their strengths and achievements that render them thoroughly human and believable. The fact that the story is told in first person from the point of view of Asha allows Divakaruni to expose Asha's opinions and hidden feelings, while she misreads Mrinal's appearance and what she knows about Mrinal's life. This point of view works to emphasize the story's point: people judge other people's outsides by comparing them to their own inner reality, often at their own expense.

Symbolism

Preparing elaborate meals from fresh ingredients for the family is an important part of Indian culture, one that Asha fully embraced in her married life with Mahesh. For her, cooking has come to symbolize the unity and nourishing quality of family life; it also signifies her investment in relationships with Mahesh and Dinesh. Now that Mahesh has left, Asha cooks differently. She relies on fast food and takeouts, reflecting her new, independent life: "I've decided that too much of my life has already been wasted mincing and simmering and grinding spices."

However, when Asha faces a crisis of confidence, worrying about the negative influence of "failing grades, drugs, street gangs, AIDS" on Dinesh, she takes refuge in cooking once more, as if there were some protection in that very ritual, "As though the translucent rings of onions and the long curls of carrots could forge a chain that would hold him to me, close, safe forever." Similarly, after Asha's argument with Dinesh, which is prompted by his anger at her lying to Mrinal about the state of her marriage and family life, she tries to win him over by cooking his favorite meal. Unable to face the truth or to discuss it openly with her son, she takes refuge in the motherly rituals, casting him as a child by using his baby name, Dinoo. The tactic fails miserably, since it is also a kind of lie; Dinesh has already eaten out, is no longer a child, and sullenly refuses to be drawn into the charade. The turning point for Asha comes after she poisons herself with fumes and then vomits—a reversal of nourishing oneself with food. During this incident, she is finally able to let go of her motherly role and allow Dinesh to look after her. Only then does Asha forgo her deceptions and decide to tell Dinesh and Mrinal the truth.

With mother and son communicating openly once more, they are able to share some pistachio milk that Asha prepares. Pistachio milk is a traditional Indian drink. The final scene in which Asha and Dinesh drink to their "precious, imperfect lives" with the pistachio milk symbolizes Asha's acceptance of her Indian tradition; Dinesh's acceptance of his mother (he accepts her offer of the milk, unlike his previous hostile response when she cooked him his favorite meal); and Asha's and Dinesh's acceptance of each other as they are, not as they might be expected to be in some illusory, presumably perfect family.

Historical Context

Immigration from India to the United States

Indian immigration to the United States was uncommon before 1900; Hindu beliefs discouraged it, as did the British colonizers of India, who restricted the movements of the Indian people. In 1946, the Luce-Celler bill was signed into law. This law permitted one hundred Indians per year into the United States and allowed them to become citizens. The following year, India gained independence from Great Britain, marking the second wave of Indian immigration; between 1948 and 1965, over six thousand Indians entered the United States. In 1990, the number of Indian-born persons living in the United States was 450,000. By 2004, India had become the second highest source of legal immigration to the United States, second only to Mexico. As of 2006, ethnic Asians made up 4.2 percent of the United States population.

Arranged Marriages

Traditionally, many Indian women (and women of other Asian countries) have their marriages arranged through relatives, so-called marriage bureaus, or paid matchmakers called bride brokers. Many Indian families living in the United States retain this practice. The 1990s saw a surge in classified advertisements placed by parents looking for prospective brides and grooms in Indian newspapers circulated in India and the United States. In the late 1990s, the growing Internet provided a variety of matrimonial websites to replace the traditional matchmaker.

The advantages and disadvantages of arranged marriages are much debated in Asian communities. Defenders of arranged marriage point out that great care is taken by the families to match the bridegroom and bride according to social background, education, and interests. They say that most young people are not forced into an arranged marriage, that love usually grows between spouses after marriage, and that such marriages have a far higher rate of success and a lower divorce rate than marriages that arise from courtship and love that are more usual in the West, which may be based on short-lived infatuation or sexual desire.

Opponents of arranged marriage claim a high incidence of incompatibility and various types of spousal abuse. Some commentators in India or Asia draw a link between arranged marriage and the growing phenomenon of bride burnings and dowry

Compare & Contrast

- **1990s:** In 1990, the number of Indian-born people living in the United States is 450,000. By 1995, there is a 160,000-strong Indian community in California alone.

  Today: India is the second highest source of legal immigration to the United States, second only to Mexico. In 2003, legal immigration from India to the United States totals 50,379. As of 2006, ethnic Asians make up 4.2 percent of the U.S. population.

- **1990s:** Arranged marriage is common among Indian and other Asian immigrants to the United States. A 1994 opinion poll of 1,715 adults in five urban centers in India finds that 74 percent of men and women believe arranged marriages are more likely than non-arranged marriages to succeed.

  Today: Arranged marriage is the prevailing trend among Indian and other Asian immigrant families. However, some commentators say that the custom has changed, having become primarily an introduction service where the children have the final say. This shift is especially true of those who are brought up in the United States.

- **1990s:** Arranged marriages among Indian immigrants are organized by relatives or professional marriage brokers. Throughout the 1990s, the number of marriages arranged through classified advertisements placed by parents in newspapers and through Internet-based matrimonial agencies increases.

  Today: As many Indian immigrants lose contact with family members and marriage brokers based in India because of the length of time away from the home country and geographical dispersal, the role of newspaper classified advertisements and Internet agencies in arranged marriages grows more prominent.

- **1990s:** Classified matrimonial advertisements are often organized by community, caste, language, or religion.

  Today: Reflecting the increasingly ambitious nature of the Asian American community, classified matrimonial advertisements gain new categories relating to profession, such as specifying doctors, lawyers, and so on.

---

deaths. They point out that arranged marriages are commonly between a man of higher caste (class) with limited money and a woman of lower caste whose family has money, with the incentive to the bridegroom being a lucrative dowry provided by the bride's parents. In some cases, once the man has pocketed the dowry, or if the family has failed to make the dowry payments, he kills his wife, often by dowsing her with gasoline and setting fire to her. He then claims that she died in a cooking accident. Because many cases of bride burnings are covered up, the number of victims can only be estimated. In 2003, the National Crime Records Bureau of India gave the number of reported dowry deaths, including bride burning, as 6,208. In 2004, the bureau reported the number at 7,026, an increase of 13.2 percent.

Proponents of arranged marriage comment that spousal abuse is as common in non-arranged marriages. They say that all family members share responsibility for an arranged marriage, so victims of such abuse can take refuge in the homes of relatives.

Critical Overview

The award-winning poet Chitra Banerjee Divakaruni's first collection of short stories, *Arranged Marriage*, was published in 1995, and in 1996, it won the American Book Award, the Bay Area Book Reviewers Award for Fiction, and the PEN Oakland Josephine Miles Prize for Fiction. The collection

Indian brides and their husbands on their wedding day   AFP/Getty Images

was well received by the public, quickly becoming a bestseller, and met with critical acclaim. Paul Nathan's review in *Publishers Weekly* is typical of those who affirmed Divakaruni's first foray into prose: "The name Chitra Divakaruni is one that more and more people are going to learn to recognize, pronounce and remember."

Donna Seaman, in her *Booklist* review of *Arranged Marriage*, hails Divakaruni as "a virtuoso short story writer" and comments that "these are ravishingly beautiful stories, some profoundly sad, others full of revelation, all unforgettable." Seaman draws attention to the main theme of the collection (and of "Meeting Mrinal"), "the vast differences between women's lives in India, the country of her birth, and in the U.S., her country of choice." An anonymous *Publishers Weekly* reviewer's description of the central conflict of these stories applies to "Meeting Mrinal": "Divakaruni places her characters at the volatile confluence of two conflicting pressures: the obligation to please traditional husbands and families, and the desire to live modern, independent lives."

For Seaman, the message of the stories is predominantly feminist and pro-Western society, as they "revolve around the attempt to maintain traditional gender roles in the free-wheeling U.S., where even the most obedient and self-negating Indian

women discover they can live a far more fulfilling life." This theme is echoed by Robbie Clipper Sethi in *Studies in Short Fiction*. Sethi notes that the women in the stories, far from being defeated by their ordeals, "prepare to battle the conventions they have left behind to take full advantage of their new lives in America."

Francine Prose, writing in *Women's Review of Books*, observes a more ambiguous tone in the stories, commenting that the young Indian protagonists are "learning to cope with the unsettling novelties of life in the United States," performing a "strenuous balancing act." Sandra Ponzanesi, in the *Cambridge Guide to Women's Writings in English*, notes that Divakaruni "does not offer readymade solutions" to the confused roles and emotional turmoil of her heroines. She cites the final line of "Meeting Mrinal" about "Drinking to our 'precious, imperfect lives'" and comments, "No real catharsis is found but only adjustments and compromises."

Prose cautions against what she perceives as a weakness of some of the stories—that they depend too heavily on a certain sort of "hot-button, up to the minute, highly contemporary and instantly recognizable" social problem, rather than on character. Examples of such problems featured in the stories include divorce, abortion, and spousal abuse. But she adds, "Divakaruni's work is strongest when her characters exhibit a surprising and truly moving intensity of response to their situations." The anonymous *Publishers Weekly* reviewer is one of many critics who see much emotional intensity in the stories, calling them "emotionally fraught" and singling out "Meeting Mrinal" as "particularly poignant." Seaman, in her *Booklist* review, also notes that Divakaruni "conveys emotions with stunning accuracy," calling the collection "deeply affecting."

Criticism

Claire Robinson

Robinson is a former teacher of English literature and creative writing and, as of 2006, is a full-time writer and editor. In the following essay, she examines how the mirage of the perfect life is explored in "Meeting Mrinal."

Chitra Banerjee Divakaruni's "Meeting Mrinal" opens on a scene in which Indian-born and newly divorced Asha prepares a meal for herself and her teenage son, Dinesh. Food and cooking identify a central theme of the story. Here, they symbolize how far Asha has departed from her accustomed wifely practice of preparing elaborate Indian meals from fresh ingredients. Now, Asha and Dinesh make do with ready-made pizza and whatever remnants of moldy vegetables Asha can find in her refrigerator. Dinesh often eats at Burger King, where he works. The scene is loaded with significance. It is traditional for an Indian wife to cook complex meals from scratch for her family and for the family to sit down to eat together. Now that Asha's husband, Mahesh, has left her for a younger white woman, Asha has left off cooking in the old way: "I've decided that too much of my life has already been wasted mincing and simmering and grinding spices." Instead, she is spending her time training for a new full-time job, which she will need as a single mother who is trying to build an independent life.

Another aspect of the scene is that the limp and moldy vegetables that Asha finds in her refrigerator suggest the rot that, unnoticed by Asha, had set into her marriage and that now threatens to infect what remains of her family life, her relationship with Dinesh. The convenience food and lifeless vegetables that she now serves up, somewhat guiltily, also reflect the lack of time, attention, and nourishment she is giving to her relationship with Dinesh. Since his father left, Dinesh has withdrawn to his room and

into his music and now looks at her with "a polite, closed stranger's face." Asha's omissions regarding Dinesh will soon prompt a crisis between mother and son—not relating to food, but to the truth in and substance of their relationship.

The barrier between Asha and Dinesh is the same as that which arises between Asha and Mrinal: Asha's inability to openly acknowledge the failure of her marriage. When Mrinal telephones Asha, Asha cannot bring herself to tell her the truth about her situation. Instead, she keeps up the pretence of a happy family life, complete with invented, respectable activities for Dinesh. Witnessing his mother constructing a fake veneer of perfection over the ruins of his family life is too much for Dinesh to bear. He angrily demands, "I'm not good enough for your friend just the way I am, is that it?" This is an unintentional, yet relevant comment on Asha's feelings about herself: She does not feel good enough for Mrinal, for Dinesh, or for society in general, just the way she is. She has worked hard at being the perfect wife and mother and feels that she has failed. Her feelings of shame deepen when, in fury at Dinesh's challenge to her to tell the truth—that Mahesh "got tired of you and left you for another woman," she slaps him. However, she loses the opportunity to be truthful with Dinesh when she falsely claims that her anger stems from his swearing rather than the uncomfortable truth that he voiced. In the ensuing coldness between Asha and Dinesh, she tries to win him round by cooking his favorite food and calling him by his baby name, Dinoo. This tactic fails miserably because it is another lie; Asha is no longer the all-capable, all-nourishing mother, and Dinesh is a young man, not a child.

Asha's situation is particularly perilous because she has no firm foothold in her old life or in her new life. Though she has made her first brave steps towards establishing an independent life in a harsh and alien Western culture in the form of her training and her fitness classes, she feels that she is not up to the task. When she drives to her meeting with Mrinal, she finds that she is not used to negotiating city traffic, a reference to her uncertainty about negotiating her way through Western culture. When she arrives at the plush restaurant, she feels dowdy and awkward. She reflects, "I knew I didn't belong here, and that every person in the room, without needing to look at me, knew it too."

Asha's feelings of inadequacy are strengthened by the images of perfection against which she has chosen to measure herself. First, there is the image of wifely perfection that, it is suggested, comes with the territory of traditional Indian marriage. Asha pursues this ideal even after Mahesh has told her that the marriage is over, buying a sexy negligée to try to tempt him back. When Mahesh leaves, she blames herself, as is clear from the shame that prevents her from speaking openly about his decision.

The second image of perfection that plagues Asha is her idealized picture of her friend Mrinal: "*She has the perfect existence—money, freedom, admiration . . . and she doesn't have to worry about pleasing anyone.*" It is easy for Asha to project an idea of perfection onto Mrinal because Mrinal has succeeded in the areas in which Asha feels weak: She is glamorous, has a successful career, a lovely home, and power over men in her work. The competitive nature of their relationship is given an added edge by the fact that Mrinal warned Asha against contracting an early arranged marriage, advising her instead to finish college and get a job, but Asha ignored her friend's suggestion. Not only does Asha think that she has failed to measure up to Mrinal, but she is convinced that she has been proved wrong and, understandably, is reluctant to admit it.

The third image of perfection is James Bond, who, with his "golden guns and intricate machines and bikini-clad beauties," represents an idealized Western image of male sophistication and success that young Asha and Mrinal admired while they were growing up in India. They vowed that if they got to the West, they would celebrate with Bond's favorite drink, vodka martini, shaken, not stirred. Indeed, when Mrinal meets Asha in the restaurant, she orders this drink for them both. For Asha, Mrinal is part of James Bond's world, with her perfect grooming and sophisticated manners. What Asha fails to bear in mind is that Bond is a fictional character.

The edifice of perfection that Asha has created crumbles when Mrinal bursts into tears and admits that she is unhappy and lonely. She envies Asha her husband and child as much as Asha has envied her. Once again, Asha avoids telling the truth, but inside, she is plunged into a crisis by Mrinal's revelation: "I feel like a child who picks up a fairy doll she's always admired from afar and discovered that all its magic glitter is really painted clay." In Chitra Banerjee Divakaruni's "Meeting Mrinal," it transpires that for Asha, images of perfection are not only her torment, but her sustenance, compensating for her own messy and confused life. She wonders, "What would I live on, now that I knew perfection was only a mirage?"

In despair, Asha drives home and makes a half-hearted attempt at suicide by gassing herself with

> " In Chitra Banerjee Divakaruni's 'Meeting Mrinal,' it transpires that for Asha, images of perfection are not only her torment, but her sustenance, compensating for her own messy and confused life."

car fumes in the garage. When she changes her mind and staggers out of the garage, Dinesh appears and helps her to the bathroom where she vomits; he looks after his mother as if he were the adult and she were the child. He seems, she remarks, "*motherly.*" Allowing Dinesh to see her at this, her lowest point, and to help her, is a breakthrough for Asha. She finally lets go of her need to be perceived as the perfect wife and mother and realizes that her role models were (unhelpfully) the superhuman heroines of Indian mythology and a hero of Western mythology. She thinks with compassion of Mahesh, noting that perhaps he had the same idealized notions when they married. She sums up her situation in brutally honest words: "I've lost my husband and betrayed my friend, and now to top it all I've vomited all over the sink in my son's presence." Far from sounding like a defeat, her words have an air of integrity. At last, Asha has allowed herself to be helped and faced her frailty; she can move forward into a future guided by truth and self-knowledge rather than false images of external perfection.

In her moment of resolution, Asha has a vision of a simple clay bowl from her art appreciation class. She remembers her teacher explaining that the master potter who made it always left a flaw in his later works, in the belief that it made them more human and more precious. The image is a positive transformation of the negative image she held in her disillusionment about the "painted clay" of Mrinal's life. The clay bowl, beautiful yet flawed, is a symbol of Asha's life, and, by extension, of Mrinal's and Dinesh's and Mahesh's life—indeed, of everyone's life: far from perfect, but infinitely precious.

What Do I Read Next?

- *Arranged Marriage* seems to have developed from the poem, "Arranged Marriage" in Divakaruni's collection of poems *Black Candle: Poems about Women from India, Pakistan, and Bangladesh* (1991), though the short story collection examines a much wider selection of themes.

- In "Uncertain Objects of Desire," an essay published in the March 2000 issue of *Atlantic Monthly* magazine, Divakaruni examines the Indian tradition of arranged marriage and comments on how it is being adapted to modern realities.

- Divakaruni's first novel, *The Mistress of Spices* (1997), draws on the rich mystical and cultural traditions of India to tell the story of Tilo, a woman who is trained in the ancient art of healing through spices and ordained as an immortal through a rite of fire. She travels through time and takes the form of a wizened old woman to set up a shop in California, from which she prescribes spices as remedies to customers.

- A 1998 interview with Divakaruni entitled "Chitra Divakaruni explains how her family, her childhood and the stories she was told have all influenced her writing," can be found at http://www.bookbrowse.com/author_interviews/full/index.cfm?author_number=338 (accessed May 4, 2006).

- Bharati Mukherjee's collection of stories *The Middleman and Other Stories* (1988) explores the meeting of East and West through the experiences of Third World immigrants to the United States and Canada. These include people of Indian origin but also people from Italy, Trinidad, Israel, Vietnam, Afghanistan, the Philippines, and elsewhere.

- The travelogue of American journalist Elisabeth Bumiller, *May You Be the Mother of a Hundred Sons: A Journey among the Women of India* (1990), is the fruit of Bumiller's four-year residence in India in the 1980s. Bumiller takes a look at Indian women, considering the custom of arranged marriage, the outlook of village women, India's evolving feminist movement, bride burning, population control, and female infanticide.

- In Thomas Dublin's book, *Immigrant Voices: New Lives in America, 1773–1986* (1993), immigrants to the United States from the time of the American Revolution to 1986 tell in their own words what it is like to move to the United States and become Americans. The stories show why they leave their original countries, why they choose to move to the United States, and what they find when they get there.

The resolution unfolds into a new truthfulness in Asha's relationship with Dinesh. She freely admits that she "made a mess" of her meeting with Mrinal and offers to tell him about it over a glass of pistachio milk. It is significant that Asha is here breaking her new habit of convenience food and returning on this occasion to a nourishing and traditional Indian drink; it is a reconciliation with her Indian roots and with the motherly role that she turned her back on after Mahesh's departure. Dinesh smilingly accepts her offer, a sign that he is ready to be reconciled with his mother. As Asha and Dinesh solemnly raise their glasses to their "precious, imperfect lives," the final image that readers are given is optimistic: "The glasses glitter like hope." Asha recognizes and, more importantly, accepts that she and Dinesh will have other arguments. Liberated from false notions of perfection, Asha plans the letter she will write to Mrinal to tell her the truth.

Source: Claire Robinson, Critical Essay on "Meeting Mrinal," in *Short Stories for Students*, Thomson Gale, 2007.

Somdatta Mandal

In the following essay, Mandal gives a critical analysis of Divakaruni's life and work.

Belonging to the group of young Indian writers that emerged on the literary scene with a postcolonial diasporic identity after Salman Rushdie, Chitra Banerjee Divakaruni's position as a South Asian writer in English is distinct and well established. As someone who has spent more time outside India than in it, she has been accepted as an Asian American writer, living with a hybrid identity and writing partially autobiographical work. Most of her stories, set in the Bay Area of California, deal with the experience of immigrants to the United States, whose voice is rarely heard in other writings of Indian writers in English. She has been published in more than fifty magazines, including the *Atlantic Monthly* and *The New Yorker*, and her writing has been included in more than thirty anthologies. Her works have been translated into eleven languages, including Dutch, Hebrew, Portuguese, Danish, German, and Japanese.

Chitra Banerjee was born in Calcutta on 29 July 1956 and spent the first nineteen years of her life in India. Her father, Rajendra Kumar Banerjee, an accountant by profession, and her mother, Tatini Banerjee, a schoolteacher, brought up their four children in modest middle-class ambience. As the second-born child and only girl among three brothers, Partha, Dhruva, and Surya, Chitra spent her childhood days in sibling rivalry and camaraderie. She studied at Loreto House, a convent school run by Irish nuns, from where she graduated in 1971. In 1976 she earned her bachelor's degree in English from Presidency College, University of Calcutta. At the age of nineteen she moved to the United States to continue her studies as an English major and got her master's degree from Wright State University in Dayton, Ohio, in 1978. Working under Stephen Greenblatt on the topic "For Danger Is in Words: A Study of Language in Marlowe's Plays," she received her Ph.D. in English from the University of California at Berkeley in 1984. She held different kinds of jobs to pay for her education, including babysitting, selling merchandise in an Indian boutique, slicing bread at a bakery, and washing instruments at a science lab. She did not begin to write fiction until after she graduated from Berkeley, when she came to realize that she loved teaching but did not want to do academic writing: "It didn't have enough heart in it. I wanted to write something more immediate." In 1979 in Dayton she married Murthy Divakaruni, an engineer by profession. Her two sons, Anand and Abhay, were born in 1991 and 1994.

Divakaruni and her husband moved to Sunnyvale, California, in 1989. For several years she was interested in issues involving women and worked with Afghani women refugees and women from

> **Divakaruni's first volume of short stories, *Arranged Marriage* (1995), explores the cross-cultural experiences of womanhood through a feminist perspective, a theme that continues to inform her work."**

dysfunctional families, as well as in shelters for battered women. In 1991 she became founder-member and president of Maitri, an organization in the San Francisco area that works for South Asian women in abusive situations. She also associated herself with Asians against Domestic Abuse, an organization in Houston. Her interest in these women grew when she realized that there was no mainstream shelter for immigrant women in distress—a place where people would understand their cultural needs and problems—in the United States. Because of the experience she gathered from counseling sessions, the lives of Asian women opened up to her, revealing unimaginable crises.

For all the years Divakaruni lived in the Bay Area, she taught at Foothill College in Los Altos Hills. She turned to writing as a means of exploring the cultural differences she encountered as a newcomer to the United States. Initially, she started writing for herself, and during the mid 1980s she joined a writer's group at Berkeley University. She wrote poems during that time, and, as she told Roxanne Farmanfarmaian in *Publishers Weekly* (14 May 2001), her venture into serious poetry writing began after she received the news of her grandfather's death in her ancestral village in India: "Poetry was closest to my psyche. Poetry focuses on the moment, on the image, and relies on image to express meaning. That was very important to me, that kind of crystallization, that kind of intensity in a small space."

As he has been with the publications of many Indian writers in English, Professor P. Lal of the Writers Workshop in Calcutta was instrumental in publishing Divakaruni's first book of poetry, *Dark Like the River* (1987). She had already established herself as a poet by the time she published *The*

Reason for Nasturtiums (1990), her first verse collection published in the United States. The subtitle of the volume explains her primary interest and indicates that her main focus is the immigrant experience and South Asian women. She shows the experiences and struggles involved in Asian women's attempts to find their own identities, as her poem "The Arranged Marriage" illustrates:

The night is airless-still, as
before a storm. Behind the wedding drums,
cries of jackals from the burning grounds.
The canopy gleams, color
of long life, many children.
Color of bride-blood . . .

. . . The groom's father
produces his scales and in clenched silence
the dowry gold is weighed. But he smiles
and all is well again. Now it is godhuli,
the time of the auspicious seeing.
Time for you, bride of sixteen,
mother, to raise the tear-stained face
that I will learn so well,
to look for the first time into
your husband's opaque eyes.

As the title suggests, Divakaruni's volume of poems *Leaving Yuba City: New and Selected Poems* (1997) includes new poems as well as ones from *Dark Like the River*, *The Reason for Nasturtiums*, and *Black Candle: Poems about Women from India, Pakistan, and Bangladesh* (1991). These poems draw on similar subject matter to her fiction: womanhood, family life, exile, alienation, exoticism, ethnicity, domesticity, love, and romance. *Leaving Yuba City* is a collection that explores images of India and the Indian experience in the United States, ranging from the adventures of going to a convent school in India run by Irish nuns to the history of the earliest Indian immigrants in the United States. The opening poem, "How I Became a Writer," describes an abusive father ("the gorilla with iron fingers") and the suicide of a mother who puts the poet to bed and locks her in "so I would not be the first to discover her body hanging from the ceiling." The poem concludes, however, with the ironic affirmation "I *know* I'm going to be / the best, the happiest writer in the world."

Leaving Yuba City comprises six sections of interlinked poems. Although they feature many of the same characters, they explore a variety of themes. Divakaruni is particularly interested in how different art forms can influence and inspire each other. The series of poems based on paintings by the American artist Francesco Clemente is of particular interest. In a section devoted to his "Indian Miniatures" series, Divakaruni's words enter into Clemente's dreamscapes and reveal moments of startling visual clarity. She also takes equal inspiration from other artists' interpretations of her native land—photographs by Raghubir Singh and Indian motion pictures, including Mira Nair's *Salaam Bombay!* (1988) and Satyajit Ray's *Ghare-Baire* (1984). As with all of her writing, these poems deal with the experiences of women and their struggle for identity. Her persistent concern with women's experience often deepens as it is arrayed against varying cultural backgrounds. As Meena Alexander, another poet of Indian origin, states: "Chitra Divakaruni's *Leaving Yuba City* draws us into a realm of the senses, intense, chaotic, site of our pleasures and pain. These are moving lyrics of lives at the edge of the new world."

The group of poems about the immigrant experiences of the Sikhs is especially poignant. Because of immigration restrictions, most of the original Sikh farmers who settled in Yuba City, California, could not bring their families with them or, in the case of single men, go back to get married until the 1940s. As a result, in the 1920s and 1930s several men married local women from Mexico. This section imagines the lives of the farmers who arrived in 1910 and takes on their voices in lush, novelistic prose poems: "I lay in bed and try to picture her, my bride, in a shiny gold salwar-kameez, eyes that were black and bright and deep enough to dive in." The poem "The Brides Come to Yuba City" describes the reunion of the long-separated lovers:

Red-veiled, we lean to each other,
press damp palms, try
broken smiles. The man who met us at the ship
whistles a restless *Angrezi* tune
and scans the fields. Behind us,
the black wedding trunks, sharp-edged,
shiny, stenciled with strange men-names
our bodies do not fit into:
. . . .
He gives a shout, waves at the men, their slow
uneven approach. We crease our eyes
through the veils' red film, cannot breathe. Thirty
    years
since we saw them. Or never,
like Harvinder, married last year at Hoshiarpur
to her husband's photo,
which she clutches tight to her
to stop the shaking. He is fifty-two,
she sixteen. Tonight—like us all—
she will open her legs to him.

This volume of poetry won a Pushcart Prize, an Allen Ginsberg Prize, and a Gerbode Foundation Award.

After three books of poetry, Divakaruni realized that there were things she wanted to say that would be better expressed in prose. "My poetry was becoming more and more narrative," she admitted to Farmanfarmaian, "and I was becoming more interested in the story element, and the nuances of character change." In 1992 she enrolled in an evening fiction-writing class at Foothill College, where she had started teaching twentieth-century multicultural literature the year before. In 1993 she edited *Multitude: Cross-Cultural Readings for Writers*, an anthology she uses in her own classroom; it is also used at many major universities in the United States. Her criterion for selection, as quoted by Elizabeth Softky in her article "Cross-Cultural Understanding Spiced with the Indian Diaspora" (1997), was "quality, but also stories that focused on problem solving, not just how terrible things are." The anthology includes stories about communication across cultures, expectations of friendships, the 1992 Los Angeles riots, and prejudice against gay people. The book includes works by a variety of authors, some of them her own students. Divakaruni's first volume of short stories, *Arranged Marriage* (1995), explores the cross-cultural experiences of womanhood through a feminist perspective, a theme that continues to inform her work. "It was while I was at Berkeley that I became aware of women's issues and the need for me to do something for them," she has said. Although her outlook has softened and her interest has shifted to more general human themes of memory and desire, at that time she felt militant: "I really wanted to focus on women battling and coming out triumphant."

How changing times affect the cherished Indian institution of arranged marriage is the theme of the eleven stories of *Arranged Marriage*. Most of the stories are about Indian immigrants to the United States from the author's native region of Bengal and are told by female narrators in the first-person-singular point of view, often in the present tense, which imparts to the stories a sense of intimacy. They capture the experience of recent immigrants, mostly from professional classes, such as electronic engineers and businesspeople, but also a few from the working class, such as auto mechanics and convenience-store clerks. There are several immigrant brides who "are both liberated and trapped by cultural changes," as Patricia Holt puts it in her "Women Feel Tug of Two Cultures" (1995), and who are struggling to carve out an identity of their own. Though references to local attractions, postgraduate education, and her Bengali culture are sprinkled liberally throughout the tales, Divakaruni says the stories themselves—which

deal with issues such as domestic violence, crime, racism, interracial relationships, economic disparity, abortion, and divorce—were the result of her own imaginings and the experiences of others.

Arranged Marriage received considerable critical acclaim and the 1996 American Book Award, the Bay Area Book Reviewers Award, and the PEN Oakland Award for fiction. Only two of the stories of this collection had been published previously: "The Bats" appeared in *Zyzzyva* (Spring 1993), and "Clothes" in the anthology *Home to Stay: Asian American Women's Fiction* (1990). Some critics have accused Divakaruni of tarnishing the image of the Indian community and reinforcing stereotypes of the "oppressed" Indian woman, but as Julie Mehta quotes the author in "Arranging One's Life" (*Metro*, 3-9 October 1996), her professed aim was to shatter stereotypes: "Some just write about different things, but my approach is to tackle these sensitive topics. I hope people who read my book will not think of the characters as Indians, but feel for them as people."

At once pessimistic and filled with hope, Divakaruni creates contradictory as well as connected fictional worlds through the stories in *Arranged Marriage*. In "Silver Pavements, Golden Roofs," the protagonist—a graduate student newly arrived in the United States, which she considers a land of illusion—is brought face to face with harsh reality when she is assaulted on the mean streets of Chicago. "The Ultrasound," which deals with the issue of female feticide, was later enlarged into the novel *Sister of My Heart* (1999). In "Affair" two temperamentally ill-matched Indo-American couples, whose marriages had been arranged on the basis of their horoscopes having matched "perfectly," divorce after many years of affluent living in Silicon Valley. In "Doors" the character Preeti, after moving to the United States, has come to love the western idea of privacy. She faces a dilemma when her husband's cousin wants to come to live with them. She expresses her discontent with the situation, which shows her newfound decisiveness and her determination to oppose her husband's view of the traditional Indian wife. In "Clothes" the husband of the narrator, Sumita, dies, and she is faced with deciding whether to stay in the United States or to go back to India to live with her in-laws. Sumita calls widows who are serving their in-laws "doves with cutoff wings."

One common theme that runs through all the stories is that Indian-born women living new lives in the United States find independence a mixed blessing that involves walking a tightrope between old beliefs and newfound desires. Though the characters vary, the themes of the short stories are essentially the same—exploration of the nature of arranged marriages as well as the experience of affirmation and rebellion against social traditions.

Divakaruni's first novel, *The Mistress of Spices* (1997), is distinct in that it blends prose and poetry, successfully employing magic realist techniques. Its heroine, Tilo (short for Tilottama), is the "mistress of spices." Born in India, she is shipwrecked on a remote island inhabited by women. Here she encounters an ancient woman who imparts instruction about the power of spices. Ordained after a trial by fire, each new mistress is sent to a far-off land. Tilo heads for Oakland, California, disguised as an old woman, and sets up a shop where she sells spices. While she supplies the ingredients for curries and *kormas*, she also helps her customers to gain a more precious commodity: whatever they most desire. The chapters of the novel are named after spices such as cinnamon, turmeric, and fenugreek, common ingredients of Indian cuisine. Here, however, they have special powers, and Tilo practices her magical powers of healing through them. Through those who visit and revisit her shop, she catches glimpses of the local Indian expatriate community, which includes an abused wife, a naive cabbie, a sullen teen, a yearning young woman, and an old man clinging to dignity, all of whom lack balance. To each, Tilo dispenses wisdom and the appropriate spice, for the restoration of sight, the cleansing of evil, the pain of rejection. When a lonely American ventures into the store, however, a troubled Tilo cannot find the correct spice, for he arouses in her a forbidden desire—which if she follows will destroy her magical powers. Conflicted, she has to choose whether to serve her people or to follow the path leading to her own happiness. Tilo has to decide which part of her heritage she will keep and which part she will choose to abandon.

The Mistress of Spices has a mystical quality to it, and, as Divakaruni puts it in "Dissolving Boundaries," an essay for the on-line journal *Bold Type* (May 1997), "I wrote it in a spirit of play, collapsing the divisions between the realistic world of twentieth century America and the timeless one of myth and magic in my attempt to create a modern fable." She drew on folktales of her childhood memories such as that of a sleeping city under the ocean and speaking serpents, but she changed them almost completely. "The speaking serpents are a different kind of magic that I only partially understand. They represent the grace of the universe, and

by that, I mean they are not governed by logic but come to us mortals as a blessing we cannot understand." Unlike in her short stories, the immigrant experience in the novel is dealt with obliquely. Her own immigrant experience in Ohio helped her express the feelings of loneliness and cultural separation that suffuse the novel. Thus the book also becomes a kind of metaphor for the struggle between social responsibility and personal happiness. When asked by Morton Marcus, in an interview for *Metro* (8-14 May 1997), why she had taken the risk of plunging into fantasy when she had already secured a large following and critical praise with the realistic *Arranged Marriage*, Divakaruni replied candidly: "First, I believe a writer should push boundaries, and I wanted to try something new, take risks. But more to the point, the risk-taking came of a near-death experience I had two and a half years ago with the birth of my second child, Abhay, who was born of a Caesarian operation that went wrong." That experience inspired her to create Tilo, who moves back and forth between one existence and another. As she explained to Marcus, "Looking at this question from another perspective, you could say that I took three 'literary risks' in the book. I bridged the purely realistic world and the mythic one; I extended my subject matter from dealing exclusively with the Indian-American community to include three other ethnic groups living in the inner city—Latinos, African Americans and Native Americans—and finally, I tried to bring together the language of poetry and prose so the idiom of the book has a lyric quality appropriate to the genre of magic realism." The concept of boundaries falling away leads the reader to the main theme of the novel, that "happiness comes from being involved in our human world."

The Mistress of Spices is also a love story, the outcome of which keeps the reader in suspense. Interestingly, when Tilo makes her decision, she changes her name to Maya, the Hindu term that defines the everyday world of desire, pain, and joy as the world of illusion, a place of inevitable sorrow from which one is trying to escape. The novel was named one of the best books of 1997 by the *Los Angeles Times* and one of the best books of the twentieth century by the *San Francisco Chronicle*, and was nominated for the Orange Prize in England in 1998.

From mid 1997 to early 1998, Divakaruni also wrote a regular column, "Spice of Life," for the online magazine *Salon*, in which she focused upon the issues she knows best. In a column titled "My Fictional Children" (28 January 1998) she notes that everything she ever tried to write about her children has been a failure but that the fictional mothers in her stories have become much more complex and full:

> My writing is made more complicated by the fact that I'm exploring the experience of being Indian, of being brought up in a culture where many still consider motherhood a woman's supreme destiny, and the inability to get pregnant her supreme failure. This is one of the major themes of the novel I'm working on right now. I think I'm not exaggerating when I say . . . that I wouldn't be writing this book had I not had children myself.

In 1998, commissioned by the New England Foundation, Divakaruni also wrote a play called *Clothes*, which was performed by the New World Theater at Amherst College and at the International Drama Festival, Athens, Greece, in 1999.

Unlike her first novel, *Sister of My Heart* is written in the realist mode and describes the complicated relationships of a family in Bengal. Born in a big, old Calcutta house on the same night when both their fathers mysteriously disappeared, Sudha and Anju are distant cousins and are brought up together. Closer than sisters, they share clothes, worries, and dreams. The Chatterjee family fortunes are at a low ebb, as there are only widows at home—the girls' mothers and their aunt. The forty-two chapters of the novel comprise a sort of extended, multitiered dialogue. The chapters themselves are alternately titled "Anju" and "Sudha" and utilize techniques that are epistolary and exclamatory, with transcultural settings, a tone that is adjectival and highly lyrical, italicized stream-of-consciousness passages, and a romantic style. Slowly the dark secrets of the past are unveiled and test the cousins' mutual loyalty. A family crisis forces their mothers to start the serious business of arranging the girls' marriages, and the pair is torn apart. Sudha moves to her new family's home in rural Bengal, while Anju joins her immigrant husband in California. Although they have both been trained to be perfect wives, nothing has prepared them for the pain, as well as the joy, that each will have to face in her new life. In the novel Indian discrimination against women stands exposed: the cousins consider themselves inferior beings because they are female. Feminist views—both overt and covert—are present in many passages of the novel. The story line, however, becomes predictable. Anju saves Sudha from the machinations of her husband and in-laws, who want to kill the girl child she has conceived, and brings her to the United States.

Reception of *Sister of My Heart* was overwhelmingly positive. For most western readers, the novel provided a new look at female bonding. Divakaruni's impetus was to write about a female-centric theme in a South Asian setting. The novel is her perception of an utter lack of emphasis on women's independence in South Asian literary genres. She identifies the novel as ultimately about storytelling. Influenced by her grandfather, who told stories from South Asian epics, she has woven those childhood folktales into her novel. She explains that the "aloneness" of epic heroines seemed strange to her even as a child. In a 28 February 1999 *San Francisco Examiner* article, she declares that in South Asian mythological stories, "the main relationships the heroines had were with the opposite sex: husbands, sons, lovers, or opponents. They never had any important friends. Perhaps in rebellion against such thinking, I find myself focusing my writing on friendships with women, and trying to balance them with the conflicting passions and demands that come to us as daughters and wives, lovers and mothers." Divakaruni shares the emotions of her protagonists and finds in them a mode of feminist expression. "In the best friendships I have had with women, there is a closeness that is unique, a sympathy that comes from somewhere deep and primal in our bodies and does not need explanation, perhaps because of the life-changing experiences we share." She has denied in interviews, however, that she has attempted to create a comprehensive picture of South Asian family life, likening such an assumption to the idea that one can understand all Americans by reading Flannery O'Connor.

Though *Sister of My Heart* is set in Calcutta, Divakaruni admits that the rest of the story is far from autobiographical and is based on observation and imagination. Around the time the novel was published, she also over the course of about a year wrote a column for the magazine *India Today*. Titled "Stars and Spice," the column dealt with immigrant issues.

Apart from her poems and fictional writing, Divakaruni has also established a reputation for herself with her nonfiction pieces. In "Foreign Affairs: Uncertain Objects of Desire," which appeared in the March 2000 issue of the *Atlantic Monthly*, she sifts through several hundred carefully categorized matrimonial advertisements in *The Times of India*, surmising that in India, a country that straddles the old and the new, they are a good place to look for signs of shifting values. Usually the ads and responses are handled by parents—proof that the practice of arranged marriage is alive and well in India. Reading between the lines of two ads typical of their eras, one from 1969 and one from 1999, she concludes that a great deal about the nature of desired partners, and the protocol for finding them, has changed. Apart from other factors, Divakaruni suggests that perhaps "this echoes a larger pattern of social movement in which the Indian woman's role is changed more rapidly than the Indian man's." In a short article she wrote for the Internet site *Rediff on the Net*, "Wheat Complexion and Pink Cheeks" (2 April 2001), she deplores the Indian obsession for fair-skinned women.

The female protagonists of eight of the nine stories in Divakaruni's sensuously evocative collection *The Unknown Errors of Our Lives* (2001) are caught between the beliefs and traditions of their Indian heritage and those of their, or their children's, new homeland, the United States. Seven out of the nine stories collected in the anthology had been published earlier in various journals and anthologies. The diverse range of the stories of this volume is noteworthy. Most of them depict life in East and West perceptively. The problem of acculturation is deftly dealt with in "Mrs. Dutta Writes a Letter," a story in which a widow discovers that her old-fashioned ways are an embarrassment to her daughter-in-law. A young American woman's pilgrimage in Kashmir is the subject of "The Lives of Strangers." Miscommunication and distancing in a brother-sister relationship is the theme of "The Intelligence of Wild Things." Ruchira, the protagonist of "The Unknown Errors of Our Lives," while packing up in preparation for her forthcoming marriage, discovers her childhood "book of errors," a teenage notebook in which she wrote down ways of improving her life.

"The Names of Stars in Bengali" is the nuanced story of a San Francisco wife and mother who returns to her native village in India to visit her mother, in which each understands afresh the emotional dislocation caused by stepping into "a time machine called immigration" that subjects them to "the alien habit of a world they had imagined imperfectly." All of the stories in *The Unknown Errors of Our Lives* are touching tales of lapsed communication, inarticulate love, and redemptive memories. They illuminate the difficult process of adjustment for women in whom memory and duty must coexist with a new, often painful, and disorienting set of standards. In an interview with Esha Bhattacharjee published in *The Sunday Statesman* on 2 February 2003, when asked what she felt she was—an Indian, an American, or an Indian living in the United States, she confessed: "I have to live with a hybrid identity. In many ways I'm an Indian, but living in America for 19 years has taught

me many things. It has helped me look at both cultures more clearly. It has taught me to observe, question, explore and evaluate."

In 2002 Divakaruni moved to Houston, Texas, where she began to teach in the creative-writing program at the University of Houston. In that same year she published *The Vine of Desire*, a novel of depth and sensitivity that can be seen as a sequel to *Sister of My Heart*. It continues the story of Anju and Sudha, the two cousins of the earlier book. The young women now live far from Calcutta, the city of their childhood, and after a year of living separate lives, are rekindling their friendship in the United States. The deep-seated love they feel for each other provides the support they need: it gives Anju the strength to survive a personal tragedy and Sudha the confidence to make a life for herself and her baby daughter, Dayita, despite not having her husband. The unlikely relationships they form with men and women in the world outside the immigrant Indian community as well as their families in India profoundly transform them, especially when they must confront the deep passionate feelings that Anju's husband has for Sudha. Sudha, seeking a measure of self-worth and trying to assuage loneliness, succumbs to Sunil's need for her and then flees from home to be a nursemaid to an old and ailing man. Sunil also moves out and away. Anju sticks to studies and makes it to the dean's list. The novel ends with her metaphorical declaration, "I've learned to fly." Divakaruni deals with a new facet of immigrant experience in the sense that the movement is not necessarily a physical one or from East to West. By making Sudha decide that she is not interested in the United States anymore and would like to go home, the author treads new ground. Through the eyes of people caught in the clash of cultures, Divakaruni reveals the rewards and the perils of breaking free from the past and the complicated, often contradictory emotions that shape the passage to independence. *The Vine of Desire* was named one of the best books of 2002 by the *San Francisco Chronicle* and the *Los Angeles Times*. Also in 2002, Divakaruni was also chosen as a literary laureate by the San Francisco Public Library.

Divakaruni's versatility as a writer was confirmed by her first children's book, *Neela: Victory Song* (2002). Part of the "Girls of Many Lands" series, featuring books and dolls based on young girls from various historical periods and cultural traditions, it is the story of a twelve-year-old girl caught up in the Indian Independence movement. In 1939, while her family is preparing for the wedding of her older sister, Neela Sen becomes interested in the world around her. When her father is jailed following a march against British rule, Neela takes matters into her own hands and goes to Calcutta to find him.

Published in September 2003 and chosen as one of the best books of the year by *Publishers Weekly*, Divakaruni's second book for children, *The Conch Bearer*, blends action, adventure, and magic in a kind of quest fantasy. The story opens in a poor section of Kolkata, as Calcutta was renamed in 2001, where twelve-year-old Anand is entrusted with a conch shell imbued with mystical power. Anand's task is to return the shell to its rightful home high in the mountains. Accompanied by a mysterious stranger and a resourceful street urchin, he encounters good and evil both in himself and in those around him.

Divakaruni's sixth novel, *Queen of Dreams* (2004), again utilizes the magic realist mode. Like Tilo of *The Mistress of Spices*, who uses spices to help customers solve their problems, in *Queen of Dreams* Mrs. Gupta is an Indian immigrant who dreams the dreams of others so she can help them in their own lives. This gift of vision and ability to foresee and guide people through their fates fascinates her daughter, Rakhi, who as a young artist and divorced mother living in Berkeley, California, is struggling to keep her footing with her family and with a world in alarming transition. Rakhi also feels isolated from her mother's past in India and the dreamworld she inhabits, and she longs for something to bring them closer. Burdened by her own painful secret, Rakhi finds solace in the discovery, after her mother's death, of her dream journals. "A dream is a telegram from the hidden world," Rakhi's mother writes in her journals, which open the long-closed door to Rakhi's past.

As Rakhi attempts to divine her identity, knowing little of India but drawn inexorably into a sometimes painful history she is only just discovering, her life is shaken by new horrors. In the wake of the terrorist attacks of 11 September 2001 she and her friends must deal with dark new complexities about their acculturation. The ugly violence visited upon them forces the reader to view those terrible days from the point of view of immigrants and Indian Americans whose only crime was the color of their skin or the fact that they wore a turban. As their notions of citizenship are questioned, Rakhi's search for identity intensifies. Haunted by her experiences of racism, she nevertheless finds unexpected blessings: the possibility of new love and understanding for her family.

Divakaruni's journey from being a young graduate student to a mature writer seems to have come full circle. She believes that there are both pluses and minuses to belonging to the growing body of Asian American writers. The interest in Asian American literature makes it easier to get published now than ten or fifteen years ago, as she told Neela Banerjee of *AsianWeek.com* (27 April–3 May 2001): "The best part is that your writing is now available to so many people, both within and outside of the community. Young South Asians have come up to me and said, 'I really relate to this story. This story has helped me understand my mother, helped me understand my culture.' That's a really good feeling." Divakaruni also admits, however, that being pigeonholed as an Asian American writer can be stifling: "You are expected to be a spokesperson for the community, and that is just an unfair kind of burden. I always try to make it clear that I am presenting one vision about what is true about the Indian American community. It is a very diverse community, and mine is just one angle of looking at it."

As Divakaruni has changed, her style of writing has changed accordingly. For example, *Arranged Marriage* includes a detailed glossary of Bengali and Hindi words, which were italicized in the stories. In *The Vine of Desire* she not only does away with italics and glossaries but uses many Bengali and Hindi words within the text. Through this means she seems to be attempting to get the reader to accept these as a natural part of the characters' world and of their language. When asked by Bhattacharjee as to how she has matured as a writer, she replied that with each new book, she found a "new challenge." Whatever the narrative technique of each of her books might be, she hoped it would connect with the readers.

The critical acclaim and increasing recognition that Chitra Banerjee Divakaruni has received has established her as a promising writer interested in the immigrant experience, not simply that of those who move from East to West. It is a cross-cultural scenario where, through her writings, the diversity of Indian writing in English is revealed.

Source: Somdatta Mandal, "Chitra Banerjee Divakaruni," in *Dictionary of Literary Biography*, Vol. 323, *South Asian Writers in English*, edited by Fakrul Alam, Gale, 2006, pp. 112–122.

Arthur J. Pais

In the following essay, Pais profiles Divakaruni and discusses the portrayal of Indian women in her work.

> **"** But there was also sadness for her in California. For she began to discover that there were hundreds of fellow expatriate women who were trapped in abusive marriages or relationships or who did not know how to cope with the more free-wheeling Western society.**"**

Long before she founded Maitri, a women's self-service group in San Francisco, and before she wrote her magical 1997 novel, *The Mistress of Spices*, Chitra Banerjee Divakaruni was intrigued and fascinated by the bond between women.

"I have been watching how Indian women were forced to do certain things—as the stories of sacrifice and devotion in the mythology demand from them," Divakaruni says, taking a break from her teaching chore at the University of Houston. "And then there are inspiring stories about women like the Rani of Jhansi that offer women refreshing role models—and the strength to fulfill their own destinies."

And now in "Sister of My Heart," Divakaruni, poet, teacher, wife, and mother of two boys, continues mining the imaginary lives of her characters, exploring their world of duty and sacrifice. She also introduces them to the world of self-fulfillment.

"Hers is one of the most strikingly lyrical voices writing about the lives of Indian women today," says novelist Amitav Ghosh in a pre-release review. And the influential *Publishers Weekly* in a starred review calls Divakaruni "an inspired and imaginative reconteur." And like her previous novel, *The Mistress of Spices*, which was translated into 12 languages and is being filmed for a division of Walt Disney—and *Arranged Marriage*, a collection of stories, the new novel has "emotions that are very recognizable," says fellow novelist Rosellen Brown.

Friendship with women were very important to Chitra Banerjee when she grew up in Calcutta, and then moved to Dayton, Ohio, to study at Wright State University in 1977. In Dayton, she would meet Murthi Divakaruni, brother of her close friend, and marry him a few years later. Her husband, who is an engineer, is also her best friend, faithful reader and critical angel, she says. "He understands women as few men do," she says in her gentle, flowing voice.

Divakaruni knew from her Wright State days that there were hundreds of interesting stories in her own life—and those of her friends that needed to be retold in poems (*Leaving Yuba City*) and prose. But first she had to learn something about America—and the Indian immigrants living there. "There were not that many Indians, so I was a curiosity," she recalls her student days in Dayton. "When I walked down the streets in a sari or salwar kameez, people would stop their cars and whisper and point." She laughs at her own misconceptions of America. "I came to plain fields of Ohio with pictures painted by Hollywood movies and the works of Tennessee Williams and Arthur Miller . . . None of them had much to say—if at all—about Dayton, Ohio."

It was a different world in California where she would earn a doctorate in English literature from the University of California at Berkeley. "The (San Francisco) Bay Area is definitely the best part of this country and is most cosmopolitan and the most multicultural," she says of her home for nearly 20 years—she moved to Houston about six months ago. But there was also sadness for her in California. For she began to discover that there were hundreds of fellow expatriate women who were trapped in abusive marriages or relationships or who did not know how to cope with the more free-wheeling Western society.

Many years later, when she plotted *The Mistress of Spices*, her protagonist will also fear and care for the expatriates and other hurt people. Maitri, she says, also taught women how to be self-sufficient and acquire the skills to meaningfully live in America. "Many women who came to Maitri needed to know simple things like opening a bank account or getting citizenship," she says, nodding her head in disbelief. "Some of them had lived in America for a decade but knew no life outside their homes." They also need to have friends to share their emotions—just the way Divakaruni's literary characters do. "Many women in Maitri spoke English," she explained in an interview with *San Francisco Examiner*. "But their English was functional rather than emotional they needed someone who understands their problems and speaks their language . . ."

Chitra, daughter of an Esso oil company officer, wanted to follow in her mother's footsteps and be a teacher. While her mother taught kindergarten and elementary classes, Divakaruni taught English and multicultural literature at Foothill College in Los Altos Hills in California. She became serious about writing about 10 years ago when she joined a writing group in Berkeley and went on to publish four books of poetry. She also edited two cross-cultural anthologies, *Multitude* and *We, Too, Sing America*. "In many ways, being an expatriate increased my desire to write for publications that were not confined to academia," Divakaruni says. "Expatriates have powerful and poignant experiences when they live away from their original culture and this becomes home, but never quite, and then you can't really go back and be quite at home there either. "So you become a kind of outsider to both cultures. This is very good for writers-to be in a position of looking in from the outside"

While she enjoyed doing her dissertation on Christopher Marlowe and studying Renaissance literature at Berkeley, she was also "feeling very dissociated from life." "I needed to do something intellectually connected to my life as an immigrant woman in America." She wonders whether she would have also thought seriously about fiction had her husband remained cool to her poems but marveled at her story ideas. "I realized then that fiction is in a way more gratifying to write because it appeals to a wide range of people." "Poetry often scares people, I think," she adds with a big chuckle.

Her publisher, Doubleday, is giving a high profile treatment to her newest book. Starting Feb. 20, it is sending Divakaruni to more than 20 cities to publicize her book. Similar publicity for *The Mistress of Spices* netted rich results for Doubleday. The book, which was hailed by international bestselling novelist Pat Conroy "as a splendid novel," was on the bestseller lists in California for over a year. Its recognition brought her invitations to write poems and short stories for such publications as *The New Yorker* and *Harper's*.

She chafes when some readers—often Indians—ask her if she writes with Western readers in mind who want to read either about an exotic and mythical India or about a deprived India.

"I have always loved writers from other cultures who create a world where I may not know every single reference but I understand the feel of

it," she said last year in discussing the magical realism in *The Mistress of Spices*.

She offers her readers a window into the multicultural world of her characters, she says. "I have no particular reader in my mind but a passionate desire to tell a honest, moving story," she adds. "If it is good literature, I know as all sensitive writers know, the reader and the writer will connect. It is inevitable."

Source: Arthur J. Pais, "Essay on Chitra Banerjee Divakaruni and Some of Her Works," in *South Asian Journalist's Association Online*, February 1999, pp. 1–3.

Francine Prose

In the following review, Prose discusses Divakaruni's ability to portray characters that move easily between cultures and her use of detail but has little enthusiasm for the "readily-grasped social problems" depicted in her work.

Not long ago I happened to read the minutes of a public meeting held by a state arts foundation. One item on the agenda concerned who should sit on the selection committees which award grants to individual artists. Some members of the audience argued that the selection committees should be composed exclusively of members of minorities. White artists, it was claimed, know only how to interpret and evaluate the art of the dominant culture, whereas minority artists—schooled in their own culture as well as that of the more powerful majority—would be able to understand the artistic expressions of both groups.

Reading this, I felt so breathless that I had to sit down and stop a moment while I wondered when our definition of art had become—almost without our noticing—so fragmented, so narrow, so chillingly xenophobic. Foolishly, I had always imagined that one of the definitions of great—or merely good—art was that it translated more or less easily not only between cultures, but between languages, classes, countries, generations, centuries: across the deep divisions of time.

Chitra Banerjee Divakaruni's new collection of stories, *Arranged Marriage*, makes it clear that fiction can speak the language and address the concerns of highly disparate cultures. Indeed, many of Divakaruni's characters are performing the strenuous balancing act of having one foot in one country, the other foot in another. Though perhaps it would be more accurate to say that the chasms her protagonists straddle have less to do with the ground beneath their feet than with the gap between past and future, between the heart and the head.

"

Typically, the sympathetic heroines of these fictions are young Indian women learning to cope with the unsettling novelties of life in the United States, and others who have adapted so well that now they must reconcile their new lives with the old ways--and the loved ones-- left behind, halfway around the planet."

Typically, the sympathetic heroines of these fictions are young Indian women learning to cope with the unsettling novelties of life in the United States, and others who have adapted so well that now they must reconcile their new lives with the old ways—and the loved ones—left behind, halfway around the planet. So in "The World Love" a Berkeley graduate student is obsessed with the question of what will happen if her unforgivingly traditional, widowed mother, back home in Calcutta, should find out that the daughter is living in sin with her boyfriend:

> The first month you moved in with him, your head pounded with fear and guilt every time the phone rang. You'd rush across the room to pick it up while he watched you from his tilted-back chair, raising an eyebrow . . . At night you slept next to the bedside extension. You picked it up on the very first ring, struggling up out of layers of sleep heavy as water to whisper a breathless hello, the next word held in readiness, mother.

In "Silver Pavements, Golden Roofs" an Indian student, studying in the United States, comes to stay with her uncle and aunt—only to find her aunt in a seclusion stricter than any purdah at home, while her uncle takes on American griefs and new American vices. And in yet another story, "Doors," a thoroughly assimilated Indian woman marries a less Americanized young man who is, as her mother

warns her, "straight out of India," where men are still brought up with "a set of prehistoric values." In fact, the marriage turns out wonderfully, amicable and romantic, until the husband's boyhood friend moves in as a long-term house guest and makes the couple aware of an unbridgeable distance between the American sense of entitlement to privacy and space and the Indian comfort with a public communal life, the belief in hospitality and in not "losing face."

The stories are full of the details of Indian and Indian-American life: the little pots of make-up, of "kumkum and sindur and kajal," the marriage dots on the forehead, the saris, the curries, the Hindi musical films, the marriages contracted after just a few modest minutes of "bride-viewing." But the problems and conflicts presented in nearly all of these fictions exist, all too commonly, in countless other cultures.

So in the volume's initial story, "The Bats," we realize, considerably earlier than the child-narrator, that her Bengali mother is a victim of spousal abuse:

> One morning when she was getting me ready for school, braiding my hair into the slick, tight pigtail that I disliked because it always hung stiffly down my back, I noticed something funny about her face. Not the dark circles under her eyes. Those were always there. It was high up on her cheek, a yellow blotch with its edges turning purple. It looked like my knee did after I bumped into the chipped mahogany dresser next to our bed last month.

And the wife's fear, in the story "Affair," that her husband is sleeping with her best friend, is by no means restricted to wives whose husbands watch MTV while they stay in the kitchen, "fry[ing] the samosas I'd made from scratch or put[ting] the finishing touches on a particularly fine qurma."

Indeed, the weaker of the stories may make one realize how much our global culture—despite the exterior trappings of custom, diet and tradition—is being reduced to the mass fascination with a certain sort of problem: hot-button, up to the minute, highly contemporary and instantly recognizable, the sort of problem that can inspire weeks and months of TV talk shows. The trouble with *Arranged Marriage* is that so many of its stories seem to be about such problems, to center on these problems, to have started with the idea of these problems— rather than from aspects of character (like the best fiction) or even, strictly speaking, from plot. The reader may feel that Divakaruni is not so much observing human nature—in all its various national costumes—as jogging around a track, dutifully touching the bases of our most up-to-the-minute "issues."

Divakaruni's work is strongest when her characters exhibit a surprising and truly moving intensity of response to their situations. The heroine of "The Word Love" gets very close to the edge when she loses the affections of both her mother and her lover. Yet these fictions are less assured when we feel their author pushing her plot and people around, struggling to get them to various popular destinations that we see coming a long time in advance. In fact, the reason we recognize them so readily is that they are so familiar and (however little we know about other cultures) that we've most likely heard of the relevant social problem before.

"The Ultrasound" is a perfect example of what goes wrong with these stories. We're informed early on that an Indian woman in America and her beloved cousin in India are pregnant at the same time; both are scheduled to have prenatal tests that will determine the health and sex of the baby. Readers of daily newspapers and fans of network "news-magazines" may instantly intuit that before the story is over the Indian mother-to-be (like many women in her country) will be pressured into aborting the foetus of an unwanted girl child—and the story seems more intent on getting to this point than on delineating the characters of the two women. Likewise, the minute we learn that the husband in "Clothes" is the proprietor of a 7-Eleven, managing the graveyard shift in a dangerous urban neighborhood, we may feel dismayingly certain that he is to suffer the violent fate shared by too many immigrants working at convenience stores, those all-night invitations to petty or serious crime.

Throughout, there is too much of that sort of signalling, as if the author is making gestures over the characters' heads to inform the attentive reader about something a protagonist is too innocent or dim to know. In "The Disappearance," we're quick to grasp some answers to the mystery of why a submissive wife took the jewelry and wedding gifts and left her husband and son. We realize as soon as he tells us:

> That was another area where he had to be firm. Sex. She was always saying, Please, not tonight, I don't feel up to it . . . Surely he couldn't be blamed for raising his voice at those times . . . or for grabbing her by the elbow and pulling her to the bed, like he did that last night.

And yet this often obvious story ends with a burst of emotion so deep that even the reader who's been invited to patronize the insensitive narrator is shocked by a rush of feeling for him, and for the sorrow that lasts his whole life.

Chitra Banerjee Divakaruni can move us, and she can tell a story. "The Maid Servant's Story," among the best in the collection, is a complex and engaging narrative about sex and betrayal, caste and social class. She needs to learn to trust her characters and to realize that the most mystifying human complexities are ultimately far more interesting than readily-grasped social problems. She can capture the deepest hopes and fears of young women caught halfway between two equally alien and familiar cultures, and I am eager to see what she does next.

Source: Francine Prose, Review of *Arranged Marriage*, in *Women's Review of Books*, Vol. 13, No. 6, March 1996, pp. 20–21.

Sources

Divakaruni, Chitra Banerjee, "Chitra Banerjee Divakaruni Readers' Group Companion," http://www.randomhouse.com/resources/bookgroup/divakaruni_bgc.html (accessed May 4, 2006).

———, "Meeting Mrinal," in *Arranged Marriage*, Black Swan, 1997, pp. 273–300.

———, "Writing," http://www.chitradivakaruni.com/about/writing/ (accessed May 4, 2006).

Nathan, Paul, "Rising Star: Author Chitra Divakaruni's Books Are Very Successful," in *Publishers Weekly*, Vol. 243, No. 46, November 11, 1996, p. 27.

Ponzanesi, Sandra, Review of *Arranged Marriage*, in *Cambridge Guide to Women's Writings in English*, edited by Lorna Sage, Germaine Greer, and Elaine Showalter, 1999, p. 21.

Prose, Francine, Review of *Arranged Marriage*, in *Women's Review of Books*, Vol. 13, No. 6, March 1, 1996, p. 20.

Review of *Arranged Marriage*, in *Publishers Weekly*, Vol. 242, No. 23, June 5, 1995, p. 53.

Seaman, Donna, Review of *Arranged Marriage*, in *Booklist*, Vol. 391, No. 21, July 1995, p. 1860.

Sethi, Robbie Clipper, Review of *Arranged Marriage*, in *Studies in Short Fiction*, Vol. 33, No. 2, Spring 1996, pp. 287–88.

Further Reading

Adler, Bill, and Stephen Sumida, eds., *Growing Up Asian American*, Perennial Currents, 1995.
This collection of fiction and non-fiction pieces presents stories of childhood, adolescence, and coming of age in the United States. The stories feature immigrants from several Asian countries, including Korea, China, Japan, and India, from the 1800s to the 1900s, and show how this population had a great impact on American life.

Daniels, Roger, *American Immigration: A Student Companion*, Oxford University Press, 2001.

This book was written specifically for use in schools and colleges as a resource for research in American history, ethnic and multicultural studies, and genealogy. It covers many aspects of immigration, including an examination of different ethnic groups and their historical background; key immigration legislation; different categories of immigrants, such as refugees, children, and exiles; and religious groups.

———, *Coming to America: A History of Immigration and Ethnicity in American Life*, HarperCollins, 1990.

Roger Daniels illustrates how, despite racial conflicts, immigrants to the United States, including Hispanics and cold war refugees, have adapted and contributed to American society. He describes the reactions of Americans to the various waves of immigration, from the rise of anti-foreign groups such as the Ku Klux Klan, to the restrictive immigration laws of the 1920s, through the World War II imprisonment of Japanese Americans in so-called resettlement camps.

Muller, Gilbert H., *New Strangers in Paradise: The Immigrant Experience and Contemporary American Fiction*, University Press of Kentucky, 1999.

Muller discusses the historical forces that have shaped immigration, including changes in the immigration laws in 1965 and shows how immigration has been treated in American fiction. Authors discussed include Isaac Bashevis Singer, Oscar Hijuelos, Jamaica Kincaid, Amy Tan, and Bharati Mukherjee.

Wheeler, Thomas C., *The Immigrant Experience: The Anguish of Becoming American*, Penguin, 1971, reprint, 1992.

This book provides a compilation of stories from a wide range of immigrants and describes their struggles to survive in a United States that turned out to be much harsher than they expected.

Melon

Julian Barnes
1996

Julian Barnes's short story "Melon" is divided into three sections, covering three ages in the life of a British nobleman of the late eighteenth century: before, during, and after the French Revolution. Dividing his life into segments without explanation may be confusing for readers at first, but Barnes's precise imagery and thoroughness of detail make his story credible and compelling. Even readers who are unfamiliar with the time period in which this work is set can lose themselves in Barnes's lush rendering of a very specific life.

The characters of this story live lives of privilege; they have no idea where food comes from or what difficulties most people face just trying to provide basic sustenance for themselves and their families. Over the course of the story, the main character grows from a child of privilege to a prisoner of war, but he does not necessarily learn about humanity.

"Melon" was published in Barnes's 1996 short story collection *Cross Channel*. The stories in this collection, like many of his other works, are concerned with the relationship between France and England, two countries separated by just a few miles of water whose histories have been intertwined.

Author Biography

Julian Barnes was born in Leicester, England, on January 19, 1946. His parents were teachers. He attended Magdalen College, Oxford, earning a B.A. with

Julian Barnes © Jerry Bauer. Reproduced by permission

honors in 1968. After college, he held a variety of freelance writing positions. He wrote entries for the *Oxford English Dictionary Supplement* in the early 1970s then became a reviewer for the *Times Literary Supplement*. In 1977, he became a contributing editor for the *New Review*. He has been a literary editor for the *New Statesman* and the *Sunday Times of London* and has been a television editor for the *New Statesman* and the *Observer*. From 1990 to 1995, he was the London correspondent for the *New Yorker*, writing a regular column. He was also a contributor to the *New York Review of Books*.

Barnes published his first novel, *Metroland*, in 1980, followed by *Before She Met Me* in 1982. At the same time, he began writing detective fiction, which he published under the pseudonym Dan Kavanagh, using his wife's maiden name. He had married Pat Kavanagh, a literary agent, in 1979. In 1984, he published *Flaubert's Parrot*, which established his international literary reputation. It was shortlisted for the Booker Prize and won the Geoffrey Farber Memorial Prize in England, and in France, it was awarded the Prix Medícis. He went on to write ten more novels, two under his pen name.

In 1996, Barnes changed the course of his writing, publishing his first collection of short stories, *Cross Channel*, which contains "Melon." He published essays frequently, including those collected in

Something to Declare: French Essays, which dwell on his fascination with Britain's long relationship with France, a theme that is prevalent in *Cross Channel*. In fact, Barnes's work is so well accepted in France that he was made an Officier de l'Ordre des Artes et des Lettres. He has also won the Somerset Maugham Award and the E. M. Forster Award from the American Academy and Institute of Arts and Letters. A collection published in 2004, *The Lemon Table*, centers on the theme of aging. He published *George and Arthur* in 2005, an historical tale in which Sir Arthur Conan Doyle, the creator of Sherlock Holmes, plays a prominent role.

Plot Summary

First Section

The first section of "Melon" is presented as a letter that a young British nobleman, Hamilton Lindsay, writes to his cousin Evelina, in 1774. Lindsay is traveling in Europe and is on his way to Rome with his tutor, Mr. Hawkins, when, at Evelina's suggestion, they change direction and stop at Montpelier, a city in the south of France (now spelled Montpellier). Lindsay makes observations about French food and French culture, noting, for instance, that the people of France seem to have no particular sport that they follow and that the women of the country strike him as homely: he says that pretty women are so rare that once, when one walked into an inn near Lyons where they were dining, everyone stood and applauded. Being a member of the nobility, he makes a distinction between those he refers to as "people of quality," who are even more pampered than they are in England, and commoners, whom he finds to be dirtier and more poorly mannered than the English people of the same, landless class.

His description of France ends with his praise for the melons that are grown in the southern French countryside. Unlike the melons grown in England, which need to be carefully cultivated, the melons of France grow abundantly and have a superior flavor. Lindsay reports that he has been eating these melons often.

Second Section

The second section of the story picks up in August 1789, the first year of the French Revolution, although that fact is not revealed for some time. Sir Hamilton Lindsay is no longer the narrator, though he is still the subject. He is an adult aristocrat, fattened, with his own estate to manage. He has been married to Evelina for ten years.

The narrative follows Sir Hamilton as he is traveling to Dover to join a team of cricket players who are scheduled to cross the English Channel to play a goodwill competition against a French team. The English team is comprised of both aristocrats and commoners, which cricket enthusiasts such as Sir Hamilton approve since it allows them to recruit the best players. But others of the nobility, particularly the wives of some of the nobles on the cricket team, feel that blurring the class lines by letting servants treat their masters as equals on the cricket field sets a confusing precedent.

Sir Hamilton and his assistant gardener, Samuel Dobson, travel to Chertsey on August 6, 1789, to join other members of the British team. Dobson is required to ride on top of the coach in the rain because Sir Hamilton feels that the wooden cricket bats are more likely to be damaged by the water than Dobson is. During the trip, Hamilton Lindsay reflects on Evelina's opposition to this trip: people in England know that there is trouble in France between ordinary citizens and the aristocracy. Still, Sir Hamilton is not afraid.

The cricket match between the English and French teams has been arranged by John Sackville, third Duke of Dorset. Ever since being appointed ambassador to France six years earlier, Dorset has returned every summer for the cricket season, but this year the political tensions have made his return impossible. To address the bad feelings between the French and the British aristocrats, Dorset has arranged a match on the Champs-Elysée. The British players are traveling to Dover at which point they will sail across the English Channel to France for the game.

As the band of British players approach Dover, they meet Dorset and his followers on the road. The cricket match is called off: a few days earlier, mobs of angry citizens forced the British ambassador to flee from his home in Paris and, presumably, looted the place. Dorset has escaped across the English Channel to England. He hopes that enough of the aristocrats he had arranged to play for the French team have managed to flee to England to enable him to arrange a match there.

Third Section

The events of this section take place years later. The French government has fallen. King Louis XVI and Queen Marie Antoinette have been incarcerated and then, in 1793, are beheaded. Many

Media Adaptations

- Barnes's official web site at http://www.julian barnes.com offers biographical information, background about his many books, interviews, links, and more.

of the people who knew Sir Hamilton Lindsay through cricket have died fighting the French. Sir Hamilton himself has been a prisoner of the government established by Napoleon Bonaparte and has been held for years until he can be traded for a French officer held by the British, a General de Rauzan. Three years into his captivity, Lady Evelina Lindsay was allowed to join him, along with Dobson, who is now the majordomo of the household. Barnes also refers to Dobson as the "chief forager" of the household, indicating that the government does not provide a decent standard of living for the Lindsays but that they must live on whatever can be scrounged.

Sir Hamilton and Lady Lindsay are allowed to walk about the town freely, followed by a French army guard. They attend the Catholic Church every Sunday afternoon, even though Sir Hamilton does not think of himself as a Catholic. The town was sacked by angry peasants during the revolution. They have taken out their anger at the Catholic Church, which supported the aristocracy, by forcing priests to either flee or marry; by dressing mules in religious vestments and parading them in the streets; and by using the Catholic Church for target practice with canons.

Sir Hamilton's mind is as devastated as the town. His thoughts continually turn to the line-up of the cricket team that gathered in Chertsey in 1789, intent on playing against the French, listing each member, each time forgetting the name of one of the players, which Lady Evelina gently supplies for him.

The story ends with their having dinner one Sunday after church service. While Sir Hamilton mutters about the cricket team, Lady Evelina tries to focus his attention on pleasant thoughts. While he talks incoherently about past events, about the people who are gone, and about his theory that the entire revolution might have been avoided had the cricket game between the French and English nobles been played, she points out what a delicious melon they have with their meal.

Characters

William Bedster

Bedster appears in this story as an example of the flexibility of the English class system: at one time the butler to the Earl of Tankerville, Bedster is described as having been able to rise in society to become a publican, or tavern manager, in Chelsea.

Samuel Dobson

Dobson is the second under-gardener at Sir Hamilton Lindsay's estate. He is not a very good gardener, but Sir Hamilton hired him away from his previous employer because he is a good cricket player. When he travels with Sir Hamilton to Dover in August 1789 to participate in the match against the team of French nobles, he is required to ride outside the coach in the rain. Sir Hamilton's reasoning is that Dobson can survive the extreme weather better than the wooden cricket bats.

In the later years of Sir Hamilton's life, when Hamilton is mentally unstable and being held by the French government, Dobson is brought from England to live with him. The doctor caring for the nobleman thought "it might be advisable to send for the man Dobson, to whom the General made such frequent allusion that the doctor had at first taken him to be the patient's son." It is clear that Sir Hamilton places great importance on Dobson's participation in the game, which illustrates the way that cricket can be used to bridge class distinctions.

Dorset

In the story, John Sackville, the third Duke of Dorset, was appointed the ambassador from Great Britain to France in 1783. He is rumored to have been romantically involved with Marie Antoinette, the French queen, referred to here as Mrs. Bourbon after the family name of King Louis XVI. The way Dorset runs his home in Paris scandalizes several proper British matrons. Being an avid cricket enthusiast, he returns each year to England for the cricket season.

In 1789, the intensifying French Revolution makes it difficult for him to travel, so Dorset devises a new plan: in response to some slanderous remarks made against England by some French nobles, he arranges a cricket match between British and French teams to be played in Paris.

The players for the British team are on their way to Dover, the port from which they will sail to France, when they run into Dorset and his party, who have been put off their Parisian estate on August 8, 1789, in the midst of the French Revolution. Despite his brush with death and race to get out of the country, Dorset is still cheerful, ready to try to arrange the same match in England with French nobles who, like him, have been driven from the country.

A few years after his return to England, Dorset is thrown into depression when he hears that the French royalty have been arrested. There are rumors that he gave his cricket bat to Mrs. Bourbon and that she kept it hidden in her closet until the palace was ransacked by revolutionaries. He locks himself in his room and never ventures outside again.

General du Rauzan

Du Rauzan is a French general who was captured by Sir John Stuart at Maida. He is being held by the English army, and so the French army is holding Sir Hamilton Lindsay as a bargaining piece for an exchange. The exchange, however, is on hold indefinitely. The problem seems to be that du Rauzan is not held in much favor by Napoleon, so there is no urgency to get him back.

Mr. Hawkins

In the first section of the story, Mr. Hawkins is tutor and companion to the young Hamilton Lindsay, on his trip through Europe. Hawkins is presented as a stern, unpleasant man, though that characterization might just be the perspective of a boy in his care.

Later, when the revolution is underway in France, Sir Hamilton invites Hawkins to join him in traveling to that country for a cricket match, but Hawkins says that he would rather remember France as the peaceful place it had been fifteen years earlier.

Mrs. Jack Heythrop

Mrs. Heythrop defends the traditional class structure. She disapproves of the way that Dorset has lived in Paris during his six years as ambassador to France, with gamblers and prostitutes coming and going freely from his house. She is also a source for the argument against letting commoners play on the same cricket teams as aristocrats, supporting racing as a good sport instead because all of the participants—owners, trainers, jockeys, and grooms—know their social place and stay separated.

Lady Evelina Lindsay

The first part of the story is presented as a letter from young Hamilton Lindsay to his cousin Evelina. She is explained as being the reason that he travels to France in the first place, as she is living in Nice and has encouraged him to see the country. He refers to her as a cultivated woman whom he greatly admires and wants to impress, feeling that she will tease him for his awkwardness as a letter writer.

Evelina does not appear in the second section of the story either, but she is mentioned. By this time, Hamilton Lindsay and she have been married for ten years. Sir Hamilton believes that she does not approve of his passion for cricket. When he leaves for France, which coincides with the start of social upheaval, she is crying and whispering instructions to Dobson, who is making the trip with her husband. Although he feels badly about her crying, particularly because she has never cried before when he has gone off to play cricket, he does not realize that she understands the perilous situation in France better than he does.

Lady Evelina is an important presence in the third section of the story. She and her husband are living in a French village under the guard of one of Napoleon's soldiers. Sir Hamilton's mind wavers between past and present events. Still, Lady Evelina has come to France to be with him and take care of him. She speaks to him as rationally as she can but also tries to pull his mind away from melancholia and toward more pleasant thoughts.

Sir Hamilton Lindsay

This story follows Sir Hamilton through three phases of his life, focusing on his relationship with France as a measure of his maturity.

In the first section, Hamilton Lindsay is a young man, traveling with his tutor and relating his impressions of the country to his cousin Evelina in a letter. Because he is young, he reports on issues, such as the suppression of religion, that are important causes of the coming French Revolution without recognizing their significance. Because he has only known a life of privilege, he does recognize the class distinctions between the aristocracy and the common people, but his observations about these distinctions lack depth. For instance, he tells the story of a coachman who whipped his horse and then was in turn whipped by his master, a story that ends with the coachman hugging the horse; Hamilton

Lindsay admits in his letter, "I draw no lesson from this."

In the second section of the story, Sir Hamilton is a jaded, callous aristocrat. He is married to Evelina, but his real passion is cricket. He treats his cricket bats better than he does his servants, although he is well aware that other aristocrats feel that he treats his servants too well because he treats Dobson, an assistant gardener, as an equal on the cricket field. Sir Hamilton is aware that there is political strife in France, but he does not take it seriously. He still believes in the class system and cannot even conceive of the idea that lower-class people might want to harm the aristocracy. He is so wound up in his passion for cricket that he and his friends are in the process of traveling to France for a cricket game when they find out that the some French aristocrats are just barely escaping the country with their lives and others have not been so lucky.

In the third section, Sir Hamilton is a broken man with a damaged mind. He has been a general in the war against France, and the war has ruined him. He is held as a prisoner of the new French government, though they do not think him much of a threat and have him watched by a guard as a token gesture. A doctor has advised that his wife and valet should be allowed to come from England to be with him, to soothe his troubled mind. Much of the time, he does not make sense when he talks, blurring the past and the present, sometimes talking about people who have died as if they are still around and at other times showing himself to be well aware of his and his friends' situation. In between his periods of inchoate verbal wandering, he is still fixated on the cricket game that was called off by the revolution, feeling that if it had occurred, all of the social turmoil of the country might have been avoided.

John Sackville

See Dorset

Lumpy Stevens

Stevens, a gardener for the Earl of Tankerville, is a common man who has earned Sir Hamilton Lindsay's respect with his cricket prowess: once he won a bet for the earl by hitting a feather on the ground with a cricket ball one in four times. Later in his life, when his mind is snapped by the ravages of war, Sir Hamilton often refers to Stevens's feat, especially when he is considering the damage done to the Catholic Church by revolutionaries who have used it for target practice, musing that Stevens's aim was much, much better than theirs.

Themes

Aristocracy

"Melon" focuses on a particular member of the English aristocracy, showing different facets of him over the course of years, highlighting the different perspectives that one can have as a member of the ruling class. When he is young, he is not the master of his world but instead is watched over by his tutor, Hawkins. Hawkins does not have control over his youthful employer, as might be expected of an older, experienced man: for instance, it is young Hamilton Lindsay who dictates the route of their trip, telling Hawkins where they are to go without asking his permission. At the same time, Lindsay is not autonomous but must rely on Hawkins's guidance, even if he does so begrudgingly. At this point of his life, he is trying to understand the social order by affecting a knowing tone that does not sound entirely convincing. He tells his cousin Evelina his views about "the people of quality" and the "common people" in France and how they compare to comparable social classes in England. Still, when he sees a man beat another man like a horse, it is so beyond his experience that he cannot explain it.

Fifteen years later, Sir Hamilton, now an estate holder, has grown into a comfortable aristocrat. He is so secure with his servants that he does not feel the need to actively enforce the differences between the social classes; he is not worried about allowing them to play as equals to him on the cricket field. More significantly, he does not concern himself at all about politics, feeling that his hobby, cricket, is more important. His unshaken faith in his own entitlement makes him sure that his rank and privilege will remain constant.

By the end of the story, Sir Hamilton Lindsay is an example of the powerless, clueless aristocracy that the social revolutions of the late eighteenth century attempted to cast aside. He is kept from knowing how powerless he is by a new ruling class that still has some respect for his type. He is allowed to have his wife come and live with him in captivity and is told that he may be useful in a prisoner trade, justifying his existence. Because he has known mostly leisure for his whole life, his only point of reference is his favorite leisure activity, cricket.

Obsession

One reason that Sir Hamilton Lindsay cannot comprehend the political reality of the coming French Revolution is that he focuses obsessively on cricket. Because of this obsession, he fails to see the importance of the historic events occurring around him. He does not properly understand his wife's concern about his proposed trip into France at a time when mobs are rising up against the nobility, interpreting her objection as prompted by a dislike of his favorite sport. He does not note the evacuation of French aristocrats, but he does note that his friend, the Duke of Dorset, has missed the cricket season for the first time in years. At the end of the story, as Sir Hamilton looks back on the events, he asserts the naïve belief that the whole revolution could have been avoided by a good cricket match.

To some extent, his final theory might be more than just the enthusiasm of a man with an obsession. While England has a class system at the time of this story, the ruling class's obsession with cricket overrides some of its more conservative members' commitment to hierarchy. On the cricket field, noblemen commingle with servants and come to recognize them as people. In a perfect world, such an obsession might have caused the French aristocracy to mix with the peasantry and have created a sense of familiarity between the two sides that may have prevented bloodshed.

Religion

During the French Revolution, religion came to signify the breach between the established Catholic Church, which had been the largest landowner in the country, and the self-determination available to ordinary people through Protestantism. In Sir Hamilton Lindsay's personal story, though, religion represents the status quo in a much more specific way. In his later years, after having witnessed brutal fighting between social classes, he becomes a regular churchgoer, even though, as Barnes explains, "he would as soon step inside a mosque or a synagogue as inside a papist shrine." The revolutionaries in this small French town have created an alliance between the Protestant aristocracy of England and the French Catholic peasantry: the same people who sacked the church and humiliated the priests are the ones who burned down the *hôtel* of the Duke of Dorset. In this case, the religious convictions of the commoners have been strong enough to overcome the revolutionaries and keep the church standing. Sir Hamilton relies on the same residual respect for authority to keep him in the villagers' good graces and to protect him from the revolutionaries' hostility. Though religion is a small, almost inconsequential matter to him and a symbol of the hated aristocracy to the revolutionaries, it is a source of potential change for the working people.

Topics For Further Study

- Make a poster showing the kinds of clothing gentlemen of the late 1700s wore while playing cricket. If you cannot find any sources showing the exact outfits for cricket, then show what would be considered casual clothes of the time.

- Research the ways that Napoleon spent his time when he was held in exile at St. Helena, a situation that parallels Sir Hamilton Lindsay's at the end of this story. Write a short story in which melons from the south of France lead Napoleon to a realization about his life.

- The first section of this story is presented as a letter from young Hamilton Lindsay to his cousin. Find an old letter that someone wrote to you and analyze it, pointing out things that you did not know when the letter was first sent and how they are hinted at within it. Write an essay on your conclusions.

- Barnes hints at an affair between the Duke of Dorset and the queen of France, Marie Antoinette. Read a biography of Marie Antoinette and write an explanation that either takes the position that her reputation has been slandered or that the story captures the sort of person she actually was.

- Sir Hamilton Lindsay agrees that nobles and commoners ought to play together on the cricket field. Find a movie that shows people in contemporary times crossing class lines, perhaps in order to engage in sports, and write a comparison that shows how much and how little that story has in common with this one. The movie, *Chariots of Fire*, may be one possible choice for a recent film.

Revolution

Shielded by privilege and money from the harsh realities of the hungry working classes, Hamilton Lindsay is unaware of the bitter ferocity with which the French peasants are willing to revolt against the prevailing class system. Although he is aware that something is going on in France in August 1789, it does not seem like anything serious enough to interrupt the cricket game planned for the Champs-Élysées in Paris. He naively feels that a squad of eleven noblemen, armed with cricket bats, has nothing to fear by entering a country that is in the throes of violent social upheaval.

In fact, the French Revolution was the culmination of great frustration with the prevailing social order and, like other political revolutions, was exceedingly brutal. Violence was aimed indiscriminately against anyone who had benefited from the old social order—nobles, aristocrats, landowners, and the clergy, most notably. Also like other revolutions, the change, long in the making, came suddenly. Social observers who were aware of the mood of the majority could see the change coming and could predict that government's efforts to suppress the revolution would only serve to make it more violent.

However, powerful individuals denied being at risk for as long as they could. The Bourbons had been on the throne of France for nearly three hundred years; they could not see the mayhem of revolt coming.

In the last part of this story, Barnes shows an aspect of revolution that is seldom described: the rational side, once the rampant bloodshed has ended. The people of the French town where Sir Hamilton is held know that they have no grievance against him, an Englishman, and so they allow him to go about his days in peace. The new government of Napoleon Bonaparte even allows his wife and servant to join him in confinement. In this interlude, before Wellington's defeat of Bonaparte at Waterloo and the return of the Bourbons to the throne with Louis XVIII in 1814, the French people do not recognize the English as their enemy.

Style

Symbolism

Barnes conveys the significance of the story through the use of symbols. One of the most obvious symbols is the game of cricket. To Sir Hamilton, cricket represents a community of rich and poor, brought together by individual skills. Barnes uses the game as a means of revealing social assumptions. The privileged aristocrats enjoy the leisure activity. Sir Hamilton mulls over the various ways that he and his friends care for their cricket bats, while his gardener is forced to ride outside of their coach in the rain. Sir Hamilton could consider the real needs of the working poor around him, but nothing in his education or lifestyle encourages him to do so. He occupies himself with the game instead.

Melons, too, are given special attention in this story, so that readers can hardly avoid pondering their possible symbolic significance. They appear in the first section as a local delicacy, a natural wonder that represents the best of southern rural France. Their sweetness is so remarkable that even a young nobleman who is trying to affect a cool attitude raves about them. In the story's last segment, Lady Evelina tries to keep Sir Hamilton from slipping into depression by urging him to focus on the wonderful melons they have with their lunch. He finds himself unable to concentrate, though: for him, the melons resemble such things as the cannonballs that have been used to smash the Catholic Church (representing the wanton violence that escalated throughout the revolution) and, of course, cricket balls (representing, for Sir Hamilton, humanity's potential for excellence). The connection is in the layered meanings: the wealthy aristocrats ate melon and played cricket while other human beings starved; the revolution hurled at them in response, changing their personal worlds permanently, though not permanently removing upper classes from power.

Epistolary Fiction

Barnes establishes the character of Hamilton Lindsay by having him speak for himself in the first section of the story. Given the type of person he is, it is effective to have him express himself in a letter. A work of fiction that is presented as if it is a letter written by one character to another is called "epistolary."

There are several reasons why the epistolary style works well for this character. For one thing, he is literate and thus has the means to record his thoughts and ideas effectively. For another, as a gentleman, he would use this formal form of communication. Finally, as an apparently historical document, the letter comes to the reader as an artifact of that era, a way of seeing the aristocratic lifestyle prior to the revolution and the attitudes that incited lower classes.

Later in the story, Barnes drops the epistolary form with its first person point of view and adopts the third person to describe Sir Hamilton's mind. This shift gives readers some distance from the character, enabling them to see the level to which he falls, against the backdrop of massive social and political change.

Historical Context

The Reign of Louis XVI

The first part of this story takes place around the year 1774, or roughly the time when Louis XVI ascended to the throne. For more than a century before Louis XVI's reign, France had suffered under the rule of the self-indulgent monarchy. Wars and poor management of the country's wealth had burdened the population with increasing debt. Those in power—the nobles and the clergy—benefited from the status quo, and so they worked to suppress any measures to make the system more fair. Heavy taxes were imposed upon the peasantry, with attempts to revise the tax codes, such as increasing taxes on property owners, defeated by aristocrats. Religious worship other than in the Catholic Church was severely punished, such as the episode young Hamilton Lindsay describes in "Melon," in his letter to his cousin, about seeing a Protestant minister hanged in the marketplace for the crime of conducting religious services.

By 1788, the country was bankrupt. Louis XVI, who was not a strong king, was forced to take some step to address the social inequality that made life miserable for the majority of the population. He convened the Estates-General in 1789 for the first time since 1614. This group consisted of the clergy (First Estate), the nobility (Second Estate), and the bourgeoisie (Third Estate). Though the Third Estate included commoners in theory, they were in practice excluded.

The Revolution

The Estates-General convened in May 1789. After fighting off challenges to structure and methods to be used, the body eventually decided to vote themselves a National Assembly, answerable not to the ruling establishment but to the people. They agreed to remain in session until France had a new constitution. The king reacted by locking them out of the hall where they met and then restructuring his ministry on July 11.

Violence broke out in Paris three days later, when angry mobs forced their way into the Bastille

Compare & Contrast

- **1780s:** A young aristocrat can travel with his entourage across France, knowing that the peasants will not dare interfere with someone of his social class.

  Today: Wealthy people travel with security details, knowing that the possibility of kidnapping is a threat.

- **1780s:** Cricket is the craze among the British aristocracy. Though the game has historical roots dating back to the 1300s, the organization of teams and leagues in the second half of the eighteenth century propels the game to become Britain's national pastime.

  Today: Soccer, a game that is played by people of all social classes around the world, has more popularity, though Britons still recognize cricket as connected to their national identity.

- **1780s:** Local delicacies, such as melons, strawberries, or oranges, are only enjoyed by people with the means to travel to exotic places.

  Today: Modern methods of refrigeration and transportation make it possible for people in developed countries to enjoy fruits and vegetables that are not indigenous.

- **1780s:** The idea of democracy is new to Western culture, with revolutions in the United States and France replacing monarchies with governments run by the citizens.

  Today: The fledgling democracies of the Middle East are in the same early stages that the Western democracies were in during the 1790s.

- **1790s:** Sir Hamilton Lindsay's trip by horse-drawn coach across England to Dover, where he will depart for France, takes three days.

  Today: Sir Hamilton could leave his estate in the early morning and, traveling by airplane, be at de Gaulle Airport in Paris before noon.

---

prison. They only released seven prisoners, but the symbolic act of defiance against the established regime ignited the passions that had been seething for so long. The mob went on to take the city hall and kill several government officials, including the mayor of Paris.

After this, the king and his followers backed down, and tensions subsided for a few weeks. The spirit of revolution began, though, and violence broke out in various places throughout the country. On August 4, 1789, the old political order collapsed when the National Assembly declared an end to feudalism: those who had been in power, such as clergymen, and certain politicians, lost their standing and were forced to flee for their lives (the story specifies August 8 as the day that the Duke of Dorset abandoned his embassy and headed back to England). Louis XVI, his family, and his supporters, were held under arrest at Tuileries Palace. They lived there for two years, escaping in June 1791 by dressing in peasants' clothes, but they were recaptured before they could reach Varennes. Their attempt to escape made it clear that, despite their proclamations, they opposed the revolution. In January 1793, Louis XVI, was executed; his wife, Marie Antoinette, a regal woman who openly disdained the common people, was beheaded before a cheering crowd on October 16 of that year, her body thrown into an unmarked grave.

The French Republic

In 1793, the other monarchies of Europe, fearing that the revolutionary spirit that overran the French government would spread, opposed the new order in France. The new government went to war against Great Britain, the United Netherlands, Austria, and Spain, losing in each. To keep up military strength, conscription laws required military duty of hundreds of thousands of Frenchmen: this, along with the rejection of the Catholic clergy, fueled the counter-revolutionary spirit.

The government responded in June 1793 with actions so repressively brutal that they came to be known as the Reign of Terror. New laws were passed to punish those who opposed the centralized government, and tribunals were convened across the country with the power to sentence insurgents to death. People were as likely to be executed for suspicion of crimes as for actual treason. The government that had fought against the injustices of the old feudal system was only able to stay in power by its own injustices.

In 1799, General Napoleon Bonaparte, the commander of the army and one of the most brilliant military strategists the country had ever known, staged a coup, taking control of the French government, seizing control of the legislature, and having himself appointed First Consul. Later, after suppressing a coup against him by the Bourbons, the relatives of Louis XVI, Napoleon crowned himself emperor of France, a position that he held until he was forced to abdicate in 1815. Louis XVIII, the brother of the former Louis XVI, took the throne after the fall of Napoleon.

West Indies cricket player George Headley batting against England at Old Trafford, Greater Manchester, 1939 Photograph by Fox Photos. Getty Images

Critical Overview

Julian Barnes has been long considered one of England's finest novelists, and his reputation grew to international acclaim with the 1993 publication of his breakout novel, *Flaubert's Parrot*. Still, as of 2006, he had not established much of a reputation as a short story writer. *Cross Channel*, the book that contains "Melon," was his first collection of short stories, published at a time when his reputation as a fiction writer was already well established. Reviews of the stories were mixed, but generally positive. Barbara Hoffert, writing in the *Library Journal*, refers to Barnes's "typically luminous, literate, restrained prose," noting, "Throughout, Barnes exhibits a wonderful sense of time and place and an exactitude of detail." She recommends it for most library collections. A brief review in the *Virginia Quarterly Review* expresses the opinion that Barnes proved with *Flaubert's Parrot* that he is the rightful heir to Russian novelist Vladimir Nabokov. The review states of *Cross Channel*: "This smart collection of stories only adds to his patrimony. Barnes's prose is always a delight to read, not only for the imagination and simplicity of the tale, but for the sheer lyricism and intelligence of the page. This writer, clearly, is a master." The *New Yorker*, one of the most influential of American publications, praised

Barnes in a light-hearted way, noting, "In his first collection of stories Barnes again proves that there will always be an England."

Though Barnes has published short stories infrequently, his reputation as a short story writer did continue with the publication of his next collection, *The Lemon Table*, in 2004. The *San Francisco Chronicle* called that collection "stunning," assessing it in much the same manner that *Cross Channel* had been portrayed. "Playful, angry, wry or humorous," the reviewer notes, "his tone is right on. Everywhere he ventures, Barnes is sure-footed: Each word, each tone, each nuance of phrase is just right."

Criticism

David Kelly

Kelly teaches creative writing and literature at two colleges in Illinois. In this essay, Kelly explains that the life of the story's protagonist, Hamilton Lindsay, is organized backwards, slipping increasingly away from maturity.

Julian Barnes's short story "Melon" has many political implications. It is the tale of an English nobleman's encounters with French culture at three distinct times in his life, giving readers his view of that country before, during, and after what is arguably the most significant event of the country's history, the revolution that transformed it from a monarchy to a republic. Still, this history lesson might have less impact if it were not attached to the personal story of a credible protagonist. Barnes makes his readers think, as they piece together the dates and places mentioned in the story into a recognizable timetable that corresponds with the French Revolution. But putting too much emphasis on the external events, the researchable aspect of the story, can distract readers from an important part of its design. The French Revolution adds highlights to the story of Hamilton Lindsay, the protagonist of "Melon," but it should not be allowed to eclipse the story entirely: without a basic structure that can stand on its own without historical events, this story would be less meaningful.

The primary story, told in three distinct segments, concerns how Hamilton Lindsay, a man of leisure, seems to age backwards, going from maturity when he is young, through a decidedly adolescent middle age, and ending up his final years in infancy. Barnes makes this a story that could happen to anyone, really, regardless of their historic period or social class. It helps that Lindsay is a member of the upper classes, of course, because that gives him the luxury of focusing on frivolous matters that a lower-class working person could not afford.

In the first phase of the story, Hamilton Lindsay is probably a teenage boy or young man. He is too young to travel on his own and tours the continent with his tutor, Mr. Hawkins, whom he criticizes for treating him like "some feeble-minded boy." It also becomes clear that this trip—originally intended for Italy and rerouted at Lindsay's discretion—is meant to be educational, a grand tour of Europe intended to broaden his knowledge of culture and history. Hamilton is not yet considered mature enough to act independently.

Even so, he is mature enough to write a letter to his cousin Eveline, giving a detailed account of his trip that includes acute observations and even some sharp reflection on himself, indicating that he is smart enough to know what is lacking in his own education. Of course, he has some childish ways about him, but he also has an eagerness to look at the world and learn from experience. His tone with his cousin has the sort of sniping, faux-angry flirtatiousness that might be expected of a boy but that balances nicely with his formal closing, including

> It is no coincidence that 'Melon' crosses a time when the world is undergoing an unprecedented growth spurt with the story of one individual who is devolving from maturity to infancy."

regards to her parents and an appropriately expressed desire to see her again.

In the first section, Hamilton Lindsay clearly knows his limitations. He may complain that his chaperone holds old-fashioned ideas, but he is smart enough to evolve, to change his assessment of French customs when he can see that he has been wrong: "I have come to a warmer understanding about such things," he explains about the local oddities of dog barbers and open-air lemonade stands. It is made clear throughout his letter that he is willing to see things anew. At this stage in his life, certain outside experience can change him. Unaware of the degree to which privilege blinds him to the realities of the working classes, he nonetheless is perceptive and recognizes cultural differences.

The same cannot be said of Lindsay in middle age. In the second section of the story, when he is most likely in his thirties, Hamilton Lindsay, now titled, is no longer interested in exploring strange lands, different cultures, unfamiliar foods, or the relative differences between nationalities. His attention is so narrowly focused on the game of cricket that he can dismiss the distant rumblings of the French Revolution; the sort of issue pressing on his mind is whether butter, ham fat, or urine might be best for curing the wood of a cricket bat. Thus focused on entertainment and game, he is slow to realize that the French peasantry is capable of violence against the country's aristocracy. When he senses this threat, he locates it away from himself, among the French, and with denial well rooted in noble privilege, he assumes the political and social upheaval in a neighboring country has nothing to do with him: the only adjustment he makes in light of the news of difficulty in France is to consider

What Do I Read Next?

- Barnes wrote the introduction to a collection of essays called *Paris and Elsewhere: Selected Writings*, by fellow Englishman Richard Cobb. The first essay in the book, "Experiences of an Anglo-French Historian," speaks of the kind of research one would do to write a story like "Melon." This collection was first published by the *New York Review of Books* in 1998.

- Most critics agree that Barnes's greatest novel is *Flaubert's Parrot* (1984), which chronicles the travels of a British doctor who follows the life of Gustav Flaubert, author of *Madame Bovary*, in order to determine if a stuffed parrot he has obtained was actually once owned by the famous French novelist.

- Christopher Hibbert's historical narrative *The Days of the French Revolution* covers the time from the meeting of the Estates-General in 1789 to Napoleon's triumphant conquest of the country ten years later. It was first published in 1990 and is available as of 2006 from Harper Perennial.

- Barnes's essay collection *Something to Declare: Essays about France* covers a range of topics, from Flaubert and Baudelaire to the Tour de France (the subject of two essays: "Tour de France 1907" and "Tour de France 2000"). His insights are enlightening, and his writing is always clear and delightful.

- Martin Amis is another London novelist, whose career has paralleled that of Barnes. Amis focuses on subjects that are more contemporary and more politically charged. A good example of his work is the novel *Time's Arrow*, concerning a doctor who participated in torture at a Nazi concentration camp, looking back over his life. The book was first published in 1991 and is as of 2006 available from Vintage.

- Barnes discussed the publication of *Cross Channel*, as well as other aspects of the writing life, with Kate Kellaway, in an interview, "The Great Fromage Matures." It was published in the London *Observer Review* on January 7, 1996.

---

a new venue for the match that was scheduled for Paris.

As an adult, Hamilton Lindsay focuses on playing a game. He has the attention span and ego of a child. Affluence has indulged him and blinded him to the wider world. He was born into the world he now enjoys, one that has existed with little alteration for generations. Its origins are medieval; its system is feudal. If it is unfair, the ones favored by it would be the last to notice. The upper classes, people of Sir Hamilton's social circle, have the luxury to live for the day, not to think about what tomorrow brings, since all the tomorrows they have known provided for all their needs and desires and then some. In this section of the story, which takes place in England, France is described through John Sackville, the third Duke of Dorset, who, as Great Britain's ambassador, is placed as close to the revolution's epicenter of French ruling groups as an

Englishman can be. Lindsay views the revolution through Dorset's description. But the trouble can be put out of mind; upon his return to England, Dorset immediately directs his attention to rearranging cricket matches. Leisure is a mindset and over time generates blind spots.

In the last section, Hamilton Lindsay is a prisoner in France, circumstances which should bring about a sense of one's own mortality that would turn a person's thoughts toward the serious. The town in which he lives is burned out: the church has been damaged, and food is scarce. People he knows have died. Still, it is cricket that consumes Sir Hamilton's thoughts. Unlike his middle-aged self, though, he does not live in the present plan for the game. Now, he lives in the past, struggling to keep clear about his all-star cricket team. Mentally unstable, Sir Hamilton cannot list the members of his team correctly, even though the same eleven names have been with him for, perhaps, decades. His wife attempts to distract him from morbid thoughts of his fallen station by directing his attention to a sweet melon, but he is not able to remain in touch with reality for any length of time. He has the mind of a child, frustrated at times because he can at times recognize his limitations but cannot master them.

It is no coincidence that "Melon" crosses a time when the world is undergoing an unprecedented growth spurt with the story of one individual who is devolving from maturity to infancy. The shielded, privileged lifestyle that enabled a man to concentrate on a game throughout his adult life was bound to fall someday in the face of a massive shift in political thinking. Against a distant backdrop of the French Revolution, Barnes creates a representative of an endangered specie in Sir Hamilton Lindsay: a man so addled by privilege that his entire life is a backward slide toward an infantilized state. This story is about a person, not an age: unlike many stories, though, it is tempting to read "Melon" as a history lesson, rather than a lesson about the workings of the mind.

Source: David Kelly, Critical Essay on "Melon," in *Short Stories for Students*, Thomson Gale, 2007.

Contemporary Authors Online

In the following essay, the critic gives an overview of Barnes's work.

"Julian Barnes," wrote *Dictionary of Literary Biography* contributor Merritt Moseley, "is one of the most celebrated, and one of the most variously rewarding, of Britain's younger novelists." His work, the critic continued, "has been acclaimed by readers as different as Carlos Fuentes and Philip Larkin; reviewers and interviewers sum him up with praise such as Mark Lawson's claim that he 'writes like the teacher of your dreams: jokey, metaphorical across both popular and unpopular culture, epigrammatic.'" In addition to novels such as *Flaubert's Parrot, A History of the World in Ten and One-Half Chapters*, and *The Porcupine*, Barnes has also won a reputation as a writer of innovative detective fiction and an essayist. "Since 1990," Moseley concluded, "he has been the London correspondent of the *New Yorker* magazine, contributing 'Letters from London' every few months on subjects such as the royal family and the quirkier side of British politics." Barnes was also one of many writers—among them Stephen King and Annie Proulx—invited to read from their works at the first-ever New Yorker Festival in 2000.

> A collection of ten short stories that span centuries, each tale is also linked by its depiction of a Brit heading for the far bank of the Channel, lured by the pleasures of neighboring France."

Barnes published four novels, *Metroland, Before She Met Me*, and the detective novels *Duffy* and *Fiddle City*—both written under the pseudonym Dan Kavanagh—before he completed *Flaubert's Parrot*, his first great success. Critics have acclaimed these early books for their comic sensibility and witty language. *Metroland* tells the story of two young men who "adopt the motto *epater la bourgeoisie*," explained *New Statesman* contributor Nicholas Shrimpton. "But this grandiose ambition is promptly reduced to the level of 'epats,' a thoroughly English field-sport in which the competitors attempt to shock respectable citizens for bets of sixpence a time." "After this vision of the Decadence in short trousers," the reviewer concluded, "it is hard to take the idea of outrage too solemnly." *Before She Met Me* is the tale of an older man who falls into an obsession about his actress wife's former screen lovers. The book, stated Anthony Thwaite in the *Observer*, presents an "elegantly hardboiled treatment of the nastier levels of obsession, full of controlled jokes when almost everything else has got out of control."

Barnes's detective fiction also looks at times and characters for whom life has gotten out of control. The title character of *Duffy* is a bisexual former policeman who was blackmailed out of his job. "The thrillers are active, louche, violent, thoroughly plotted," stated Moseley. "*Duffy* shows the result of serious research into the seamy world of London's sex industry; in *Duffy*, as in its successors, the crime tends to be theft or fraud rather than murder, though Barnes successfully imbues the book with a feeling of menace." *Fiddle City*, for instance, takes place at London's Heathrow airport and looks at the smuggling of drugs and other illegal items.

It was with the publication of *Flaubert's Parrot*, though, that Barnes scored his greatest success to date. The novel tells of Geoffrey Braithwaite, a retired English doctor, and his obsession with the great French novelist Gustave Flaubert. After his wife's somewhat mysterious death, Braithwaite travels to France in search of trivia concerning Flaubert; his chief aim is to find the stuffed parrot that the writer kept on his desk for inspiration while writing *Un coeur simple*, the story of a peasant woman's devotion to her pet. Barnes "uses Braithwaite's investigations to reflect on the ambiguous truths of biography, the relationship of art and life, the impact of death, the consolations of literature," explained Michael Dirda in the *Washington Post Book World*.

Far from a straightforward narrative, *Flaubert's Parrot* blends fiction, literary criticism, and biography in a manner strongly reminiscent of Vladimir Nabokov's *Pale Fire*, according to many critics. *Newsweek* reviewer Gene Lyons called it "too involuted by half for readers accustomed to grazing contentedly in the best-seller list," but recommended it to readers "of immoderate literary passions." Other reviewers stressed that, while a complex and intellectual work, *Flaubert's Parrot* is also "endlessly fascinating and very funny," in the words of London *Times* contributor Annabel Edwards. Dirda concluded that this "delicious potpourri of quotations, legends, facts, fantasies, and interpretations of Flaubert and his work . . . might seem dry, but Barnes' style and Braithwaite's autumnal wisdom make the novel into a kind of Stoic comedy . . . Anyone who reads *Flaubert's Parrot* will learn a good deal about Flaubert, the making of fiction, and the complex tangle of art and life. And—not least important—have a lot of rather peculiar fun too."

Of Barnes's more recent works, *A History of the World in Ten and One-Half Chapters* and *The Porcupine* are probably best known to U.S. readers. *A History of the World in Ten and One-Half Chapters* "builds on Barnes' reputation as one of Britain's premier postmodernists," stated *Village Voice Literary Supplement* contributor Rob Nixon. "The anti-novel that emerges attempts to double as a novel of ideas—never Brit lit's forté . . . The principal concern of the novel, which begins with corruption on the Ark and ends in the tedium of heaven (pretty much like life with lots of shopping), is to debunk religion and that most seductive of theologies, History." Barnes conceives of history in the book as a series of different, mostly unrelated events, and the connections individuals invent to link them together. "One of Barnes's characters rather improbably describes her supposed mental condition—imagining that she has survived a nuclear disaster, which, as it turns out, she has—as 'Fabulation. You keep a few true facts and spin a new story about them,'" declared Frank Kermode in the *London Review of Books*. "This is what Barnes himself, in this book, attempts. He fabulates this and that, stitches the fabulations together, and then he and we quite properly call the product a novel." "As a 'historian,'" stated Anthony Quinn in the *New Statesman and Society*, "he is unlikely to dislodge Gibbon or Macaulay; but as satirist and story-teller he has few equals at present."

The Porcupine is a short novel set in a fictional Eastern European country in the post-Communist era. "Stoyo Petkanov, the former president, a cross between [former Rumanian premier] Nicolae Ceaucescu and Bulgaria's Georgi Dimitrov," explained *New York Times Book Review* contributor Robert Stone, "is on trial in the courts of the shakily democratic successor government." His prosecutor is Peter Solinsky, born into a family prominent under the Communists. Solinsky is shaken by Petkanov's sincere belief in the principles of Communism. Contrasting them with the poverty and lack of respect that the reforms have brought, Solinsky begins to turn away from his new democratic ideals. "In the end," Mary Warner Marien declared in the *Christian Science Monitor*, "nothing is resolved except a clearer vision of the stupendous obstacles facing the former communist country." "Admirers of the earlier, Francophile Julian Barnes may regret that in his latest work . . . the author of *Flaubert's Parrot* and *Talking It Over* has shed his brilliance and dandyism to become a rather somber recorder of his times," stated *London Review of Books* contributor Patrick Parrinder. "The grayness seems inherent in his subject-matter, but it has not infected his acute and spiny prose."

England, England, a darkly satiric novel set in the twenty-first century, incorporates conflicting world situations and their connectedness to greed for power and money. Protagonist and businessman Sir Jack Pitman plots to replace England with a replica island—a Disneyland-type fantasy world—intending to reap huge financial rewards. John Kennedy, writing for the *Antioch Review*, concluded that the book falls short because the characters are underdeveloped. Even so, he commended Barnes's writing style, adding that he "cleverly puts his finger upon a central issue: how do we find our personal uniqueness and salvation when 'memory is identity' and everywhere history and heritage are being manipulated for profit." Philip Landon, in the *Review of Contemporary Fiction*, dubbed *England, England* "a novel of downright Swiftian darkness and ferocity." Comparing the fantasy island to Lilliput, Landon called the work a "stinging caricature" that "chills with the bleakness of its cultural panorama."

Commenting on *Love, etc.* for *Yomiuri Shimbun/ Daily Yomiuri*, a reviewer called Barnes a "sensitive writer, whose specialty is a down-to-earth lucidity about the sad paradoxes of love and marriage." *Love, etc.* is a ten-years-later look into the lives of the characters of *Talking It Over*, although reading the latter is not a prerequisite to enjoying the former. Steven Rea, reviewing the book for *Knight-Ridder/Tribune News Service*, noted that *Love, etc.* "is penned in confession mode—in the voices of its protagonists, a knotty triangle of love, loathing, trust and betrayal known as Stuart, Gillian and Oliver." He called Barnes's prose "lively, lucid, ricocheting with wryly observed commentary on the human condition," adding that Barnes "pokes and prods into the dark corners of contemporary relationships." Dale Peck in the *New Republic*, however, found the writing clever but the story ultimately "soulless." As Peck explained, "Barnes is a terribly smart man, a terribly skilled writer . . . [but] intelligence and talent in the service of a discompassionate temperament are precisely the opposite of what one seeks from a novelist, or a novel."

In a departure from his longer fictional works, Barnes experimented with the short-story form in 1996's *Cross Channel*. A collection of ten short stories that span centuries, each tale is also linked by its depiction of a Brit heading for the far bank of the Channel, lured by the pleasures of neighboring France. Drawing on the similarities between the British and their Gallic cousins, Barnes's "imagination seems to work comfortably in a historical context, building fiction on bits of fact," according to Chicago's *Tribune Books* reviewer Bruce Cook. Among the stories—each set on French soil—are "Junction," which revolves around the perception of the French-born Channel-spanning railroad's builders' perception of their British co-workers during the railroad's 1840s construction. "Melon" finds a cross-cultural cricket match interrupted by the French Revolution, much to the dismay of the story's high-born protagonist who had hoped to sideline the populace's rush to rebel by sparking a far more healthy interest in sport. And in "Inferences," an older-than-middle-aged English musical composer now living in France awaits the performance of his latest composition on the radio, hoping to surprise his young mistress with its magnificence.

Slipping back and forth between the centuries, Barnes's "prose slips quietly back from its modern cadences into those of the early nineteenth century, into the cherished foreignness of the past," noted Michael Wood in a *New York Times Book Review* critique of *Cross Channel*. The author also slips back and forth between outlook, between the way the British view the French and vice versa, understanding the French perspective yet clearly aligned with the British. "*Cross Channel* reconfirms Barnes' sympathy for those characters whose Englishness accompanies them, like a sensible mackintosh, into the unpredictable depths of France," quipped critic Gerald Mangan in his review of the collection for the *Times Literary Supplement*. Praising the volume for its sensitive portrayal of a myriad of cultural subtleties, Cook had particular praise for the dry wit that imbues the collection. Barnes "may indeed be a comic writer at heart—and that may be why he appeals to French readers," surmised the critic. "His humor is the sort that translates well. It travels."

Returning again to the short-fiction format in *The Lemon Table*, Barnes combines eleven unique short stories that focus on individuals whose lives are connected through the unnerving themes of death and aging. As readers plunge into the lives of the characters, dark secrets are revealed, along with chilling answers to much-feared questions. Barbara Love in *Library Journal* called *The Lemon Table* a "superb collection" and added: "This is Barnes at his best." A reviewer for *Publishers Weekly* commented that the short tales "are as stylish as any of Barnes's creations, while also possessed of a pleasing heft . . . the reader is taken for a delightful ride."

Source: Contemporary Authors Online, "Julian Barnes," in *Contemporary Authors Online*, Thomson Gale, 2006.

Peter Childs

In the following essay, Childs presents the function of art and history in Barnes's writing.

Barnes is sometimes considered a postmodernist writer because his fiction rarely either conforms to the model of the realist novel or concerns itself with a scrutiny of consciousness in the manner of modernist writing. He has been said to stretch the bounds of fiction in his novels but it has just as often been suggested that he is an essayist rather than a novelist and his experimental books do

> 'History', this suggests, is a way of constructing reality, of explaining what happens, of tracing patterns in events, of creating a form, a narrative structure, from what has happened in the world."

not question the bounds of the novel but fall outside them.

With regard to his own practice, Barnes rarely discusses fictional technique in his novels, except through Braithwaite's meditations in *Flaubert's Parrot*, and instead uses painting and other kinds of imaginative and imitative art to discuss indirectly the function of writing, as well as to address wider issues of aesthetics and criticism that are common to a range of cultural practices. This goes from the debates between Toni and Chris in *Metroland* through to the imitative world created by Jack Pitman in *England, England*. Chris explains that his and Toni's reason for constantly visiting the National Gallery in London is because they agreed that 'Art was the most important thing in life' (M, 29). The boys consider it rewarding and ameliorative: 'It made people not just fitter for friendship and more civilized ... but *better*— kinder, wiser, nicer, more peaceful, more active, more sensitive. If it didn't what good was it?' (M, 29). Their 'constructive loafing' is exemplified by studying the ways in which people are 'in some way improved' when they see works of art in the Gallery.

The belief in the supremacy of art is reinforced by Geoffrey Braithwaite quoting Flaubert: 'Superior to everything is—Art' (F, 108); yet the idea that art is the most important thing 'in life' is partly paradoxical because in Barnes's books art and life are often contrasted: 'Books are where things are explained to you; life is where things aren't' (F, 168). This partly expresses the attraction of art—there is its beauty but its intellectual value lies in its attempt

to make sense of the world. This is also the argument of the 'Shipwreck' chapter of *A History of the World*, but in *Flaubert's Parrot* the differences between life and art are brought out in Braithwaite's attempt not just to understand his own life but that of the nineteenth-century writer who famously claimed that the life of novelists has nothing to do with their writing.

Braithwaite asks early on: 'Is the writer much more than a sophisticated parrot?' (F, 18), and there are many intimations in *Flaubert's Parrot* that the reader cannot reliably get to 'know' the writer any better than Braithwaite can get to 'know' which of many parrots was the Loulou of Flaubert's *Un Coeur Simple*. 'How do you compare two parrots, one already idealized by memory and metaphor, the other a squawking intruder? My initial response was that the second seemed less authentic than the first. Mainly because it had a more benign air' (F, 21). Braithwaite goes on to say: 'The writer's voice—what makes you think it can be located that easily? Such was the rebuke offered by the second parrot' (F, 22). So, though the novel's facts about the French author are not in dispute even the first image of Flaubert encountered in the book is potentially misleading: 'The statue isn't the original one', Braithwaite laconically assures us (F, 11).

Biography is ultimately considered a string of words designed to encompass the writer just as a fish net is a tool to catch fish; but, argues Braithwaite, a fish net can be logically deemed a collection of holes tied together with string: and so can a biography (F, 38; cf. Barnes use of the metaphor in interview, *Cercles*, 263). This description also fits well with Barnes's view of history. 'History isn't what happened. History is just what historians tell us. There was a pattern, a plan, a movement, expansion, the march of democracy; it is a tapestry, a flow of events, a complex narrative, connected, explicable' (H, 242). Historiography is a narrative composed of connections, threads that reach across the gaps in knowledge and understanding where most of the past falls through the net. History emerges for Barnes as a kind of tapestry, a text(ile) woven out of other texts and strands of memory.

But what are his books' objections to the ways in which history is understood? They seem to focus on gaps: what falls through history's net: 'How do we seize the past? How do we seize the foreign past? We read, we learn, we ask, we remember, we are humble; and then a casual detail shifts everything' (F, 90). For Braithwaite, it is only distance, the passage of time that enables us to feel we are able to understand history: 'So how do we seize the past? As it recedes, does it come into focus? Some think so. We know more, we discover extra documents, we use infra-red light to pierce erasures in the correspondence, and we are free of contemporary prejudice; so we understand better. Is that it? I wonder' (F, 100).

Braithwaite's scepticism seems to be based on the view that distance enables us to understand history better only because with the passing of time some events and perspectives are forgotten while others, those that fit our theory of history, remain: 'what a curious vanity it is of the present to expect the past to suck up to it' (F, 130). So theories that fit our present beliefs arise to turn history into a process, a force, a pattern, but Barnes is sceptical: 'And does history repeat itself, the first time as tragedy, the second time as farce? No, that's too grand, too considered a process. History just burps, and we taste again that raw-onion sandwich it swallowed centuries ago' (H, 241).

In Barnes' *History of the World*, what we find throughout the book is a number of parallels, between occurrences of boats, beetles, and behemoths. The reason for this is not because history has a number of parallels, but because the past is habitually perceived in a certain way—stories lead on to other stories and human beings always look for patterns, for systems, for explanations. 'History', this suggests, is a way of constructing reality, of explaining what happens, of tracing patterns in events, of creating a form, a narrative structure, from what has happened in the world.

Barnes has said that against history bearing down on us we can put three things: religion, art, and love. Religion, he thinks, is not true, art does not satisfy everyone, and so love is the final 'fallback position' (Moseley, 120). History does not give us truth, it just finds things out (H, 242), whereas 'love and truth: that's the vital connection' (H, 240, 245). For Barnes, and this is in many ways the story of Braithwaite's explorations in biography too, 'The history of the world becomes brutally self-important without love' (H, 240). History is therefore seen as impersonal; it leaves out the most important human elements—faith, art, love— and its march of progress, power, and politics leaves many casualties: 'when love fails, we should blame the history of the world. If only it had left us alone, we could have been happy' (H, 246).

Source: Peter Childs, "Julian Barnes: 'A Mixture of Genres,'" in *Contemporary Novelists: British Fiction since 1970*, Palgrave Macmillan, 2005, pp. 86–88.

Painting of Napoleon by Jacques-Louis David

Corbis/Francis G. Mayer

Merritt Moseley

In the following essay, Moseley gives a critical analysis of Barnes's life and work.

Julian Barnes is one of the most celebrated and most variously rewarding of Britain's younger writers—that is, those who were born in the late 1940s and began publishing in the late 1970s or the 1980s, a group that also includes Martin Amis and Ian McEwan. The author of seven novels under his own name—*Flaubert's Parrot* (1984) and *A History of the World in 10 1/2 Chapters* (1989) are probably the ones best known in the United States—he has also published four exceptional detective novels under the pseudonym "Dan Kavanagh" and a book of short stories. Furthermore, he is a busy and knowledgeable journalist. From 1990 to 1995 he was the London correspondent for The *New Yorker*, contributing the "Letter from London" column every few months on topics such as the royal family and the quirkier side of British politics. These pieces, which were published in book form in 1995, demonstrate his skill as an interpreter of British culture to a foreign audience; in his other writings he has often been an interpreter of, or guide to, France for his own countrymen.

> " Themes include the wars of religion, the nature of the artist, the trickery of memory, and sexual infidelity."

Barnes's fiction has been acclaimed by readers as different as Carlos Fuentes and Philip Larkin; reviewers and interviewers sum him up with praise such as Mark Lawson's claim that he "writes like the teacher of your dreams: jokey, metaphorical across both popular and unpopular culture, epigrammatic." On the other hand, he has been subjected to a persistent argument that the books he calls novels are really collections of short stories or essays or some other nonfiction genre and are only "marketed" as novels. Although he is regularly called "erudite" and "philosophical," he is also witty and humane; as David Coward explains in the *Times Literary Supplement* (5 October 1984), "The modern British novel finds it easy to be clever and comic. Barnes also manages that much harder thing: he succeeds in communicating genuine emotion without affectation or embarrassment." Barnes's work has stimulated considerable critical discussion over its allegedly postmodern traits, including questions about whether it is dangerously relativistic or nihilistic. That his novels have never won the Booker Prize, the most prestigious award for British fiction—although Flaubert's Parrot was one of the six finalists for the prize in 1984—has baffled some observers. His *Metroland* (1980) won the William Somerset Maugham Prize, which is given for an outstanding first book; he has won other English literary awards, and *Flaubert's Parrot* was honored in France with the Prix Medicis. Barnes has also been named an Officer de l'Ordre des Arts et des Lettres.

Partly because of comparisons with his slightly younger contemporary Amis, a famously precocious author, Barnes sees himself as a late starter: he was thirty-four when *Metroland* was published. It was, however, the product of a long gestation period, and he published another book—his first Dan Kavanagh detective thriller, *Duffy* (1980)—that same year. Since then his output has been impressive in quantity as well as quality.

Julian Patrick Barnes was born in Leicester, an industrial city in England's East Midlands, on 19 January 1946; his parents, Albert Leonard and Kaye Scoltock Barnes, were teachers of French. The family moved to the London suburb of Northwood when Barnes was quite young; he attended the City of London School on a scholarship, commuting on the Metropolitan Line of the London Underground—an experience that helped to produce *Metroland*. He studied languages at Magdalen College, Oxford, teaching in France in 1966-1967 and receiving a B.A. with honors in 1968. He took a job as editorial assistant at the *Oxford English Dictionary*. As a man working mostly with women, he explained in a 1989 interview with Amanda Smith, he was assigned most of the "rude words and sports words."

In 1972 he moved to London, where he studied law and passed his final bar exams. He also became involved in journalism, reviewing novels and then serving as assistant literary editor and television critic of *The New Statesman*, contributing editor of the *New Review* (where he published under the name "Edward Pygge"), deputy literary editor of the *Sunday Times*, and television critic for *The Observer* (London). During this period he also wrote a restaurant column for the *Tatler* under the pseudonym "Basil Seal," named for one of Evelyn Waugh's characters. He left *The Observer* in 1986 to become a full-time writer, but he wrote the "Letter from London" column for *The New Yorker* for five years and still reviews and comments regularly for such journals as the *Times Literary Supplement* and the *New York Review of Books*. Since 1979 he has been married to Pat Kavanagh, a prominent literary agent. His pseudonym Dan Kavanagh seems to be a tribute to his wife, to whom many of his novels are dedicated.

Mira Stout has called Barnes "the chameleon of British letters" because each of his "mainstream" novels is distinctive. This is less true of the detective novels: as Dan Kavanagh he seems able to satisfy any need he may feel for predictability, formula, and generic continuity, while as Julian Barnes he is careful not to repeat himself. In the interview with Amanda Smith he speaks contemptuously of some reviewers' expectation that after *Flaubert's Parrot*, his first great success, he would repeat himself by writing "Victor Hugo's Dachshund."

Barnes's first novel took him eight years to write. The deceptively calm *Metroland*, like many first novels, is a story of adolescence and coming-of-age; but a mark of the work's maturity is that it shows coming-of-age as involving a coming to terms with lowered expectations. *Metroland* demonstrates certain features that will be constants in Barnes's fiction: wit, familiarity with French culture, shapeliness and high finish, and a delicate concern with love and jealousy.

In the first part of this three-part novel, "Metroland (1963)," the teenage Christopher Lloyd, who lives in one of the London suburbs served by the Metropolitan Underground line, and his friend Toni are disdainful of school, sports, and, especially, the English middle-class culture represented by their parents. The values they treasure are art, sexual liberation (which is entirely theoretical to them as yet), and France. They spend much of their time in art museums making fun of the bourgeois families they see there. They wish to affront the smooth mediocrity of their times, but their rebellion is mostly verbal and quite funny. Barnes presents Christopher as a young man who is sufficiently unusual to be interesting while sufficiently typical to be a representative of the intelligent, urban adolescent filled with longing and dissatisfaction. Part 2, "Paris (1968)," finds Christopher in the French capital during the May 1968 student rebellion—of which, ironically, he is completely unaware. He has come to France ostensibly to write a thesis but really to satisfy his youthful fascination with French culture and to take advantage of the opportunities for sexual liberation he associates with Paris. He does achieve a sexual initiation with a French girl, Annick, who eventually leaves him because of his dishonesty about his attraction to an English girl whom he later marries. As for art, Christopher does some desultory writing; it is, predictably, derivative—in this case, of Charles-Pierre Baudelaire. In the third part, "Metroland II (1977)," Christopher is back in metropolitan London. He has settled down into marriage, gone into business, and forgotten about the artistic life. His bourgeois existence is complicated by arguments with Toni, who is not nearly as assimilated to middle-class "adulthood," and by stresses in his mainly happy marriage.

Metroland is a short, unexciting, but highly accomplished study of becoming adult—with all that that implies about narrowing horizons, settling down, and accepting one's ordinariness. Although it is possible to argue, as Paul Bailey did in an unsympathetic review in the *Times Literary Supplement* (28 March 1980), that *Metroland* is a "prig's progress" and that it is about "settling for suburbia," Christopher is no prig. Barnes allows the reader to choose between Christopher's realistic accommodation to normal life and Toni's embodiment of the artist as untameable wild man.

Barnes's first Dan Kavanagh novel, *Duffy*, published the same year as *Metroland*, is a tense thriller set in London's sleazy Soho district; the title character is a bisexual private detective who is no longer with the police because he was blackmailed by crooked cops. Barnes went on to write three more *Duffy* novels: *Fiddle City* (1981), *Putting the Boot In* (1985), and *Going to the Dogs* (1987). Not only are these louche, violent, thoroughly plotted thrillers published under the Kavanagh pseudonym quite different from the mainstream novels published under his real name, but he also writes them in a different place (in the country; he writes the mainstream novels of his home in the city) and on a different typewriter. There has been considerable speculation about the reason for this split career; perhaps the conventional plot-making that some critics miss in *Metroland* or *Flaubert's Parrot* is held over for the *Duffy* books. The first two *Duffy* novels appeared in the United States in 1986 as paperbacks in the Pantheon International Crime series; *Putting the Boot In* has not yet received an American publication.

Nick Duffy is a complicated man, rather tormented in his bisexuality. He loves a woman, Carol, but is currently impotent with her as a result of trauma, while he is perfectly capable of performing in his casual affairs with men. As the series moves through the 1980s the rise of AIDS is reflected in Duffy's fear of the disease and in his less promiscuous behavior. All of the books are firmly anchored in what feels like reality. While the central crime in each book tends to be theft or fraud rather than murder, Barnes imbues the novels with a mood of menace. There is, to be sure, plenty of overt violence in the series: Duffy is beaten up, motorists are run off the road, women are tied up and slashed, thugs throw paraffin (kerosene) heaters into shops. Sometimes the criminals commit imaginative sorts of violence against animals, such as cooking a cat in an oven; such incidents are perhaps more troubling to the animal-loving British readership than are acts directed against people.

In the tradition of hard-boiled American detectives, Duffy is no paragon of respect for the law, partly because he was driven from the force by dishonest policemen and still has dealings with "bent coppers" and partly because he pursues moral rather than legal justice. In *Fiddle City* the narrator explains this ethos:

> Duffy's moral outlook had always been pragmatic. Three years in the force had made it more so, and it wasn't going to change now. He wasn't idealistic

about the law, or about how it was implemented. He didn't mind a bit of give-and-take, a bit of blind-eye, a bit of you-naughty-boy-on-yer-bike and forget it. He didn't think the ends justified the means—except that sometimes, just occasionally, they did. He didn't believe all crimes were equal; some he couldn't get worked up about. But always, at the back, there were absolutes. Murder was one, of course, everyone agreed on that. Bent coppers was one; but then, Duffy had a little private experience of that, and could be expected to feel strongly. Rape was one; Duffy was disgusted how some coppers thought it was little more than a mild duffing up with a bit of pleasure thrown in. And heroin was one as well.

In the first three Duffy books the detective does not so much "solve" crimes—he usually already knows who the malefactor is—as restore some sort of moral balance. In *Duffy*, for instance, in pursuing the question of who slashed Mrs. McKechnie he enters the slimy world of the Soho sex industry, with his client turning out to be a pornography merchant and his opponent a Maltese Mr. Big. The action includes a harrowing assault on Duffy in a massage parlor. At the end Duffy exacts a sort of rough justice, aware that the police—especially those in his old beat, Soho, who are shown as particularly corrupt—are not likely to achieve justice of any kind.

The next installment in the Duffy series is set at Heathrow Airport, called "Fiddle City" because of the enormous opportunities it provides for crime (*fiddle* is British slang for cheating or graft). The novel's beginning is reminiscent of that of *Duffy*, which opens with the laconic sentence "The day they cut Mrs. McKechnie, not much else happened in West Byfleet." *Fiddle City* begins, "The day they crashed McKay, not much else happened on the M4 [highway]." Duffy takes over the investigation McKay had been conducting; through a series of developments, including a one-night stand with a man he meets in a bar, he goes underground at a shipping concern. Most of the menace to Duffy in this book comes from his coworkers and supervisors at the warehouse. He solves the mystery of who ran McKay off the road (McKay did not die but was seriously injured) and the much bigger one that involves a major heroin-smuggling ring. The solution brings him great satisfaction, both because he is able to gain revenge against the sadist who ripped the stud out of his ear with a pair of pliers and because his friend Lesley died as a result of heroin abuse. He reflects, "At one end of the chain there were dead babies in Thailand"—a reference to an account he has been given of women hollowing out dead babies to carry heroin across borders; "at the other end there were Lesleys fixing themselves to death."

Almost all of Barnes's novels, whatever their main themes may be, are partly about love and jealousy. A relatively understated, tender, but penetrating treatment of infidelity and jealousy appears in the last section of *Metroland*, but Barnes's next mainstream novel, *Before She Met Me* (1982), displays the strongest, grimmest, and most menacing kind of jealousy. Graham Hendrick, a dull university lecturer, is married to Ann, a former actress for whom he left his first wife, Barbara. Still bitter, Barbara urges their daughter, Alice, to ask Graham to take her to see a certain movie; as he soon realizes, the point is for him to see Ann, in a minor role, "committing adultery" with an actor in the picture. Although Ann has been totally faithful to Graham since their marriage, he becomes obsessed with her sex life before they met. He neglects his work to travel all over London to see all of her movies again and again, studying the actors with whom she had love scenes and worrying about whether she had slept with any of them in real life (she had); he goes to the other movies of the actors with whom Ann had worked; he cross-examines her and makes exhaustive mental notes. Clearly he has become unbalanced. For consolation and advice he consults Jack, a novelist friend; unbeknownst to him, Jack is another of Ann's former lovers. The novel ends extremely violently.

Before She Met Me is gripping, disturbing, and moving. It is comparable to the macabre, unsettling novels Barnes's contemporaries Amis and McEwan were writing—for instance, Amis's *Dead Babies* (1974) and McEwan's *The Cement Garden* (1978), which deals with oedipal and incest themes. In the interview with Smith, Barnes calls *Before She Met Me*

> a rather nasty book about unpleasant sexual feelings, jealousies and obsessions. It was meant to have had a rather sour and hard-driving edge to it. I think it's my funniest book, though the humor is rather bleak and in bad taste usually.

The novel certainly is funny, and its black humor survives even its growing horror. It is this book, perhaps more than any other, that has led critics to oversimplify Barnes as a writer obsessed with obsession, but Graham Hendrick is obsessed in a way that none of Barnes's other characters is. Barnes's recurrent subjects of infidelity (in this case, wholly imaginary) and jealousy occur here in their starkest form. He will go on to revisit and refine these themes.

In a 1987 interview with Patrick McGrath, Barnes emphasizes the novel's social commentary:

> In a way it's a sort of anti-'60s book. It's against the idea that somehow the 60s sorted sex out, that

everyone was all fucked up beforehand. Queen Victoria was still in charge—and then along came the Beatles, suddenly everyone started sleeping with everyone else, and that cured the lot. That's a rough plan of English sexual history, as seen by many people. And I just wanted to say, it's not like that; that what is constant is the human heart and human passions. And the change in who does what with whom—that's a superficial change.

Obviously it is not a superficial change for Graham Hendrick or for some of Barnes's other troubled and cuckolded men; but this affirmation is important to keep in mind in considering Barnes's central novelistic concerns.

In 1984 Barnes published his "breakthrough" novel, *Flaubert's Parrot*. He says that he feels "enormous affection" for it "because it's the book that launched me." Experimental in both form and content, *Flaubert's Parrot* presents itself as a non-fiction book about Gustave Flaubert written by a widowed English doctor, Geoffrey Braithwaite. Braithwaite's book grows out of the discovery that there is more than one stuffed parrot in Normandy that is identified as the bird Flaubert borrowed while he was writing "Un Coeur Simple" (1877; translated as "A Simple Heart," 1923) and develops into a subtle, witty speculation on the relationship between life and art, the knowability of the human personality, the nature of fame, and many other topics. There are also a sly but increasing emphasis on Braithwaite's autobiography and, as usual with Barnes, serious discussions of the nature and meaning of married love. The book is eclectic in form: it includes alternative chronologies of Flaubert's life, a dictionary of received ideas about the author, an examination paper on Flaubert by Braithwaite, and an account of Flaubert as it might have been written by his mistress, Louise Colet. It is an erudite and playful work; in Coward's words, it is "an extraordinarily artful mix of literary tomfoolery and high seriousness."

It is also the first of Barnes's novels to be thought of as some sort of "case," or even as a "problem." For some critics it was distinguished from Barnes's earlier works by its postmodernism—a tendency that was welcomed or rejected, depending on the critic's point of view. John Bayley disapproved of the "modish"—that is, slippery postmodern or poststructuralist—notions that he believed the novel espoused:

> The conscious implication of Flaubert's Parrot is that since one cannot know everything about the past, one cannot know anything; but its actual effect—and its success—is to suggest something different: that the relative confirms the idea of truth instead of dissipating

it, that the difficulty of finding out how things were does not disprove those things but authenticates them. It may be that few things happened as they are supposed to, and many things did not happen at all, but why should this be a reason for abandoning traditional conceptions of history, of art, of human character?

James B. Scott, on the other hand, approved of the postmodern skepticism about truth and knowability he, like Bayley, saw in the novel:

> reality and truth are the illusions produced when systems of discourse (especially artistic discourse) impinge on human consciousness. In practice, this has led postmodern novelists to strive to undermine hermeneutic responses to art by foregrounding the discourse that informs their artifact, thereby implying that not only is the final "meaning" of a work of art forever unknowable, but also any orthodox truth is actually a discourse-generated fluke.

Bayley's theory is probably closer to what Barnes is trying to suggest in the novel: that is, he is not endorsing the idea that all truths are contingent, discourse-generated, and unreliable.

Some reviewers and literary journalists suspected *Flaubert's Parrot* of not being a novel at all. One line of argument was summed up by David Sexton in the *Sunday Telegraph* (11 June 1989): "Barnes writes books which look like novels and get shelved as novels but which, when you open them up, are something else altogether. *Flaubert's Parrot* was for the most part a set of studies of Flaubert and his parrot." A burlesque by Eric Metaxas, titled "That Post-Modernism," pretended to describe "Flaubert's Panda," by "Boolean Jarnes," as "part biography, part literary criticism, part fire hydrant, and part decayed wolf's pelt—in short, the post-modernist novel at its best." Defending his claim that the book is, indeed, a novel, Barnes is quoted by Sexton as invoking the more experimental Continental novelists and showing that his work fits the definition of the genre: "It's an extended piece of prose, largely fictional, which is planned and executed as a whole piece."

Questions of the knowability of truth are important in Barnes's later novels *A History of the World in 10 1/2 Chapters* and *Talking It Over* (1991), and *A History of the World in 10 1/2 Chapters* was subjected to even sharper challenge on the grounds that it was not a proper novel. So *Flaubert's Parrot* helped to create the critical atmosphere in which Barnes's novels would be received, not least by making him a celebrated novelist whose works henceforth would receive a great deal of attention—not all of it admiring.

Barnes's next book was another Dan Kavanagh Duffy mystery, *Putting the Boot In*, set in the world of minor-league professional soccer. Like his first two detective books, it shows a command of the conventions of the genre and the kind of authority that comes from getting the details right. The soccer scenes are quite well done; this authenticity may, in fact, explain why the book has never been published in the United States, where the sport does not have a large following. Duffy, previously a moderately promiscuous bisexual, is so terrified of AIDS that he is now celibate (though he and Carol share a bed).

The first, third, and fifth parts of the novel, titled "Warm-Up," "Half-Time," and "Extra Time," respectively, are an amusing account of a soccer match played by the Western Sunday Reliables, for whom Duffy keeps goal. Geoff Bell is a member of the team and uses his electronics skills to eavesdrop on the other team's plans. Framed by the match is a story of small-town corruption and mayhem centering around a lower-division soccer club, the Athletic, whose run of bad luck turns out to be part of a scheme to ruin the club and make its property available for development. Although Duffy uncovers the conspiracy, nobody is arrested or even discomfited; and the novel ends without even the rough balance between the forces of right and wrong that was restored in the first two Duffy books.

The next novel published under Barnes's real name was *Staring at the Sun* (1986), an understated study of a woman named Jean Serjeant from her childhood during World War II to the 2020s. The main character, while she is quietly strong, enduring, and even heroic, is an "ordinary," "private" woman. The events of her life are not particularly exciting; the high points are a game of golf, a visit to the Grand Canyon, some other tourism, and an airplane flight that gives rise to the central image of the novel: by diving his plane dramatically at dawn, the pilot can see the sun come up twice. This phenomenon is described as an "ordinary miracle," and Jean Serjeant's life is meant to be the same sort of miracle. Barnes wants to reveal the heroism that exists within the ordinary; in the interview with McGrath he pointed out that people "tend to think of courage as a male virtue, as something that happens in war . . . but there are 85,000 other sorts of courage." In this book Barnes, who was reared without religion and has never been a churchgoer, delves into ultimate questions about death, an afterlife, and God; in a 1989 interview with Kate Saunders he described the contents of *Staring at the Sun* as "DIY [do it yourself] theology."

Although it received many positive reviews, *Staring at the Sun* disappointed some readers; after the tour de force of *Flaubert's Parrot* they found it tame, even a bit dull. Barnes clearly has been nettled by this reaction. In a 1991 interview with Andrew Billen he said: "As soon as you say you were disappointed, I get deeply protective about the novel. I say: Carlos Fuentes [who reviewed it in *The New York Times*] liked it—so sod you. This is the writer's response. It's like criticising your fourth child."

In 1987 Barnes published what he has claimed is his last Duffy book, *Going to the Dogs*; in a 1991 interview he told Mark Lawson that a "recyclable hero" had proved to be "more tiresome than he expected," and this Duffy novel is weaker than its predecessors. The title refers both to greyhound racing, which plays a minor role in the book, and rich people's pets, one of which comes to a violent end in the novel. Duffy is called in to solve a crime for an old acquaintance, a not entirely honest but successful man whose wealth has permitted him to live the country life and make friends with snobs and pretentious idlers. In this novel Duffy's class consciousness comes strongly to the fore. There is also some self-referential humor as Duffy, flirting with a beautiful socialite, derides the restaurant column in the Tatler written by "Basil Berk." In fact, the restaurant columnist for the Tatler at the time, writing as "Basil Seal," was Barnes himself.

In 1989 came the novel that, in ambition, complexity, and experimental quality, seemed to be the real successor to *Flaubert's Parrot*. *A History of the World in 10 1/2 Chapters* is really a history of the world: the first chapter is about Noah's ark, the last about heaven. In between are chapters on a medieval church prosecution of termites, an American astronaut's quest for the remnants of the ark, the making of a movie in a South American jungle, and Théodore Géricault's painting *The Raft of the Medusa* (1819). The chapters are as variable in form as in content, including art criticism, letters, a journal, the records of a trial, and a dream.

Like *Flaubert's Parrot*, *A History of the World in 10 1/2 Chapters* challenges conventional definitions of the novel. It lacks a unified plot, developing characters, consistent fictionality, and consistent verisimilitude. In the interview with Lawson, Barnes responded to critics who say that he is really an essayist who disguises his essays as fiction for commercial reasons: "My line now is I'm a novelist and if I say it's a novel, it is. . . . And it's not terribly interesting to me, casting people out of the realm of fiction."

One of the characters in *A History of the World in 10 1/2 Chapters* announces that "Everything is connected, even the parts we don't like, especially the parts we don't like." Although she may be delusional, her comment is true, at least, of the novel in which she appears. Its parts are connected by a network of motifs, the most obvious one being voyages of salvation by water: Noah and his ark recur in most of the chapters. Another striking motif is woodworms; a slightly less important one is reindeer.

Like most of Barnes's books, this one is philosophically rich. There is meditation on the meaning of human life, on religion and the afterlife, on the nature of history—is there History, or are there only various "histories"?—and, most prominently, on love. The "half chapter" is about love, and its message is that in a universe where history is an unreliable set of stories of disasters, salvation is to be found in love: "We must believe in it, or we're lost." Perhaps the voice that speaks these words is, like the other voices in the book, wrong; perhaps this chapter is ironic. But such does not seem to be the case. Love is set against history and connected with truth. As in *Flaubert's Parrot*, the possibility of truth is contested in this novel: is there a truth, or are there merely competing truths? The first chapter—the unorthodox story of Noah's ark as told by a stowaway woodworm—seems to suggest that there are only alternate versions. And yet the claim that people tell the truth when they are in love implies that some truth exists for them to tell, and it justifies Joyce Carol Oates's description of Barnes as a "quintessential humanist, of the pre-post-modernist species."

Barnes's next book, *Talking It Over*, returns to the territory of *Metroland*: it is a study of love, sex, and marriage set in contemporary London. The rather dull but worthy Stuart feels, and is treated as, inferior to his witty and flashy friend Oliver. Soon after Stuart marries Gillian, Oliver decides that he loves Gillian and dedicates his life to making her fall in love with him; eventually he succeeds. *Talking It Over* is a story of how love works and how jealousy feels. The two men and the woman are artfully distinguished, particularly stylistically: Stuart writes dully; Oliver has a clever, allusive style, to which Barnes has added some of his own favorite turns of phrase. Each of the three addresses the reader much more directly than is common in novels, pleading with the reader, asking questions about the other characters, suggesting ways to test the truth of the story, asking for belief and even assistance; each has his or her own

version of the story, none of which is completely reliable. One minor character, a discarded girlfriend of Stuart's, provides a unique perspective on the plot—she is highly dubious of Gillian's motives, for instance—but is "thrown out" of the novel through the combined efforts of Stuart and Oliver and despite an appeal to the author. *Talking It Over* is both moving and funny.

The Porcupine (1992) is set in a fictional country clearly based on Bulgaria; it was first published in that country and in Bulgarian. An overthrown dictator, Stoyo Petkanov, justifies himself, resists the attempts of his accusers (many of whom were formerly his supporters) to change the rules by which Stalinist societies measure successful government, and tweaks his prosecutor, the anguished former communist Peter Solinsky.

Although Petkanov is a monster, he is given arguments that are by no means easy to dismiss; in their disputes he often seems to get the better of Solinsky. As Solinsky's obsession with convicting Petkanov—on charges other than the ones of which he is really guilty—grows, his own self-doubts strengthening his determination, his wife loses her respect for him and leaves. Solinsky gives himself to evil means for a good end; were Petkanov's crimes any different? The apparent convergence of Solinsky and Petkanov raises questions about the moral superiority of the reformed system over the communist regime.

Letters from London: 1990-1995 (1995) is a collection of Barnes's columns from *The New Yorker*. There are essays on garden mazes, on the financial problems of Lloyd's of London, on Harrods, and on literary topics, including former prime minister Margaret Thatcher's memoirs. Barnes, a Labour Party supporter, is at his best when writing about politics. His account of himself campaigning with Glenda Jackson for Parliament is engaging, but his language becomes richest in satire: he describes Thatcher at Prime Minister's Question Time, standing "rather stiffly at the dispatch box, with swept-back hair, firm features, and an increasingly generous embonpoint thrusting at her tailored suit of Tory blue or emerald green; there, butting into the spray and storm of Her Majesty's Loyal Opposition, she resembles the figurehead on the prow of some antique sailing ship, emblematic as much as decorative." For one who is often characterized as a postmodernist mandarin playing intellectual games, he is solidly in touch with the real world, and he always finds something unusual to report (for example, changing fashions in pictures on currency) or a new approach to a familiar topic (such as Thatcher or her successor as prime minister, John Major) and a witty way of expressing it.

As a prepublication announcement in *Granta* (Spring 1994) put it, Barnes's *Cross Channel* (1996) is "a collection of short stories occasioned by historical meetings between the English and the French." Three of the stories were originally published in *The New Yorker*, another in *Granta*; the others appear for the first time in the book. Themes include the wars of religion, the nature of the artist, the trickery of memory, and sexual infidelity. In "Interference" an aging English artist living in France thinks about the problem of belonging:

> He was an artist, did she not see? He was not an exile, since that implied a country to which he could, or would, return. Nor was he an immigrant, since that implied a desire to be accepted, to submit yourself to the land of adoption. But you did not leave one country, with its social forms and rules and pettinesses, in order to burden yourself with the parallel forms and rules and pettinesses of another country. No, he was an artist. He therefore lived alone with his art, in silence and in freedom.

In "Experiment" the narrator recounts some sexual experiments among the Surrealists, with whom his English uncle Freddy became involved in 1928. The story is full of delightful wordplay—Freddy may have said "je suis, sire, rallyiste," meaning that he was in town for a motor rally, and been misunderstood as declaring himself to be a Surrealist— and deepening levels of complexity as the narrator discovers truths Freddy could not have known.

In a 1996 interview with Carl Swanson for the on-line magazine *Salon*, Barnes claimed that he is "the one middle-class English writer who loves France but doesn't have a house there." He spends much time there, however, and is sometimes accused by English friends of being too French. He explained to Swanson:

> I think everybody needs another country. . . . You need another country on which to project, perhaps, your romanticism and idealism. I think this is a good idea, but I don't think it happens to most people. Most people think mostly about their own country, and idealize their own country, and I think that's dangerous. I think one's own country should be scrupulously and skeptically examined [as in Letters from London, perhaps]. And you should allow your idealism and romanticism to be projected onto something else.

It is a telling comment, both about Barnes's attitude toward France and about his combination of skepticism with romanticism and idealism.

Lawson, trying to encapsulate Barnes's style, offers the phrase "alternative versions." It is an apt

characterization of a writer whose characters Stuart and Oliver in *Talking It Over* present alternative versions of how Oliver ended up with Stuart's wife; who depicted, in the same year, the ironic domesticity of *Metroland* and the desperate and squalid vice of *Duffy*; and who offers with each new book a different approach, even a new and distinctive voice. There are constants in his fiction: high craft, verbal brilliance, a determination to deal in ideas without giving way to didacticism, frequent experimentation in subject or form or both; but another constant is variation itself. His career illustrates his adherence to his maxim that a novel should be *novel;* "what is constant," as he told McGrath, "is the human heart and human passions."

Source: Merritt Moseley, "Julian Barnes," in *Dictionary of Literary Biography*, Vol. 194, *British Novelists Since 1960, Second Series*, Gale Research, 1998, pp. 27–37.

James Wood

In the following review, Woods compares Barnes to Willa Cather and E. M. Forster, attributing Barnes with a penchant for tidiness in writing, an "addiction" to facts, and weaving mysteries into his stories. He describes Barnes's books as "a picnic of the mind."

Two landscapes, one American and one English, from roughly the same period. The American landscape is seen by Willa Cather in *My Antonía* (1918), and the English landscape is seen by E. M. Forster in *The Longest Journey* (1907).

Cather's narrator sits by a window in Lincoln, Nebraska. "My window was open, and the earthy wind blowing through made me indolent. On the edge of the prairie, where the sun had gone down, the sky was turquoise blue, like a lake, with gold light throbbing in it." The man is reading Virgil's *Georgics*. He is bluntly halted by a line of the poetry: "for I shall be the first, if I live, to bring the Muse into my country." This is a moment of soft revelation for the narrator. It is also the means by which Cather establishes her own originality, the obligation she might feel, as a novelist of the West, to bring the Muse into her country; but at no point does Cather say this, or even play with direct statement. Instead she rustles with suggestion, letting us know, as if this moment were like the prairie itself, that we are on the verge of a discovery that can hardly be voiced. "We left the classroom quietly, conscious that we had been brushed by the wing of a great feeling . . ."

Forster's hero, Rickie, sits on a hill in Wiltshire. Forster comments: "Here is the heart of our island: the Chilterns, the North Downs, the South Downs radiate hence. The fibres of England unite in Wiltshire, and did we condescend to worship her, here we should erect our national shrine." Rickie reflects on how much he loves "these unostentatious fields." Then he pulls out a volume of Shelly and recites a poem. The poem annoys him, but it is clear that in some way Shelley consecrates this moment and this piece of land.

Both passages are characteristic of their authors, and of the literary traditions that produced them. Cather's land is ancient—as ancient as Virgil's soil—but anciently unknown. It is unliterary. If literature is brought to plow it, then this imposition will be a strenuous and artisanal task, with "an earthy wind blowing through." Just as Cather's narrator leaves the classroom quietly, so does her writing. It swerves away from the academic, away from knowledge, away from cleverness, away from the merely known. Its window is open. Yet the writing trembles hugely, with an earnestness toward truth, and an aroused plainnes.

Forster's English landscape is not unknown, it is already sacred. Forster can condescend to the idea of erecting a national shrine precisely because the land is already its own shrine, hallowed and binding. England is known, named, literary. Forster's writing is cozy, prissy-clever. It has a contract with the reader, to whom Forster makes direct address ("our island"). It is slackly written: the word "fibres" is at once lame, in a literary sense, and awkwardly hints at moral fiber or backbone. Cather is suggestive, stroking the not-said; Forster is explicit, and eager to clear things up. Where Cather respects a mystery, Forster engulfs one.

Despite his reputation as "a novelist of ideas," his interest in France and his Anglo-American suavity, Julian Barnes is a very English writer who is squarely in Forster's descent. Like Forster, he is brisk with mystery, a little fussy, undeniably clever and certainly cozy. He is Forster without the grand liberalism, and without the triumphant uncertainties of *A Passage To India*. He has adapted Forster's penchant for interrupting his texts (Virginia Woolf complained that Forster was like a light sleeper who was always getting up to come into the next room) into a mode of direct address with his readers. He is thoroughly literary, and fond of literary sports. Like Forster, he has an essentially neat mind. He clears up his intellectual mess as he goes along.

Life, in Barnes's books, is a picnic of the mind. Barnes spreads a cloth and presents riddles and

> **But his fiction is addicted to fact, to the tidiness and undistress of the known. His novels and stories propose mysteries which then, in a quiet spirit of self-congratulation, they solve. Of course, the solutions are not announced as such. Often they are announced as further complications."**

games for our ingestion. Actually, under skeptical investigation, these riddles and games begin to look like simplicities that are merely camouflaged as fiendish complexities. His fiction is beguiling because it is confident about the known and jauntily undaunted by the unknown.

Barnes is famous for the bright and waxy health of his "ideas." But his fiction is addicted to fact, to the tidiness and undistress of the known. His novels and stories propose mysteries which then, in a quiet spirit of self-congratulation, they solve. Of course, the solutions are not announced as such. Often they are announced as further complications. But, in Barnes's world, mysteries are clearer for their enunciation as such. Perplexity need never cause real pain. Talk clears the air, and is preferred to silence. And so, when Barnes tells us that something is complicated, or paradoxical, it does not sound complicated or paradoxical any longer. "But then the quotidian is often preposterous, and so the preposterous may in return be plausible," as the narrator of one of the stories in *Cross Channel* helpfully offers. Barnes smoothes his world into summation. Nothing in this world escapes summation, not least those moments which, he tells us, are escaping summation.

Is this the gift of hard simplicity? Or is it not the trick of easy difficulty? Barnes is a master of the first half of the escape artist's act, when he elaborately imprisons himself. Certainly, Barnes likes to entangle himself. His usual method is to select a simplicity and to turn it into a riddle. What he seems to do, in such a circumstance, is to complicate something. But his complications do not cross his simplicities at any moment; they run parallel to them. His novel *A History of the World in 10½ Chapters* is a concertina of riddles, but it is dedicated, in all its smart expansions and contractions, to the production of a facile and solving music.

One of its contractions—its half-chapter—is called "Parenthesis," and it has become celebrated as a full-throated contemporary song of love, when such proclamations are rare. In "Parenthesis," the novel's narrator, speaking with the authority and the range of the real Julian Barnes, attempts to probe the mystery of love. The probing is entirely typical of Barnes's procedures. First, we must overpower something that we take for granted, and make it seem more difficult to itself. "Let's start at the beginning. Love makes you happy? No. Love makes the person you love happy? No. Love makes everything all right? Indeed no." So love is not the simplicity we thought it was, says Barnes. (Of course, this simplicity is his making, not ours. His repeated "No's" are stern corrections to unasked questions. How many of Barnes's readers think that "love makes everything all right"?)

Next Barnes fakes—the word is not too strong—the motions of argument. Having established his mystery, Barnes offers deeper mysteries. But the mysteries that he offers are as simple as the simple misapprehensions that he thinks he is defeating. We think that the heart is a simple organ, Barnes asserts. (Do we?) But "the heart isn't heart-shaped." Barnes provides some stubborn facts about the heart, such as that in a child, "the heart is proportionately much larger than in an adult," and that "after death the heart assumes the shape of a pyramid." Barnes's narrator visits the butcher and buys an ox's heart. He dissects it "with a radiologist friend." The result of these labors? The heart is not a simple organ. Internally, it is complex and bloody and messy.

One should note the motion here: we are being warned against simplicity in a manner that is itself simplifying. That the final message about love is, at the end of these mental labors, childishly solving, and cozily fenced, is not a surprise: "Love won't change the history of the world . . . but it will do something much more important: teach us to stand up to history, to ignore its chin-out strut. . . . How you cuddle in the dark governs how you see the history of the world." "How you cuddle"! But that is precisely what Barnes offers his readers: a kind of intellectual cuddle, not in the dark, but in good, cleansing daylight.

This is not a prose of discovery, but a prose of the idea of discovery. That is why, although he loves metaphor, and uses it abundantly, his metaphors do not deepen or complicate his world. Comparing his wife's easy sleep with his own restlessness, the narrator in "Parenthesis" confesses: "I admire her because she's got this job of sleeping that we all have to do, every night, ceaselessly, better worked out than I have. She handles it like a sophisticated traveller unthreatened by a new airport. Whereas I lie there in the night with an expired passport, pushing a baggage trolley with a squeaking wheel across to the wrong carousel." But curiously, although Barnes wants us to compare the order of one approach to sleep with the disorder of the other, both are subsumed within the simplifying order of his metaphor. The wife's serenity sounds as easy as the husband's anarchy, because both have been trivialized.

This is one of Barnes's intellectual habits, and it is in evidence in his new book of stories. Two opposing ideas are selected; but as they collide, they each expose the absurdity and the vulnerability of their opposing extremity. This is neat enough to watch, but it seems easy, for what is really difficult is not the vulnerability of extremity, but the troublesome solidity of what is in the middle, of what is not extreme. As the Fool warns Lear, "Thou hast pared thy wit on both sides and left nothing i' th' middle." So has Barnes.

One of the new stories, "Junction," is about the building of the Rouen-Paris-Le Havre railway line in the 1840s. Like most of the stories in this book, it tidily deploys and tidily solves, while pretending not to. The rail-building interests Barnes because the line was largely built by English navvies, and is thus one of the "Cross Channel" entanglements of the French and the British that provides this volume with its title-theme. The story generates a collision between the opposition of scientific triumphalism (the railway) and religious obscurantism (a local *curé*'s belief that the line is preparing not the path of French travelers, but the way of the Lord). Barnes nicely exposes the weakness and the comedy of both extremities. The story is charming, and zany with fact.

Cross Channel ends with a story called "Tunnel," which is about an "elderly English gentleman" who takes the Chunnel train from London to Paris, in the year 2015. He reflects on many of the themes and some of the situations in the book's preceding stories. We suspect that this reflective gentleman may well be Barnes himself. As indeed he is. The story ends: "And the elderly English gentleman, when he returned home, began to write the stories you have just read."

Earlier in the story, Barnes meditates on something that one of his narrators has already announced: the preposterousness of ordinary reality, and hence the ordinariness of the preposterous. The elderly author, thinking about the trick that reality plays on the creative imagination, remembers a woman seen frantically searching her handbag at an airport. What had she lost? Surely, the writer thinks, it could not be something humdrum, like lipstick or film. Perhaps it is a "contraceptive item whose absence would imperil the holiday"? The woman is in his party, and days later, after obsessing about it, he asks her what she had lost at the airport. Her boarding card, she replies.

The author is deliriously happy at the foolishness of the quotidian. He is uncertain which delights him more, "the excess of his misprisions or the primness of the truth." This is nicely phrased. But note that both positions, his misprisions and the truth, are excessive. The imagination, which invented all kinds of disasters for the frantic lady, is excessive; and the truth, which bested imagination, is excessive. Both are a bit ridiculous, and somewhat trivialized. Both have been caricatured, and what is being enjoyed here is not the comic surprise of ordinariness, but the pantomime of banality.

Barnes's fiction caricatures truth while playing games with it. Many of these games have to do with fact. Barnes is in love with facts: true facts, false facts, funny facts, ironic facts. *Flaubert's Parrot*, Barnes's first great success, is an attractive meditation on fact. Barnes takes the details of Flaubert's life and stretches them until they no longer have the dependable silence of facts, but the smart reply of riddle or paradox. He likes to enslave facts with a sense of their own constructedness. It is well-known, for example, that when Flaubert and his friend Du Camp climbed the largest pyramid in Giza to watch the dawn, Flaubert found, attached to the top of the pyramid, a calling card that said *Humbert, Frotteur* and an address in Rouen, Flaubert's own town. Barnes notes that this seems to us one of the great modern ironies. But Flaubert's friend Du Camp had planted the card there the night before; and Flaubert had himself brought the card from Rouen to Egypt. Was Flaubert planning his own traveler's ironies? Barnes, it seems, makes the familiar less stable than we had imagined it to be.

But despite Barnes's post-modern compound eye—the writer, locust-like, seeing around and behind all truths—he is old-fashionedly in love with the surety of fact. In this, he displays his Englishness. He is not a European Pyrrhonist, he is an English empiricist—more precisely, a rogue empiricist, for whom facts, real ones and faked ones, are all pieces of information. *Le Figaro* (of course) has praised Barnes for "the abundance of original thought, the wealth of information" in his work. (Who reads fiction for a "wealth of information"? Original thought puts "information" on a diet, rations it.) For many of Barnes's readers, however, it is hard to tell if he is feeding true or false information. And that is the point. Some of Barnes's somewhat preening details seem benignly verifiable, such as the information that Flaubert likened himself to a camel, and that "*chameau*, camel, was slang for an old courtesan. I do not think this association would have put Flaubert off." And noting that Flaubert also likened himself to a bear, Barnes's narrator gushes forth bear-information: "William Scoresby, the Arctic explorer, noted that the liver of the bear is poisonous—the only part of any quadruped known to be so. Among zookeepers there is no known test for pregnancy in the polar bear. Strange facts that Flaubert might not have found strange."

But some of Barnes's facts are more obscure. The elderly English gentleman in "Tunnel" remarks, as the train passes through Lille, that he could get off and visit "the last surviving French slag-heap." But the story is set in 2015. Is this Barnes's prediction of where France's last slag-heap will be situated? Much of the rest of this new book deals in historical information—about Victorian railways, or an English cricket team that was preparing to travel to France in 1789, while revolution was breaking. Most readers will be sure about the Rouen-Paris railway, but unsure about the eighteenth-century cricket team. In Barnes's style of narrative, however, there is no such thing as ruined facts, for all that he goes around happily destroying them. For the facts that Barnes explodes or complicates have the same status as the true facts (like the building of the French railways) that he leaves alone. All his facts startle so as to soothe.

How? First, they offer the riddle of their strangeness—cricket was last played at the Olympics, in 1900, in Los Angeles, according to one of the stories here—and then the impregnability of their existence, which is itself a kind of solution to their strangeness. Even when we suspect the accuracy of certain facts, they are still soothing, because they connect us to the known world. Even inaccurate facts have a kind of empirical electricity for Barnes, since they connect him to a larger informational zealousness. Wrong facts contain within themselves the ghost of their own accuracy, in the same way that a good parody says something true about its object.

Barnes has made knowingness into an aesthetic. For him, the world is, despite his games, old-fashionedly knowable. When we learn, in *Flaubert's Parrot*, about the complicating ironies of that calling card at the top of the Egyptian pyramid, we complicate our knowledge; but not very much, and it is always better, in Barnes's world, to know more than to know less. In the end, Barnes always wants to help, to inform, to solve, to charm, to boast. However he muddies the waters, he always ferries us across. He points out helpfully that the waters are now very muddy, because he has stirred them up, but he is still ferrying us.

Of course, all fictional description contains fact, and description is explanation. The writer must then make a revolution with this description-explanation. In Barnes's fiction, however, facts are separated from description and handed out like coins to the reader. Barnes's writing does little with them, descriptively. All this information comes from the known world, and merely passes through Barnes's writing on its way to the reader, who is also in the known world. It is as if Barnes's prose is merely a host to this passage.

As a result, his fiction is one of tidy statement. He likes to order his themes even as he proclaims that he is scattering ideas all over the floor. In the story "Experiment," in this new book, Barnes has fun with the jauntiness of his empirical load: a young man tells us about the strange tale of his Uncle Freddy, who as a young man in Paris in 1928 once took part in André Breton's Surrealist Group's researches into sexuality. The hearty Englishman, sitting next to Breton and Queneau, and forced to intellectualize about the commonsensical business of sex, is a fine *donnée*, and amusing. But it is precisely the jauntiness of Barnes's fact—did an Englishman really participate in these famous sessions?—which imprisons the story, and makes it a revolving conceit rather than a grasped truth. "Experiment" is itself an experiment, a controlled experiment, sealed and finite.

This tidiness is a peculiar problem of English fiction in this century. A writer such as D. H. Lawrence, who bullies his reader but who also bullies himself, whose prose is a violent bloom of awkwardness—such a writer is the exception in modern English fiction. Formal neatness, a fondness for over-explicitness or direct statement, and a fat hand with symbolism, are more characteristic. One sees this in early Forster, in William Golding, in Angus Wilson, in Doris Lessing; and in our own age, in Ian McEwan and Julian Barnes.

Kipling, whose stories have a vigorous reticence (even as his poems are ideological ballads), is a different exception to the English zeal for plain-speaking. Barnes's best story in this new book, "Evermore," about a woman's lifelong mourning for her brother, who was killed in the First World War, is strongly reminiscent of two Kipling stories on a similar theme, "The Gardener" and "Mary Postgate." In "Evermore," we learn of Miss Moss, an aging proofreader, who makes obsessive visits in her antique Morris Minor car to the French war cemetery where her brother lies. She cannot forget him, and has dedicated her life to remembrance.

This is a touching story. Here Barnes comes closest to defeating his own intellectual tidiness, and to producing something that discovers grief, rather than something that tells us about grief. But even here Barnes will not let his material flow its own way. He cannot resist bustling around. Where Kipling's two stories about a woman's grief subtract, Barnes's story over-supplies. Kipling seems to tell us everything about Mary Postgate, except about her obsessive hatred of the Germans. Barnes cannot help informing us that Miss Moss's life was "devoted . . . entirely to her own commemorations." Miss Moss is given to ask herself the kinds of rhetorical questions, perfectly expressed, that only characters in stories asks themselves, such as: "Was it a vice to have become such a connoisseur of grief?" We are told about her "voluptuous selfishness of grief," a phrase whose own luxuriousness condescends, somewhat, to Miss Moss. And this sentimentality of explicitness: "She claimed no understanding of military matters. All she claimed was an understanding of grief."

The story is themed. Its own devotion to commemoration does not make clearer its protagonist's devotion, but drowns it. By the end, Barnes is interrupting, like Forster, and talking directly to the reader—making his own appeal, literalizing the theme of remembrance: "if this [forgetting the First World War] happened to the individual, could it not also happen on a national scale?"

Narrative must discover. The facts that it "discovers" already exist, of course; but great fiction is not daunted by the prior existence of the world. Great fiction appears to discover facts by giving us the impression that our reading of the text completes the bottom half of a discovery whose plaintive top stalk the writer has merely uncovered. Fiction should seem to offer itself to the reader's completion, not to the writer's. This whisper of conspiracy is one of fiction's necessary beauties. Perhaps this illusion of discovery, the uncovering of a world which is related to, but not continuous with, the known world, is fiction's greatest beauty: fiction's false bottom.

It cannot be said enough: this is not, as in the fiction of Julian Barnes, the false bottom of fact, by which we learn one certainty only to have it replaced by another, brighter or more complicated certainty. It is the false bottom of truth, whereby we learn many things, all of them bottomless. Fiction must not stroke the known. It must distress the undiscovered. A literature of fact, of knowingness, a fiction like Barnes's, knows too much and speaks too much. But a literature that discovers, that dares to know less, is always on the verge of what is not sayable, rather than at the end of what has just been said.

In such quietness, we may attend to Cather's large hush, as we wait for the message-carrying air to blow through our open window.

Source: James Wood, "The Fact-checker," in *New Republic*, September 25, 1977, pp. 40–43.

Sources

Barnes, Julian, "Melon," in *Cross Channel*, Vintage Books, 1996, pp. 65–87.

Hoffert, Barbara, Review of *Cross Channel*, in *Library Journal*, March 15, 1996, p. 98.

Review of *Cross Channel*, in *New Yorker*, December 16, 1996, p. 109.

Review of *Cross Channel*, in *Virginia Quarterly Review*, Vol. 73, No. 4, Autumn 1996, p. 132.

Review of *The Lemon Table*, in *San Francisco Chronicle*, July 25, 2004, Sunday Final Edition, p. M2.

Further Reading

Binton, Craig, *The Anatomy of Revolution*, Vintage, 1965.
  Binton's book, considered a classic in its field, explores the American, French, and Russian Revolutions, explaining their similar structural patterns.

Guignery, Vanessa, *The Fiction of Julian Barnes*, Palgrave Macmillan, 2006.
  Guignery has written extensively about Barnes and here gives a comprehensive overview of criticism on Barnes's works.

Kempton, Adrian, "A Barnes Eye View of France," in *Franco-British Studies*, Vol. 2, Autumn 1996, pp. 92–101.
  Basically reviewing *Cross Channel*, Kempton focuses on the importance of French themes throughout the book.

Moseley, Merritt, *Understanding Julian Barnes*, University of South Carolina Press, 1997.
  Though this book touches on only a few of the stories from *Cross Channel*, it offers extensive explication of Barnes's fiction dating from the time that this story was published.

Pateman, Matthew, *Julian Barnes*, Northcote House, 2002.
  Pateman's focus is on Barnes's novels, but his analysis gives a good understanding of the writer.

Sesto, Bruce, "Julian Barnes and Postmodernist Fiction," in *Language, History, and Metanarrative in the Fiction of Julian Barnes*, Peter Lang, 2001.
  This book focuses primarily on Barnes's novels, but Sesto's introduction offers a good way for readers to place Barnes in a literary context.

The Middleman

Bharati Mukherjee

1988

"The Middleman" is the title story in Bharati Mukherjee's collection, *The Middleman and Other Stories* (1988). Told by an Iraqi Jew who is a naturalized American citizen, it is set in an unnamed Central American country in the throes of a guerrilla insurgency. The idea for the story came to Mukherjee when she was writing an incomplete novel about a Vietnam veteran who becomes a mercenary soldier in Afghanistan and Central America. The novel featured a minor character named Alfie Judah, a Jew who had relocated from Baghdad to New York, via Bombay, India. Alfie became such a strong presence in the writer's mind that, as she reported in an interview with Alison B. Carb in *Massachusetts Review*, he "took control and wrote his own story." "The Middleman," then, is the story of Alfie, a cynical man who "travels around the world, providing people with what they need—guns, narcotics, automobiles." It is a story of lust, betrayal, and murder, featuring American expatriates, a beautiful woman, and ruthless guerrillas.

Author Biography

American novelist and short-story writer Bharati Mukherjee was born on July 27, 1940, in Calcutta, West Bengal, India, to wealthy parents, Sudhir Lal and Bina Mukherjee. Her father co-owned a pharmaceutical factory and later became director of research and development of a large chemical complex.

Even as a child, Mukherjee knew she was going to be a writer. She learned to read and write at the age of three, and she later reported that as a child, the fictional worlds she discovered in stories were more real to her than the world around her. She started her first novel when she was nine or ten, and at high school in Calcutta, she started writing short stories for school magazines.

Mukherjee received her bachelor of arts from the University of Calcutta in 1959, and a master of arts from the University of Baroda in 1961. Wanting to pursue a career as a writer and encouraged by her father to do so, Mukherjee then left India to attend the Writers' Workshop at the University of Iowa. She received a master of fine arts in 1963, and a Ph.D. in comparative literature, also from the University of Iowa, in 1970.

While studying at the Writers' Workshop, Mukherjee met the Canadian, Clark Blaise, who was also a student on the same program. The couple married in 1963, and from 1966 to 1980, they lived in Canada, first in Toronto and then Montreal, where they both held teaching positions.

Mukherjee became a Canadian citizen but was unhappy living in that country because of the racial prejudice she encountered. She was refused service in stores and was sometimes followed by detectives in department stores who assumed she was a shoplifter. It was in Canada that Mukherjee wrote her first two novels, *The Tiger's Daughter* (1972) and *Wife* (1975), but her work received little attention from critics or the public.

In 1980, Mukherjee resigned her professorship at McGill University and moved with her husband and two sons to the United States, where she became first a permanent resident and then a U.S. citizen. Living in New York, she taught at Skidmore College, Mountain State College, Queen's College of the City University of New York, and Columbia University. In 1984, she was writer in residence at Emory University. She felt that being in the United States was a great relief after the discrimination she had suffered in Canada. In New York City, she was able to blend in with people on the street, and she believes that attitudes toward Indian immigration are healthier in the United States than in Canada. Mukherjee chose to identify fully with her new country of choice, and she regards herself as an American, not an Indian-American or an Indian in exile.

Mukherjee's first short story collection, *Darkness*, was published in 1985. This was followed by a second collection, *The Middleman and Other*

Bharati Mukherjee AP Images

Stories (1988), which won the National Book Critics Circle Award for Best Fiction. Like much of Mukherjee's work, the stories deal with the experience of new immigrants to the United States. This is also the theme of one of her most popular novels, *Jasmine*, which was published the following year. The title character, Jasmine, is a young Indian woman who comes to the United States as an illegal immigrant.

Mukherjee has also written *The Holder of the World* (1993) and *The Tree Bride: A Novel* (2004), as well as several nonfiction works, including some co-authored with her husband. As of 2006, Mukherjee was a professor in the Department of English at the University of California, Berkeley.

Plot Summary

"The Middleman" is told in the first person by Alfie Judah, a Jew who is a newly naturalized American citizen originally from Baghdad, Iraq. He has temporarily left the United States because he has been involved in some shady financial dealing and is fighting extradition. He is currently living in an unnamed Central American country, where he has just started employment on the ranch of an expatriate American named Clovis T. Ransome. Ransome fled the United States with fifteen million dollars in cash that he appears to have appropriated illegally in some kind of financial scam. Alfie has attached himself to Ransome in the hope that he can gain some advantage from the situation. He is the "middleman" of the title; he manages to make a living "from things that fall." There appears to be plenty of opportunity for such graft; an insurgency is going on in the country, and the president, a corrupt man named Gutiérrez, pays retainers to various armed groups, and also to Ransome, to protect him.

Alfie sits at the side of the swimming pool and confesses that he has a weakness for women. He mentions that a young woman named Maria, Ransome's wife, lives on the ranch. At the pool, Alfie chats briefly with Ransome, who is waiting for his crony Bud Wilkins to drive over in his pickup. They plan to go on a deep-sea fishing trip. Ransome invites Alfie to go with them, but Alfie declines. Maria, who has been swimming in the ocean, comes to join Alfie, while Ransome loads up the jeep with beer.

Bud arrives, and he and Ransome drink beer together. Eduardo, the houseboy, loads up Bud's pickup with crates which Alfie suspects contain rifles, ammunition, and possibly medicine. Then Bud and Ransome drive off into the jungle in Ransome's jeep.

Eduardo kills two ocean crabs that have found their way into the kitchen. He is upset over something, and Maria and Alfie take him to his room. Eduardo has crates under his bed, and Alfie wonders what is in them. But Maria replies that she respects Eduardo's privacy, and Alfie should, too.

Alfie sets the table, and Maria brings a tray of cheese and biscuits. She says she is hoping he will drive her to San Vincente, a small market town, in Bud's pickup. Alfie does not want to, but he agrees. He does not want to know what is in the crates that are piled up in the pickup. The crates are labeled "fruits," but Alfie knows he has been recruited for a gunrunning operation, when all he wanted to be was a bystander.

They drive the rough road through the jungle to San Vincente. After about forty minutes, Maria tells Alfie to turn off and head for a village called Santa Simona. She says she was born there. Alfie knows Santa Simona is not a village; it is a guerrilla camp.

Alfie and Maria get out of the truck and make their way to some shacks. Alfie knows that this is not the intended destination for Bud's arms shipment; the load has been hijacked. He would have preferred that Maria had not involved him in this little adventure.

A tall guerrilla soldier comes toward them; he and Maria embrace. Maria then introduces Alfie to the guerrilla soldier, whose name is Andreas. The three of them go inside one of the shacks, which is the command post for the guerrillas. Maria offers Alfie a beer, and then she and Andreas leave. Alfie opens his beer and takes it with him to the back porch. There is a caged bird by the laundry tub, and a boy of ten is teasing it. The boy, who later turns out to be Andreas's son, asks him for gum. Alfie gives him a cheap pen to keep him quiet and returns inside to drink his beer.

About an hour later, Maria returns and wakes him up. She says they have finished unloading the guns and it is time to go. Alfie, Maria, and Andreas, who is carrying the bird cage, go to the truck. On the drive back to Ransome's ranch, Maria explains what is going on. She indicates that Bud has been killed because he refused to let Ransome in on his illicit arms-dealing business.

They arrive back at the ranch, where Ransome is sitting on the love seat on the porch. Alfie asks him where Bud is, and Ransome replies that a gang of guerrillas shot him only half a mile down the road. He wonders how he got away, but Alfie knows that the guerrillas were in Ransome's pay. Alfie observes that Ransome notices the crates are gone from Bud's truck, so Ransome knows he has been betrayed.

Maria sits down on the love seat next to her husband while Alfie goes to the kitchen for a beer. When he returns, Ransome, who has been drinking heavily, is snoring. His hand is inside the bird cage, and the bird is pecking him, but this does not awaken him. Maria asks Alfie to kill the bird.

At eleven o'clock that night, Alfie carries Ransome up the stairs to the spare bedroom and leaves him fully clothed on the bed. Alfie then returns to his room. Maria comes to him and they make love, and Maria tells him of the beatings she received from Ransome.

At about three o'clock in the morning, a man rides up on a scooter. Maria thinks it is Andreas, but it is another man, a tall Indian, who enters Alfie's room. Maria says something to the man and he steps outside. She and Alfie quickly get dressed; the Indian comes back into the room with two more Indians. They demand to know where Ransome is, and Alfie tells them. A group of guerrillas, including Andreas, open Ransome's door. Ransome is awake; he keeps cool and tries to bargain with the men. He says they can take Maria, and he also of-fers them money. He says they can take Alfie, too.

Andreas has three Indians and Eduardo take a large stash of dollar bills from a trunk. He says he will take Maria as well, but he does not want Alfie. While Ransome remains politely defiant, Andreas hands his pistol to Maria. She shoots Ransome, killing him instantly. After aiming the gun at Alfie's genitals, she smiles and returns the gun to Andreas. Alfie is relieved. Maria and Andreas leave, and Alfie plans his next move. He decides that in a few days, he will walk to San Vincente and befriend the Indians there. He is sure that some-one will be interested in the information he has to offer about the guerrilla camp and about Bud and Ransome. He thinks, "There must be something worth trading in the troubles I have seen."

Characters

Andreas

Andreas is the guerrilla leader. A tall, hand-some man, he is Maria's lover. When Alfie meets him, he realizes that Andreas is the man on the poster that Eduardo has placed on the wall of his room. It shows a man in beret, black boots, and bandolier who looks as if he might have "played Che Guevara in some B-budget Argentine melodrama."

Eduardo

Eduardo is the houseboy at Ransome's ranch. He seems rather nervous and overreacts when he has to kill two stray ocean crabs in the kitchen. It appears that he hates his employers and other grin-gos, or Americans. Maria and Alfie have to take him to his room to calm him down. Eduardo's sym-pathies are with Andreas and the other guerrillas, and he is present when they confront and kill Ransome.

Alfie Judah

Alfie Judah, the narrator of the story, is a Jew who is originally from Baghdad, Iraq, but is now a naturalized U.S. citizen. He appears to be a widely traveled man, having lived in Bombay, India, but he is also someone who does not really fit in wher-ever he goes. His American home is in Flushing, in the borough of Queens, New York, and he has an American wife. Alfie is a wheeler-dealer and a hustler who is not too fussy about how he makes his money. He gets people what they need, whether

it is guns, drugs, or cars, and he knows how to survive in a rough world. He was forced to flee the United States, however, because the authorities discovered an illicit fund he was maintaining for New Jersey judges. "My dealings can't stand too much investigation," he says. So he ends up in Central America and attaches himself for the time being to Ransome, although he expects to be able to return to the United States eventually. Alfie is dark-skinned, which means that he is spared the ha-tred the local people have for Americans. No one knows how to place him; to some he is an Arab, to others an Indian. Alfie's weakness, he confesses, is women. He lusts after Maria and somehow man-ages to win her favors, if only for one night, and he suffers no consequences for this act of adultery. He also survives when the guerrillas come to kill Ransome. No one cares much about Alfie, so the guerrillas do not bother to kill him. As a result, he survives and seems to relish the prospect of walk-ing in to San Vincente, the capital city, talking to people, and finding some other way of keeping himself afloat.

Clovis T. Ransome

Clovis T. Ransome is an expatriate American who, according to Alfie, has "spent his adult life in tropical paradises playing God." Ransome fled Waco, Texas, with fifteen million dollars in petty cash that he had obtained fraudulently. He just managed to escape the investigators from the Se-curities Exchange Commission (SEC). Ransome is a player in the ruthless political game that operates in the unnamed country. It appears that he runs a protection racket to shield President Gutiérrez from his many enemies. This may have been how he ac-quired the beautiful Maria as his wife, since Maria was formerly the president's mistress. Maria hates her husband and claims that he beats her. Ransome is a violent, amoral man who arranges for the guer-rillas to kill his friend Bud Wilkins, because Bud had refused to allow Ransome to become part of his gun-running operation. But Ransome also falls foul of the guerrillas, for reasons unstated, and when they confront him in his room, Maria shoots and kills him with Andreas's pistol.

Maria Ransome

Maria Ransome is a beautiful young, dark-skinned woman, mostly Indian, who is married to Clovis T. Ransome. It is a loveless marriage, how-ever. When she was a girl, Maria planned to marry Andreas, but Gutiérrez, now president but then minister of education, came to her school when she was fourteen and took her for himself. Later, Maria was, so the talk goes, "partially bought and partially seduced" by Ransome. There is a rumor that Maria comes from an aristocratic family and is a former beauty queen. She is the object of all men's lust, including that of Alfie and Bud Wilkins. She allows Alfie to spend the night with her when they return from the guerrilla camp and her husband is in a drunken sleep. However, her loyalty is to Andreas. She helps the guerrillas acquire the armaments that are loaded in Bud Wilkins's pickup, and when the guerrillas confront Ransome, Maria coolly shoots her husband.

Bud Wilkins

Bud Wilkins is a Texan and possibly a former CIA agent who has built up a business in the Central American country. He owns a fleet of trucks, planes, and buses, which form the legitimate side of his business. But since he has the means of transportation, he also makes a fortune selling arms. He and Ransome appear to be friends, but Ransome arranges for Bud to be killed by the guerrillas because Bud refused to give him a cut of his profits in arms trading.

Themes

Amorality, Deceit, and Self-interest

The world depicted in the story is a brutal, violent, cynical one. With the possible exception of Andreas, the guerrilla leader, the characters are concerned only with how they can exploit the situation for their own benefit. The finer qualities of love and friendship and behavior guided by moral standards are absent. It is a dog-eat-dog world, in which ruthlessness and selfishness are rewarded. Cynical betrayal is the order of the day, and loyalty has no place. No one has any ideals that they are prepared to live by. Clovis T. Ransome, for example, is nothing more than a swindler who likes to live in luxury with his trophy wife, whom he abuses. It also appears that he cynically tries to play one group off against another, a strategy that eventually costs him his life. Ransome will not be mourned, though; it is clear that the indigenous Indians whom he employs to clear the jungle hate him, as they do all Americans.

The other American in the story, Bud Wilkins, is no better. He makes a profit from dealing in arms; he will, no doubt, supply the arms to the highest bidder, weapons that will be used to bring further

devastation on this poor country. He cares nothing for peace. Bud's violent nature is shown in the small incident when he first arrives at the ranch. He backs his pickup truck hard against a tree and disturbs a bird, at which he "lines it up with an imaginary pistol and curls his finger twice in its direction." The incident shows the thoughtless violence that lurks everywhere in this environment. Life is cheap, whether human or wildlife. Another example occurs at the guerrilla camp, when the one-armed guerrilla asks Maria, indirectly, if he should kill Alfie. For men such as these, the killing of a man (even one who has done them no harm) is of no more consequence than the killing of a bird or a rat.

Of course, it is Alfie who is the embodiment of the cynicism that is at the heart of the story. Like Bud, he is only concerned with "outfitting the participants" in the civil war. He knows the "rules of survival," and it is these that govern his life, not any moral code about how to behave. In fact, Alfie has no concept of right and wrong and does not even acknowledge that such things exist; in his world, "There's just supply and demand running the universe." This must be a chilling world in which to live, in which there is neither God nor moral law in charge, but only an economic principle that Alfie is determined to exploit. Nonetheless, it is a world to which Alfie, even though he is an outsider, is well attuned. He is a shrewd operator. "I calculate margins," he says, as he speculates about whether a night with Maria would be worth any consequences that might result. Everything for Alfie is a profit-and-loss calculation, even when it comes to lust and adultery.

Lust

The theme of lust centers on the alluring Maria. She is at once the object of lust and lustful herself. Sexual tension is injected into the story on Maria's first appearance, when she emerges from the ocean in her pink bikini. Alfie watches as the water beads on her shoulders, and he thinks "how cool her flesh will be for just a few more minutes." Alfie is constantly aware of Maria's body and its sexual power: "She shrugs, and her breasts are slower than her shoulders in coming down." Later, he observes that "The way her bottom bounces inside those cutoffs could drive a man crazy." He admits that he would kill for her. This is not really a surprise, since Alfie confessed earlier that his dominant passion is lust, and he described the sexual frustrations of his youth in Baghdad.

At one point, Alfie elevates Maria to an importance similar to that of Helen of Troy in ancient Greek mythology, over whom supposedly the Trojan War

Topics For Further Study

- Research historical patterns of immigration to the United States. How did those patterns change during the twentieth century, in terms of which countries the majority of immigrants came from? What effect did the change in immigration policy in 1965 have? Where do the majority of immigrants come from today? What effect does that have on the racial and ethnic composition of the United States? Write an essay in which you present your findings.

- Write a short story in which the protagonist is a second-generation teenage immigrant whose parents are foreign-born. Your protagonist was born and raised in the United States and is attuned to American values. Bring out in the story the cultural conflict between the two generations. What is the conflict about? The way the young person speaks or dresses or behaves? Why does this create conflict with the person's parents?

- Tape record an interview with some immigrants in your school or town. Find out their story. Why did they come to the United States? What are their dreams? Have they experienced prejudice here? Make a class presentation, playing portions of the tape, and putting their experiences in a social context. For example, how many immigrants from that country come to the United States? What sort of occupations do they take up?

- Think of another character, from a television show, book, or movie, like Alfie Judah in the sense that the reader/viewer likes him in spite of the fact that he does not behave well, lacks conscience or morality, or other virtues. Why do characters such as this sometimes appeal to us more than the virtuous or good characters? Try and be specific about the appeal of the character(s) you select. What qualities do they embody and why do we like them? Write an essay which explains how immoral characters can be more attractive than moral ones.

---

was fought. He suggests that the entire civil war in the country is due to a quarrel between men over who should possess Maria: "It's all a family plot in countries like this; revolutions fought for a schoolgirl in white with blunted toes." If lust is at the root of what moves men to war, Alfie is also aware, from his childhood in Baghdad, of the extent to which a society—a male-dominated one—may go in order to punish the expression of lust outside approved channels. This is apparent from his graphic description of an incident he witnessed as a child, in which a beautiful young woman was stoned to death in the village for adultery.

Style

Setting

The unnamed Central American country is evoked in full sensory detail. The weather is hot and soon the rains will come, but at the moment it is "so dry it could scratch your lungs." The wildlife is exotic: "Bright feathered birds screech, snakeskins glitter, as the jungle peels away. Iguanas the size of wallabies leap from behind macheted bushes."

The Spanish-speaking society depicted is strongly Catholic. Maria went to a convent school. The houseboy, Eduardo, has posters of saints on his bedroom walls. At the guerrilla camp, above the cot in the main shack, is a "sad, dark, plaster crucified Jesus."

In addition to being religious, the local people are strongly anti-American. They hate Americans even more than they hate the president of their own country. Paradoxically, however, the Indian population seems saturated with American popular culture. They know all the Hollywood names and the names of the automakers in Detroit; they imitate the signs they see American baseball fans making on television, and they wear their Braves baseball caps. At the guerrillas' rundown camp—a mere clearing in the jungle—sits a 1957 two-tone Plymouth with fins and chrome. It seems that the reach of American culture is ubiquitous. But the effects of the American presence are not presented as benign. In this respect, Ransome's swimming pool is symbolic. He fills it with chemicals so toxic that if a toad falls into it, the water blisters its skin. Eduardo's hysterical complaint about his employer, "He kills everything," can be seen as a comment on the effects of the presence of the Americans.

Historical Context

East Asian Immigration to the United States

Immigration to the United States from India and other South Asian countries greatly increased following the 1965 Immigration and Naturalization Act. By the mid-1970s, there were over 175,000 Indian immigrants in the United States, with four states, California, New York, New Jersey, and Illinois, developing sizable Indian American populations. The majority of these new immigrants already spoke fluent English and adjusted well to life in the United States, becoming one of the most prosperous of immigrant groups. Many were of professional status, such as doctors, engineers, and experts in the emerging information technology. However, Indian Americans also faced incidents of racism. In New Jersey in the 1980s, a number of Indians were murdered by young white men, who deliberately targeted them because of their race and the fact that as professionals they had attained material success.

Indian Americans, as well as those Indians who settled in Canada, soon produced a generation of writers who documented their experience as immigrants. Such writers included Mukherjee, Ved Mehta, A. K. Ramanujan, Suniti Namjoshi, Michael Ondaatji, and Rohinton Mistry. These writers explored issues such as racism, nostalgia for home, and the question of identity. Should they attempt to preserve their distinct Indian identity or assimilate with mainstream U.S. culture? In "Two Ways to Belong to America," an article published in the *New York Times* in 1996, Mukherjee described how she had made the decision to become an American citizen and wholeheartedly embrace her new identity, whereas her sister, Mira, who had been in the United States since 1960 as a permanent resident alien, still identified strongly with India and planned to return to her native country on retirement. Mukherjee believed that the majority of Indian immigrants had attitudes closer to those of her sister than her own.

Civil War in Central America in the 1980s

Although the country in which "The Middleman" is set is not named, it clearly alludes to the situation in the Central American countries of El Salvador and Nicaragua in the 1980s.

In El Salvador, a country marked by great social inequalities, there was a civil war in which a leftist guerrilla insurgency attempted to overthrow the government. The government was dominated by the wealthy elite, while the majority of citizens lived in poverty. Supported by billions of dollars in aid from the United States, the El Salvadoran government was ruthless in attempting to suppress the insurgency, establishing death squads that carried out assassinations of prominent individuals who spoke out against the government. Many atrocities were committed. In 1980, the archbishop of San Salvador, Monsignor Oscar Arnulfo Romeroy Galdámez, was celebrating mass in a chapel when he was shot dead by a professional assassin. In another incident in the same year, three U.S. Roman Catholic nuns and a lay worker were raped and killed by El Salvadoran National Guard troops. During 1982 and 1983, approximately eight thousand civilians a year were being killed by government forces. In another infamous incident, in 1989, El Salvadoran soldiers murdered six Jesuit brothers and two female co-workers. By 1992, when a peace was brokered by the United Nations, the civil war had taken approximately seventy thousand lives.

In Nicaragua, one of the poorest countries in the world, the leftist Sandinista Party government faced an insurgency from guerrillas known as the contras. The Sandinistas took power in 1979, when a revolution overthrew the dictator Anastasio Somoza. The Sandinistas legitimately won a national election in 1984, but they faced hostility from the United States and turned to the Soviet Union and Cuba for support. The United States offered aid to the rebel contras, enabling them to attack the Sandinistas from bases in Honduras. The United States also imposed trade sanctions and mined Nicaraguan harbors. In 1987, a U.S. plane carrying guns for the contras was shot down in Nicaragua. The only survivor was an operative of the Central Intelligence Agency (CIA) named Eugene Hassenfuss who was captured by the Sandinistas and later released. This incident may have been what inspired Mukherjee's creation

Compare & Contrast

- **1980s:** Immigration to the United States from Asian countries continues to grow as a result of the 1965 Immigration and Nationalization Act. Immigrant communities from India, the Philippines, Korea, Vietnam, China, and other Asian countries all experience rapid growth.

  Today: There are 1.7 million Indian immigrants in the United States, according to the 2000 census. This represents an increase of 106 percent since 1990, with an annual growth rate of 7.6 percent. Indian Americans are the third largest Asian minority in the United States, after Chinese and Filipinos. Indian Americans are above the national average in terms of education and income levels.

- **1980s:** Immigration to the United States is higher than at any point since the early twentieth century. During the 1980s, ten million immigrants, both legal and illegal, arrive in the United States. Four million of these come from Mexico. The problem of illegal immigration, most of it across southern U.S. borders, also rises. Estimates of the number of illegal immigrants in the country range from three million to twelve million.

  Today: The problem of illegal immigration from Mexico and other Central American countries becomes a major political issue. Illegal immigrants

mount large demonstrations for their rights in many American cities. President George W. Bush favors the creation of a new category of guest workers to address the problem. This arrangement would legalize the status of millions of illegal immigrants but would be for a limited time period, after which the guest worker would have to return to his or her country of origin.

- **1980s:** Violent conflict occurs during much of the decade in the Central American countries of Nicaragua and El Salvador. In Nicaragua, the left-wing governing Sandinistas battle an insurgency by the U.S.-backed contras, while in El Salvador, the right-wing government, with financial aid from the United States, attempts to put down a guerrilla insurgency.

  Today: Nicaragua is no longer governed by the Sandinistas, but it remains one of the poorest countries in the Western Hemisphere. It has high unemployment and large external debt and relies on international assistance. In 2005, Nicaragua ratifies the U.S.-Central America Free Trade Agreement (CAFTA), which it believes will attract investment and create more jobs. El Salvador, at peace after a decade of war, tries to boost its sluggish economy by encouraging foreign investment and modernizing its tax and healthcare systems. In 2006, El Salvador implements CAFTA.

---

of the character Bud Wilkins in "The Middleman," since Wilkins is rumored to be a former CIA agent and is involved in arms dealing. There were also allegations at the time that the CIA was involved in drug-trafficking to aid the contras.

In 1990, as part of a peace agreement, the contras were disbanded in exchange for free elections in Nicaragua. In the election, the Sandinistas were unexpectedly defeated by a coalition of opposing forces. The eight-year civil war had badly damaged the country. Unemployment stood at 30 percent of the workforce, and Nicaragua's national debt was

seven billion dollars, the highest per capita debt in Latin America.

Critical Overview

Mukherjee's collection, *The Middleman and Other Stories*, was well received by reviewers. In *New York*, Rhoda Koenig describes the stories as "sharp and resonant." She points out that "the displaced persons" who form the subjects of the stories "adapt

Young El Salvadoran anti-government guerrilla soldiers after attacking the village of San Francisco Javier, El Salvador © Bill Gentile/Corbis

surprisingly well to circumstances, though not all of them become model citizens." She had Alfie Judah of "The Middleman" in mind, commenting that "A foreign middleman—middlemen come out the winners in any revolution—stays with a Latin American dealer in dubious commodities."

In the *New York Times Book Review*, Jonathan Raban notes that the immigrants depicted in the stories are dispersed over a huge territory, "from Toronto in the north down to a steamy Central American republic." Noting that Alfie Judah is a Jew, Raban comments that Mukherjee "hijacks the whole tradition of Jewish-American writing and flies it off to a destination undreamed of by its original practitioners." Raban also seems to be commenting on Alfie in his observation about Mukherjee's "new Americans—their guiltlessness, bounce, sexual freedom, their easy money and the lightness of their footsteps on the American landscape. . . . [They] are no more tormented by conscience than butterflies." As a final point, Raban notes that "Every story ends on a new point of departure. People are last seen walking out through an open door, planning an escape, or suspended on the optimistic brink of a blissful sexual transport." He quotes one of the closing lines of "The Middleman,"

"I will walk down the muddy road," in support of this observation. These characters, Raban writes, again neatly describing Alfie Judah, "keep aloft on luck and grace."

Criticism

Bryan Aubrey

Aubrey holds a Ph.D. in English and has published many articles on twentieth-century literature. In this essay, Aubrey discusses "The Middleman" in the context of the experience of recent immigrants to the United States.

Bharati Mukherjee is known for her compelling stories about the experience of recent immigrants to the United States from the Third World. Although "The Middleman" takes place not in the United States but in an unnamed Central American country, it features the same theme. Alfie Judah is a naturalized American citizen who found his way to the United States via Baghdad and Bombay. He has learned many American ways, although he remains an outsider wherever he goes. In fact, the very term "middleman" is a metaphor of the immigrant experience, suggesting someone who is caught between two cultures, a full member of neither. Alfie, despite the American-style informality of the shortened version of his first name by which he introduces himself, is an outsider several times over. First, he is a Jew, and if there are any people in the world who have become familiar, over the course of many centuries, with what it means to be outsiders, it is the Jews. Alfie grew up as a Jew in Baghdad, an Arab city dominated by Muslims. He refers to the different, "lenient" nature of his upbringing in Baghdad when he recalls how he was taken as a child to "see something special from the old Iraqi culture," the stoning to death of a woman for adultery. As a member of a minority group, Alfie was clearly set apart from the dominant culture of his society.

Then when Alfie immigrated to the United States, he became a double outsider, so to speak. As a dark-skinned Iraqi Jew, he would have been regarded by many as a foreigner, and possibly a foreigner not to be trusted. Of course, given Alfie's chosen method of making money in his newly adopted homeland—he got involved in some kind of financial scam which landed him in trouble with the authorities—this mistrust might have been justified. But it is not quite as simple as that.

An immigrant such as Alfie cannot come to the United States and straightaway become president of the local bank, join the country club, and volunteer at Little League. Yes, Alfie is the kind of man who makes no distinction between a moral and an immoral way to live, but in his defense, the path to success in the United States did not lie as wide open to him as it would have done to his WASP neighbors. (WASP is an acronym for White Anglo-Saxon Protestant and refers to the American elite who occupy the vast majority of positions of power in the country.) Mukherjee herself came to the defense of Alfie, her character, in an interview she gave to Alison B. Carb in *Massachusetts Review*. "He [Alfie] attracted me because he was a cynical person and a hustler, as many immigrant survivors have to be." Her comment suggests that it is too easy to make moral judgments about Alfie and the way he chooses to survive in an alien environment. As an immigrant herself, Mukherjee has the ability to see things from the immigrant's point of view. Indeed, she once commented, in an interview with Beverley Byers-Pevitts, that "The Middleman" was the most "autobiographical" of her stories. She explained that the origin of the story lay in a trip she made to Costa Rica, where she was "stuck . . . among rather complicated, difficult people." She tried writing the story with a Bengali woman in it but realized that this was implausible. Switching from third-person to first-person point of view, she discovered the character of Alfie, who fitted the story perfectly. With that in mind, it is easy to see some common ground between Mukherjee and her character Alfie in the sense that they both gave up a rich cultural heritage in order to come to the new world. Mukherjee was raised in a Hindu Bengali Brahmin family. She wrote in "Two Ways to Belong in America" of "surrendering those thousands of years of 'pure culture,'" to become an "immigrant nobody." So it is with Alfie Judah, as he recalls the "once-illustrious" Judahs whose family heritage goes back to places such as Smyrna, in Turkey, where there has been a large Jewish population since the seventeenth century, and Aleppo, an ancient city in northern Syria which traditionally had a large Jewish population, one which shrank drastically during the mid-twentieth century. In those two allusions to cities known for their Jewish communities, Mukherjee creates a sense of a rich cultural identity extending back hundreds of years or more, which has been lost by Alfie Judah as the price he pays for his decision to come to the United States. (Although, it must be said, Alfie shows no regret at all about this. He has learned to

> Alfie, therefore, wins a kind of grudging tolerance born of indifference. He may be a middleman, but in this society, he is a kind of nowhere man, his origins, nationality, and allegiances unknown."

adapt—and he did manage to land in the immigrant-rich city of Flushing, in the borough of Queens, New York City, which in the 1980s had a large Asian-American population.)

When from a legal point of view, life gets too hot for Alfie in Queens and he ends up in a strife-torn Central American country, he becomes even more of an outsider. Technically, he is an American citizen, but he is not American in the way that Clovis T. Ransome and Bud Wilkins, the two white Texans, are American. Although he has learned some "New World skill[s]" such as how to open a beer bottle by hitting the cap against a metal edge, he cannot share the easy camaraderie of Clovis and Bud—before the one betrays the other, that is. Alfie is forever outside their world. When he tries to explain Ransome's fanatical devotion to the Atlanta Braves baseball team, for example, Alfie says, "There are aspects of American life that I came too late for and will never understand." This is the puzzled statement of the immigrant everywhere. There are some things about every society that a person cannot understand unless he or she has been born and raised in it. Quasi-tribal allegiances to particular sports teams that go back generations and are rooted in local pride and sense of place are among the most noticeable examples. The immigrant may try hard to understand; he may learn all the rules of, say, baseball, and all the players' names and all the baseball statistics, but compared to the lifelong fan, his understanding will always be superficial, lacking in real emotional depth.

But Alfie Judah is no more at home with the indigenous population of this unnamed country

What Do I Read Next?

- Mukherjee's novel *Jasmine* (1989) emerged out of the short story of the same title published in *The Middleman and Other Stories*. *Jasmine* follows the life of a courageous young woman who leaves her native India and learns how to survive in the alien environment of the United States.

- Jhumpa Lahiri was named by the *New Yorker* magazine as one of the twenty best young writers in the United States. In her first collection of nine stories, *Interpreter of Maladies* (1999), Lahiri writes about the Indian American experience in all its variety.

- *Contours of the Heart: South Asians Map North America* (1996), edited by Sunaina Maira and Rajini Srikanth, is an award-winning anthology of poems, stories, photographs, and essays that explores many aspects of the South Asian experience in North America. Many of the writers discover that they do not have to choose between identifying with South Asian or American cultures, but they can create their own culture that values heritage yet is also new.

- *Living in America: Poetry and Fiction by South Asian American Writers* (1995), edited by Rustomji-Kerns, is an anthology of Asian American authors, some native-born, others immigrants and refugees. It contains poetry and short fiction by established and new writers. Many of the contributions reflect the concerns of a predominantly middle-class, educated South Asian community as it comes to terms with a new culture and defines its identity.

- Lan Samantha Chang's critically acclaimed *Hunger* (1998), consisting of the title novella and some short stories, explores the experience of Chinese immigrants in the United States, some of whom find that their offspring, raised in America, are more attuned to American values than traditional Chinese ones.

---

than he is with the Americans. The Indians regard him with puzzlement. Because of his dark skin, he is spared the hostility extended to white Americans, but the locals cannot place him. When Maria introduces him to Andreas, the guerrilla leader, Andreas looks him over and says, "Yudah?" and frowns. Maria just shrugs, and Alfie is more or less left alone. When the guerrillas come looking for Ransome in order to kill him, Maria has to explain the presence of Alfie to one of them. Alfie hears her say, "Jew" and "Israel," which apparently is enough to make the guerrilla lose interest, since his target is the *gringo*, the American. Alfie, therefore, wins a kind of grudging tolerance born of indifference. He may be a middleman, but in this society, he is a kind of nowhere man, his origins, nationality, and allegiances unknown. Alfie, a born survivor if ever there was one, is used to this outsider status, and it does not disturb him. To some, he says, he is an Arab, to others an Indian. (Of course, he is neither.) For his part, he is content just to observe this new country from the outside and pick up whatever knowledge he needs that will serve his purposes. A cunning man, he knows more than he lets on, as when he understands some of the Spanish spoken around him but pretends he does not.

Denied the social connections provided by a shared culture, Alfie appears to seek only one connection to compensate for the lack, and that is the temporary, emotionally meaningless coupling provided by a woman's body in the heat of desire. The language of lust transcends all differences, if only for a short while. The fact that Alfie, himself a married man, has just seduced another man's wife, in the man's own home, does not trouble his conscience. He lives without morality or guilt, on the margins of society, picking up whatever scraps happen to fall his way.

Despite all Alfie's faults, Mukherjee presents him in a sympathetic light, and the reader warms to this character. What is likable about Alfie is that he does not self-consciously play the role of expatriate; nor does he particularly care about embracing American culture and the American dream. There is insouciance about him, a kind of casual indifference to the things that seem so important to others. He does not cling to the past—and Alfie Judah, one senses, has had many pasts—but is ready to reinvent himself, as the American expression goes, whenever the need arises. Wily to the last, he is a match for any situation.

In the interview in *Massachusetts Review*, Mukherjee identified Alfie as a character typical of her stories about immigrants. These are characters, she said, who

> want to make it in the new world; they are filled with a hustlerish kind of energy . . . Although they are often hurt or depressed by setbacks in their new lives and occupations, they do not give up. They take risks they wouldn't have taken in their old, comfortable worlds to solve their problems. As they change citizenship, they are reborn.

Source: Bryan Aubrey, Critical Essay on "The Middleman," in *Short Stories for Students*, Thomson Gale, 2007.

Teri Ann Doerksen

In the following essay, Doerksen gives a critical analysis of Mukherjee's life and work.

Bharati Mukherjee has developed a reputation for exploring, through her writings, the meeting of the Third World and the First from the perspective of the immigrant to North America—to Canada and to the United States. Although she is well known for her novels, she has received critical acclaim for her two volumes of short stories, as well; several stories from her first collection, *Darkness* (1985), were singled out for awards, and her second collection, *The Middleman and Other Stories* (1988), earned a National Book Critics Circle Award. Her stories focus on the immigrant experience, but she resists attempts to categorize her as a "hyphenated" writer whose appeal is limited to certain ethnic groups; instead, she characterizes herself as an American writer in an established American tradition. She says in the introduction to *Darkness*:

> I see my "immigrant" story replicated in a dozen American cities, and instead of seeing my Indianness as a fragile identity to be preserved against obliteration (or worse, a "visible" disfigurement to be hidden), I see it now as a set of fluid identities to be celebrated. I see myself as an American writer in the tradition of other American writers whose parents and grandparents had passed through Ellis Island.

Mukherjee is one of a growing number of authors who resist efforts to push to the sidelines

> " *Alfie has an affair with the businessman's wife, who is also the president's mistress. When--to his -surprise--he survives the discovery of the affair, he decides to see how much money he can make from his inside information about his former bosses. This jaundiced view of entrepreneurship in the Western world is echoed in 'Danny's Girls.'"*

literature featuring the richness of immigrant and ethnic communities and who redefine through their works what it means to be American. Along with the Native Americans Paula Gunn Allen and Leslie Marmon Silko and the Chinese American Amy Tan, Mukherjee depicts a United States that can no longer imagine itself in monolithic terms, that "is about diversity, not uniformity," as Allen was quoted as saying in an article in the *Chicago Tribune* (17 March 1991). In the same article Mukherjee said that "The ethnic voices were always there, but there wasn't a recognition of a community of writers until the de-Europeanization of our country became physically evident in the mid-80s." Mukherjee's short stories reflect her growing interest in representing a more and more inclusive view of what it means to be American. While most of the stories in both volumes are set in the United States or Canada, the first collection focuses primarily on Indian immigrants; the second presents a kaleidoscope of perspectives, including those of an Anglo Vietnam veteran, a newly arrived Ugandan American, and a third-generation Italian American introducing her family to her Afghanistani refugee boyfriend.

Mukherjee's renderings of interracial tensions, of the encounters between East and West, and of the experience of expatriation to Canada and immigration to the United States are drawn from her personal history. Mukherjee was born in Calcutta on 27 July 1940 to Sudhir Lal Mukherjee, a wealthy chemist who had traveled and studied in Germany and Britain, and Bina Barrejee Mukherjee. Both parents were Bengali Brahmins, members of the highest Hindu caste. Although Bina Mukherjee had not had an advanced education, she, like her husband, believed that their three daughters should be educated. In a 1987 interview with Geoff Hancock, Mukherjee said that her father "wanted the best for his daughters. And to him, the 'best' meant intellectually fulfilling lives. . . . My mother is one of those exceptional Third World women who 'burned' all her life for an education, which was denied to well-brought-up women of her generation. She made sure that my sisters and I never suffered the same wants."

Although Mukherjee's first language was Bengali, she was taught English at a bilingual Protestant missionary school in British-ruled Calcutta. Soon after India gained its independence in 1947, the Mukherjee sisters left with their parents for their first trip outside the country; Mukherjee attended boarding schools in England and Switzerland for three years before returning to Calcutta and enrolling at Loreto House, an English-speaking school run by Irish nuns. In a 1990 interview with *The Iowa Review* she recalled:

> There was an instilling of value systems, cultural value systems, which now strikes me as so ironic. The nuns were Irish to begin with, but in the outpost, they became more British than the British. And during the schooldays we were taught to devalue . . . Bengali plays, Bengali literature, Bengali music, Bengali anything. And then we went home—I came from a very orthodox, traditional family—so we had to negotiate in both languages. But, as I'm sure happens with minority children who are being channeled into fancy prep schools and all, it created complications within the Hindi community, within the Indian upper-class community of my generation.

Tensions between Third World and First World values became the foundation for much of Mukherjee's writing.

After graduating from Loreto House, Mukherjee attended the University of Calcutta, where she received a B.A. in English, with honors, in 1959. At about that time her father had a dispute with a business partner and moved the family to Baroda in western India, where he worked for a large chemical firm. Mukherjee received an M.A. in English and ancient Indian culture from the University of Baroda in 1961.

After Mukherjee finished her M.A., her father arranged for her to attend the University of Iowa Writer's Workshop. She received an M.F.A. from Iowa in 1963. On 19 September 1963—during their lunch hour—she married Clark Blaise, a Canadian novelist, whom she had met at the university. They have two sons, Bart and Bernard.

Mukherjee became an instructor in the English department at Marquette University in Milwaukee in 1964; in 1965 she took a similar position at the University of Wisconsin at Madison. In 1966 she and Blaise accepted positions as lecturers at McGill University in Montreal. Mukherjee received her Ph.D. in English and comparative literature from the University of Iowa in 1969 and was promoted to assistant professor.

While teaching at McGill, Mukherjee wrote her first novel. In *The Tiger's Daughter* (1972) Tara Banerjee Cartwright returns to India to find that her childhood memories of wealth and Brahmin gentility do not jibe with the dirt, poverty, and political upheavals she encounters. Tara's father, "The Tiger," is closely based on Mukherjee's father. In 1973 Mukherjee became an associate professor and went to India on sabbatical. In her second novel, *Wife* (1975), Dimple Dasgupta, an Indian woman, moves with her Indian husband to New York City. The gap between her husband's expectations of her and those of the culture in which she finds herself are so large, and her mental state is so shaky, that she finds herself torn between killing herself and killing her husband; she chooses the latter alternative, stabbing him in the neck as he eats a bowl of cereal.

Mukherjee and Blaise spent 1976-1977 in India, where Mukherjee was directing the Shastri Indo-Canadian Institute in New Delhi. They had contracted with a publisher to record their experiences independently, Blaise as a Westerner visiting the country for the first time and Mukherjee as a returnee whose perspective had been shifted by ten years in North America. The result was *Days and Nights in Calcutta* (1977). Mukherjee became a full professor at McGill in 1978. She also served as the chair of the writing program and as director of graduate studies in English.

In the 1990 interview with *The Iowa Review* Mukherjee noted that after the Canadian government allowed Ugandan Asians with British passports to enter the country in 1973, "I started to notice on a daily basis little incidents in my corner Woolworth's in Montreal, or in hotel lobbies, on buses, things just not being quite right. Then it ballooned into very vicious physical harassment by 1977, 1978." Soon after *Days and Nights in Calcutta* was published, Mukherjee and Blaise moved to Toronto, a hotbed of racist violence in Canada, and learned of people of color being thrown onto railroad tracks and run over intentionally on the streets. Paralyzed by anger over her encounters with racism in her adopted home, Mukherjee stopped writing for almost ten years, and she and Blaise decided to leave Canada permanently. They resigned their tenured positions and took part-time, temporary teaching jobs at colleges around New York City. When Mukherjee began to write again, she chose a new genre: the short story.

Mukherjee's first book of short stories, *Darkness*, published in 1985, reveals her outrage at the racism she had encountered in Canada and the optimism she associates with living in the United States. Most of the twelve stories in the collection were written while she was writer-in-residence at Emory University in Atlanta in the spring of 1984, although some had been written in Canada. The tone of the stories moves from bitterness about the difficulty of maintaining Indian identity in Canada to a cautious hopefulness about the potential for successful assimilation into the culture of the United States.

The stories in *Darkness* feature characters from Southern Asia and provide a mosaic of perspectives on this kind of immigrant experience. Several stories are either set in Canada or involve characters who live there and depict the overwhelming racism encountered there by people of Indian origin. "The World According to Hsü" is told from the point of view of Ratna Clayton, an Indian woman married to a white Canadian academic in Montreal. The couple is on vacation on an island off the coast of Africa; the uprising and coup that occur during their visit correspond to the internal upheaval Ratna feels at the news that her husband wants to take a position in Toronto: "In Montreal she was merely 'English,' a grim joke on generations of British segregationists. It was thought charming that her French was just slightly short of fluent. In Toronto, she was not Canadian, not even Indian. She was something called, after the imported idiom of London, a Paki. And for Pakis, Toronto was hell."

Other stories extend beyond the middle and upper classes to the experience of poor immigrants—who are almost always assumed by those in

authority to be in Canada illegally. In "Tamurlane" a Toronto restaurant is raided by Royal Canadian Mounted Police officers who are looking for illegal immigrants. Gupta, a lame cook who has his papers, at first resists the unjust arrest in the only way he knows how—with his cleaver—then reaches for his passport; but one of the Mounties shoots him through the very document that proves that they should not have tried to arrest him in the first place. In the award-winning "Isolated Incidents" a young white Toronto social worker is made aware of the vast gap between classes when a visit to an old school friend, who is now a famous pop singer, coincides with an incident in which an Indian immigrant is pushed in front of a subway train and an encounter with a plaintive Hispanic client who wants her to save his sister from being deported.

In "Nostalgia" the reader is introduced to Dr. Manny Patel, who is proud of his white wife, Camille; his young son; and the money he has earned in the United States. At the same time, however, he longs for the familiarity of the culture he left behind in India. Patel's nostalgia takes on substance in his lust for an Indian girl he meets at the market and romances at an expensive restaurant. Patel ignores the waiter's plea for help in getting a visa for his nephew, because "he didn't want this night to fall under the pressure of other immigrants' woes," only to find, in an ironic twist, that the entire experience was engineered: the girl he is romancing is the waiter's niece, and he is blackmailed into helping with the visa and giving them money, as well. Patel, suddenly aware of his disconnectedness from his Indian heritage, reacts in a way that proves that he is also disconnected from his family: as the story ends he is planning to bribe his wife with a cruise to make up for his infidelity and humiliation. A story later in the volume, "Saints," illustrates the long-term repercussions of Patel's detachment. Many years later Camille and Manny have divorced; their son, Shawn, cannot understand his father's coldness or his mother's attraction to men who cheat on her and batter her, and at the end he is walking the midwinter streets "like a Hindu saint," peering through the windows at Indian families and hoping for a glimpse of his own identity.

The most pervasive theme in the volume, appearing in some form in nearly all of the stories, is the tension between the changed cultural and sexual expectations confronting Indian women immigrants to North America and the unchanged values of their traditional Indian parents and husbands.

"A Father" is a particularly vivid illustration of this theme. Mr. Bhowmick discovers that his daughter is pregnant and is overjoyed by his visions of a grandson and by the notion that his intelligent but awkward daughter is loved by a man. He is willing to forgive the fact that she is pregnant out of wedlock; after all, he reasons, "Girls like Babli were caught between the rules." He congratulates himself on his progressive ideas; but the brittleness of his position becomes apparent when he discovers that his daughter was impregnated by artificial insemination rather than by a boyfriend. His self-congratulatory acceptance explodes into rage and violence, and he beats his daughter with a rolling pin until his wife calls the police.

"Visitors" also plays on immigrant uncertainty about how much acceptance of Western culture is allowable. Vinita, a young immigrant bride, is receiving visitors on her first afternoon in her new home. She is faced with a difficult decision when a young man she has met comes to the door: in Calcutta it would be inappropriate to be with him unchaperoned, but the rules are different in New Jersey. He, however, judges her by Calcutta rules, taking her invitation to tea as an acknowledgment of her desire for him. She repulses his attack, but the experience has made her long for something more than she has. She finds herself longing to "run off into the alien American night where only shame and disaster can await her."

Darkness received generally favorable reviews. Mahnaz Ispahani commented in *The New Republic* (14 April 1986): "Mukherjee has created some complicated inner lives, and evoked the sensations and the traditions and the combustion of two very different cultures. Unlike many writers about the immigrant experience, Mukherjee does not succumb to guilt or to maudlin memories about the past. Instead her work soberly celebrates resilience. Like most of her characters, she has no thoughts of turning back."

After *Darkness* was sent to the publisher, Mukherjee acquired a National Endowment for the Arts grant and took time off from teaching to begin writing another series of stories about Indian immigrants to the United States. This work was interrupted by an event that led to another nonfiction book: the 23 June 1985 bombing off the Irish coast, apparently by Sikh terrorists, of Air India flight 182, en route from Toronto to New Delhi via London, in which 329 people were killed. In 1987 Mukherjee and Blaise published *The Sorrow and the Terror: The Haunting Legacy of the Air*

India Tragedy, in which they argued that ultimate responsibility for the disaster lay with misguided Canadian government policies on immigration and multiculturalism.

After the completion of *The Sorrow and the Terror* Mukherjee returned to the stories she had begun earlier, but in a much different frame of mind. During the intervening years she had settled permanently in the United States, and as she wrote the last of the stories for her second collection she was preparing to become a citizen. She continued to be concerned with the racism facing Indian immigrants to Canada, but she began to approach the issue from a more hopeful perspective. Early in 1988 she took her citizenship oath in New York City; a few months later *The Middleman and Other Stories* was published.

The Middleman and Other Stories reflects an exuberance that contrasts with the uncertainty and sense of betrayal that pervades many of the pieces in *Darkness*; Mukherjee said in the 1990 interview that "by the time I came to write *The Middleman*, I was exhilarated, my vision was more optimistic. I knew that I was finally where I wanted to be." The stories also shift away from her earlier focus on Indian immigrants to include new arrivals from Uganda, the West Indies, and Afghanistan. Except for a few darker stories, the collection celebrates the kaleidoscopic nature of the new American population. Finally, Mukherjee adopts a new narrative perspective in the stories: while *Darkness* explored the immigrant experience from a third-person-omniscient standpoint, *The Middleman and Other Stories* allows many of these new American voices to speak for themselves; some of the narrators are native-born Americans who are learning to live with the changes brought to the country by the recent arrivals. All of the stories address the tensions and hopes produced when "new" Americans meet "old" ones.

As diverse as the stories are, they fall into definable categories. The first is a new one for Mukherjee: stories told from the point of view of white Americans who are seeking, with differing degrees of success, to make sense of the new America emerging around them. In "Loose Ends" the Vietnam veteran Jeb Marshall has become an assassin-for-hire in Florida. Bitter and unable to accept the changes that immigrants have brought to the United States, he sees people of Hispanic and East Indian descent as threats and views himself and his wife as "coolie labor in our own country." In Vietnam, he thinks, he sacrificed to "barricade the front door" and protect his country; now he wonders, "who left the back door open?" Checking into a cheap motel run by an East Indian family, he is enraged when he realizes that to them he is unimportant: "They've forgotten me. I feel left out, left behind. While we were nailing up that big front door, these guys were sneaking in around back. They got their money, their family networks, and their secretive languages." He rapes and murders the young Indian woman who shows him to his room, believing that by doing so he is taking back "his" America. In "Fathering" another veteran, Jason, faces a power struggle between his common-law wife, Sharon, and his daughter, Eng, whom he fathered in Vietnam and who has just arrived in the United States.

The largest group of stories consists of those that are told from the point of view of first- and second-generation Asian immigrants as they become acculturated in the West. In the title story, "The Middleman," Alfie Judah, an Iraqi who has just become a United States citizen, is employed by an arms-dealing syndicate in a Central American republic; the syndicate is secretly run by an American businessman and the president of the country. Alfie has an affair with the businessman's wife, who is also the president's mistress. When—to his surprise—he survives the discovery of the affair, he decides to see how much money he can make from his inside information about his former bosses. This jaundiced view of entrepreneurship in the Western world is echoed in "Danny's Girls." The unnamed narrator, a teenage Ugandan refugee, admires Danny Sahib, another boy in his building, whose business is "selling docile Indian girls to hard-up Americans for real bucks." But when he becomes infatuated with Rosie, a Nepalese mail-order bride, he realizes "what a strange, pimpish thing I was doing, putting up pictures of Danny's girls, or standing at the top of the subway stairs and passing them out to any lonely-looking American I saw—what kind of joke was this? How dare he do this, I thought, how dare he make me a part of this?"

Two stories explore meetings between new immigrants and families who are well established in the United States. In "Jasmine" an illegal emigrant from Trinidad finds a job in Michigan caring for the daughter of the Moffitts. The feminist Lara Hatch-Moffitt is blithely unaware of the hypocrisy of her exploitation of the teenage immigrant to further her own career; Bill Moffitt also exploits Jasmine by having an affair with her. (The explosive potential of the situation established in "Jasmine"

led Mukherjee to expand it into a novel of the same title, which was published in 1989.) In "Orbiting," one of the strongest pieces in the collection, a second-generation Italian American family gathers for that most traditional of American holidays, Thanksgiving, at the home of the eldest daughter, Rindy. The dinner is complicated by the introduction of Rindy's new boyfriend, Ro, an Afghan refugee. Ro's presence changes the way the more-established Americans see the holiday they are celebrating, and the assumptions they have about what it means to be an American. When Ro explains the politics that forced him to leave his country and the torture he suffered in jail, Rindy's father and brother are shocked out of their complacent belief that "only Americans had informed political opinions—other people staged coups out of spite and misery." As Ro's story continues, Rindy observes that her father is beginning to look ill; she notes with acerbity that "The meaning of Thanksgiving should not be so explicit." Victoria Carchidi calls the story "a comedy of manners worthy of Jane Austen, whom Mukherjee has acknowledged as an influence on her work. We see misunderstandings, and correct understandings, where least expected as the characters enact in miniature the ballet of complementary moves that is America."

The last group of stories encompasses a category that is familiar from Mukherjee's previous work: stories of Indian women who have immigrated to the United States or Canada and are struggling with the distance between their cultural background and the new society in which they find themselves. In "A Wife's Story" Panna Bhatt is studying for a doctorate in special education in New York City. When her husband, who manages a cotton mill north of Bombay, arrives for a visit, he asks why she has not worn his mother's gold and ruby ring to the airport. She explains that it is not safe to do so: "He looks disconcerted. He's used to a different role. He's the knowing, suspicious one in the family. . . . I handle the money, buy the tickets. I don't know if this makes me unhappy." By the end of the story she knows that she will not return to India with him. The final image is of a woman discovering a new sense of herself: "I watch my naked body turn, the breasts, the thighs glow. The body 's beauty amazes. I stand here shameless, in ways he has never seen me. I am free, afloat, watching somebody else." In "The Tenant" a young professor from India is torn between her desire for a connection with her Indian heritage and her desire for independence. She has dinner with the family of an Indian colleague; afterward, he drives her home and then masturbates at the wheel of the car while she watches, aghast. She turns to personal advertisements for Indian companionship, then to her armless landlord, and, finally, back to the man she had met through the personals. It is a story of searching without finding, but without the bleakness that might have pervaded a similar story in *Darkness*.

The most powerful work in the collection, "The Management of Grief," grew out of Mukherjee's experience researching the Air India crash. Mrs. Bhave's husband and two sons are killed in the disaster, and in the following weeks she becomes a focal point for misunderstandings between the Canadian government and the grieving families. She is disappointed in herself for being unable to show the emotion she should, for not wailing for the dead; others in her community wonder if she really loved her family, since she can take their loss so silently. The Canadian authorities, on the other hand, try to use her to inspire a similar stoicism in the other bereaved Indian families. The authorities also assume that the survivors will be comforted by the identification of the bodies of their loved ones, while Mrs. Bhave and the others take their only solace in the belief that somehow their families might have survived: *"In our culture, it is a parent's duty to hope."* When Judith Templeton, a social worker, asks for Mrs. Bhave's help with the other families, she reluctantly agrees; but Templeton's ignorance is too much to bear. Not only does Templeton want Mrs. Bhave to talk with a Sikh family—members of the ethnic group responsible for bombing the plane in which Mrs. Bhave's family died—but she also confides that the "stubbornness and ignorance" of two survivors "are driving me crazy." Finding herself more in sympathy with her traditional enemies than with the Canadian social worker, Mrs. Bhave asks to be let out of the car at a subway stop. This strong declaration of self is followed by eventual release from grief: after many months, she hears her family 's voices telling her to *"Go, be brave,"* and she begins a new life, a new "voyage."

The Middleman and Other Stories was a commercial and critical success, garnering the National Book Critics Circle Award for Fiction. Eleanor Wachtel noted in *Maclean's* (29 August 1988): "In *The Middleman*, Mukherjee has plunged herself into the throes of American society. In return, she offers acute insights into the clashes that mark a nonwhite's entry into that culture."

At the time of the publication of *Jasmine* Mukherjee was invited to become a distinguished professor at the University of California at Berkeley. Since then she has published two nonfiction books, *Political Culture and Leadership in India: A Study of West Bengal* (1991) and *Regionalism in Indian Perspective* (1992), and two novels, *The Holder of the World* (1993) and *Leave It to Me* (1996). Critics have found Mukherjee's work to be a shaping force in a new American literature that reimagines the United States as a multifaceted rather than a monolithic entity, and her work is beginning to be the focus of scholarly inquiry. She speaks to an America that is culturally rich and diverse; while she acknowledges that such diversity comes with discomfort and sacrifice, she shows that it also provides tremendous rewards.

Source: Teri Ann Doerksen, "Bharati Mukherjee," in *Dictionary of Literary Biography*, Vol. 218, *American Short-Story Writers Since World War II, Second Series*, edited by Patrick Meanor and Gwen Crane, Gale Group, 1999, pp. 228–234.

Bharati Mukherjee, Michael Connell, Jessie Grearson and Tom Grimes

In the following interview, Mukherjee discusses her upbringing, how she incorporates metaphysics in her work, where she draws inspiration for her characters, the violence and the love that appear in her later work, the feminist response to her work, and the writing process.

This interview took place over a two day period just after Thanksgiving, 1989, in Iowa City, where Bharati Mukherjee had come to read from her latest novel, *Jasmine*, and also to spend the weekend with her husband, Clark Blaise, who was teaching at the Iowa Writers' Workshop. It was a hectic period for her. *The Middleman and Other Stories* had recently won the 1988 National Book Critics Circle Award for Fiction; Berkeley had offered her a Distinguished Professorship, which she accepted; and she was promoting the new book, which was critically praised when it appeared earlier that fall . . .

Bharati Mukherjee was born into a well-to-do Indian family—her father was a prize-winning chemist—in 1940. Since coming to the Writers' Workshop in 1962, she has lived largely in the U.S. and Canada, returning home to India every summer for a visit. After earning her MFA, she completed a PhD in English Literature, taught at McGill for several years following their move to Canada, and recently has taught in New York at Queens College and Columbia University. Her teaching has limited her writing time. Nevertheless, she has produced three novels, *Jasmine* (1989), *Wife* (1975), and *The Tiger's Daughter* (1972); two story collections, *The Middleman* (1988), and *Darkness* (1985); as well as two works of nonfiction, *Days and Nights in Calcutta*, about her return to India, and *The Sorrow and the Terror*, an investigative report into the 1985 Air India bombing in which 323 people were killed. The nonfiction books were written in collaboration with Clark Blaise, who is the author of *A North American Education* (stories), *Lust, Lunar Attractions* (both novels), and *Resident Alien*, a recent collection of short stories and autobiographical essays. *Days and Nights in Calcutta* is currently being made into a movie, and the two of them were working on the screenplay and on a piece about Salman Rushdie, when we met.

For all the incarnations Bharati Mukherjee has gone through—from Bengali Brahmin to workshop student, from working mother to celebrated author—she is a woman who seems unshakably sure of who she is. But the idea of transformation, of life being a process of almost constant and radical evolution, has been one of the major themes of her work.

[*The Iowa Review*:] *You said at one point, "There are no harmless, compassionate ways to remake one's self . . . we murder who we were so we can rebirth ourselves in the images of our dreams." Do you see violence as necessary to a transformation of character?*

[Bharati Mukherjee:] Yes. And I can see that in my own life it's been psychic violence. In my character Jasmine's case it's been physical violence because she's from a poor farming family. Plus terrorism is a virus of the '80s, so there is the initial violence of the village, where her husband dies in a fire bombing. Because she is an undocumented, poor alien, she necessarily goes through a kind of physical harassment that someone like me was exempt from. But just growing up in my Calcutta, the daughter of a very rich factory owner in a time when West Bengal, and especially Calcutta, was becoming Communist, I had to personally experience a great deal of labor violence and unrest. There were many times when I went to school with what we used to call "flying squads." Military policemen in vans in front, special policemen in vans in back, our car, with chauffeur and bodyguard in between so we could, the three sisters, take part as pretty maidens in gondoliers. Gilbert and Sullivan light operas, etc. I'm coming out of a 19th-century world, and have witnessed a lot of violence for myself which didn't physically scar me—I mean,

> **"** For some nonwhite, Asian women, our ways of negotiating power are different. There is no reason why we should have to appropriate—wholesale and intact—the white, upper-middle-class women's tools and rhetoric."

no one threw acid on my face as was feared. But Jasmine actually encountered it, because it's not a realistic novel. It's meant to be a fable.

Can we talk about your upbringing for a bit?

Certainly.

Is Bengali your native language?

Yes.

You spoke it before you spoke English?

Yes. I was unilingually Bengali for the first three years of my life. This was before Independence in 1947, the tail end of the British Raj, when the Raj already knew it was crumbling and there were a lot of nationalistic struggles in and around Calcutta.

I went at age three to a school run by Protestant missionaries and that was a sort of bilingual school for elementary schoolchildren. The courses were taught in Bengali, but they introduced English. That's how I knew mat, bat, cat—more complicated sentences, actually—by the time I went to school in England at age eight. And that was the three years in England and Switzerland when I felt I was totally bilingual. I could operate in both languages equally well. And I could speak English like a Cockney when necessary, or establishment English because it was a fancy Sloane Square school that I was sent to. When I came back to India, to Calcutta, to a very special girls' school called Loretto House run by Irish nuns in independent Calcutta, I became less Bengali-speaking.

Your English had taken over?

Yes.

Was this a matter of choice, or had you just lost the Bengali by then?

I hadn't lost it, but there was an instilling of value systems, cultural value systems, which now strikes me as so ironic. The nuns were Irish to begin with, but in the outpost, they became more British than the British. And during the schooldays we were taught to devalue—I was going to say sneer at, but that's putting it a little too strongly—Bengali plays, Bengali literature, Bengali music, Bengali anything. And then we went home—I came from a very orthodox, very traditional family—so we had to negotiate in both languages. But, as I'm sure happens with minority children who are being channeled into fancy prep schools and all, it created complications within the Hindi community, within the Indian upper-class community of my generation. It wasn't until I became a graduate student at Baroda (where, if I wanted to get a Master's degree in English, I also had to take either a regional Master's in a regional Indian language, or in ancient Indian culture) that I really came to know the marvels of Hinduism. No, I knew Bengali, but the culture itself I hadn't really studied formally until then. I just imbibed it by osmosis. . . .

That sense of the metaphysical and the literal seems to run through your work. Do you see immigration as an experience of reincarnation?

Absolutely! I have been murdered and reborn at least three times; the very correct young woman I was trained to be, and was very happy being, is very different from the politicized, shrill, civil rights activist I was in Canada, and from the urgent writer that I have become in the last few years in the United States. I can't stop. It's compulsive act for me. It's a kind of salvation, and the only thing that prevents me from being a Joyce Carol Oates, and I'm not talking about quality, but just that need to create, is schedule.

You seem to write about similar characters leading different lives. Does this tie into your idea of reincarnation?

I must be interested in certain types of characters (Maya/Angela/Jasmine) and so they keep recurring to me in different ways. Or what she thinks is the right thing to do has changed as I have changed, as a person. . . .

The kinds of women I write about, and I'm not generalizing about women in the South Asian community here, but the kinds of women who attract me, who intrigue me, are those who are adaptable. We've all been trained to please, been trained to be adaptable as wives, and that adaptability is working to the women's advantage when we come over as immigrants. The males function very well as engineers or doctors or whatever, and they earn good money, but they have locked their hearts against mainstream culture. They seem to be afraid of pollution. Their notion of India seems to have frozen in the year in which they left India and they don't want to change. Change is frightening; they are like mini-Ayatollahs in some way. They don't want to be part of history and flux. Whereas the women are forced to deal with Americans in the small daily business of life. They have to go to the grocery store and actually interact with real Americans, so they have to attend PTA meetings, be in car pools, and so on. For an Indian woman to learn to drive, put on pants, cash checks, is a big leap. They are, as Clark was saying, exhilarated by the change. They are no longer having to do what mother-in-law tyrannically forced them to do. And they are free to set up businesses, which they are doing throughout the country. And these new Indian wives are apparently heavy duty users of day care centers, so they can run their boutiques and businesses.

The men always seem to be translating dollars into rupees, and thinking, "Well, I can always go back and buy this condominium and I'll be safe." But the women seem to be going further and further into America. From Darkness *through* Middleman *and into* Jasmine, *there seems to be this flight into the American experience.*

I don't know if all my women characters make that flight into American successfully though. I think of Maya as a very lost, sad character, who really went out and married a white man and is so well attuned to women intellectuals, her colleagues, but at the same time there is that desire for a wholeness, nostalgia, that India and Indian traditions promised. And so, she's the one who is going out and seeking an advertised, perfect Indian groom, and it works out in strange ways for her. For her, the turn comes when the guy without arms, the lover without arms, calls her May. Suddenly, she snaps. No, I'm not May, I'm Maya, and people from the outside don't understand me. Whereas a Jasmine, in the short story, is someone who wants to make—is hurtling into an unknown America . . .

You were talking earlier about different forms of power, acquiring and expressing power, the different forms of power for women, and it struck me that in your work there is power even in the re-straining and pouring of tea.

Well, certainly all my life, I realize now, all my writing life, I've been interested in the ways people acquire power, exercise power, and even more importantly, I realize, relinquish power or are forced to relinquish power. One of the novels I started but never finished, is about an Idi Amin kind of figure. The title of this unfinished manuscript is *The Father of His Country*. I guess in different ways I am always trying to find a metaphor, the right character to tell the story, or variants of the story of how to acquire power, exercise it and then have it taken away from you, or voluntarily give it up. For some of the women characters in my stories, fasting is a way of exercising that power. When you have nothing really, withholding food can become the only way to exercise power. What is regarded as passivity, or was regarded in *Wife* as passivity, by feminist *Ms.* magazine-type readers in 1975, was meant to be read very differently. My women are utilizing the tools at hand. I did not build, deliberately build into the center of *Wife*, the *Ms.* magazine way as the "right" way with everyone else defective in their ways of fighting domination, whether it is male or class or poverty. I want to think that power is my central obsession. . . .

There seems to be a resistance to a Western idea of feminist thought or philosophy in your work.

Yes, I think a resistance does run through my work. For some nonwhite, Asian women, our ways of negotiating power are different. There is no reason why we should have to appropriate—wholesale and intact—the white, upper-middle-class women's tools and rhetoric. Especially rhetoric. I think that 1975 was a very dogmatic, prescriptive year in American feminism and they could not stand any deviations or any rebellions. There were a lot of run-ins. I had a lot of run-ins. I'll give you a small example of the kinds of misinterpretations, in terms of feminism, that my stories go through. "Jasmine," the story in *The Middleman*, ends with young Jasmine, this Caribbean-Indian girl, making love to her white boss on a Turkish rug in front of the fire, in a room which she cleans during the day. Reviewers loved that story generally and loved that scene, but they saw Jasmine as an exploited young woman, and the white male, her employer, as a sleazy boss who is taking advantage of this poor, innocent, put-upon, au-pair girl. Whereas I meant for Jasmine to know exactly what

it is she wants and what she is willing to trade off in order to get what she wants. She is in charge of the situation there. The man has succumbed to lust and to her sexuality. Jasmine is a woman who knows the power, is discovering the power of her sexuality. If there is a villain in that story, it is Lara, the wife, whose feminism and professionalism are built on the backs of underemployed Caribbean or Hispanic au-pair girls. But no one got that, you see. It was meant to be a very political ending. . . .

There seems to be a move toward an acceptance of the inevitability of violence in your later work. We go from hesitancy in Wife *to the resolute action in* Jasmine.

It's a natural part by then. Having written the book on the Air India terrorism, I realized how pervasive violence is in this country. It's just under the skin of real life. It doesn't seem exotic, or external, anymore. I was coy, or decorous, a person of great decorum, when I was writing *The Tiger's Daughter*. Should I allow the main character in the novel to be deflowered, I had to ask myself. I absolutely didn't want that. And Clark said, when I showed him my manuscript, "The novel demands it, and you have to go through with it." And I thought, Oh, my God. Even though it's not autobiographical, people are going to assume that the same thing happened to me. It's that kind of violence that I was reluctant to write of in the early books. . . .

There is a sense of great love in your later works, for the characters and for the landscape, the New World.

That happened somewhere between *Darkness* and *The Middleman*. *Darkness* was a breakthrough book in the sense that I was writing about changes among the immigrants. It was still darkness, after all, and I was coming out of that whole Canadian mess. I want to think that writing that book was invigorating for me. But for many of the characters, things didn't work out when they transplanted themselves into a new culture. But by the time I came to write *The Middleman*, I was exhilarated, my vision was more optimistic. I knew that I was finally where I wanted to be. And though I was moving in degrees of acculturation, the overall authorial vision is, I hope, consistent. . . .

How does your work begin to happen for you?

When the writing is going well, the characters take over, and they dictate what is going to happen to them in the scene. In "Buried Lives," for instance, I thought, when I started out, that the Sri Lankan, Tamil, was going to die off the coast of Nova Scotia. There had been two boatloads of refugees who had been put by unscrupulous captains into boats which sank there. They just deserted them when they saw the Coast Guard coming. So I assumed that this would be how this man would end in my story. But the guy wouldn't get on the boat. He found ways of hanging around, staying on in Germany. Then he found a girlfriend and she gave him his necessary visa papers. So I really do hear a voice when things are going well. Then I read something about athletes being "in the zone." And I said, "My God, that's really what's happening in the best of my work." I immediately identified with that idea. I find that I throw away the stuff I've written when I have not entered "the zone." I am like a medium. I am both inside and outside the character. I'm hearing this voice that's writing itself. The scenes work themselves out, and each project has its own momentum. I am forced to write so fast, and with such intensity, because it's always during vacations. I'm working twenty-one hour days with everything bubbling in my head. So in the middle of the night these things are working themselves out. Though I may have gotten up out of my chair.

During that time you're sensitive to absorbing things, like photographs?

Yes. Everything works its way in. And I don't waste, it seems. Any overheard conversations, any faces seen—I never know when they're going to work their way into my fiction. I don't keep notebooks, but these details just pop up in the work.

The book becomes like a magnet?

Yes. Maybe that's exactly what I've been saying about how scraps of conversation during certain periods will feed themselves into the book. It all seems appropriate; I know how to use it all. Or every face will suggest a compulsive story.

Earlier in your career you talked about "voice" being your prime aesthetic.

Finding the right voice, right. That's something that I came to as a result of talking to, or listening to, Clark. The sense of voice being the way one controls fiction. Voice can be the sum total of every artistic trick in your bag. It's how to use texture, how to use metaphor, how to choose the right point of view, the point of view character, and

therefore the idioms, the language. Knowing when to withhold information, when to disclose, etc. Now I realize that in addition to that, voice, for me, is the physical, or actual, hearing of the main character speak. The rest happens automatically. It is all happening without my having to think about it.

What about essay writing? Is "the zone" involved in that kind of writing, too?

No. I know when I'm doing well, and when the ideas are simply not clear. But it's not the same physiological change that happens to me when I'm writing fiction that I'm really satisfied with. Essays seem to me to be coming out of a different part of my brain. It's not the same internal compulsion. I won't take on a subject that doesn't interest me. I will only do it if I feel I have a special angle on it, and the subject matter is sufficiently interesting to me. I don't come in with preconceived notions of what I'm going to find. But it's a very different kind of writing. It's Mukherjee writing, and Mukherjee assessing and analyzing, rather than something else. I don't have that intermediary. I haven't become someone else. I must not become someone else when I'm writing an essay. . . .

Maxine Hong Kingston has talked about our needing a "global novel." Do you see your fiction going that way?

Maybe fiction is going that way, but I would never start out with an agenda that I must sit down and write a "global novel." A character has to come to me urgently—a scene, a sentence. The fiction itself must seem urgent to me. I don't like to have the social prescription, or the political prescription, that I am then trying to flesh out. I think there's a propaganda novel or thesis novel that can be important, but the concept strikes me as necessarily lacking life. It doesn't come from the guts, the heart, of the writer. And I don't see at all why good fiction has to be global fiction. It's the lot of some writers, who are—because of the accidents of history—forced to be on the move. Then there are the Richard Fords and the Russell Banks who may be writing of small town America, but with great gifts, and great compassion. It's making life important, making a single life important, rather than having to have a prescription for the global ills which afflict us.

Source: Bharati Mukherjee, Michael Connell, Jessie Grearson, and Tom Grimes, "An Interview with Bharati Mukherjee," in *Iowa Review*, Vol. 20, No. 3, Fall 1990, pp. 7–32.

Uma Parameswaran

In the following review, Parameswaran discusses Mukherjee's exploration of the "celebration of being American" through the author's exaggerated characters, touch of cynicism, and "curious mix of voices and experiences."

Bharati Mukherjee's second volume of short fiction consists of eleven stories that are wide-ranging in both settings and themes. Following her self-proclaimed American identity stated in her first volume of stories, *Darkness* (1985; see *WLT* 60:3, p. 520), she explores the American experience through various personae or protagonists, four of whom are white American males and six of whom are females (only three of the women are of Indian origin). The result is a curious mix of voices and experiences that go to make up the celebration of being American (as she states in *Darkness*) as opposed to being Canadian.

Mukherjee's explorations of male attitudes and diction are interesting as experiments. Alfred Judah, the protagonist of the title story, is a macho operator in the rough-and-tumble world of smugglers: "Me? I make a living from things that fall. The big fat belly of Clovis T. Ransome bobs above me like whale shit at high tide." This image from the Florida scenery seems to have impressed her deeply, for in the next story we find "python turds, dozens of turds, light as cork and thick as a tree, riding high in the water." One is led to see a metaphorical streak that runs through the volume: these characters may be full-blooded Americans racing with both hands grabbing at all that life has to offer, but what they grasp is rather obnoxious all the way. More disturbing is the fact that Mukherjee's control of language is as devastating as ever, but now geared to a kind of cynicism that was absent in her earlier works. The characters who appear in the American stories, especially those from India, are stark caricatures of individuals: motel owners who use underpaid fellow Indians whenever possible; highly educated professionals whose linguistic idiosyncrasies are laughed at; a Vietnam veteran who brings home his daughter Eng and "rescues" her from "our enemies," the doctor and the hospital that terrify her; a ruffian who, we are asked to believe, is driven to auto theft and rape by his feeling of betrayal by some larger entity, the state.

The final story in the collection is "The Management of Grief." It has clearly come out of Mukherjee's scintillating and controversial documentary *The Sorrow and the Terror* (coauthored

> **More disturbing is the fact that Mukherjee's control of language is as devastating as ever, but now geared to a kind of cynicism that was absent in her earlier works. The characters who appear in the American stories, especially those from India, are stark caricatures of individuals....**

with Clark Blaise), on the crash of Air India flight 182 on 23 June 1985, which killed 329 passengers, most of whom were Canadians of Indian origin. There are minor questions that come to the reader's mind. Would the Stanley Cup have been played so late in June? Would the two young Sikhs have left for India within a month of having brought over their parents, who did not know the language and had no other family members? However, the story is very poignant and improves on E. M. Forster's idea of the failure of disparate cultures to connect. Though the families of the victims manage their grief in their own ways, the Canadian government finds itself in a quandary of communication, trying ineffectually to get paperwork done through translators. Shaila, who has lost her husband and two sons in the crash, is a volunteer interpreter; when the government agent Judith takes Shaila to the old Sikh couple who had been in Canada only a month before losing both their sons, we see their intractability clashing with Judith's impatience. No amount of explanation will persuade them to accept aid, because such acceptance might "end the company's or the country's obligations to them." Or, as Judith perceptively concludes, "They think signing a paper is signing their sons' death warrants." As Judith and Shaila leave, Judith talks about the next woman, "who is a real mess." At this, Shaila asks Judith to stop the car, gets out, and slams the door, leaving Judith to ask plaintively, "Is there anything I said? Anything I did . . . Shaila? Let's talk about it." The story would have been more effective if it had ended here, but Mukherjee follows her more traditional storytelling form of tying up loose ends.

The title of the volume goes beyond the title story to imply that many of Mukherjee's personae are middlemen, moving between cultures or events that pull others or themselves in opposite directions.

Source: Uma Parameswaran, Review of *The Middleman and Other Stories*, in *World Literature Today*, Vol. 64, No. 2, Spring 1990, p. 363.

Sources

Byers-Pevitts, Beverley, "An Interview with Bharati Mukherjee," in *Speaking of the Short Story: Interviews with Contemporary Writers*, edited by Farhat Iftekharuddin, Mary Rohrberger and Maurice Lee, University Press of Mississippi, 1997, p. 190.

Carb, Alison B., "An Interview with Bharati Mukherjee," in *Massachusetts Review*, Vol. 29, No. 4, Winter 1988–1989, pp. 648, 654.

Koenig, Rhoda, Review of *The Middleman and Other Stories*, in *New York*, Vol. 22, No. 27, July 3–10, 1989, p. 142.

Mukherjee, Bharati, "The Middleman," in *The Middleman and Other Stories*, Grove Press, 1988, pp. 3–21.

————, "Two Ways to Belong in America," in *Away: The Indian Writer as an Expatriate*, edited by Amitava Kumar, Routledge, 2004, p. 273, originally published in *New York Times*, September 22, 1996.

Raban, Jonathan, "Savage Boulevards, Easy Streets," in *New York Times Book Review*, June 19, 1988, pp. 1, 22.

Further Reading

Alam, Fakrul, *Bharati Mukherjee*, Twayne's United States Authors Series, No. 653, Twayne, 1996.

This is an analysis of Mukherjee's fiction and nonfiction. Alam's conclusion is that Mukherjee has created original and valuable fiction about the immigrant experience in North America; she has taken American fiction in new directions and can claim to be a major ethnic writer of contemporary America.

Chua, C. L., "Passages from India: Migrating to America in the Fiction of V. S. Naipaul and Bharati Mukherjee," in *Reworlding: The Literature of the Indian Diaspora*, edited by Emmanuel S. Nelson, Greenwood Press, 1992, pp. 51–61.

This essay discusses the work of Mukherjee and V. S. Naipaul, another expatriate Indian writer. Chua traces Mukherjee's evolution as a writer, from her early period when she used Naipaul as a model to the mature, self-confident writer who is firmly in the American immigrant tradition of writers such as Henry Roth and Bernard Malamud.

Drake, Jennifer, "Looting American Culture: Bharati Mukherjee's Immigrant Narratives," in *Contemporary Literature*, Vol. 40, No. 1, Spring 1999, pp. 60–84.

Drake argues that Mukherjee's stories do not simply celebrate assimilation of the immigrant into U.S. culture but represent both the pleasure and the violence of cultural exchange. Mukherjee both discovers and creates multicultural myths and histories and rejects the expatriate's nostalgia for home.

Kalita, S. Mitra, *Suburban Sahibs: Three Immigrant Families and Their Passage from India to America*, Rutgers University Press, 2005.

This nonfiction work tells the story of three immigrant families from South Asia living in Middlesex County, New Jersey, which as of 2005 had a large Indian population. The book explores how immigration has altered the U.S. suburbs and how the suburbs have altered the immigrant.

The Necessary Grace to Fall

Gina Ochsner's story, "The Necessary Grace to Fall," is the title story in her award-winning collection published in 2002. It tells the story of Howard, a well-meaning but mediocre man who works in the claims department of an insurance company. As he processes insurance claims made on behalf of the dead, Howard becomes morbidly fascinated by death. He is trapped in a bad marriage, and his life seems to be going downhill, but at the end of the story, he is granted a moment of illumination that gives him a new sense of purpose. This is typical of Ochsner's stories, many of which end on a positive note in which the protagonists find new strength to continue with their lives. Ochsner stated in an interview with Rob Felton that she thinks of herself as a writer of faith. She commented that "I have a deep abiding and intense faith in a benevolent and personal God who's in charge. I do think it comes through." Most readers would agree that her spiritual orientation makes itself felt in "The Necessary Grace to Fall," as well as in her other stories, but Ochsner's writing is never overtly religious or Christian. She prefers to brings out in a general way the notion that life, even in difficult and painful situations, is more about hope and unexpected inspiration than hopelessness and despair.

Gina Ochsner

2002

Author Biography

Gina Ochsner was born in 1970 and was adopted as an infant by Dick and Gayle Withnell. She acquired

her love of literature as a child from her mother, a substitute English teacher.

Ochsner majored in language arts teaching at George Fox University, in Newberg, Oregon, and began writing short stories as an undergraduate. But during her senior year, in which she taught in a high school, she decided that she wanted to be a writer not a teacher. She graduated in 1992 and enrolled in a master's degree program in English at Iowa State University. After that she returned to the northwest to pursue a master of fine arts degree in creative writing at the University of Oregon.

In 1996, when she was twenty-five years old, Ochsner had a brush with death. After giving birth to her son, Connor, complications caused extensive bleeding, and two weeks later her doctor told her she was dying. She recovered after surgery. The experience made her reconsider the purpose of her life and may have contributed to the subject matter of her stories, in which death is often prominent.

Ochsner received her MFA from the University of Oregon in 1997, but at that point she did not have any stories that she thought were worth submitting for publication. In 1999, however, Ochsner won an international short-story contest sponsored by an Irish publishing company for her story "From the Bering Strait." From that point on, her stories began to be published regularly in literary magazines. In 1999, she sent all the stories she had available to the Flannery O'Connor Award for Short Fiction competition, the winner of which would receive automatic publication. She won the competition, and her eleven stories were published by the University of Georgia Press in 2002, under the title *The Necessary Grace to Fall*, the name of the first story in the collection. In addition to the Flannery O'Connor Award, the book won the Oregon Book Award for Short Fiction and the Pacific Northwest Booksellers Association (PNBA) Book Award, 2003.

Ochsner's second collection of stories, *People I Wanted to Be*, was published by Houghton Mifflin in 2005. Many of these stories are set in Russia or the countries of the former Soviet Union. As part of her research for the book, Ochsner traveled to Prague, the capital of the Czech Republic; St. Petersburg, Russia; and Poland.

As of 2006, when she was in her mid-thirties, Ochsner had won an astonishing number of literary awards, twenty-three in all, including the William Faulkner Award, the Robert Penn Warren Fiction Prize, the Raymond Carver Fiction Prize, the Fish Short-Story Prize, and the Ruth Hardman Award for Fiction.

Ochsner believes that writers should support other writers, and she has had teaching positions in creative writing at George Fox University, the University of Oregon, Western Oregon University, and Chemeketa Community College.

As of 2006, she and her husband, Brian, lived with their four children in Keizer, Oregon, a suburb of Salem.

Plot Summary

"The Necessary Grace to Fall" begins on an August day in an office in the Hope and Life Insurance Company in an unnamed American city. The main character, Howard, works in this office with Leonard, his immediate supervisor, who is a physical fitness fanatic. Howard has only recently switched to his current position in which he investigates the insurance claims of the deceased. Before this, he worked in the data coding department. Howard is a little disappointed in the work. He had thought it would be more exciting, akin to investigating a crime, but Leonard told him on his first day that he was an investigative assistant only, and his work would be mostly routine. Leonard then told him the routine for handling claims following suicide and natural and accidental deaths. Howard had hoped for a little more murder. The only excitement he had found was working with Ritteaur, the coroner's assistant, who would tell him over the phone all the gory details of the more interesting cases. Sometimes Howard visits the coroner's lab, too. He is fascinated by a case in which a wife killed and dismembered her husband.

Howard's wife, Carla, calls him at work, suggesting they have lunch together. She works on another floor of the same building, in the medical coding department. Howard does not want to meet his wife, and he makes an excuse. It is apparent that their marriage is not all it should be.

Howard gets interested in the file of a woman named Svea Johnson who has recently died after jumping or falling from a bridge. She was about his age and lived in the neighborhood in which he grew up. He thinks they must have gone to high school together, and he wishes he could remember something about her.

He takes a phone call from Carla telling him not to be late for dinner then leaves work early, at about four o'clock in the afternoon, and drives into the neighborhood where Johnson lived. He plans to take a look at her house. He drives around the neighborhood, going past the house where he lived as a boy. But he does not feel right about looking at the Johnson house and drives home without looking at the house numbers.

He returns late for dinner, and Carla demands to know where he has been. She is not satisfied with his response and is spoiling for a fight. But Howard does not have the energy to respond. Carla reminds him that his attendance is required at the Y the following night. Her eight-year-old son, Kevin, from a previous marriage is taking a karate test there.

The next morning Howard tries to avoid looking at the Johnson file. During a coffee break he tells Leonard that he has a strange feeling in his chest, and he thinks something may be wrong with him. Later that morning, he tries to focus on processing the Johnson file. But he suspects that the case was a suicide, and this depresses him. He still feels some physical discomfort. He calls Ritteau for the autopsy results on the woman, and the coroner's assistant invites him to come over and take a look for himself.

In the coroner's lab, Howard sees the body of the dead woman. He observes that she had been beautiful, and he regrets going to the lab. The coroner has found no bruises on the body, which might indicate suicide (since there is no sign of a struggle), but he has also found bits of moss under the woman's nails, which might indicate she fell. However, it might indicate that she intended to jump but changed her mind at the last minute. Ritteau has to do some more work before he can record a verdict, but he suspects the verdict will be accidental death. Howard expresses some thoughts about the dignity of the dead, saying that accidental death sounds better than "botched suicide."

After Howard leaves the lab, he once again drives into the neighborhood of the dead woman and stops two doors down from her house. He sits in the car, thinking about his unhappy school days. When he returns to his office, Carla calls him to remind him of Kevin's green belt karate test. Howard does not want to go.

After work he again goes to Madison Street, where Johnson lived. He sits in his car, planning to knock on the door and ask if Johnson's parents could tell him a little about their daughter. But he does not carry out his plan. Instead, as he drives slowly past the Johnson house, he sees Carla's car in his rear-view mirror. She is at the end of the street, turning the corner.

Howard returns to the office. At seven-thirty, Carla calls him from the Y. She says she saw him on Madison Street, and she reproaches him. Then she says that she forgives him, although she does not know what he was doing in that neighborhood. She tells him to be sure to be at the Y for Kevin's test.

Howard starts for the Y, but stops and parks near the bridge from which Johnson fell or jumped to her death. He walks to the bridge then stands on it and leans over the railing. He wonders how the woman must have felt at that moment and what kind of sadness had brought her there. He removes his shoes and stands on the cement handrail. He sees how easy it would be to decide to commit suicide and jump off the bridge. He feels like laughing. Then he stops himself and cautiously climbs down from the ledge. He realizes he has small things to live for, including Kevin's test, and he tells himself he should try harder to get along with the boy. He also thinks of other things that might happen in the future that would be worth living for. He slips his shoes on and walks back to the car.

Characters

Carla

Carla is Howard's wife. She has an eight-year-old son, Kevin, by a previous marriage, and she works for the same insurance company that employs Howard. She is an aggressive woman who gets angry when Howard is late for dinner and reproaches him for his unreliability when she sees him in an unfamiliar neighborhood when he should be preparing to go to the Y. Howard thinks she maintains a long list of grievances against him, and he secretly fears her.

Howard

Howard is the main character in the story. He works in the investigations department of Hope and Life Insurance, processing claims. He is bored because his job lacks excitement, his marriage is unsatisfactory, and he does not get along with his wife's son. He seems fascinated by the morbid details about death he reads in coroner's reports. He also suffers from unusual physical symptoms and may have undiagnosed chronic depression. He often feels divided against himself, as if he is split into two people, "the Howard who wanted to arrive home in time for dinner so as to please his wife and the Howard who knew even as he promised that he would, he wouldn't." In other words, part of him wants to do the expected thing, while the other part seems in the grip of some other unpredictable impulse that he does not fully understand. His interest in the Svea Johnson case seems to indicate his own suicidal tendency, which he finally overcomes at the end of the story.

Kevin

Kevin is Carla's eight-year-old son. Howard tries to get along with him but fails, in spite of Carla's insistence that Kevin needs a father figure in his life.

Leonard

Leonard is Howard's supervisor at Hope and Life Insurance company. He is a muscular, physical fitness fanatic who consumes large quantities of power bars, energy drinks, and vitamins.

Ritteaur

Ritteaur is the coroner's assistant who keeps Howard informed about interesting cases and invites him over to the lab to view the corpse of Svea Johnson.

Themes

Mortality, Suicide, and the Affirmation of Life

The characters vary greatly in the extent to which the life force and the desire to live flows through them. Leonard, with his physical fitness, well-defined muscles and constant munching of "energy bars," has a strong hold on life, as does the aggressive Carla, with her desire to dominate and control her husband. Howard, by contrast—uncertain, diffident, trapped in a bad marriage and an unsatisfying job—has a much weaker grip on life, and Svea Johnson, who appears in the story only as a corpse, has lost her hold on life altogether.

In this story that is saturated with the sense of human mortality, often presented in explicit ways, the characters represent extremes of affirmation and negation of life. As a waverer, a man who seems unsure of his path and his purpose for living, Howard must acquire some of the trust in life that will enable him to keep going. As the story unfolds, it seems unlikely that he will succeed. His is the clear case of a man who is suffering from undiagnosed depression, a kind of mental illness that can in severe cases lead to suicide. This depression is strongly suggested by Howard's recollection of

the time he spent volunteering at a suicide hotline. He wanted to tell the callers that he understood how they felt and that "*I'm just like you.*" When they hung up, he felt he had failed again, the word "again" suggesting that Howard has a habit of blaming himself when things go wrong. He is, he knows, "full of guilt and too many character faults to count." Howard even feels that Svea Johnson's suicide represents a failure on his part, simply because he and the dead woman were about the same age, went to the same high school, and lived in the same neighborhood. This inappropriate sense of guilt can be one of the symptoms of depression.

Howard's unhealthy mental state is also indicated by his morbid fascination with death, as shown by his visits to the coroner's lab and his more than professional interest in the fate of Svea Johnson. He feels responsible for her, whether her death was a suicide or an accident. Although Howard and Svea Johnson are of different genders, she is in a sense his *doppelgänger*, or double, a kind of ghostly second self that haunts the first self. It is she who gave in to the desire to die that Howard himself also feels. It seems to manifest in him as a longing to escape from the confines of the physical body, that "menagerie of flawed parts . . . [that] could and would fail." Because Svea Johnson has acted out his secret desire, she is a figure of fascination for him, which explains his need to see the house that she lived in and talk to her parents, as well as the guilt he feels that he cannot remember her from his schooldays.

Just as he imagines Svea Johnson doing, Howard also—driving around the neighborhood, stopping, going to the bridge from which the woman jumped or fell—seems to be waiting for the right moment to extricate himself from the sorrow and the difficulty of life. He imagines that it takes a moment of "necessary grace to fall," as if picking the moment to die, even in this manner, requires a sense of timing, a knowledge of when such an act may be permitted.

But what he finds at the crucial moment, when he seems about to emulate Svea Johnson, is something else altogether, not the necessary grace to fall but the necessary grace to live. Suddenly, at that crucial moment of decision, he finds value in the small opportunities that life offers that he had formerly dismissed as unimportant or irritating. He also regains a sense of the mystery of life and its infinite possibilities ("the appearance of new suns"). No explanation is offered of how or why this happens, since by definition a moment of grace

Topics For Further Study

- Team up with one other student and act out for the class a conversation on a suicide hotline. Your partner is desperate and wants to take his or her life. You must talk her out of it. You can prepare a script in advance or do the scene from notes or improvise as you go along. The class votes on whether they think you did enough to save the person's life.

- Should terminally ill people have the right to end their lives at a time of their choosing? Should a doctor or relative be allowed to assist such as person? Research the right-to-die movement and compare the law on assisted suicide in Oregon to the law on assisted suicide in the Netherlands. Write an essay in which you compare these laws and argue for or against the right to die.

- What are the legal aspects of suicide in the United States? Why was it once considered a crime to commit suicide? Examine past and present attitudes to suicide in some non-Western societies, such as China and Japan, and in ancient Greece and Rome. Under what circumstances was suicide considered an honorable death? Write an essay in which you present your findings.

- Watch the movie, "It's a Wonderful Life" (1947), starring James Stewart, in which an angel helps a suicidal businessman by showing what life would have been like if he never existed. Make a class presentation summarizing the plot and the theme of the movie and then discuss real-life suicide prevention strategies employed by medical professionals in emergency situations. What are some of the ways that people who want to take their own lives are persuaded not to do so?

has no discernible cause and is certainly not the result of any effort put out by the beneficiary. It is a mysterious sign of the benevolence at the heart of the universe that affirms life rather than death.

Alienation

Howard is alienated from his wife and from his co-workers. He is self-absorbed, aware of his own conflicted feelings, and also aware of disconnecting from the relationships he has with his wife and her son and with his physical fitness pro of a supervisor. While he is detached from the living, he seems to gravitate toward the dead and toward the past. He wants to visualize Svea Johnson as a student in his high school, wants to see her house in his own neighborhood, wants to view the water from the bridge where she fell or jumped to her death, wants to see her body. It is as though just as he pulls back from interacting with people around him, he is drawn toward the dead, toward imagining the dying process, toward experiencing the kind of moment when one chooses to jump. The monotony

of his job, his wife's nagging, his failure to connect with her son, all of these contribute to his inability to relate to his work and familial context. The resolution of this pattern happens in the moment when he has his shoes off and steps up on the railing of the bridge; through an act of grace, he has an inexplicable change of heart, and he turns from his obsession with death to a willingness to see what life has yet to offer him. The story seems to suggest that no matter how much one is drawn to suicide, the anodyne lies in considering what life has yet to offer.

Style

Imagery of the Human Body

The story contains much imagery of the human body in its different forms. Leonard's muscular physique is emphasized, as is the physical presence of the corpse of Svea Johnson. But the main examples are in reference to Howard. Unlike Leonard, who is extremely comfortable inside his own skin, Howard is frequently aware of unusual and sometimes disturbing sensations in his body. At one point he feels a strange sensation in his chest, like he is "gulping sky"; another time he feels "an itch in [his] arteries." Several times he has an expansive feeling, as if there is an empty space inside his chest: "Howard's shoulders slumped and he could feel a space widening inside his rib cage." Sometimes this space seems to get wider, and it pushes at his lungs. These images suggest Howard's discomfort with the limitations of the physical body and his desire to escape its confines, either into some kind of vague state of spiritual transcendence or perhaps in death. This is especially clear in the following image, which occurs after he presses his hand against his heart and then his chest: "He hoped his internal organs would just disappear and he could give himself over to his internal gases and float, balloon-like, up and out of the office." These images suggesting a kind of floating out of the body culminate in the moment Howard stands on the bridge, apparently ready to jump. He "felt light, giddy in this feeling of anti-gravity." But his willingness to escape the demands of life and the physical body suddenly recede; as he steps down from the ledge, although he still feels a sense of physical lightness, this feeling is allied to a sense of the need for purposeful action in the world. His slipping into his shoes again symbolically represents his decision to ground himself in the responsibility of living a useful life, to bear the burden and not seek to escape it.

Historical Context

Suicide in the United States

Suicide is a widespread social problem that occurs in all human societies. In the United States in 2000, suicide was the eleventh leading cause of death. The total number of suicides was 29,350, or 1.2 percent of all deaths. In 2001, the figure was 30,622. Suicide is more common than murder. The problem goes even deeper than the statistics state, since it is estimated that for every death by suicide, there may be from eight to twenty-five attempted suicides.

Risk factors for suicide vary. More than 90 percent of people who kill themselves suffer from depression or some other mental disorder or from substance abuse. Suicide as well as depression are associated with lower levels of a brain chemical called serotonin. Medication aimed at relieving depression boosts serotonin levels.

Depression and suicide may also be a response to adverse and stressful life events, such as loss of a job or spouse, although experts point out that suicide is not a normal response to stressful situations. Suicide may happen when the pain the person is experiencing overwhelms the coping strategies and resources they have for dealing with it.

Other risk factors for suicide include a family history of mental disorder or substance abuse; family history of suicide; family violence, including physical or sexual abuse; firearms in the home; incarceration; and exposure to the suicidal behavior of others, including family members and peers.

Suicide is more common among men than women. In the United States in 2000, suicide was the eighth leading cause of death for males and the nineteenth leading cause of death for females. More than four times as many men as women die by suicide, although women report attempting suicide about three times as often as men.

Suicide is more common among whites than other racial groups. In 2000, white men accounted for 73 percent of all suicides.

Suicides rates differ according to age groups. In 2000, suicide was the third leading cause of death among ten- to fourteen-year-olds, as well as among fifteen- to twenty-four-year-olds. Amongst teenagers, five times as many boys die from suicide as girls.

Older adults are also at risk for suicide. People age sixty-five and over comprise 13 percent of the U.S. population but accounted for 18 percent of all suicides in the United States in 2000. In 1999, 84 percent of suicides in this age group were men. The risk is especially high among white men age eighty-five and older. Divorced and widowed people are more at risk than those who are married, since being single can often lead to loneliness, social isolation, and depression.

Suicide prevention efforts rest largely on the identification and treatment of mental problems, including depression. Most forms of depression can be successfully treated, but sometimes the illness can be hidden behind other symptoms and go unrecognized. Reducing access to means of suicide, such as toxic substances and handguns, may also be a way of reducing suicide.

One aspect of suicide prevention is the existence of crisis hotlines, such as the one Howard volunteered for in "The Necessary Grace to Fall." A crisis hotline is a phone number people can call to get emergency counseling, usually by trained volunteers. Such hotlines have existed in most major cities of the United States since the mid-1970s. Initially set up to help those contemplating suicide, many now deal more generally with emotional crises. However, there is no evidence that the existence of such hotlines has reduced the number of suicides.

Critical Overview

Although Ochsner's first collection of stories, *The Necessary Grace to Fall*, won literary awards, it attracted little attention from reviewers. This is not unusual for a first collection from a young, unknown writer. However, Ochsner's second collection of stories, *People I Wanted to Be* (2005), did attract some notice. Interestingly, many of the comments of the reviewers about these stories might equally be applied to "The Necessary Grace to Fall." The reviewer for *Publishers Weekly*, for example, describes Ochsner's characters as "a host of oddballs whose touchingly resilient hopes and small leaps of faith fly in the face of almost certain disappointment." This well describes Howard's sudden and unexpected moment of grace at the end of the story, set against the accumulated tensions and disappointments of his life. The reviewer also mentions as a notable feature of Ochsner's stories, "the tension between small, improbable miracles and the damp, chilly world in which they suddenly occur," which likewise might be applied to "The Necessary Grace to Fall."

Ochsner's character Howard can again be recognized in the following comment made by Gillian Engberg in a review of *People I Wanted to Be*, for *Booklist*: "Ochsner's flawed, wholly sympathetic characters miraculously stumble into small moments, shaped with a delicious sense of the absurd, which connect them to a world that's magical, merciful, and infinite."

In England's *Guardian*, reviewer Maya Jaggi notes that Ochsner's stories typically end in optimism rather than despair, and her comment also can be taken as applying to "The Necessary Grace to Fall": "Despite, or because of, the insistent presence of death, these stories end on a sudden high, in intimations of flight, or stomach-fluttering hope."

Young person crouched on the edge of a bridge

© Corbis-Bettmann. From a photograph in *Suicide*, by Adam Woog.

Lucent Books, 1997. Reproduced by permission of Corbis.

Criticism

Bryan Aubrey

Aubrey holds a Ph.D. in English and has published many articles on contemporary literature. In this essay, Aubrey discusses Ochsner's characterization of her protagonist and the way she crafts his moment of transformation at the end of the story.

Many of Ochsner's short stories, including "The Necessary Grace to Fall," are informed by a spiritual vision that offers moments of unexpected redemption to troubled characters. Ochsner's commitment to an optimistic view of the possibilities latent in even the most despairing of lives is an unusual, some would say refreshing, quality in a young American writer of literary short stories. She is no Raymond Carver, committed to a relentlessly bleak view of human life and human nature. Although she does not turn a blind eye to the sadness of life and the small hells that people create for themselves, and subjects such as death, suicide, violence, and terminal illness feature quite often in her stories, it seems as if she is looking always for

> " Howard turns his back
> on those moments when he
> seems to expand beyond his
> body. It seems that those
> experiences are, after all,
> more the expression of a
> secret longing for death
> and annihilation, the desire
> not to be, than an
> intimation of potential
> spiritual freedom."

the moment when the dark door opens, the clouds part, the oppressive weight is lifted, and a pure beam of light pours into the world.

Howard—poor, well meaning, mediocre—Howard in "The Necessary Grace to Fall," is a case in point. There are so many things wrong with Howard's life that it would hard to list them all. A bad marriage and a boring job would probably top the list and would be enough to drive stronger men than Howard to distraction. Howard is probably in early middle age, but the years have already worn him down. He is an odd, lonely man, apparently with no love or affection in his life, who longs for someone to show him kindness. He likes to perform acts of kindness himself mainly because "He desperately hoped his good intentions would bring back to him some small act of kindness in return, he didn't care how small." There is a world of rejection and pain in that last phrase. Howard is like a starving man who would be overwhelmed by gratitude if someone were to take pity on him and toss him a crust of bread. Perhaps not surprisingly, Howard does not feel in control of his life. He is not even in control of himself. He decides to do one thing but ends up doing another, for reasons he does not understand.

But in spite of all these failings, Ochsner ensures that Howard wins the reader's sympathy. She treats him rather gently, as if she likes him and wants to help him out. The more confident characters, Leonard and Carla, are treated more ruthlessly.

They are hard, with firm ideas about the way life is and should be, and untroubled by any deep thoughts or speculations. In this sense, they are more limited than Howard, who at least has an inquiring mind, and Ochsner enjoys a little satire at their expense. But Howard she has marked for redemption from the beginning. He is a little man who would do good in life if he knew how, so Ochsner, as author, allows herself the license to play God and decides to give him the boost he needs.

The key to Howard's eventual moment of salvation is contained in the unusual, expansive images of inner and outer space that are placed at regular intervals in the story. They are always tied to some physical sensation that Howard is feeling. It is as if something inside him is tired of being cramped up in a small physical body with five limited senses and wants to experience freedom. He wants to shed the weight of physical existence and experience the lightness of a new mode of being, although he does not conceptualize it in this way, since he has no firm idea of what he is looking for. These images can either be interpreted as a longing for mystical, spiritual experience or a longing for death and the dissolution of the body. Ochsner does not make it clear until the end of the story which interpretation she intends.

The first time the space metaphor appears is early in the story, when he is first disappointed with the routine nature of his job: "Howard's shoulders slumped and he could feel a space widening in his rib cage." Having seeded the story with this image, Ochsner works with it until it seems to signify something transcendent, a state of being without boundaries that is quite the opposite of little Howard's constant petty fears and imaginings. When Howard thinks of the family of the dead woman, for example

> [H]e felt acres and acres of empty space growing inside of him, pushing everything else out of the way. His heart, his lungs—none of it mattered—and he could swear he felt them shrinking to the point where he could see himself reflecting pure sky, the vastness of that inner space.

Another example of the space image comes when Howard presses on his rib cage, "lightly fingering the spaces between the bones, feeling as spacious inside as before, if not spacier." As in the earlier passage, this is immediately followed by the image of the infinite expanse of the sky: "Outside, the sky was a cloudless blue, so pure Howard had to look away." By dint of repetition, Ochsner will not allow the reader to miss the significance of these images. They seem to hammer home the message

What Do I Read Next?

- Ochsner's second collection of eleven short stories, *The People I Wanted to Be* (2005), is set in Eastern Europe and Russia as well as Ochsner's native Oregon. Like many of the stories in *The Necessary Grace to Fall*, these stories feature sympathetic, long-suffering characters who suddenly find a kind of spiritual redemption in unlikely circumstances.

- *Will's Choice: A Suicidal Teen, a Desperate Mother, and a Chronicle of Recovery* (2005), by Gail Griffith, is the story of one mother whose seventeen-year-old son tried to commit suicide by overdosing on an antidepressant. The author also discusses her own struggle with depression. The book shows that depression is a treatable illness, since both mother and son recovered from it.

- Sylvia Plath's autobiographical novel, *The Bell Jar* (1963), is based on Plath's final college year in New York as a guest editor for a women's magazine. Like Plath, the protagonist, Esther Greenwood, suffers from depression and tries to commit suicide by taking an overdose of sleeping pills. She is given electric shock treatment and eventually recovers. Plath herself, however, committed suicide in 1963.

- Just as "The Necessary Grace to Fall" ends in a moment of illumination in which a troubled protagonist finds peace and a sense of renewal, so too does the protagonist in William Trevor's short story "After Rain," which appears in his collection of the same title (1996). In a moment of redemptive grace, a thirty-year-old Englishwoman, on vacation in Italy, is granted a crucial insight into why she has been unable to retain love in her life.

- "Paul's Case" (1906), by Willa Cather, is a character study of a boy who leaves school, goes to another city and spends all his money, and then commits suicide by jumping in front of a train. The story is told from the point of view of teachers and other authorities who review what happened and try to explain what caused this teenager to take his own life. The story is available in *Willa Cather's Collected Short Fiction 1892–1912* (1970), edited by Virginia Faulkner and published by the University of Nebraska Press.

---

that the small human self that is contained in one human body is not the entire being of the person. There are other states of being possible that substitute freedom for enclosure, infinity for the finite—or perhaps these images merely signify death, the dissolution of all things, and escape from the heavy responsibilities of being human.

There is a parallel in Ochsner's use of these expansive, inner-outer images in the work of Leo Tolstoy, in his novel *War and Peace*. In that novel, one of the main characters, the Russian aristocrat Pierre Bezuhov, is held prisoner by the French and is forced to take part in Napoleon's retreat from Moscow. One night under the stars, he sees the absurdity of the situation, realizing that his "immortal soul" cannot be confined in this way. There is a full moon, and as he gazes up at the stars and the vastness of the sky, he thinks, "And all that is mine, all that is in me, and all that is *me*. And they took all that and shut it up in a shed barricaded with planks." He smiles and lies down contentedly to sleep, having realized that the essential self, who he in reality is, cannot be enclosed by anything or imprisoned by anyone.

This seems to be close to the experience to which Ochsner is pushing Howard—the breaking of the bonds of the finite. And yet when that image of inner and outer expansive space occurs once again, as the story builds to its climax, it seems to carry another connotation. Howard arrives at the bridge from which Svea Johnson fell to her death and wonders what she felt at that moment. He asks himself, "Did she give herself over to the collapsing arms of the air, to all that space within and without, a falling between the ribs and then here between the arms, between fingertips and sky?"

Here those images seem to be associated with imminent death rather than with the expansion of consciousness.

And so in the end, Howard turns his back on those moments when he seems to expand beyond his body. It seems that those experiences are, after all, more the expression of a secret longing for death and annihilation, the desire not to be, than an intimation of potential spiritual freedom. He realizes now that he must ground himself in a more firm appreciation of life in the here-and-now, with an awareness of what he can contribute to it. He must stay in his body, so to speak, rather than encourage experiences that lead him away from it. Significantly, in that moment, he finds himself thinking of someone other than himself. He becomes outer- rather than inner-directed, thinking of how he might be able to help eight-year-old Kevin. The mystery of the infinite possibilities in life also takes hold of him, indicating that in this moment the smallness of his selfhood no longer defines him completely. He can reach beyond it to a way of transcendence not through the cultivation of unusual psychological or spiritual experiences but through a more simple wonder, engagement, and fascination at the miracle of continually unfolding life.

Source: Bryan Aubrey, Critical Essay on "The Necessary Grace to Fall," in *Short Stories for Students*, Thomson Gale, 2007.

Anna Maria Hong

Hong is a poet and the editor of a fiction and memoir anthology. In the following essay, Hong discusses how Ochsner humorously and empathetically explores the drives toward life and death through characterization and by employing the motifs of water and air, as well as the tension between falling and flying.

Ochsner begins the title story of her acclaimed collection with the intriguing sentence, "All summer had been a medley of jumpers and fallers." In doing so, the author establishes one of the central themes of "The Necessary Grace to Fall": death, and specifically the difference between intentional and accidental dying. She follows the opening sentence with grisly examples of ways to die: "The previous spring, simple dismemberment, and the winter before that, freakish hurricane-related deaths and injuries—deaths by debris, Leonard, Howard's immediate supervisor and cubicle-mate, called them." Although the context for this morbid list is not obvious from the opening sentences, Ochsner soon clears up the mystery by establishing that they emanate from the thoughts of the protagonist,

Howard, an investigative assistant at a company called Hope and Life Insurance. Not incidentally, Howard is obsessed with death, suicide, and the like, and the story focuses on Howard's coming to terms with the twin impulses toward life and death. In relating this darkly humorous tale, Ochsner lightly satirizes the deadening effects of contemporary, American society, while exploring deeper, more universal themes.

The central character, Howard, embodies the story's primary tensions. A middle-aged, white-collar worker, Howard is noticeably uncomfortable in his body. Unlike Leonard, his supervisor at Hope and Life, Howard is clearly out-of-shape, a desk-jockey who eats cinnamon rolls, as opposed to the stockpiles of power bars Leonard consumes. The type of guy who does crunches for his oblique muscles at his desk during the daily coffee-break, Leonard represents Howard's antithesis, providing a physical and philosophical counterpoint to Howard's more introspective, passive way of being. In one early scene, Leonard offers Howard a Tiger bar, which Howard declines while pointing to the sticky baked good on the corner of his desk. Leonard responds by saying, "'Treat your body like a temple, and it'll take care of you.'"

Bewildered by this statement, Howard merely blinks, pushes up his glasses, and says nothing, while he thinks about bodies and ruminates on how Svea Johnson, the case he's currently handling, actually fell to her death. As an investigative assistant, Howard makes sure the paperwork for insurance claims is filed properly by following-up on police reports. The job is not as exciting as he would like it to be, and he craves "a little more murder" as well as a deeper connection with the people who have died and their families. He wants to know the story behind the deaths that come across his desk as files.

Howard is sometimes helped in this quest for personal information on the deceased by Ritteaur, the coroner's assistant. Ritteaur conducts the autopsies to determine the cause of death. Although he knows it is morbid and weird, Howard finds these lab investigations fascinating, and he pumps Ritteaur for details, even when the information is not technically required for his job. Howard seems to especially enjoy hearing about the more gruesome cases, such as Pietrzak, the man whose wife chopped him up into little bits and flushed him down the toilet "one flush at a time."

Howard solicits Ritteaur's macabre reports partly to jolt himself out of boredom and partly to avoid his wife, Carla, who also works at Hope and

Life Insurance. An employee in the medical coding department, Carla telephones Howard every day to see if he wants to have lunch, and although they used to have lunch together regularly in the break room, Howard now finds himself avoiding both lunch with her and, if possible, her phone calls. Rather than refusing her directly, however, Howard eludes her by either being on the phone himself or being out of the office during lunch hour. He notes to himself that neither hatred nor malice accounts for his desire not to meet Carla, as he thinks,

> In fact, there was no particular reason why he wanted to avoid his wife. He just got tired of their regular lunches that over time began to feel forced, wearing on him like a habit that needed breaking. People need space, he reminded himself, though he knew she'd never let him get away with such a flimsy reasoning.

Like Leonard, Carla is also a character who contrasts with Howard, and their interactions highlight Howard's dilemma, which lies in his inability to express openly his feelings. Howard wants more excitement, empathy, and action than he can muster. A believer in human kindness, he also desperately wants to be good and do good for others. However, although he feels he should perform small acts of kindness whenever he can, he is frustrated by not quite knowing how. Prior to working at Hope and Life, Howard had volunteered at a suicide hotline where he had tried to dissuade people on the verge of suicide. His desire to help them stemmed from his ongoing need for reciprocal kindness as well as his identification with people in distress. He recalls trying to cheer the callers up by telling them about his high school summers doing the grim job of chicken picking on his grandparents' farm. The job entailed picking up the chickens by their feet and loading them in cages onto a truck to be delivered to their deaths. Once loaded, the chickens would start squawking with fear, and Howard relates that "Though he hated that job, hated what he had to do, somehow sending those birds to their deaths validated his own life."

Although Howard does not completely understand why the odious work had this effect on him, he recalls telling the suicide callers about the job and what it meant to him, in a desperate attempt to make a connection with the callers. Inevitably, however, Howard would fail to make this connection. Even his suggestion that the caller get a pet or a goldfish to care about seemed useless. At that point, the callers would hang up, and Howard would be left feeling overwhelmed by his own sense of failure, of letting the other person down.

> **"** Here, as elsewhere, the air motif signals a longing for freedom away from mundane and bodily concerns. The motif also sets up the tension between floating away and falling, as floating upward may be the opposite of tumbling downward to death."

The recalled anecdote about Howard's stint as a volunteer at the suicide hotline illustrates the crux of his problem, which is the gap between his noble desires and the reality of his life. At the heart of his immobility lies the tension between what Howard sees as two sides of himself: the bodily or physical Howard and his consciousness or will. He recognizes that there are two aspects of him that frequently seem to pull him in opposing directions, as they want different things. A pensive character, Howard understands that this opposition between his consciousness and his body accounts for his continual failure to please Carla, as part of him wants to please her and part of him wants something different from the usual marital and family routine.

Unlike Leonard, who solves this body/mind dilemma that all human beings face by making his body an impervious, muscular "temple," Howard has to take another route to resolving these antipathies. In one humorous scene, a distressed Howard seeks Leonard's advice on what his problem is by lifting up his shirt and showing Leonard his torso, where he feels the anxiety. Leonard responds by saying his problem lies in Howard's nonexistent oblique muscles and drinking too many beers. Uncomforted, Howard replies, "I think it's more serious," and indeed it is. Howard's problems intensify as he becomes obsessed with the Svea Johnson case.

From the outset, Howard identifies with Johnson, who either fell or jumped from the local bridge. She is exactly the same age as Howard, and they grew up in the same neighborhood. He worries that she was a jumper, an intentional suicide, rather than someone who fell off the bridge accidentally. He worries because he wants to believe she was not so depressed about life that she killed herself, a personal fear for him, as he, too, suffers from chronic depression. Howard is also upset by the idea that he might have known Johnson in high school and then forgotten her. This possibility distresses him because he knows he's capable of forgetting things, and yet for some reason, he feels responsible for her, which entails knowing who she was.

As his anxiety over the Johnson case increases, Howard finds himself driving to the neighborhood where Johnson and he grew up, intending to find her home and her family. Though he knows Carla will be angry if he is late for dinner, he goes anyway, leaving work early to seek out some clue about Johnson's life. However, the trip is not successful because while he drives around his old neighborhood, Howard becomes distracted by memories of delivering newspapers as a boy. He turns home without finding Johnson's house or gaining a sense of satisfaction about the case.

On his drive home to the anticipated conflict with his wife, Howard experiences the sense of

> empty space growing inside of him, pushing everything else out of the way. His heart, his lungs—none of it mattered—and he could swear he felt them shrinking to the point where he could see himself reflecting pure sky, the vastness of that inner space.

As the story continues, Howard feels that inner space expand whenever he thinks about the Johnson case, as the two sides of him vie for dominance. In an effort to allay his discomfort, Howard calls Ritteaur, who offers to show him Johnson's corpse, which he is currently analyzing. In the lab, Ritteaur notes that it is either a suicide or an accident, and that it is possible that she intended to jump but then changed her mind at the last minute. The visit ends inconclusively, as Ritteaur has not completed the investigation, and Howard leaves the lab feeling nauseated and more puzzled about Johnson, wondering how he perhaps could have helped her. He attempts again to drive to the old neighborhood to find the Johnson house but is again distracted from his purpose, this time by memories of his own miserable elementary school experiences.

Throughout the story, Ochsner invokes the motifs of air and water to reinforce the themes. Back at work, Howard again feels the air-filled space in his chest, and though he tries to thump it away with his hand, he also hopes "his internal organs would just disappear and he could give himself over to his

internal gases and float, balloon-like, up and out of the office." Here, as elsewhere, the air motif signals a longing for freedom away from mundane and bodily concerns. The motif also sets up the tension between floating away and falling, as floating upward may be the opposite of tumbling downward to death.

Ochsner employs the motif of water in a similar way, and throughout the story, she makes several references to water. In the scene in which he seeks Leonard's opinion, Howard describes his feeling in his chest by saying, "Like I'm gulping sky, can't get enough of it. Other times I feel I'm drowning on air." When he asks if a person can do that, Leonard points out that fish do that "all the time." Both Howard and Svea Johnson are compared to fish, as her dead eyes look like those on dead fish, and at one point Howard wishes he could tell suicide victims how unforgiving water is when one jumps from a height into it. In the story, water is the element of life for good and for bad; it is the emotional element, and it sustains and connects the characters to one another. There is the anecdote about the woman attempting to flush her husband away, and when Carla follows Howard on his third attempt to find the Johnson house, he sees her car in his rearview mirror "fishtail" away.

Carla tells him she caught him doing something suspicious and that she forgives him but that he needs to stop because people count on him. She reminds him to be at Y later that day when his stepson Kevin takes a karate test, which Howard would rather avoid. Howard agrees to be there, but as he approaches the Y, he detours and heads for the bridge where Johnson and others have fallen to their deaths. The bridge represents the line between life and death, and by going to the bridge, Howard accomplishes several things. He parks his car and walks to the thick cement rail, and then he stands on top of rail, re-enacting what Johnson might have done. As he does this, he is finally able to imagine her life and what may have compelled her to fall or jump. This identification with her gives him a sense of completion as he feels compassion for the dead woman and thus gains insight into his own sadness and challenges. These insights in turn enable Howard's two selves to coalesce, and at the end of the story, his will to live saves his body.

By standing on the rail, his corporeal self has finally acted to satisfy his wishes, and once that happens, his consciousness steps in as Howard tells himself to stop and get down from danger. After climbing down, he realizes that the people he has failed were not strangers like Johnson but those people close to him, Carla and Kevin, and he realizes, too, that their love and obligation is what kept him from jumping himself—that and myriad other pleasures and interesting phenomena life offers. Ochsner illustrates how the protagonist's mind and body work together at the end, as Howard triumphs and wants to really live, to see among other things "distant limbs of the galaxy." He desires the fusion of the corporeal with the celestial and knows how he can provide solace to the living.

Source: Anna Maria Hong, Critical Essay on "The Necessary Grace to Fall," in *Short Stories for Students*, Thomson Gale, 2007.

Sources

Engberg, Gillian, Review of *People I Wanted to Be*, in *Booklist*, Vol. 101, No. 14, March 15, 2005, p. 1266.

Felton, Rob, "Gina's Gift," in *LIFE*, Vol. XXXII, No. 3, July 2002, pp. 1, 5, http://www.georgefox.edu/life/archives/LIFE_Vol_32_No_3.pdf (accessed May 11, 2006).

Jaggi, Maya, "A Ghost of a Chance," in *Guardian*, December 10, 2005, http://books.guardian.co.uk/reviews/general fiction/0,6121,1663557,00.html (accessed May 11, 2006).

Ochsner, Gina, "The Necessary Grace to Fall," in *The Necessary Grace to Fall*, University of Georgia Press, 2002, pp. 1–21.

Review of *People I Wanted to Be*, in *Publishers Weekly*, Vol. 252, No. 14, April 4, 2005, p. 42.

Tolstoy, Leo, *War and Peace*, Vol. 2, translated and with an introduction by Rosemary Edmonds, Penguin Books, 1969, p. 1207.

Further Reading

Hendin, Herbert, *Suicide in America*, Norton, 1996.
  Hendin, a psychiatrist, casts new light on the problem of suicide. He demonstrates that treatment of seriously suicidal people is possible. He shows how American social policy toward suicide is marked by misconceptions. He also evaluates the right-to-die movement.

Jamison, Kay Redfield, *Night Falls Fast: Understanding Suicide*, Vintage, 2000.
  Jamison, a psychiatrist, explores the psychology of those who commit suicide, especially people under the age of forty. She discusses manic-depression, suicide in different cultures and eras, suicide notes, suicide methods, preventive treatments, and the devastating effects of suicide on loved ones. The book includes many anecdotes about people who have committed suicide.

Marcus, Eric, *Why Suicide?: Answers to 200 of the Most Frequently Asked Questions about Suicide, Attempted Suicide*, HarperSanFrancisco, 1996.
  Marcus, whose father committed suicide when Marcus was twelve, examines suicide from a variety of angles in a question-and-answer format. This is a practical book with much advice for anyone who is dealing with the suicide of a loved one. It includes a discussion of doctor-assisted suicide, as well as some cross-cultural comparisons.

Miller, John, *On Suicide: Great Writers on the Ultimate Question*, Chronicle Books, 1993.
  This anthology features passages from novels, short stories, essays, and poems that deal with suicide. Authors represented include Plato, Sylvia Plath, Albert Camus, Gustave Flaubert, Virginia Woolf, Langston Hughes, Cynthia Ozick, Primo Levi, Graham Greene, William Shakespeare, Emily Dickinson, John Donne, Jorge Luis Borges, Leo Tolstoy, and William Styron.

Paris 1991

Kate Walbert

1998

Kate Walbert's *Where She Went* is a collection of fourteen connected stories about a mother and a daughter, Marion and Rebecca, who are searching for a place where they can establish roots and find contentment. "Paris 1991" opens the collection. This story focuses on Rebecca's trip to Paris with her husband, Tom, where she hopes to conceive a baby. Rebecca had chosen Paris as the setting for becoming pregnant as the city is considered romantic, a city she has read about in books. She is not sure that this is the right time to get pregnant, but she determines that a child might provide her with the sense of fulfillment that she seeks.

Rebecca's imaginative visions of this exciting and romantic city, however, fade on its cold, rainy streets. There is little romance between her and her husband as they sit in cafés with nothing to say, feeling disconnected from the city as well as from each other. As Walbert arranges the imagistic scenes of the couple's few days in Paris, she conveys the tensions between romantic illusions and indifferent reality in this portrait of one woman's search for meaning.

Author Biography

Ann Katherine Walbert was born in 1961, in New York City to J. T. and Donna Walbert. Her family moved frequently around the country, and between 1963 and 1965, they lived in Japan. She notes the

Kate Walbert AP Images

influence that this had on her writing in an interview with Alyssa Colton-Heins, concluding, "that sense of being new, having to size up a situation immediately, having to hang back at the same time and read the scene as quickly and efficiently as you can really does a lot to strengthen the powers of observation." She notes the visual nature of her fiction and claims, "that's the result of looking and going from one place to another in radically different landscapes."

Her first book, *Where She Went*, a collection of interlinked stories about a mother and daughter and their travels and relationships, which includes "Paris 1991," was published in 1998 and received positive reviews. Her literary reputation was solidified by her next two novels. *The Gardens of Kyoto: A Novel*, published in 2001, focuses on the experiences of two cousins prior to World War II. *Our Kind*, published in 2004, chronicles the lives of a group of women in the 1950s who struggle with traditional attitudes about women's roles.

Walbert has also written a one-person play, *Year of the Woman*, based on the life of Jeannette Rankin, who in 1917 became the first woman to serve in Congress. The play was produced at Yale University in 2001. Walbert has also contributed articles

and fiction to various publications, including *Nation*, *Paris Review*, *DoubleTake*, *Fiction*, *Antioch Review*, *Ms.*, and the *New York Times*.

Walbert was awarded the Connecticut Commission on the Arts grant in 1994 and a Creative Writing fellowship from the National Endowment for the Arts in 1998. The *New York Times Book Review* named *Where She Went* one of its notable books for 1998. An early version of *The Gardens of Kyoto* won the Pushcart Prize and O. Henry Award, and she was nominated for the National Book Award for *Our Kind* in 2004. As of 2004, she was teaching at Yale University.

Plot Summary

In the opening scene of "Paris 1991," Rebecca and her husband, Tom, fly into Paris at night where they hope to conceive a baby. They take a taxi to their room, which is so small that by stretching out his arms Tom can touch the walls on both sides of the bed. Rebecca leans out the window and listens to the street sounds.

They walk in the rain because "there is nothing else to do," talking little as they wait for Rebecca's temperature to rise, indicating that she is fertile. After wandering through the galleries in the Bibliotèque Nationale looking at manuscripts, they go into a café that looks romantic. Rebecca wonders if children can choose their parents. Her mother, Marion, died of cancer months ago, and Rebecca has this weird feeling of seeing her in the street or in doorways.

As they sit in the back of a café and eat, "they have nothing to say" to each other. After her mother died, Rebecca determined "to live in the moment. No regrets, no sorrow. Only the next day and the next." She decided to get pregnant, so she cut up her diaphragm. Tom wanted to talk about the decision to have children, but Rebecca insisted that they already had, and "anyway, there's no good time, really." When Tom asked if she was sure, she remained silent.

Back in the café, Rebecca shows Tom a postcard of devils that she has bought in the gift shop, concluding, "Marion would have loved this." She "would have thought it very cosmopolitan." As the day fades, Rebecca is overcome with melancholy, thinking of Marion.

That night Rebecca observes a woman lighting candles in a room across the street from the hotel. She tells Tom that she wants to go out, but he thinks it is too late. She chides him, noting that Parisians are having dinner and that they should adopt their customs while there. As she looks at the woman across the way, she imagines romantic details in the other woman's room. Again, she suggests to Tom how nice it would be to go out for a drink and some fruit and cheese, and he acquiesces.

In the morning, as they wait for a church to open, Rebecca asks Tom what they should name the baby. At first, he says that he does not know and that it is bad luck to choose names before becoming pregnant. Tom notes that it could take a year or perhaps never. When he will not talk to her about it anymore, she feels "rebuked." She also "feels dowdy, old," compared to stylish Parisian women. In response, she imagines herself making colorful new curtains for their apartment and thinks about how handsome Tom is. When he asks if she likes the name Sophie, she admits that she never would have thought of that name.

After they enter the church and gaze at a famous portrait of the Virgin and Child, Rebecca notes that the face of the Virgin looks like a child while the Child looks like an old man. She lights a candle in front of an altar and declares, "Poor Marion . . . Poor Sophie."

Time shifts back to the period when Rebecca and Tom first started dating. They often spent time playing an imagining game, thinking about "all the other lives they could have led," a game she learned from her mother. She imagined living in Florence or in Rajasthan or in Greece. Tom thought he could have been a passenger on a train across Canada had he not learned the route was disconnected.

Rebecca admitted that she fell in love with his name first because she liked the way it sounds and noted that people liked Tom. After remembering the hikes they went on when she visited his home in California, she thinks that they felt adventurous then, but now they feel awkward and self-conscious in Paris.

At dinner, Tom eats oysters, hoping they will make him sexually more potent. It seems as if arguments are erupting at all of the tables in the dark restaurant. Yet the wine makes Tom happy. Rebecca thinks of how her mother always wanted to go to Paris and tries to imagine her there, but Tom insists that she would have hated the food.

Back in the hotel, as they have sex, Rebecca does not look at his face. Recalling an earlier mentioned idea that the unborn choose their parents, she imagines someone watching, "a soul hovering, debating whether to come back into this world." She then imagines a carriage that contains a woman, "a mother, a daughter, a goddess" and babies and devils, "hovering . . . waiting for their chance to be born." In this lyrical ending, Rebecca's thoughts of a child mix with thoughts of herself and her mother.

Characters

Marion

Marion, Rebecca's mother, died of cancer months before Rebecca and Tom go to Paris. She still has a profound influence, however, on her daughter. Rebecca seems to feel pressure to live an exciting, adventurous life that her mother could not have. When Rebecca buys the devil postcard and muses about how Marion would respond, she suggests that her mother had lived vicariously through Rebecca's chronicles of her travels. Twice during her stay in Paris, she declares, "poor Marion," expressing sorrow over her mother's lack of fulfillment. Yet she seems also to resent Marion's influence on her life when she cannot admit to Tom that she would have chosen her as a mother. Perhaps she blames her mother for her inability to find her own satisfaction in one place.

Rebecca

Rebecca, Tom's wife and Marion's daughter, is probably in her mid-thirties and feeling her biological clock ticking. Hesitant until now to start a family, she comes to Paris with her husband in 1991 intent on becoming pregnant. She and Tom appear to have traveled quite a bit and to be cosmopolitan in their tastes and references. Rebecca has an eye for detail and a refined imagination; watching a woman in a neighboring building, Rebecca imagines the woman setting a table with yellow pears on a wooden plate, having cut the fruit with heirloom pearl-handled silverware. Poetically aware of color, texture, and sound, Rebecca describes the "five-story buildings painted the color of old teacups and women with black hair." She hears "a crowd far away, pushing at the seams of quiet." Yet she is dissatisfied with herself; if her mother had come to Paris, she would have worn her "kelly green coat," but comparing herself to the Parisians, Rebecca feels "dowdy." She and Tom have difficulty trying to ignite their relationship and find the enthusiasm to start a family.

Rebecca's references to how her mother would have responded to Paris reveal Rebecca's sympathy for her and her unfulfilled dreams. She envisions her mother in Paris in better weather, meeting a dashing Frenchman. By contrast to this image, Rebecca's own experiences there leave her detached and empty.

Rebecca has an aloof relationship with her husband. While she sometimes tries to be affectionate with him, she often regards him as a stranger and finds little to say to him. She also exhibits a sense of detachment from others. When they sit next to the four old men playing cards in the restaurant, she does not try to interact with them, claiming, "it's like we're in a painting." Her sense of separation is heightened in the museum where "everyone reads a brochure, or listens to tapes hung around their necks."

Her search for meaning reveals her self-absorption. She never considers the needs of her husband and often overrides his wishes. She makes the decision to come to Paris just as she has made the decision to have a baby, even though her husband voices his concern about the timing and their hesitancy. When Paris does not fulfill her romantic visions, she turns inward, withdrawing from everyone, including Tom.

Tom

Tom, Rebecca's husband, is tall, thin, and has large hands. He seems amiable and pliable, perhaps somewhat passive. Although he suggests that they should talk about having a baby, Rebecca is the one who cuts up her diaphragm, deciding to "live in the moment." In asking repeatedly if she is "sure," Tom may suggest his own uncertainty. Yet Rebecca is the one who envisions the impregnation, in Paris when her temperature "rises point six degrees." When she wants to go out late at night and eat like Parisians, he balks but eventually agrees. He consistently avoids confrontation and gives into Rebecca's desires, yet he never points out her lack of attention toward him.

People like Tom because he appears "quaint" and most likely because of his amiability. Rebecca falls in love initially with the sound of his name, and she sympathizes with him over a difficult relationship he had in the past.

He appears more content with their lives but also seems to experience the same sense of disconnection that Rebecca feels. When they play the imagining game, he envisions he might have ridden on a train that crossed Canada except for discovering "that recently they disconnected the route." At one point, the narrator notes that while Rebecca holds his hand, he holds an umbrella, perhaps suggesting that he does not respond to her offer of affection. This lack of connection extends to their sexual relationship as well, as Tom feels the need to eat oysters to help him prepare for being sexual, and Rebecca drifts off into a fantasy during intercourse.

Themes

Self-fulfillment

Although readers do not get many details about Marion's life, Rebecca suggests that her mother experienced the same kind of discontentment as does she. When she buys the devil postcard, Rebecca implies that Marion lived vicariously though her daughter's travels, ones that she, as a married woman during the 1950s and 1960s in the United States, could not enjoy. The suffering her mother endured causes her daughter twice to declare, "Poor Marion."

Ironically, Rebecca experiences the same sense of meaninglessness even though she suffers none of the conventional restrictions that her mother faced. Rebecca appears to have the upper hand in her marriage when she convinces Tom that the time is right to have a baby and that Paris is the perfect setting in which to become pregnant. She also has been able to convince him to leave his home in California and relocate to the East Coast.

Walbert suggests that Rebecca's freedom prevents her from finding fulfillment. Because she is able to take off for Paris on a whim, or perhaps to Italy or Greece, she imagines that each locale promises her the exciting, adventurous life that eludes her at home. When her fantasies are dispelled, she is compelled to invent another dream of another place where she may attain happiness. The longing and pursuit of something that resides elsewhere contributes to her dissatisfaction with the immediate.

Ironically, Rebecca envisions that her life will be fulfilled not necessarily by hopping from one location to another, but through motherhood, a conventional role for a woman. Yet she expresses uncertainty about whether it is the right time to have a baby. This indecision, coupled with her inability to find satisfaction through her travels, suggests that Rebecca will not find the sense of meaning she seeks.

Topics for Further Study

- Rebecca briefly mentions her mother, Marion, in the story. Read some of Marion's chapters in *Where She Went*, enough to get a sense of her character, and write an essay discussing her influence on Rebecca, which is only hinted at in "Paris 1991."

- Imagine Rebecca five years after the story ends. Write a scene for a play or a screenplay that focuses on dialogue between her and her husband, illustrating whether she has found meaning in her life.

- Choose a place that you would like to visit and do some research about the culture of the area. Write a short story about a character who takes a trip to this chosen place, suggesting the significance the trip comes to have on the character's subsequent life.

- Note all of the colors Walbert uses in her descriptions of specific scenes in the story. Draw one of the scenes using her colors. Be ready to explain why you think she chose those colors and what meaning they seem to convey given the story's themes.

Connection and Disconnection

Ironically, Rebecca appears to be more connected to her dead mother than to her husband. When her mother was alive, she communicated to Rebecca her desire to travel to other countries and experience exciting, romantic adventures. This connection remains strong as shown by Rebecca's buying a postcard that she thinks her mother would like and imagining her wearing her green coat sitting in outdoor cafés and meeting dashing Frenchmen. Rebecca tries to live the life her mother envisioned not only to find personal fulfillment but to compensate for her mother's lack of freedom.

Though written in third person point of view, the story is seen from Rebecca's perspective; readers do not have access to Tom's private thoughts.

He does not discuss them with Rebecca, and he acquiesces to her. Yet he has been unable to help her find fulfillment because she has not been able to articulate clearly the connection she has with her mother and what effect that has had on her life. Dependable, pliable Tom is not a part of her romantic fantasies other than his ability to impregnate her. By the end of the story, she withdraws from him into her vision of motherhood, which includes her mother and her child but not Tom.

Style

Imagery

Walbert uses selected images to convey a scene, focusing on certain details to describe a street or view through a window. Her style is reminiscent of the Imagists, including Ezra Pound and Amy Lowell, a group of American and British poets in the second decade of the twentieth century who were noted for the exactness and clarity of the concrete details they employed in their work.

Rebecca has a photographic or painterly way of seeing and elaborating on details in the setting. In one instance, she sees a woman through a window in a building across the street from her own hotel room. She imagines the woman carrying cognac and sliced pears in from the kitchen to set on a table beautifully arranged amidst antique chests covered in velvet. These elegant and homey visions contrast with the gray Paris street and the bare hotel room, but ultimately, they seem to promise that someday she, too, can establish this sense of place and home.

At other points, Rebecca's visions become blurred. When she initially thinks of Paris before the trip, "the name is enough" to conjure images of excitement, but they are only hazy bits of historic events and springtime blooms since "she can't remember" the details. A picture on the wall of a café vaguely reminds her of a poem she read in school, but she cannot name it. This juxtaposition between photographic and blurry images reinforces the tension between reality and illusion in the story.

The title of the story juxtaposes the city name and the year. It provides two facts: one of place, the other of time. The suggestion is that the story is located in the past, that in the intervening cities and years between the setting of this story and the reading of it much has happened. But readers are not told about what follows or given hints about it.

Historical Context

A Woman's Place and Purpose

During the first few decades of the twentieth century, feminist thinkers on both sides of the Atlantic engaged in a rigorous investigation of female identity as it related to all aspects of women's lives. Some criticized the institution of marriage, identifying patterns and inequities within the traditional sex roles arrangement and suggesting ways of achieving parity. Others questioned the traditional notion of maternal instinct, rejecting the notion that motherhood is the ultimate goal of all women or that biology is destiny.

The early feminists in the United States, such as Margaret Sanger (1883–1966) who led a crusade to legalize birth control, fought for certain rights for women, including the right to vote. They were not able, however, to change widespread assumptions about a woman's place within the home. During World War II, American and British women were encouraged to enter the workplace where they enjoyed a measure of independence and responsibility. After the war, though, they were encouraged or forced to give up their jobs to the returning male troops. Hundreds of thousands of women were laid off and expected to resume their domestic and family roles in the home.

In the 1950s, special emphasis was placed on training girls to seek and conform to a feminine ideal of perfect wife and mother. Women who tried to gain self-fulfillment in other ways, for example through graduate education and careers, were criticized and deemed dangerous to the stability of the family. They were pressed to find fulfillment exclusively through their support of their husbands. Television shows such as *Ozzie and Harriet* and *Father Knows Best*, popular magazines such as *Good Housekeeping*, and advertisements that featured women happily cleaning their homes, all encouraged the image of woman-as-housewife throughout the 1950s. The small number of women who did work outside the home often suffered discrimination and exploitation as they were relegated to low-paying clerical and service jobs or positions in traditionally female-dominated careers of teaching and nursing. The 1970s, however, brought this history and persistent social and economic patterns under the harsh scrutiny of the women's rights movement.

The restricted 1950s life of Rebecca's mother, Marion, exerts one pull on Rebecca. It urges her toward settling down and having children. But Marion's example also urges Rebecca toward a wider sphere of travel and exotic experiences. Rebecca's visiting Paris suggests that wider sphere; the fact that it occurs in 1991 pinpoints the time at which Rebecca confronts the decision to become pregnant and commit herself to the life of a mother. The title of the story seems to suggest the convergence of two plots or patterns in a woman's life, leaving that intersection unresolved.

Critical Overview

Reviews of the collection have been generally positive. Nancy Pearl, in *Booklist*, announces, "This collection of linked short stories introduces a writer we should watch for in years to come." She finds the stories graceful and insists that Walbert's "use of a fractured narrative works like a prism to reveal the broken lives of her two main characters." Don Lee in *Ploughshares* concludes that Walbert "gives us haunting portraits of two women, "while her "prose [is] always lyrical, [with] images and phrases recurring to great effect."

A *Publishers Weekly* reviewer praises "Walbert's meticulous, unshakably sad collection" but determines that "sometimes these enigmatic stories are precious and overworked, straining toward a hush of despair." More frequently, however, "they resonate with surprising pathos, and these moments establish Walbert as one of the season's most promising, idiosyncratic new writers."

While Christine DeZelar-Tiedman in the *Library Journal* admires the stories that center on the mother, she finds that "the Rebecca stories are less compelling; what we get are mostly fragmented accounts of bizarre happenings in foreign countries." Criticizing the structure of the work as a whole, she concludes, "We assume that Rebecca's upbringing, along with a family tragedy, has left her unable to commit or find direction, but this connection is never made clear, and the character's self-absorption makes her unsympathetic."

Molly Giles, in her review for the *New York Times Book Review*, suggests a different view. Although "Rebecca's more poetic narratives rely on interwoven segments that often form an uneven collage," Giles finds solid connections between her stories and those pertaining to Marion, the mother. Giles writes that "their stories are small, elegiac and inconclusive" with "many quick flashes of beauty." She argues that at its best moments, the collection "goes far, and takes us with it."

Couples sitting outside a café in Paris © Owen Franken/Corbis

Criticism

Wendy Perkins

Perkins is a professor of American and English literature and film. In this essay, Perkins examines the tensions between illusion and reality in the story.

In her short story "Paris 1991," Kate Walbert immediately contrasts light and dark. The story opens with Rebecca's arrival by plane "into the city of light [where] she descends in darkness." This first juxtaposition of light and dark imagery illustrates the tension between illusion and reality in the story, as Rebecca's fanciful imagination clashes with the evidence of her emotional emptiness. Paris's "gray storm-ridden sky" colored "a strange mauve" forecasts a confirmation of her sense of meaninglessness rather than the prospect of a significance for which she has been searching.

Rebecca believes that the famously romantic city is a perfect setting for conceiving a baby. She yearns for something to provide her with a sense of meaning, to alleviate the ennui of her life. She decided impulsively to cut up her diaphragm one evening, waving off her husband's desire to discuss

the idea of having children. Yet, despite her dramatic decision, she remains apparently uncertain.

Rebecca tries to convince Tom to start a family through negation, insisting "there's no good time, really," and telling him, "you either do it or you don't. And we know we don't want to don't, so we might as well do, right?" When he asks if she is sure, she first says no and later refuses to answer him.

While she hopes that a child will make a positive change in her life, her indecision becomes apparent after she and her husband arrive in Paris when, she estimates, "it is the right time, more or less" to try to conceive, a comment that becomes appropriate not only for her hormonal cycle but also for her feelings about getting pregnant. Tom appears indecisive, too, as he twice eats oysters to "get him in the mood." Their obvious ambivalence suggests that her hopes will go unrealized.

The decision to have a baby becomes more of a staged "moment" for Rebecca as she cuts up her diaphragm, part of a move toward making a permanent commitment and giving her life meaning. Another part of the staging is having a romantic Parisian setting for the procreation. Rebecca's active imagination has conjured an image of perfect marital harmony in the city of lights, which should inevitably lead to a purposeful, fulfilled life.

Rebecca frequently creates fictive worlds that are more exciting and adventurous than her own. She determines that "she would like to run through a rainstorm or hunt big game somewhere," One of her favorite games with Tom when they first met was to imagine other lives that they could have led. She saw herself living with a man in Florence or riding elephants in Rajasthan or sitting under the shade of grapevines at the edge of the Aegean. In Paris, she imagines shops with brightly colored clothing and rooms with trays of cognac and "ripe yellow pears, sliced with pearly-handled silver." The city's beauty, the "silver church domes of unimaginable heights," are all meant to convey a thrill, an intense feeling, in which as she becomes pregnant, Rebecca can begin to live the adventure she envisions.

Reality, however, quickly dissolves the fantasy. Before Paris, Rebecca had felt "distracted always, often alone." As soon as they arrive, the sense of disconnection between her and her husband becomes apparent. In the cab ride, Tom speaks without looking at her, and later, when she tells him she is hungry, Tom is asleep. Often "she finds herself looking at [Tom] as if he is entirely unfamiliar to her, a blind date, or somebody's cousin she has agreed to meet."

Rebecca and Tom "came to [Paris to] find conversation, a way of being two together," but after they arrive, they sit in cafés and "have nothing to say" to each other. Rebecca acknowledges "the city of light's gone dark" for them. "She had thought that to be in Paris with a husband meant to be bent, head to head, in discussion" as they walked the streets. "She would like to tell him certain things, what she has done or imagined she has done before this moment in her life, but every time she opens her mouth to start a conversation she feels tired." The setting does not change their relationship or the detachment she feels from him.

Rebecca's impulse to focus on foreign locales comes from her mother, Marion, who has recently died. With her mother much in her thoughts, Rebecca admits that she often sees Marion "in doorways, crossing the street." Marion taught Rebecca her favorite imagining game and had herself dreamed of coming to Paris, which suggests that she had similar fantasies of finding happiness through adventure. After buying a fanciful postcard with swooning devils, "sharp-eared men with pointy noses, tiny fingernails, hovering on the

> **" Rebecca frequently creates fictive worlds that are more exciting and adventurous than her own."**

shoulders of gentle women," Rebecca insists to Tom, "Marion would have loved this. I could have sent it with a note, Having a devilish good time. She'd think we were running nude in fountains or something." She "would have thought it very cosmopolitan." These remarks suggest that Rebecca is evaluating her present experience in light of Marion's likely assessment of them.

The fictive nature of Rebecca's fantasies for her mother, however, becomes evident when Rebecca tries to imagine her there. When she suggests that Marion "would have come to the city in better weather, and would have sat out in the cafés and watched the people and met some dashing Frenchman," Tom counters with a note of reality, insisting, "Marion would have hated the food." Similarly, Rebecca's illusions about what the city will provide for her are eventually dispelled by the reality of her experience there.

Faced with their inability to connect with each other, Rebecca and Tom determine that "there is nothing else to do" but walk in the rain, which becomes "tiny tears" to her. "[T]hey both feel awkward, as if they are watched from every window, their actions exaggerated, their voices loud and shrill." The romance of the city becomes impossible to find when they must bundle up in long underwear and heavy coats to try to ward off the cold, "aware of their numb feet and runny noses, aware of the bare trees."

The story ends with an elusive description of the couple having intercourse, Rebecca drifting away from the moment, imagining herself "borne out of this place to another." Though she had resolved to "live in the moment," in this moment of hoped-for impregnation, she locates herself elsewhere, trying to imagine the unborn waiting for the chance to be born.

Fantasy and the reality of the moment merge in Rebecca's final vision of a carriage containing

What Do I Read Next?

- Walbert's *The Gardens of Kyoto: A Novel* (2001) focuses on the experiences of two cousins prior to World War II.

- Walbert's *Our Kind* (2004) chronicles the lives of a group of women in the 1950s who struggle against the social restrictions of the age.

- *The Awakening*, first published in 1899, is Kate Chopin's long-suppressed novel of a young woman who struggles and fails to resolve the conflicting roles of wife and artist. This novel depicts the upper-class social roles of Creole wives living in New Orleans at the end of the nineteenth century.

- "To Room Nineteen" (1963), by Doris Lessing, follows a British housewife's slow descent into madness as she confronts what she sees as the meaninglessness of life in the suburbs as a wife and mother. This story appears in Doris Lessing's *A Man and Two Women* (1963).

a woman, "a mother, a daughter, a goddess," suggesting her unborn daughter, her mother, and herself, "all of them hovering, waiting to descend, waiting to be asked." The problem Rebecca has faced during her time in Paris is the conflict between her desire to fulfill her mother's romantic illusions of travel and her own desire to establish roots. The merging of these three images at the close of the story suggests Rebecca's persistent tendency to entertain the fantasy rather than take concrete steps to change her life. Here, she imagines attaining meaning through the advent of a child, meaning that eluded her in seeing Paris with her husband.

The story ends inconclusively. As she and her husband have sexual intercourse, Rebecca's fantasy images are described, a composite of female figures in a carriage. All the images, along with babies and devils, present a notion of possi-

bility and expectation, but what actually those images have to do with Rebecca and Tom's future remains undetermined. The tension between desire and fulfillment remains, with Rebecca's focus on potential.

Source: Wendy Perkins, Critical Essay on "Paris 1991," in *Short Stories for Students*, Thomson Gale, 2007.

Anna Maria Hong

Hong is a poet and the editor of a fiction and memoir anthology. In this essay, Hong discusses how Walbert uses the motifs of color and light to portray her protagonist's inner and outer landscapes.

As the title indicates, Walbert's short story "Paris 1991" takes place in Paris in 1991, with a couple flashbacks to New York and California during the immediate years before. Setting the story in Paris, the city of light, enables Walbert to invoke the motif of light, which she does to several effects. Walbert also makes use of Paris's reputation for romance and its fame as a center of the arts and a magnet for imaginative, artistic people. Using the city's unique history and visual qualities, Walbert is able also to employ a motif of color. The author uses both light and color to elucidate her protagonist's state of mind and desires and to show the difference between those longings and the reality the protagonist experiences.

The protagonist of the story is Rebecca, an American woman, probably in her mid-thirties, who has come to Paris from New York with her husband, Tom, to try to conceive a baby. They have apparently flown to Paris on a whim, assuming the city to be the best place in which to become pregnant. The decision to have the baby is a bit sudden for the couple, who debated the issue for a while, and the choice is partly driven by the recent death of Rebecca's mother, Marion. In the wake of her mother's death, Rebecca wants to live spontaneously with "no regrets, no sorrow. Only the next day and the next." Rebecca thinks of Marion often while on the trip, as her grief about her is still fresh.

Walbert makes it clear that the couple is trying to revitalize their relationship. Their growing apart over the years has impelled the decision to try to have a baby, something new. Toward the beginning of the story, the narrator says, "They came to Paris impromptu; this is how Rebecca would tell it. In truth, they came to find conversation, a way of being two together."

The couple is no longer young, and the evidence for their aging lies in the gray streaks in Rebecca's hair and in Tom's beard. Walbert uses a palette of colors to signal different things. Gray, unsurprisingly, shows up in the story as a sign of age and also of grim reality, contrasting sharply with the reds, blues, and yellows that appear at key points.

Walbert employs colors in a painterly way; the striking use of color is apparent from the story's opening paragraph in which she describes Rebecca and Tom's arrival in Paris:

> Into the city of light she descends in darkness. Or this is how Rebecca hears it: I descend on the city of light in darkness. A gray storm-ridden sky, clouds bunched in fat grape colors, a strange mauve. The city of stone streaked with pigeon [sh——t], ripped rock-and-roll posters. A poet's place.

Unfortunately for Rebecca, Paris continues to thwart her expectations for it to be utterly romantic, and again Walbert shows Rebecca's disappointment through her descriptions of the city's colors. Many of the things Rebecca sees in Paris are gray toned. In addition to the sky and the stone, she sees a gray river, gray steps going to the national library, and pigeons with wings that are "white and gray-speckled." The grayness is also apparent in the fading of the famous Parisian light, and Rebecca frequently notices light waning during the visit.

This waning light reinforces the state the couple is in, as they have arrived at a point in their relationship when excitement has to be summoned, and they find being together somewhat challenging. After looking for a café "that looks romantic," they settle into a place only to find that they have nothing to say to each other. Distressed by this fact, Rebecca looks out the window and remarks, "The city of light's gone dark." As in the opening paragraph, Walbert invokes the motif of light to point up the difference between what Rebecca longs for and what she knows in her heart is true.

However, the couple is also not entirely doomed, and as they work to regain a sense of connection and bonhomie with each other, Rebecca also experiences moments suffused with bright, intense colors whose life and vitality contrast with the depressing urban grays she sees in the Parisian landscape. Notably, she sees these vivid colors while either looking upon an actual scene in Paris or imagining some extension of what she sees. Watching a woman across the street from their

> **In the story's last paragraph, as elsewhere, Walbert employs the well established motifs of light and color to depict Rebecca's longings and the richness of the character's imaginative capacities."**

apartment, Rebecca sees her lighting candles, as well as "Red geraniums in clay pots, cobalt blue shutters."

The scene is one of domestic warmth, and after the woman closes the shutters, Rebecca imagines the woman preparing the table as for a sensual late meal with cognac, "ripe, yellow pears, sliced with pearly-handled silver. Heirlooms passed down in worn wooden chests, kept in corners covered in maroon velvet; everything draped with a soft worn fabric." The colors are vibrant, the fabrics supple, and as she continues her reverie, Rebecca also envisions the woman's black hair shining in the light, as well as a succession of women. Rebecca imagines that the woman has learned to brush her hair in a certain way from her mother who learned it from her grandmother and on and on back through the generations.

In this scene and several others, Walbert employs light and vivid colors to illustrate Rebecca's desire for a richer, warmer life. The colors and light signify how she wants things to be and her wish to join a maternal line of women. In the story's penultimate scene, Rebecca tells Tom how she imagines her mother would be in Paris. She pictures her in a "kelly green coat," enjoying a romance with a French stranger. Although Tom dryly circumvents Rebecca's fantasy for her mother by saying she would have hated the food, Rebecca here again succeeds in imbuing her inner life with a kind of intensity and colorful passion that goes beyond her reality. Green appears nowhere else in the story.

In another scene, she lights white candles in a church and thinks of both her mother and her possible future baby, mourning and conflating both female relatives as she says, "'Poor Marion, poor Sophie.'" (Sophie is the name Tom suggested for their baby.) In this scene, light again suggests life, while white suggests neutrality and the place life may come from.

The shade of white is different both from the vitality of colors and the dullness of gray, and as with the other colors in the spectrum, white appears both in the landscape of Paris and in Rebecca's memory. Tom's socks are white, as were the walls of his stucco house in California—the house he lived in while they were courting. In addition to the church candles and the wings of birds and their droppings, Rebecca's skin after her arrival in Paris is described as white "mottled with pink from cold, from rain."

Pink suggests possible pregnancy for Rebecca, as the color is often associated with babies (especially the baby pink of female babies) and is only mentioned again at the end of the story after the couple has had sexual intercourse. As she lies in bed, Rebecca thinks of babies as "cherubs pink as the angels in the illuminated manuscripts," and she feels a soul debating whether to become her child.

In the story's last paragraph, as elsewhere, Walbert employs the well established motifs of light and color to depict Rebecca's longings and the richness of the character's imaginative capacities. She imagines the cobblestones outside shining beneath the window and "a carriage, a woman behind the shuttered carriage windows, her hand gloved in white velvet, her body swathed in fresh silk: a princess, a saint, a mother, a daughter, a goddess borne out of this place to another." She thinks of the other place as the world where babies, devils, and everyone else resides while waiting to be born. It is a kind of eternity.

The concluding passage echoes the earlier one, in which Rebecca imagines a line of women passing on knowledge to their daughters. The unnamed woman in this passage wears white, symbolizing the other world, and as in all of Rebecca's imaginings, the fabrics are glamorous and soft, contrasting with the itchy wool the characters actually wear throughout the story. This third motif of texture or the tactile further enriches the themes Walbert expresses by invoking light and color—the themes of individual longing, loneliness within marriage, and the sometimes painful gap between what people desire and what they experience.

Source: Anna Maria Hong, Critical Essay on "Paris 1991," in *Short Stories for Students*, Thomson Gale, 2007.

Contemporary Authors Online

In the following essay, the critic gives an overview of Walbert's work.

Kate Walbert, who teaches writing at Yale University, is the author of *Where She Went*, a collection of fourteen interconnected stories focusing on a mother and a daughter. The first half of the book is the story of the mother, Marion, who moves to New York City from Indiana and works as a secretary with an insurance firm. After a year she meets Robert Clark, an efficiency expert, and they become engaged after three dates. "Niagara Falls 1955" begins Marion's story and describes the couple's honeymoon. Marion's life becomes rootless, forced as she is to relocate from city to city as her husband's career dictates. They have a daughter Rebecca, and a second daughter who dies while an infant, causing Marion to suffer depression and to attempt suicide.

The second half of the book details Rebecca's travels to Europe and her love affairs. Marion lives vicariously through postcards she receives from Rebecca detailing her adventures. "A reluctant surrogate, Rebecca wanders through France, Jamaica, Italy and Turkey obediently trying to experience the glamour, romance and adventure her mother feels she has missed," wrote Molly Giles in the *New York Times Book Review*, which named the collection one of its notable books for 1998 and praised its many "quick flashes of beauty." Rebecca returns to New York, takes a job as a typist at a newspaper, and edits children's books. A second trip to Europe is disappointing, but she fabricates news to send back to the expectant Marion. Rebecca eventually marries a California sculptor. "Rebecca, like her mother, is unable to articulate the root of her unhappiness," commented critic Don Lee, reviewing the novel in *Ploughshares*. "Travel and marriage have only accentuated the sadness of mislaid, unrealized lives." Reviewer Nancy Pearl, writing for *Booklist*, felt that "Walbert's use of a fractured narrative works like a prism to reveal the broken lives of her two main characters." A *Publishers Weekly* reviewer felt the vignettes to sometimes be "precious and overworked. . . . At their frequent best . . . they resonate with a surprising pathos," and considered Walbert to be "one of the season's most promising, idiosyncratic new writers."

Source: Contemporary Authors Online, "Kate Walbert," in *Contemporary Authors Online*, Thomson Gale, 2004.

Sources

Colton-Heins, Alyssa B., "Kate Walbert: Writing and Reading Women and War," in *Women Writers*, December 1, 2001, http://www.womenwriters.net/Winter2001/walbert.html (accessed May 7, 2006).

DeZelar-Tiedman, Christine, Review of *Where She Went*, in *Library Journal*, June 15, 1998, p. 110.

Giles, Molly, "Wanderlust," in *New York Times Book Review*, October 11, 1998, p. 19.

Lee, Don, Review of *Where She Went*, in *Ploughshares*, Vol. 24, No. 2–3, Fall 1998, pp. 233–34.

Pearl, Nancy, Review of *Where She Went*, in *Booklist*, Vol. 94, No. 19–20, June 1, 1998, p. 1730.

Review of *Where She Went*, in *Publishers Weekly*, June 15, 1998, pp. 42–43.

Walbert, Kate, "Paris 1991," in *Where She Went*, Sarabande Books, 1998, pp.13–25.

Further Reading

Coen, Stephanie, ed., *American Theatre Book of Monologues for Women*, Theatre Communications Group, 2003.
The monologues included in this text were selected from plays by authors such as Wendy Wasserstein, Edward Albee, and Sam Shepard, published in *American Theatre* magazine.

Downie, David, *Paris, Paris: Journey into the City of Light*, Transatlantic Press, 2005.
This exploration of Paris, written by an American expatriot, looks at the sites and the culture of Paris.

Friday, Nancy, *My Mother/My Self*, Delta, 1997.
Nancy Friday explores the often complex relationship between mothers and daughters, seeking to show the mirroring that occurs in many of these relationships.

Millet, Kate, *Sexual Politics*, Doubleday, 1970.
This work outlines women's fight for equality during the middle of the twentieth century as well as the history and dynamics of feminism.

Someone to Talk To

Deborah Eisenberg

1993

Deborah Eisenberg's "Someone to Talk To" first appeared in the *New Yorker* magazine on September 27, 1993. Four years later, it was included in her fourth collection of short stories, entitled *All Around Atlantis*. The story chronicles the journey of concert pianist Aaron Shapiro, fresh from a breakup with his longtime girlfriend, to an unspecified Latin American country where he is scheduled to perform his first concert in many years. When he arrives, he learns that the concert promoters are affiliated with the oppressive military regime that is currently in power.

Deborah Eisenberg traveled extensively throughout Central America in the 1980s, and several of her short stories are set in this region, exploring themes of oppression, persecution, and the indifference that allows these things to continue. The relationship between the powerful and the powerless is examined through the eyes of Shapiro, who is powerless himself, unable to halt the downward spiral of his career or the failure of his relationship.

Author Biography

Deborah Eisenberg was born in Chicago, Illinois, on November 20, 1945. She grew up in Winnetka, a middle-class Chicago suburb. Her father, George, was a pediatrician, and her mother, Ruth, was a housewife. As one of the few Jewish students at her school, wearing a full-torso brace to correct her

scoliosis, Eisenberg was a misfit and, according to Dinitia Smith, a self-admitted "behavior problem." Her parents responded by sending her to boarding school in Vermont in the early 1960s. Afterwards, she stayed on in Vermont to attend Marlboro College, studying Latin and Greek. Then Eisenberg left Vermont for New York City, where she earned a B.A. at the New School for Social Research in 1968.

Eisenberg worked in New York for seven years as a secretary and waitress before she became a writer. It was during this time that she met actor Wallace Shawn, whose father was then the editor of the *New Yorker*. They fell in love, and Shawn encouraged her to begin writing. At first, she concentrated on writing for the stage; her play, *Pastorale*, was produced by the Second Stage Theatre in 1981. In the mid-1980s, Eisenberg traveled throughout Latin America, an experience that influenced her work for years to come. She claims to have traveled to every country in Central America except Costa Rica and Belize. These were turbulent political times in Latin America, and Eisenberg witnessed firsthand the stark contrast between the privileged classes and the oppressed native peoples, a contrast that features prominently in many of her stories, including "Someone to Talk To."

Transactions in a Foreign Currency, Eisenberg's first collection of short stories, was published in 1986, earning many favorable reviews. The title story won Eisenberg the first of her four O. Henry Awards. In 1987, she received the PEN Hemingway Citation, the Mrs. Giles Foundation Award, a Guggenheim fellowship, and the Whiting Foundation Award. In the late 1980s and early 1990s, she also spent several years teaching, first at Washington University in St. Louis and later at the University of Iowa, as part of the Iowa Writers' Workshop.

In 1992, Eisenberg published her second short-story collection, *Under the 82nd Airborne*. Though some critics felt it lacked the intensity of her first collection, this new volume garnered Eisenberg more awards; in 1993, she was given the Friends of American Writers Award, the Ingram-Merrill Foundation Grant, and the Award for Literature from the American Academy of Arts and Sciences.

During the mid-1990s, Eisenberg continued to teach, both at the City College of New York and New York University. In 1997, her first two collections were re-released in one volume, entitled *The Stories (So Far) of Deborah Eisenberg*. Later the same year, she published a new collection, entitled *All Around Atlantis*, in which the story "Someone to Talk To" appeared. Many critics considered this

Deborah Eisenberg   Paul Hawthorne/Getty Images

collection to be her best yet, and the stories "Across the Lake" and "Mermaids" were both O. Henry Award winners (in 1995 and 1997, respectively).

In 1999, Eisenberg took on a new role: actress. She appeared in the play "The Designated Mourner," written by her longtime companion, Wallace Shawn. She did not abandon writing for acting, however. In 2000, she won the Rea Award for the Short Story, and in 2002, her story "Like It or Not" won her yet another O. Henry Award. In January 2006, she released her fifth collection of stories, *Twilight of the Superheroes*, which includes "Like It or Not" and a story entitled "Some Other, Better Otto," which was originally published in the *Yale Review* and chosen for *Best American Short Stories 2004*.

As of 2006, Eisenberg was continuing to write and was teaching writing each fall at the University of Virginia. When she was not teaching in Virginia, she was living in Manhattan with Wallace Shawn.

Plot Summary

The story begins as Caroline, Aaron Shapiro's live-in girlfriend of six years, is leaving him for another man (identified only as "Jim"). She leaves him with both a broken heart and her cat, ironically named

Lady Chatterley ("Jim, evidently, was allergic"). As she walks out the door, she tells Aaron, "I'll always care about you, you know."

In the next scene, Aaron wakes up in a shabby hotel somewhere in Latin America, and as he reminisces about his relationship with Caroline, the reader learns that Aaron is a concert pianist who was once hailed as a star on the rise, but lately he has been forced to make ends meet by giving piano lessons to "startlingly untalented children." Shapiro's growing depression over his failing career (and the related financial difficulties) gradually eroded his relationship with Caroline, whose privileged background made it difficult for her to understand Shapiro's anxieties about money. Ironically, it was when the relationship was already damaged beyond repair that Shapiro received an invitation to play his first big concert in years in Latin America. (The country is not specified but bears a strong resemblance to Guatemala.)

Still reeling from Caroline's departure, Aaron leaves his tiny hotel room and heads to the hotel restaurant to meet with Richard Penwad, a representative of the group staging the concert. Pompous and elitist, Penwad is clearly uncomfortable in Shapiro's presence, as though he considers him one of the lower classes, like the ragged, emaciated native Indians who wait on them in the restaurant. During his conversation with Penwad, Aaron learns that the group sponsoring the concert is affiliated with the military government in power, the same government that has brutally oppressed and persecuted these native people. Uncomfortable with this knowledge, Shapiro reminds himself of his money woes: "Fee plus lessons, minus rent, minus utilities."

After breakfast, Penwad drives Aaron to the Arts Center for rehearsal. As the orchestra begins to play, Shapiro is horrified; "the sound was so peculiar that he feared he was suffering from some neurological damage." However, once Aaron himself begins to play, he realizes the problem is the acoustics of the concert hall. He struggles with the concerto, a piece written by a Latin American composer; Shapiro had premiered the concerto himself seventeen years earlier at the height of his career.

After the discomfiting rehearsal, Shapiro proceeds to an interview (arranged by Penwad) with an English journalist named Beale. He meets Beale at a large, ostentatious hotel where, Shapiro realizes, "they'd put an *important* musician." Beale is an odd-looking character, described as having a spaceship-shaped head, wearing a stain-spattered suit and a tie made of rope. Though he is supposed

to be interviewing Shapiro, he does most of the talking himself, espousing his personal theories on a variety of topics, most notably the beauty of the country and the tragedy of what has happened to the native Indians. He gets increasingly drunk throughout the "interview"; at one point, he implies that Shapiro is gay, and at another, he takes him to task for being American: "Dare I mention whose country it was that killed *all* their Indians?"

Beale is so insufferable that Shapiro excuses himself to use the phone, just to get away from him. When he returns to the table, he finds Beale speaking urgently into his tape recorder; when Shapiro arrives, he turns it off "with a bright smile, as though he'd been apprehended in some mild debauchery." With Aaron back at the table, Beale continues his monologue, this time waxing rhapsodic over the wonders of radio: "You haven't a friend in the world, then you turn on the radio, and someone's talking to *you*."

Though the pompous Penwad and his wife are scheduled to pick him up and show him around the next morning, Shapiro slips out early to avoid them and see the city himself. He wanders through the grand neighborhoods of the wealthy and then through poor parts of the city where the starving and destitute live on the streets. He is reminded of the homeless in the city where he lives, who terrify him. The more he struggles to pay his bills, the less unimaginable their plight appears. He searches their faces "for proof that each was in some reliable way different from him."

As he continues his walk, he thinks of Caroline, who would choose to simply ignore the existence of such people. Finally, he stops at a small restaurant for a bowl of soup. At the next table are three large men all carrying pistols. When they see Shapiro staring at them, one of the men reaches up and unscrews the light bulb from the lamp over their table.

Later that evening, Shapiro performs the concerto at the acoustically challenged hall. When he had performed the piece seventeen years earlier, his performance was described as "*affirming*." Now, in this hall, though he does his best, "it had simply sat over them all—a great, indestructible, affirming block of suet."

Outside the hall after the concert, Penwad and his wife approach Aaron and point out notable dignitaries and other members of elite society, including the woman who is hosting a reception for Shapiro at her home that evening. Her haughty son stops to talk to Shapiro, and in the midst of their conversation, the journalist Beale approaches, sloppily eating an orange. He apologizes to Shapiro for getting drunk during their interview. The pompous youth with whom Shapiro has been talking makes a rude comment, indicating that Beale is not welcome at the reception. Shapiro is appalled, and Beale is livid, calling the boy a "Little putrid viper." Joan, Penwad's snobbish wife, beckons to Shapiro, saying it is time to leave for the reception. He joins her, but before he leaves, he wants to find Beale, feeling bad for him. He searches and finally locates him, "crouched in the corner of a concrete trough that must have been intended as some sort of reflecting pool." He is talking into his tape recorder, describing the elegant party to which he has not been invited. He speaks tenderly, almost as if talking to a lover, describing the Indian children of the servants playing a game near the fountain and reminiscing about the beauty of the country before the war. Finally, he puts the tape recorder behind his head like a pillow, and stretches out in the trough for a nap. The last thing he tells the recorder is, "everyone has something, some little thing, my darling, they've been waiting so long to tell you."

Characters

Beale

Beale is the English radio journalist who interviews Shapiro. Actually, he does very little interviewing and spends most of the time voicing his own opinions. Though at first Beale appears to be a minor character, the author uses him as a spokesperson for her views on the oppression of the native people and the beauty of the country. By having these weighty themes voiced by such an odd, buffoonish character, Eisenberg is able to avoid sounding pedantic.

Psychologically, Beale appears to be a bit unstable. He rambles uncontrollably, drinks too much, and holds tender, clandestine conversations with his tape recorder. At the interview lunch with Shapiro, Beale wears a "tie that appeared to be made of rope," a noose-like image that adds to his unhinged persona. Yet it is Beale who gives the story its title: he is so desperate for "someone to talk to," he has invented his own listener. This basic human need, the need to be heard, is an important theme in the story.

Caroline

Aaron Shapiro's longtime girlfriend, Caroline, who leaves him in the opening scene, represents the kind of benign indifference often shown to the oppressed and suffering in this story. As Eisenberg describes her: "She despised no one. Those who were not nice, pleasant, happy simply ceased to exist." Not surprisingly, as Aaron's star began to fade and he became troubled and depressed, Caroline became uncomfortable. Rather than real empathy, she offered Aaron empty platitudes, such as "Things will work out," and "Something will turn up."

Caroline comes from a privileged background, and her attitude matches that of the wealthy patrons of the arts who attend Shapiro's concert. They live in grand mansions just moments away from the neighborhoods of native Indians who are starving and destitute. They ignore the plight of these people because they are not pleasant or happy.

Umberto García-Gutiérrez

García-Gutiérrez, a fictional Latin-American composer, wrote the concerto Shapiro performs at the concert. He is a "great tree of a man," powerful and imposing. He is also apparently gay and interested in Shapiro. The fact that Shapiro premiered García-Gutiérrez's concerto seventeen years earlier, when his star was still on the rise, drives home the vast difference between Shapiro's career now and his career then.

Native Indians

The native peoples of this country, who have been oppressed, tortured, and massacred by the government, are a constant presence in the story. Ironically, the only person in the story who refers to them directly is Beale. When Shapiro notices the "fuming slums" while surveying the landscape with Penwad, Penwad blames the conditions on a recent earthquake then quickly turns the conversation back to the architecture of the Center for the Arts, which "survived intact." Penwad's wife, Joan, appears to be repulsed by the Indians, yet she is eager to show Shapiro the city's Institute of Indigenous Textiles.

Joan Penwad

Richard Penwad's snobbish wife, Joan, is more openly derisive towards the native Indians than her husband; when Richard mentions that they left Shapiro messages at the desk of his hotel, Joan excuses Shapiro by commenting, "Well . . . those *people* at the desk." Apparently unaware of her own hypocrisy, she is enthusiastic about the Institute of Indigenous Textiles and the "cross-fertilization" of native and modern motifs in the work of local architect Santiago Mendez.

Richard Penwad

Penwad is the pompous representative of the group sponsoring Shapiro's concert. He carefully avoids any mention of the native Indians or what is happening in the country. He seems wary of Shapiro as well; he grimaces when Shapiro shakes his hand and afterward "glanced at his palm," as if Shapiro might pass on some sort of contaminant.

There are hints that Penwad is a bit dominated by his wife; he voices her opinions of the center's architecture, rather than his own, and when offering to show Shapiro the area, he says, "Joan has her own ideas, but you must say what interests *you*." He does not offer any suggestions of his own.

Aaron Shapiro

Aaron Shapiro, the story's main character, is a concert pianist who once was considered a star on the rise; however, this potential was never realized. His career peaked in his twenties, and now he frets constantly about paying his bills, going over figures in his head: "Rent, plus utilities, plus insurance, minus lessons, plus food."

Though the reader is privy to Aaron's thoughts and emotions, he says very little throughout the story. He is continually interrupted or overshadowed by the words of those around him—the verbose Beale, pompous Richard Penwad and his wife, even the haughty son of his hostess. He talks to Caroline, but to no avail; "If he spoke truthfully to her, she couldn't hear him." Even when he has an opportunity to speak, he is unable to seize it. When Beale stops talking for a rare moment during their interview, "Shapiro opened his mouth; a blob of sound came out." Though to Penwad and others in the story the lines between classes are distinctly drawn, Shapiro has begun to realize how little separates him from the homeless people on the street, and it terrifies him.

Themes

Loneliness and the Need to Be Heard

The main character of "Someone to Talk To," Aaron Shapiro, is coping with the departure of his live-in girlfriend of six years. In addition, he is far from home, in an unfamiliar country torn by years of civil war. As the story progresses and the reader learns more of Aaron's history, it becomes clear that even when Caroline was still living with him,

he was dealing with loneliness of a different form—the loneliness of not being heard or understood. Caroline did not want to hear anything from Aaron that contradicted her view of the world as a happy, benign place where troubles are temporary and easily remedied.

To compound this sense of isolation and impotence, not a single character in the story really listens to Aaron Shapiro. Penwad and his wife are too wrapped up in themselves to care, especially since they consider Shapiro to be beneath them, socially. Ironically, Beale is so consumed by his own need to be heard and understood that he talks almost incessantly, leaving Shapiro few opportunities to speak at all. The reader gets a sense of Beale's lonely childhood from the speech he makes about the wonders of radio: "It's raining outside, your mum's still working in the shop, you haven't a friend in the world, then you turn on the radio, and someone's talking—to *you*." Perhaps this is why Shapiro feels sympathetic towards Beale at the end of the story, when Beale is insulted by the haughty young man at the concert; Shapiro recognizes that he and Beale are searching for the same thing: someone to talk to, someone who will actually listen and understand.

Shapiro is even thwarted when he attempts to express himself through his music. The acoustics of the hall are so poor that the sound "sloshed and bulged, gummed up in clumps, liquefied, as though the air were full of whirling blades."

On a larger scale, the persecuted native peoples of this country are also without a voice. As Shapiro walks through the poor neighborhoods of these people, they are described as "People who were almost invisible, almost inaudible. People to whom almost anything could be done: *other* people." Their cries for help are unheeded by the wealthy elite, who choose, as Caroline would, to ignore them and their unhappy, unpleasant situation.

Indifference

The attitude that Caroline takes towards Aaron's despair is similar to the attitude that the wealthy elite takes towards the poor and suffering in their country. Caroline is described as being "deeply sympathetic with, and at the same time deeply insensitive to, the distress of others." In the same way, the wealthy people here employ the native people as servants, admire their art and textiles in museums, and yet choose to ignore their desperate living conditions and starving children. Even

Topics For Further Study

- Why is the name of Caroline's cat, Lady Chatterley, an ironic choice by Eisenberg? Research the name and write a paragraph explaining the meaning behind it. Can you think of other names for the cat that would be equally ironic, given Aaron's situation?

- The country and political problems described strongly resemble Guatemala, but Eisenberg does not specify this country in her story. Research the geography and history of some other countries in the region. Choose another country in which the story could take place, and write a paragraph explaining why you chose that particular location. Find a map of the country and include it with your writing.

- Beale criticizes the United States for its treatment of its own native people. Compare the treatment of the native Mayans in this story with the way Native Americans have been treated in the United States. In what ways are the two situations similar and/or different? Make a side-by-side chart comparing the two situations. Include the different rationales given for the persecution of the native people.

- While people know that the number of homeless people in the United States rose dramatically during the 1980s, definite statistics concerning the exact number of the homeless are not available. Why do you think it is so hard to count the homeless population? List three reasons. Then find statistics estimating the homeless population in the United States in the 1970s, 1980s, 1990s and 2000s, and draw a graph showing the changes.

Beale, who laments the plight of the native Indians at length, does not mention any plans or theories for improving the situation.

On a more political scale, this criticism is extended to the United States. First, Beale makes his comment about how Americans "killed *all* their Indians." Secondly, if readers assume that the country in this story is Guatemala, much of the suffering in that country was aggravated by the aggressive U.S. support of any non-communist government that sought power. In an effort to keep communism off America's doorstep, the United States aided ruthless political groups that persecuted, tortured, and murdered thousands and thousands of native Indians from the 1950s through the 1980s. Yet few Americans were aware of or interested in the situation. As Eisenberg says in an interview included in the paperback version of *All Around Atlantis*, "In what way can we be said to 'not know' or 'not understand' certain things that are happening very much within the compass of information available to us?"

Class Distinctions

Within the story, there are definite distinctions between classes of people. At the top are wealthy elite who support the arts, such as Penwad and his wife, and the hostess of Shapiro's reception. Penwad's discomfort in dealing with Shapiro indicates that he considers him a step below him on the class scale, perhaps because Shapiro is Jewish, or simply because he is a musician, and not a particularly prominent one. Beale, with his odd way of dressing and his slovenly manners, is clearly lower on the scale than Shapiro, so low that even the son of Shapiro's hostess has no qualms about insulting him to his face. At the very bottom of the scale are the native Indians, whom the elite consider so insignificant they never even mention them directly, even though they encounter them often as servants. Only Joan refers to them at all, and she calls them "those *people*."

Shapiro realizes where he stands with the elite group; after the concert when Joan summons him to leave for the reception, tugging the lapel of his tuxedo, he reflects that "He might just as well be wearing grease-stained overalls with his name embroidered on the pocket." To them, he is an employee, one more servant, summoned for their amusement.

Even the locations where people live are arranged according to class, from lowest to highest. Down at the bottom are the ravines, "encrusted with fuming slums," where the native peoples live. Further up on the hills are the homes of people like Penwad and his wife, and then, highest on the slope is the "Gold Zone," where the most powerful and wealthy reside.

Style

Point of View

"Someone to Talk To" is written in the third person limited omniscient; however, because the reader has access to only Aaron Shapiro's thoughts and emotions, and no one else's, the effect is similar to that of a first-person narrative. This is important, because otherwise readers would not experience the psychological upheaval that Aaron is going through, thrown from an emotionally jarring situation—his breakup with Caroline—straight into the physical and mental disorientation of traveling to a foreign country. For example, Aaron's performance at the concert is satisfactory—the composer himself commends Aaron afterwards—but to Aaron it is all a confusing blur: "Shapiro felt as though he'd awakened to find himself squatting naked in a glade, blinking up at a chortling TV crew that had just filmed him gnawing a huge bone. Had he played well or badly? He hardly knew." Similarly, when he is sitting in the small restaurant after walking through the poor neighborhoods of the Indians, he falls into a reverie and sees Caroline in his mind's eye. He says, "Caroline," but afterward, he is unsure whether he has actually spoken the name aloud or just thought it. Because only Aaron's thoughts are expressed, the reader experiences the same uncertainty.

Setting

The Latin American country to which Aaron travels figures prominently in the story. In particular, seeing the abject poverty of the native Indians forces Aaron to confront his own terror about his failing career and precarious finances and to realize the fine line between "ordinary" people like him and the homeless people camped out near his own home in the city. Moreover, he realizes that in the minds of the wealthy snobs who have hired him, that line is even finer, in terms of class distinction.

The beauty of the countryside provides a stark contrast to what is happening to its native people. Though Eisenberg uses few words to describe the landscape, more than one character refers to its beauty. When Shapiro takes his long walk through the city, he notes that "beyond the surrounding slopes lay the countryside—the gorgeous, blood-drenched countryside." Later, the hostess of Shapiro's reception is described as having a "blood-red mouth," linking her and the other wealthy concert goers to the war and strife brought about by the oppressive government.

Travel is a common theme in Eisenberg's work, often throwing her characters off-balance. In a 1992 interview in the *New York Times Book Review*, Eisenberg describes this disorientation: "The thing that guides you in the ordinary round of your day is not there—the stability that carries you from one moment to the next is gone." This disruption underscores the unsettled and vulnerable feelings of people who are financially at risk or who have been financially stable and now experience abject poverty because of an oppressive governmental takeover.

Humor

Though "Someone to Talk To" is by no means a comedy, Eisenberg uses humor throughout to leaven its weighty themes. Sometimes the humor is more subtle, as in her wry description of Shapiro's piano students: "startlingly untalented children who at best thought of the piano as a defective substitute for something electronic." In her description of the relentlessly chipper Caroline, she writes, "He'd once overheard her saying thank you to a recorded message." Later, Eisenberg describes Shapiro's performance of the concerto, once hailed as "affirming," as "a great, indestructible, affirming block of suet."

Not all of the humor is couched in descriptive passages, however. The interview with Beale contains moments broad enough for vaudeville, such as when Beale takes offense at Shapiro's question regarding how dangerous the country is:

> "I mean, this place is hardly in the league of—I mean, one's forever reading, isn't one? How some poor tourist? Who's saved his pennies for years and years and years. Who then *goes* to New York, to see a show on your great Broad*way*, and virtually the instant he

arrives gets stabbed in the . . .." He took a violent gulp of his drink. "The—"

"Liver," Shapiro said.

"*Sub*way," Beale said.

The humor with which Eisenberg describes Beale and his behavior, and his rambling, loony way of talking, allows her to give Beale the task of voicing some serious themes—persecution of the Indians, for example—without dragging the story down.

Tone

Critics have commented on the dreamlike quality of Eisenberg's stories. In "Someone to Talk To," Aaron Shapiro literally dreams his way through much of the story, due to his preoccupation with Caroline and their breakup. He frequently falls into reveries about their days together. Eisenberg uses language that accentuates his dreamlike state: "The night had been crowded with Caroline and endless versions of her departure—dreamed, reversed in dreams, modified, amended, transfigured, made tender and transcendently beautiful as though it had been an act of sacral purification." Later, when he escapes to a phone booth for a few moments away from the journalist Beale, Eisenberg writes, "Shapiro sat down inside it, shutting himself into an oceanic silence. Beyond the glass wall people floated by—huge, serene, assured, like exhibits." This distorted, surreal feeling is common in Eisenberg's work. In a review of *Under the 82nd Airborne* in the *New York Times Book Review*, reviewer Gary Krist writes that "the overall atmosphere of beleaguered disorientation" is an "Eisenberg trademark."

Historical Context

Guatemala

Though other Central American governments have mounted violent counterinsurgency campaigns, the description of the Indians' persecution in "Someone to Talk To" bears a strong resemblance to the history of Guatemala in the 1980s. Though the Guatemalan army had used death squads to quash insurgents since the 1960s, the slaughter of political dissidents and their alleged supporters reached a bloody peak in the early 1980s, due in part to the strong support of the Reagan administration. In 1983, Reagan lifted an earlier ban on military aid to Guatemala. The United States provided the Guatemalan army with millions of dollars' worth of military assistance, including trucks, jeeps, and aircraft parts, all in an effort to keep communism out of Central America. (Interestingly, it was also Reagan who helped bring about the end of the cold war later in the 1980s, rendering such precautions obsolete.)

The Guatemalan army was quick to label citizens as insurgents; in many cases poor native Indians were simply assumed to be supporters of the Guerilla Army of the Poor (known as the EGP) without proof or investigation, and hundreds of Mayan villages were systematically destroyed. Thousands of Indians were killed, but some managed to escape to the hills, homeless.

The true extent of the atrocities committed by the Guatemalan army, and the complicity of the U.S. government, did not become known to the general American public until the late 1990s, when the Clinton administration declassified a large number of secret documents pertaining to this sad chapter in Guatemalan and U.S. history.

Homelessness in America

An economic recession in the early 1980s, plus large cuts in funding for the Department of Housing and Urban Development (HUD), precipitated a huge increase in the number of homeless people during the 1980s. The rise of crack cocaine, a much cheaper form of the drug than had been available before, further aggravated the problem. Some estimates put the number of homeless during this time as high as two million. While the overall economy improved throughout the 1980s, homelessness remained a problem.

The problem of homelessness was set in sharper relief by the growing gap between the richest and poorest Americans. After the Reagan administration took office in 1981, it relaxed government regulations and taxes for big business, which led to a boom for large corporations. Coupled with the aforementioned cuts made in social programs, the result was that the rich got richer, and the poor got poorer. The social activism of the 1960s had been largely abandoned during the 1970s (dubbed the "Me Decade" by author Tom Wolfe), and this trend continued into the 1980s. Americans became less interested in the ills of society and more focused on their personal ambition and financial success. Consumption of luxury items increased, conspicuous symbols of their owner's success. This attitude was summed up by the evil

Compare & Contrast

- **1980s:** The early 1980s are some of the bloodiest years of the thirty-six-year civil war in Guatemala. Violent counter-insurgency measures taken by the army rage out of control, resulting in the killing of over 100,000 people, including thousands of indigenous Mayan Indians. The violence is aggravated by the financial and military support of the United States, which helps the oppressive government in an effort to keep communism out of Central America.

  Today: The signing of a peace treaty in 1996 ends the civil war. Guatemala is governed by a parliamentary system. The president and parliament are democratically elected every four years, and though corruption still exists in the government, conditions have improved greatly since the 1980s.

- **1980s:** The United States and the Soviet Union are still engaged in the cold war, making the presence of communism in Central America a matter of great concern to the U.S. government.

  Today: The collapse of the Soviet Union in 1991 ends the cold war, making communism in Central America a matter of less importance to the U.S. government. In the 1990s and early 2000s, the United States turns its attention to economic threats posed by volatile governments in the Middle East.

- **1980s:** According to census data, in 1980, 6.4 percent of the U.S. population is Hispanic.

  Today: The percentage of Hispanic Americans in the United States nearly doubles between 1980 and 2000; in 2000, the percentage was 12.5. In 2003, the Census Bureau announces that Hispanics now outnumber blacks in the United States. If Hispanics had constituted such a large segment of the population in the early 1980s, the U.S. government may have found it more difficult politically to aid oppressive governments in Central America.

- **1980s:** Of five Central American countries—Guatemala, El Salvador, Honduras, Costa Rica, and Nicaragua—only Costa Rica has a stable democratic government. Both Guatemala and El Salvador are in the throes of civil war, and Nicaragua's new Sandinista government is undermined by the United States beginning in 1981. The government of Honduras keeps changing hands in the 1970s through coups and then in the 1980s becomes a base of operations for rebels against the Sandinista government in Nicaragua.

  Today: All five Central American countries are democratic republics, with leaders elected by popular vote every four to five years.

Gordon Gecko, a character in the popular 1987 movie *Wall Street*: "Greed is good."

Critical Overview

All Around Atlantis, the short-story collection in which "Someone to Talk To" appears, was critically well received. Two of the stories from the collection, "Across the Lake" and "Mermaids," won O. Henry Awards. "Someone to Talk To," though not considered the best story of the collection by many critics, was occasionally mentioned in reviews.

A reviewer from *Kirkus Reviews* calls the story "superb," and R. Z. Sheppard, in a review for *Time* magazine, specifically praises the character Beale: "In 'Someone to Talk To,' a journalist who won't stop gabbing about himself long enough to ask a question is worthy of Evelyn Waugh." Gail Caldwell of the *Boston Globe*, however, felt that the three stories in the collection set in Central America "suffer from a pedantic overkill on the displaced-imperialist theme." Referring specifically to "Someone to Talk To," she writes, "I felt I was reading a workshop exercise by someone who loved Graham Greene, without being anything like Graham Greene." Jim Shepard of the *New York Times*

Van Cliburn plays the piano during his concert in Moscow, on September 21, 2004

© Dmitry Khrupov/Novye Izvestia/epa/Corbis

Book Review, in an otherwise positive review of the collection, complains briefly of Eisenberg's "fondness for pointedly illuminating chance encounters with eccentrics, who through their ramblings focus the stories' themes while bringing the usually somewhat baffled protagonists up to speed." Though he does not mention the character Beale by name as one of these eccentrics, the description certainly fits.

Many reviews of the collection as a whole, however, were glowing. David Wiegand of the *San Francisco Chronicle* writes, "Deborah Eisenberg . . . seems incapable of writing a bad short story." Shepard affirms, "These stories are spirited and masterly road maps through sad and forbidding and desolate terrain." Eisenberg is known for her offbeat characters, and reviewers often praised her skill in making them both believable and sympathetic. As Wiegand puts it, "So skilled is Eisenberg at developing these characters as engagingly 'ordinary' that we find ourselves identifying with them without realizing how we got there." Caldwell of the *Boston Globe* agrees: "Much of the emotional weight and delivery of Eisenberg's stories owes a debt to her characters. . . . people just two inches weirder than the strange guy next door, or slightly more lunatic than all of us know ourselves to be."

Eisenberg began her writing career as a playwright, and this is most noticeable in her deft handling of dialogue. Her characters speak in short, pithy fragments, pausing to grope for words, sometimes changing subjects in mid-thought, just as people do in real life. As Wendy Brandmark writes in her review of *All Around Atlantis* in the *Times Literary Supplement*, "Her characters speak with the cut and thrust of a taut screenplay; yet they sound completely natural and real." Caldwell says in her review, "The dialogue, reflecting those early dramatist's skills, is crisp and revelatory."

All Around Atlantis, which was released in 1997, was considered by many critics to be Eisenberg's best collection yet. After that she continued to write award-winning short stories, and in 2006, she released another collection entitled *Twilight of the Superheroes*.

Criticism

Laura Pryor

Pryor has a B.A. from the University of Michigan and twenty years experience in professional and creative writing with special interest in fiction. In this essay, Pryor compares the characters Aaron Shapiro and Beale regarding how they communicate with others.

Aaron Shapiro, the protagonist of "Someone To Talk To," has a communication problem. From the opening of the story—an awkward farewell with his longtime girlfriend—to the final scenes of the story outside the concert hall, Shapiro is alternately unable to communicate or prohibited from communicating. When in the course of the story, he is interviewed by a journalist who cannot stop talking, Shapiro's inability to speak up is dramatized literally. In fact, through juxtaposition with Beale, the journalist, Aaron Shapiro's sense of being eclipsed becomes more obvious.

It begins with Caroline's departure. In the opening scene, Aaron is watching the woman with whom he has spent six years of his life walk out his door for the last time. In the entire scene of farewell, Aaron manages just ten words, two of which are spoken to the cat. As he reminisces about the downward spiral of their relationship, the reader learns that "Recently, he'd been silent for whole evenings." When Caroline would call him from work to say she would be late, "her words floated in the air like dying petals while he listened,

"

**Many parallels can be
drawn between Shapiro and
the poor native Indians in
the story."**

reluctant to hang up but unable to think of anything to say." He finally lashes out at her and her hollow reassurances ("Things will work out"), the first honest communication of his feelings, but it comes out far more harshly than he intended: "Was that his voice? Were those his words? He could hardly believe it himself." Ironically, Caroline sounds the death knell for the relationship when she utters the words, "Listen Aaron. . . . We have to talk."

Relocation to Latin America does nothing for Aaron's communication skills. To complicate matters, he finds himself surrounded by people who, like Caroline, really do not care for anything he has to say, unless it is complimentary and positive. Richard Penwad is so eager to be free of him altogether, that when he speaks of Aaron's departure, "he already, Shapiro noticed, looked relieved."

Enter Beale, the English radio journalist. Beale is Shapiro's opposite in terms of communication; while his listening skills could use some improvement, he is never at a loss for words. He speaks almost incessantly throughout the interview with Aaron, who is hard-pressed to fill even the few brief gaps Beale allows him in the conversation. Even the physical description of Beale makes him sound like some sort of communication device: "Beale's head was an interesting space-ship shape. Colorless and sensitive-looking filaments sprouted from it, and his ears looked like receiving devices. Sensors, transmitters, Shapiro thought."

Interestingly, Beale possesses something else that Shapiro seems to lack: passion. While one tends to think of concert pianists as people with a passion for, even obsession with, their art, Aaron is obsessed only with the money he is not making with his career. Aaron enjoys playing the Garcia-Gutierrez concerto, but what he enjoys are "the athletic challenge of its surface complexities. . . . the response of the audience." Beale, on the other hand, is all passion and little reason, clearly unconcerned with appearances (as evidenced by his stained suit).

He delights in the sensual: the food and drink at lunch with Shapiro cause him to burst into joyous little exclamations ("oh! . . . pork pie!"). He waxes poetic about the beauty of the country, its history, its people.

Shapiro's lack of passion is likely the cause of his stalled career. "The qualities he greatly admired and envied in other pianists—varieties of a profound musicianship which focussed the attention on the ear, hearing, rather than on the hand, executing—were ones he lacked." Diligent practice brings him "just the faintest flicker of heat in his crystalline touch." This flaw in his musicianship is, in its own way, one more failure to communicate, to command the attention of his audience and help them feel the music.

Though Shapiro seems deeply affected by Caroline's departure, his reveries about her are not those of a man passionately in love; he reflects more on her failings than her positive qualities. As with his career, he seems to be mourning the loss of the relationship not because he was so passionate about it, but simply for the status it brought him. Because Caroline was initially attracted to him because of the glamour of his ascending career, losing her is one more indication "that success, the sort of success Penwad's letter seemed to promise for him again, was something he could just, finally, forget about."

Shapiro's choice of Caroline as a partner indicates that he is actually avoiding passion in his life. The descriptions of Caroline paint a picture of a woman who is delicate, frail, pale, and patrician, with a cool elegance about her. It is ironic that straight from his breakup with the icy Caroline, Shapiro travels to Latin America, a region known for the fire and passion of its people.

Many parallels can be drawn between Shapiro and the poor native Indians in the story. The Indians have no voice in the society in which they live; they have been silenced by the oppressive military regime in power. Just as the hall in which Shapiro plays—a hall built by the government in power—distorts and suppresses the music he performs, the government of this country has done everything in its power to prevent the rest of the world from hearing the full story of what has been done to these people. In addition, this is not the first time these people have been robbed of their voice; as Beale explains to Shapiro: "You know, the Indians here had simply everything at one time. A calendar. A written language—centuries, centuries, *centuries* before the Spanish came. . . . and the Spanish

What Do I Read Next?

- Deborah Eisenberg's first two short story collections, *Transactions in a Foreign Currency* and *Under the 82nd Airborne*, were released together in 1997 in one volume entitled, *The Stories (So Far) of Deborah Eisenberg*. The collection includes other stories set in Latin America.

- Eisenberg's Latin America–based stories have been compared to works by Graham Greene and Robert Stone. *The Portable Graham Greene* (1994), which includes two complete novels, excerpts from other novels, short stories, essays, and more, is a good introduction to Greene's work. *A Flag for Sunrise* (1981) is Stone's political thriller about Americans in a fictitious Central American country run by a right-wing military government.

- *A Brief History of Central America* (1989), written by Costa Rican scholar Hector Perez Brignoli, summarizes the history, describes the geography of the region, and analyzes the political and social problems of the five Central American countries (Guatemala, Honduras, El Salvador, Nicaragua, and Costa Rica).

- Novelist Kathy Reichs tackles the subject of massacres by the Guatemalan military in her mystery novel, *Grave Secrets* (2002). The disappearance of four girls and the murder of a human-rights investigator makes Reichs's heroine, Temperance Brennan, believe that the same atrocities of the 1980s are happening again in 2002.

---

actually destroyed it all. . . . The written language was actually destroyed, do you see." Every attempt by the Indians to communicate their plight is thwarted, even in this description of the city on the night of the concert: "A slow continuous combustion of garbage sent up bulletins of ruin from the hut-blistered gorges, which were quickly snuffed out by the fragrance drifting from the garlanded slopes of the Gold Zone." The wealthy patrons of the arts follow Caroline's example, with a stubborn insistence that all is happy and pleasant and a determination to ignore any evidence to the contrary.

Though Shapiro is repulsed by Beale's slovenly manners and lack of tact, at the same time, he is drawn to him, perhaps fascinated by the ease with which Beale expresses himself, the stream-of-consciousness monologue he maintains almost continuously. Shapiro recognizes in Beale the passion for life that has eluded him in both his art and his relationships. As he listens to Beale speak into his tape recorder at the end of the story, he seems to experience, vicariously, the same sensations that Beale is experiencing: "Beale stretched himself out in the trough, tucking the tape recorder under his head like a pillow, and a delicious sensation of rest poured into Shapiro's body." Similarly, when Beale describes a scene from his imagination, Shapiro

closes his eyes and experiences it himself: "Yes, he could hear it, the chatter, the pointless chatter. And smell the orange-scented garden." The reader begins to feel that with Beale as his coach, Shapiro could break out of the numb trance he has been wrapped in and experience the emotion and passion he has been avoiding for so many years.

Source: Laura Pryor, Critical Essay on "Someone to Talk To," in *Short Stories for Students*, Thomson Gale, 2007.

Claire Robinson

Robinson is a former teacher of English literature and creative writing and, as of 2006, is a full-time writer and editor. In the following essay, Robinson examines how Eisenberg gives a voice to what is left unsaid in "Someone to Talk To."

In her review of Deborah Eisenberg's *All Around Atlantis* in the *Houston Chronicle*, Paula Friedman writes that Eisenberg's "uncannily wise stories give haunting voice to what is often left painfully unsaid." Friedman's observation aptly describes the interactions between the characters in "Someone to Talk To."

The opening scene sets the tone for the story. Aaron Shapiro's girlfriend Caroline is leaving him. In this potentially raw moment, the emotion is both

"
Beale, a prophet in spite of himself, unwittingly answers an unspoken question that tortures Aaron regarding his role as an artist."

unexpressed and displaced. Displacement is a psychological defense mechanism in which there is an unconscious shift of emotions from the original object to a more acceptable substitute. In this instance, the recipient of Aaron and Caroline's emotions is the cat. It is clear that Aaron still loves Caroline, as he is painfully aware of her fragrance and terrified of the possibility that she might touch him. But the two characters treat each other with excruciating politeness. Instead of touching each other, they touch the cat. Caroline asks the cat to take care of Aaron, a roundabout way of expressing her love for him and of acknowledging that she will not be taking care of Aaron herself. Though Aaron says that he will be fine, the fact that he feels the cat's leaning against his leg "thuggishly" suggests that Caroline's leaving him is an onslaught against his feelings.

The description of Aaron seeing himself "as if in a dream, standing on a dark shore," suggests a state of shock (people suffering shock often find themselves standing outside their body) and of disorientation. He has reached the end of this piece of dry land but cannot see his way ahead. His desolation and disorientation is made concrete when in the next scene, he wakes in a country far away from Caroline, in an unfamiliar hotel room that "wobbled into place around him." The wobbling motion expresses his emotional state.

It becomes clear that Aaron has long been divorced from any real direction in life. His early virtuosity as a pianist depended on his technical ability, focusing the attention on the hand and the execution, rather than the ear and the hearing of the piece. He is present in body (to execute the piece) but not in soul (to breathe life into it). Aaron lacks vital heat in his cold, hard, "crystalline touch." His name, "once received like a slab of precious metal,

was now received like a slip of blank paper"—another image suggestive of someone who is not vitally present.

Just as Aaron is disconnected from his music and from his early sense of purpose, so he fails to form a firm connection with Caroline. Even when the two met, they were at cross-purposes. She was starry-eyed at his apparently brilliant musicianship, unaware that he had already admitted defeat. He had moved to the margins of the city, symbolic of his abandonment of commitment to his role as a musician and of his alienation from the mainstream. As their relationship progressed, it was characterized not by increasing connection, but by disconnection. She touched him less often, and he remained silent, worrying about finances.

In both speech and music, Aaron has nothing to say. He has become "exiled" from "the bower of celebrity." The metaphor of exile is picked up in his later, literal exile to an unnamed Latin American country to play at a concert and in the British expatriate journalist, Beale, whom he meets there. Both Aaron and Beale are exiles in the sense that they are marginalized characters who do not belong. The question of whether either can still make any meaningful connection with the rest of the world is answered later.

Aaron's relationship with Caroline reaches a crisis when he challenges her reassuring platitudes that "Things will work out." Breaking his silence, Aaron replies harshly that things will undoubtedly work out, "for some other species. Or on some other planet." While Caroline has a bright outlook that springs from her idyllic childhood, Aaron has a darker outlook that Caroline cannot accept. Aaron's view is that "he, like most humans, was an experiment that had never been expected to succeed, a little padding around some evolutionary thrust, a scattershot nubbin of DNA." He feels that he, as an individual within the great scheme of things, does not matter. Life and evolution do matter, but he is irrelevant to both. In this most extreme disconnection, Aaron is divorced from life itself.

These disconnections foreshadow a major disconnection in the narrative, enacted in Aaron's visit to the Latin American country. The government of this country, in league with the U.S. Embassy, has invited him to play one of his signature pieces. Aaron, the innocent, believes he is simply going to play music. The truth turns out to be quite different.

In the hotel, Aaron meets Richard Penwad, the contact to whom he has been assigned. Eisenberg's description of the meeting is a satirical masterpiece, succeeding largely because of what is left unsaid. The change of setting reflects a widening of the story's focus. The disconnection previously explored on a personal level is expanded to the political, to show a disconnection between spin and reality.

Penwad explains that he and his fellow organizers of the music festival (an unidentified "we") hope to attract more North American musicians and that Aaron is to play a piece by the composer García-Gutiérrez, who is being featured because he is local. Though Penwad does not say as much, his words show that the invitation to Aaron is not a recognition of his genius, but a political maneuver. The gap between political spin and reality is shown in the juxtaposition of the pictures of regal, smiling Indians on the hotel walls and the skinny, grief-raddled Indians working there as waiters. In addition, Aaron is aware that the country's Indians are being massacred by the government. Penwad says that he hopes "our" sponsorship of the festival "will help to . . . rectify the, ah, perception that we're identified with the military here." In spite of this political doublespeak, Aaron suddenly realizes that he is here as part of a propaganda campaign on the part of the United States government and its client regime in this country. When Penwad asks who "we" are, Penwad replies evasively but reveals that he is connected to the U.S. Embassy.

The very buildings in this country are the instruments of politicians in their attempts to control the populace. The Arts Center, far from being an organic expression of the people's love for the arts, is divorced from the people, to the extent that the taxi drivers do not know where it is. It is a crude defense against social breakdown imposed on the people by politicians, at a time when it was feared that increased leisure time and economic wealth would "cause humanity to devolve into a grunting mass sprawled in front of blood-drenched TV screens." In a satirical comment, Eisenberg points out that poverty accomplished this devolution by itself.

The Arts Center is a piece of political spin even in its design: Penwad praises it to Aaron for its "cross-fertilization" of indigenous Indian and modernistic Western motifs. Such architectural symbolism implies that the two populations are happily integrated. But it is clear to Aaron that the Indians live in slums in ravines that have been hit by a recent earthquake, whereas the English-speaking community and the business center are safe in their own parts of town. The word "cross-fertilization"

gains a heavy ironic weight, reinforced by Aaron's baffled question, "Of what . . . does *Joan* . . . say 'cross-fertilization?'" In the context of plant breeding, the word refers to sexual reproduction between different types of plants. In this city, cross-fertilization between the populations does not happen; ghettoization and segregation would be more accurate terms.

While the Indians suffer most in this region of dictatorships, the educated classes also live in fear. Part of what Penwad has avoided saying is conveyed in the picture of the members of the orchestra that accompanies Aaron. The musicians are of "startled appearance, as though a huge claw had snatched them from their beds and plonked them into their chairs." They are cowed victims, the prey of a predator. The Arts Center, in keeping with its history as an instrument of a tyrannical state, joins in the victimization process by means of its "demonic" acoustics, which turn into "whirling blades." Aaron dislikes the concerto even as he is playing it, though the audience enjoys it because the fact that the composer is local makes them feel that their worth has been recognized. The scene reveals that art, far from being pure, has become corrupted by politics. Aaron was not invited as a musician, but as a propagandist; the audience are not there to enjoy music, but to feel affirmed.

Seemingly, the only chance Aaron has of boosting his battered self-image is the interview that Penwad has arranged with the British journalist Beale. The hotel where Aaron is to meet Beale is grander than the one in which Aaron has been installed, and in yet another humiliation, he notes that "this was where they'd put an *important* musician."

In theory, the interview with Beale should provide Aaron with a chance to express what he has to say. But it transpires that listening to Aaron is low on Beale's list of priorities. His first priority is getting a free meal on expenses; his second is, as the story's title puts it, having someone to talk to. He talks so relentlessly about his own concerns that it does not occur to him to ask a question. Nevertheless, Beale's appearance—Eisenberg describes him as looking like a radio receiver—and the fact that he is a radio journalist alert the reader to the fact that Beale has absorbed information about his adopted country. He spends his interview time with Aaron revealing the sordid underside to the spin and diplomacy of Penwad. In an ironic understatement, Beale says that this country is not a "favorable climate" for the arts, as it is better at killing

The historic center of Guatemala City © Lynsey Addario/Corbis

students than producing artists. Beale's obsession is the plight of the Indians, who had a sophisticated culture until the Spanish arrived and destroyed it. Indeed, the Spanish are still slaughtering the Indians, but news reports remain silent about it, so officially, the problem does not exist. Beale's fascination with the Indians led to his trying desperately to be posted to this country. In an instance of dramatic irony, Beale says, "fortunately, there were all these insurrections and whatnot, and that created demand, and so now I've been here over fifteen years!" Unwittingly, he has become reliant on the oppressive regime that he hates. This is also the situation in which Aaron and García-Gutiérrez find themselves: shown off by the government as exhibits, they have been drafted into the ranks of the oppressors.

Beale causes a crisis in Aaron's soul when he almost says that the musician is the instrument of the composer. Before Beale can utter the word "instrument," Aaron rushes out and shuts himself into the merciful silence of a phone booth. The reader must fill in the blanks. Perhaps Aaron cannot bear to hear the full truth of what Beale is suggesting: that he is not only an instrument of the compromised government exhibit, García-Gutiérrez, but an instrument of the governments of the United States and the military regime in this country.

Beale, a prophet in spite of himself, unwittingly answers an unspoken question that tortures Aaron regarding his role as an artist. Unlike Aaron, who has come merely to regurgitate an empty piece of music that happens to be in his repertoire, Beale retains his sense of wonder, spontaneity, and love of communicating. His words concern radio, but they could equally apply to music:

> Oh my darling! Someone is talking to you, and you don't know . . . what thing they've found to tell you on that very day, at that very moment. Maybe someone will talk to you about cookery. Maybe someone will talk to you about a Cabinet Minister. And then that particular thing is *yours*, do you see what I mean? Who *knows* whether it's something worth hearing? Who *knows* whether there's someone out there to hear it! It's a leap of faith, do you see? That both parties are making. Really the most enormous leap of faith.

These scenes contrast starkly with the scene after the concert, which displays the glossy veneer that the ruling powers like to present. The radiance of the spotlights and the glitter of diamonds contrast with the lack of light in the gloomy, threatening restaurant. In the light of what has been revealed about the plight of the Indians, Joan's enthusiasm for "our Institute of Indigenous Textiles" and her contempt for the Indians who staff Aaron's hotel seem patronizing. This tone continues when the hostess's son adopts a contemptuous attitude towards the scruffy Beale and later at the reception, which is held at a house that the army guards against a resentful populace.

The glittering world of the reception has lost its attraction for Aaron, even when he receives the adulation he has craved for so long in the form of people calling out for him. Instead, he seeks out Beale near the Indian servants' quarters. Beale is describing into his tape recorder the understated beauties of the remnants of the Indian culture: a fragment of pottery; children joining hands in an almost-forgotten game. Beale recalls a happier and more prosperous time for the Indians, when he first arrived here. He had seen a crowd of Indian women walking down a mountain to do their washing. He had longed to speak to them and make the sort of connection that has proved so elusive throughout this story. He retains a hope that he may still make that connection. He says, "I know they're still there—they'll always be there, beyond the curtain of blood." He plans to return the following morning:

> And finally we'll speak. Please be there with me. They'll be so happy. . . . Because everyone has something, some little thing, my darling, they've been waiting so long to tell you.

Source: Claire Robinson, Critical Essay on "Someone to Talk To," in *Short Stories for Students*, Thomson Gale, 2007.

Robin A. Werner

In the following essay, Werner gives a critical analysis of Eisenberg's life and work.

The characters in Deborah Eisenberg's stories are often lost. Whether they travel through a foreign country or their own equally alien, familiar worlds, they are on quests of discovery. Throughout her three volumes of short fiction, this theme is consistently honed and refined. Employing vivid descriptions and poignant symbols, Eisenberg takes her readers along into a world that is strangely familiar. Her witty prose and dramatic delineation of character deepen the sensations of confusion and loss that pervade her fiction.

Deborah Eisenberg was born on 20 November 1945 to George and Ruth Eisenberg in Chicago, Illinois. Her father was a pediatrician, her mother a housewife. Eisenberg has described her childhood in the Chicago suburb of Winnetka as a "hermetically sealed" middle-class existence. In the early 1960s Eisenberg left suburban Illinois for Vermont, where she attended boarding school and later studied Latin and Greek at Marlboro College. Then, in

" [These stories] examine the conflict between the worlds of the pampered tourist and the impoverished locals, adding in politics and war as grim reminders of the world outside the individual's search for understanding."

the mid 1960s, Eisenberg moved to New York City, where she earned her B.A. in 1968 from the New School for Social Research in the New School College. For the next seven years she remained in New York, holding a variety of secretarial and waitressing jobs, until in 1975 she "stopped smoking and started writing."

In 1981 her play, *Pastorale*, was produced by the Second Stage Theatre in New York and was published in 1983. The switch from writing for the stage to writing short fiction seems to have been a movement centered on Eisenberg finding her voice. Explaining why she likes the short-story form best, Eisenberg said in a 1992 interview: "I like the bristling, sparky, kinetic effect you can get from condensing something down to the point where it almost squeaks."

During the mid 1980s Eisenberg traveled sporadically throughout Latin America. These travels have had a tremendous impact on her writing. She claims to have visited every Central American country with the exceptions of Costa Rica and Belize. In the 1992 interview Eisenberg explained why she loves travel: "even though there are always horrible experiences . . . the thing that guides you in the ordinary round of your day is not there—the stability that carries you from one moment to the next is gone." In 1986 Eisenberg published her first collection of short stories, *Transactions in a Foreign Currency*, and received the first of three O. Henry Awards (the others followed in 1995 and 1997).

Eisenberg's writing is dreamlike; it projects a great variety of moods different from the narrow focus of many short-story writers. The seven stories that comprise *Transactions in a Foreign Currency* deal with protagonists who, in some way, are alienated from their surroundings. Travel, a major theme throughout Eisenberg's writing, surfaces here both in actual movement into new surroundings and in the inward journeys of her troubled heroines. The narratives reveal the dysfunctional world, and the epiphanies the characters achieve generally center on self-awareness.

"Flotsam," the first story in this collection, depicts a woman's struggle to define herself rather than constantly viewing her identity in relation to others' perceptions. The story opens in a flashback; the narrator displays herself in a relationship that has grown sour. Her academic boyfriend begins to grow more and more fastidious, ultimately lashing out with a phrase typical of Eisenberg's occasionally florid prose: "You're like the Blob. You remember that movie *The Blob?* You're sentient protoplasm, but you're as undifferentiated as sentient protoplasm can get. You're devoid of even taxonomic attributes." In this early volume such passages seem to break up the narrative flow; however, Eisenberg's wit and her vivid characters make such moments humorous rather than distracting. The narrator of "Flotsam," Charlotte, then travels to New York City to live with a stranger, dramatically altering her surroundings and associates. New York is described vividly through a stranger's eyes as the problems of Eisenberg's heroine are brought out in this alien environment. The subway itself becomes mystical: "How gaudy and festive it was, like a huge Chinese dragon, clanking and huffing through its glimmering cavern." Despite the vast differences in the people and places that now surround her, Charlotte continues to define herself through her former boyfriend's dismissive assessment, living under a smiling picture of him that she has hung prominently in the apartment.

The narrator's new roommate, the stunning, scintillating, and drug-addicted Cinder, leads Charlotte into a new realm. Through her encounters with two men Charlotte begins to break her identification with her former boyfriend and her dependence on Cinder. After-work drinks with her married employer and an impromptu date with Cinder's castoff boyfriend begin to guide Charlotte to a new view of her life. Finally Cinder bursts out in anger at Charlotte, and Charlotte realizes the extent to which her life has been molded by her perceptions. As she prepares to leave Cinder's apartment she notices the picture of her former boyfriend:

> And, Lord—I'd almost forgotten my photograph of Robert. What was it doing up there anyway—as if he

were the president of some company? I yanked it from the wall with both hands, and it tore in half . . . to my surprise, I didn't care. Robert had never looked like that picture anyhow. That was how I'd wanted him to look, but he hadn't looked like that.

"A Lesson in Traveling Light" is also about a female protagonist's growing awareness of herself and those around her, but this narrative is framed in a seemingly endless cross-country journey by van. Through this story of a relationship on the verge of self-destruction Eisenberg illuminates the ways in which people understand their intimates through their interactions with others. Despite having lived with Lee for several years, the narrator knows little about him. Through his interactions with old friends, whom they stay with at various intervals in their random journey, the narrator sees her lover and their relationship in a new way. The first moment of this insight is presented almost supernaturally: "Lee and I had always drunk wine out of the same glasses we drank everything else out of, and it was not the kind of wine you'd have anything to say about, so Lee with his graceful raised glass was an odd sight. So odd a sight, in fact, that it seemed to lift the table slightly, causing it to hover in the vibrating dimness."

The story becomes one of watching and waiting. As they travel, rootless, the narrator philosophizes: "'It's incredible,' I said, 'how fast every place you go gets to be home,'" and Lee replies, "That's why it's good to travel . . . It reminds you what life really is." Travel in Eisenberg's stories brings the human relationships into sharp relief, and nowhere is this more apparent in *Transactions in a Foreign Currency* than in this story. "A Lesson in Traveling Light" ends, as do many of Eisenberg's narratives, on an ambiguous down note as the narrator stands alone in a parking lot realizing that one day soon she will be there boarding a bus, her relationship with Lee finally finished. Despite the loneliness of her final musing there is a sense of greater strength and self-knowledge in the final moments:

> I watched the van glide out onto the road, and I saw it accelerate up along the curve of the days ahead. Soon, I saw, Lee would pull up in front of Kathryn's house; soon he would step through the door and she would turn; and soon—not that afternoon, of course, but soon enough—I would be standing again in this parking lot, ticket in hand, waiting to board the bus that would appear so startlingly in front of me, as if from nowhere.

In the end the relationship itself is what must be shed in order to truly travel light.

The title story, "Transactions in a Foreign Currency," appears near the end of the collection. This story, like "A Lesson in Traveling Light" and so much of Eisenberg's work, examines relationships and the effect of travel on a woman's ability to see herself. "Transactions in a Foreign Currency" presents the reader with a heroine enmeshed in a destructive on-again-off-again nine-year-old relationship. As the story opens, the narrator's lover, Ivan, calls to ask her to come visit him in Montreal:

> I turned with the receiver to the wall as I absorbed the fact of Ivan's voice, and when I glanced back at the man on my sofa, he seemed like a scrap of paper, or the handle from a broken cup, or a single rubber band—a thing that has become dislodged from its rightful place and intrudes on one's consciousness two or three or many times before one understands that it is just a thing best thrown away.

Eisenberg's vivid description immediately sets the tone of this relationship. The unnamed narrator puts her own life on hold while she flies to Ivan. When her relationship with Ivan began, the narrator had hoped for marriage. Despite Ivan's claim that she has "just as much power as I do" in the relationship, it appears to have been rather one-sided for some time. The narrator describes being with Ivan as feeling "as if I were standing in the sun, and it never occurred to me to hesitate or to ask any questions." This story is not so much about a relationship, however, as about a woman finding her own power.

Soon after the narrator's arrival in Montreal, Ivan decides to fly home to spend Christmas with his son and former wife. Left alone in Ivan's world, the narrator confronts her own loneliness and questionable self-sufficiency: "I felt I had been equipped by a mysterious agency: I knew without asking how to transport myself into a foreign city, my pockets were filled with its money, and in my hand I had a set of keys to an apartment there." This feeling is only the beginning of her quest for self-identification. The narrator descends first into sleep, unconsciously fasting, and then goes on a grocery-shopping spree in the clothes that some other woman has left in Ivan's closet. When she returns to Ivan's apartment she finds it inhabited by a waiflike man who claims that Ivan owes him money. This man, Eugene, offers her drugs, but what makes an impression on the narrator is Eugene's beauty: "He was beautiful, I saw. He was beautiful. He sparkled with beauty; it streamed from him in glistening sheets, as if he were emerging from a lake of it." They sleep together, and the narrator uses the remainder of her foreign currency to pay off Ivan's debts.

By the time Ivan returns, the city has become, somehow, no longer foreign, and the story ends with a sense that the narrator is beginning to claim her power in their relationship. She realizes her relationship with Ivan is hollow: "How I wished I could contain the golden wounding hope of him. But it had begun to diverge from me—oh, who knew how long before—and I could feel myself already reforming: empty, light." As she and Ivan walk along the street, the same way she had walked on her quest for groceries, the city ceases to be foreign:

> How familiar it was, as if I'd entered and explored it over years. Well, it had been a short time, really, but it would certainly be part of me, this city, long after I'd forgotten the names of the streets and the colors of the light, long after I'd forgotten the feel of Ivan's shirt against my cheek, and the darkening sight separated from me now by a sheet of glass I could almost reach out to shatter.

These final words, with Eisenberg's enigmatic symbolism, flow into the title of the final story, "Broken Glass," and recall the major thematic connections between the stories of this collection: how the foreign becomes familiar and the ways in which people see themselves through relationships with others.

Transactions in a Foreign Currency was greeted with a generally positive critical reception. Michiko Kakutani of *The New York Times* (5 March 1986) wrote that in Eisenberg's first collection of short fiction "she delineates her characters' lives with a full palette of colors, using not just the earth tones of fashionable alienation, but also the pastel brights of comedy and the darker, more luminous shades of an artist blessed with emotional wisdom." Kakutani's criticism is couched in flattery: "at times, Miss Eisenberg's ease in capturing the way we speak today combined with her sure sense of craft, can result in 'slice of life' studies that suffer from a certain patness."

Bob Shaccochis's review in *The New York Times Book Review* (9 March 1986) focuses on the element of travel, both literal and figurative, in these narratives. Characters are "made to travel outside the native land of their inner selves into a world that appears astonishingly regulated, where ostensibly enlightened men collect women the way superpowers assert spheres of influence." Many of her characters seem lost, a fact pointed out in Richard Panek's more critical article for *The Chicago Tribune* (13 July 1986). Panek complained that the "balance between introspection and overstatement is delicate, especially in first-person fiction, and sometimes Eisenberg slips." Lynne Sharon Schwartz's review for *The Washington Post*

(11 May 1986) began by praising Eisenberg as "a writer of considerable talent—she has wit, deftness and grace, and she can cut through her characters' trivial and overlong conversations with an arresting, illuminating metaphor." Schwartz goes on to complain, however, that Eisenberg's gifts "do not, for the most part, relieve the spell of monotony cast by the voice of enervated sophistication."

Virtually all of the criticism focuses on Eisenberg's language, relating it to her early success as a playwright. Kakutani began by saying that Eisenberg "writes with a playwright's quick, bristling ear for dialogue and a painter's affection for nuance and image." Most of the critics, even those who pointed out flaws, praised *Transactions in a Foreign Currency* for Eisenberg's use of dialogue, her wit, and her character depiction.

From the mid 1980s through the early 1990s Eisenberg held a series of academic appointments. In 1987 she was awarded the PEN Hemingway citation, the Mrs. Giles Writing Foundation Award, a Guggenheim Fellowship (1987–1988), and the Whiting Foundation Award (1987–1988). She served the first of her two terms as the visiting Hurst professor at Washington University in St. Louis in 1989. In 1991 she served as the Shirley Sutton Thomas visiting writer and was awarded the Deutscher Akademischer Austauschdienst Stipendium. She participated in the Iowa Writers' Workshop at the University of Iowa in the fall semesters of 1990, 1992, and 1993.

Her second collection of short stories, *Under the 82nd Airborne*, was published in 1992. One of the most striking of the seven pieces in the volume is the title story, which appears second. "Under the 82nd Airborne," like much of Eisenberg's work, is set in Latin America, and Eisenberg's travels in the area obviously contribute to the vivid descriptions. The heroine of this story, Caitlin, is older than many of Eisenberg's protagonists and works as an actress. She has traveled to the small town of Tegucigalpa, in Honduras, in order to spend time with her daughter, Holly, who is accompanying her fiancé on a business trip. Caitlin's need to connect with her daughter is motivated by her dissatisfaction with her normal round of auditions and casting calls in New York City. Caitlin is searching for understanding, trying to know her daughter who is now, almost miraculously, "as old as Caitlin and Todd had been" when Holly was born. Caitlin has just broken up with her live-in boyfriend, and her life has suddenly taken a downturn. Thus, this story is also about her attempt to reconnect with herself.

Caitlin's age becomes a significant factor as she tries to assess the woman she has become:

> Her gray-blue eyes were still clear and wide, her pale-brown hair still gave off light. From a distance she could have been a girl, but tonight her face was disfigured by the meaningless history of a stranger. Surely her intended self was locked away somewhere, embryonic and protected. She searched the mirror, but the impostor on duty there stared bafflingly back.

As her trip progresses, the story moves back and forth between the present and Caitlin's reflections on her past: how she became pregnant with Holly, the dissolution of her marriage, and how her husband managed to limit her contact with their daughter after the divorce.

Instead of connecting, however, Caitlin and her daughter just fight: "Jesus, Caitlin thought. How idiotic. Holly would be sorry later—she always was. But in the meantime . . . Oh, well. Out for adventures." As she travels out into the foreign world around her, she realizes there are troops and many Americans present. A "burly, red-faced boy who was drinking a beer as he walked" bumps into her and says "Gramma's looking good."

As in "Transactions in a Foreign Currency," this woman's fevered walk through the city becomes a significant turning point. She meets up with a businessman (who may actually be a CIA agent) whom she had encountered on the plane. Over drinks they discuss the city. As they talk, it becomes clear that the country is on the brink of war, a strategic point that the Americans and the communist countries are about to fight over. The tensions in the country contrast sharply with the world of the Americans in the bar as it fills with journalists, "All waiting to watch the 82nd Airborne Division fall out of the sky." The bitterness of the men and the emptiness of the journalists there to document the aerial attack lead Caitlin's thoughts back to Holly and what has brought her here. Eisenberg offers no concrete resolution in this story. It ends with reflections: the memory of the day she left Holly and her husband and the sight of a fish "darting and circling in the flickering light, bumping against the glass as though at any moment its cloudy little bowl could be a great fresh pond, strewn with leaves and flowers." The reader is left to contemplate whether in fact Caitlin has moved through the tale like the fish in its bowl.

"The Custodian" is the most acclaimed story in *Under the 82nd Airborne* and was chosen for the *The Best American Short Stories of 1991*, edited by Alice Adams and Katrina Kenison. In this story

Eisenberg repeats her focus on the confrontation of past and present by opening the story with two women who meet again in the small town in which they grew up. The narrator, Lynnie, confronts her memories of Isobel all around her, but when the two actually meet, their discussion is stiff and awkward. After the opening the story moves fluidly back into the past to narrate the events that led to Isobel being sent away—her seduction by a married professor for whom the girls baby-sat.

Lynnie and Isobel were friends more from a lack of anything better to do than from any real affinity for one another. Lynnie idolized the beautiful, wealthy, and slightly older Isobel. During summer bike rides they often visited a wonderful house that becomes central to the rest of the story:

> The house is stone, and stands empty on a hill. Clouds float by it, making great black shadows swing over the sloping meadows below with their cows and barns and wildflowers. Inside, in the spreading coolness, the light flows as variously clear and shaded as water. Trees seem to crowd in the dim recesses. The house is just there, enclosing part of the world. . . . The girls walk carefully when they visit, fearful of churning up the delicate maze of silence.

One day this silence is broken by the arrival of a family. Through Ross, Claire, and their children, the family who come to inhabit this house, Lynnie and Isobel obtain a glimpse into an intellectual and artistic world quite different from their small-town existence. The idyllic life they are allowed brief glimpses of, however, is ultimately threatened. Lynnie witnesses Ross visiting Isobel at night when her parents are not home:

> It is the following week that Isobel leaves. Lynnie watches from her window as Isobel and her mother and father load up her father's car and get into it. They are taking a trip, Lynnie thinks; they are just taking a trip, but still she runs down the stairs as fast as she can, and then, as the car pulls out into the street, Isobel twists around in the back seat. Her face is waxy with an unhealthy glow, and her hair ripples out around her. Lynnie raises her hand, perhaps imperceptibly, but in any case Isobel only looks.

It is never made clear who is responsible for the anonymous letter that informed Isobel's parents of her improper relationship with Ross.

After Isobel's departure, life changes for Lynnie. Isobel's mother barely contains her distaste when she passes Lynnie on the street, and suddenly, Lynnie sees herself as the woman must see her:

> an impassive, solid, limp-haired child, an inconveniently frequent visitor, breathing noisily, hungry for a smile—a negligible girl, utterly unlike her own daughter. And then Lynnie sees Isobel, vanishing

brightly all over again as she looks back from her father's car, pressing into Lynnie's safekeeping everything that should have vanished along with her.

Only in this final line does the significance of the title become clear.

"The Custodian" is followed by another story set in Central America: "Holy Week." The style of this story is unusual for Eisenberg. It begins under the heading "Sunday" with a breathless list: "Everything as promised: Costumes, clouds of incense—processions already begun; town tingly with anticipation." This style continues for the first three paragraphs and then resolves itself into the notes that Dennis, the narrator, is taking for his travel article. This note-taking is interrupted by Sarah, the girl he has brought with him on this trip. The rest of the story progresses with the narrative periodically interrupted by another heading and more notes. Generally this stylistic device is interesting, but it does become strained at points as Dennis takes notes on his crumbling relationship. The inclusion of the travel-article notes, however, shows the difference between how the reality of foreign cities differs from the fantasy fed to tourists. The notes waver between descriptions obviously intended for the article and Dennis's own reflections:

> Indians impenetrable as they watch Jesus pass by, ribs showing through white plaster skin, trickling red plaster blood; they watch so intently, holding their babies up to look. Unnerving, the way they watch, way they walk, gliding along in those fantastical clothes of theirs. Silent emissaries from a vanished world, stranded in ours.

Once again, as in "A Lesson in Traveling Light," Eisenberg uses the foreign setting to throw the relationships between her characters into relief. Dennis muses on the advantages and disadvantages of his relationship with the much younger Sarah: "On the one hand, the intensity, the clarity (generally) of Sarah's reactions. On the other, her impatience, stubbornness, unwillingness to see the other point of view. Fundamentally youth's refusal to acknowledge the subtlety, complexity of a situation; at worst, adds up to a sort of insensitivity." The more time he spends in this foreign town, the more lovely it seems. Once more, Eisenberg's description evokes powerful emotions:

> Gets more beautiful as the eye adjusts. So high, so pale, so strange. Flowers astonishing—graceful rococo shapes, sinuous, pendant, like ornamentations on the churches. Every hour of the day, in every changing tint of air, new details coming forward. The ancient stillness. All the different ancientnesses— Spain, Rome, themselves so new compared to the

Indians. All converging right here in the square. Concentrated in the processions, in every dark eye.

As in the title story of this collection, the military forces its presence into the heady existence of the tourists. This time it is the local militia: "The soldiers—the hard-eyed, ravenous-looking boys." They rule over the parade, seemingly unnoticed by the locals.

By "Friday" Dennis's notes begin to reveal a portrait of himself as a self-deluded, rapidly aging man, and he comes to the realization that his time with Sarah will soon be over. Dennis pictures her at a future cocktail party discussing "her first involvement with a mature man," comforting himself that he will not have meant nothing to her. As their trip comes to a close, the combination of evidence of a secret guerilla war and Dennis's brooding over the foreseeable demise of their relationship spoils their enjoyment of the elegant restaurants and hotels. Sarah, with her youthful enthusiasm, cannot forget what she has seen or understand why it has not appeared in newspapers. Dennis, however, puts the conflict between the rich and the poor out of his mind and begins to return to his normal life. After all, he thinks:

> would it improve, the world, if Sarah and I stay in and subsist on a diet of microwaved potatoes? Because I really don't think so . . . I suppose—that by the standards of any sane person it could be considered a crime to go to a restaurant. To go someplace nice. After all. Our little comforts—The velvet murmur, the dimming of the street as the door closes, the enfolding calm of the other diners . . . that incredible moment when the waiter steps up, smiling, to put your plate before you.

At this enigmatic point Eisenberg leaves the reader, pondering the distinctions between places so close and yet so distant.

Criticism of *Under the 82nd Airborne*, focused on the occasional lack of warmth evinced by these technically brilliant stories. In his laudatory review for *The New York Times* (9 February 1992) Gary Krist claims that this second collection is "darker, more complex and more thematically opulent than their predecessors, suggesting a conscious attempt on the author's part to thicken the psychological texture of her fictional world." If this "conscious attempt" to write a more psychologically complex work occasionally leads to descriptions that are "abstract, cold, even unapproachable," he concludes, this detraction is less important than the evidence that Eisenberg "is a writer who is not afraid to extend her range."

In a review for *The Chicago Tribune* (31 March 1992) Bill Mahin wrote that Eisenberg "creates vibrant, vivid characters that linger in memory long after reading." Mahin's review is unabashedly glowing, but other reviews critiqued this second collection as lacking in some of the virtues of her first. According to Richard Eder in his 13 February 1992 review for *The Los Angeles Times*, Eisenberg's first collection had a "fierceness in the insult and an energy in the sensibility." In *Under the 82nd Airborne*, however, "that urgency, that insistent wind pressure, has died down . . . In some of the stories, the characteristic voicing remains, but it is underpowered, and as a result is a sporadically successful ornamentation." Yet, even Eder must admit, at times these stories display the fact that "Eisenberg has her own authentic sharpness, and the narration is perfectly done." Overall, the response to this second collection was laudatory, and in 1993 Eisenberg received three awards: the Friends of American Writers Award, the Ingram-Merrill Foundation Grant, and the Award for Literature from the American Academy of Arts and Sciences.

After *Under the 82nd Airborne*, Eisenberg devoted herself to a variety of projects while working on her third short-story collection. She served as a visiting professor at the City College of New York in the spring of 1993 and 1994. In 1994 Eisenberg published *Air, 24 Hours: Jennifer Bartlett*, a 167-page monograph on a series of paintings. In the summer of 1995 she participated in the Prague Summer Writers' Workshop. She served as an adjunct professor at New York University in the spring of 1995 and 1996. In 1997 Eisenberg's first two collections were published together as *The Stories (So Far) of Deborah Eisenberg*. Her third volume of short stories, *All Around Atlantis*, was published in 1997.

The story that opens *All Around Atlantis*, "The Girl Who Left Her Sock on the Floor," vividly illustrates how far beyond her two earlier collections this volume has moved. It is a witty, moving depiction of a girl's search that begins with the death of her mother and ends on the verge of meeting the father she thought had died before she was born. The central character, Francie, immediately engages the reader. In some ways, Francie, like most of Eisenberg's protagonists, is lost, but her situation is deeper and more complex, more of a comment on the current state of the world. The opening pages range back and forth between beautiful descriptions of the snowy world outside her boarding-school dorm window and humorous commentary to her roommate: "'You know,' Francie said, 'there are people in the world—not many, but a few—to whom the most important thing is not whether there happens to be a sock on the floor. There are people in the world who are not afraid to face reality.'" This passage provides not only a rapid-fire character study but also hints at the deeper themes evoked in this tale. Left alone in the world by her mother's death, Francie must travel home musing on the ephemeral nature of life:

> If you were to break, for example, your hip, there would be the pain, the proof, telling you all the time it was true: *that's then and this is now.* But this thing—each second it had to be true all over again; she was getting hurled against each second. *Now. And now again—thwack!* Maybe one of these seconds she'd smash right through and find herself in the clear place where her mother was alive, scowling, criticizing.

Francie does not grieve and hurt because her relationship with her mother was idyllic. In fact, it seems to have been rather strained, but it was her only link, her only connection. As she travels to the hospital, Francie believes that she is orphaned.

The mortician, to whom her mother's body has been sent for cremation, reveals that Francie's father is alive and living in New York City. Francie furthers her odyssey, almost out of money and carrying her mother's ashes, desperate to find this man who may not even know she exists. In the end Eisenberg holds back from this confrontation. Instead of her father, Francie finds a man named Alex who invites her in to wait for her father's return. Sitting on the sofa, clutching the box of ashes, Francie does not dare reveal the reason for her visit. She imagines her father, walking down the street: "He fished in his pocket for change, and then glanced up sharply. Holding her breath, Francie drew herself back into the darkness. *It's your imagination*, she promised; he was going to have to deal with her soon enough—no sense making him see her until he actually had to."

"Rosie Gets a Soul" is in some ways a continuation of the themes in "The Girl Who Left Her Sock on the Floor." It also examines the precarious place of humanity in the world and the fragility of identities. In this story Rosie's quest begins by quitting the heroin that has kept her in a dreamlike existence and leaving her boyfriend and drug dealer, Ian. Depending on the mercies of a high-school friend, Jamie, Rosie finds herself caught up in his world. Jamie is an artist who supports himself by painting and stenciling on the walls of the extremely rich, and as the story opens, Rosie has

been hired as his assistant: "almost thirty years old, Rosie thinks, and this is where she finds herself—on someone's bedroom ceiling." Throughout this story the conflict between the dull business world of the rich and the colorful yet far less privileged world of artists presents a vivid social commentary. Rosie's motivation to get off the drugs is prompted by just such a comparison: "Those people had treated their lives so well, tending them and worshipping then and *using* them (however moronically), and she had just tossed hers into the freezer, like some old chunk of something you didn't exactly know what to do with."

As the story progresses and Rosie gains a sense of herself, she begins to fixate on the couple whose apartment she is painting. After meeting Elizabeth, the wife, Rosie is tempted by a silk slip that has been hanging tantalizingly in the bathroom for some time: "when Rosie gives the slip just the gentlest tug, it tumbles down, twinkling, into her hands. The slip pours tremblingly around her body, transforming it into a thrilling landscape, all gleams and shadows." This one item, casually left by the owners, is a clear symbol for the world of privilege. After meeting the husband, however, Rosie is drawn into their lives. One evening they exchange a serious flirtation and a passionate kiss; but then his failure to call, or even acknowledge their connection, prompts Rosie to assert herself and enact a small form of revenge: "The slip glimmers as though it's been waiting for her; it tumbles into her arms as she touches it. A rescue? Oh, no, not at all." She muses that the owners will be forced to think about her, to think about what she has done, in stealing the slip but she will just shove it on a back shelf and never think of them again—in this way she will get her revenge.

Three of the stories in this collection continue Eisenberg's focus on Latin America: "Across the Lake," "Someone to Talk To," and "Tlaloc's Paradise." All three continue the thematic thread begun in the earlier collections by stories such as "Broken Glass," "Under the 82nd Airborne," and "Holy Week." They examine the conflict between the worlds of the pampered tourist and the impoverished locals, adding in politics and war as grim reminders of the world outside the individual's search for understanding. The title story of the collection also examines these themes, but from a different perspective: that of the daughter of Holocaust survivors who is trying to come to terms with her own past and her relationship with her troubled mother.

All Around Atlantis is Eisenberg's most polished collection of short fiction. Eisenberg herself has said that her stories need to be read slowly—carefully—because each includes far too much meaning for a casual or cursory reading. R. Z. Shepard commented on this depth in his 15 September 1997 review for *Time:* "Powerful currents of the subconscious run beneath Eisenberg's winsome surfaces."

In her review of *All Around Atlantis* titled "City of the Drowned," Wendy Brandmark commented in *The London Times Literary Supplement* (13 March 1998):

> Deborah Eisenberg writes with the lucidity of a wise child who pushes aside the excuses of adults and yet understands their ambivalence and hypocrisy. We may not identify with her characters, but we are pulled into the stories by their emotional accuracy and the ease and economy with which she reveals people and their relationships.

This statement is telling, particularly since some of the most impressive stories in this collection, such as "The Girl Who Left Her Sock on the Floor," "Mermaids," and "All Around Atlantis" focus on children and adolescents.

Jim Shepard commented on this fact in his review for *The New York Times* (21 September 1997). Shepard compares Eisenberg's treatment of children and teenagers to that of Henry James, whom he quotes: "Eisenberg uses children to make seemingly ignoble people worthy of our attention . . . by the play of their good faith, these children make their parents 'concrete, immense and awful.'" This review is not entirely favorable; Shepard pointed out that "not all the strategies that recur in Eisenberg's stories are endlessly pleasing. Occasionally, the noticed detail is too flatfootedly an object correlative . . . and there's a fondness for pointedly illuminating chance encounters with eccentrics, who through their ramblings focus the stories' themes while bringing the usually somewhat baffled protagonists up to speed." Overall, however, the critics seem to have deemed *All Around Atlantis* the best collection that Eisenberg has yet produced. As Shepard said in his concluding sentence: "these stories are spirited and masterly road maps through sad and forbidding and desolate terrain."

Eisenberg continues to be read by a growing audience: her fiction has been translated into six languages. She has held a variety of collegiate positions and served as contributing editor for *Bomb Magazine*. Eisenberg currently splits her time between Manhattan and Virginia, teaching fiction writing every fall at the University of Virginia. Her short stories continue to appear in such periodicals as *The New Yorker*, *The Yale Review*, and *The Voice Literary Supplement*. In the fall of 1999 Eisenberg began to pursue a new interest—acting—rehearsing the role of Judy in Wallace Shawn's *The Designated Mourner* under the direction of André Gregory.

In the worlds Eisenberg creates, humanity is viewed through interrelationships, and the characters' surroundings, no matter how exotic, all include a certain familiar pang. Throughout her three volumes of short fiction, Eisenberg presents witty and urbane characters on voyages of self-discovery. As her style has matured, Eisenberg's prose has become increasingly sharp and symbolic. Eisenberg's vivid and intense reflections on characters juxtaposed against their surroundings have gained her a place among the most accomplished short-story writers of the late twentieth century.

Source: Robin A. Werner, "Deborah Eisenberg," in *Dictionary of Literary Biography*, Vol. 244, *American Short-Story Writers Since World War II, Fourth Series*, edited by Patrick Meanor and Joseph McNicholas, The Gale Group, 2001, pp. 92–100.

Sources

Brandmark, Wendy, Review of *All Around Atlantis*, in *Times Literary Supplement*, March 13, 1998, p. 23.

Caldwell, Gail, Review of *All Around Atlantis*, in *Boston Globe*, October 5, 1997, p. C1.

Eisenberg, Deborah, Interview, in *All Around Atlantis*, Washington Square Press, 1998, pp. 247–48.

———, "Someone to Talk To," in *All Around Atlantis*, Washington Square Press, 1998, pp. 59–89.

Friedman, Paula, "Characters Grow through Silences," in *Houston Chronicle*, December 14, 1997, p. 25.

Krist, Gary, Review of *Under the 82nd Airborne*, in *New York Times Book Review*, February 9, 1992, p. 11.

Review of *All Around Atlantis*, in *Kirkus Reviews*, July 1, 1997, n.p.

Sharkey, Nancy, "Courting Disorientation," in *New York Times Book Review*, February 9, 1992, p. 11.

Shepard, Jim, Review of *All Around Atlantis*, in *New York Times Book Review*, September 21, 1997, p. 9.

Sheppard, R. Z., Review of *All Around Atlantis*, in *Time*, September 15, 1997, p. 108.

Smith, Dinitia, "Achieving Grand Attention with a Fifth Book of Stories," in *New York Times*, February 28, 2006, p. E3.

Wiegand, David, Review of *All Around Atlantis*, in *San Francisco Chronicle*, October 5, 1997, p. 1.

Further Reading

Dubal, David, *Reflections from the Keyboard: The World of the Concert Pianist*, Summit Books, 1984.

This book contains a collection of interviews with famous concert pianists, including Murray Perahia, Andre Watts, and the late Glenn Gould and Vladimir Horowitz. In each interview, Dubal and the pianist discusses performance, technique, and interpretation.

Remnick, David, comp., *Wonderful Town: New York Stories from the "New Yorker,"* Modern Library, 2001.

This anthology of stories originally published in the *New Yorker* includes Eisenberg's story "What It Was Like, Seeing Chris," as well as stories by Philip Roth, Dorothy Parker, James Thurber, and Isaac Bashevis Singer.

Rossi, Peter H., *Down and Out in America: The Origins of Homelessness*, University of Chicago Press, 1991.

Rossi presents an academic analysis of the homeless and extremely poor, including demographic data, along with an interpretation of what the data means and suggestions for solutions.

Wilkinson, Daniel, *Silence on the Mountain: Stories of Terror, Betrayal, and Forgetting in Guatemala*, Houghton Mifflin, 2002.

Through personal interviews with Guatemalan citizens, Wilkinson tells the story of the country's thirty-six-year civil war from many different viewpoints. Included are accounts of atrocities committed by the army against entire communities and disturbing descriptions of the CIA's involvement with the Guatemalan government.

What We Cannot Speak About We Must Pass Over in Silence

John Edgar Wideman

2003

"What We Cannot Speak About We Must Pass Over in Silence" by John Edgar Wideman was first published in the December 2003 issue of *Harper's*. It is also available in a collection of Wideman's stories, *God's Gym* (2005). This disturbing story features an anonymous black, middle-aged male narrator who becomes obsessed by the imprisoned son of a dead friend. He spends much time struggling with prison bureaucracy in order to track the man down to a prison in the Arizona desert. The story, which is told in a stream-of-consciousness style, reflects Wideman's concerns about the high levels of incarceration of African American men (as of 2006, Wideman's younger brother and son were serving life sentences). Themes include the dehumanizing nature of the prison system, the political and economic division between the races, and the social isolation and fear felt by many African Americans. Also emphasized are the broader human difficulties of gaining reliable knowledge and of forming connections with, and knowledge of, other people in a society characterized by disconnection, fragmentation, and mechanization.

Author Biography

The African American writer John Edgar Wideman was born on June 14, 1941, in Washington, D.C., the eldest of five children of Edgar and Bette Wideman. The family moved to Pittsburgh, Pennsylvania, where he was later to set much of his fiction (especially in the Homewood ghetto). He attended Peabody High School, excelling in his studies and being made captain of the basketball team. He won a scholarship to the University of Pittsburgh, where he began to study psychology but soon changed to English, graduating in 1963. During his undergraduate career, Wideman made the Big Five Basketball Hall of Fame, won the university's creative writing prize, and earned membership of Phi Beta Kappa. He received a Rhodes scholarship to study philosophy at Oxford University in England, becoming only the second African American to receive such recognition. He gained a B.Phil. in eighteenth-century literature from Oxford's New College in 1966.

After returning to the United States, Wideman began writing and teaching at such institutions as the University of Pennsylvania and the University of Wyoming. His first novel, *A Glance Away*, was published in 1967. The story of a day in the life of a drug addict, the novel reflects Wideman's experiences during his youth in Homewood. Wideman soon gained critical acclaim for his use of an erudite and experimental literary style to describe ghetto experiences. His subsequent novels include *Hurry Home* (1970), *Hiding Place* (1981), *Sent for You Yesterday* (1983), *Philadelphia Fire* (1990), *The Cattle Killing* (1996), and *Two Cities* (1998). His short story collections include *Damballah* (1981), *Fever* (1989), *The Stories of John Edgar Wideman* (1992), and *All Stories Are True* (1993).

Wideman is also the author of a memoir, *Brothers and Keepers* (1984), which juxtaposes his life and that of his younger brother Robby, who was sentenced to life imprisonment for taking part in a robbery and for murder. In 1988, Wideman's son Jacob, aged eighteen, was sentenced to life imprisonment after pleading guilty to murder. Wideman has written numerous articles and given speeches on race, social deprivation, and the criminal justice and prison systems. His short story collection *God's Gym*, which includes "What We Cannot Speak About We Must Pass Over in Silence," was published in 2005.

As of 2006, Wideman was a professor of English at the University of Massachusetts, a post to which he was appointed in 1986. Wideman was living in Amherst with his wife, Judith Ann Goldman, whom he married in 1965, and three children: Daniel, Jacob, and Jamila. Daniel was a published writer, and Jamila a professional basketball player for the L.A. Sparks; Judith was working as a lawyer specializing in death penalty cases.

John Edgar Wideman © Jerry Bauer. Reproduced by permission

Wideman's work has won numerous awards. He is the only writer to have been awarded the PEN/Faulkner Award for Fiction twice—once in 1984 for *Sent for You Yesterday*, and again in 1991 for *Philadelphia Fire*, which also won an American Book Award from the Before Columbus Foundation. *Brothers and Keepers* was nominated for a National Book Critics Circle Award. Wideman was awarded the James Fenimore Cooper Prize for historical fiction in 1996 for *The Cattle Killing*. He won the New England Book Award and a Black Caucus Award of the American Library Association in 2002 for his memoir *Hoop Roots: Basketball, Race, and Love* (published in 2001).

Plot Summary

"What We Cannot Speak About We Must Pass Over in Silence" begins with the anonymous fifty-seven-year-old narrator announcing that he has a friend with a son in an Arizona prison. About once a year, this friend visits his son. The friend says that the hardest part of visiting is leaving, in the painful knowledge that his son is left behind, trapped in prison.

The narrator has just received a letter from a lawyer announcing the death of his friend, who is called Donald Williams. Inside the lawyer's envelope is a sealed letter that the friend has addressed to the narrator. The narrator is surprised that Williams thought him significant enough to be informed of his death. They had not known each other well and had been acquaintances rather than friends. Because of their not being close and because he accepts death as inevitable, the narrator has no strong emotional response to Williams's death. However, he finds himself grief-stricken over the plight of the son, who, according to Williams, never had any other visitors. The narrator wonders if his grief is partly due to the fact that he himself is, metaphorically speaking, imprisoned, interacting less and less with others.

He writes to the lawyer asking for the son's mailing address. The lawyer's office replies saying that while it executed Williams's will, it has no knowledge of any son. The narrator researches prisons in Arizona in an attempt to track down the son. He finds that there are many prisons and retirement communities in that state and wonders if the skills required in managing retirees translate to managing prisoners. This human "traffic" is processed by a huge number of computer specialists who input and retrieve information all day.

The narrator is motivated in his search by curiosity about the son and anger that though the system has the information he requires, it refuses to divulge it. He observes that if a person ever reaches a human voice, its hostile tone implies that the caller has done something wrong.

Finally, he locates the son. He writes to the son offering sympathy on his father's death. The son replies curtly, saying that he knew nothing of his father until he received the narrator's note. The narrator wonders if this is a case of mistaken identity or whether father or son was lying, or even hallucinating.

He goes to the lawyer's office and talks to the lawyer's paralegal, a young Asian woman called Suh Jung. Suh Jung has a brutally short haircut. She had her long hair cut after her domineering father, who had forbidden her to cut it, committed suicide by hanging himself. Suh Jung confirms that her office has no information on the son, but she offers to help the narrator in his search. The narrator flirts with Suh Jung and gets her telephone number. Though the narrator has now obtained information

on where and how to visit the son, he delays his visit while he and Suh Jung begin a sexual relationship. He finds himself breaking through his usual timidity by taking small risks, such as bathing her and smoking marijuana with her. He imagines how it would be if the son, not he, were with Suh Jung, as the son would be a more appropriate age for her partner.

Traveling one day on a bus, the narrator notices fresh blood on one of the seats and sits as far away from it as possible. He recalls an exhibit of works he visited by the Swiss sculptor and painter Alberto Giacometti (1901–1966). He reflects on Giacometti's belief that "art always failed" because it "lied" and also on the notion that people's eyes lie, in the sense that "No one ever sees the world as it is." Indeed, the narrator cannot even remember his dead friend's face and tries to reconstruct it from his own reflection in the mirror. He recalls some research showing that most people do not see accurately what is around them. As he gazes into the mirror, he is amazed at how beaten-up he looks and concludes that he prefers to see nothing.

In order to ease the narrator's passage through prison bureaucracy, the son tells him to claim on the form that he is the son's father. As the narrator waits for the prison to authorize his visit, he is afraid that this lie has been discovered. He calms himself with the thought that it is no crime to believe one is someone's father, even if it is not true. With Suh Jung's help, he gathers more information on the son. He learns that the son has done "the worst kinds of things" and that as the state cannot execute him, it will never let him go. Suh Jung says she would think twice about visiting, but the narrator tells her that everyone has crimes to answer for and that innocence or guilt is sometimes irrelevant in deciding who ends up behind bars.

The narrator arrives at the prison two days later than scheduled, and there is a delay while the prison authorities check up on him. He hears two guards laughing as they discuss a coyote that came scavenging near the prison's perimeter fence and that had been casually shot by a guard. The narrator imagines that the guard was having a bad day and took out his frustration on the coyote.

The narrator must go through a metal detector and various locked doors to get into the visiting area. Every step of his security progress is watched and monitored by machines. He is held in an open-air wire cage, exposed to the baking sun. Hot and silently furious, he waits as the prison staff shuffle papers and punch buttons on a computer console. He fears he might be trapped there forever and forced to confess his sins. Finally, one of the staff arrives and tells him his visit has been canceled and that according to the computer the inmate he seeks is not at this facility. The story ends with the narrator being told to come back on another day and to make way for the next visitor.

Characters

Friend

The narrator's friend is already dead when the story opens. He is only once referred to by his name, Donald Williams. Before he died, the friend told the narrator that he had a son in prison, whom he visited about once a year. The friend said that the hardest part about visiting was walking away from the prison, knowing that his son was still trapped inside.

After the friend's death, the narrator is surprised to receive a lawyer's letter with a note from the friend inside it. His surprise stems from the fact that he thought of the friend as only a casual acquaintance. The narrator becomes obsessed with the idea of visiting the son in prison. His failure to achieve this meeting raises the question that perhaps the friend, the son, or the narrator was lying or even hallucinating.

Suh Jung

Suh Jung is a young Asian female paralegal who works in the lawyer's office that informs the narrator about his friend's death. She helps the narrator track down his friend's son in prison. Like the narrator, Suh Jung is a frightened person who lives in an internalized prison. She was victimized by her brutal father, who dominated her and the rest of his household, and seems not to have given her any love. After he committed suicide by hanging himself, she cut off the long hair that he had insisted she not cut. Her stated aim in doing so was to protect herself from the submissive Asian female stereotype.

At the narrator's instigation, Suh Jung starts a sexual relationship with him and opens him up to new experiences, such as mutual bathing. The relationship does not appear to be founded on deep love or even strong attraction, and Suh Jung soon begins to taunt the narrator about his obsession with the son. She takes a more conventional view of the criminal justice system than the narrator, believing the records that accuse the son of terrible crimes and cautioning the narrator against becoming involved.

Narrator

The narrator is a fifty-seven-year-old African American man with a timid, nonconfrontational nature. He is acutely aware of being a member of "America's longest, most violently reviled minority," but unlike his hero, the poet Amiri Baraka, he is neither an activist nor a fighter. He uses expressions that suggest that he feels as if he is locked in an internal prison. When his friend dies, he becomes obsessed with the idea of visiting his son in prison. He tries to track down the son, frustrated at every step by bureaucracy. Along the way, he expresses many observations and criticisms of the prison system that Wideman himself has also voiced in his non-fictional writings. The narrator's failure to achieve the long-awaited meeting raises the question that perhaps the friend, the son, or the narrator was lying or even hallucinating.

Instead of forming a relationship with the son, the narrator begins a sexual relationship with Suh Jung, the young Asian paralegal who helps him in his search. Though there is no strong spark of attraction between them, he finds himself taking small risks in his relationship with her that appear to shift him out of his habitual timidity. Her bathing him appears to him to be a ritual cleansing, preparing him for the meeting with the son.

Though the narrator fails in his stated purpose of visiting the son, his bearing witness to the prison experience (both in terms of external and internal, psychological prisons) may represent his real achievement. In the simple act of telling his story, he has become an artist-activist like his hero, Baraka.

Son

Very little information is given about the son. He remains a shadowy character who never appears in person in the story. According to the official records, the son has done "the worst kinds of things," and since the state cannot execute him, it will never let him go. When the narrator writes to the son in prison telling him of the death of his father, he replies in a curt note, indicating he has no knowledge at all of his father, not even that he had died. The narrator sees him as "A smiling leopard in a cage," an image suggesting stored-up rage. The narrator fails to meet the son, and finally, the reader is left in doubt about the son's whereabouts or even existence.

Themes

Imprisonment

"What We Cannot Speak About We Must Pass Over in Silence" features the narrator's obsession with the imprisoned son of his dead friend. The story offers a critique of the prison system, reflecting the author's activism on the subject. As of 2006, Wideman's son and younger brother were both serving life sentences for murder, and Wideman has given speeches and written stories and articles questioning the prison system and the high rates of incarceration for black males in the United States.

In the story, Wideman's narrator emphasizes the dehumanization of the prison system, in which vast numbers of people are processed and monitored by equally vast numbers of computer specialists punching keys. He presents Arizona, where the son is held, as a state in which the economy depends upon prisons and other sorts of holding facilities (retirement homes, senior centers, hospices, and so on). The inmates are treated not as people, but as commodities, "a steady stream of bodies" or "traffic." Humane and ethical concerns have vanished, just as the son has vanished beyond the sight and reach of the narrator, beyond the knowledge of the prison's computer system. The system is dominated by the economic concerns of filling vacancies, collecting fees, and making sure the dead are replaced by the living with maximum efficiency. The absence from this picture of human values is emphasized by the narrator's description of the "eerily vacant" streets during "heatstroke daylight hours." He imagines the people who do the counting as "sequestered in air-conditioned towers or busy as bees underground in offices honeycombed beneath the asphalt." In the Arizona "gulags," each prisoner has ceased to be a person and has become "a single speck with its unique, identifying tag." Not only are the kept (the prisoners) stripped of their humanity by such a system, but so are the keepers (the computer operators), who have been reduced to the status of insects living underground. Wideman raises the question: in such a system, arising from society's terrified determination to keep criminals out of sight and out of reach, who are the prisoners, and who are the free?

Suh Jung represents the conventional view, that prison walls separate the dangerous people (the prisoners) from the decent people (the free), as is suggested by her warning the narrator against becoming involved with the prisoner. She believes the

records, which say he is guilty of terrible crimes. The narrator is more ambivalent, replying, "Everyone has crimes to answer for." He says that people can end up in "Situations when nothing's for sure except some of us are on one side of the bars, some on the other side, but nobody knows which side is which." He goes on to tease Suh Jung with the possibility that he himself could be a serial killer. The narrator's stance echoes the words of African American radical activist and prison abolitionist, Angela Y. Davis (born 1944), in her essay, "A World Unto Itself: Multiple Invisibilities of Imprisonment," in *Behind the Razor Wire* (a book to which Wideman also contributed): "to hear the stories of incarcerated women and men is to recognize that little more than the luck of the draw—or rather, of one's socioeconomic birthright—separates 'us' from 'them.'"

Indeed, the narrator's experiences of the adversarial prison system lead him to feel like a criminal. During his research, when he finally extracts information on the son's whereabouts, the automated and the human administrators of the prison system make him feel that he has done something wrong. During his visit to the prison, he is held in a wire cage under a burning sun until he is desperate to flee, fearing that he will be trapped there forever, knocked to his knees, and "forced to recite my sins, the son's sins, the sins of the world." Apart from the narrator's dealings with the prison system, even in his daily existence, he is a kind of prisoner. His life, restricted by his timidity, is a "prison I've chosen to seal myself within," with "fewer and fewer visits paid or received."

Imprisonment and Race

In his essay, "Doing Time, Marking Race" in *Behind the Razor Wire*, Wideman writes that incarceration is a form of apartheid. This judgment is based on the disproportionately large numbers of incarcerated black males, the perceived racism of the criminal justice system with its heavy sentencing for so-called black crimes, and the exploitation of society's fears by politicians who promise to get tough on the crimes perpetuated by some "other" group (by implication, black people). Wideman writes that he has an intimate knowledge of prisons due to the fact that "From every category of male relative I can name—grandfather, father, son, brother, uncle, nephew, cousin, in-law—at least one member of my family has been incarcerated." He adds, "I am a descendant of a special class of immigrants—Africans—for whom arrival in America was a life sentence in the prison of slavery."

Topics For Further Study

- Read about John Edgar Wideman's views on prison, social exclusion, and race, and write an essay showing how "What We Cannot Speak About We Must Pass Over in Silence" explores these views.

- Research African American and white people's views of aspects of the criminal justice system, such as interactions with police, the courts, and prisons. You may use written sources and/or interviews in your research. Write a report comparing African American views with white views.

- Research the criminal justice systems of other cultures, whether historical or current. Write a report analyzing the advantages and disadvantages of the different systems, saying which aspects, if any, you would like to see adopted by current society.

- Study the writings of people who are currently working for reform of the criminal justice system. Write a report on their views of what should be changed, and how, and finally, give your own views.

- Research the correlations between poverty and crime. Write a report on your findings, drawing charts where appropriate.

- Many people who work for reform of the criminal justice system draw attention to what they see as unfair differences in treatment of so-called black crime and white crime. Research this topic and write a report on your findings.

- Study the work of a contemporary or historical writer or artist who is/was also a social activist. Write an essay analyzing their views and how their work relates to it. Discuss any of the social changes they pressed for which may have been brought about by the artist's work or other factors.

In the same essay, Wideman comments: "To be a man of color of a certain economic class and milieu is equivalent in the public eye to being a criminal." One possible response to such treatment is to protest loudly; another, that adopted by the narrator of "What We Cannot Speak About We Must Pass Over in Silence," is to keep one's head down. The narrator compares himself unfavorably with the outspoken black activist poet Amiri Baraka (born 1934), describing himself "as quietly integrated and nonconfrontational a specimen as I seemed to be of America's longest, most violently reviled minority."

In line with Wideman's accusation that incarceration is a form of apartheid, "What We Cannot Speak About We Must Pass Over in Silence" shows the desire of white middle and upper classes to separate themselves from prisons and their inmates by hiding prisoners in far away places like the Arizona desert. This desire, however, seems doomed to backfire. Just as Wideman's story blurs the line between those locked in literal prisons and those on the outside who inhabit psychological prisons, Wideman suggests in "Doing Time, Marking Race" that for an African American underclass, the distinction between prison and the urban street is increasingly hard to define. Prison itself is being transformed by the street values of young prisoners to mirror urban war zones, revolving around drugs and gang affiliations. Prisons now "accommodate a fluid population who know their lives will involve inevitable shuttling between prison and the street." Wideman's story confirms that because prisons are products of attitudes of those inside and outside the prison walls, they cannot effectively be separated from the general society.

The Problem of Knowledge

The sense of isolation, alienation, and imprisonment felt by the two main characters in the story is compounded by the seeming impossibility of gaining accurate knowledge about anybody or anything in a world that is fragmented and dehumanized. The first line of the story, "I have a friend with a son in prison," turns out to be open to doubt in its every aspect: the friend is not so much a friend as an acquaintance, the friend may or may not have a son, and the son may or may not be in prison. The narrator muses on his inability to remember his dead friend's face or even to recognize his own face and points out that nobody knows for sure who their father is. His attempts to trace the son are frustrated by an almost impenetrable bureaucracy administered by computers and automated systems. The narrator's small successes in gaining information are punished by an adversarial, hostile stance conveyed by these systems that makes him feel like a criminal. Even the narrator's relationship with Suh Jung is characterized by a failure to achieve a meaningful connection, partly because of her frightened defensiveness about her true nature.

The only successful attempts at both seeing and showing truth are achieved by two artists featured in the story, the Swiss sculptor and painter Alberto Giacometti (1901–1966) and the African American poet Amiri Baraka (born 1934). Giacometti's picture of a dog awakens a passionate response in the narrator, who, contrary to his habit, both sees and recognizes its truth. Baraka's courageous activism inspires the narrator to take small risks in his relationship with Suh Jung. The narrator, in spite of his timidity, joins the ranks of the artists when he creates his own piece of art, the story he is telling. Through the story, he shows something of the truth about society's external and internal prisons.

Style

Stream of Consciousness

In this story, Wideman uses a stream-of-consciousness and experimental language, both reminiscent of the work of the Irish novelist James Joyce (1882–1941). Stream-of-consciousness presents an interior monologue of the narrator, allowing us to see inside the mind of the character as it associates ideas and moves along in a flow of thoughts. Writing in stream-of-consciousness allows rapid and apparently unrelated (but in reality, carefully crafted) jumps in focus. This kind of narrative gives no objective information about external events, and readers are forced to rely on and evaluate the narrator's thoughts which may or may not be reliable. It is left up to readers to decide if the narrator's thoughts are aligned with objective reality or delusional. For example, when the story ends, readers may wonder where the son is or whether he even exists.

Word Order and Rhythm

Wideman's experimental use of language has been likened to the improvised rhythms of modern American jazz. It adds to the density and relative difficulty of Wideman's prose style, but it also creates remarkable effects. For example, in one place, the story presents a letter from the narrator to the son. The letter is a mosaic of original and revised wording juxtaposed without explanation:

> Please allow me to express my sympathy for your great loss I don't claim to know to have known him well but I your father fine man good man considered him a valuable friend heartfelt he spoke of you many times always quite much good love.

Elsewhere is a passage in which the narrator imagines Suh Jung making love with the imprisoned son: "Would it be the same woman in both places at once or different limbs, eyes, wetnesses, scents, like those tigers whirling about Sambo." The insistent, frantic rhythms of this passage reflect both the whirling tigers and the imagined sexual excitement of the scene. In these and other stylistic ways, Wideman locates the action of the story very much in the internal language of a particular person, this narrator, words jumbled together oftentimes as only that person would think of them.

Metaphors

Wideman uses metaphors of imprisonment to describe the free lives of those outside prison, blurring the line between the so-called innocent and the so-called guilty. The narrator's experience of extracting information about the son from the adversarial prison system makes him feel that he has "done something stupid or morally suspect by pursuing it to its lair." The metaphor raises the question of who is the hunter and who is the hunted, in a society whose terror of criminals leads to locking them up physically and to isolating them even further behind a mesh of mechanization and computerization.

A metaphor emphasizing the narrator's restricted, prisoner-like existence is used to describe his home. He lives "in a building in the bottom of somebody's pocket. Sunlight never touches its bricks." His life itself has become restricted; it is a "prison I've chosen to seal myself within. Fewer and fewer visits paid or received." He likens himself to a prisoner about to be executed: After he has finished looking at himself in the mirror, he switches off the light, letting "the merciful hood drop over the prisoner's head."

The Asian character Suh Jung is also described in images that compare her to a criminal, a prisoner, or more particularly, a prisoner of war. She tries to cover up her fear with an "unsuccessful theft" of her father's blank eyes. She is her father's victim and his prisoner, "relentlessly, meticulously hammered into an exquisitely lifelike, flawless representation of his will, like those sailing ships in bottles or glass butterflies in the museum." After her father's suicide, she tries to protect herself against the Asian female cliché of submissiveness by having her hair cut into a "helmet," an item of military defense. Her nipples are "twin sentry towers." When the narrator makes love to her, he describes her in terms of a vanquished enemy: she is "easy to . . . subdue"; he is "capturing her, punishing her." He realizes that in his power over her, he has become her brutal father and her jailer, "the steel gate dropping over the tiger pit in which she's naked, trapped, begging for food and water. Air. Light."

This image of the steel gate dropping over the tiger pit is a terrifying one, suggesting not love, but power exercised over someone who is angry yet helpless. Coming from the narrator, it also blurs the line between abuser and victim, just as Wideman blurs the line between those inside the prison and those outside. The narrator is a victim when faced with those in power, such as the prison authorities, but a potential abuser when faced with those weaker than he is, like Suh Jung. Wideman seems to suggest that to whatever extent a person feels himself to be a victim, he victimizes, passing on the prison experience, just as a beaten dog does not bite his tormentor but finds a smaller dog to bite.

Another metaphor pattern uses big cats. When the narrator imagines Suh Jung making love to the imprisoned son, he pictures her as a tiger whirling about him, suggesting both the clichéd expression, the Asian tiger, and the unleashed sensuality that he himself never achieves with her. When the narrator is making love to her, he likens her to a tiger trapped in a pit, suggesting anger denied free expression. The same meaning is implied by his description of the imprisoned son as "A smiling leopard in a cage," except that the son is in a literal prison, whereas Suh Jung is in a psychological one.

Symbols

The coyote that prowls around the prison is given significant emphasis in the story. It is a predator, but harmless to the guards. They laugh at it until one of them, who is evidently having a bad day, casually shoots it. The coyote symbolizes both the narrator, in his cautious and fearful approach to the prison, and black people, who are mercilessly hunted down if they encroach on white territory. Their lives, like the life of the coyote, are seen as cheap and disposable.

Plot

Wideman deliberately breaks one of the conventions of fiction by denying the reader the long-expected outcome—the meeting between the narrator and the imprisoned son. This inconclusive ending achieves a number of effects. One is to emphasize the frustration of dealing with the prison system: the narrator's frustration is mirrored by the reader's. Another is to indicate that the story is not really about this meeting but something else entirely. Possible interpretations of the story include the difficulty of making meaningful connections in a dehumanized, disconnected world and the narrator's artistic achievement in shining a light into the dark world of the prison system.

Setting

The setting of the prison, in the Arizona desert, emphasizes the way in which the prison system is removed and hidden from the U.S. population at large. Also, as the narrator points out, Arizona is the national choice for institutions that house those it would rather forget: the criminals, the retirees, the dying, and the dead. It confirms Angela Y. Davis's comment in *Behind the Razor Wire*, that the prison creates an "illusion of inaccessibility," which

> works two ways: on the one hand, it is designed to persuade those on the outside that those who are locked away cannot reach into our homes, our neighborhoods, or, for that matter, our society; on the other hand, however, we in the 'free' world rarely imagine ourselves being able to reach into the imprisoned world—that is, to enter into this world—without ourselves being arrested and imprisoned.

Wideman wants readers to be aware of the system that is in place to handle prisoners and what that system does to prevent those on the outside from making contact with inmates. More than that, he wants readers to understand that what distinguishes insiders from outsiders may be more matters of race and class than of free will and law infringement. Finally, bondage and entrapment take various forms. So while Wideman focuses on Arizona for its role in the prison industry, he also makes clear that other settings, both urban and psychological, play their parts in the various kinds of incarceration people experience.

Post-Aesthetic Movement

John Edgar Wideman's work is considered as falling in the literary category of the post-aesthetic movement. This movement is an artistic response made by African Americans to the black aesthetic movement of the 1960s and early 1970s, which attempted to produce works of art that would be meaningful to black people. Since that time, writers of the post-aesthetic movement have placed less emphasis on the disparity between black and white in the United States. African Americans are portrayed as looking inward for answers to their own questions. In "What We Cannot Speak About We Must Pass Over in Silence," the focus is as much on the internal, psychological prisons of the characters, as on the external prisons.

Historical Context

Race, Imprisonment, and the Socioeconomic Divide

In the later half of the nineteenth century, some American states passed laws restricting privileges given to emancipated African Americans after the Civil War. These so-called Jim Crow laws segregated African Americans from the white population and denied them equal status with whites in all aspects of their lives, including the use of public services, public places, schools, poling regulations, and so forth. These local laws remained in place until the civil rights movement, which gained momentum in the 1940s, pushed the Supreme Court to declare segregation laws illegal in a series of decisions beginning in 1954. In 1964, the U.S. Congress passed the Civil Rights Act which outlawed state laws requiring segregation. However, this law did not end the practice of segregation, which continues unofficially, mostly due to the economic factor of poverty. Thus, in many parts of the United States, African Americans live and attend schools separately from whites. In a 2003 speech, "The American Dilemma Revisited: Psychoanalysis, Social Policy, and the Socio-cultural Meaning of Race," published in *Black Renaissance*, Wideman gives some revealing statistics: Poverty has continued to increase for African Americans since the 1980s. Forty-four percent of black children live below the poverty line, compared with 20 percent of all American children. A black baby is three times more likely to die than a white one.

Black people's experiences with, and attitudes toward, the criminal justice system often differ from those of white people, prompting racial tensions. In 1991, the beating of an unarmed black man, Rodney King, by four Los Angeles police officers was captured on videotape. An all-white jury acquitted the police officers, prompting riots in Los Angeles and widespread protests. In 2001, fifteen black men were killed by police or died in police custody over a period when no men from other races died in comparable circumstances. No police officers were found guilty in criminal or civil courts. This sequence of events provoked rioting in Cincinnati, Ohio.

The statistics on African Americans caught up in the criminal justice system give an idea of the extent of the problems. In "The American Dilemma Revisited," Wideman notes that 781,000 black males are incarcerated, 200,000 more than are enrolled in colleges and universities. Every day, a black male aged between eighteen and thirty-four has a one-in-ten chance of finding himself locked up; one in three are under custodial supervision; each year, each has a one-in-three chance of being imprisoned. Possession of the cheap drug crack, widely used in poor African-American communities, carries much heavier jail time than luxury drugs such as cocaine. An analysis of 141,000 traffic citations written between 1999 and 2000 by Cincinnati police found black drivers were twice as likely as whites to be cited for driving without a license, twice as likely to be cited for not wearing a seat belt, and four times as likely to be cited for driving without proof of insurance.

The Privatization of Prisons

The 1990s saw a debate about the growing privatization of prisons, which previously were run by the government. The argument for privatization emphasizes cost reduction. Arguments against it claim that cost-cutting results in lower standards of care and that privatization leads to a market demand for prisoners and prison labor, which is fed by tougher sentencing. Wideman's story, "What We Cannot Speak About We Must Pass Over in Silence," critiques the dehumanizing aspects of what the author terms the "prison industry," which flourishes from human "traffic."

Critical Overview

The work of John Edgar Wideman arouses strong responses in readers, and critics are no exception.

Saguaro cacti in the Sonoran Desert, Arizona Corbis/David Muench

His work, too demanding to achieve mass popularity, is largely read in colleges and universities, where he enjoys a distinguished reputation as a black intellectual who is steeped in Western culture but who is gradually rediscovering his African roots. It has been remarked that a college education is needed to negotiate his complex prose style and understand his erudite references to various artists and philosophers. His stories and novels combine ghetto experiences with experimental fiction techniques and quasi-autobiographical material to explore social, racial, and cultural conflicts.

Revealingly, with each publication of a Wideman work, a multitude of articles appear in newspapers and magazines about the man. His early years as a basketball player and the contrast between his extraordinary academic reputation and the fact that both his younger brother and his son are serving life prison sentences make him an intriguing subject for journalists. However, there is relatively little in-depth criticism of his work. This is possibly because critics are wary of its intellectually challenging nature and its uncomfortable tendency to frustrate readers' expectations. It must be emphasized, though, that Wideman's work strongly repays patient attention and rereading, perhaps with the help of an encyclopedia for checking references.

After John Edgar Wideman's story, "What We Cannot Speak About We Must Pass Over in Silence," appeared in *Harper's* in 2003, it was chosen for *The Best American Short Stories 2004* (edited by Lorrie Moore, published 2004). The story was published again in the collection, *God's Gym* (2005). Critical response to the collection was mostly admiring. Earni Young, in *Black Issues Book Review*, writes that Wideman's stories are "alive with passion, intelligence and the electric rhythm that has twice won him the PEN/Faulkner Award."

Several reviewers warn the more timid sort of readers about the difficulty of Wideman's experimental style. Playing on the title *God's Gym*, Ed Nawotka, writing in *People Weekly*, cautions that the collection is "a mental workout" that may leave the reader fatigued. In similar vein, the anonymous reviewer for *O, The Oprah Magazine* comments that *God's Gym* "is so brazenly and lyrically experimental, so charged with emotion and restless intellect, that a reader gets winded just trying to keep up with him." John Freeman, writing in *Seattle Times* and making reference to Wideman's stint as a basketball player, comments, "No American writer dribbles a sentence quite like John Edgar Wideman. Watching him thread language between his legs and around his back is a bit like watching a Harlem Globetrotter vamp." He terms the collection "dazzling." Terrence Rafferty, writing for the *New York Times Book Review*, also uses a basketball analogy, noting Wideman's practice in the stories of aborting developing scenes or abruptly shifting the direction of the narrative, "backpedaling like a basketball player in transition from offense to defense—for all sorts of reasons."

Referring to Wideman's withholding of the expected meeting between the narrator and the imprisoned son, Rafferty acknowledges that some readers may find "Wideman's persistent refusal to fulfill the requirements of well-made fiction" to be "willfully perverse." But Rafferty cautions, "it would be a mistake to think he's just messing with our heads"; Wideman violates the conventions of narrative and language itself because "they can't take him where he wants to go."

An anonymous reviewer for *Kirkus Reviews* notes, "The best of the stories are charged with deep feeling," singling out "What We Cannot Speak About We Must Pass Over in Silence" as a "wrenching tale." A *Publishers Weekly* reviewer admires the way Wideman pushes the boundaries of narrative and form but was one of several critics who object to his treatment of the coyote, pointing out that "the detour is so long it stops the story dead" and robs it of its power. Jeffrey Severs, in his review for the *Austin American-Statesman*, points out that while the coyote seems to symbolize black people being hunted down by a hostile society, Wideman's real topic is "the fear that twists black people's minds in many other, less dramatic moments."

Rebecca Stuhr, in her review for *Library Journal*, calls the stories "feasts of language offering up new metaphors and original imagery." Stuhr remarks on an important aspect of Wideman's work, which can at first meeting seem inaccessible and opaque: "Each story is a gem that grows more brilliant with rereading." In sum, reviewers seem to agree that reading Wideman's prose is well worth the effort.

Criticism

Claire Robinson

Robinson is a former teacher of English literature and creative writing and, as of 2006, is a full-time writer and editor. In the following essay, Robinson explores how the problem of finding truth in a world dedicated to avoiding it is examined in

John Edgar Wideman's "What We Cannot Speak About We Must Pass Over in Silence."

John Edgar Wideman took the title of his story, "What We Cannot Speak About We Must Pass Over in Silence," from the last line of a work by an Austrian philosopher: *Tractatus Logico-Philosophicus* (1921) by Ludwig Wittgenstein (1889–1951). A possible interpretation of Wittgenstein's sentence and the argument that leads up to it is that the essence of the world is beyond the reach of human thought and words. Words can describe known facts about the world, but that is all. Among the many things that lie beyond words are ethics, aesthetics, the meaning of life, the immortality of the soul, the nature of language and logic, and the fundamental structure of the universe. Wittgenstein asserts that most philosophical confusion arises from trying to speak about things that can only be shown. Having dismissed even his own philosophical propositions as nonsense, Wittgenstein concludes, "What we cannot speak about we must pass over in silence."

Wittgenstein's statement alerts the reader to an important theme of Wideman's story: the difficulty of knowing anything about anything and anybody. This eternal philosophical problem is given added weight in modern society as Wideman portrays it. Here is a world in which computers, which were designed to facilitate communication between people, often serve only to dehumanize and fragment society. It is a world in which huge resources are poured into the prison industry and ever-increasing numbers of people are moved out of sight in an effort to make the rest of the people feel safe. This social fragmentation is reflected in the isolation and alienation felt by the narrator. His attempts to extract meaningful information from his limited interactions with others are largely marked by frustration and failure.

In this respect, the first sentence of the story is revealing: "I have a friend with a son in prison." As the story progresses, it turns out that every aspect of this simple statement is open to doubt. The narrator's friend, he later reveals, is not really a friend, but an acquaintance with whom he has only fleeting contacts. The friend may or may not have a son, and that son may or may not be in prison. The question of the son is made even more opaque when he writes to the narrator asking him to pose as his father, apparently to smooth his way through the prison bureaucracy, though this is not certain. The narrator agrees, since nobody can prove that he does not believe himself to be the son's father.

Indeed, he reflects that most children go through a phase in which they do not believe that the adults raising them are their real parents. The episode suggests that nobody can know for certain who their father is.

The narrator never learns the truth about the son. In fact, in a reversal of the usual story format, the truth seems more elusive at the story's end than at the beginning: "Computer says the inmate you want to visit is not in the facility." Frustratingly, the narrator cannot question the computer further.

Thus, the expected meeting with the son never happens. Instead, the narrator forms a relationship with Suh Jung. But even this, the only person-to-person relationship presented in the story, is characterized by a lack of truth and meaning. It does not spring from attraction, but an embarrassment on the part of the narrator at seeing weak and indecisive. There is always a distance between them, which grows more obvious when she begins to taunt him about his obsession with the son in prison. The narrator admits that he uses her in order to obtain information about the son, but he justifies himself by saying that all relationships are about using people. He does not mention love.

Suh Jung is also disjointed or lacking in congruence. She has cut her hair into a brutal style that does not suit her in order to protect herself from a stereotype. She is in reality a terrified girl but hides her fear with a pretended coolness. She has stolen this coolness from her father, whose attitude toward her is characterized by a "blankness" behind his eyes and a determination to hammer all around him into "an exquisitely lifelike, flawless representation of his will." To him, she is not a human being, but an artifact.

Compounding the sense of uncertainty and disorientation is the narrator's inability to recall the face of his friend, the son's father. When he tries to reconstruct it by gazing at his own reflection in the mirror, he is shocked by the time-battered, frightened face that gazes back. He does not even recognize himself: "Who in God's name was this person," he asks. Recalling scientific research that shows that people do not really look at what is around them, he suggests that this is an unconscious way of avoiding taking responsibility: "Instead of staring without fear and taking responsibility for the unmistakable, beaten-up person I've apparently become, I prefer to see nothing."

This comment resonates in the story. The narrator describes how the Arizona prison is situated in a "Vast emptiness," and how the computer operators

> **"** Like the narrator of Wideman's "What We Cannot Speak About We Must Pass Over in Silence," who prefers not to see his frightened, battered face, people on the outside prefer not to see the prisons or their inmates; they cannot speak about them, and they pass over them in silence."

who administer it and the other facilities are "sequestered" in towers or in underground offices. The aim is to keep the inmates safely apart from outsiders, out of sight and out of mind. This aim is supported by the impenetrable prison bureaucracy that is reluctant to give up any information to the narrator about the imprisoned son. So successful is it that by the end of the story, the narrator has no idea where the inmate is or even if he exists at all.

Like the narrator of Wideman's "What We Cannot Speak About We Must Pass Over in Silence," who prefers not to see his frightened, battered face, people on the outside prefer not to see the prisons or their inmates; they cannot speak about them, and they pass over them in silence. Angela Y. Davies, in her essay in *Behind the Razor Wire*, "A World Unto Itself: Multiple Invisibilities of Imprisonment," calls prisoners "invisible populations" living in "invisible worlds." In his essay "Doing Time, Marking Race" in the same book, Wideman elaborates on this theme: "Prisons do their dirtiest work in the dark. The evil they perpetrate depends on a kind of willed ignorance on the part of the public." As a potential remedy to this state of ignorance, Wideman suggests that "The truth of art. . . . can throw light on what occurs inside prisons. This light, whether a source of revelation for millions, a spur to political reform, or simply one more candle burning, will help to dispel the nightmare we've allowed our prisons to become."

Even this modest degree of certainty about the power of art to reveal the truth seems to be thrown into doubt by the bleak vision of "What We Cannot

What Do I Read Next?

- John Edgar Wideman's autobiographical work, *Brothers and Keepers* (1984), includes a portrait of his brother Robby, who is serving a life prison sentence for a murder committed during a robbery. Wideman seeks to understand how he and his brother could have such disparate lives after a childhood together in the ghetto of Homewood, Pittsburgh.

- Nathan McCall's autobiographical work, *Makes Me Wanna Holler: A Young Black Man in America* (1994), recounts his life as a boy in a black neighborhood, his participation in violent crime, and his imprisonment for armed robbery. While in prison, he worked as a librarian, and on his release, he became a successful writer.

- Michael Jacobson-Hardy's *Behind the Razor Wire: Portrait of a Contemporary American Prison System* (1998) is a book of uncompromising and revealing photographs and essays on the prison system. Included are essays by Angela Y. Davis ("A World Unto Itself: Multiple Invisibilities of Imprisonment") and John Edgar Wideman ("Doing Time, Marking Race").

- Alan Elsner's *The Gates of Injustice: The Crisis in America's Prisons* (2004) is a devastating exposé of the prison industry. It recounts aspects of prison life, including drug and alcohol abuse, disease, rape, murder, and racism, and shows how a huge prison-industrial complex promotes imprisonment over other solutions.

- *Prison Nation: The Warehousing of America's Poor* (2003), edited by Tara Herivel and Paul Wright, makes the case that the United States has an in-justice system at work which operates largely out of sight of the public. Shocking brutalities and mistreatments are recounted, as well as racist bias, inadequate medical care, abuses of prison labor, and the use of the restraint chair.

Speak About We Must Pass Over in Silence." The narrator says that the artist Giacometti, who, unlike the willfully and complacently blind, actively sought the truth, "didn't trust what was in front of his eyes": "He understood art always failed. Art lied to him. People's eyes lied. No one ever sees the world as it is." Giacometti found that if he glanced away from his model, when he looked back, "it would be different, always different, always changing."

However, it would be a mistake to identify the narrator with Wideman's own view. The narrator is self-confessedly timid, simultaneously "begging and fearing to be seen," imprisoned by a "lack of directness, decisiveness, my deficiency of enterprise and imagination." While this timidity is understandable in humanity in general, it is perhaps especially so in a member of an ethnic minority. But the narrator's timidity is not the way to truth.

The two artists featured in the story, Giacometti and the African American poet Amiri Baraka (born 1934), who is known for his activism in black causes, are braver. While no character in the story manages to see or speak the whole truth, these artists do manage to show something of the truth. Showing is the one way that Wittgenstein believed truth could be revealed; in Wideman's story, the people who show are the artists. While Giacometti sees the limitations of art to capture a changing world, he does not allow that to stop him from creating it. The narrator, in spite of his focus on Giacometti's statements about the failure of art, cannot fail to respond to the artist's famous picture of a dog. The truth of this picture produces a heartfelt passion in him that Suh Jung fails to inspire: "I loved the slinky dog. He was so . . . so . . . you know . . . *dog*." It is characteristic of the narrator that he fails to see it at the exhibit, as he is overwhelmed by all the objects. Instead, he sees it at one remove, in the catalog. But this man who has made a habit of not seeing his own face or the faces of those around him at last does see, with great immediacy and immediate recognition, and he is moved.

The narrator also loves Baraka, not so much for what he writes but for "the chances he'd taken, chances in his art, in his life." The narrator is thankful for the "Sacrifices of mind and body he endured so I could vicariously participate, holed up in my corner." It is significant that the narrator's praise of Baraka comes just before his account of the tiny risks he takes, the "low-order remarkable things" he experiences with Suh Jung. These risks, if he were able to magnify them many times, could make a difference in his life and perhaps in the lives of others. Baraka and Giacometti have embraced risk. Through their art, they show a truth that can illuminate the invisible, the hidden, that which is passed over by most people in silence. The final twist is that, in telling his story, the narrator has abandoned his timid existence on the sidelines and has, largely in spite of himself, become an artist. His obsession about the imprisoned son has led him to create a piece of art that shows us a part of the truth about our external and internal prisons.

Source: Claire Robinson, Critical Essay on "What We Cannot Speak About We Must Pass Over in Silence," in *Short Stories for Students*, Thomson Gale, 2007.

Timothy Dunham

Dunham has a master's degree in communication and a bachelor's degree in English. In the following essay, Dunham examines the debilitating effects of the narrator's spiritually imprisoned soul in "What We Cannot Speak About We Must Pass Over in Silence" and the violent means God uses to free it.

T. S. Eliot's *The Waste Land* opens with an epigraph that John Edgar Wideman could just as easily have used to open "What We Cannot Speak About We Must Pass Over in Silence": "For on one occasion I myself saw, with my own eyes, the Cumaean Sibyl hanging in a cage, and when some boys said to her, 'Sibyl, what do you want?' she replied, 'I want to die.'" This passage, which Eliot took from Petronius's *Satyricon*, refers to the Sibyl of Cumae, a prophetess of the ancient world to whom Apollo granted a single wish. She wished to live as many years as the number of grains she could hold in her hand, but she forgot to ask for eternal youth; as a result, she suffered increasing decrepitude as the years wore on, only she did not die. In the context of *The Waste Land*, the Sibyl hanging in her cage is an image of the soul imprisoned, an apt metaphor for the monotonous, lonely, and empty lives of the poem's characters. The image is especially befitting the narrator and main character of "What We Cannot Speak About We Must Pass Over in Silence," an unnamed man

> " Using prison as an overarching metaphor, Wideman depicts how relationships, living conditions, and the natural world reflect the entrapped state of the narrator's soul...."

who sees everything in his experience as a kind of prison. Like the people who inhabit *The Waste Land*, he lives a life emotionally cut off from others and is unable to find joy or fulfillment; but unlike the narrator of *The Waste Land*, he is not aware that there is a way out of the cage, that is, until the very end. "What We Cannot Speak About We Must Pass Over in Silence" is the chronicle of a man's journey from a confining life of empty routine to the cusp of a new life in which the possibility exists for value and renewal.

Throughout the story, no philosophical or theological interpretation is given for the narrator's imprisoned soul, and no explanation is provided for how it became imprisoned. Wideman seems to be in accordance with the postulation Eliot puts forth in *The Waste Land*: an imprisoned soul is part of the natural order of things and can only be freed by a spiritual force. (The Christian term for this is original sin.) Many people, like those in *The Waste Land*, are unaware of their predicament, while others are aware and try to do something about it. The narrator of "What We Cannot Speak About We Must Pass Over in Silence" is one of the latter, his awareness being triggered by the manner in which he responds to the news of his friend's death. When he receives the manila envelope containing the information, he feels no shock, sadness, or remorse; in fact, it "move[s] [him] not a bit." After all, this was a friend in the loosest sense of the word, an acquaintance whom he had met on occasion for coffee or a movie but never got to know very well; in fact, he cannot even remember what he looked like. The narrator describes the nature of their relationship in chillingly impersonal terms:

> He's the kind of person you could see occasionally, enjoy his company more or less, and walk away with no further expectations, no plan to meet again. If he'd moved to another city, months might have

passed before I'd notice him missing. If we'd lost contact for good, I'm sure I wouldn't have regretted not seeing him. A smidgen of curiosity, perhaps. Perhaps a slight bit of vexation, as when I discover I haven't restocked paper towels or Tabasco sauce. Less, since his absence wouldn't leave a gap I'd be obliged to fill.

The action the narrator takes is different from that which he normally takes when faced with a personal dilemma. He is used to stepping away from it, "escap[ing] into a book, a movie, a vigorous walk," or simply laughing it off. This time, however, he faces the dilemma head-on, energized by the sympathy he feels for the imprisoned son. He writes to the attorney who sent the envelope and asks for the son's mailing address, but the attorney is unable to provide it, so he calls the Arizona correctional system and endures one bureaucratic nightmare after another before he is finally able to get it. He sends the son a letter expressing his condolences, to which the son replies, in essence, that he never knew his father. Rather than stop there, the narrator goes to the attorney's office in an effort to find out where he had been led astray. He pursues the matter with the attorney's paralegal, Suh Jung, and suddenly, what was once a wholehearted effort becomes halfhearted and lackadaisical. The pursuit of information becomes the pursuit of Suh Jung and thus begins yet another empty relationship that brings no comfort and leaves him "more alone now . . . than when [he] arrived spanking brand-new on the planet." The only difference between this and former relationships is that now he is aware of the emptiness and loneliness. This awareness, first triggered by his response to the contents of the envelope, has become a permanent part of his consciousness. He continues to act on behalf of the imprisoned son, writing to him and trying to arrange a visit, but as he dawdles with Suh Jung, he becomes a brooder as never before and begins to see all that surrounds him as a reflection of his imprisoned nature.

The first thing the narrator notices is the oppressive nature of his living conditions. He says the building he lives in is "in the bottom of somebody's pocket," a pocket "deep and black" where "a hand may dig in any moment and crush [him]"; he describes its physical appearance as one might describe a prison: "Sunlight never touches its bricks. The building's neither run-down nor cheap. Just dark, dank, and drab." The narrator portrays the confines of his small apartment in much harsher terms: "Water, when you turn on a faucet first thing in the morning, gags on itself, spits, then gushes like a bloody jailbreak from the pipes." Such imagery brings to mind Dostoevsky's underground man, the sick and wicked brooder who lives holed up in his little compartment, shut off from society and reflecting on his sorry condition. Words such as "gag," "spit," "gush," and "bloody jailbreak" suggest states of illness and imprisonment; but, interestingly enough, they also suggest possibilities—although violent—of escape. At this point in the story, these words act as a foreshadowing (a hint for what will come later), since the narrator is not yet aware that the possibility for escape exists.

Within his cell of an apartment, the narrator "dallies" (his word) with Suh Jung: they smoke marijuana and stimulate each other sexually by various means. However, the narrator quickly loses interest in Suh Jung. Her sarcastic remarks get on his nerves, and her boyish body disappoints him. Their relationship, like the apartment, is oppressive, the essence of which is perfectly detailed in the brutal entrapment image the narrator uses to describe them while having sexual intercourse: "I'm aware of my size, my strength towering over her squirming, her thrashing her gasps for breath. I am her father's stare, the steel gate dropping over the tiger pit in which she's naked, trapped, begging for food. And water. Air. Light." Comparing sexual intercourse to the violent capture and caging of an animal is one of the story's most powerful metaphors and a precise encapsulation of the story's theme: the human soul is in bondage and needs to be freed. The objectification of others, as the narrator does with Suh Jung, is a facet of this bondage that "What We Cannot Speak About We Must Pass Over in Silence" explores. To the narrator, Suh Jung is not a human being to be loved and cared for but an object to be conquered and confined. A loving relationship is simply not part of his experience, nor the rest of the world's, for that matter; as he says when describing the expedient nature of the relationship he had with his friend, "Most of the world fits into this category now." He is a product of the wasteland in which he lives, where giving is replaced by taking and sexual expression is a matter of entrapment. The image of the caged animal, in which he is the objectifying captor, suggests that he too is a "selfish, greedy animal."

After much delay that is partly his fault and the partly the fault of the bureaucratic prison system, the narrator flies to Arizona to visit his friend's son. One might think that the trip itself would provide temporary relief from his oppressed state, but such is not the case; he carries it with him everywhere and it distorts all he sees. No sooner is he in the air, free of his apartment and Suh Jung, than the natural world begins to encroach on him. He looks down at the land far below and observes mountains and farmland but recognizes beauty in none of it. The mountains are simply "rugged," the farmland looks like a flat desert, and the rest is an "undramatic nothingness beyond the far edge of wrinkled terrain." Instead of bringing him joy, the landscape makes him think of hell: "Upside-down mountains are hollow shells, deep, deep gouges in the stony waste, their invisible peaks underground, pointing to hell."

For reasons even he cannot explain, the narrator arrives at the prison two days late, causing confusion and unwelcome shuffling on the part of certain prison personnel. As the narrator waits for them to make the necessary phone calls and fill out the additional paperwork, he overhears two guards talking about a coyote that had, for an undisclosed period of time, been scavenging around he prison's perimeter fences. That very morning, however, one of the tower guards trapped the unsuspecting creature in his sights and killed him. The guards' discussion hearkens back to the narrator's description of his sex act with Suh Jung in that it depicts an image of animal entrapment, but it also adds something to it: an image not of death (as one might anticipate) but of release. Like the phrase "bloody jailbreak," this new image foreshadows the story's final moments. The narrator passes through various checkpoints and locked doors before being told to wait in a wire holding pen while more prison personnel perform more bureaucratic shuffling. He waits and waits. The heat becomes so oppressive that sweat gushes out of him, but the heat is purgatorial rather than injurious. It is what Eliot and Dante (alluding to the words of the prophet Zechariah in Zechariah 13:9) refer to as "the fire that refines." In a manner reminiscent of Flannery O'Connor, the narrator describes his experience in the cage in both violent and redemptive terms:

> Would I be knocked down to my knees, forced to recite my sins, the son's sins, the sins of the world. If I tried to escape, would my body—*splat*—be splashed and pulped on the razor wire or could I glide magically through the knives glinting like mirrors, not stopping till I reach a spot far, far away where I can bury my throbbing head in the coolness miles deep below the sand, so deep you can hear the subterranean chortle of rivers on the opposite face of the planet.

Using prison as an overarching metaphor, Wideman depicts how relationships, living conditions, and the natural world reflect the entrapped state of the narrator's soul, then reveals how a trip to a literal prison in the Arizona desert can serve as a means to free it. In this collection of stories,

Visiting day in women's jail in Mexico City
© Hulton-Deutsch Collection/Corbis

entitled *God's Gym*, the prison and the gym function as metaphors for the same thing: they are both places where God causes spiritual growth in His people. The God of John Edgar Wideman works in mysterious ways. He reveals Himself in the dark corners and gritty crevices where one would least expect to find Him, using prisons and gyms as instruments of mercy and violence as a means of grace. He is tough and stern, yet also just and merciful. The narrator of "Weight," the first story of the collection, describes Him best: "My mother believes in a god whose goodness would not permit him to inflict more troubles than a person can handle. A god of mercy and salvation. A sweaty, bleeding god presiding over a fitness class in which his chosen few punish their muscles. She should wear a T-shirt: *God's Gym*." The narrator of "What We Cannot Speak About We Must Pass Over in Silence" should wear one as well.

Source: Timothy Dunham, Critical Essay on "What We Cannot Speak About We Must Pass Over in Silence," in *Short Stories for Students*, Thomson Gale, 2007.

Wilfred D. Samuels

In the following essay, Samuels gives a critical analysis of Wideman's life and work.

> "Form is also important to Wideman's *Damballah*, for each story, as his narrator tells us, is a letter. Addressed to Robby, whose incarceration forces him to lose touch with family, heritage, and culture, Wideman's stories/letters, like *Hiding Place*, focus on the people of Homewood who are Sybela Owens's relatives, giving Robby an intimate understanding of his legacy and family."

During the 1960s, the architects of the black arts movement—Imamu Baraka (LeRoi Jones), Larry Neal, Haki R. Madhubuti (Don L. Lee), Addison Gayle, and others—demanded that black writers use their talents and works for the betterment of the black community and black life, for "the liberation of black people." Arguing that the black arts movement was the "aesthetic and spiritual sister of the black power concept," for example, Neal admonished black artists to speak directly to the needs and aspirations of black Americans. Simultaneously, the black arts prophets called for a rejection of Western ethics and aesthetics and for the establishment of a black value system based on an African concept of art which would be used to evaluate the creative works of Americans of African descent.

Although it had some impact, the black arts movement did little to alter the fundamental direction of the Afro-American literary tradition, which remained firmly in the grips of those writers with a more conventional view of art. Led by writers such as Ralph Ellison and James Baldwin, who were more interested in craftsmanship than politics, this tradition moved closer toward the mainstream rather than away from its salient values.

Although he was among the cadre of young black writers that emerged during the 1960s, John Edgar Wideman did not align himself with the politically oriented black arts movement. Instead, from the beginning, he demonstrated an interest in an art that carefully and logically resulted from the creativity, expertise, and ability of the artist, rather than one that sought to announce the political convictions of its creator. His intricate style, which includes experimentation with form, the use of surrealism and stream of consciousness, and multiple allusions to literary masterpieces—coupled with the absence of a focus on racial or cultural experience—brought him immediate attention from critics who felt he had successfully established himself in a vein of contemporary American, rather than Afro-American, fiction. In 1978, Robert Bone, the author of *The Negro Novel in America*, declared that Wideman was "perhaps the most gifted black novelist of his generation."

John Edgar Wideman was born on 14 June 1941, in Washington, D.C., to Edgar and Betty French Wideman. Almost a year after his birth, young Wideman survived a near-fatal crash while en route to Pittsburgh, Pennsylvania, where his family has deep roots. Wideman spent the first ten years of his life in Homewood, but later moved with his parents to Shadyside, a predominantly white, upper-middle-class district in Pittsburgh, where he completed primary and secondary education at Liberty School and Shadyside High School. Nevertheless, Wideman remembers fondly his early years in Homewood School, and he remembers well the summer days spent at his grandmother's home in Homewood. His mobility in both worlds—one that was predominantly black, the other white—was facilitated in part by his interest in sports, particularly basketball.

Because of his athletic and scholastic achievements, Wideman won a Benjamin Franklin Scholarship to the University of Pennsylvania in Philadelphia, where he majored first in psychology and then in English, and became a basketball star. Graduating Phi Beta Kappa, Wideman, in 1963, won a Rhodes Scholarship, bringing him international attention, as Alain Locke had been the only Afro-American to do so some fifty-five years earlier. Wideman went to Oxford University, where he spent three years pursuing an academic degree in eighteenth-century studies and wrote a thesis on four eighteenth-century novels. He played on Oxford's basketball team, including one that won the amateur championship of England. Wideman, who served as captain and coach, was voted the most valuable player.

Leaving Oxford with a bachelor of philosophy degree in 1966, Wideman, who had married Judith Ann Goldman of Virginia in 1965, returned to the United States and as a Kent Fellow attended the Creative Writing Workshop at the University of Iowa from 1966 to 1967. He left Iowa to begin a six-year stint at the University of Pennsylvania as a lecturer and later professor of English. While there, he was responsible for initiating Penn's first Afro-American studies program, which he chaired from 1972-1973, although he had no interest in administrative work. It was during his first years as a member of Penn's faculty that Wideman, at twenty-six, published his first novel, *A Glance Away* (1967).

Primarily concerned with the main characters' search for self, *A Glance Away* focuses on one day in the life of Eddie Lawson, a thirty-one-year-old rehabilitated drug addict and former postal clerk who struggles to remain clean, and Robert Thurley, an English professor whose personal conflicts result in part from his homosexuality. The day of Eddie's homecoming, Easter Sunday, symbolizes his resurrection and rebirth, as it marks his return after a year's stay in a narcotic rehabilitation center, as well as his reassociation with his mother and sister, Bette; his sometime lover, Alice; and his best friend, Brother Small. Although convinced of his ability to find new meaning and desirous of making sense out of his life, Eddie discovers a Camus-like world, one that is ephemeral and unpredictable—one that is absurd. The fulfillment that he expects does not materialize because his world remains unsympathetic. He finds that his paraplegic mother continues to expect him to take the place of his dead brother, Eugene; his sister remains locked in a silent and meaningless world that is controlled by their mother, who detests her; and his lover, psychologically damaged by Eddie's affair with her white girl friend, wallows in unforgiveness and refuses his love. For him, the only tangible element that remains in his former environment is his friendship with Brother Small (Alice's brother), an albino and addict, who supports his habit in part through his homosexual relationship with Thurley.

Thurley, too, finds that he leads an unfulfilled life in an ephemeral world. His memory is riddled by a past that includes a dominating mother, a failed marriage, and homosexual activities with black youths. He is able to find satisfaction only when he frequents a bar in the black section of town that is patronized by social pariahs like himself. It is through Brother that Eddie meets Thurley, who sees himself as "an aesthetic Catholic, in politics a passive communist." At the end of the novel, Eddie has decided to return to drugs as an escape from his meaningless existence. But rather than let him commit suicide through drugs, Thurley successfully engages Eddie in a dialogue, allowing him to become victorious over his hopeless fate—at least for one day.

In his first novel, Wideman reveals at concern with themes which continue to dominate his work: the significance of history, both personal and collective; the presence of a working imagination; the isolation of twentieth-century man; the sacredness of family and culture; and the importance of friendship, especially the fraternal relationship between men. For example, sensing alienation in their struggles for meaning, both Lawson and Thurley probe their pasts to find who and what they are. It is their reflections and assessments of their pasts that reveal logical minds trying to comprehend the meaning of existence in a world that seems unsympathetic and chaotic.

A Glance Away was greeted enthusiastically by critics. Declaring in the *New York Times Book Review* that Wideman had "written a powerfully inventive novel," Harry Roskolenko wrote that Wideman "has all sorts of literary gifts, including a poet's flair for taut, meaningful, emotional language." Stephen Caldwell wrote in *Saturday Review*: "What moves us is Wideman's artistry, his one-and-two paragraph evocations of joy and sorrow that first appear in his fine prologue and are echoed and revised time and again through the course of the book." And Kurt Vonnegut, Jr., wrote to Wideman, "You have written an American book. . . . The language is handsome."

Appearing two years after *A Glance Away*, *Hurry Home* (1969), Wideman's second novel, depicts the main character's search for identity and meaning. At thirty-one, Cecil Otis Braithwaite remains cradled in a sense of absence. Although he has a law degree, he works as a janitor and later as a hairdresser. Supported by Esther while he is in law school, Cecil, out of a sense of obligation, marries her on his graduation day; but aware that he does not love her and haunted by the memory of their stillborn son, Simon, he walks out on their wedding night. He meets Webb, who, seeking to compensate for his failure to acknowledge the son he had fathered with his black mistress, takes him to Europe. While there, Cecil seeks to come to grips with the strife that results from his suspension between two worlds; he seeks to transcend what W. E. B. Du Bois calls "double consciousness," an identity that is rooted in two cultures—one that is

European (American) and the other which is African. Although Cecil's search finally leads him to Africa, he is unable to accept wholeheartedly his African self or heritage. After three years, he returns to his ghetto apartment in Washington, to a wife whose life remained unchanged for the most part, and to menial employment outside of his profession.

In *Hurry Home*, Wideman is again concerned with history, with the past. By frequenting the museums and galleries of France, Italy, and Spain, Cecil seeks cultural roots and meaning in a white, European world—a world in which, as a lawyer, he is expected to be mobile. Failing to do so, he travels to Africa to gain a sense of past and meaning for his present, but he remains on the threshold. Similarly Webb is haunted by his past, and the guilt which he suffers because he has failed to acknowledge his black offspring controls his every thought and reflection, rendering his effort as a writer totally useless.

By focusing as he does on both Braithwaite's and Webb's consciousness, Wideman again highlights in *Hurry Home* the working imagination, extensively utilizing surrealistic techniques. The inner workings of the characters' minds are revealed through thoughts, letters, journals, and diaries. Again, the friendship that Webb is able to establish with Braithwaite, and the companionship that he shares with Albert, gives him the only real sense of fulfillment that he has. Like Eddie, who finds meaning through his friendship with Brother, Webb grows to depend on Cecil and Albert, who are the only tangible sources of life in his immediate environment.

Critics welcomed *Hurry Home* and showered Wideman with accolades. Writing in the *Philadelphia Bulletin*, M. L. Stone concluded that it firmly established Wideman "in the front rank . . . of contemporary black literature." Stating in his *New York Times Book Review* that Wideman's second novel reveals a "formidable command of the techniques of fiction," Joseph Goodman described the work as a "dazzling display": "we can have nothing but admiration for Mr. Wideman's talent." Describing *Hurry Home* as a "rich and complicated novel," John Leonard, like other critics, compared Wideman to James Joyce and T. S. Eliot, finding similarity between Eliot's Prufrock and Wideman's Webb.

It would not be farfetched to say that both *A Glance Away* and *Hurry Home* are not black novels, for although written by a black author and developed around characters who are of African descent, neither novel is specifically or solely concerned with race, racial issues, or unique aspects of the black experience. For the most part, Eddie Lawson's and Cecil Braithwaite's conflicts do not emerge solely from the fact that they are Afro-American and know oppression as a result. Although both men are ghetto dwellers, their lives, unlike Bigger Thomas's of Richard Wright's *Native Son*, are not controlled by socioeconomic conditions that render them powerless. When Eddie reflects on his childhood experiences in an integrated middle-class neighborhood, there is not the sense of distinction and separation of races that the young Wright was forced to acknowledge and accept in *Black Boy*. Cecil does not seem irreversibly bound by his ghetto community and becomes a lawyer in spite of his economic status. Both Eddie's and Cecil's sense of absence results to a great degree from weaknesses in their own personalities. Cecil becomes an exile as much from his desire to escape a loveless marriage as from his desire as a professional to find meaning in a world that remains fragmented.

Equally significant is the presence of major white characters in both *A Glance Away* and *Hurry Home*. Unlike Frank Yerby, Willard Motley, and Ann Petry, who sought to demonstrate to the mainstream their competence by writing novels peopled mostly by white characters and centered around themes which, for the most part, were not related to the black experience, Wideman blends the two racial experiences, reducing them in the process to one basic human experience. Consequently, there is parallel development in Wideman's treatment of Eddie and Thurley in *A Glance Away* and Cecil and Webb in *Hurry Home*. What is true of the black characters is also true of the white ones: they, too, suffer from a sense of absence and alienation, which is due mostly to choices and decisions made by them early in life. Together, Eddie, Thurley, Cecil, and Webb are individuals who seek to understand and assess their past in order to best resolve, if possible, the conflicts that they presently face. Race remains secondary to their problems.

Beginning with the third novel, *The Lynchers* (1973), Wideman's emphasis shifts, and race, though it does not supersede his interest in form, language, and experimental techniques, becomes more important to his fundamental theme. Set in Philadelphia, *The Lynchers* develops around the main characters' desire to change the life of urban dwellers. Intended as a "fulcrum turning history," their planned lynching of a white policeman is conceived by Willie Hall ("Littleman"), a crippled social activist who views the lives of black

Philadelphians as a process of slow death. Walking down South Street, he says, "This street means they're killing us, whittling away day by day a man, woman, a baby at a time. And most of us just sitting on our asses wasting our time." Supported by Wilkerson (who becomes morally disturbed by his impending participation), Saunders, and Rice, the executioners of his plan, Littleman masterminds the murder not only of the white officer but also of his black prostitute concubine. The scheme is aborted, however, when, considering himself used and abused by the other lynchers, Rice kills Wilkerson.

In *The Lynchers*, setting becomes an important theme for the first time in Wideman's fiction. With its street vendors who remain aloof and unfriendly, schoolchildren who are more interested in their street lives than in books, filthy streets and roach-infested ghetto buildings within the sight of the more fashionable Lombard Street and Society Hill, where the wealthy climb marble steps to find refuge in the history left as legacy by the Age of Reason, Philadelphia emerges as a character in the novel. It renders its black inhabitants helpless in a life of meaninglessness and brutality. Equally important in this novel is the fraternal relationship between male characters. Most notable is the deep friendship that is shared by Orin Wilkerson and his father, Thomas, alias "Sweetman." Although the younger Wilkerson reveals a deep love and attachment for his mother, he also exhibits a sincere understanding of his alcoholic father. When Sweetman accidentally kills his best friend, his schoolteacher son is the first to visit him in jail. From behind bars, the father pours out, for the first time, his innermost feelings and fears: "I wanted to hide in him. I wanted all that was still alive in me to fall off my shoulders and give him back his life. I wanted to be dying in his arms, but all I could do was cry like a baby."

Although history remains important in *The Lynchers*, Wideman employs the aggregate history of blacks rather than the personal history of an individual. He begins his novel by chronicling lynching in the United States, listing over one hundred accounts that span more than three hundred years— a way of juxtaposing fact and fiction. Wideman isn't successful, as some critics noted, at showing the relevance of the lengthy chronicle to the rest of the novel. *The Lynchers* was not widely acclaimed. Richard P. Brickner wrote in the *New York Times Book Review* that although it was done "with enormous care and intelligence," *The Lynchers* "is often frustrated in a manner related to the frustration it concerns . . . it has trouble acting." Yet, the noted

black critic Saunders Redding declared: "I think *The Lynchers* is far and away the and away the truest, the most moving, and the most brilliantly crafted novel of Negro life in almost a quarter of a century—that is, since Ellison's *Invisible Man*, which in some ways it surpasses."

After an eight-year silence in which Wideman and his wife, Judith, and children (Danny, Jacob, and Jamilla) exchanged Philadelphia for the open prairie of Wyoming, where he took a position as professor of English at the University of Wyoming at Laramie, Wideman, who spent some of that time steeping himself in his personal culture and history, published two more works. *Hiding Place* and *Damballah* (a collection of short stories) were both published in October 1981 by Avon Books. Each reveals a crystallization of Wideman's concern with history, culture, and heritage; but now he is concerned with the culture and heritage of Sybela Owens, his maternal great-great-great-grandmother.

In *Hiding Place* and *Damballah*, Wideman returns to Homewood, the Pittsburgh community that nurtured him through early childhood. Amid its landscape and cityscape, he weaves his tales around the fascinating offspring of Sybela Owens, who more than a hundred years ago helped to settle Homewood with her husband, Charles Bell, her master's son whose love led him to steal her before she could be sold by his father.

In *Hiding Place*, Tommy, Sybela's great-great-great-grandson, fails in his attempt to rob a local merchant and is wanted for the murder of his partner in crime. Though innocent, he flees Homewood and as a fugitive seeks sanctuary in Brunston Hill, where Mother Bess, the family's matriarch, who had known Sybela, has lived as a recluse since the deaths of her husband and son. At first Bess rejects Tommy, but she takes him in. When boredom drives Tommy back to Homewood, he is discovered and pursued. He returns to Bess while in flight, but he is captured and killed before she can offer him a hiding place.

In many ways, *Hiding Place* represents the zenith of the concern with the basic themes that have dominated Wideman's work. History, the sacredness of family, and culture, all present in his earlier novels, merge in this novel. They are powerfully presented through Mother Bess, who as a griot, in the traditional African sense, knows and recites the family's history. She knows *who* Tommy is: "You Lizabeth's son, Thomas. Your grandmother was my sister's girl. You wasn't even close to born when my sister Gert died. Freeda was her oldest. And some say the prettiest in her quiet way. John French your granddaddy. Strutting around in that big brown hat like he owned Homewood. . . . You a Lawson now. You and your three brothers and your sister in the middle."

With Tommy, Wideman reaches the peak of his treatment of his black male characters. As he did with Eddie and Cecil, Wideman burrows beneath the surface of Tommy's external and internal conflicts. Most intense and sensitive is his examination of Tommy's efforts to come to grips with his desire to be a husband to Sarah and a father to Clyde, and at the same time know a certain degree of freedom. He tells Sarah, "Loved you and loved that boy more than anything. But I wouldn't do right. Just couldn't do right to save my soul. Love him [his father] and love you and here I sit like some goddamn stranger drinking coffee at your table. He [his father] had to die to get us in the same room. Now what kind of sense that make?" Speaking about his son, Tommy says:

> Sonny's upstairs, woman. Wasn't for me he wouldn't be here. Ain't much but it's something. Say what you want about me. I'm still his daddy. I was a wrong nigger. Sometimes I knew I was fucking up and sometimes I didn't know. Sometimes I cared about fucking up and sometimes I didn't give a damn. Now that's a wrong nigger. That's me and I'm dealing with that. Got to deal with it. Look back sometimes and I want to cry. But I ain't crying. No time to cry. Don't do no good no way.

Wideman's treatment of Tommy reveals a continued interest with the physical alienation of twentieth-century man who seeks meaning and fulfillment.

Wideman reveals in these two works that he remains interested in a work that is experimental in form. In fact, he is not at all interested in conventional narration. He says, "Form for me, is a kind of adventure. Any writing is a kind of adventure, a form of play, very serious play, but something that I just like to do." In *Hiding Place* he fuses his interest in experimental form with his unending interest in the working imagination. The result is a novel dominated by stream of consciousness and interior monologues. Wideman's Clement demonstrates that the inarticulate's world is more complex than it appears on the surface.

Form is also important to Wideman's *Damballah*, for each story, as his narrator tells us, is a letter. Addressed to Robby, whose incarceration forces him to lose touch with family, heritage, and culture, Wideman's stories/letters, like *Hiding Place*, focus on the people of Homewood who are Sybela Owens's

relatives, giving Robby an intimate understanding of his legacy and family. As he does in *Hiding Place*, Wideman begins *Damballah* with Sybela's family tree.

Perhaps the most important story in the collection is the last one, "The Beginning of Homewood," in which the foundation of the family's history is unraveled by Aunt May and Mother Bess. "This woman, this Sybela Owens our ancestor, bore the surname of her first owner and the Christian name, Sybela, which was probably a corruption of Sybil, a priestess pledged to Apollo." In other stories which provide his kaleidoscopic view of Homewood and Sybela's progeny, Wideman spotlights Elizabeth, whose weekly visits to her imprisoned son, Tommy, cause her to lose, for a brief moment, her faith in God ("Solitary"). But also sensitively drawn are the grandmother, Freeda, whose premonition about death comes true ("The Chinaman"), and the father, Mr. Lawson, who though a waiter is a very proud and loving man ("Across the Wide Missouri").

Sybela Owens was born twenty years after David Walker admonished the black readers of his "The Appeal" to strike a blow against slavery, eleven years after Nat Turner and his men rebelled in Southampton County, Virginia, and ten years before William Wells Brown's *Clotel* first appeared, in which the heroine chooses death over slavery. One hundred and one years later, John Edgar Wideman was born, and forty years after his birth he found in his work a voice to celebrate her life and legacy.

For his most recent novel, *Sent for You Yesterday* (1983), which is once again set in Homewood, Wideman received the P.E.N./ Faulkner Award. The jury for this major literary award chose this novel as the best volume of fiction published in 1983 over books by better-known writers such as Bernard Malamud, Cynthia Ozick, and William Kennedy. Scheduled for publication in autumn 1984 is Wideman's first nonfiction book, *Brothers and Keepers*, which he calls "a personal essay about my brother and myself." Wideman is said to hope that the book will lead to parole for his brother, who is in prison.

What Wideman brings to Afro-American literature and culture is a validation and celebration of Afro-American life. He continues to work to master the techniques of the novel. Additionally in part by having his three most-recent books published as paperback originals, he seeks a wider (black) audience than he has reached. His receiving the P.E.N./ Faulkner Award may well enhance his visibility. More important, Wideman has a desire to utilize in his daily life the message his grandfather gave him: "Give them the benefit of the doubt." To Wideman, this means always taking a longer, slower look at people and situations before acting or speaking or writing.

Source: Wilfred D. Samuels, "John Edgar Wideman," in *Dictionary of Literary Biography*, Vol. 33, *Afro-American Fiction Writers After 1955*, edited by Thadious M. Davis and Trudier Harris, The Gale Group, 1984, pp. 271–278.

Sources

"Biblio: Recommendations from Our Shelf to Yours," in *O, The Oprah Magazine*, Vol. 6, No. 2, February 2005, p. 144.

Davis, Angela Y., "A World Unto Itself: Multiple Invisibilities of Imprisonment," in *Behind the Razor Wire: Portrait of a Contemporary American Prison System*, by Michael Jacobson-Hardy, New York University Press, 1998, pp. xiv–xvi.

Eliot, T. S., *The Annotated Waste Land with Eliot's Contemporary Prose*, edited by Lawrence Rainey, Yale University Press, 2005, pp. 57, 75.

Freeman, John, "Wideman Short Stories Hit Nothing but Net," in *Seattle Times*, February 27, 2005, p. J10.

Nawotka, Ed, Review of *God's Gym*, in *People Weekly*, Vol. 63, No. 6, February 14, 2005, p. 60.

Rafferty, Terrence, "Pumping Irony," in *New York Times Book Review*, March 20, 2005, p. 20.

Review of *God's Gym*, in *Kirkus Reviews*, Vol. 72, No. 23, December 1, 2004, p. 1115.

Review of *God's Gym*, in *Publishers Weekly*, Vol. 252, No. 2, January 10, 2005, p. 36.

Severs, Jeffrey, "John Edgar Wideman's Treadmill of Racism," in *Austin American-Statesman*, February 6, 2005, p. K5.

Stuhr, Rebecca, Review of *God's Gym*, in *Library Journal*, Vol. 130, No. 1, January 1, 2005, p. 104.

Wideman, John Edgar, "The American Dilemma Revisited: Psychoanalysis, Social Policy, and the Socio-Cultural Meaning of Race," in *Black Renaissance*, Vol. 5, No. 1, Spring 2003, pp. 32–45.

———, "Doing Time, Marking Race," in *Behind the Razor Wire: Portrait of a Contemporary American Prison System*, photographs and text by Michael Jacobson-Hardy, New York University Press, 1998, pp. 13–17.

———, "Weight," in *God's Gym*, Houghton Mifflin, 2005, p. 2.

———, "What We Cannot Speak About We Must Pass Over in Silence," in *God's Gym*, Houghton Mifflin, 2005, pp. 93–119.

Young, Earni, "The Art of Brevity: Collections from Two Masters Raise the Question: Whatever Happened to Short Stories?" in *Black Issues Book Review*, Vol. 7, No. 4, July-August 2005, pp. 32–33.

Further Reading

Coleman, James W., *Blackness and Modernism*, University Press of Mississippi, 1989.
    While this book was written long before Wideman wrote "What We Cannot Speak About We Must Pass Over in Silence" and many of his other stories and novels, it remains a major critical source on his work.

Davis, Angela Y., *Are Prisons Obsolete?* Open Media, 2003.
    In this book, African American activist and prison abolitionist Angela Y. Davis questions why two million Americans are behind bars and looks for her answer at the corporations that profit from prisons. Davis explores the question of racial bias in the criminal justice system, which has the effect of politically disenfranchising large numbers of ethnic minority voters.

Dyer, Joel, *The Perpetual Prison Machine: How America Profits from Crime*, Westview Press, 2001.
    Dyer argues that the growing practice of turning over the running of prisons to private enterprise has led to cost-cutting, resulting in negligence, danger, violence, and escapes. He points out that the privatized prison industry has a vested interest in incarcerating ever-increasing numbers of people.

Ferranti, Seth M., *Prison Stories*, Gorilla Convict Publications, 2005.
    This book, written by a prisoner, gives vivid, first-hand accounts of various aspects of prison life.

Mbalia, Doreatha D., *John Edgar Wideman: Reclaiming the African Personality*, Associated University Presses, 1995.
    Mbalia argues that Wideman's earlier voice was characterized by the white Western culture in which he was immersed by his education but that in his later work he has rediscovered his African voice.

Ross, Jeffrey Ian, and Stephen C. Richards, *Behind Bars: Surviving Prison*, Alpha, 2002.
    Protest groups often issue leaflets to their supporters, offering advice on what to do if they are arrested during a demonstration. This book, written by two criminologists, is a guidebook for surviving the criminal justice system, loosely modeled on those kinds of leaflets, though it covers crimes more serious than civil disobedience. The legal system the authors portray bears no resemblance to the one depicted in textbooks.

TuSmith, Bonnie, ed., *Conversations with John Edgar Wideman*, University Press of Mississippi, 1998.
    In a series of interviews and articles spanning thirty-five years, Wideman discusses a variety of topics, from postmodernism to genocide, from fatherhood to basketball. He also reveals his artistic aims, techniques, and sources of inspiration.

Wice, Paul, B., *Rubin Hurricane Carter and the American Justice System*, Rutgers University Press, 2000.
    Wice takes the famous story of Rubin Carter, a man sentenced to life in prison for a murder he did not commit, and scrutinizes the U.S. justice system as it handled his case. Of the many books about Rubin Carter's case, this one particularly works to show both the strengths and weaknesses of the American legal system.

Glossary of Literary Terms

A

Allegory: A narrative technique in which characters representing things or abstract ideas are used to convey a message or teach a lesson. Allegory is typically used to teach moral, ethical, or religious lessons but is sometimes used for satiric or political purposes. Many fairy tales are allegories.

Allusion: A reference to a familiar literary or historical person or event, used to make an idea more easily understood. Joyce Carol Oates's story "Where Are You Going, Where Have You Been?" exhibits several allusions to popular music.

Analogy: A comparison of two things made to explain something unfamiliar through its similarities to something familiar, or to prove one point based on the acceptance of another. Similes and metaphors are types of analogies.

Antagonist: The major character in a narrative or drama who works against the hero or protagonist. The Misfit in Flannery O'Connor's story "A Good Man Is Hard to Find" serves as the antagonist for the Grandmother.

Anthology: A collection of similar works of literature, art, or music. Zora Neale Hurston's "The Eatonville Anthology" is a collection of stories that take place in the same town.

Anthropomorphism: The presentation of animals or objects in human shape or with human characteristics. The term is derived from the Greek word for "human form." The fur necklet in Katherine Mansfield's story "Miss Brill" has anthropomorphic characteristics.

Anti-hero: A central character in a work of literature who lacks traditional heroic qualities such as courage, physical prowess, and fortitude. Anti-heroes typically distrust conventional values and are unable to commit themselves to any ideals. They generally feel helpless in a world over which they have no control. Anti-heroes usually accept, and often celebrate, their positions as social outcasts. A well-known anti-hero is Walter Mitty in James Thurber's story "The Secret Life of Walter Mitty."

Archetype: The word archetype is commonly used to describe an original pattern or model from which all other things of the same kind are made. Archetypes are the literary images that grow out of the "collective unconscious," a theory proposed by psychologist Carl Jung. They appear in literature as incidents and plots that repeat basic patterns of life. They may also appear as stereotyped characters. The "schlemiel" of Yiddish literature is an archetype.

Autobiography: A narrative in which an individual tells his or her life story. Examples include Benjamin Franklin's *Autobiography* and Amy Hempel's story "In the Cemetery Where Al Jolson Is Buried," which has autobiographical characteristics even though it is a work of fiction.

Avant-garde A literary term that describes new writing that rejects traditional approaches to literature in favor of innovations in style or content. Twentieth-century examples of the literary avant-garde include the modernists and the minimalists.

B

Belles-lettres: A French term meaning "fine letters" or" beautiful writing." It is often used as a synonym for literature, typically referring to imaginative and artistic rather than scientific or expository writing. Current usage sometimes restricts the meaning to light or humorous writing and appreciative essays about literature. Lewis Carroll's *Alice in Wonderland* epitomizes the realm of belles-lettres.

Bildungsroman: A German word meaning "novel of development." The *bildungsroman* is a study of the maturation of a youthful character, typically brought about through a series of social or sexual encounters that lead to self-awareness. J. D. Salinger's *Catcher in the Rye* is a *bildungsroman*, and Doris Lessing's story "Through the Tunnel" exhibits characteristics of a *bildungsroman* as well.

Black Aesthetic Movement: A period of artistic and literary development among African Americans in the 1960s and early 1970s. This was the first major African-American artistic movement since the Harlem Renaissance and was closely paralleled by the civil rights and black power movements. The black aesthetic writers attempted to produce works of art that would be meaningful to the black masses. Key figures in black aesthetics included one of its founders, poet and playwright Amiri Baraka, formerly known as Le Roi Jones; poet and essayist Haki R. Madhubuti, formerly Don L. Lee; poet and playwright Sonia Sanchez; and dramatist Ed Bullins. Works representative of the Black Aesthetic Movement include Amiri Baraka's play *Dutchman,* a 1964 Obie award-winner.

Black Humor: Writing that places grotesque elements side by side with humorous ones in an attempt to shock the reader, forcing him or her to laugh at the horrifying reality of a disordered world. "Lamb to the Slaughter," by Roald Dahl, in which a placid housewife murders her husband and serves the murder weapon to the investigating policemen, is an example of black humor.

C

Catharsis: The release or purging of unwanted emotions—specifically fear and pity—brought about by exposure to art. The term was first used by the Greek philosopher Aristotle in his *Poetics* to refer to the desired effect of tragedy on spectators.

Character: Broadly speaking, a person in a literary work. The actions of characters are what constitute the plot of a story, novel, or poem. There are numerous types of characters, ranging from simple, stereotypical figures to intricate, multifaceted ones. "Characterization" is the process by which an author creates vivid, believable characters in a work of art. This may be done in a variety of ways, including (1) direct description of the character by the narrator; (2) the direct presentation of the speech, thoughts, or actions of the character; and (3) the responses of other characters to the character. The term "character" also refers to a form originated by the ancient Greek writer Theophrastus that later became popular in the seventeenth and eighteenth centuries. It is a short essay or sketch of a person who prominently displays a specific attribute or quality, such as miserliness or ambition. "Miss Brill," a story by Katherine Mansfield, is an example of a character sketch.

Classical: In its strictest definition in literary criticism, classicism refers to works of ancient Greek or Roman literature. The term may also be used to describe a literary work of recognized importance (a "classic") from any time period or literature that exhibits the traits of classicism. Examples of later works and authors now described as classical include French literature of the seventeenth century, Western novels of the nineteenth century, and American fiction of the mid-nineteenth century such as that written by James Fenimore Cooper and Mark Twain.

Climax: The turning point in a narrative, the moment when the conflict is at its most intense. Typically, the structure of stories, novels, and plays is one of rising action, in which tension builds to the climax, followed by falling action, in which tension lessens as the story moves to its conclusion.

Comedy: One of two major types of drama, the other being tragedy. Its aim is to amuse, and it typically ends happily. Comedy assumes many forms, such as farce and burlesque, and uses a variety of techniques, from parody to satire. In a restricted sense the term comedy refers only to dramatic presentations, but in general usage it is commonly applied to nondramatic works as well.

Comic Relief: The use of humor to lighten the mood of a serious or tragic story, especially in plays. The technique is very common in Elizabethan works, and can be an integral part of the plot or simply a brief event designed to break the tension of the scene.

Conflict: The conflict in a work of fiction is the issue to be resolved in the story. It usually occurs between two characters, the protagonist and the antagonist, or between the protagonist and society or the protagonist and himself or herself. The conflict in Washington Irving's story "The Devil and Tom Walker" is that the Devil wants Tom Walker's soul but Tom does not want to go to hell.

Criticism: The systematic study and evaluation of literary works, usually based on a specific method or set of principles. An important part of literary studies since ancient times, the practice of criticism has given rise to numerous theories, methods, and "schools," sometimes producing conflicting, even contradictory, interpretations of literature in general as well as of individual works. Even such basic issues as what constitutes a poem or a novel have been the subject of much criticism over the centuries. Seminal texts of literary criticism include Plato's *Republic,* Aristotle's *Poetics*, Sir Philip Sidney's *The Defence of Poesie,* and John Dryden's *Of Dramatic Poesie.* Contemporary schools of criticism include deconstruction, feminist, psychoanalytic, poststructuralist, new historicist, postcolonialist, and reader-response.

D

Deconstruction: A method of literary criticism characterized by multiple conflicting interpretations of a given work. Deconstructionists consider the impact of the language of a work and suggest that the true meaning of the work is not necessarily the meaning that the author intended.

Deduction: The process of reaching a conclusion through reasoning from general premises to a specific premise. Arthur Conan Doyle's character Sherlock Holmes often used deductive reasoning to solve mysteries.

Denotation: The definition of a word, apart from the impressions or feelings it creates in the reader. The word "apartheid" denotes a political and economic policy of segregation by race, but its connotations— oppression, slavery, inequality—are numerous.

Denouement: A French word meaning "the unknotting." In literature, it denotes the resolution of conflict in fiction or drama. The *denouement* follows the climax and provides an outcome to the primary plot situation as well as an explanation of secondary plot complications. A well-known example of *denouement* is the last scene of the play *As You Like It* by William Shakespeare, in which couples are married, an evildoer repents, the identities of two disguised characters are revealed, and a ruler is restored to power. Also known as "falling action."

Detective Story: A narrative about the solution of a mystery or the identification of a criminal. The conventions of the detective story include the detective's scrupulous use of logic in solving the mystery; incompetent or ineffectual police; a suspect who appears guilty at first but is later proved innocent; and the detective's friend or confidant—often the narrator—whose slowness in interpreting clues emphasizes by contrast the detective's brilliance. Edgar Allan Poe's "Murders in the Rue Morgue" is commonly regarded as the earliest example of this type of story. Other practitioners are Arthur Conan Doyle, Dashiell Hammett, and Agatha Christie.

Dialogue: Dialogue is conversation between people in a literary work. In its most restricted sense, it refers specifically to the speech of characters in a drama. As a specific literary genre, a "dialogue" is a composition in which characters debate an issue or idea.

Didactic: A term used to describe works of literature that aim to teach a moral, religious, political, or practical lesson. Although didactic elements are often found inartistically pleasing works, the term "didactic" usually refers to literature in which the message is more important than the form. The term may also be used to criticize a work that the critic finds "overly didactic," that is, heavy-handed in its delivery of a lesson. An example of didactic literature is John Bunyan's *Pilgrim's Progress.*

Dramatic Irony: Occurs when the reader of a work of literature knows something that a character in the work itself does not know. The irony is in the contrast between the intended meaning of the statements or actions of a character and the additional information understood by the audience.

Dystopia: An imaginary place in a work of fiction where the characters lead dehumanized, fearful lives. George Orwell's *Nineteen Eighty-four,* and Margaret Atwood's *Handmaid's Tale* portray versions of dystopia.

E

Edwardian: Describes cultural conventions identified with the period of the reign of Edward VII of England (1901–1910). Writers of the Edwardian Age typically displayed a strong reaction against the propriety and conservatism of the Victorian Age. Their work often exhibits distrust of authority in religion, politics, and art and expresses strong doubts about the soundness of conventional values. Writers of this era include E. M. Forster, H. G. Wells, and Joseph Conrad.

Empathy: A sense of shared experience, including emotional and physical feelings, with someone or something other than oneself. Empathy is often used to describe the response of a reader to a literary character.

Epilogue: A concluding statement or section of a literary work. In dramas, particularly those of the seventeenth and eighteenth centuries, the epilogue is a closing speech, often in verse, delivered by an actor at the end of a play and spoken directly to the audience.

Epiphany: A sudden revelation of truth inspired by a seemingly trivial incident. The term was widely used by James Joyce in his critical writings, and the stories in Joyce's *Dubliners* are commonly called "epiphanies."

Epistolary Novel: A novel in the form of letters. The form was particularly popular in the eighteenth century. The form can also be applied to short stories, as in Edwidge Danticat's "Children of the Sea."

Epithet: A word or phrase, often disparaging or abusive, that expresses a character trait of someone or something. "The Napoleon of crime" is an epithet applied to Professor Moriarty, archrival of Sherlock Holmes in Arthur Conan Doyle's series of detective stories.

Existentialism: A predominantly twentieth-century philosophy concerned with the nature and perception of human existence. There are two major strains of existentialist thought: atheistic and Christian. Followers of atheistic existentialism believe that the individual is alone in a godless universe and that the basic human condition is one of suffering and loneliness. Nevertheless, because there are no fixed values, individuals can create their own characters—indeed, they can shape themselves—through the exercise of free will. The atheistic strain culminates in and is popularly associated with the works of Jean-Paul Sartre. The Christian existentialists, on the other hand, believe that only in God may people find freedom from life's anguish. The two strains hold certain beliefs in common: that existence cannot be fully understood or described through empirical effort; that anguish is a universal element of life; that individuals must bear responsibility for their actions; and that there is no common standard of behavior or perception for religious and ethical matters. Existentialist thought figures prominently in the works of such authors as Franz Kafka, Fyodor Dostoyevsky, and Albert Camus.

Expatriatism: The practice of leaving one's country to live for an extended period in another country. Literary expatriates include Irish author James Joyce who moved to Italy and France, American writers James Baldwin, Ernest Hemingway, Gertrude Stein, and F. Scott Fitzgerald who lived and wrote in Paris, and Polish novelist Joseph Conrad in England.

Exposition: Writing intended to explain the nature of an idea, thing, or theme. Expository writing is often combined with description, narration, or argument.

Expressionism: An indistinct literary term, originally used to describe an early twentieth-century school of German painting. The term applies to almost any mode of unconventional, highly subjective writing that distorts reality in some way. Advocates of Expressionism include Federico Garcia Lorca, Eugene O'Neill, Franz Kafka, and James Joyce.

F

Fable: A prose or verse narrative intended to convey a moral. Animals or inanimate objects with human characteristics often serve as characters in fables. A famous fable is Aesop's "The Tortoise and the Hare."

Fantasy: A literary form related to mythology and folklore. Fantasy literature is typically set in non-existent realms and features supernatural beings. Notable examples of literature with elements of fantasy are Gabriel García Márquez's story "The Handsomest Drowned Man in the World" and Ursula K. Le Guin's "The Ones Who Walk Away from Omelas."

Farce: A type of comedy characterized by broad humor, outlandish incidents, and often vulgar subject matter. Much of the comedy in film and television could more accurately be described as farce.

Fiction: Any story that is the product of imagination rather than a documentation of fact. Characters and events in such narratives may be based in real life but their ultimate form and configuration is a creation of the author.

Figurative Language: A technique in which an author uses figures of speech such as hyperbole, irony, metaphor, or simile for a particular effect. Figurative language is the opposite of literal language, in which every word is truthful, accurate, and free of exaggeration or embellishment.

Flashback: A device used in literature to present action that occurred before the beginning of the story. Flashbacks are often introduced as the dreams or recollections of one or more characters.

Foil: A character in a work of literature whose physical or psychological qualities contrast strongly with, and therefore highlight, the corresponding qualities of another character. In his Sherlock Holmes stories, Arthur Conan Doyle portrayed Dr. Watson as a man of normal habits and intelligence, making him a foil for the eccentric and unusually perceptive Sherlock Holmes.

Folklore: Traditions and myths preserved in a culture or group of people. Typically, these are passed on by word of mouth in various forms—such as legends, songs, and proverbs—or preserved in customs and ceremonies. Washington Irving, in "The Devil and Tom Walker" and many of his other stories, incorporates many elements of the folklore of New England and Germany.

Folktale: A story originating in oral tradition. Folk tales fall into a variety of categories, including legends, ghost stories, fairy tales, fables, and anecdotes based on historical figures and events.

Foreshadowing: A device used in literature to create expectation or to set up an explanation of later developments. Edgar Allan Poe uses foreshadowing to create suspense in "The Fall of the House of Usher" when the narrator comments on the crumbling state of disrepair in which he finds the house.

G

Genre: A category of literary work. Genre may refer to both the content of a given work—tragedy, comedy, horror, science fiction—and to its form, such as poetry, novel, or drama.

Gilded Age: A period in American history during the 1870s and after characterized by political corruption and materialism. A number of important novels of social and political criticism were written during this time. Henry James and Kate Chopin are two writers who were prominent during the Gilded Age.

Gothicism: In literature, works characterized by a taste for medieval or morbid characters and situations. A gothic novel prominently features elements of horror, the supernatural, gloom, and violence: clanking chains, terror, ghosts, medieval castles, and unexplained phenomena. The term "gothic novel" is also applied to novels that lack elements of the traditional Gothic setting but that create a similar atmosphere of terror or dread. The term can also be applied to stories, plays, and poems. Mary Shelley's *Frankenstein* and Joyce Carol Oates's *Belle fleur* are both gothic novels.

Grotesque: In literature, a work that is characterized by exaggeration, deformity, freakishness, and disorder. The grotesque often includes an element of comic absurdity. Examples of the grotesque can be found in the works of Edgar Allan Poe, Flannery O'Connor, Joseph Heller, and Shirley Jackson.

H

Harlem Renaissance: The Harlem Renaissance of the 1920s is generally considered the first significant movement of black writers and artists in the United States. During this period, new and established black writers, many of whom lived in the region of New York City known as Harlem, published more fiction and poetry than ever before, the first influential black literary journals were established, and black authors and artists received their first widespread recognition and serious critical appraisal. Among the major writers associated with this period are Countee Cullen, Langston Hughes, Arna Bontemps, and Zora Neale Hurston.

Hero/Heroine: The principal sympathetic character in a literary work. Heroes and heroines typically exhibit admirable traits: idealism, courage, and integrity, for example. Famous heroes and heroines of literature include Charles Dickens's Oliver Twist, Margaret Mitchell's Scarlett O'Hara, and the anonymous narrator in Ralph Ellison's *Invisible Man.*

Hyperbole: Deliberate exaggeration used to achieve an effect. In William Shakespeare's *Macbeth,* Lady Macbeth hyperbolizes when she says, "All the perfumes of Arabia could not sweeten this little hand."

I

Image: A concrete representation of an object or sensory experience. Typically, such a representation helps evoke the feelings associated with the object or experience itself. Images are either "literal" or "figurative." Literal images are especially concrete and involve little or no extension of the obvious meaning of the words used to express them. Figurative images do not follow the literal meaning of the words exactly. Images in literature are usually visual, but the term "image" can also refer to the representation of any sensory experience.

Imagery: The array of images in a literary work. Also used to convey the author's overall use of figurative language in a work.

In medias res: A Latin term meaning "in the middle of things." It refers to the technique of beginning a story at its midpoint and then using various flashback devices to reveal previous action. This technique originated in such epics as Virgil's *Aeneid.*

Interior Monologue: A narrative technique in which characters' thoughts are revealed in a way that appears to be uncontrolled by the author. The interior monologue typically aims to reveal the inner self of a character. It portrays emotional experiences as they occur at both a conscious and unconscious level. One of the best-known interior monologues in English is the Molly Bloom section at the close of James Joyce's *Ulysses*. Katherine Anne Porter's "The Jilting of Granny Weatherall" is also told in the form of an interior monologue.

Irony: In literary criticism, the effect of language in which the intended meaning is the opposite of what is stated. The title of Jonathan Swift's "A Modest Proposal" is ironic because what Swift proposes in this essay is cannibalism—hardly "modest."

J

Jargon: Language that is used or understood only by a select group of people. Jargon may refer to terminology used in a certain profession, such as computer jargon, or it may refer to any nonsensical language that is not understood by most people. Anthony Burgess's *A Clockwork Orange* and James Thurber's "The Secret Life of Walter Mitty" both use jargon.

K

Knickerbocker Group: An indistinct group of New York writers of the first half of the nineteenth century. Members of the group were linked only by location and a common theme: New York life. Two famous members of the Knickerbocker Group were Washington Irving and William Cullen Bryant. The group's name derives from Irving's *Knickerbocker's History of New York*.

L

Literal Language: An author uses literal language when he or she writes without exaggerating or embellishing the subject matter and without any tools of figurative language. To say "He ran very quickly down the street" is to use literal language, whereas to say "He ran like a hare down the street" would be using figurative language.

Literature: Literature is broadly defined as any written or spoken material, but the term most often refers to creative works. Literature includes poetry, drama, fiction, and many kinds of nonfiction writing, as well as oral, dramatic, and broadcast compositions not necessarily preserved in a written format, such as films and television programs.

Lost Generation: A term first used by Gertrude Stein to describe the post-World War I generation of American writers: men and women haunted by a sense of betrayal and emptiness brought about by the destructiveness of the war. The term is commonly applied to Hart Crane, Ernest Hemingway, F. Scott Fitzgerald, and others.

M

Magic Realism: A form of literature that incorporates fantasy elements or supernatural occurrences into the narrative and accepts them as truth. Gabriel Gárcia Márquez and Laura Esquivel are two writers known for their works of magic realism.

Metaphor: A figure of speech that expresses an idea through the image of another object. Metaphors suggest the essence of the first object by identifying it with certain qualities of the second object. An example is "But soft, what light through yonder window breaks? / It is the east, and Juliet is the sun" in William Shakespeare's *Romeo and Juliet*. Here, Juliet, the first object, is identified with qualities of the second object, the sun.

Minimalism: A literary style characterized by spare, simple prose with few elaborations. In minimalism, the main theme of the work is often never discussed directly. Amy Hempel and Ernest Hemingway are two writers known for their works of minimalism.

Modernism: Modern literary practices. Also, the principles of a literary school that lasted from roughly the beginning of the twentieth century until the end of World War II. Modernism is defined by its rejection of the literary conventions of the nineteenth century and by its opposition to conventional morality, taste, traditions, and economic values. Many writers are associated with the concepts of modernism, including Albert Camus, D. H. Lawrence, Ernest Hemingway, William Faulkner, Eugene O'Neill, and James Joyce.

Monologue: A composition, written or oral, by a single individual. More specifically, a speech given by a single individual in a drama or other public entertainment. It has no set length, although it is usually several or more lines long. "I Stand Here Ironing" by Tillie Olsen is an example of a story written in the form of a monologue.

Mood: The prevailing emotions of a work or of the author in his or her creation of the work. The mood of a work is not always what might be expected based on its subject matter.

Motif: A theme, character type, image, metaphor, or other verbal element that recurs throughout a single work of literature or occurs in a number of different works over a period of time. For example, the color white in Herman Melville's *Moby Dick* is a "specific" motif, while the trials of star-crossed lovers is a "conventional" motif from the literature of all periods.

N

Narration: The telling of a series of events, real or invented. A narration may be either a simple narrative, in which the events are recounted chronologically, or a narrative with a plot, in which the account is given in a style reflecting the author's artistic concept of the story. Narration is sometimes used as a synonym for "storyline."

Narrative: A verse or prose accounting of an event or sequence of events, real or invented. The term is also used as an adjective in the sense "method of narration." For example, in literary criticism, the expression "narrative technique" usually refers to the way the author structures and presents his or her story. Different narrative forms include diaries, travelogues, novels, ballads, epics, short stories, and other fictional forms.

Narrator: The teller of a story. The narrator may be the author or a character in the story through whom the author speaks. Huckleberry Finn is the narrator of Mark Twain's *The Adventures of Huckleberry Finn*.

Novella: An Italian term meaning "story." This term has been especially used to describe fourteenth-century Italian tales, but it also refers to modern short novels. Modern novellas include Leo Tolstoy's *The Death of Ivan Ilich,* Fyodor Dostoyevsky's *Notes from the Underground,* and Joseph Conrad's *Heart of Darkness.*

O

Oedipus Complex: A son's romantic obsession with his mother. The phrase is derived from the story of the ancient Theban hero Oedipus, who unknowingly killed his father and married his mother, and was popularized by Sigmund Freud's theory of psychoanalysis. Literary occurrences of the Oedipus complex include Sophocles' *Oedipus Rex* and D. H. Lawrence's "The Rocking-Horse Winner."

Onomatopoeia: The use of words whose sounds express or suggest their meaning. In its simplest sense, onomatopoeia may be represented by words that mimic the sounds they denote such as "hiss" or "meow." At a more subtle level, the pattern and rhythm of sounds and rhymes of a line or poem may be onomatopoeic.

Oral Tradition: A process by which songs, ballads, folklore, and other material are transmitted by word of mouth. The tradition of oral transmission predates the written record systems of literate society. Oral transmission preserves material sometimes over generations, although often with variations. Memory plays a large part in the recitation and preservation of orally transmitted material. Native American myths and legends, and African folktales told by plantation slaves are examples of orally transmitted literature.

P

Parable: A story intended to teach a moral lesson or answer an ethical question. Examples of parables are the stories told by Jesus Christ in the New Testament, notably "The Prodigal Son," but parables also are used in Sufism, rabbinic literature, Hasidism, and Zen Buddhism. Isaac Bashevis Singer's story "Gimpel the Fool" exhibits characteristics of a parable.

Paradox: A statement that appears illogical or contradictory at first, but may actually point to an underlying truth. A literary example of a paradox is George Orwell's statement "All animals are equal, but some animals are more equal than others" in *Animal Farm.*

Parody: In literature, this term refers to an imitation of a serious literary work or the signature style of a particular author in a ridiculous manner. A typical parody adopts the style of the original and applies it to an inappropriate subject for humorous effect. Parody is a form of satire and could be considered the literary equivalent of a caricature or cartoon. Henry Fielding's *Shamela* is a parody of Samuel Richardson's *Pamela.*

Persona: A Latin term meaning "mask." Personae are the characters in a fictional work of literature. The persona generally functions as a mask through which the author tells a story in a voice other than his or her own. A persona is usually either a character in a story who acts as a narrator or an "implied author," a voice created by the author to act as the narrator for himself or herself. The persona in Charlotte Perkins Gilman's story "The Yellow Wallpaper" is the unnamed young mother experiencing a mental breakdown.

Personification: A figure of speech that gives human qualities to abstract ideas, animals, and inanimate objects. To say that "the sun is smiling" is to personify the sun.

Plot: The pattern of events in a narrative or drama. In its simplest sense, the plot guides the author in composing the work and helps the reader follow the work. Typically, plots exhibit causality and unity and have a beginning, a middle, and an end. Sometimes, however, a plot may consist of a series of disconnected events, in which case it is known as an "episodic plot."

Poetic Justice: An outcome in a literary work, not necessarily a poem, in which the good are rewarded and the evil are punished, especially in ways that particularly fit their virtues or crimes. For example, a murderer may himself be murdered, or a thief will find himself penniless.

Poetic License: Distortions of fact and literary convention made by a writer—not always a poet—for the sake of the effect gained. Poetic license is closely related to the concept of "artistic freedom." An author exercises poetic license by saying that a pile of money "reaches as high as a mountain" when the pile is actually only a foot or two high.

Point of View: The narrative perspective from which a literary work is presented to the reader. There are four traditional points of view. The "third person omniscient" gives the reader a "godlike" perspective, unrestricted by time or place, from which to see actions and look into the minds of characters. This allows the author to comment openly on characters and events in the work. The "third person" point of view presents the events of the story from outside of any single character's perception, much like the omniscient point of view, but the reader must understand the action as it takes place and without any special insight into characters' minds or motivations. The "first person" or "personal" point of view relates events as they are perceived by a single character. The main character "tells" the story and may offer opinions about the action and characters which differ from those of the author. Much less common than omniscient, third person, and first person is the "second person" point of view, wherein the author tells the story as if it is happening to the reader. James Thurber employs the omniscient point of view in his short story "The Secret Life of Walter Mitty." Ernest Hemingway's "A Clean, Well-Lighted Place" is a short story told from the third person point of view. Mark Twain's novel *Huckleberry Finn* is presented from the first person viewpoint. Jay McInerney's *Bright Lights, Big City* is an example of a novel which uses the second person point of view.

Pornography: Writing intended to provoke feelings of lust in the reader. Such works are often condemned by critics and teachers, but those which can be shown to have literary value are viewed less harshly. Literary works that have been described as pornographic include D. H. Lawrence's *Lady Chatterley's Lover* and James Joyce's *Ulysses.*

Post-Aesthetic Movement: An artistic response made by African Americans to the black aesthetic movement of the 1960s and early 1970s. Writers since that time have adopted a somewhat different tone in their work, with less emphasis placed on the disparity between black and white in the United States. In the words of post-aesthetic authors such as Toni Morrison, John Edgar Wideman, and Kristin Hunter, African Americans are portrayed as looking inward for answers to their own questions, rather than always looking to the outside world. Two well-known examples of works produced as part of the post-aesthetic movement are the Pulitzer Prize–winning novels *The Color Purple* by Alice Walker and *Beloved* by Toni Morrison.

Postmodernism: Writing from the 1960s forward characterized by experimentation and application of modernist elements, which include existentialism and alienation. Postmodernists have gone a step further in the rejection of tradition begun with the modernists by also rejecting traditional forms, preferring the anti-novel over the novel and the anti-hero over the hero. Postmodern writers include Thomas Pynchon, Margaret Drabble, and Gabriel Gárcia Márquez.

Prologue: An introductory section of a literary work. It often contains information establishing the situation of the characters or presents information about the setting, time period, or action. In drama, the prologue is spoken by a chorus or by one of the principal characters.

Prose: A literary medium that attempts to mirror the language of everyday speech. It is distinguished from poetry by its use of unmetered, unrhymed language consisting of logically related sentences. Prose is usually grouped into paragraphs that form a cohesive whole such as an essay or a novel. The term is sometimes used to mean an author's general writing.

Protagonist: The central character of a story who serves as a focus for its themes and incidents and as the principal rationale for its development. The protagonist is sometimes referred to in discussions of modern literature as the hero or anti-hero. Well-known protagonists are Hamlet in William Shakespeare's *Hamlet* and Jay Gatsby in F. Scott Fitzgerald's *The Great Gatsby*.

R

Realism: A nineteenth-century European literary movement that sought to portray familiar characters, situations, and settings in a realistic manner. This was done primarily by using an objective narrative point of view and through the buildup of accurate detail. The standard for success of any realistic work depends on how faithfully it transfers common experience into fictional forms. The realistic method may be altered or extended, as in stream of consciousness writing, to record highly subjective experience. Contemporary authors who often write in a realistic way include Nadine Gordimer and Grace Paley.

Resolution: The portion of a story following the climax, in which the conflict is resolved. The resolution of Jane Austen's *Northanger Abbey* is neatly summed up in the following sentence: "Henry and Catherine were married, the bells rang and every body smiled."

Rising Action: The part of a drama where the plot becomes increasingly complicated. Rising action leads up to the climax, or turning point, of a drama. The final "chase scene" of an action film is generally the rising action which culminates in the film's climax.

Roman a clef: A French phrase meaning "novel with a key." It refers to a narrative in which real persons are portrayed under fictitious names. Jack Kerouac, for example, portrayed various friends under fictitious names in the novel *On the Road.* D. H. Lawrence based "The Rocking-Horse Winner" on a family he knew.

Romanticism: This term has two widely accepted meanings. In historical criticism, it refers to a European intellectual and artistic movement of the late eighteenth and early nineteenth centuries that sought greater freedom of personal expression than that allowed by the strict rules of literary form and logic of the eighteenth-century neoclassicists. The Romantics preferred emotional and imaginative expression to rational analysis. They considered the individual to be at the center of all experience and so placed him or her at the center of their art. The Romantics believed that the creative imagination reveals nobler truths—unique feelings and attitudes—than those that could be discovered by logic or by scientific examination. "Romanticism" is also used as a general term to refer to a type of sensibility found in all periods of literary history and usually considered to be in opposition to the principles of classicism. In this sense, Romanticism signifies any work or philosophy in which the exotic or dreamlike figure strongly, or that is devoted to individualistic expression, self-analysis, or a pursuit of a higher realm of knowledge than can be discovered by human reason. Prominent Romantics include Jean-Jacques Rousseau, William Wordsworth, John Keats, Lord Byron, and Johann Wolfgang von Goethe.

S

Satire: A work that uses ridicule, humor, and wit to criticize and provoke change in human nature and institutions. Voltaire's novella *Candide* and Jonathan Swift's essay "A Modest Proposal" are both satires. Flannery O'Connor's portrayal of the family in "A Good Man Is Hard to Find" is a satire of a modern, Southern, American family.

Science Fiction: A type of narrative based upon real or imagined scientific theories and technology. Science fiction is often peopled with alien creatures and set on other planets or in different dimensions. Popular writers of science fiction are Isaac Asimov, Karel Capek, Ray Bradbury, and Ursula K. Le Guin.

Setting: The time, place, and culture in which the action of a narrative takes place. The elements of setting may include geographic location, characters's physical and mental environments, prevailing cultural attitudes, or the historical time in which the action takes place.

Short Story: A fictional prose narrative shorter and more focused than a novella. The short story usually deals with a single episode and often a single character. The "tone," the author's attitude toward his or her subject and audience, is uniform throughout. The short story frequently also lacks *denouement*, ending instead at its climax.

Signifying Monkey: A popular trickster figure in black folklore, with hundreds of tales about this character documented since the 19th century. Henry Louis Gates Jr. examines the history of the signifying monkey in *The Signifying Monkey: Towards a Theory of Afro-American Literary Criticism,* published in 1988.

Simile: A comparison, usually using "like" or "as," of two essentially dissimilar things, as in "coffee as cold as ice" or "He sounded like a broken record." The title of Ernest Hemingway's "Hills Like White Elephants" contains a simile.

Socialist Realism: The Socialist Realism school of literary theory was proposed by Maxim Gorky and established as a dogma by the first Soviet Congress of Writers. It demanded adherence to a communist worldview in works of literature. Its doctrines required an objective viewpoint comprehensible to the working classes and themes of social struggle featuring strong proletarian heroes. Gabriel Gárcia Márquez's stories exhibit some characteristics of Socialist Realism.

Stereotype: A stereotype was originally the name for a duplication made during the printing process; this led to its modern definition as a person or thing that is (or is assumed to be) the same as all others of its type. Common stereotypical characters include the absent-minded professor, the nagging wife, the troublemaking teenager, and the kind-hearted grandmother.

Stream of Consciousness: A narrative technique for rendering the inward experience of a character. This technique is designed to give the impression of an ever-changing series of thoughts, emotions, images, and memories in the spontaneous and seemingly illogical order that they occur in life. The textbook example of stream of consciousness is the last section of James Joyce's *Ulysses.*

Structure: The form taken by a piece of literature. The structure may be made obvious for ease of understanding, as in nonfiction works, or may be obscured for artistic purposes, as in some poetry or seemingly "unstructured" prose.

Style: A writer's distinctive manner of arranging words to suit his or her ideas and purpose in writing. The unique imprint of the author's personality upon his or her writing, style is the product of an author's way of arranging ideas and his or her use of diction, different sentence structures, rhythm, figures of speech, rhetorical principles, and other elements of composition.

Suspense: A literary device in which the author maintains the audience's attention through the buildup of events, the outcome of which will soon be revealed. Suspense in William Shakespeare's *Hamlet* is sustained throughout by the question of whether or not the Prince will achieve what he has been instructed to do and of what he intends to do.

Symbol: Something that suggests or stands for something else without losing its original identity. In literature, symbols combine their literal meaning with the suggestion of an abstract concept. Literary symbols are of two types: those that carry complex associations of meaning no matter what their contexts, and those that derive their suggestive meaning from their functions in specific literary works. Examples of symbols are sunshine suggesting happiness, rain suggesting sorrow, and storm clouds suggesting despair.

T

Tale: A story told by a narrator with a simple plot and little character development. Tales are usually relatively short and often carry a simple message.

Examples of tales can be found in the works of Saki, Anton Chekhov, Guy de Maupassant, and O. Henry.

Tall Tale: A humorous tale told in a straightforward, credible tone but relating absolutely impossible events or feats of the characters. Such tales were commonly told of frontier adventures during the settlement of the west in the United States. Literary use of tall tales can be found in Washington Irving's *History of New York,* Mark Twain's *Life on the Mississippi,* and in the German R. F. Raspe's *Baron Munchausen's Narratives of His Marvellous Travels and Campaigns in Russia.*

Theme: The main point of a work of literature. The term is used interchangeably with thesis. Many works have multiple themes. One of the themes of Nathaniel Hawthorne's "Young Goodman Brown" is loss of faith.

Tone: The author's attitude toward his or her audience may be deduced from the tone of the work. A formal tone may create distance or convey politeness, while an informal tone may encourage a friendly, intimate, or intrusive feeling in the reader. The author's attitude toward his or her subject matter may also be deduced from the tone of the words he or she uses in discussing it. The tone of John F. Kennedy's speech which included the appeal to "ask not what your country can do for you" was intended to instill feelings of camaraderie and national pride in listeners.

Tragedy: A drama in prose or poetry about a noble, courageous hero of excellent character who, because of some tragic character flaw, brings ruin upon him- or herself. Tragedy treats its subjects in a dignified and serious manner, using poetic language to help evoke pity and fear and bring about catharsis, a purging of these emotions. The tragic form was practiced extensively by the ancient Greeks. The classical form of tragedy was revived in the sixteenth century; it flourished especially on the Elizabethan stage. In modern times, dramatists have attempted to adapt the form to the needs of modern society by drawing their heroes from the ranks of ordinary men and women and defining the nobility of these heroes in terms of spirit rather than exalted social standing. Some contemporary works that are thought of as tragedies include *The Great Gatsby* by F. Scott Fitzgerald, and *The Sound and the Fury* by William Faulkner.

Tragic Flaw: In a tragedy, the quality within the hero or heroine which leads to his or her downfall. Examples of the tragic flaw include Othello's jealousy and Hamlet's indecisiveness, although most great tragedies defy such simple interpretation.

U

Utopia: A fictional perfect place, such as "paradise" or "heaven." An early literary utopia was described in Plato's *Republic,* and in modern literature, Ursula K. Le Guin depicts a utopia in "The Ones Who Walk Away from Omelas."

V

Victorian: Refers broadly to the reign of Queen Victoria of England (1837–1901) and to anything with qualities typical of that era. For example, the qualities of smug narrow-mindedness, bourgeois materialism, faith in social progress, and priggish morality are often considered Victorian. In literature, the Victorian Period was the great age of the English novel, and the latter part of the era saw the rise of movements such as decadence and symbolism.

Cumulative
Author/Title Index

Cumulative
Nationality/Ethnicity Index

African American

Baldwin, James
  The Rockpile: V18
  Sonny's Blues: V2
Bambara, Toni Cade
  Blues Ain't No Mockin Bird: V4
  Gorilla, My Love: V21
  The Lesson: V12
  Raymond's Run: V7
Butler, Octavia
  Bloodchild: V6
Chesnutt, Charles Waddell
  The Sheriff's Children: V11
Ellison, Ralph
  King of the Bingo Game: V1
Hughes, Langston
  The Blues I'm Playing: V7
  Slave on the Block: V4
Hurston, Zora Neale
  Conscience of the Court: V21
  The Eatonville Anthology: V1
  The Gilded Six-Bits: V11
  Spunk: V6
  Sweat: V19
Marshall, Paule
  To Da-duh, in Memoriam: V15
McPherson, James Alan
  Elbow Room: V23
Toomer, Jean
  Blood-Burning Moon: V5
Walker, Alice
  Everyday Use: V2
  Roselily: V11
Wideman, John Edgar
  The Beginning of Homewood:
    V12
  Fever: V6

  What We Cannot Speak About
    We Must Pass Over in
    Silence: V24
Wright, Richard
  Big Black Good Man: V20
  Bright and Morning Star: V15
  The Man Who Lived
    Underground: V3
  The Man Who Was Almost a
    Man: V9

American

Adams, Alice
  Greyhound People: V21
  The Last Lovely City: V14
Agüeros, Jack
  Dominoes: V13
Aiken, Conrad
  Silent Snow, Secret Snow: V8
Alexie, Sherman
  Because My Father Always Said
    He Was the Only Indian Who
    Saw Jimi Hendrix Play "The
    Star-Spangled Banner" at
    Woodstock: V18
Allen, Woody
  The Kugelmass Episode: V21
Anderson, Sherwood
  Death in the Woods: V10
  Hands: V11
  Sophistication: V4
Asimov, Isaac
  Nightfall: V17
Baldwin, James
  The Rockpile: V18
  Sonny's Blues: V2

Bambara, Toni Cade
  Blues Ain't No Mockin Bird: V4
  Gorilla, My Love: V21
  The Lesson: V12
  Raymond's Run: V7
Barrett, Andrea
  The English Pupil: V24
Barth, John
  Lost in the Funhouse: V6
Barthelme, Donald
  The Indian Uprising: V17
  Robert Kennedy Saved from
    Drowning: V3
Beattie, Ann
  Imagined Scenes: V20
  Janus: V9
Bellow, Saul
  Leaving the Yellow House: V12
  A Silver Dish: V22
Benét, Stephen Vincent
  An End to Dreams: V22
Berriault, Gina
  The Stone Boy: V7
  Women in Their Beds: V11
Bierce, Ambrose
  The Boarded Window: V9
  An Occurrence at Owl Creek
    Bridge: V2
Bisson, Terry
  The Toxic Donut: V18
Bloom, Amy
  Silver Water: V11
Bowles, Paul
  The Eye: V17
Boyle, Kay
  Astronomer's Wife: V13
  Black Boy: V14
  The White Horses of Vienna: V10

Antiguan

Cumulative Nationality/Ethnicity Index

Mexican

Paz, Octavio
  My Life with the Wave: V13

Native American

Alexie, Sherman
  *Because My Father Always Said
    He Was the Only Indian Who
    Saw Jimi Hendrix Play "The
    Star-Spangled Banner" at
    Woodstock:* V18
Erdrich, Louise
  Fleur: V22
  The Red Convertible: V14
Ortiz, Simon J.
  The End of Old Horse: V22
Silko, Leslie Marmon
  Lullaby: V10
  The Man to Send Rain Clouds: V8
  Storyteller: V11
  Yellow Woman: V4

Nepalese

Upadhyay, Samrat
  The Good Shopkeeper: V22

New Zealander

Mansfield, Katherine
  Bliss: V10
  The Garden Party: V8
  Marriage à la Mode: V11
  Miss Brill: V2
Sargeson, Frank
  A Great Day: V20

Nigerian

Achebe, Chinua
  Civil Peace: V13
  Vengeful Creditor: V3
Okri, Ben
  In the Shadow of War: V20

Peruvian

Vargas Llosa, Mario
  The Challenge: V14

Philippine

Santos, Bienvenido
  Immigration Blues: V19

Polish

Borowski, Tadeusz
  *This Way for the Gas, Ladies and
    Gentlemen:* V13
Conrad, Joseph
  Heart of Darkness: V12
  The Secret Sharer: V1
Singer, Isaac Bashevis
  Gimpel the Fool: V2
  Henne Fire: V16
  The Spinoza of Market Street: V12

Portuguese

Saramago, José
  The Centaur: V23

Russian

Asimov, Isaac
  Nightfall: V17
Babel, Isaac
  My First Goose: V10
Chekhov, Anton
  The Darling: V13
  Gooseberries: V14
  The Lady with the Pet Dog: V5
Dostoevsky, Fyodor
  The Grand Inquisitor: V8
Gogol, Nikolai
  The Overcoat: V7
Nabokov, Vladimir
  A Guide to Berlin: V6
  That in Aleppo Once . . . : V15
Pushkin, Alexander
  The Stationmaster: V9
Solzhenitsyn, Alexandr
  *One Day in the Life of Ivan
    Denisovich:* V9
Tolstaya, Tatyana
  Night: V14
Tolstoy, Leo
  The Death of Ivan Ilych: V5
Yezierska, Anzia
  America and I: V15

Scottish

Doyle, Arthur Conan
  The Red-Headed League: V2
Scott, Sir Walter
  Wandering Willie's Tale: V10

South African

Gordimer, Nadine
  Town and Country Lovers:
    V14
  The Train from Rhodesia: V2
  The Ultimate Safari: V19
Head, Bessie
  Life: V13
  Snapshots of a Wedding: V5
Kohler, Sheila
  Africans: V18
Mphahlele, Es'kia (Ezekiel)
  Mrs. Plum: V11

Spanish

Unamuno, Miguel de
  *Saint Emmanuel the Good,
    Martyr:* V20
Vargas Llosa, Mario
  The Challenge: V14

Swedish

Gustafsson, Lars
  *Greatness Strikes Where It
    Pleases:* V22
Lagerlöf, Selma
  *The Legend of the Christmas
    Rose:* V18

Welsh

Dahl, Roald
  Lamb to the Slaughter: V4

West Indian

Kincaid, Jamaica
  Girl: V7
  What I Have Been Doing Lately:
    V5

Subject/Theme Index